Mary Baker Eddy

MARY BAKER EDDY

The Years of Authority

Robert Peel

Holt, Rinehart and Winston

New York

Acknowledgments

For permission to reprint copyright material, grateful acknowledgement
is made to the following: The Christian Science Board of Directors for
quotations from Mrs. Eddy's published and unpublished works; Trustees of The
Christian Science Publishing Society for quotations from works published by
them; Viking Press, Inc. for passages from *The Portable Mark Twain*, ed.
Bernard De Voto; Random House, Inc. for three lines from *Poems* by W. H.
Auden © 1934 and renewed 1962 by W. H. Auden; Dodd, Mead & Company
for quotations from Leon Burr Richardson, *William E. Chandler: Republican*
© 1940; Columbia University for part of a letter by Hart Crane from *Letters of
Hart Crane and his Family*, ed. Thomas S. W. Lewis © 1974 by Columbia
University Press; Harold J. Dies, trustee of The Dreiser Trust, for passage from
Theodore Dreiser, *The Color of a Great City* © 1923 by Boni and Liveright;
Yale University Press for passages from Jonathan Edwards, *Images or Shadows
of Divine Things*, ed. Perry Miller, and Margaret M. Elder, *The Life of Samuel
J. Elder;* Charles Scribner's Sons for passages from Edwin F. Dakin, *Mrs. Eddy*
© 1957, 1958; Harper & Row, Inc. for a passage from Hamlin Hill, *Mark Twain,
God's Fool* © 1973 by Harper & Row, and passages from Samuel L. Clemens,
Christian Science © 1907 by Harper & Brothers; and E. P. Dutton & Co., Inc.
for a passage from Van Wyck Brooks, *Helen Keller: Sketch for a
Portrait* © 1954, 1956 by Van Wyck Brooks.

Library of Congress Cataloging in Publication Data

Peel, Robert, 1909–

Mary Baker Eddy.

Third vol. in the author's 3-vol. biography,

the 1st and 2d of which are Mary Baker Eddy: the

years of discovery, and Mary Baker Eddy: the years

of trial.

Includes bibliographical references and index.

1. Eddy, Mary Baker, 1821–1910.   2. Christian

Scientists—United States—Biography.   I. Title.

BX6995.P38   289.5′092′4 [B]   66-14855

ISBN Hardbound: 0-03-021081-X
ISBN Paperback: 0-03-056709-2
First Holt Paperback Edition—1980
Printed in the United States of America

1 3 5 7 9 10 8 6 4 2

Contents

Prefatory Note

Prefatory Note

The present volume completes a trilogy begun almost twenty years ago. Like the others, it does not assume the reader's prior familiarity with the subject but allows him to become acquainted with Mary Baker Eddy at a significant stage of her career as though he were coming upon her for the first time.

The trilogy as a whole has involved the exploration of largely unmapped terrain—a landscape assumed by some to be an uninviting wasteland, by others to be an indescribable paradise. The rewards of the enterprise have been commensurate with the hazards. In retrospect, I find that the sequence of discovery, trial, and authority sums up the methodological ideal of the three volumes as well as the major phases of Mrs. Eddy's experience.

I am well aware how many of the heights and depths of the subject lie beyond the book's topography. No life of magnitude can be captured in its full variety, let alone its limitless subjectivity, by even the most searching biographer. But I have tried at every step to convey the true proportions and suggest the inner dimensions of a life story which, in both its public and its private aspects, has been misrepresented so often by sanctified legend and scandalous fable.

My debt of gratitude to others is beyond repayment, but I warmly thank all those who have contributed in any way to the enrichment or the accuracy of this work. I am especially grateful to the Christian Science Board of Directors for the free access they have given me to the church archives and their permission to quote abundantly from unpublished materials. To Dr. Lee Zeunert Johnson, Archivist of The Mother Church, and his always cooperative staff I am indebted for their inexhaustible patience and cheerful help. And for his early encouragement of the project I continue to be grateful to the late Perry Miller of Harvard, whose own combination of objective scholarship and sympathetic insight into the Puritan background of American thought enabled him to recognize the Christian roots of Mrs. Eddy's teaching.

Finally, a word of gratitude to two people who have been intimately connected with the writing of the trilogy. For two decades my secretary and assistant, Ethel G. Adelman, has brought to the work incalculable virtues of care and judgment. The undertaking has also benefited throughout from the vision, counsel, and penetrating criticism of my colleague, Allison W. Phinney. To borrow Mrs. Eddy's words, I am bankrupt in thanks to such associates.

ROBERT PEEL
Boston, Massachusetts

Prologue

Prologue

When Mary Baker Eddy at the age of seventy moved from a house in the center of Concord, New Hampshire, to a tidy estate on the outskirts of that overgrown country town, it was a matter of local note but caused no flutter in Paris, Rome, or Omsk. Nor, for that matter, in Battle Creek or Sioux Falls.

There was little to indicate on the unremarkable June afternoon in 1892 when Mrs. Eddy drove up to the reconditioned farmhouse for which she had chosen the bland though accurate name of Pleasant View that, before she moved away some fifteen years later, the name of her estate (not to mention her own name) would be headline fare for millions of newspaper readers.

To be sure, she was already a minor celebrity as the secluded though still active leader of the vigorous young Christian Science movement, whose converts were to be found forming churches and healing the sick in cities across the United States. Yet on the day she moved in as mistress of Pleasant View she was still far from being the controversial figure whose quasi-legendary comings and goings the general public would follow with fascination in only a few more years. Outside the United States she was still hardly known at all.

At that time the most productive period of Mrs. Eddy's life lay just ahead of her. Some ten years later Mark Twain would be describing her as in some ways "the most interesting woman that ever lived, and the most extraordinary . . . already as tall as the Eiffel tower . . . adding surprisingly to her stature every day." To which he would add, with tongue notably absent from cheek though perhaps with a slight gritting of teeth, that it was "quite within the probabilities that a century hence she will be the most imposing figure that has cast its shadow across the globe since the inauguration of our era"[1]—i.e., the Christian era.

Mark Twain, for all the fierce glooms of his later years, never guessed how close to extinction the Christian era and even human history itself might move "a century hence." While he indulged in fantasied threats of authoritarian Christian Science rule for the twentieth century, the real menace to humane values might soon enough turn out to be a voracious scientism committed to the invalidation of every remnant of spiritual transcendence in human life, every moral or cultural sanction inherited from a prescientific past.

In this development, institutionalized religion would increasingly be rated as a casualty. An era which saw the dogma of papal infallibility emerge from the First Vatican Council of 1870 could hardly have anticipated the collapse of ecclesiastical authority that would follow the secularization of values a century later. And the optimists of scientific secularism could hardly have anticipated the devaluation of human life that would follow the draining away of religious ideals and disciplines.

It would be one thing to get rid of sacerdotal authoritarianism; it would be quite another to allow no place at all for the authority of spirit in the affairs of men.

In an age of innovative technology riding to power on sheer performance, long-cherished Christian ideals might be expected to have no more weight than outgrown nursery fables. The power to make things happen would be honored far above the power of established office and tradition. Even charismatic leadership would tend to yield to bureaucratic management as the growing complexity of affairs would make more evident the inadequacy of the simplistic myths from which great leaders have traditionally drawn support. Organized religion would become increasingly indistinguishable from business enterprise on the one hand and social engineering on the other.

In the vast transition from the traditional past to the empirical future, Mary Baker Eddy stands at the crossroads between Christianity and science, between faith based on revelation and authority based on demonstration. Regarded by society in general as a special rather than a typical case, her life nevertheless speaks directly to the dilemma of Christianity as a whole.

Planting herself on the example rather than the historicity of the Founder of Christianity—himself reputed to have astonished the people of his day because he taught them "as one having authority, and not as the scribes"[2]—she was discerning enough to recognize that Christian authority must rest not only on the truth of its message but also on its validation by practical, repeatable results. This involved a new concept of both revelation and demonstration.

In challenging the authority of religious tradition, Mrs. Eddy put herself squarely on the side of what might be called spiritual democracy, as when she wrote:

All revelation (such is the popular thought!) must come from the schools and along the line of scholarly and ecclesiastical descent, as kings are crowned from a royal dynasty. In healing the sick and sinning, Jesus elaborated the fact that the healing effect followed the understanding of the divine Principle and of the Christ-spirit which governed the corporeal Jesus. For this Principle there is no dynasty, no ecclesiastical monopoly. Its only crowned head is immortal sovereignty. Its only priest is the spiritualized man. The Bible declares that all believers are made "kings and priests unto God." The outsiders did not then, and do not now, understand this ruling of the Christ; therefore they cannot demonstrate God's healing power. Neither can this manifestation of Christ be comprehended, until its divine Principle is scientifically understood.[3]

Yet this emphasis on principle and rule pointed straight back to the issue of authority. Democracy without constituted law would soon become anarchy, as science without agreed methodology would be mere guesswork. For the last two decades of her life, Mrs. Eddy addressed herself to this problem not in theoretical terms but as a woman facing the need both to implement and to safeguard her vision for the world.

At the time of her move to Pleasant View, few even of her followers would have thought of her as exploring the relationship of authority to democracy, any more than the world at large regarded her as having anything significant to say about the relationship of Christianity to science. It was easier to see her simply as either a saint or a fraud.

Even a century later most people would be in doubt as to what she actually was. She herself insisted that her life could not be understood apart from her lifework, or her character apart from the religion she founded. Certainly her experience remains incomprehensible without serious reference to the currents of thought which swept through, around, out from and beyond it.

This is especially true of the final chapters of her life, in which she consciously confronted both the challenge and the verdict of the coming centuries. But the mild opening chapter in 1892 gave little evidence of the greater drama still to come.

Chapter I

Pleasant View, Varying Views

Pleasant View, Varying Views

With a characteristic absence of any sense of history, Mrs. Eddy's close-mouthed secretary and steward, Calvin A. Frye, wrote in his dry little diary for June 20, 1892: "Moved this P.M. to new house Pleasant St. Concord."[1]

The street, the house, the view—all were "pleasant." Writing to a new acquaintance two years later, Mrs. Eddy described the place as having been, when she moved there, "a cow pasture with a captivating view."[2] In remodeling the old farmhouse into a comfortable if still unpretentious dwelling where she could receive visitors from all over the world, she had added a little tower with her study in it and a three-tiered rear veranda that ran the width of the house.

The study was, in fact and in figure, "a room with a view." From the balcony outside it she would address ten thousand Christian Scientists on a June day eleven years later, greeting them with a mild bit of wordplay: "Welcome to Pleasant View, but not to varying views."[3] In point of fact, nothing could vary more dramatically than the views that her contemporaries and later history would take of the half-hidden life in those placid surroundings.

To casual visitors through the years the scene was unexceptional enough, as Mrs. Eddy pointed out to them with obvious pleasure the pastoral charms of the shallow river valley spread out beneath their gaze in a tranquil panorama of meadow and woodland. One needed, perhaps, to see Pleasant View in blizzard or squall or hurricane to catch even a hint of the struggles that sometimes raged within the house.

From the rear veranda the viewer could see the distant Bow Hills where, seventy years earlier, Mary Baker had been born to a respected New Hampshire family on a windswept upland farm. Now the farmer's daughter had become a religious leader who held all things earthly to be "type and shadow" of eternal spiritual truths, and who consequently found sermons in storms and theological lessons even in the ornamental fishpond donated to the new estate by some of her followers.

In thanking them for this large pond constructed on the broad rear lawn, the mistress of Pleasant View showed that her roots were in the soil of New England Puritanism. A simple thank-you for a nonutilitarian gift took the characteristic form of an article entitled "Pond and Purpose"[4] which, after a few initial pleasantries, developed into a strongly felt disquisition on the metaphysical significance of baptism. The article grew as naturally in the mental atmosphere of Pleasant View as the full-grown elms which Mrs. Eddy had transplanted to the front lawn flourished in their congenial new surroundings.

First, in the article, came a bit of realistic psychology which showed its author's debt to the tough-minded Calvinism of her girlhood teachers, a way of thinking which found its most eloquent expression in that earlier typologist and metaphysician, Jonathan Edwards.[5] This was the unpleasant view, the bitter medicine which the founder of Christian Science always kept handy for those who were inclined to drift off into transcendental tenuities:

> The baptism of repentance is indeed a stricken state of human consciousness, wherein mortals gain severe views of themselves; a state of mind which rends the veil that hides mental deformity. Tears flood the eyes, agony struggles, pride rebels, and a mortal seems a monster, a dark, impenetrable cloud of error; and falling on the bended knee of prayer, humble before God, he cries, "Save, or I perish." Thus Truth, searching the heart, neutralizes and destroys error.

After describing a second state of religious development, the "baptism of the Holy Ghost," which brought "new motives, new purposes, new affections" and permeated "with increased harmony all the minutiæ of human affairs," the article moved to a third state which, at least to the ordinary earthling, might seem as far removed from the minutiæ of human affairs as the Atlantic Ocean at the end of the Merrimack River was removed from the fishpond at Pleasant View:

> The baptism of Spirit, or final immersion of human consciousness in the infinite ocean of Love, is the last scene in corporeal sense. . . . Mortal man's repentance and absolute abandonment of sin finally dissolves all supposed material life or physical sensation, and the corporeal or mortal man disappears forever. The encumbering mortal molecules, called man, vanish as a dream; but man born of the great Forever, lives on, God-crowned and blest.

Whatever this beatific vision might mean in practical terms, the man to whom it referred was not to be looked for in molecular structures, in genes and chromosomes. Presumably he was to be glimpsed in the quality of spiritual-mindedness—and in the actions that issued from such a state of mind. This last point was vitally important to Mrs. Eddy. Though everything at Pleasant View was transposable into thought, thought was expected at all times to be translated into action.

Both Calvinist and pragmatist elements entered into the work ethic of Christian Science, but essentially it was rooted in the basic proposition that "All is infinite Mind and its infinite manifestation."[6] In Mrs. Eddy's view the necessary corollary of such a proposition was that every area of human experience—including Pleasant View—must be treated as the proving ground of ideas.

Soon Calvin Frye's diary was reporting new items:

> *Begin to fill the pond this* A.M. . . . *Grass seed sown east and south of house.* . . . *Picking apples.* . . . *Took up Dalliahs* [*Frye, like Mrs. Eddy, was never a good speller; this was one area that escaped their metaphysics*]. . . . *Pond full and a little ran over dam.* . . . *Commenced to put up Wind Engine.* . . . *Started windmill.* . . . *Had Gene and Jerry* [*horses*] *clipped today.* . . . *12 bales of hay.*[7]

Later, additional boggy acres on both sides of the estate were acquired and reclaimed, so that Pleasant View before long had its own adjoining farm, as well as a cottage where the caretaker and the coachman lived. Mrs. Eddy's voluminous correspondence, largely concerned with things of the mind and spirit, occasionally reflected her satisfaction with the tangible fruits of her field in such passing remarks as, "We are having the *best corn* cucumbers peas and raspberries you ever tasted."[8] She also issued crisp directions for planting an orchard, trimming the shrubs around the fountain, moving the azaleas where the double buttercups had been, replacing the bittersweet on the front piazza with woodbine, caring for the lawns, bringing in the hay, painting the barn, buying an express wagon, and carrying out a thousand small improvements on the estate. As an almost incessant worker herself, she had a taste for homespun aphorisms to the effect that hard work never hurt anyone.

At the same time, she believed in keeping life simple. As a setting for spiritual revolution, Pleasant View should be run with economy of means and effort. To be sure, it was important for it to express visibly the beauty of Mind's "invisible universe," but undue time should not be given to the cultivation of mere "materiality." When the highly successful farming operations tended to absorb too much attention, Mrs. Eddy sent a note to William Clark, who was at that time in charge of them:

Tilling the ground came with the curse. *The Garden of beauty and harmony was before that. You know I said at first only raise vegetables enough for me. Now I return to what I said. Only cultivate ground enough for this end, and for my family—and give your labor to the beautifying of Pleasant View.*[9]

The "family" referred to consisted of Calvin Frye; the cook, Martha Morgan; an aide and housekeeper, Laura Sargent, who alternated during the next few years with Clara Shannon of Montreal; and, on his frequent visits from Boston, Mrs. Eddy's adopted son, Dr. Ebenezer J. Foster Eddy. These devoted regulars, all of whom had studied Christian Science with her when she taught in the Massachusetts Metaphysical College in Boston, were augmented by a few locals who served as needed in various indoor and outdoor capacities and who were consequently the objects of fascinated interrogation by their fellow townsmen.

The indoor household was run on the same basis as the outdoor estate: strict order and neatness, close attention to detail, a simplified and systematized way of life—and a reckless, breathtaking genius for improvisation. "As of old," Mrs. Eddy wrote her students in Boston, "I stand with sandals on and staff in hand, waiting for the watchword and the revelation of what, how, whither."[10]

She might take her morning walk around the pond or, in sterner weather, up and down the rear veranda of the house, followed by her regular afternoon drive through the streets of Concord, bowing politely to her acquaintances and waving smilingly to the children she passed, but her inner life was one of almost total unpredictability.

Only three years before, in a series of smashing moves, she had undone in a few months the work of ten years—dissolving the church organization she had built up with immense labor and sacrifice, closing the flourishing Massachusetts Metaphysical College from which she was sending out practitioners of Christian Science healing all over the United States, dismissing into a three-year limbo of adjournment the National Christian Scientist Association which had brought together annually all her leading students, withdrawing personally from Boston and from active supervision of the loosely organized movement through which Christian Science now found expression.

Nor were any of these moves, as events were to show, a sign of the timidity or retrenchment of old age. This was not the "Let us cultivate our own gardens" of a tired Candide retreating from the cosmic optimism of Leibniz into the Voltairean cynicism of a comfortable maxim. Mrs. Eddy's "retirement" to Concord in 1889 had been quite simply the preparation for a journey greater than any she had taken before.

She was literally and very actively waiting for the "what, how, whither" of a move that would carry Christian Science around the globe. She was thinking in terms of continents and centuries, of a world that was hovering on the edge of inconceivably vast changes, of the role that Christian Science could play in that tremendous drama if somehow, *somehow,* it could escape the common fate of institutionalized religion. Her church—and Mrs. Eddy had never surrendered the idea of her church, but only its organization—must be structured into the underlying reality of things. It must lend itself so radically, so responsively, to the shaping and transforming power of spirit that it would not be left stranded on its own temporal triumphs, only to crumble away with all the other relativities of human life.

The year before, she had written, "All things earthly must ultimately yield to the irony of fate, or else be merged into the one infinite Love."[11] While her knowledge of history as an academic discipline was sketchy, her sense of the impermanence of all human institutions was fairly overwhelming. On the other hand, this same strain of hard-headed realism kept her sharply aware that religion as pure subjectivity, without discipline, without organization, without demonstrable authority, could no more regenerate society than it could morally absolve the individual of his corporate responsibilities. Inspiration needed instrumentality, yet the useful instrument became a fatal hazard when it took on a life of its own.

For three years now, her wrestling with this dilemma had been visible in both her published writings and her private correspondence. To the good people of Concord, however, who saw her drive by in her carriage each day—a slim, white-haired figure with a fresh complexion, a pleasant smile and, on occasion, a far-away look on her face—there was nothing to suggest exactly *where* she was looking.

2

In the weeks preceding her move to Pleasant View, Mrs. Eddy had been engaged in a running conflict with a minority faction among her followers. These were the trustees responsible for building a church in Boston on property which she had conveyed to them for that purpose. Chief among them was a brisk young businessman from South Dakota named William G. Nixon.

When Nixon and his wife had studied with Mrs. Eddy in 1889, the two had had a short talk with her at the end of the last session. In the course of their conversation, she had remarked thoughtfully to the young man, "If you should ever turn from Christian Science you would become one of the strongest enemies it ever had."[12]

Two months later she brought him to Boston as publisher of her monthly periodical, *The Christian Science Journal.* Soon afterward she gave him the additional and still more responsible task of publishing the Christian Science textbook, *Science and Health with Key to the Scriptures.* Before the end of the year she had made him one of the three trustees who held title to the parcel of land in Boston's Back Bay on which they were to start building a church as soon as they received $20,000 in subscriptions.

Her choice of Nixon was an interesting example of her policy of taking calculated risks. In this case the dangers finally outweighed the gains.

Isaiah had described as "beautiful upon the mountains" the feet of one "that publisheth salvation." To Mrs. Eddy the business of publishing, like the business of building, fell within the category of what the Founder of Christianity had called "my Father's business."[13] It had its own rules, its own aims, its own methods, which might in some cases be as diametrically opposite to those of the world as Christian Science healing was to ordinary medical treatment.

Publishing, seen this way, was a matter of healing the world's opposition to spiritual truth, not merely a matter of selling copies of *Science and Health*—necessary as that activity might be in the larger process.[14] Mrs. Eddy liked to point out that the very words "science and health" had been used by Wyclif where the King James Version of the Bible used "knowledge of salvation,"[15] and she saw the publisher of her book as literally publishing salvation, as bringing the healing power of Christianity down from the mountaintops of inspiration to the urgencies of common life.

This did not obviate the need for businesslike methods. Mrs. Eddy had turned to Nixon for his very skill in this direction; but she soon made it clear that his motivation needed thorough reorienting and he must be ready wherever necessary to subordinate his past experience to the new light of revelation.

Nixon, who enthusiastically accepted Christian Science as a healing system in the narrow sense, was in all other respects a businessman whose feet were firmly planted on what he considered to be intelligent commercial practice. Business was business. Advertising, promotion, publicity were the obvious tools of selling. When some of his carefully thought-out campaigns along this line failed to produce results, the reason seemed to him clear: it was Mrs. Eddy's feminine instability, her arbitrary orders and sudden changes of direction.

What she thought of the matter is revealed in a letter which she sent him after one of his plans to increase the sales of *Science and Health* brought about the opposite result. The trouble was, she wrote him, that he was allowing himself to be misled into giving his time to *schemes*:

> . . . and in these schemes [you] use the means that God has forbidden. If you believe that my writings are inspired, you certainly can read them and thus learn that you are instigating means and measures contrary to the divine directions. This must stop, or you will force me to take the side of God . . . which is opposed to your worldly material means and maintain it against you.[16]

She went on to say that the only possible alternative to this would be to leave God and her "out of this question of publishing His [God's] word," and instead "let Mr. Nixon rule my students and have in business the same material motives that the world acts from."

In an undated talk that was probably given between 1889 and 1892 Mrs. Eddy extended this same distinction to the whole question of forming a church. One passage in particular seems to draw up the battle lines on which the struggle with the church trustees was to be fought—and, by implication, on which the age-long war between religious idealism and religious institutionalism has been waged:

> *The smartest business man is not scientifically a safe business man. He is not as smart as God, while he thinks himself smarter and is quite unconscious of this thought.*
>
> *If you have more faith in establishing Christ's Church by material organization than upon the spiritual Rock of Christ, then you build upon matter instead of Spirit and build upon sand. Personal combinations, human thought and effort, material ways and means whereby to establish and maintain the Church of Christ are weak, vacillating, temporal, subject to divisions, factions, feuds, and all the etcetera of mortal and material phenomena.*
>
> *The church created, founded and erected on the Rock against which the winds and waves prevail not, is the Church triumphant, the indwelling temple of God; it is the mind that has consecrated its affections, its aims, ambitions, hopes, joys and fruition in Spirit,*

whose methods and means, plans and successes are secure; they cannot be separated from success. . . .

What is your model business man—the real Scientist who plants in Mind, God, who sows in Mind and reaps in Mind, or he who begins with political economy, human plans, legal speculations, and ends with them, dust to dust?[17]

As a smart businessman and the dominant figure among the three trustees whom Mrs. Eddy was urging to proceed with the building of a Boston church, Nixon was insistent that without a properly organized church body the trustees were legally powerless to start building. The immediate necessity, he insisted, was for a church reorganized under state law, with ultimate authority vested in the membership.

This would mean, as Mrs. Eddy saw it, a church without protection from that innate proclivity of American Protestantism which Matthew Arnold ironically characterized as "the dissidence of dissent."[18] It could lead to a renewal of the very factionalism that had caused her to dissolve the earlier form of organization in 1889. While Nixon and his colleagues held with tenacious masculine logic to the need to reorganize along the old lines, Mrs. Eddy's thinking took unforeseeable twists and turns as she explored her way toward a new form of church polity. Her undefined ideal at the time seems to have been to avoid both the spiritual anarchy of the Protestant diaspora and the centralized absolutism which Lord Acton—himself a faithful son of Rome—saw as subject to the universal "tendency or . . . certainty of corruption by authority."[19]

At the heart of Mrs. Eddy's hesitations lay her deep distrust of what she called "material" organization.

In the years between 1889 and 1892 she had kept alive a sort of shadow government for the Boston congregation. In addition to the trustees charged with collecting funds for a church building, she had appointed a loosely defined five-man board of directors to maintain regular services and "to organize a Church in the usual form"[20] when the time was ripe. With less business experience than the trustees, the directors had more faith in Mrs. Eddy's leadership and consequently resisted Nixon's pressure for reorganization along the old lines.[21]

As the matter hung in suspension through the spring of 1892, she wrote the directors on March 23, asking them not to "change your present materially disorganized—but spiritually organized—Church, nor its present form of Church government."[22] About the same time she wrote the Christian Science church in Denver, Colorado, which was dedicating its new building, "Exercise more faith in God and His spiritual means and methods, than in man and his material ways and means, of establishing the Cause of Christian Science."[23]

During this time, however, she continued to encourage Christian Scientists in various cities to organize and build churches, nor was there ever any doubt that she wanted a church building erected in Boston on the land purchased by its former members for that purpose.

The March *Journal* had as a frontispiece the combined publishing house and church which the trustees proposed to build, despite the fact that the property had been deeded to them for the exclusive purpose of constructing a church edifice. Opposite this pictorial symbol of cross-purposes and organizational muddle was a statement by Mrs. Eddy which undercut the trustees' demand for reorganization as the necessary condition for their proceeding with the church building. In answer to the question, "If not ordained, shall the Pastor of the Church of Christ, Scientist, administer the Communion,—and shall members of a Church not organized receive the Communion?" she wrote, in part:

> It is not essential to materially organize Christ's Church. It is not absolutely necessary to ordain Pastors, and to dedicate Churches; but if this be done, let it be in concession to the period, and not as a perpetual or indispensable ceremonial of the Church. If our Church is organized, it is to meet the demand, "suffer it to be so now." The real Christian compact is love for one another. This bond is wholly spiritual and inviolate.[24]

The trustees, however, through a vigorous campaign convinced a majority of the Boston Christian Scientists that reorganization of the church was the only way of remedying certain undoubted legal defects in the deed under which they had solicited building funds.[25] Mrs. Eddy, who held that the defects could be cured easily by agreement between the directors and trustees, nevertheless wrote the latter at once: "Let the church reorganize . . . let her pass on to her experience, and the sooner the better. When we will not learn in any other way, this is God's order of teaching us. His *rod alone* will do it."[26]

Shaken by this somber warning, the Boston congregation withdrew their support from the trustees, and all was again fluid and uncertain. To Ira Knapp, chairman of the board of directors, Mrs. Eddy wrote just before she moved to Pleasant View that there were two ways of resolving the conflict: one was through "a material hard fought battle," the other was summed up in the Bible verse, "Be still, and know that I am God."[27] The second way, she said, was her course and should be his. Her view of her leadership in relation to Knapp was expressed in another letter written to him about the same time:

God will keep you, and when you hear His voice and can distinguish between the highest false sense that means well and the "still small voice" of God you will follow. Till then, God will lend me to you to distinguish for you what is the false and what the true direction.[28]

Within a week she had written an article reviewing the history of the way in which she had acquired and conveyed the lot of land for the Boston church. It was a complex process in which over several years she had had to take each step on faith, without precedent to guide her or evidence to convince her own legal advisors that she knew where she was going.[29] The article contained an admonition obviously directed to the troubled and resistant trustees:

As the ambassador of Christ's teachings, I admonish you: Delay not longer to commence building our church in Boston; or else return every dollar that you yourselves declare you have had no legal authority for obtaining, to the several contributors,—and let them, not you, say what shall be done with their money.[30]

In sending this article to *The Christian Science Journal* for publication, Mrs. Eddy assured the editor, Julia Field-King, that she had written it because she had to: "God seemed (as many times He has under severe need) to deprive me of all peace until I wrote it and then my sweet peace returned."[31]

Two days later she moved to Pleasant View, with the last words of the article she had just written ringing in her ears:

Of our first church in Boston, O recording angel! write: God is in the midst of her: how beautiful are her feet! how beautiful are her garments! how hath He enlarged her borders! how hath He made her wildernesses to bud and blossom as the rose![32]

The metaphor seemed to speak of an accomplished fact rather than an unresolved situation, but it was evidently referring to something more basic to her than the envisioned church building in Boston. This was the kind of imagery, drawn from the millennial prophecies of Scripture, with which Mrs. Eddy habitually clothed her vision of the supramundane Church—that Church which, in abstract metaphysical terms, she defined in *Science and Health* as: "The structure of Truth and Love; whatever rests upon and proceeds from divine Principle."[33]

The practical problem before her remained, however, the translation of her vision into the structural form, the base of authority, and the rules of procedure suitable for a temporal institution.

On a quiet summer afternoon at Pleasant View, Mrs. Eddy could feel that she had come home to a familiar world. Here were the broad vistas, the gentle contours, the green tranquilities of her childhood. Enhanced, to be sure, by additional minor charms, like the rambler roses spilling over the gazebo and the small pleasure boat on the pond. Yet almost literally she was living in a different universe from the one she had known as a child. Though she referred often to "the universe, including man," she was to refer also to "man, including the universe," and in the first edition of *Science and Health* had written of man as epitomizing the universe.[34] Time has made unmistakably clear that the universe she carried within her included not merely the placid landscape visible to the most casual visitor to Pleasant View but a good deal of unexplored wilderness and rugged mountain territory. It was a test of such visitors whether they saw only the Bow Hills or also the invisible crags and chasms. Even to some who met her a number of times over the years, the latter remained unsuspected.

So it was with William Dana Orcutt who, fresh from Harvard College, had gone to work in 1891 at the University Press in Cambridge. This well-bred young man, full of ideas of "the beautiful" which he had imbibed from Charles Eliot Norton at Harvard, soon became almost a son to John Wilson, head of the press and a highly regarded figure in his profession.

For ten years the University Press had been printing Mrs. Eddy's *Science and Health with Key to the Scriptures,* and Wilson had become a stout supporter of the author, though never quite accepting Christian Science himself. Through this association young Orcutt also came to know James Henry Wiggin, a Boston literary figure who had helped Mrs. Eddy extensively as editorial advisor on two major revisions of *Science and Health.*[35]

From the conversations of Wilson and Wiggin, Orcutt gained some sense of her formidable strength of character but he was unprepared for the quality that struck him most when, in the summer of 1892, he was sent to Pleasant View to go over some proof sheets with her. This quality, he later recorded, was her "motherliness."[36]

After their business was over, she had asked him to stay on for a little and tell her more about himself. Before he knew it, he was confiding to her his most ardent hopes and aspirations. "When I left Pleasant View that day," he wrote more than fifty years later, "I felt as if I had known her all my life."[37]

During the course of a friendly business association that lasted for eighteen years, Mrs. Eddy made no effort to turn the Episcopalian Orcutt into a Christian Scientist, although—in the book he wrote about her in his last years—he almost succeeded in making her out to be a neo-Renaissance humanist.

This dexterous if aberrant feat started with an early conversation between the two. When Mrs. Eddy one day asked young Orcutt why he was not interested in becoming John Wilson's successor at the University Press, he explained his dissatisfaction with American printing as compared with the typographical masterpieces of the fifteenth century, and concluded, "I want to devote myself to something in which there is beauty."

All the more reason for considering the opportunity offered by Wilson, Mrs. Eddy suggested. "Have you never realized that if a man has beauty in himself, he can put it into anything?" The conversation that followed played a large part in guiding Orcutt into his subsequent career as printer, writer, and bibliophile.

Many years later came a conversation with Dr. Guido Biagi, librarian of the Riccardi and Laurentian Libraries in Florence, custodian of the Medici, Michelangelo, and da Vinci Archives, a Dante scholar of some reputation, and subsequently Orcutt's close friend. Biagi's partial definition of a humanist, ancient or modern, as "one who holds himself open to receive truth unprejudiced as to its source," led Orcutt at their first meeting to tell him about Mrs. Eddy and *Science and Health*. This Harvard-Episcopalian description brought courtly approval from Biagi. "I am greatly interested in what you tell me," he commented. "We in Italy would surely consider Mrs. Eddy a humanist."

Probably no more misinformed though well-intentioned characterization of the Christian Science leader has ever been made. The gap between Mrs. Eddy's metaphysics and a philosophy grounded in faith in human culture would seem to be fairly conclusive. Yet a sentence in *Science and Health* that Orcutt singled out as especially significant to him does point to an essential though subordinate humanist element in her theism: "The divinity of the Christ was made manifest in the humanity of Jesus."[38]

It was obviously Mrs. Eddy's humanity rather than her spiritual leadership that attracted the humanistic Orcutt, and in a 1926 book he summed up his personal impression of her character in two paragraphs:

> *At first one might have been deceived by her quiet manner into thinking that she was easily influenced. There was no sug-*

gestion to which she did not hold herself open. If she approved, she accepted it promptly; if it did not appeal, she dismissed it with a graciousness that left no mark; but it was always settled once and for all. There was no wavering and no uncertainty. . . . To many her name suggests a great religious movement, but when I think of her I seem to see acres of green grass, a placid little lake, a silver strip of river, and a boundary line of hills; and within the unpretentious house a slight, unassuming woman,—very real, very human, very appealing, supremely content in the self-knowledge that, no matter what others might think, she was delivering her message to the world.[39]

It was quite a different matter with James F. Gilman. This self-taught artist from rural Vermont cannot properly be described as a young man at the time he turned up at Pleasant View in 1892, yet it is difficult not to think of him as such.

Actually he was forty-two and for almost twenty years had been teaching art at local academies and in the summertime traipsing the back roads as a roving painter, earning his room and board at prosperous farms by his drawings of the homesteads and his portraits of the family members. With a characteristic mixture of naïveté and introspective analysis, he later described himself as first appearing to Mrs. Eddy with a "childlike state of thought engendered by the sequestered way of art-practice in the country by-ways."[40]

Today his pictures enjoy a more sophisticated vogue among Vermonters, as a record—"affectionately rendered, exact and appealing"[41] —of the rural settings, houses, and life of the eighties in that attractive state. Gilman himself is described as a lanky redhead with a fiery temper—and also as a gentle, cheerful soul who loved talking with children and was always content with small and simple things: "a boy fishing, pigeons flying round a dovecote, the look of light on roofs."[42] The two descriptions are not incompatible, and both aspects are suggested in his later relations wth Mrs. Eddy.

In 1884 Gilman had become interested in Christian Science and was soon responding to it with all the eagerness of his idealistic temperament. In 1892 he felt "led" to come to Concord. Looking for something to do, he was engaged by Mrs. Eddy's photographer, S. A. Bowers, to make several sketches of Pleasant View which could be included with some photographed interiors and presented to her as a gift.[43]

So it was that on a fine day in mid-December he sat sketching details of the house from the rear lawn at a distance of about three hundred yards. But Gilman, for all the primitive simplicity of his art, was the sort of person who could sense chasms and caves hidden from the sight of less intuitive people. At one point as he sketched, "a *dark* figure"[44] came onto the upper veranda from the tower room, which he later learned was Mrs. Eddy's study. For more than fifteen minutes, as he continued his work, the black-clad figure walked vigorously back and forth the length of the veranda.

When he finished and started for the front of the house, Gilman found as he neared the balcony and looked up again at the figure walking there that, in the words of a letter he wrote to a friend the next day, "the impressiveness of the blackness, as blackness, grew upon my sense." He was especially struck by the Quaker-type bonnet, which was "so large and bent so around the head that no face was visible to me," and "the depth of the black to my sense seemed beyond description and left an impression upon my mind of sackcloth and ashes." This gave him "a weird feeling," he wrote his friend, "such as I have sometimes felt in dreams. . . . It has suggestions of work for me that I trust will find expression in appropriate action."

When he was introduced to Mrs. Eddy a few days later inside the house, she appeared to him to be "a small, bright, graceful appearing woman of sixty or sixty-five with white hair and with a small, slender, delicate hand with which she greeted me at the introduction."[45] After commenting on the wonderfully fine December weather, she remarked laughingly that he must have been astonished at the strange black garb he had seen her in a few days before, but it was so comfortable she liked to wear it for walking on the veranda. He replied, like a good New England typologist, that he "had been regarding it as a type of the darkness of materiality which she was contending with." This flash of insight into her own deepest feelings obviously struck a note for which she was not prepared, for at once she "turned away walking to a window and showed signs of being affected to tears." Gilman, puzzled, concluded that he must have "blundered."

After a minute, however, Mrs. Eddy returned, sat down, and began talking cheerfully with him about the beauties of the surrounding landscape and her acquisition of Pleasant View. Later she showed him the view from the upper veranda, took him around her study and living quarters, and even brought out the black garb so that he could see it was "perfectly harmless."

"She showed me everything with the pleasure of a child," Gilman wrote in his diary that night, then added:

> Her childlikeness impressed me the most, while the magnetic sense of personal presence is so little that it scarcely seemed I was

in the presence of anyone who could write Science and Health. *This state of things I have been studying on all the day since, and this evening I just begin to see that the impressive magnetic sense of presence is not to be looked for in one of high attainments in Christian Science, but just the opposite.*

This conclusion was reinforced when he and Bowers, the photographer, had Sunday night supper with Mrs. Eddy on New Year's Day. Bowers, who was not a Christian Scientist, said to her at one point, "Christian Scientists call *Science and Health* a kind of revelation from God, but I think you originated it from your own superior talent." "Oh dear, no!" Mrs. Eddy demurred. "I could not originate such a book. Why, I have to study it myself in order to understand it."[46]

After supper she explained Christian Science very simply to Bowers and impressed both men so deeply with a sense of God as Love that, according to Gilman, it became plain to them that "that glorious state of mind included all goodness, all reality, being perfectly satisfying, making lesser possessions, aims, or desires appear paltry and poor indeed."[47]

Her notes to Gilman show that Mrs. Eddy felt a special interest in this ingenuous but oddly percipient "young" man who had come to her, in his own words, as "a lonely, homeless wanderer." She even spoke of wanting to have him study with her if she should hold another Normal class for a select group of students.[48] But it was her adopted son, E. Foster Eddy, who took action and snapped Gilman up for a class which he himself taught in Boston at the end of January, 1893.

Gilman assumed that Foster Eddy was doing this at Mrs. Eddy's request, whereas the class was actually being held without her knowledge or authorization. When it was over and Gilman had returned to Concord, Mrs. Eddy at her next interview found his mental attitude so changed, so "material," that she dismissed him after fifteen minutes with a copy of "Pond and Purpose" to take back to his boardinghouse to study.

The following evening she summoned him to Pleasant View again. Then for the first time he looked for an hour or two into the darkness he had sensed at his first glimpse of her.

It began with her questioning him about the seven-day study of Christian Science he had just completed with Foster Eddy—and which she had just learned about. "Mr. Gilman," she asked him with what he later described as a mixture of anxious solicitude and tender reproachfulness, *"do you feel an added sense of consecration since you have been through the class?"* The answer was a reluctant no. Gradually she drew him out until finally he spoke with frankness. The first four evenings on which the class was held, he told her, Foster Eddy had seemed to grow in spiritual impressiveness with each lesson. Then, with the last three, the inspiration had drained away, until the final lesson had "nothing to it to speak of."

Mrs. Eddy began to pace the floor. Gradually her anguished concern for the whole movement came to the surface. Would it not be better, she asked almost despairingly, if there were no teaching at all and people were instructed simply through their own study of *Science and Health?* Her mounting distress went far beyond the Foster Eddy episode. "It isn't the personal feeling that agitates me," she explained. "I could take the dear boy to my arms and forget it all." But her momentarily overwhelming dread, she told Gilman, was for "the effect upon the Cause" of such spiritual immaturity and irresponsibility.

This seems to have been even more than a concern for a cherished movement. Mrs. Eddy had written of Christian Science as an ontological discovery before she had ever thought of it as an organized movement. Her primary commitment, as she had shown in the dissolution of the first organization, was to the sharing of a vision of ultimate reality rather than the perpetuation of a particular human enterprise. The vision, to be sure, was far from being the God-intoxicated metaphysical geometry of a Spinoza or any other system of pure essences and celestial abstractions—without practical consequences or behavioral implications. In Christian Science, divine being implied human redemption, revelation implied development, the vision of good implied a revision of effort. But it was no accident that Mrs. Eddy defined the word "Church" first in terms of ideal structure, or the intrinsic nature of being, and only secondarily as a useful institution.

She was as likely to speak and write of "the Cause of Truth" or "the Cause of Christ" as of "the Cause of Christian Science." The dread she had to face and outface was not merely that a healing movement might fail but that the key to real being might be lost. The thing which seems to have lifted her out of this consuming *angst* time and again was the conviction that "the Cause" was Truth's, not hers.

So it was that when Gilman saw her the next week, he found her at the same time resigned, serene, and "joyous" as she quoted to him the Psalmist's words: "Commit thy way unto the Lord; trust also in him; and he shall bring it to pass."[49]

4

Nothing in Mrs. Eddy's life has been more astonishing to most people than her adoption in 1888 of a forty-one-year-old ex-homeopathic doctor as her son. This has been considered all the more remarkable because she had an actual son of almost the same age—living, to be sure, with a family of his own in the far-off Black Hills of South Dakota. Behind this unusual situation lay Mrs. Eddy's unusual history.

In the major revision of *Science and Health* which appeared in 1891, the first chapter opened by announcing her discovery of Christian Science in 1866, then went on to state that for many years God had been graciously "fitting" (later changed to "preparing") her for that event.

The gracious preparation included a series of disasters. One of these was her early widowhood six months after marriage. Then came the invalidism that followed the birth of her son three months later. Because she lacked both the health and the means to support him, the boy was subsequently taken away from her and entrusted to the care of another family, who afterward moved to what was then the Wild West.

Not until he was thirty-five did they meet again. Good-hearted, illiterate, rough and ready, the bearded stranger who came to see her in Boston at that time belonged to a world that was spiritually even farther from hers than his unsuccessful mining properties in the Black Hills were, geographically, from the thriving Massachusetts Metaphysical College where she was then teaching.

Despite the love they never ceased to feel for each other,[50] and a six-month attempt by the son and his family to settle down in Boston in 1887–88, it was clear that their paths were unalterably set in different directions. It was too late to combine either their modes or their views of life, so George and Nellie Glover and their four children returned to the Black Hills for good.[51]

Mrs. Eddy continued to correspond with them, sent money and advice to George from time to time, concerned herself with the education of her grandchildren, and concealed her disappointment as best she could. When George in 1891 sent her as a Christmas present a heart-shaped locket filled with gold dust from his mine, she thanked him warmly for his "heart," then sighed, "But dear son, I wish it was full of love for God, and I hope that it is."[52]

In this same letter she went on to send love to her "dear granddaughter, Mary," whose "letter was read with delight," and to "sweet Evelyn" and George's "dear wife," and told him to "take a good share for yourself, with a Mother's tender wish for the welfare and happiness of all." There was no lack of affection in her letters but a rather worried concern for the way the Glovers were bringing up their children. This was evident when, shortly after moving into Pleasant View, she wrote George with a touch of initial amusement in regard to his winning the last of several lawsuits over mining affairs:

> *I should think you would be the terror of the West in such matters. But dear child, when will you have a house for your family in a pleasant location and such an one as young ladies would feel pleasantly over inviting into it the highest toned society?*[53]

The family in Lead, South Dakota, may have had its own moment of amusement, or bewilderment, over her desire to export to their easygoing community the social standards of the eastern seaboard. There seems to be a hint of intended reassurance in fifteen-year-old Mary Baker Glover's letter to her a week or two later:

> *This is Sunday evening, and Father is away from home it is very lonsome without him for he makes our home so happy with his smiling face. . . . When he comes home he always kisses us all and says what would Grandmother give to see us all to gether again.*[54]

There was good will aplenty on both sides, but no possibility of the sort of mother-son intimacy for which both Mrs. Eddy and George Glover longed. On her side, a further element intensified the disappointment. During her last year or two in Boston her thoughts were turning toward her need for an executive assistant who might serve as both a spiritual aide and an eventual successor to her. Obviously, to have had a son who could fill that role would have satisfied a deep maternal craving on her part, not to mention the hope more often found on the father's side that an only son will carry on a cherished family enterprise.

In view of the bleak actualities of the Glover situation, Mrs. Eddy as usual did the unexpected thing, looked elsewhere for a surrogate relationship that would give her, personally, a "son" and, organizationally, an "heir," and settled on Ebenezer Foster.

Benny, as she soon came to call him, had a genuine devotion to her, a certain buoyancy and kindliness—and a fatally soft core. Following his study in the Massachusetts Metaphysical College he had made himself useful to her in many ways. But with the prestige conferred on him by his new position and the concurrent discovery that it demanded of him a total subordination of his personal inclinations to the needs of the movement, a conflict was set up in him that wrought havoc in what seems to have been a naturally sweet disposition.

Mrs. Eddy's letters show that she lavished upon him all the frustrated love of a long-deprived mother. He was her "darling Benny," her "dearest and sweetest of all the earth." To J. Henry Wiggin she wrote early in 1891, "He has some of the freshest, rarest qualities of mind I have ever found"—though she added that "one must know him to find this out, for they lie not on the surface of his character."[55] This last remark seemed necessary, since other people generally found him less enchanting than she did.

William Dana Orcutt, who had dealings with Foster Eddy while the latter held the post of Mrs. Eddy's publisher, wrote later:

> *I shall never forget the first time I saw him. He arrived at the University Press in a cab, which he had wait for him. This in itself was sensational, for our other clients, including Mrs. Eddy, made use of the less luxurious horsecars from Scollay Square. He was immaculately dressed, the climax being his magnificent fur-lined coat, fur cap, and the stunning diamond in his shirtfront. We found in him an agreeable personality, with a gratifying willingness to accept suggestions and make promises to co-operate; but there it stopped. Over and over again we had to refer details direct to Mrs. Eddy because Dr. Foster-Eddy was not in his office, and could not be located for days at a time.*[56]

At first Mrs. Eddy delighted in using him as her spokesman and giving him responsible tasks, but soon her realism began to sound the alarm to her affections. This she passed along to Foster Eddy in stern warnings against the beguilements of animal magnetism—her name for the material-mindedness which, as she saw it, would try to stop or reverse the action of the Christ in human affairs.

Mrs. Eddy's rebukes were never easy to take, and Foster Eddy found them unbecoming to his status as heir presumptive. When she wrote him in December, 1892, either to go to New York and take care of some urgent business or "let me know that you *will not* so that I can save the Cause through some other means,"[57] he replied with offended dignity:

> *A letter in your handwriting addressed to nobody, signed Mother, presumably intended for me is at hand. This is a very strange letter and to sense the most insulting one I ever received.*[58]

Mrs. Eddy immediately sent him a conciliatory note explaining that she had only wanted him to let her know one way or the other instead of keeping her in total ignorance of the situation, and in turn he came back at her with a letter both patient and patronizing:

Dearest Mother when will you know your child? There is no one in this world that has your interest and welfare and that of the cause that God has given to the world through you as I your own child has. I know more than you think I do and see farther than you think I see. . . . And my dearest Mother when you have demonstrated over those in your own household you have demonstrated over "the world, the flesh and the devil."[59]

The barb in the last sentence was obviously directed at such household members as Calvin Frye and Laura Sargent, whom he believed to be undermining his position with Mrs. Eddy. It is unlikely that these well-drilled soldiers would actually have dared to criticize Foster Eddy to his mother; but, leading the sort of garrison life they did at Pleasant View, it would be surprising if they never resented his getting away with major insubordination while they were held responsible for every slightest dereliction of duty.[60]

The episode recorded by James Gilman in regard to Foster Eddy's unauthorized Boston class is a case in point. Frye's diary records the acute physical suffering Mrs. Eddy went through on the night the class began, though neither he nor she at that time knew it was being held. When they later learned of it, they both connected the night's distress with Foster Eddy's clandestine defiance in taking a teaching position for which Mrs. Eddy felt he was quite unready. (It was generally accepted in the household that because of her extreme mental sensitiveness she often felt in her own body the needs and crises of the movement.[61]) Consequently, it was an undoubted shock to Frye that Foster Eddy went unscathed for the anguish he had caused her.

The fact is that Mrs. Eddy was determined to save her son for the great work she still hoped he might do, and when he gave her his excuse for holding the Boston class she accepted it. It was "not a good excuse," she told Gilman,[62] but it seemed the lesser of two evils not to make an issue of it. Later she wrote to another member of the class, one J. W. Keyes, M.D., who had been troubled by the quality of the teaching:

> *His teaching at that time was unexpected to me but by no means intended on his part to infringe upon my College rules. He is deeply read and taught in "Science and Health", has a classical education, has an excellent record in Homeopathic Practice, is a highly sensitive, affectionate, conscientious young man, and as such I have great anticipations for him and the blessing he will be to our Cause and the race.*
>
> *His mistake was, to accomodate others before consulting me.*

But my best students have gained their highest positions through mistakes and my strong corrections thereof. And he, it seems, is not an exception. The joy is to know as I do that each error seen, is overcome, *by him. Let us my dear Sir, be patient, be charitable, be willing to wait for the age to give us* experienced *Christian Scientists, taught of God by the things they suffer, then shall we have the true disciple and you and I will rejoice.*[63]

Several more years were to pass before Mrs. Eddy would have to make a conclusive choice between her adopted son and the movement she had hoped to see him serve. Few episodes in her life were to cause her more anguish and wavering, but her final decision was never basically in doubt. In an obvious sense, the Christian Science movement was her real "child." Through the early 1890's Christian Scientists were increasingly calling her "Mother," and to the Denver church at the time of its dedication in 1892 she wrote:

I, as a corporeal person, am not in your midst: I, as a dictator, arbiter, or ruler, am not present; but I, as a mother whose heart pulsates with every throb of theirs for the welfare of her children, am present, and rejoice with them that rejoice.[64]

Yet even this metaphorical motherhood would turn out to be less than an absolute value in her final resolution of the problem. In another ten years she would surrender the term "Mother" for the more impersonal title of "Leader." Just as the ultimate issue was not human motherhood but spiritual leadership, so the critical need, she came to feel, was not a mother figure but a Mother Church. For the Christian Science churches that were springing up around the country clearly needed a central organization that would strengthen, cherish, and coordinate their infant steps.[65]

5

In Boston, through the summer of 1892, the church that was and was not a church still wrangled over the form of its prospective embodiment. At one point the trustees, who had continued to solicit building funds from Christian Scientists even while refusing to build, returned this money to the donors at Mrs. Eddy's urging. It was their anomalous solicitation of funds that caused her in a letter to her attorney to refer to William Nixon, the moving spirit in the operation, as "a Western sharper."[66]

But all this was only surface turbulence. Underneath, the tide was running quietly and inexorably toward the formation of the sort of church organization that would lend itself, by her reckoning, to the transformation of its members' lives rather than the mere enlistment of their loyalties.

The great necessity, as Mrs. Eddy saw it, was a church that would be a training ground in the science and art of living Christianity—and of communicating this same ability to others. There would need to be at least the minimal machinery for developing practitioners and teachers, for it was the practice or demonstration of Christian Science through healing that would most effectively convey to others the vision of Christian perfection as operative truth rather than as mere insubstantial yearning.

Ideally, every Christian Scientist would be a practitioner or demonstrator of spiritual truth to the degree that he had grasped it, but to communicate the what, how, and why of his faith would require a good deal more than evangelistic fervor. The discipline of working with others at different levels of spiritual development would be at least as necessary as the discipline of cultivating increased spirituality in his own subjective experience.

To Mrs. Eddy it became increasingly clear that a corporate church body which would be the servant rather than the foe of its members' inner spiritual life was quite as essential as was, at this stage of experience, an articulated, organic body responsive to the government of Mind for the outward expression of individual identity.[67]

Not that she held it necessary or desirable for the church to reincorporate legally, as Nixon and his associates insisted must be done. On July 16, in an effort to prevent further strife, she did indeed consent to have the directors apply to the state for a new charter, but sometime in August she set her lawyers to search the Massachusetts statutes for an alternative method, convinced that a legal way would be found to form a church free of corporate limitations.

The search uncovered a provision in Section One, Chapter 39, of the Public Acts of Massachusetts that seemed providential in the circumstances:

> *The deacons, church wardens, or other similar officers, and the trustees of the Methodist Episcopal churches, appointed according to the discipline and usages thereof, shall, if citizens of this commonwealth, be deemed bodies corporate for the purpose of taking and holding in succession all grants and donations, whether of real or personal estate, made either to them and their successors, or to their respective churches, or to the poor of their churches.*[68]

Without wasting any time, Mrs. Eddy moved to form her church. The building site in Boston which had been returned by the trustees to Knapp (acting as unacknowledged agent for Mrs. Eddy) was quitclaimed by him to her—the first time she had held it in her own name. Three days later, on August 22, she wrote to Alfred Lang, treasurer of the building trust fund:

> *The First Church of Christ, as a title, is not allowed us by the Com. on Corporations in Boston.*
> *I will not give my land to a name that sinners suggest.* . . . *All that I have done or advised doing in the direction of organizing a church at this time has been at the beck of lawyers and infants in Christian Science. Now I shall deed my land* today, *and to certain persons that I know to be seeking and finding Christ's Church in their hearts, and let them use it for the benefit of Christian Science, for building thereon a Church edifice in which to preach Christ, Truth, and to* demonstrate love for one another.
> *I shall give a* sound *title or deed, and this way of donating my land is just as legal as to give it to a church that must organize.*
> *God meant* much *when he moved me to recommend the disorganization of the Church in Boston and His terrible meaning will be* fulfilled. *With love to you and the other Trustees.*[69]

On the same day she wrote to William B. Johnson, member of the board of directors and clerk of the church, a letter which indicated the basic direction of her thought. The church would seek legal status this time not by means of a charter but through the creation of a picked body of officers who by statutory law could be deemed a body corporate for the purpose of holding property and receiving donations for the church:

> *Drop all further movements towards chartering a church in Boston! God is not pleased with this movement that has been forced on me to attempt.*
> *Let there first be a Church of Christ in* reality—*and in the hearts of men before one is organized.* . . .
> *Now* incorporate AT ONCE *by whatever name you please.*[70]

How the final injunction was to be carried out was made clear by the series of events that followed. On the same day, at Mrs. Eddy's request, a letter was sent to twelve of her most trusted students by Johnson—who himself had served her with rocklike devotion for eight years. These students were invited to meet together on August 29 to form a corporation to be known as First Church of Christ, Scientist. The meeting was held in the Dartmouth Street rooms of Julia Bartlett, the earliest of Mrs. Eddy's students still to be active, loyal, and prominent in the movement. Present, in addition, were Ira Knapp and his wife Flavia, William B. Johnson, Stephen A. Chase, Captain Joseph Eastaman (an old salt, turned practitioner), his wife Mary, Foster Eddy, Mary W. Munroe (wife of the third trustee but thoroughly faithful to Mrs. Eddy), Janet Colman, Ellen Clarke, and a lady rejoicing in the name of Eldora O. Gragg.

There was a feeling of quiet excitement at the meeting. The fact that Mrs. Eddy had chosen twelve of her followers for the occasion was not lost on them, and the implied parallel might have seemed even stronger if they had known that one of them, Foster Eddy, was to prove something of a Judas before too long. On the whole, they were simple but vigorous people with strong convictions of their own. If they were willing to do Mrs. Eddy's bidding without question, it was because they were convinced that she spoke with the authority of revelation, but, except for Knapp,[71] there seems to have been little of the mystic in any of them.

Foster Eddy, straight from Pleasant View, had been entrusted with a message from Mrs. Eddy: in accordance with the new turn of events, they were to form the church *without* organizing as a corporation after all. He then read them the draft of a trust deed conveying the lot for the church building to a four-man board which would combine the functions formerly divided between the trustees and directors. This board was to be composed of three Boston men who were already serving as directors of the local congregation— Knapp, Johnson, and Eastaman— plus Stephen Chase of Fall River, Massachusetts. By virtue of the statute so conveniently found for this purpose, the new board of directors would be legally entitled to proceed with the building of the church and the conducting of its services.[72]

The small assemblage voted to accept the four men named as the "Christian Science Board of Directors" who should constitute "a perpetual body"[73] that would fill any vacancy occurring on its own board by vote of the remaining members. It was an act of startling faith—or, to those who felt like Nixon, an unconscionable leap into the authoritarian blue.

Mark Twain would see it as the beginning of "the Christian Science Trust" which he expected to absorb most of the American churches in the next century. A more sober eye might have seen it as the beginning of a significant experiment in the development of a federal system of church government, lay in character, theocratic in aim, but depending for effectiveness on a creative tension between powerful central authority and democratic self-government at the local level.

On September 2, after the trust deed had been formally executed, Mrs. Eddy wrote Mrs. Nixon, whose heart at the moment was divided between her husband and her leader:

> *I have settled the legal question for the Church, rather, God has. I tried to incorporate anew, but the legal arm said no! "We could not be chartered by our former name." I would not quarrel, but took the pacific step and God has done great things for us in giving us a church independent of religious or civil oppression.*[74]

By this time it was clear that Mrs. Eddy's strictures on "material" organization were strictures not on organization per se but on the sort of organization that would permit or invite control by material-mindedness or what she called "mortal mind." It was this, in her view, that had wrecked the church in its earlier congregational form. She was proceeding now, not by private mental blueprint but by a kind of intuitive empiricism, to take advantage of each new development that would permit her to shape the nascent organization toward a union of those who were prepared to accept her leadership as one of proven merit rather than of arbitrary power. Her authority, so far as these followers were concerned, rested on her understanding of divine Principle and was not to be confounded with personal domination.

At the time she wrote Mrs. Nixon, however, the church was still in the paradoxical position of having a self-perpetuating board and a congregation but no actual members. This extraordinary situation was rectified three weeks later when, at her request, the same students who had acted earlier met again at Miss Bartlett's. Before this meeting, William B. Johnson wrote solemnly in his diary, "Friday, the 23rd of September is a day of great moment in the history of Christian Science, the date of the founding of the Mother Church."[75]

This time, again in accordance with Mrs. Eddy's request, the students present voted themselves and twenty additional students "First Members of The First Church of Christ, Scientist, in Boston, Mass." New additions were made at succeeding meetings, both of invited First Members and of the applicants for regular membership who constituted the bulk of the growing church body.

The First Members, who participated until 1901 in the government of The Mother Church,[76] represented the vestigial element of congregationalism from the earlier organization—an element which continued in full force, however, in the self-governing "branch churches" throughout the country. All members of The Mother Church might also belong to local branch churches, but membership in the mother organization identified them more fully with the movement as a whole.

The church was to pass through further evolution before it took its final form, but its main lines of development were now set once and for all. Without historic model or consultation with others, Mrs. Eddy had found—by what later historians would describe variously as shrewdness, inspiration, or mere chance—a form of church government uniquely adapted to the growth of the new movement. "Every organization," she wrote a student on November 5, "every educational measure civil and religious, I have founded in Christian Science on a purely original plan—for God, not man, has suggested it to me."[77]

The intimate relations with Deity implied by such a statement raised the question not only for astounded outsiders but also for devout Christian Scientists: Who *was* Mrs. Eddy? And what, for that matter, was the nature of the directing power she referred to as God? As the world approached a century in which the authority of Christian dogma would drain steadily away, what was to be made of her claim to restore to the Christian Church the authority of practical demonstration?

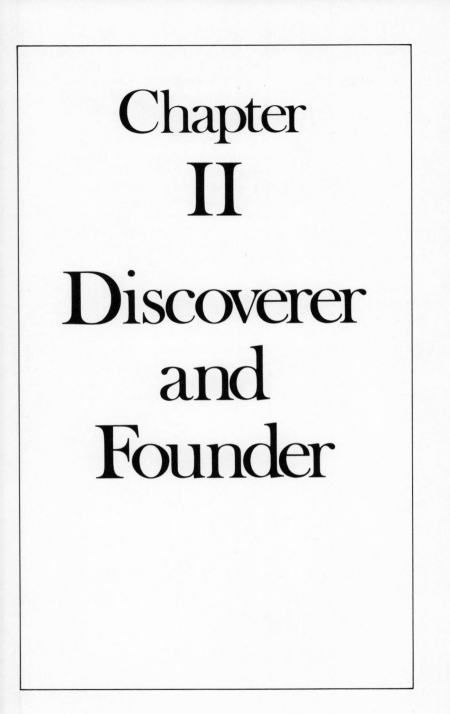

Chapter II

Discoverer and Founder

Discoverer and Founder

During 1892 Mrs. Eddy settled on the title that was to describe her relation to Christian Science. Henceforth she was to be known officially as its Discoverer and Founder. "Only," she wrote Julia Field-King, editor of *The Christian Science Journal,* "I beg of you to be *temperate* in using it."[1]

The double term implied the discovery of a truth and the founding of a system. Discovery suggests exploration and investigation, not merely passive recipience; it suggests that the fact or truth discovered exists independent of the discoverer, yet, once having been made, is historically inseparable from him. Hence Boyle's law, the Pythagorean theorem, the Heisenberg uncertainty principle.

If, in addition, the discoverer is able to systematize his discovery, establish rules for its practical application, perhaps institutionalize it, he may be said to have founded a system, discipline, or practice on what he has discovered. In such a case technology (in the original Greek sense of τέχνη as a kind of art) is not merely the child of pure research but is, rather, its alter ego.

A further point was involved in Mrs. Eddy's choice of the word "discoverer."

Christian Science, as she saw it and as its name implied, was to be recognized as not only a scientific discovery but also a Christian revelation.[2] As a consequence, some of her followers were persistently drawn to refer to her as the revelator rather than the discoverer of Christian Science. In her own writings, however, she rigorously abstained from using the word in this way.[3] Instead, in dozens of different contexts she wrote, "Science reveals . . ." and with that small phrase indicated a concept of revelation far removed from traditional supernaturalism.

If, as she believed, revelation was the ceaseless self-disclosure of a God who was infinite Mind and Principle, then it must be open to all; yet historically the fact seemed evident that it broke through only to those spiritual explorers who pushed beyond second-hand theological formulations to the direct confrontation of ultimate Truth. In this sense the biblical concept of revelation through chosen prophets[4] could be reconciled with the facts available to rational inquiry—as one might say that the rising sun "chose" the highest peak on which to shine first, though the choice was in fact the operation of laws quite oblivious of particular geological formations.

Using a similar metaphor, Jesus could speak of being sent by his Father to lighten the darkness of the world, as a ray of light is "sent" by the sun to do its "appointed" work on earth.[5] Again, when he prophesied (John 14:16) that God would send the Holy Ghost, Comforter or "Spirit of truth" to guide his followers "into all truth," he was foretelling, in Mrs. Eddy's view, that the truth he had exemplified in his own life would come as a universal, divine Science, demonstrable by all who accepted and practiced its revelation of the true nature of being.[6]

Because Mrs. Eddy interlaced the metaphoric language of biblical prophecy with the analytic language of metaphysics, it was easy to attribute to her a mysticism[7] that was more apparent than real—more a matter of religious temperament than of conceptual judgment. There was, however, an undoubted tension between the two, sometimes even a war, and some of her severest struggles during the next ten years would be to clarify for herself and others her place in the history of Christian thought and revelation.

One victory of reason over mysticism was her choice, after some deliberation, of the words "discoverer" and "founder" to define her relation to Christian Science. In the same letter to Mrs. Field-King in which she made this announcement, she wrote, "A moderate reminder of this great point of history is needed and will be so long as time lasts."[8]

The emphasis on moderation and temperate statement was necessary, for Mrs. Field-King was so intemperate in her adulation of her leader that she fell privately into virtual apotheosis, addressing her in such terms as "the divinely chosen of Divine Principle for a present Saviour."[9] It soon became clear that she herself had been less than divinely chosen as editor of the *Journal,* and she left her post at the end of August after only five months of active editorship. But the tendency she represented remained a factor in the background of Christian Science thinking for many years to come.

Mrs. Field-King's successor as editor was a man who was to play a prominent though sometimes uncomfortable role in the clarification of this issue. He was also to bring the *Journal* to a level of competence at which it would win a widening international audience of educated readers considerably more demanding than its early modest supporters.

At Nixon's suggestion as publisher, Mrs. Field-King had spent the first two or three months of her editorship traveling around the country to raise new subscriptions. Finally Mrs. Eddy had written to Nixon objecting to this and warning: "If she gets *10000* subscribers for the Jour. it will not change my views. They will be lost again unless the Jour. deserves them. You look at effects, I at *cause.*"[10] Septimus J. Hanna, the new editor, was a man who, she felt, would also look at cause.

Appointed, in his own words, "at the venerable age of 23"[11] to fill out an unexpired term as judge of the county court at Council Bluffs, Iowa, he was known thereafter as Judge Hanna, through a law career that included quasi-judicial public office in Colorado, where he went for his health in 1879. After careful study and investigation of Christian Science, he became profoundly convinced of its truth, experienced its healing, turned to its practice, and found an entirely new life opening up for him.

At the time he was called to Boston by Mrs. Eddy, he was forty-eight, a man of intelligence and character, with a distinction that drew comment without being exactly definable. When he had begun writing for the *Journal* a year or two earlier, Mrs. Eddy had detected an unusual talent, had invited him and his wife, Camilla, to visit her, and was at once drawn to them strongly. So it was natural for her to choose him as editor and Camilla as assistant editor when both posts fell vacant.

At the time Hanna had little idea of what the call meant. Only a few months before, he had written Mrs. Eddy:

> *Ever since I set aside false pride and made, so far as I knew how, the complete surrender to Truth, my pathway has been strewn with more flowers than, it seems to me, I deserve. The yoke has been, relatively, easy, and the burden light. I have been, I believe, willing to carry the cross. Have I not yet truly taken it up, or has it been in large part carried for me by another? Has the new interpretation of the Christ Love given through Science & Health measurably lifted from our shoulders the cross-bearing burden? Can it be that this is sacrificing all for Christ? If so, it is the sacrifice of exchanging pebbles for pearls, dross for gold.*[12]

Mrs. Eddy's reply led Hanna a step further toward understanding the demand that lay ahead of him:

> *Many thanks for your pleasant far reaching thoughts. You will find the cross is light—and sometimes heavy. Both conditions*

are the weight we, not God, give it. Jesus said "my burden is light"—again he fainted under it.[13]

During his first visit to Concord in 1891, Hanna had come face to face with the question that was to lie behind all that he did as editor for the next ten years: Who *was* Mrs. Eddy? Afterward he had written her of the great lesson he had learned from the visit. He had seen most clearly defined "Mrs. Eddy, the personal, and Mrs. Eddy, the impersonal," or "Mrs. Eddy on the human plane, and Mrs. Eddy on the Mount."[14] What this meant in practical terms is not clear from his letter, but his evident intention was to draw a distinction between Mrs. Eddy acting as an inspired leader and Mrs. Eddy reacting as a human personality from the demands of her own leadership.

A few months after the Hannas were installed in Boston, Mrs. Eddy picked up this distinction in a letter she wrote them in regard to getting a new pastor for the recently formed church. The Reverend Lanson P. Norcross, an ex-Congregational minister who had been serving as pastor for the Boston congregation for two years, was not altogether satisfactory, she felt, and her thought was turning to her student John Linscott of Chicago as a possibility—but she was not very enthusiastic about having his wife, Ellen, come.[15] To the Hannas she wrote:

> *Here you see the personal and impersonal Teacher again. The personal says have Mr. Linscott come to Boston free to act [as Pastor] untrammeled and have his wife stay in Chicago. The impersonal rebukes me for this and says, As ye would that others should do etc.*[16]

A fortnight later she wrote them again:

> *The personal Mrs. Eddy is pliant as wax, the impersonal impregnable to wind and wave. In the spiritual altitude of the latter I stand alone, none can see from my standpoint there. . . .*
> *The Boston pulpit needs just the right man, one who "is more than a prophet." Such an one would hear and obey the divine order. No matter if he could not stand face to face with the Father, he would obey without it.*[17]

The following day Hanna replied with a letter which struck the keynote of his thirty-year service to Mrs. Eddy and her church:

> *He would be a poor general who did not issue his orders and place his men, to meet the tactics of the enemy. And he would be a worse than useless subaltern who did not promptly obey those orders though they changed an hundred times a day.*

We either have a Godgiven *Leader, or we have* none. *This is the issue. We must meet it.*

When I enlisted in this Army I enlisted to obey orders. We are under divine orders, and you are their interpreter. I have but to discern your wish to know what my orders are.[18]

About the same time—March, 1893—Mrs. Eddy wished to replace Captain Eastaman on the Board of Directors with Joseph Armstrong, the Kansas banker whom she had already made publisher of the *Journal* in place of Nixon. Simple soul and outstanding healer that Eastaman was,[19] it was becoming all too clear that he lacked the qualities for the new responsibilities of the directorship, and so she sent him a letter with what General Douglas MacArthur might have described as a hint with the force of an order:[20]

The healing of my students changes its stages as they learn from experience. It starts a marvel of power and then becomes a marvel of grace. *The latter is gained by the spiritualization of practice which acts on the moral more than the physical degree of healing, but is sure to produce the latter which never relapses. More of the spirit than letter is required to reach this Christ-stage of healing sickness and sin. This, dear one, is what I want you to attain. Holding an office in Christian Science would be a hindrance rather than a help in the practice of healing.*[21]

Eastaman resigned. Comforting him over the stir of gossip surrounding the other Directors' dissatisfaction with him, she assured him that she did not believe the gossip, that it would kill itself, but that she knew it would "die sooner after your present resignation that will quiet the *envy* at your success in healing."[22] And to William B. Johnson as Clerk of the church, she wrote: "My hope is fulfilled and Capt. Eastaman is a *great-hearted honest man.* I thank God for this."[23]

At the same time Mrs. Eddy had found the pastor she needed for Boston—another ex-Congregational minister, the Reverend D. A. Easton, to whom she wrote on March 10:

In consequence of the hungry calls for spiritual help that come to me from Boston . . . I feel it is my duty to state to you the special need of my old church in that city. It is in short a revival. An outpouring of love, of the Spirit *that beareth witness. I found it essential, when the pastor of this church, to lead them by my own state of love and spirituality. By fervor in speaking the Word, by tenderness in searching into their needs—and specially by feeling myself and uttering the spirit of Christian Science—together with the letter. . . .*

Have your sermons not at all commonplace but well chosen, eloquent, and adapted to the Boston high culture.[24]

With the formation of the new organization, the question of authority had taken on a new urgency, almost a new dimension. As if to keep the matter in perspective, Mrs. Eddy published in the March *Journal* an article which reminded her readers that scientific progress demanded obedience to Principle, to the impersonal law of Love. "Obedience," she wrote, "is the offspring of Love; and Love is the Principle of unity, the basis of all right thinking and acting."

This, as she developed the theme, was something very different from a demand for personal bootlicking or an encouragement to run to her for advice in every contingency:

It is difficult for me to carry out a divine commission while participating in the movements, or modus operandi, of other folks. To point out every step to a student and then watch that each step be taken, consumes time,—and experiments ofttimes are costly. According to my calendar, God's time and mortals' differ. The neophyte is inclined to be too fast or too slow: he works somewhat in the dark; and, sometimes out of season, he would replenish his lamp at the midnight hour and borrow oil of the more provident watcher. God is the fountain of light, and He illumines one's way when one is obedient. The disobedient make their moves before God makes His, or make them too late to follow Him. Be sure that God directs your way; then, hasten to follow under every circumstance.[25]

The tone of authority in such a passage was obvious enough; its validity would have to be tested by what she—and her followers—did.

2

While Boston affairs particularly engaged Mrs. Eddy's attention, Concord was the laboratory in which she distilled her messages. In life at Pleasant View were to be found the simple elements of her developing leadership.

Nothing in her largely rural background had prepared Mrs. Eddy for the command of a world movement. At times she was almost overcome by the wonder as well as the responsibilities of the task. Only God, she repeatedly insisted, could possibly make her equal to such unpredictable demands, as only He had enabled her to write so unaccountable a book as *Science and Health*.

She found a precedent for her sense of dependence on divine

power in the Hebrew prophets and the words attributed to Jesus: "The Son can do nothing of himself, but what he seeth the Father do. . . . I can of mine own self do nothing."[26] In a poem entitled "Christ and Christmas," which she wrote early in 1893, the link between the mission of Jesus and the writing of *Science and Health* was made explicit in one stanza:

> As in blest Palestina's hour,
> So in our age,
> 'Tis the same hand unfolds His power,
> And writes the page.[27]

Early in March Mrs. Eddy conceived the idea of enlisting James Gilman[28] to work with her on illustrations for this poem, in an effort to translate its rather mystical and cryptic language into a graphic symbolism that would reinforce the basic meaning of the verse. Other poems of hers were later set to music as hymns; this was her sole experiment in matching verbal metaphor to visual symbol.

What seems to have suggested the project to her was the publication of Phillips Brooks's "O little town of Bethlehem" in an illustrated version.[29] Gift books of this sort were very much in vogue at the time, with illustrators ranging from Aubrey Beardsley to Edwin Abbey, but Mrs. Eddy's aim went far beyond producing an attractive gift book, as Gilman's execution fell far short of acceptability at the critical level.

In the diary he kept during the months they worked together,[30] Gilman frequently noted the "childlike" eagerness with which Mrs. Eddy discussed ideas for the illustrations and examined his preliminary sketches. Both of them were in some sense primitives in relation to the arts of poetry and painting, but in moral earnestness they might have been Dante Alighieri and Gustave Doré working out illustrations for the *Divine Comedy*. Except that the heart-searchings recorded in Gilman's journal--the painful struggles to attain the purification of motive that would make him "worthy" of his assignment—belonged unmistakably to the world of Puritan introspection, of Bunyan's *Grace Abounding* and Edwards's *True Awakening*. And Mrs. Eddy's demand that "Art must not prevail over Science"[31] shared the Calvinist theologian's scrupulous insistence on the sovereignty of God's will.

The finished product of their collaboration would be described variously as a revelation of God's purpose in history, a worthless piece of amateurism, a blasphemous attempt to exalt Mrs. Eddy to the level of Jesus, a pleasant Christmas gift, a work of art comparable to that of "the oldest of the old masters," an example of Victorian kitsch, a noble experiment that ended up as a denominational embarrassment, a book of profound hidden wisdom, a helpful aid in understanding Christian Science healing in relation to primitive Christianity.[32]

While the more scornful critics have used "Christ and Christmas" to discredit the seriousness of Mrs. Eddy's work as a whole, some Christian Scientists have professed to find in its visual symbolism intimations of a higher truth than is set forth in the reasoned metaphysics of *Science and Health*. A middle-ground view holds it simply to be Mrs. Eddy's exploration of the possibility of embodying spiritual truths in material symbols, the question that came to a focus for all Christians in the historical centrality of the incarnation.

It was all very well to say in the "scientific statement of being" that Spirit was real and matter unreal, but the abstract statement had to be translated into concrete living—and that demanded art as well as Science. Christianity, one might say, was the art of living divine Science in human circumstances. It was the Word made flesh. By analogy, must it not be possible also to convey the "scientific" reality behind the shadow-play of material appearances by art forms and figurative representations drawn from the world of shadows, but under the control of spiritual sense?[33]

These were large issues to be raised in connection with the production of a Christmas gift book by a self-taught artist from rural Vermont and an untrained theologian from rural New Hampshire. To Mrs. Eddy and Gilman the undertaking seemed a spiritual enterprise more gripping than any of the adventure-strewn voyages recorded by Captain Eastaman. This one was carefully logged by Gilman during the six-month course of alternating calm and storm, and the log revealed a Mrs. Eddy so various as to escape neat psychological pigeon-holing.

There were days when she clapped her hands with delight over the drawings he showed her, when the two of them laughed lightheartedly over an unintentional comic effect,[34] when she could hardly wait for his arrival to take him out on the veranda to show him a freak of light on the distant landscape, when in general she seemed so childlike and unremarkable in her attitude that Gilman afterward was beset with sudden doubt as to how she could be the chosen vessel of truth or the writer of *Science and Health*.

Then there were times when she stood over him like Wordsworth's "Stern Daughter of the Voice of God"[35] and made him sharply aware that unless he could learn to obey her explicit directions with the understanding that they were not personal commands but logical necessities, she would have to call the whole thing off. Under the storm cloud of her displeasure, he would have long hours of despair or rebellion: despair at what he felt to be his own spiritual obtuseness, rebellion against what seemed to him needless exactions or undeserved rebukes—based, so he sometimes felt, on her own failure to remember what she had said earlier or to recognize the practical requirements of his situation.[36] But always he came at last to the conclusion that there was a necessary lesson for him to learn, a purification of character to go through, and when he returned to her in that spirit, as the next diary entry repeatedly shows, the cloud would be gone.

There were sessions when Mrs. Eddy confided to him some of the problems in Boston and elsewhere that were troubling her, others when she talked to him with authority on the metaphysics of Christian Science, still others when she listened quietly to his own views of life and art. On one occasion as they discussed the details of the design for an illustration of Christian Science healing—a woman, vaguely suggestive of Mrs. Eddy, raising a man from a sickbed—Gilman held forth on the "most spiritually appropriate disposition"[37] of the woman's hands and arms:

> I reasoned that an attitude of peaceful composure and calmness born of perfect faith in omnipotent Spirit, even perfect understanding of God, should be considered as the most appropriate. I argued that the likeness of the Infinite would realize the perfect reality of all things, hence would have no agitation of mind as to the outcome of the healing thought of Divine Mind and therefore perfect repose and calm in the attitude of the healer would predominate. Mrs. Eddy's reply to this I can never forget. She said: "Yes, but Love yearns."

The incident is typical. On one side was Gilman's view—earnest, plausible, theoretical, bland—of the "appropriate" attitude to take in raising someone from a deathbed. On the other was Mrs. Eddy's practical experience—not only in healing the sick but even more in struggling to lift her students from the letter to the spirit of her teachings. This, in her own rueful words, was an experience "of patching breaches widened the next hour; of pounding wisdom and love into sounding brass; of warming marble and quenching volcanoes."[38] And all the time there was a world to be healed!

As Gilman continued with the work, the conviction grew in him that what he was experiencing was the strong discipline of a love that really yearned. Although, at low ebb and after a particularly strong difference of opinion with Mrs. Eddy, he could feel that "she was seeking my complete subjection to that point that would make me her abject slave," he ended each time by concluding that the enslaving element was actually his own self-conceit.

As an artist, Gilman was feeling in more temperamental terms what the officers of Mrs. Eddy's church felt when their cherished organizational plans ran up against her views of a necessity larger even than organization. Oddly enough, it may have been what Mrs. Eddy herself felt when her personal inclinations were forced to give way to unexpected but inexorable demands which seemed to her to come direct from God.

The small tempests that disturbed the work on "Christ and Christmas" were as much "illustrations" of the larger issue of leadership as were the sketches that produced them. After one such tempest Gilman wrote:

> Sunday was a day of great sorrow in which annihilation again seemed preferable to life in the flesh, a dark and sad day to me mentally, but it has left a sweet and sacred memory that I would not have effaced for any worldly recompense. I find that my experience in this was exactly like that described in the first of the three states in "Pond and Purpose." . . . Toward Sunday evening I began to be able to appropriate God's promises to those who exercise faith and humility. . . .
>
> Monday morning I went up again, this time prepared and with my brushes, as she had before requested. I was ushered into the library as usual and awaited with confidence born of Spirit, Mrs. Eddy's appearance. Soon I heard the gentle rustle on the stairs that I had learned to know, followed by her appearance in the doorway. Instantly I felt that she perceived the state of my mind upon seeing me, as I arose and advanced a step to meet her and receive her extended hand of welcome. She retained the hold upon my hand . . . and with earnest solicitation said yearningly like a mother, "It seems hard to bear, I know. You won't feel hard toward me, will you? I felt I must be severe because you needed it; but it was hard for me to be so. . . . Oh!" she said with great feeling, "You don't know what burdens I have borne through the necessity I have felt for rebuking students, but who could not receive my rebuke as coming from Love for them. This is the great test of the true student."

Like the Gandhi disciple who remarked of his master, "He is more right when he is wrong than we are when we are right,"[39] Gilman's final faith extended even to those occasions on which Mrs. Eddy was clearly wrong by any reading of the external facts.

There was, to take a trivial but revealing instance, the time she approved a preliminary sketch of some cherubs he had roughed out for one of the illustrations. When he brought her the finished picture she at once denied ever having seen or approved the design. Gilman was understandably incensed—until he realized that in the time following her acceptance of the preliminary sketch, he had become so absorbed in the pleasure of developing the cherubic little figures as to lose sight completely of the glimpsed qualities of thought they were meant to symbolize. Ergo, to Mrs. Eddy's eyes the end result was literally a different picture, as someone viewing a presumptively abstract painting might see a "different" work of art if he suddenly recognized it as a straight representation of patterned fields long familiar to him.

However one looked at it, working with Mrs. Eddy was a very strict discipline. It was not the discipline that Gilman would have received in a first-class art school, but it was the kind that was standard at Pleasant View.

3

Chicago had played a special part in the development of Christian Science. Like the vigorous young architect from Boston, Louis Sullivan, who had stepped off the train in Chicago, looked around him, stamped the ground, raised his hand, and announced with the vatic aplomb of a junior Whitman,

THIS IS THE PLACE FOR ME[40]

Christian Science found in the energetically growing city an unabashed expectancy that took the new to its bosom and made any good thing seem possible.

In 1884 Mrs. Eddy had taught a class of twenty-five in Chicago, then had given a public lecture on the text, "Whom do men say that I am?" to a couple of hundred people who had little idea who she was.

Four years later she had addressed a wildly acclamatory audience of four thousand in Chicago's Central Music Hall, and the press had reported in vivid detail the triumphant visit of the "Boston prophetess."

Now, early in 1893, she was receiving enthusiastic invitations from Christian Scientists in that city to stay with them when and if she came out to the great Columbian Exposition that would draw visitors from all over the world.

But world fairs had little appeal for Mrs. Eddy, and this one she quickly dubbed "Vanity Fair" in her private correspondence. In a brief notice in the April *Journal* she explained to her followers why she would not be attending:

> *I have a world of wisdom and Love to contemplate, that concerns me, and you, infinitely beyond all earthly expositions or exhibitions. In return for your kindness, I earnestly invite you to its contemplation with me, and to preparation to behold it.*[41]

There remained, however, the question of the participation of the Church of Christ, Scientist, in the exposition. Mrs. Eddy's most prominent student in New York, the eloquent and determined Augusta E. Stetson, was plumping heavily for aggressive, imaginative action. She had got in touch with some of the leading Christian Scientists in Chicago, and soon there was a concerted demand that the church should seize this unparalleled opportunity to bring Christian Science before the world.

Mrs. Eddy was at first cool to the idea, but yielded finally to the pressure. By this time, the Christian Scientists had been told by the fair officials that there was not one inch of space left for an exhibit, but they had no intention of yielding to that "negative suggestion." Edward A. Kimball of Chicago, in some ways Mrs. Eddy's most able student, was designated by her to take charge of the situation. Kimball brought to the assignment a combination of executive skill, serene common sense, and what might be called spiritual statesmanship, before which all obstacles went down. When the exposition opened, the Christian Scientists had a good-sized space in an unusually advantageous position, a well-designed exhibit built around Mrs. Eddy's books, a flood of interested visitors, and compliments from all concerned.

So far, so good, but there were issues involved that went far beyond anything the gratified Christian Scientists could see. Mrs. Eddy—permissive, even congratulatory—kept her own counsel and continued in private to refer to the exposition as Vanity Fair.

Meanwhile, a related opportunity which seemed to be even more promising had opened up for the church. This was in connection with the so-called World's Parliament of Religions, held as an auxiliary of the fair in Chicago and bringing together representatives of all the religions of the world. This was ecumenism leaping forth full-voiced if not full-panoplied, and on a scale probably not equaled until the World Conference on Religion and Peace in Kyoto seventy-seven years later.[42]

In retrospect the Parliament of Religions looks as superficial an effort to promote religious solidarity among radically divergent faiths as do the abortive attempts of a later period. At the time, however, it seemed to be ushering in a bright new era of interfaith understanding, and the Christian Scientists were eager to be a part of it. Once again Mrs. Eddy had mixed feelings; once again the ardor of her followers carried the day; once again the delay in applying for inclusion made difficulties; and once again Edward Kimball's calm intelligence won not only the cooperation of the officials but in addition their warmly expressed respect for the cause he represented.

As a result, Christian Science was the only faith invited both to hold a denominational "Congress" of its own and to make a presentation of its teachings at a plenary session of the "Parliament." No group was more conspicuous by the numbers and zeal of its attendants at these meetings. On September 20 four thousand Christian Scientists crowded into the great Hall of Washington for their own congress, and the *Chicago Inter-Ocean* reported the next day:

> One of the best congresses yet held in connection with the Parliament of Religions, judged by number and interest, was that of the Christian Scientists which took place yesterday afternoon in Washington hall.
>
> For two hours before the hall opened crowds besieged the doors eager to gain admission. At two o'clock, the time set for opening the proceedings, the house was filled to the roof, no seats being available for love or money. The delegates came from all parts of the country. Rev. Mary Baker G. Eddy, the founder of the organization, chose not to be present, but her devoted disciples were there, and the large audience sat through a programme that lasted to 7 o'clock in the evening without showing signs of weariness.

The Reverend Mrs. Eddy, however, had been finding the preparation for this and the following meeting a considerable burden. Back in May she had written to Hanna, "I see great aims and results both *pro* and *con* to this Congress business." The power of the established religions, she added, was against them—"unless it be pagan religion derived more from nature than man."[43] Some of her disaffected students who were closer to "mind cure" than to Christian Science were seeking independent representation at the fair, and she warned that they would have more psychological appeal to "the scholarly thinkers of our time" than the true Scientists, who would catch only the pagans. "This would delight priestcraft for it only waits opportunity to classify us thus."[44]

Nevertheless, once committed, she urged careful preparation for the two meetings, sending out instructions through Hanna to the speakers for the Christian Science Congress. Their remarks should be tempered to the understanding of the non-Scientists who might hear them or read the press reports of their talks, and they should "refrain from antagonizing other churches, schools, and theories."[45] The occasion was to be fraternal, not polemic.

Yet an undertone of misgiving persisted through her increasing encouragement of her students' efforts. To Mrs. Stetson she wrote that *if* fair play were given to Christian Science at the world fair, this "would do more towards Christianizing the race than all else" except the Bible and *Science and Health;*[46] but she had a lingering presentiment that the atmosphere would actually be more hospitable to the Oriental seductions of Theosophy than to the New Testament primitivism of Christian Science.

When the meeting described by the *Chicago Inter-Ocean* took place, with Foster Eddy as chairman, such anxieties seemed groundless. The welcome given by Charles C. Bonney, president of the World's Congress Auxiliary of the Columbian Exposition, was all that Mrs. Eddy could ask for:

> *No more striking manifestation of the interposition of divine Providence in human affairs has come in recent years, than that shown in the raising up of the body of people which you represent, known as Christian Scientists.*
>
> *We had come to the state of the world in which science was called infidel. . . . The Christian Scientists were therefore called . . . to restore the waning faith of many in the verities of the sacred Scriptures. . . .*
>
> *The common idea that a miracle is something which has been done in contravention of law is to be wholly discarded and repudiated. . . . It is mere ignorance of those laws that leads men to think that. . . .*
>
> *Who can doubt, in witnessing the tremendous events that are now transpiring in our midst, that the day of miracles is as surely here as it was eighteen centuries ago.*
>
> *To restore a living faith in the efficacy of prayer—the fervent and effectual prayer of the righteous man which availeth much; to teach everywhere the supremacy of spiritual forces; to teach and to emphasize the fact that in the presence of these spiritual forces all other forces are weak and inefficient—that I understand to be your mission.*
>
> *That you may so fulfil this mission that not only all Christen-*

dom, all the great bodies to which I have referred, but the whole world and all its worshippers of God and servants of man, may have cause to rise up and call you blessed, is my sincere and fervent wish.[47]

Gratifying as this and the rest of the meeting were to Christian Scientists, there was still to come the session of the Parliament of Religions two days later at which Judge Hanna would read an address by Mrs. Eddy to a formidable audience, including representatives of the Christian churches, of Judaism, Islam, Hinduism, Buddhism, and assorted lesser faiths. The address was composed of selections from her books arranged to set forth certain fundamentals of Christian Science.

When September 22 came and Hanna read the speech to an exceptionally large general audience, there were interesting undercurrents on the platform. Swami Vivekananda, who was creating something of a sensation at the parliament and introducing thousands of Americans for the first time to the world of Hindu thought, was observed to be listening to Mrs. Eddy's speech with concentrated attentiveness. On the other hand, the Reverend Joseph Cook of Boston was visibly squirming, red-faced and tight-lipped, in a state of barely suppressed outrage.

Eight years before, the conservatively Protestant but immensely popular Cook had grudgingly allowed Mrs. Eddy ten minutes at one of his famous Monday lectures at Tremont Temple to reply to a sharp attack on Christian Science made from his platform a week or two earlier.[48] At that time Cook's audience of two thousand had listened to her in silence. Now her speech was greeted with warm applause, and the Reverend J. H. Barrows of Chicago, chairman of the meeting and of the General Committee on Religious Congresses, had gracious words for her faith and her followers. On his way out of the hall afterward, Cook exploded into nonecclesiastical invective, but the Christian Scientists who overheard him exulted like Moses and Miriam that the Lord had triumphed gloriously and the horse and his rider had been thrown into the sea.

That night Kimball wrote Mrs. Eddy:

The Judge was splendid. *Mrs. Barrows said to me after adjournment that it was a noble paper—and that she was also very much interested in our Congress. . . .*

We have made a very decided impression. It is as you say "the dawn of a new day."

In the warfare against false theology and demonology, we will now work from the standpoint of an acknowledged status.

Jos. Cook who had given the orthodox or Cook's view of the Bible chemicalized terribly—and all the ministers who were on the platform were very uneasy.[49]

Letters and telegrams of rejoicing poured in to Pleasant View. The whole household, including Mrs. Eddy herself, was caught up in a tide of jubilation as reports came in of the excellent impression made by the Christian Science presentation in general and her paper in particular.

Then came a letter from Judge Hanna which changed the whole situation:

The Gospel was preached to all nations on the 22d. You did the preaching. God was with us.

Your prophecy that the theologians wd try to crowd us out at the last moment was literally fulfilled. They did try but failed. . . .

The demonstration [i.e., working out] on the whole was a grand one, but, I suppose, we could hardly hope that there wd not be some mishaps.

We had to meet this alternative. [Your] address must go into the newspapers. Their reporters were there with instructions to report; we must either rely on their garbled work, or give them copies. The Dr. [Foster Eddy], Mr. K[imball] & myself concluded it was best to give them copies, which we did in full, with the explanatory addendum attached [the brief note explaining that the paper was by Mrs. Eddy although read by Hanna]. What was my chagrin when they appeared with it left out & it appeared to be my address. . . .

The thing was another effort by M.A.M. to cut you off & set some one else up in your stead as the Leader.[50]

The effect of the letter was immediate. Like a chemical precipitant, it brought forth in definitive form the objection which had clouded her approval from the start of the enterprise.

4

Here was a small mishap, a familiar instance of the wrong attribution of a speech by the newspapers, easily if not altogether adequately corrected by a letter to the editors. Mrs. Eddy's response to the slip could be attributed either to the wounded vanity of an author or to the incident's confirmation of her initial suspicion of the whole undertaking. But what it involved at a deeper level was the complex issue of spiritual leadership in a highly expedient world.

There was, for instance, the question of obedience. Hanna had written her seven months earlier, "When I enlisted in this Army, I enlisted to obey orders."[51] But in the interest of casual common sense he had brushed her orders aside in giving her address to the reporters. Now she reminded him of her "solemn charge" to him when she gave him the manuscript that it should not pass out of his hands "until it was delivered by you to Mr. Kimball and he should promise you to *let no one see it* until it was printed in the World's Fair book."[52]

Closely related to this curious demand was the unusual labor Mrs. Eddy had put into the compilation of passages from her writings to form her address. Writing a month earlier to Mrs. Hanna about the "incredible" difficulty she was encountering in her work for "Vanity Fair," she pointed out the need to have selections that would "elucidate" and not merely state truth. "The bald statement without self evident explanation," she wrote, "is blinding to eyes not opened or to those trying to be opened."[53]

Now, following the newspapers' publication of the full text of the address, she wrote her student, Caroline Noyes, in Chicago:

> *Stop all mental effort, or any kind, to get my address in the Parliament book. Since the newspapers devoured it contrary to my solemn charge God has shown me by* signs *and* wonders *that it must not be published at this date. The dose is* too great, *the chemicalization will do incalculable harm. This is evidently why God has always kept me from concentrating portions of my works and publishing them as students have so often begged me to do.*[54]

The real bombshell was included in a letter to Kimball, to whom she had previously sent her warmest gratitude "for the wisdom, labor and success that are manifested through you in all this matter at Chicago."[55] Now she wrote him that "God has compelled me at last to do as He seemed to say plainly at first but I was turned aside,"[56] and in the letter she included two missives for Kimball to read and then send on to Messrs. Bonney and Barrows. Both enclosures took the same line, and both might well leave the recipients slightly stupefied.

The one to Barrows, who was to edit the official history of the Parliament of Religions, contained a reversal of Mrs. Eddy's promise to furnish him with the full text of her address for his book:

> *I am most grateful to you for the Christian charity and liberal sentiments you manifest to all religions. I thank you espe-*

*cially for your honorable endeavors in behalf of Christian Science
and shall cherish this memory in my heart of hearts. But I must
decline to have my address which Judge Hanna read before the
Parliament of Religions published in the World's Fair book which
is to contain these matters.*

*I was opposed to having my numerous students take part in
this World's Fair but yielded to their views on this subject. I
cannot see that it is a fit opportunity to test the heart of Christianity but I may be mistaken.*[57]

Hanna and Kimball were bewildered. Although they theoretically
accepted her view of Christianity as a science, it did not occur to
either of them that a physical scientist necessarily takes strict account
of any unruly fact which cannot be squared with his experimental
hypothesis. This was one of many occasions when Mrs. Eddy's more
exacting approach caused her to respond to failure in a detail of
performance by probing for a fundamental error in the whole approach, while her followers were content to brush aside the uncomfortable detail and sun themselves in an "approximate" success. For
her there was a clear distinction between even a useful experiment
and a successful demonstration.

In this case, her letter to Barrows indicated, it was "the heart of
Christianity" that was being tested by Christian Science participation
in the World's Parliament, and for all the outward cordiality of
reception it was clear that Mrs. Eddy's metaphysics stuck in the craw
of the orthodox churchmen present. "I have learned from bitter
experience," she wrote Kimball later, "that the head instructed before
the heart is ready, costs me and our Cause dangerous difficulties and
sore defeats."[58] Here she was getting close to the central issue: the
need for demonstrating the spirit rather than promoting the letter of
Christian Science metaphysics. But she was not yet able to define the
issue in terms that Kimball and Hanna could grasp.

Hanna was at first in a state of open rebellion. After defending
his action in giving her address to the papers, he expostulated with
her over the letters she had sent to Barrows and Bonney:

*I cannot think if you had waited until a calmer moment
governed that you would have been thus impelled. Nor do I
think that under cooler moments you would have written letters
to these gentlemen which . . . would cast the whole responsibility
upon the students who were active in this matter. This . . . places
all of us who have been laboring from what we conscientiously
believed to be your wishes and the best interests of the cause, in*

the position of subserving rather our own ambitious ends. In view of the history of this matter I feel the accusation to be unjust and cruel. It surely was not our loving Mother who said that. . . .

If I was capable of understanding anything about your wishes they were this: First, if we were to be the only Christian Scientists recognized, and second, if we were permitted to make a presentation of Christian Science to the General Parliament, we should proceed; otherwise not. This surely was the tenor of your letters; and was the effect of all the correspondence between Mr. Kimball and myself from that stage on. . . . With a faithfulness and skill which I have never known equalled, and through a chain of circumstances which seemed to me to be God-directed, he [Kimball] secured all that was required.

Now to have him placed in the attitude of a disobedient and over-ambitious student, and that too before the gentlemen with whom he labored, is so repugnant to my sense of justice, that I feel that I should be cowardly and servile not to enter my protest against it. . . . In view of all we had to meet and contend with, I am wholly unable to see that we were not fairly successful.

This, of course, was the issue at point. Hanna was quite sure that his judgment of the event's success was correct and hers was wrong. As the letter proceeded at endless length, he even seemed to be trying to force her to accept his judgment:

I believe the matter to have been God-appointed. I believe it to be fulfillment of prophecy. I believe it to have been a part of your great mission. I believe that for the first time in the world's history the Gospel was preached to all nations in a day. If one could have evidence that he was moved and protected by divine power, I had, throughout this trying ordeal. If I may not so believe, I should be inclined to question whether there is a God who moves in human affairs, and to doubt the divinity of your mission.[59]

Upon receiving this letter, Mrs. Eddy immediately wrote Hanna, "Will you publish in your next issue [of the *Journal*] an exact copy of your last letter to me and my reply as I shall write it . . .?"[60] She further indicated that if he was afraid to do this, he could resign his office as editor.

For several days Hanna struggled with his feelings, then finally he wrote her, "Last night the infernal spell was broken; the seven devils were exorcised." For days *Science and Health* had been a "stone" to him, while he had been "crying out from the belly of hell" and "reviling God." It was the same sort of turbulence Gilman had gone through when he felt Mrs. Eddy's demands to be unjust, and it ended with the same conclusion: there was something big for him to learn from what looked like a very small error.

"I did disobey your explicit orders," he wrote her, referring to his giving the text of her address to the newspapers. "The trust was a sacred one, and it was violated." Had he obeyed her, he added contritely, "I would not have been placed in a false position by being set up as the leader and author of your address, and you would not have been wronged by the attempt to crowd you out."[61]

The letter showed both dignity and humility, but it still missed the point. What it indicated was obedience rather than understanding. In her own correspondence at the time, Mrs. Eddy nowhere showed the slightest concern that anyone would think Hanna was the leader of the movement or the author of her works. In fact, her challenge to him to publish his first letter in the *Journal* implies an easy confidence that her leadership would not be threatened by anything he might say or do. Although she welcomed his contrition and wrote him a letter filled, in Hanna's words, "with the sweet oil of forgiveness,"[62] it was evident that he still had no idea of the major question that was really troubling her about the whole Parliament of Religions affair.

The real issue came to light only in the longer and in some ways more painful correspondence with Edward Kimball. On October 5 she had written him:

> You know not what you do! Since the newspapers took the heart of my works into their jaws there has an evil come from it that threatens our Cause with a blow worse than ever before befell it. . . . Already God's judgments are apparent; while you are flushed with a feeling of success.[63]

On the same day Kimball wrote her, "flushed" but not with success:

> I cannot tell you how sorry I am that everything I now say seems to be evidence of evil. . . .
>
> Whatever satisfaction I may have felt concerning the Congress has turned to bitter gall and I greatly, deeply deplore the hour when I was urged to work in its behalf.
>
> Not in one solitary particular have I ever failed to try to do what I thought you would approve of. . . .
>
> I have done the best I knew how to do and if for this I am condemned, I shall have to endure until the day of peace shall come when we shall awake in His likeness and be satisfied.[64]

After further correspondence, Mrs. Eddy agreed to allow an abridgment of her address to go into the Parliament of Religions history, explaining to Kimball that her opposition to any publication of it was based on "God's demand of me not to part the raiment of Christ"—a demand which, from her first publication of *Science and Health,* had been a "specialty, as I understand, of my mission."[65]

As complications arose and endless letters flowed back and forth in regard to other histories whose editors wanted to publish her address, her picture, and accounts of the Christian Science Congress, Kimball struggled to understand her demands, refusals, reversals—and his own evident failure to interpret her wishes and meaning to her satisfaction—while at the same time groping toward the reason for her growing objection to the whole enterprise.[66]

At Mrs. Eddy's insistence, however, he continued with the necessary chores until the business was finished, whereupon she wrote two of her students in Chicago, "Dear Mr. Kimball has got out of it *wisely* and at great toil and vexation to himself,"[67] while to the Hannas she wrote that he had shown "great business talent and Christian integrity."[68] To Kimball she sent final thanks "for the care and wisdom you have used in accomplishing your part of the World's Parliament of Religions."[69]

Why, then, all the anguish in their earlier correspondence?

More than eighty years later many of the hints in Mrs. Eddy's letters come clear. When social historians refer back to the Parliament of Religions, they almost unanimously see its chief or sole significance in its popular introduction of Oriental religion to America.[70] If Christian Science is mentioned at all—and this is rare indeed—it is in the context of the impression made by such non-Christian exotica as Vedanta, Baha'i, and those arcane forms of Oriental thought hitherto represented to Americans by Theosophy.

This is exactly what Mrs. Eddy predicted from the outset. Her letters about the World's Fair and its auxiliary Congresses are laced with concerned references to the Theosophists in particular and what she called "the Pagans" in general. Grounded as she was in Christian theism, she had a horror of a pantheism that substituted esoteric subtleties and mystical ecstasies for the simple spiritual disciplines of charity and humility.[71] Her insistence that her teachings must be understood as practical Christianity and not be turned into a set of metaphysical abstractions measured her desire to keep Christian Science from being confounded with the cosmic philosophies of the East.

That, however, is what happened at Chicago. It was a convenient way of disposing of an upstart heresy which showed such surprising and even alarming vitality. Far from making for greater unity between Christian Science and the traditional Christian churches, the Parliament of Religions crystallized opposition against Mrs. Eddy and the Church of Christ, Scientist.

At first she stood almost alone in recognizing this result. Kimball had written Calvin Frye a week after the Parliament meeting, "It is a step in the right direction and is the opening wedge which will lessen bigotry and tend to greater unity in Truth."[72] A month later, under the prodding of Mrs. Eddy's letters he had moved toward a more realistic assessment:

> There is no doubt but that the Christian (?) ecclesiastics were a good deal agitated during the progress of the Parliament. Their idea of a Parliament had been of a place where a lot of religious people of all creeds & beliefs could be gathered, and there converted to their religion. They did not like it when the orientals stood their ground and presented a high degree of morality as a rule and intimated that the Christians did not follow Christ. The Congress was a terrific uncovering to Protestantism, Catholicism, etc.[73]

At that point Kimball still showed little recognition that from now on Christian Science itself would have to endure a good deal more vigorous opposition from both Protestantism and Catholicism. The outward signs were not immediately forthcoming, but for several months Mrs. Eddy's letters were peppered with brief premonitory observations:

> I think if the address had been properly disposed of and not given to reporters . . . God would have shown me before the book went out just what to do. But now this published dose has unified parties against us in prayer that is something my students do not yet know how to meet in its effects.[74]

> The Catholic priests call at my door and demand to know if I have any Catholic help. All the help of that kind I have had they take away from me. It would seem since the World's Fair that they are afraid of the power of Christian Scientists and would exterminate the Leader.[75]

> The World's Fair cost Christian Scientists the threats and efforts of Church and state that we now are facing. But the error will have its day, unless we learn there is no error.[76]

The ministerial league growing out of the Religious Congress whereby to strengthen their failing prospects, includes among other things prayers for the heretics. This combined mental force is in belief the one that to the religious mind brings more anguish and hopelessness and hatred of me than any power before let loose.[77]

To those less preoccupied than Mrs. Eddy with the kinetics of thought, the episode nevertheless has its own sort of revelation. Here were the finest and best of her followers caught up in the optimistic American assumptions that publicity in itself is a form of blessedness, that goodwill conquers all, that declamation is equivalent to demonstration, that truth only needs an open forum in order to be recognized and divine grace a public platform in order to win men's hearts. Yet history would soon enough relegate their brief day of triumph in Chicago to the scrap heap. If the radical spirituality of Christian Science was to win its way in the face of the world's opposition, it would have to do so on the battleground of daily living rather than the parade ground of publicity.

In the November, 1893, issue of *The Christian Science Journal*, which was largely devoted to the speeches given at the Christian Science Congress at the World's Fair, Mrs. Eddy inserted a notice which indicated her own view of the matter. The need in the movement, she wrote, was for study and "daily Christian demonstration." It was the students' *materiality* that clogged their progress, and more "prayer and fasting" was called for:

> *Assembling themselves together, and listening to each other amicably, or contentiously, I have seen, is no aid to the student [in] acquiring solid Christian Science. Experience, and above all obedience, are the tests of growth and understanding in Science.*[78]

It was becoming clear to some of Mrs. Eddy's students that following her leadership required, as she had written of Christian discipleship, a willingness "to cut off the right hand and pluck out the right eye, that is, to set aside even the most cherished beliefs and practices."[79]

5

In December of 1893 *Christ and Christmas* was published in gift-book form and immediately created a small sensation among Christian Scientists. It was the illustrations rather than the poem itself that stirred the greatest interest. Most of Mrs. Eddy's followers found that the pictorial symbolism gave them an exhilarating freedom of interpretation which was not possible in pondering, say, the scientific statement of being.

Did, for instance, the aureoled female figure standing hand in hand with Jesus and bearing a scroll labeled "Christian Science" represent Truth, or did she represent Mrs. Eddy? The question was both titillating and crucial, for it bore directly on Mrs. Eddy's own concept of her role in history.

In the course of her correspondence with Kimball, she had written him in October, knowing that she could say to him what he would interpret in terms of her relationship to Science rather than as an expression of self-glorification:

> For the world to understand me in my true light, and life, would do more for our Cause than aught else could. This I learn from the fact that the enemy tries harder to hide these two things from the world than to win any other points.[80]

The comment was at least prophetic. Through the coming century nearly every extensive published attack on Christian Science would *start* with a pejorative account of Mrs. Eddy's life and character as the basis for its subsequent interpretation of Christian Science doctrine and practice.[81]

Although she herself insisted that Christian Science could be understood fully only when she was understood properly, Mrs. Eddy also insisted that the converse was equally true. Kimball, too, felt that the more deeply he penetrated into the letter and spirit of Christian Science, the more he began to understand otherwise enigmatic actions of hers. In the very midst of his struggle over the Chicago business he could write her:

> My sense of this whole effort is that so far as this age is concerned there is an identity between Christian Science and its Founder. They cannot be separated in human consciousness and have good results follow.
>
> The Message and the Messenger are so closely allied that human thought is safely poised only when it includes the delicate discernment of what "God's impartation to man" really means.[82]

What it did not mean Kimball indicated two weeks later when he reported to her with unconcealed distaste that there were students of hers "who go around saying that you are 'God's Christ,' and that you are 'greater than Jesus Christ.' "[83] These signs of the dangerous human tendency to exalt the founder of a religion to almost divine status were multiplying among some of her more emotional students, at the very time that she was trying to cultivate their "delicate discernment" in regard to following her leadership without worshiping her personality.[84]

This was the situation into which *Christ and Christmas, a Poem* was launched with accompanying illustrations, biblical texts, and a final page which announced:

REV. M. B. G. EDDY,
and
MR. J. F. GILMAN,
Artists.

First came the response to the book as an aesthetic production.

Augusta Stetson of New York, who was one of the worst offenders in respect to turning Mrs. Eddy into a quasi-deity, nevertheless wrote her a hurried and worried letter in which she announced that all to whom she showed the poem "stood aghast at the illustrations, which both critics and those who are not connoisseurs say are caricatures, having no artistic merit." Friends of the Cause had told her "that if the critics and press get this to review before Christmas they will use it against Science."[85]

The effect of her letter—possibly one of the most outspoken she ever wrote—was counterbalanced by a panegyric from another student, extensive passages from which Mrs. Eddy quoted in an article in the January *Journal.* This fulsome young lady, Miss Annie Dodge, told how in Italy "years ago" (when she must have been very young indeed) she had studied the works of the old masters "thoroughly" and so "got quite an idea of what constitutes true art," following this up with two years in Paris devoted to "music and art." With these ambiguous qualifications, she went on to say:

> *The first thing that impressed me in your illustrations was the conscientious application to detail, which is the foundation of true art. . . . The hands and feet of the figures—how many times have I seen these hands and feet in Angelico's "Jesus," or Botticelli's "Madonna"! . . .*
>
> *All that I can say to you, as one who gives no mean attention to such matters, is that the art is perfect. It is the true art of the oldest, most revered, most authentic Italian school, revived.*[86]

Neither Mrs. Eddy nor James Gilman was qualified or inclined to dispute young Miss Dodge's judgment, as she dragged Botticelli and Fra Angelico like twin red herrings across the serious questions raised by *Christ and Christmas*. The book, as Mrs. Eddy wryly wrote in her *Journal* article, was as "hopelessly original" as *Science and Health* itself. Whether it was an aesthetic triumph or disaster was less important than whether it was trying to do something that could or should be done.

Was it moving in the direction of an official iconography? Was it using visual symbols for a didactic purpose and thereby turning art into pedagogy? Could metaphysical truth be pictured to the eye as medieval artists and craftsmen had pictured biblical theology to illiterate worshipers?

There is no evidence that Mrs. Eddy specifically asked herself any of these questions or intended any of these purposes. To her the poem and its illustrations were *sui generis*. When she predicted in her *Journal* article in regard to the stir they had created that "Christian Science and its art will rise triumphant," there was no hint that she was anticipating the development of a distinctive Christian Science art form, style, or symbology. Truth was infinitely expressive, and its forms of expression must necessarily be as various as experience itself.

Yet the fact remained that whatever form it took, the art of Christian Science must always be in the broadest sense a healing art; and in the same article, abandoning apologetics for metaphysics, Mrs. Eddy announced: "The truest art of Christian Science is to be a Christian Scientist; and it demands more than a Raphael to delineate *this* art."

In a very short time she began to have doubts about the wisdom of having published *Christ and Christmas*. At first she was delighted to hear of healings—especially of children—which came from the contemplation of its illustrations, but it was soon evident that there was more blind faith than spiritual understanding in such iconotherapy. Hanna, who had emerged from his tussle with her over the World's Fair with an ardor that had an element of mysticism in it, informed her that he had memorized the entire poem and was using it to treat himself, whereupon she wrote him:

> Please tell no one how you utilize "Christ and Christmas"; used thus it is a mental opiate by which the dreamy extacy of the repeator lulls fear, nothing else. There is an axe to be used, and laid at the root. This axe is the first Hebrew commandment as explained in my works.[87]

"Thou shalt have no other gods before me"—the Hebrew commandment was still a radical corrective for hierophantic tendencies. Grieved by her criticism, Hanna wrote Mrs. Eddy in dismayed incomprehension, and she quickly replied:

There is a flower whose language is "I wound to heal." There is a physician who loves those whom he chastens. There is a woman who chastens most those whom she loves. Why? Because like a surgeon she makes her incisions on the tender spot to remove the cold lead that is dangerous there. Was not "Christ and Christmas" a good remedy when it worked well as you found? Is it not Truth and does not Truth heal? Yes, but even the truth is not to be spoken at all times. What you have to meet dear one is only a fear and what pacifies fear does not destroy it. Take your weapon that kills it,—the first commandment, and with that cut off its head no matter if you have some fighting to do . . . for done it must be to decapitate the ghost. This is our play of "much ado about nothing."[88]

This interchange of letters seems to have precipitated Mrs. Eddy's decision to withdraw her new book from circulation, and on January 10, 1894, she wrote Foster Eddy briskly:

I have stopped my book Christ & Xmas being printed! The students made a golden calf of it and therefore I pull down this dagon. Don't ever speak of it as a healer. I did in my article for our Mag. but did not know then the modus operandi *abroad. The books heal* scientifically. *The Poem is not made the healer but the pictures are . . . and the picture-healing is made by misuse of Charm-healing such as pagans use, and mind-curers mesmerists and faith-curers adopt to save learning through* growth out of *error into Truth.*[89]

Her explanation to the public followed in an article entitled "Deification of Personality" in the February *Journal.* "Idolatry is an easily-besetting sin of all peoples," she warned. Human thought must learn to turn to the divine Mind rather than to finite personality. Then she sprang her surprise:

Friends, strangers, and Christian Scientists, I thank you, each and all, for your liberal patronage and scholarly, artistic, and scientific notices of my book. This little messenger has done its work, fulfilled its mission, retired with honor (and mayhap taught me more than it has others), only to reappear in due season. The knowledge that I have gleaned from its fruitage is, that intensely contemplating personality impedes spiritual growth. . . .

My Christmas poem and its illustrations are not a textbook. Scientists sometimes take things too intensely. Let them soberly adhere to the Bible and Science and Health, which contain all and much more than they have yet learned. We should prohibit our- selves the childish pleasure of studying Truth through the senses, for this is neither the intent of my works nor possible in Science. . . .

To impersonalize scientifically the material sense of existence —rather than cling to personality—is the lesson of to-day.[90]

Empiricist that she was, Mrs. Eddy could retreat without surren- dering. In her very withdrawal of *Christ and Christmas* she made casual mention that the book might "reappear in due season." Her wording suggested that the prerequisite for its reissue would be the ability of Christian Scientists to take the poem and its illustrations with due regard for the "scientific impersonalizing" of its otherwise ambivalent message. Meanwhile she undertook to help them toward that end by her public and private instructions—and by instituting certain small but telling changes in the Gilman pictures.

One slight incident and its aftermath illustrate both these mea- sures. In May, 1894, a young woman in Toronto wrote her about the healing of a very sick child as the result of the correspondent's enrap- tured contemplation of the cherubs' faces in one of the *Christ and Christmas* illustrations. Mrs. Eddy replied firmly:

. . . the way you listen for my voice and to it is your own self mesmerism which is very harmful in the end. It . . . props your faith in person rather than Principle and the understanding of Christian Science. . . . The Cherubs were an artist's form of de- picting cherubic thoughts not children. The female figure which art uses to represent liberty means anything but a woman, it means the beauty of liberty for one thing. Beware of letting your imagina- tion control your thought.[91]

When the book was reissued unobtrusively four years later, the cherubs had virtually faded into the background, and shortly after- ward they were replaced by a new picture entirely.[92]

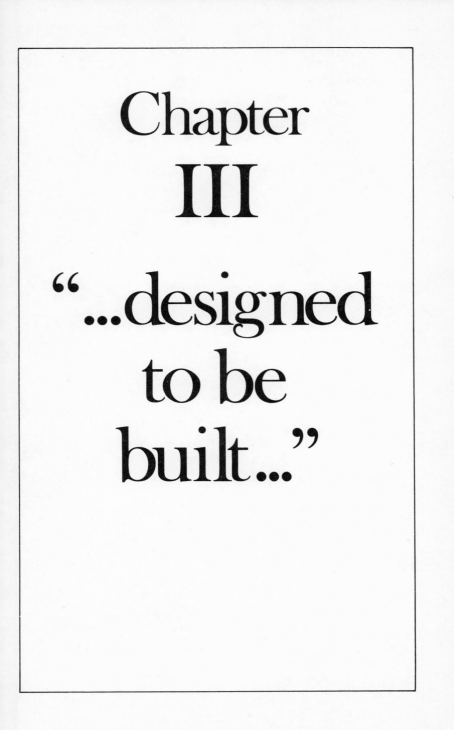

Chapter III

"...designed to be built..."

Animal magnetism might be termed Mrs. Eddy's equivalent of original sin. It represented the hard fact that thinking rooted in material appearances had no intention of acknowledging a transcendent spiritual power that challenged its own legitimacy. It might, said Mrs. Eddy, take the form either of ignorant resistance or of malicious opposition to spirituality. In either case, it aimed to confound an influence so alien to its own presuppositions and so difficult to live with.

The term, borrowed from the vocabulary of early mesmerism or hypnotism, also pointed to the nature of its operation as mental suggestion. Recognized as such, animal magnetism had only as much power, Mrs. Eddy taught, as the unwary gave it by accepting psychological tricks as substantive facts.

Christians had traditionally acknowledged this phenomenon, however they defined it. The New Testament itself furnished a vivid illustration in the story of the unclean devil crying out, "Let us alone; what have we to do with thee, thou Jesus of Nazareth? art thou come to destroy us? I know thee who thou art; the Holy One of God." So when Mrs. Eddy analyzed this enmity of the "carnal mind"[1] as operating with mistaken or criminal intent to frustrate the design of transcendent good, she was talking about something that related to conventional Christianity as well as to Christian Science. The interesting fact was that the established churches wrote off her reformulation of the problem as heresy without troubling to find out what she meant by it.

At first she had been far from wanting to start a new denomination. Her mission, as she saw it, was to Christianity and, through that, to the world. But when organized Christianity itself had treated her spiritual radicalism as an unreasonable disturbance of the religious status quo, she had seen nothing for it but to have a church of her own.

Now the time had arrived for that church to take tangible form in a building in Boston[2]—but in a way that would bear witness to the substantiality of Spirit, not of matter. It was a tall order. From the start of the enterprise, it seemed to Mrs. Eddy, animal magnetism was determined to prove that material circumstance ruled spiritual intent.

The United States had plunged into one of its worst depressions, and money was tight as a drum. The triangular plot of filled-in tideland on which the church was to be built offered special architectural and construction problems.[3] Although the dragged-out dispute over the land title had been settled, new building regulations and city ordinances sent costs up unexpectedly, while the deed of gift did not permit the property to be mortgaged. Finally, the Board of Directors, for all their faithfulness, were not particularly well equipped by experience to deal with the contractual complications, labor disputes, engineering problems, and building-supply shortages which were to plague them—or even to get the project moving in the first place.

Mrs. Eddy used all the authority at her command to stir them to decisive action. In September, 1893, she wrote them, "Why in the name of *common sense* do you not lay the foundation of our Church as GOD BIDS YOU, AT ONCE?"[4] Twelve days later she again urged them:

> Do not delay one other day to lay the foundation of our Church; the season will shut in upon you perhaps, and the frost hinder the work. God is with you, thrust in the spade Oct. 1st, 1893, and advertise in next No. of Journal that you have begun to build His temple.[5]

A month later the work had still not begun, and on October 17 Mrs. Eddy wrote the newest Director, Joseph Armstrong:

> Nothing but M.A.M. is preventing the foundation of our church being laid in this month as God has bidden it to be done! Mr. J[ohnson] & Mr. K[napp] in times past by delay at critical times would have lost my whole plan to save my church lot had not I driven them to obey. Do not wait for their movements. Now I protest against this delay to have the foundation built. Also I warn you against the mental argument for this to be done when the frost comes![6]

Two days later the contracts for excavation, pile driving, and stone foundations were signed, and the work began before the winter freeze set in.

Though the Directors troubled Mrs. Eddy with few details, she kept close mental watch on their moves, as one small incident illustrates. They were ready for the building of the walls, but the estimated cost greatly exceeded the funds on hand. To promise anything beyond their assets would have been, by the terms of their trust, to forfeit title to the land. Moreover, the Directors had made it a rule never to base their calculations on mere pledges from the potential contributors.

Into this dilemma, which they had not discussed with her, Mrs. Eddy on December 1 dropped a quiet suggestion which at once solved the problem. Could not the contract include a provision that they might order the work to stop at any time after a specified portion of it was completed? Four days after her letter was received, a satisfactory contract with just such a condition was signed.

A week or two later Mrs. Eddy wrote more than forty of her staunchest students asking them for subscriptions of $1,000 each to the building fund—a staggering figure for people who were living, for the most part, in very modest circumstances and for whom such a sum was more than $10,000 in the money values of the 1970's. With heroic good cheer, they virtually all rose to the occasion and sent in the money. Their accompanying letters recounted with awe the wonders that had come from their efforts to accomplish the seemingly impossible. In turn, their names were placed in the cornerstone of The Mother Church—and its walls of New Hampshire granite began to rise from the completed foundation.

While Mrs. Eddy's letters to the Directors contained a good deal of practical advice, the evidence is clear that she considered the whole undertaking a mental rather than a material one. The real building blocks, in her view, were spiritual.[7] When it came to her attention, for instance, that one of the students who had sent in $1,000 in response to her appeal was not a believer in the virgin birth of Jesus, she returned the money with a brief explanation:

> The virginity of Jesus' mother is a cardinal point of Christian Science. I did not know your views until after my invitation for you to contribute to our Church fund, or I would not have written as I did. Some time, dear one, you will grow to a higher sense of Divine Science, and meantime I am as ever your loving teacher.[8]

As one hindrance after another delayed each new stage of the work, Mrs. Eddy's insistence grew that the church *must* be completed in 1894. The delays *must* be handled as animal magnetism. When the cornerstone was finally laid on May 21, with a quiet little ceremony at which a special address by her was read, a revealing incident followed close on its heels.

Later that day Camilla Hanna, as assistant editor of *The Christian Science Journal,* took a proof of Mrs. Eddy's address up to Pleasant View for her final approval for publication. She found the Christian Science leader with dark rings under her eyes and apparently bowed down with weakness. Informed by Mrs. Hanna that the cornerstone had been laid that day, Mrs. Eddy replied heavily but elliptically,

"Yes . . . *I laid it.*" Too burdened to go over the proof herself, she consented to lie on a sofa and have Mrs. Hanna read it to her for the necessary sanction.

As she listened intently to her own words, a marked change came over her. At one point she exclaimed, "That's wonderful!" At the end she sprang to her feet and said, "Come on upstairs. I've got something more wonderful than this!" As Mrs. Hanna recalled later:

> *Every trace of weariness had disappeared and she was alert and full of vigor. . . . During our long association with Mrs. Eddy we saw this many times. The flash and recognition of Truth which would come to her would wipe out all sense of weariness with which she was many times oppressed.*[9]

Taking the article from Mrs. Hanna, the revived author—intent on improving it further—proceeded to work on it off and on all through the night. Three or four times Mrs. Sargent brought it into Mrs. Hanna's room for the latter to take back to Boston when she left the next morning. Then, each time, Mrs. Eddy would send for it again in order to make further revisions—a procedure characteristic of her as a writer. When Mrs. Hanna rose at dawn to catch an early train to Boston, Mrs. Eddy was still awake and alert, sending her guest various messages to deliver to her students there.

In the article itself, as it appeared in its final form, Mrs. Eddy once again reminded Christian Scientists that the church must be seen in nonmaterial terms:

> *To-day I pray that divine Love, the life-giving Principle of Christianity, shall speedily wake the long night of materialism, and the universal dawn shall break upon the spire of this temple. The Church, more than any other institution, at present is the cement of society, and it should be the bulwark of civil and religious liberty. But the time cometh when the religious element, or Church of Christ, shall exist alone in the affections, and need no organization to express it. Till then, this form of godliness seems as requisite to manifest its spirit, as individuality to express Soul and substance.*[10]

By the end of October, 1894, it looked as though six months at a minimum would be required to finish the church building. About this time Joseph Armstrong, who had been put in charge of the work by the other Directors, had a visit with Mrs. Eddy at which, he wrote later, his eyes were opened like Elisha's servant to see that "they that be with us are more than they that be with them" and he "knew as an absolute certainty"[11] that the work would be done in 1894 as she insisted.

As if to test his faith, on November 6 after months of fine weather the church—unprotected by roof, floor, or window—was full of snow, the earliest to have fallen in Boston for years. The following day Mrs. Eddy wrote two of her women students:

> What is this Church to me or to you if Mesmerism governs its Directors, as certainly it has and is still doing. . . . The Church will not be built the year that God told them to build if they go on as now. And if it is not, woe be to them who are guilty of this needless, useless, stubborn, disdain of God's command.[12]

Let them give up some of their "gods," she wrote—the mosaic flooring, the marble and onyx, the silk walls for the "Mother's Room" they were building for her in the bell tower, all the planned luxuries that would delay the completion of the church. "I would rather," she wrote in another letter, "see 5000 hearers in a plain wooden Tabernacle listening to the Scriptures and Science & Health than pride and contracted walls hemming in 1200 hungry hearers."[13]

Her student, Edward P. Bates, of Syracuse, New York, who was given the contract for heating and ventilating apparatus, brought to the whole situation in early November a vast new energy. Officially he "placed his whole time at the service of the Directors."[14] Actually he charged onto the scene like a determined bull, impelled by the conviction that whatever Mrs. Eddy ordered must, could, and would be done. What he lacked in finesse he made up in assurance, trampling down ifs, buts, and can'ts, offending susceptibilities and building up problems for the future, but getting the immediate job done.

His wife, Caroline, who worked with him during this time, was of the same mettle. When a labor dispute stopped work on the roofing of the bell tower, she twice climbed to the top by means of a series of twenty-five-foot ladders set up on loose planks inside the tower wall, and on one occasion remained there on her flimsy perch for three hours in a stiff wind until she had settled the dispute.

Mrs. Eddy's gratitude to the Bateses was unbounded. This was the sort of faith if not of comprehension that she was looking for. As Edward Bates put it a year later:

> I could have been no possible use in building the Church if I had doubted for a moment that the work would be finished. When I went into that building I saw it finished as it is today.[15]

All through December the building "from boiler room to auditorium ceiling" hummed with continuous activity. Armstrong later described the scene with gusto: materials pouring in night and day, laborers in profusion clattering up and down the unfinished stairs, painters, plasterers, plumbers, electricians working side by side, mosaic being laid in one part, concrete mixed and spread in another, artists setting stained-glass windows to the music of hammer and buzz saw. Once the workmen accepted the fact that, contrary to appearances, the church *could* be finished by the end of the year, there was remarkable cooperation among them.[16]

Mrs. Eddy's letters roused and encouraged, as well as scolded. On December 12 Knapp wrote her, "Your letter to the Directors and to Mr. Bates is the word of God and it seems as though it would raise the dead and I think it has, myself included."[17] On the same day Mrs. Eddy wrote Kimball in Chicago, "Showers of grace and glory are gently falling all around us in the midst of the battle."[18] And to the Directors a week later she sent word: "The day is well nigh won. You will soon rest on your arms." Then, with the work apparently far from completion she added: "Hold your services in the Mother Church Dec. 30, 1894, and dedicate this church Jan. 6th."[19]

On Saturday night, December 29, the building complete, workmen laid the cement sidewalk outside and covered it with a tent to keep the cement from freezing. Inside the church a host of Christian Scientists armed with dusters, mops, pails, and brooms cleaned up the auditorium. Exactly as midnight struck, the work stopped. The church was ready for the Sunday service that morning, as Mrs. Eddy had asked that it be.

2

From now on, it would be a different sort of service. In the same letter in which she set the date for the opening, Mrs. Eddy went on to say:

> The Bible and "Science and Health with Key to the Scriptures" shall henceforth be the Pastor of the Mother church. This will tend to spiritualize thought. Personal preaching has more or less of human views grafted into it. Whereas the pure Word contains only the living, health-giving Truth.

Nine months earlier, following the sudden death of D. A. Easton, Judge Hanna had been called to the pastorate of The Mother Church, while still retaining the editorship of the *Journal*. "Must I go to this Nineveh too?"[20] he had asked Mrs. Eddy with the reluctance of an overworked Jonah, and she had assured him that it would be for only a year.

Now, after nine months of resounding success in this supplementary pastoral role, he was to be superseded by what Mrs. Eddy described as the "impersonal pastor"—the Bible and *Science and Health.* Her decision to institute this form of service, which was soon to become standard for all Christian Science churches, was in line with her preference for silent over audible prayer. Personal eloquence could all too easily become a substitute for scientific instruction and practical application of Christian truths. "To my sense," she wrote a few years later, "the Sermon on the Mount, read each Sunday without comment and obeyed throughout the week, would be enough for Christian practice."[21]

Hanna remained, however, as First Reader of The Mother Church for another seven years.[22] Mrs. Eddy deplored the personal ambitions which tried to maneuver a rival candidate into even this relatively impersonal office,[23] but the virtually universal satisfaction with Hanna's subsequent readership confirmed for her the wisdom of transferring emphasis from a personal interpreter of the word to the word itself.

On similar grounds, it was logical that Mrs. Eddy should be represented at the dedication of The Mother Church on January 5, 1895, not by her personal presence but by a dedicatory sermon written by her but read by another. Early in the message she asked, "To-day, being with you in spirit, what need that I should be present *in propria persona?*" Then, permitting herself the luxury of a little biblically oriented wonderment, as she had permitted her followers at last their mosaic and marble and onyx, she exclaimed:

> *Were I present, methinks I should be much like the Queen of Sheba, when she saw the house Solomon had erected. In the expressive language of Holy Writ, "There was no more spirit in her;" and she said, "Behold, the half was not told me: thy wisdom and prosperity exceedeth the fame which I heard."*

Never one to linger unduly over present triumphs, however, she went on to remind them of mental battles still to come and of the church's function in this warfare. Drawing on the current Sino-Japanese war for analogy, she exhorted them:

> *With the mind's eye glance at the direful scenes of the war between China and Japan. Imagine yourselves in a poorly barricaded fort, fiercely besieged by the enemy. Would you rush forth single-handed to combat the foe? Nay, would you not rather strengthen your citadel by every means in your power, and remain within the walls for its defense? Likewise should we do as meta-*

physicians and Christian Scientists. The real house in which "we live, and move, and have our being" is Spirit, God, the eternal harmony of infinite Soul. The enemy we confront would overthrow this sublime fortress, and it behooves us to defend our heritage.[24]

In a reminiscence some forty years later, William P. McKenzie, by then a member of the Christian Science Board of Directors, threw light on something of the personal struggle behind the speech.

Young McKenzie, a Scottish-Canadian Presbyterian minister who had turned English professor, was an ardent idealist, poetic in both temperament and appearance. Another professor who had known him at the University of Toronto recalled him later as "the handsome fellow" who had played in a college production of *Antigone* and wrote poetry in Scottish dialect.[25] Through an equally ardent young woman, Daisette Stocking, McKenzie had become a convert to Christian Science, and on Christmas Day of 1894 he had his first visit with Mrs. Eddy, an hour-long interview. Writing to Lyman Powell in 1932 he declared that during that visit he once and for all "became her man, like a clansman giving allegiance in love to a chief."[26] Mrs. Eddy, for her part, frequently referred to him in correspondence as her "John," the most gentle and affectionate among her male disciples.

A week later, and only five days before the dedication, she asked him to come again to Pleasant View, this time with Judge Hanna. To his dismay, she looked thirty years older than the previous week.[27] In turn she asked each of them whether he would be able to read her address on the coming occasion, and in turn each declined because he too felt under intense physical and psychological strain. Probably neither of them knew at the time of Foster Eddy's fixed determination to read the speech and be the leading figure in the dedication ceremonies. Nor did they know of Mrs. Eddy's grieving conviction that nothing could be worse for either the movement or her adopted son.

Following the visit she decided that there was too great a mental stir to have any of her students read the speech, and at the last moment she engaged and rehearsed a professional elocutionist, one Henrietta Bemis Clark, who was not a Christian Scientist. According to the newspapers the latter read the address with simplicity and dignity, but most Christian Scientists present at the five consecutive dedication services on January 6 felt that she read without any real understanding of its spiritual message. It was for them the one flaw in an otherwise triumphant day.[28]

Mrs. Eddy, on the other hand, found a deeper flaw in the

unhealed materialism of some of her followers. As Knapp wrote her two or three weeks after the dedication, "Whilst evil is hating this shining work, this symbol of Christ's Church, others are worshiping the symbol more than the divine idea which made it possible."[29] Mrs. Eddy took what steps she could to correct the situation.

The room in the church known as "Mother's Room" had been built with the contributions of Christian Science children, and their continuing small gifts brought fresh flowers to it every week. Very soon Mrs. Eddy sent word that there was too much Roman Catholicism in this personal devotion for her taste, and she wanted them to give gifts to God, not to her.[30] Again, in regard to another feature of the room, she informed Captain Eastaman:

> *I never fully approved of the lamp that always burns in our church. This was a rite perpetuated by Vestal Virgins and they were interested spectators of the tortures of Christians. So the symbol is associated with unpleasant history and I have told the Directors to stop replenishing that lamp.*[31]

When Edward Bates wrote her with eminent satisfaction that the new Westminster chimes in the bell tower would remind people of Christian Science every fifteen minutes, Mrs. Eddy didn't quite take in the implications. But as soon as she read in the Boston papers that the chimes were keeping the distraught residents of Back Bay awake at night, she wrote the Directors of her astonishment at their permitting this imposition on the neighborhood to continue. To the *Boston Herald* she sent a letter of apology, with a wry explanation that it was the purpose of Christian Science to help sick people, not to give them sleepless nights, and offering to stop the chimes altogether.[32]

With all this, she felt a deep desire to see for herself the building which symbolized, however modestly, the emergence of Christian Science as a Church on the stage of world history. So on Monday, April 1, accompanied by Calvin Frye and Clara Shannon (who was temporarily replacing Laura Sargent at Pleasant View), she took a train to Boston, drove straight to The Mother Church, and stayed overnight in the Mother's Room, with no one but a handful of students knowing of her presence. As she wrote young McKenzie afterward, the Boston students had been "calculating on having a procession, chime of bells, *et cetera*" when she should choose to make a visit, but she went "without shot of gun . . . and God was manifest to me in more ways than I have time to tell."[33]

Clara Shannon in her reminiscences described the scene in which

Mrs. Eddy went alone into the auditorium of the church after her arrival. With the lights turned on—the sunburst in the center of the ceiling, the bracketed silver lamps on the wall—the whole place seemed suffused with color: the warm tones of the pews of curly birch, upholstered in rosy plush; the stained glass windows in their bronze frames; the russet walls with their frescoed borders and gold-lettered texts from the Bible and *Science and Health;* the trim of rose pink Tennessee marble; the Italian mosaics, the painted organ pipes.

While Miss Shannon watched and waited at the door, Mrs. Eddy walked slowly down the aisle. On an evening twenty-seven years before, she had been turned out of a house some forty miles from there into the pouring rain, without friends, without money, with no place to go for shelter, with nothing but a vision and an unshakable sense of mission.[34] Now she was in her own church and it was a moment for both wonder and responsibility. Standing beneath the sunburst set in the shallow dome, she paused for some time in thought, then slowly advanced to the marble steps that led to the Readers' platform and for a few moments knelt on the lowest step in silent prayer.

When she had withdrawn to the Mother's Room, where she was to spend the night, she talked with the Directors and several other students but later returned to the church auditorium. This time she mounted the platform, stood behind the first desk, and repeated aloud the words of the ninety-first Psalm—familiar words which time and again had been for her a refuge from the storm. Then, moving over to the second desk, she spoke the words of a hymn which, like so many of her own prayers, moved from petition to affirmation but looked more to the needs of the future than the gains of the past:

> Guide me, O Thou great Jehovah!
> Pilgrim through this barren land:
> I am weak, but Thou art mighty,
> Hold me with Thy powerful hand.
> Bread of heaven! Bread of heaven!
> Feed me till I want no more.
>
> Open is the crystal fountain,
> Whence the healing waters flow:
> And the fiery, cloudy pillar
> Leads me all my journey through.
> Strong Deliverer! Strong Deliverer!
> Still Thou art my strength and shield.[35]

Some weeks later Mrs. Eddy paid another unexpected visit to The Mother Church. This time she came on a Saturday (May 25), again stayed overnight in the Mother's Room, and midway through the service on Sunday morning appeared at the rear entrance of the auditorium. The Readers, who had been briefed ahead of time, stopped reading; the congregation, taken by surprise and more than a little awed, rose to its feet; and Mrs. Eddy proceeded to the platform. After a solo which gave the congregation time to settle down again, she addressed them extemporaneously, in keeping with the impromptu quality of the whole episode.

As reported by a teen-aged boy in a letter home immediately after the service, she spoke "in a quiet pleasant voice, very distinct—for you could easily hear every word—and yet she seemed to be talking as if she were in a small room sitting only a few feet from you instead of in that large church." His summing up has a certain value for its very guilelessness:

> Mrs. Eddy did not preach; she took no text, but I wish I could write you all she said. She must have spoken for twenty minutes. . . . She said it all in such a simple, loving way. . . . I don't wonder that she is loved,—she is all love. You simply feel as if she was your best friend.[36]

Oddly enough, however, the subject of her talk was sin and repentance.[37] Moreover, she had a very special reason for choosing that particular topic at that particular time. For the finishing of the church building, and the spontaneous explosion of press interest which had followed, had been the prelude to certain internal disruptions—a situation which lies behind William B. Johnson's letter to Mrs. Eddy on May 27:

> I rejoice that you were with us in bodily presence yesterday. . . .
>
> I thank you for your words, for your rebuke, for your benediction.
>
> What can I give you in return? only this—and it may be much—that you have led me to repentance.[38]

In her address Mrs. Eddy had said, "Without a knowledge of his sins, and repentance so severe that it destroys them, no person is or can be a Christian Scientist."[39] In the classical Christian tradition, she regarded sin as something very much broader and deeper than the obvious forms of immorality or dishonesty, since what was a relatively harmless failing in one person might be a dangerously culpable fault in someone at a higher stage of moral and spiritual development.

When pointing out their "sins" to some of her most devoted students she often indicated that she meant the unrecognized tendencies or suggestions that blurred their spiritual sense, tainted their judgment with personal bias, tricked them into forgetting vital duties, and opened the way for them to become the unsuspecting tool of others' more devious thinking.[40] For some time she had been complaining that both Johnson and Knapp were not sufficiently awake on this point.

Early in the year she decided that she needed the forthright business energy of Edward Bates on the Board of Directors, and she asked Knapp to resign in order that Bates might take his place as chairman. Knapp, hewn out of New Hampshire granite, a minor prophet come down from the hills with burning eyes and flowing beard,[41] was stricken by the request and figuratively cast himself at her feet in anguish. As a result, she allowed him to stay[42] and asked Johnson whether he would be willing to resign instead, though retaining his post as Clerk of the Church. Johnson at once agreed, with bleak but determined cheerfulness, and Mrs. Eddy used the opportunity to point out to him where he too had need of more grace and self-knowledge. It was to this that Johnson referred in his letter to her regarding his "repentance."

As the year went on, it became apparent that the headstrong Bates, whatever his talents as a businessman, lacked the spiritual maturity to cope with the work. Within six months everyone, including Bates himself, agreed that he should resign. Mrs. Eddy regretfully accepted the necessity, writing to Hanna, "Mr. Bates like all others has made some mistakes, but is a grand character as a friend, a man of business, and a Christian Scientist in embryo."[43] She recommended that Hanna should take his place, and on October 1, 1895, the change was made. Not surprisingly, a directorship on top of his editorship and readership was too much for Hanna, and he begged off in little more than a month. By early November, Johnson was back on the Board, to continue in that position for another fourteen years.

In building the Church, it was evident, the native granite of New England provided the safest foundation for the early formative years.

3

Mrs. Eddy seldom apologized. When she made mistakes, reversed her position, put people in office and then removed them, she felt this was a necessary form of learning and that God was giving her and them the experience they needed. She was charitable with others' mistakes so long as she felt they were learning from them, and she was equally charitable with herself. To her student Emily Meader she wrote on one occasion:

> *I have always understood . . . that the things you referred to with regret, were simply mistakes. And who of us is there, exempt wholly from mistakes? Here I always say in the words of our Master: "Let him that is without sin cast the first stone." Yes, my precious student, I have endeavored to be patient with all flesh, inasmuch as I need God's dear mercy for myself. Oh that all who profess to be Christian Scientists would remember always the blessing it is to ones self, to be charitable. "Love suffereth long and is kind."*[44]

On the face of it, Mrs. Eddy never made any greater mistake than in adopting Ebenezer J. Foster. For some years she had been struggling between hope and fear, affection and realism, the feeling that Bennie *must* be saved for the movement and that the movement would sometime have to be saved from Bennie. Far more than George Glover, he was the weak spot in her sense of motherhood, the ultimate discipline in her effort to subordinate her personal desires to the impersonal largess of spirit which she saw as the great desideratum of life.

There were times when she felt she could share her human weakness more easily with Bennie than with anyone else. On one occasion she wrote him:

> *I have nothing new to write. It is just struggle, work, pray, all the time. But Oh! how much we have to be thankful for midst all this pain, and suffering nameless . . . since God has told us that all this shall work together for good to them that love Good. This is my only comfort that I do know I love Good, and have done much to bring this great, this infinite blessing to others.*
>
> *So let me be patient, trust the love that knoweth best, and hope that I can at last overcome the world, the flesh and all evil. But this is something to do, or seemeth so to those who try it. . . .*
>
> *Dear me, how frail is our fortitude to annihilate the claims of personality! What a poor demonstrator of this am I. To resolve and re-resolve and then go on the same. Cannot Love better than the rod of Love wean us from all flesh and help us to love only the unseen, untouched, immaterialized person, the divine not human.*[45]

In battling her very human desire to elevate Foster Eddy beyond his present capacities to the level of her ideal for him, she was learning some hard lessons about her mothering of the Christian Science movement. Yearning to see him fulfill his potentialities, she was all too ready to forgive and forget the evidences of his unreadiness to accept the responsibilities she had given him. His recurrent periods of genuine concern for her and of remorse for his own indiscipline she greeted eagerly as signs of permanent reformation, writing on one occasion to Hanna, "He has seen himself and is regenerated[;] his sweetest of all natures now dominates,"[46] and on another to James Gilman:

> Rejoice with me, the glamor has fled—and my noble, loving, good boy, the Dr., is awake and busy doing good. Oh! may he and all of us be delivered from all errors or mistakes.[47]

His great weakness, she felt, was a craving for power that allowed him to be "handled by animal magnetism" and in turn to influence other people against their, her, and even his own best interests. Sometimes she felt it necessary to warn the Directors confidentially of what she believed to be his attempts to control them mentally, as when she wrote Armstrong: "He will *ruin you* unless you defend yourself mentally against his influence. . . . What shall I do to defend the cause against him?"[48]

As time went on, her warnings to Foster Eddy himself grew stronger, though her human feelings still made the task difficult, as when she wrote him:

> The last twice you were here I felt most emphatically your unspiritual condition but I love you and had not the grace to take up my cross and tell you of it.
>
> Also I cannot now bear this cross . . . as in times past. I do not feel equal to it or that it is my duty. I have done this and you must now do your work. The chemicalization of the Truth I tell is too much for me now.[49]

Foster Eddy had become more than a personal problem; he was a classical symptom. The Bennies of this world, it was increasingly apparent, craved authority without being willing to do the work, make the sacrifice, or accept the discipline that alone could justify their being given it.

Dissatisfied with his important but unglamorous post as Mrs. Eddy's publisher, Bennie had lobbied to get the more conspicuous position of First Reader when it was created at the beginning of 1895 but lost it to Hanna, for whom the acceptance of this role in addition to his other duties meant a continuing sacrifice. It could have been to the unsuccessful aspirant an object lesson in the advantage of character over ambition, but his tendency was to regard each such incident as a defeat resulting from jealousy of him in high places.

The whole situation came to something of a climax a month or two later in connection with Foster Eddy's secretary in his publishing office. Mrs. Nellie Courtney had studied with Mrs. Eddy in the late 1880's, but had gone her own way since then. Never very close to her teacher, she had maintained a questionable relationship with a maverick student, Frank Mason, who was teaching his own version of Christian Science and doing his best to discredit Mrs. Eddy.

When Foster Eddy brought Mrs. Courtney from the West to be his private secretary—a *very* private secretary, as Mrs. Eddy later wrote the Board of Directors sardonically[50]—he was careful to keep the fact from his mother, though leading the Boston students to believe that she knew and approved of the situation. After several months, during which the sales of *Science and Health* went steadily down despite the increasing numbers of people turning to Christian Science, it finally came to Mrs. Eddy's attention that the growing intimacy between Foster Eddy and Mrs. Courtney had become a matter of scandal in Boston.

Although she accepted his impassioned assurance that there was no improper conduct between them, the author of *Science and Health* was horrified at what she felt to be the duplicity of her publisher son. It was bad enough in her eyes that he had gone out of his way to conceal from her the fact that Mrs. Courtney, leaving her husband and family, had come to work for him.[51] It was still worse that he had introduced so questionable a Christian Scientist and so equivocal a situation into the office responsible for publishing the book which, together with the Bible, now had the weighty function of serving as "pastor" of her church.

When Calvin Frye rashly let his personal feelings show in a short note to Foster Eddy by referring to the latter's secretary as his "paramour," Bennie stormed up to Pleasant View, confronted Frye noisily, threatened him with a libel suit, and when his mother refused to see him, pounded with impotent rage on her locked door.[52] Though he wrote a letter of apology the next day and withdrew his threat, something had happened which in time would prove decisive.

A few days later, at Mrs. Eddy's request, the First Members of The Mother Church passed a new bylaw to the effect that any student of hers who refused to leave a place in the field which Mrs. Eddy knew it was to his interest to leave should be dropped from membership. In explaining her request, she wrote:

> I ask you to act on this By law for two reasons, viz. (1st) I cannot be your Leader unless I have the power to guide you when you need this guidance. (2d) Because I will pray earnestly and watch for God to guide me in knowing that I am right in my decision before entering a complaint against a member of this Church.[53]

Ironically enough, Foster Eddy as president of the church was the one to read aloud the communication, which was clearly directed against his continuing in Boston. Before voting, the members (with the exception of Foster Eddy) adjourned to Concord to meet with Mrs. Eddy herself, who—while defending her son from the charge of sexual misconduct—laid bare what she considered to be the tragic flaw in his loyalty to the church. This, in her view, meant loyalty not merely to a denominational organization but to "whatever rests upon and proceeds from divine Principle."[54] As a result, when the members returned to Boston they voted that each president of the church should hold office for only one year and that Edward Bates should supersede Foster Eddy in that office for the ensuing year.

That Mrs. Eddy made her "awful unveiling"[55] of her son's shortcomings with anguish rather than rancor seems clear from some of the letters she received afterward. Typical was one from Mrs. Gragg, Second Reader of The Mother Church: "I never suffered as I did after my visit to Concord. . . . How I love Dr. Eddy!—and would to God I could help him."[56]

In several subsequent meetings with the Directors, their wives, the Hannas, and Foster Eddy himself, Mrs. Eddy explored the situation with them. Her deep reproaches for their lack of love fell on Bennie's critics as well as on Bennie, but she was evidently regaining the equanimity and well-being which had been temporarily shaken. After one of these meetings on May 8, Armstrong wrote her, "I want to tell you how pleased I was to see you looking so well and beautiful," but he added that Foster Eddy "still retains that dogged look and sullen manner."[57]

It was some two weeks later that she gave her first address in The Mother Church, on the subject of sin and repentance. The subject continued uppermost in her thought for some time as she saw what seemed to her a crying need for self-correction, illustrated equally by those who wanted to gloss over destructive shortcomings and those who were satisfied to condemn the offender rather than heal the situation.

A year earlier she had urged Foster Eddy himself to take a less condemnatory attitude to a renegade student. "If you meet her treat her as you used to do," she admonished him, reminding him of Jesus' attitude to the woman taken in adultery.[58] Now she addressed 180 of her old students who had attended a meeting of the alumni of the Massachusetts Metaphysical College on June 5 and had come up to Pleasant View the next day at her invitation:

> *My dear students, guard your tongues. When you see sin in others, know that you have it in yourself and become repentant. If any of you think you are not mortal you are mistaken. I find my students in an apathy, or in a frenzy. I am astounded at your ignorance of the methods of animal magnetism. Your enemies are watching incessantly while you are not walking as you should. They do not knock, they come with a rush. They do not take me unawares. I know before they come. Would that my head were a fountain of waters and my eyes rivers of tears that I might weep because of the apathy of my students and the little they have accomplished.*[59]

In spite of the magniloquent echo of Jeremiah's lament, her words as usual seem to have had the effect of rousing rather than dispiriting her listeners. Mrs. Eddy's resilience was never more apparent than when she made her unsparing realism the propellant to new enterprise. When Foster Eddy promised her that he would leave Boston, start afresh, and this time "do right," her hope sprang up once more that now at last he was set on the path that would lead to his salvation. Calvin Frye, on the other hand, with his dourer brand of realism, noted in his diary Bennie's renewed levy on her forbearance, then burst out with unwonted vehemence: "Damnation, damnation, damnation."[60]

Actually a year later Bennie was still in Boston, still maneuvering for important church offices, and an additional nine months would elapse before Mrs. Eddy made the definitive break with him that would acknowledge at last that he was beyond reclamation.

4

When the young woman who had shepherded William P. McKenzie into Christian Science accompanied him on a visit to Mrs. Eddy early in 1895, she approached the occasion a little breathlessly. How would she *feel* and what would she say in the presence of the figure whom she venerated so profoundly that Mrs. Eddy had once or twice replied to her letters with a warning that she must put more emphasis on the Principle of Christian Science and less on the person of the Leader?[61]

Once there, however, Daisette Stocking never stopped to think how she felt, according to her later account, but only knew that she was happy:

> I recognized . . . that Mrs. Eddy had that rare gift of losing herself in ministration to another. With whomsoever she was conversing, that one was the whole world to her. It was as though she and the visitor were alone with God, and her whole attention and love given for the moment to only one consciousness. This was not a studied attitude, but the result of her deep interest in each human being, and it had a wonderful effect of calling out the very best that each individual held in his heart.[62]

One thing that Mrs. Eddy said made an especially strong impression on her two visitors. Long after Miss Stocking had become Mrs. McKenzie, she wrote that when storms such as they had never experienced before came to the couple, this instruction of Mrs. Eddy's "practically saved our lives." According to her recollection, Mrs. Eddy had told them:

> Some one said to me, "No one but a fool or a woman would have written Science and Health," and he was right; either a fool, who did not know the consequences of writing that book, or a woman who would have humility enough to go down and survive the persecution. A man would have been more apt to resist, and to resist would have been fatal. I had to learn the lesson of the grass. When the wind blew I bowed before it, and when mortal mind put its heel upon me, I went down and down in humility and waited,—waited until it took its heel off, and then I rose up.[63]

Mrs. Eddy was besieged constantly by Christian Scientists who wanted to see her, hoping to receive gratuitous bounties of inspiration and instruction from her. Those she did see came almost entirely by invitation. There was a fairly steady stream of invited guests, as Frye's diary indicates, but many other requests for interviews were turned down as either unnecessary or unduly demanding on Mrs. Eddy's time and energy.

One of the most persistent pleaders was the ex-editor of the *Journal*, Julia Field-King, who was now teaching Christian Science in St. Louis. A dramatic but unstable character, Mrs. Field-King combined a sweeping exercise of authority over her pupils with intermittent confessions to Mrs. Eddy that in everything she did she felt "a hidden self-seeking motive" and other unspecified sins which at one point she thought might even include the "unpardonable" sin.[64] This periodic abasement of herself was coupled with appeals that her adored teacher would grant her an interview. "In your presence," she wrote in a spasm of ambiguous contrition, "all these devilish suggestions that have pursued me for years will be destroyed."[65]

Evidently recognizing the unhealthiness of Mrs. Field-King's blend of lavish praise with confessional abandon, Mrs. Eddy's attitude was summed up in her reply to one of the earliest of these appeals:

In Christian Science my Rules or rather God's are written ineffaceably in my books and when I advise a student I do it most conscientiously[;] therefore if these rules are not heeded and my advice is not followed then the good I may do by an interview is problematic for it can only be my atmosphere instead of their understanding that does it and when this fades, like borrowed plumes the effect is gone.[66]

A year later in answer to a renewed appeal from Mrs. Field-King, she wrote:

I have found it does no good where my students have my works and read them for them to talk with me. It only is a soothing syrup and the error returns sometimes more severely[;] it must be cured by yourself not me.[67]

In general, Mrs. Eddy was trying to shift more responsibilities from her own shoulders to those of her followers. To Hanna she complained that while she was often called a pope, she was in fact the "household drudge" for the cause.[68] He, in turn, marveling at her capacity for detail, even to her sending sprightly little notes of gratitude for trivial services done for her, wrote, "I am seeing more and more that the infinite is also the infinitesimal."[69]

Yet there was a cost, and to Mrs. Bates in 1895 she wrote in regard to the pressure she was under:

A long article for [an] Encyclopedia. . . . Another for the Press, another for my book that is to be pub with Sermon etc. Also endless letters, and Mr. Johnson! Housekeeping etc. Old age!!! pounding into my ears but not brains, quarrels, gossip. [In] Concord, State law. Need of my articles in consideration etc.; proof reading and Mr. Frye! but he is at least honest. This is but a fractional part. . . . What is fame? Nothing. What is peace? Everything. When shall I find it, where? Not here.[70]

Increasingly, Mrs. Eddy was to refer to herself in letters as "the woman in the wilderness." To her old student Julia Bartlett, who was going through a trying period, she wrote that Julia had never been so close to her as she was then: "Hence you begin to feel my solitariness 'alone in the wilderness.' "[71]

This was not the side of Mrs. Eddy that most visitors saw. Many whom she invited to stay for dinner told afterward of the lively discussion, anecdotes, laughter at the table, with a carefree Mrs. Eddy who was interested in all that was going on in the world. Even Calvin Frye's dry Yankee humor came frequently into play, and the general impression was of a cheerful household with a serene hostess who at any moment might become gravely earnest as the conversation took a new turn.

Yet Frye knew, too, the nocturnal struggles, the exasperations and storms of the woman whom many of her followers imagined to be always on a mountaintop. During the last two or three years of Foster Eddy's association with her, the dogged Calvin found the strain almost too much for him at times. Something of the burden he carried is suggested by a deadpan entry in his diary for January 25, 1896: "Mrs. E said to me yesterday 'you have a way of dampening my hope, but Benny encourages me.' "[72] The bitterness of the entry lay in his realization that when the crunch came it was always his faithfulness rather than Benny's fickle good nature to which Mrs. Eddy would turn.

Frye strove mightily to be what Mrs. Eddy wanted and needed him to be. Earlier on, he had written in his diary:

> Another severe experience causing me to neglect & forget my work, thereby aggravating & discouraging her & causing suffering. Then I got disheartened and hid away from her instead of trying to comfort her & manifesting kindness & tenderness toward her. Remedy: If overcome with carelessness or forgetfulness to condemn it and . . . go to her & speak a kind word to encourage her and manifest an interest in her welfare.[73]

At the same time, Calvin's limitations, his recurrent taciturn stubbornness, his undeniable peculiarities of behavior, almost drove Mrs. Eddy wild on occasion. Stonily he would enter in his diary her sudden outbursts: "Mrs. E was disturbed with my driving yesterday called me an idiot insane and so forth."[74] Nothing of that sort was too ephemeral for him to record; his diary was in a very real sense his safety valve.

Yet when Foster Eddy accused Frye of turning Mrs. Eddy against him, she would always come to the rescue of the loyal figure who, she might agree for the sake of argument, was "the most disagreeable man"[75] in the world but was *honest*—which was more than could be said for Benny. "Instead of his being my enemy," she wrote the latter, "with all his disagreeableness it would seem that he is my only practical helper on earth. And he *never* tried to injure you."[76]

The last statement was equally true of Laura Sargent who, as Mrs. Eddy wrote Foster Eddy, "would no more harm you *knowingly* than I would."[77] Mrs. Sargent was a gentle soul who sometimes got things mixed when she was flustered but was all kindness at heart. Mrs. Eddy was apt at this time to refer to Laura as her "pigeon" because of the frequent confidential messages she was dispatched to carry between Concord and Boston, and the name fitted her in other less literal ways.

Where Frye unloaded into his diary the hurts and discouragements as well as the mundane trivia of the day, Laura reserved her journal for the spiritual lessons that Mrs. Eddy had given them orally. If she wept over the quota of strong reprimands that came her way on practical matters, she could always reread the passages of instruction she had copied with such evident joy from the same exalted source that launched the thunderbolts. As where Mrs. Eddy had told her:

> When I hear [students] say that they love everybody and [yet] see in their lives the evidence that contradicts their words I think of one of the last lessons that the Master gave his disciples, when he said, "Simon . . . lovest thou me, feed my sheep," as much as to say if you are sincere in what you say give me the proof of it. The sheep do not thrive well on stubble. They need the tender grass and clover tops with their blossoms of honey-dew. The pastures of the heart need the dew of heaven to moisten their dry surface and the "early and latter rain" of that Love which "thinketh no evil."[78]

To such passages—and there are many—in the Sargent diary, the half-truculent yet in the end wholly humble entries by Frye offer an instructive counterpoint. As when he wrote, as late as 1897, after his greatest moment of rebellion:

> On the evening of Aug. 29, Mrs. Eddy rebuked me severely but her accusation seemed so unjust that I told her it was not true and I would not remain in the house & hear such an accusation & as she repeated it I left the house & went to the Hotel[;] afterward she sent a letter calling me back & I returned.
> This evening she explained to me in what sense that accusa-

*tion was true and then I saw the reasonableness of it and thanked
her for her kindness. And I solemnly promised her & God that no
matter what she shd hereafter say to me I would not go & leave
her because of it.*[79]

In the last analysis, even the stubble of Pleasant View had for
Calvin and Laura a succulence not to be found in the clover and
honey-dew of lusher pastures.

5

Mrs. Eddy was above all else an author. Not a stylist, to be sure,
a belletrist, a literary professional, or a journeyman drudge, but in a
very deep sense a practitioner of the written word.

It was her books, not her person, to which she wanted her followers to turn. "Those who look for me in person," she wrote, "or
elsewhere than in my writings, lose me instead of find me."[80] The
pastor of her church was a book—or rather, two books. The government of her church was to rest finally on a book.

The completion of the new building in Boston was followed by
the appearance of two small books. The first—*Pulpit and Press*—
included Mrs. Eddy's dedicatory sermon, a few miscellanea by her,
and a selection of newspaper stories illustrating the surprised but
favorable public response to the visible evidence that a new religious
denomination had arrived on the scene. The second, her *Manual of
The Mother Church,* was to play a role in the movement second only
to that of *Science and Health.*

Mrs. Eddy's purpose in publishing *Pulpit and Press* was historical
rather than promotional.[81] She dedicated the book to the twenty-six
hundred children who had contributed to the Mother's Room, and
remarked in the preface:

*Three quarters of a century hence, when the children of
to-day are the elders of the twentieth century, it will be interesting
to have not only a record of the inclination given their own
thoughts in the latter half of the nineteenth century, but also a
registry of the rise of the mercury in the glass of the world's
opinion.*[82]

Three quarters of a century hence, when the little Romanesque
edifice seating nine hundred people would be surrounded by an
extensive complex of additional buildings forming the world headquarters of the Christian Science movement, this achievement would
still be a limited one in terms of Mrs. Eddy's expectation that by

then the influence of Christian Science would be visible far beyond its own denominational borders.[83] She was no ecclesiolater. When the First Members voted to suspend services in The Mother Church for one month in the summer, as many urban churches of other denominations did, she wrote the Directors:

> *Please read this in meeting. When you voted to adjourn all the meetings one month, you should also have voted to close the church building to all visitors during that month! Our Master asked, Which is greater, the temple or the gift that sanctifieth the temple?*[84]

In her letters of later years Mrs. Eddy warned repeatedly against the worship of church buildings, which existed solely for the sake of the religious services and functions they housed. At the same time she warned against the worship of publicity. When the first Chicago church was completed and was to be dedicated, various members wrote her of their successful efforts to get widespread publicity for the coming event. Suddenly a telegram from Mrs. Eddy told them to stop all further efforts, and she followed this with letters of explanation. To the Readers of the church, Edward Kimball and Mrs. Ruth Ewing, she wrote:

> *"His voice was not heard in the streets." It is not Christlike to act in any worldly way to promote anything. "His ways are not as ours."*
>
> *The press should act spontaneously[;] then we will know the true status of public opinion and not one gotten up. It spoke for the Mother church spontaneously.*[85]

The same decisiveness was evident in the rules and bylaws which she sent to The Mother Church for adoption as new contingencies arose. It was almost as though she were trying out Kant's categorical imperative on an experimental basis. When a certain course of action seemed to her to be dictated by Principle (the name which most clearly defined for her God's nature as lawgiver) she would put it into the form of a bylaw to govern similar church situations which might arise in the future. If later experience proved it ineffective or unsuitable for general application, she would ask to have it rescinded or amended into a new form. The aim was universal applicability but the method of arriving at that end was far removed from the logical inflexibility and—in Mrs. Eddy's own phrase—the "cold categories" of Kant.[86]

In view of the bewildering rapidity with which bylaws in the coming years would multiply, change, and disappear, there would inevitably arise a need for their codification and publication for easy reference. Once published, revised editions could be issued periodically to take account of changes made during the intervening period.

So it was that in the latter part of 1895 the first edition of the *Manual of The Mother Church* appeared. The book was then, and remained during its subsequent revisions, a slim volume setting forth the general framework of organizational government rather than a ponderous compilation of canon law.

From the outset it became the ultimate authority for all action by the church. Though it bestowed many special privileges and rights on Mrs. Eddy as Leader, she herself must obey its bylaws until and unless they were changed to permit otherwise prohibited action. While such changes were made at her request or with her approval, this very fact put upon her the responsibility of weighing each contemplated change against the possible needs and general welfare of the movement in the future.

Mrs. Eddy enlisted competent help in codifying the bylaws and consulted legal authority as to the wording of some of them. But the whole process by which the *Manual* "grew" out of experience was the reverse of normal efficient planning procedures. Her earlier distrust of organization as an end in itself had not vanished. Organization, she had long since concluded, was a useful necessity, but it must serve as the backbone of effort, not as a straitjacket for inspiration.[87]

In a letter to Hanna in September, 1895, she registered her own view of the *Manual*'s genesis and purpose:

> The Rules and By-laws in the Manual of The First Church of Christ, Scientist, Boston, originated not in solemn conclave as in ancient Sanhedrim. They were not arbitrary opinions or dictatorial demands, such as one person might impose on another. They were impelled by a power not one's own, were written at different dates and as the occasion required. They sprang from necessity, the logic of events,—from the immediate demand for them as a help that must be supplied to maintain the dignity and defense of our Cause; hence their simple, scientific basis, and detail so requisite to demonstrate genuine Christian Science, and which will do for the race what absolute doctrines destined for future generations might not accomplish.[88]

During the remaining fifteen years of her life, Mrs. Eddy did all she could to educate Christian Scientists to look to the *Manual* rather than to her personally for direction of their church affairs. More and more when the Board of Directors asked her for advice she turned them to the *Manual* and to the spiritual guidance of the Bible and her writings for their answer. While the Board was made responsible for implementing the provisions and enforcing the disciplines of the *Manual,* her aim was to have the government of The Mother Church, so far as possible, a government of laws rather than of men.

At the same time the *Manual* safeguarded the self-government of the branch churches, within the general denominational framework, by prohibiting The Mother Church from interfering with their internal polity and discipline. "In Christian Science," one of the bylaws stipulated, "each branch church shall be distinctly democratic in its government, and no individual, and no other church shall interfere with its affairs."[89]

In a more general statement which she was to make in *The Christian Science Journal* in 1904 and repeat in 1909, Mrs. Eddy would say of the Church of Christ, Scientist, as a whole:

> *Essentially democratic, its government is administered by the common consent of the governed, wherein and whereby man governed by his creator is self-governed. The church is the mouth-piece of Christian Science,—its law and gospel are according to Christ Jesus; its rules are health, holiness, and immortality,— equal rights and privileges, equality of the sexes, rotation in office.*[90]

The difference between the "distinctly" democratic government of the branches and the "essentially" democratic government she posited for the denomination as a whole was crucial.

Nothing could seem less democratic on the face of it than the responsibility vested by the *Manual* in a self-perpetuating Board of Directors, especially after the powers vested in the First Members were transferred to the Directors by a new bylaw in 1901. Yet Mrs. Eddy had written many years earlier: "Thought is the essence of an act, and the stronger element of action."[91] The mental or spiritual essence of democracy, as she saw it, lay not in the ballot box but in the capacity of individual thinking to make itself felt in the decisions and operations of government—and this was dependent on the degree of its alignment with Principle, with the ultimate power of the universe.

In her dedicatory sermon she had put this explicitly:

> *Is not a man metaphysically and mathematically number one, a unit, and therefore whole number, governed and protected by his divine Principle, God? You have simply to preserve a*

scientific, positive sense of unity with your divine source, and daily demonstrate this. Then you will find that one is as important a factor as duodecillions in being and doing right, and thus demonstrating deific Principle. A dewdrop reflects the sun. Each of Christ's little ones reflects the infinite One, and therefore is the seer's declaration true, that "one on God's side is a majority."[92]

Naturally enough, the idea that a single individual could influence church decisions through his prayers seemed as phantasmal to Mrs. Eddy's critics as the Christian Scientist's conviction that prayer could remove a malignant tumor from the body. Even some Christian Scientists found it hard to move from their experience of bodily healing to the logical conclusion that the same divine power was available to them for healing the ills and strengthening the operations of the body politic or ecclesiastic. It was an application of the Ecclesiastes parable of the "poor wise man" who "by his wisdom delivered the city."[93]

While the branch churches could act as schools of democratic procedure, the *Manual of The Mother Church* paradoxically aimed at educating church members toward a "spiritual" democracy—a "democracy of prayer," as it was later to be called[94]—through a rigorous structure of centralized authority. But because Mrs. Eddy was quite as intent upon producing a manual for Christian service as a charter for church government, she kept the skeletonic framework spare, minimal, and dependent for effectiveness on the spiritual directions built into it.

In many if not most cases, Mrs. Eddy chose not to exercise the absolute power of final decision vested in her by the *Manual*, or exercised it only as a constitutional monarch might, at the advice of his ministers. But she was quite firm that she could not surrender her commission to improve the *Manual* as an instrument of government and to oversee its implementation, until her work as founder should be completed. At that point the sole responsibility for administering the *Manual* bylaws in their final and unalterable form would rest with the Board of Directors. They would act as the trustees of her purpose, but their authority would be both conferred and circumscribed by the *Manual* itself.

"Heaps upon heaps of praise confront me," Mrs. Eddy was to write after a major revision of the *Manual* in 1903, "and for what? That which I said in my heart would never be needed,—namely, laws of limitation for a Christian Scientist." God's ways differed from men's, she indicated; hence her "disappointed hope and grateful joy." Without spelling out the ways in which limiting rules might act as the disciplines needed to achieve ultimate mastery of a skill, as in the case of the dancer or the athlete, she went on to announce with oracular confidence:

> *Truth is strong with destiny; it takes life profoundly; it measures the infinite against the finite. Notwithstanding the sacrilegious moth of time, eternity awaits our Church Manual, which will maintain its rank as in the past, amid ministries aggressive and active, and will stand when those have passed to rest. . . .*
>
> *This church is impartial. Its rules apply not to one member only, but to one and all equally. Of this I am sure, that each Rule and By-law in this Manual will increase the spirituality of him who obeys it, invigorate his capacity to heal the sick, to comfort such as mourn, and to awaken the sinner.*[95]

This statement illustrates Mrs. Eddy's emphasis on the church as an educational institution. Christian Science was a study and a practice, not merely a system of belief or of ritual. "It is sad," she wrote in *Science and Health*, "that the phrase *divine service* has come so generally to mean public worship instead of daily deeds."[96] Church disciplines, as she viewed them, were a means toward more effective living.

At first she had wanted the *Church Manual* to include a history of Christian Science up to that point, but during the upheavals of 1895 she wrote Hanna, Bates, and Johnson to drop the idea, for it was not the right time to recapitulate church history: "My present impressions are that Christian Scientists are making material history and evil altogether too real."[97] When she finally did add a short historical sketch to the first edition, it contained a statement which reflected the realism of her view of what had been accomplished so far and what remained to be done: "The First Church of Christ, Scientist, in Boston, Mass., is designed to be built on the Rock, Christ"[98]—not that it was already *built* on the Rock, but was *designed* to be so built.

She as founder had furnished the design—was, in fact, still refining and perfecting it as the founding process went on and the *Manual* drew closer to its final form. But the church, as she saw it, would no more be built with bylaws than with stones; it would be built with lives and it would not be complete until the lives of all men were lived "according to the pattern showed to thee in the mount."[99]

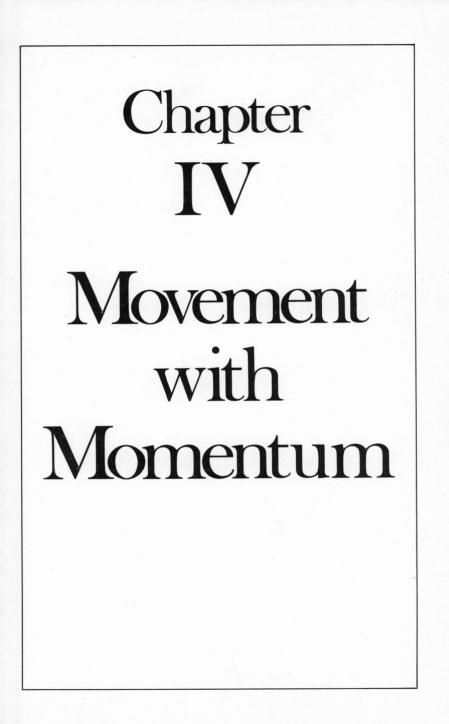

Chapter IV

Movement with Momentum

When Mrs. Eddy paid her third (and last) visit to The Mother Church on the weekend of January 4, 1896, and delivered her second (and last) address there at the communion service the next day, she wrote the Hannas afterward, "I find the general atmosphere of my church as cold and still as the marble floors."[1]

Later, she explained this a little more fully to the Armstrongs:

> My students are doing a great, good work and the meeting and the way it was conducted rejoices my heart. But O I did feel a coldness a lack of inspiration all through the dear hearts (not for me, Oh no, they are loyal to the highest degree) but it was a stillness a lack of spiritual energy and zeal I felt.[2]

Mrs. Eddy always differentiated carefully between spiritual zeal and mere enthusiasm. Nowhere in her writings did she use the latter word in a positive sense.[3] In many ways she was a child of the eighteenth-century Enlightenment,[4] and she shared its distrust of a term that suggested mere emotional excitement. Commitment to truth, in her view, included rationality, method, and verification, as well as spontaneous delight. "I make strong demands on love," she had written some years earlier, "call for active witnesses to prove it, and noble sacrifices and grand achievements as its results."[5] Above all, she called for *healing* as evidence of serious engagement with what she defined as "the problem of being."[6]

Her own talk in The Mother Church had, as usual, brought its quota of healing.[7] Her mail over the years included an increasing flow of letters telling of healings which had resulted from reading *Science and Health*, gaining a new insight into the Bible, remembering some statement of hers in a sudden crisis, listening to the "impersonal pastor" at a church service, finding through one or another of the avenues she had opened up a new sense of being. Some of these letters she passed along for publication in the *Journal*, some she answered in person.

"Testimony in regard to the healing of the sick is highly important," she wrote in the *Church Manual*.[8] At the same time, healing rather than testimony was of first importance, she held, and even the physical healing achieved took second place to the mental regeneration of which it was presumptive evidence. While the spiritual vigor she demanded was a prerequisite to healing, too much subsequent emphasis on the mere pleasing results could result in spiritual sloth. To Hanna she wrote:

> *About our Journal*[:] *Shall I say the testimonials are too numerous* [;] *they lower the standard of Principle by appeals to person and mortal mind. They are in Metaphysics much like narcotics in medicine and fiction in literature.*[9]

An excessive number of pages of testimonials, she wrote again later, was "too much like patent medicine suggestions to call attention rather than to satisfy enquiry."[10] Yet there could not be too many *healings*. Science demanded proof, and Christianity rested on works rather than words. Mrs. Eddy shared none of Luther's coolness toward the challenge of James: "Show me thy faith without thy works, and I will show thee my faith by my works."[11] In another letter she wrote: "Healing is the best sermon, healing is the best lecture, and the entire demonstration of *C.S.* The sinner and the sick healed are our best witnesses."[12]

Certainly most newcomers to Christian Science turned to it initially for healing of mind or body. Without facts to support its claims, Christian Science would have been, in Mrs. Eddy's words, "a Shakespeare without a Hamlet."[13] Twenty years earlier, the Concord philosopher Bronson Alcott had written one of her students: "A method so contrary to received opinions, and a faith so spiritual as hers, must of necessity encounter popular prejudice, and its truths proved by unquestioned facts, *and many such*."[14] The word "demonstration" had for Mrs. Eddy a far broader (and actually a more precise) meaning than the cure of disease, but this latter was the kind of healing that most tangibly demonstrated her claim to serious attention.

Alarmed as much by the successes of Christian Science practice as by the dangers of proliferating quackery,[15] the medical profession increasingly pressed for laws to restrict healing to those who were thoroughly trained in orthodox medicine and surgery—laws which, the Christian Scientists were quick to point out, would have prevented Jesus Christ himself from healing anyone. Vigorously opposing such a medical practice act in Massachusetts in 1894, William James (himself a professor at the Harvard Medical School before becoming a psychol-

ogist and philosopher) had written the *Boston Transcript* in regard
to Christian Scientists and the "mind curers" whom he lumped together with them:

> *I assuredly hold no brief for any of these healers, and must
> confess that my intellect has been unable to assimilate their the-
> ories, so far as I have heard them given. But their* facts *are patent
> and startling; and anything that interferes with the multiplication
> of such facts, and with our freest opportunity of observing and
> studying them, will, I believe, be a public calamity.*[16]

The very day after James's letter was published, Mrs. Eddy wrote
Augusta Stetson, who was seeking signatures for a petition to the New
York legislature in regard to Christian Science healing:

> *Do not, I warn you, present the petition you enclosed to me,
> it is an evidence of weakness and will injure our Cause. An evi-
> dence that is false, for we have no need of clemency on the score
> of religious toleration that is in our constitutional Bill of Rights.
> It dishonors the dignified grounds on which I have founded Chris-
> tian Science. . . . I have no fears whatever of the passage of any
> law that can injure Christian Science and only fear the dishonor
> that comes from unwise measures taken by students. Christian
> Scientists have better remedy than material means for error.*[17]

Mrs. Eddy's consistent position was that prayer was as potent in
healing legal injustice as in healing physical disease—more potent, she
implied, than political maneuver or artful propaganda. There were
increasing opportunities to put this drastic thesis to the test, for an
era of court cases was beginning in which (usually under the prodding
of the medical profession) the right of Christian Scientists to rely
wholly on spiritual means for healing was strongly challenged.

Many of these cases resulted in a parade of witnesses for the defense, giving testimony under oath to their healing by Christian Science
of diseases which had been medically diagnosed as cancer, tuberculosis,
meningitis, pneumonia, Bright's disease, and a host of lesser and
vaguer ailments.[18] The result was often not merely acquittal but an
access of new inquirers at the local branch church. One curious phenomenon was the number of physicians and members of the legal profession who became Christian Scientists at this period, and for the
next decade or two *The Christian Science Journal* and the sister periodicals which were soon to augment it were peppered with articles by
judges and ex-doctors.

Nevertheless, Mrs. Eddy continued to express her dissatisfaction with the quality and quantity of Christian Science healing. Nothing less than the New Testament record matched her expectations, and that could be realized only as Christian Scientists strove for the New Testament standard of spirituality. The theme is a constant one throughout the letters of her later years, and she reached out eagerly to those Christian Scientists who gave promise of attaining what she saw as a consistently apostolic (and scientific) level of Christian healing.

There was young James Neal, for instance, who had been a cashier in Joseph Armstrong's bank back in Kansas. When Mary Armstrong had been healed in 1886, both her husband and his fervent young cashier had come tumbling into Christian Science, devouring *Science and Health,* and going to Boston shortly afterward to study with Mrs. Eddy at the Massachusetts Metaphysical College. For Neal, as for many others, Christian Science meant not merely a new point of view but a new set of realities, and almost immediately he began healing friends and fellow townsmen. Blindness, deafness, insanity, a broken skull, tuberculosis—the list grew rapidly.[19]

On a visit to his family in Kearney, Nebraska, he was asked to treat a seriously ill child who was not responding to medical treatment. After one day's treatment from Neal without visible improvement, the fearful mother returned the case to the doctors. The child died soon afterward, and the newspapers announced that the coroner's inquest was expected to result in a charge of manslaughter against Neal—on the basis of his brief interlude as practitioner. The local paper also announced that Neal had run out of town on a freight train at night to escape arrest. Neal replied with a letter to the paper expressing his regret at the death of the child, explaining that she had been treated for twelve weeks by physicians, only one day by himself, and had died after medical treatment had been resumed; also that far from leaving Kearney, he had decided because of the criticism to stay there for six months, during which time he could be found every day at the Midway Hotel during certain hours.

At the inquest, the coroner was extremely rough with him. Had Neal ever healed a case of cancer, he asked at one point, and the answer was yes. Was it not true that he had testified to the fact that he never diagnosed disease? Yes. Then how did he know the case he healed was cancer? Because "seven regular practicing physicians" had all pronounced it cancer—and that, said Neal, was all he knew about it. At the end of the inquest, one of the jurors who had been hand-picked for his known hostility to Christian Science asked Neal for treatment, and within a few weeks the coroner was complaining to a friend that "that little devil" had got all his best practice.[20]

Later, at Mrs. Eddy's request, Neal came to Boston to assist Armstrong in his publishing activities, but his overriding love remained the work of healing. On January 28, 1897, Mrs. Eddy wrote him a letter which in time became something of a classic among Christian Science practitioners:

Your letter is my best New Year's gift. I had felt for sometime the fitness you possessed for healing I knew it when you were a member of my College class. It looked a waste of your talents to have you in a counting room. Now, thank God, I have at least one student in Boston that promises to be a Healer such as I have long waited and hoped to see. Oh may the Love that looks on you and all guide your every thought and act up to the impersonal, spiritual model that is the only ideal—and constitutes the only scientific Healer.

To this glorious end I ask you to still press on, and have no other ambition or aim. A real scientific Healer is the highest position attainable in this sphere of being. Its altitude is far above a Teacher or preacher; it includes all that is divinely high and holy. Darling James, leave behind all else and strive for this great achievement. Mother sighs to see how much her students need this attainment and longs to live to see one Christian Scientist attain it. Your aid to reach this goal is spiritualization. To achieve this you must have one God, one affection, one way, one Mind. Society, flattery, popularity are temptations in your pursuit of growth spiritual. Avoid them as much as in you lies. Pray daily, never miss praying, no matter how often: "Lead me not into temptation,"—scientifically rendered,—Lead me not to lose sight of strict purity, clean pure thoughts; let all my thoughts and aims be high, unselfish, charitable, meek,—spiritually minded. With this altitude of thought your mind is losing materiality and gaining spirituality and this is the state of mind that heals the sick. My new book will do you much good. Do not purchase one, Mother wants to give you one. I welcome you into the sanctum of my fold. God bless you.[21]

The "new book" to be published in February, 1897, bore the noncommittal title of *Miscellaneous Writings*. It marked, in a way, the watershed between the formative and the productive years of the church's history.

2

It was Edward P. Bates who suggested in 1895 that Mrs. Eddy's miscellaneous writings for *The Christian Science Journal* since its inception in 1883 should be gathered into a book. During the second half of 1896 she spent a good deal of time revising and selecting from these writings, removing from them "the pioneer signs and ensigns of war" and retaining "the privileged armaments of peace."[22]

To help her with the task she engaged a young Scottish Christian Scientist, Jessie Gorham, who acted as both assistant and advisor on all questions of style.[23] For several years Mrs. Eddy had been reluctant to call on her old literary aide, J. Henry Wiggin, whose lack of real understanding of either her purpose or her metaphysics made his work increasingly unsatisfactory to her. When she had asked his help on a small matter in 1895, she had written him, "If only you could correct my copy *without* REWRITING it then I could correct the places where you change the true statement of metaphysics."[24] On that occasion Hanna had written her:

> *In reference to Wiggin's performance, I feel almost "mean" enough to say, Serve you right! It seems to me that your submitting articles to his criticism is about like Gladstone submitting his state papers, as premier of England, to a Boston alderman, to pass upon their correctness from the standpoint of statesmanship.*[25]

With Miss Gorham—"My precious Highland Lassie," as Mrs. Eddy was prone to address her—there was a sense of awe which made her almost apologetic about offering suggestions, though Mrs. Eddy encouraged her to speak up frankly. "I liked the words added," she wrote the young woman early on. "You cannot be too critical." And again, "Your nice distinctions suit me."[26] Nevertheless, it became evident that Miss Gorham's emotions sometimes interfered with her judgments, and as a result Mrs. Eddy found it necessary to give her a little more direction as time went on. Explaining her retraction of earlier orders and change of working procedures, she wrote Miss Gorham:

> *Darling,—*
> *If as Emerson advises you "harness your wagon to a star," you look upward; but if to me, you look into strife and rise upward through great tribulation. My earthlife is that of a weathercock— it turns, veers and stops with the winds of circumstance. Your last copy shows me it is wise for me to look over the copy first and you afterwards. None but the author sees certain needs in the copy, and the less written by any other person the better. Why? Because*

*I say things from a different standpoint than another person can,
—and this person can see the grammar that I have measurably forgotten,—but cannot see my vision of the new tongue and of human
need.*[27]

It was planned for some time to call the book *Repaid Pages*,[28] and
the name was even sent to the copyright office as the anticipated title,
but at the last moment the weather vane turned again and the more
utilitarian *Miscellaneous Writings* was substituted. As was usual with
Mrs. Eddy's books, the weeks before publication were full of upsets.

To Armstrong and Bates, she wrote in January: "I have tried
two weeks to have Mr. Frye type the *Contents* of my book and each
time he did it wrong. He is trying again this morning." Two days
later, she wrote them, "Poor *good* Mr. Frye torments me, but 'the spirit
is willing.' "[29] This time Frye had had the book copyrighted as of Concord rather than Boston, thus causing legal complications.

To her "darling Jessie" Mrs. Eddy wrote: "So many varying winds
blow that the weather-vane flies hither and thither. My life-work is
never tranquil or assured except in its *finale*."[30] And when Miss Gorham felt that her own work and motives were being misrepresented to
Mrs. Eddy by Armstrong and Bates, who were publishing the book in
Boston, the beleaguered leader at Concord assured her:

> *Mother knows what cyclones, orders, counterorders, and utter
> disregard of what is the straight line, always has occurred when a
> book of great power has been published by her. So, dear one, she
> is used to it, and loves Jessie and always shall love her.*[31]

She was evidently so used to the cyclones et al. that once the book
was out she could write the Knapps:

> *I hope you do not think from what is said to you that I am
> tired with my tasks. Instead of this being the case I feel better for
> them and never was in better health. Mr. Frye and Miss Shannon
> are happy with the new book and they are growing apace.*[32]

The new book, gathering up the lessons of the past, had a good
deal more of the personal Mrs. Eddy in it than did *Science and Health*.
To Mrs. Stetson's protégé and associate, Carol Norton, she wrote, "My
heart speaks to you in my last book," whereas in *Science and Health*,
she continued, there was so much of "the divine Heart," or what she
elsewhere called "the great heart of Christ," that there was less of her
own human feelings.[33]

While the preface to *Science and Health* ended by committing its pages "to honest seekers for Truth," *Miscellaneous Writings* was dedicated "To loyal Christian Scientists," and the difference was revealing. The Church of Christ, Scientist, was nowhere mentioned by name in *Science and Health,* except for a brief reference in the preface, nor did the book anywhere speak of its author as Founder or Leader.[34] *Miscellaneous Writings,* on the other hand, contained much practical counsel for church members, recorded some of the birth throes of the organization, included sermons, addresses, and letters to The Mother Church and its branches, and referred freely to Mrs. Eddy's role as Founder and Leader as well as Discoverer. Where she resolutely avoided presenting Christian Science as a denominational teaching in *Science and Health* itself, *Miscellaneous Writings* gave practical instruction on how to be a more effective student and church member.[35]

On the day after its publication, Edward Bates wrote her, "Two years ago you gave us our Impersonal Pastor . . . and now you give us the Impersonal Teacher."[36] In the March *Journal* a signed notice by Mrs. Eddy suspended all teaching of Christian Science for one year in order to let *Miscellaneous Writings* prepare readers to understand the Christian Science textbook better. This was the culmination of her concern over the quality and accuracy of the teaching being carried on throughout the field, a concern which equaled her solicitude for the healing work.[37]

To Carol Norton she wrote:

> *Divine Science shall be taught more divinely, by the reading of Mis. Writ. The human teaching tends to liquidate the genuineness of Truth. It always has, and always will. I taught [others] to teach with great reluctance knowing this. . . . The lack of spirituality and the abundance of vainglory and tyranny in many of my students have hurt . . . our Cause.*[38]

Yet there was much in *Miscellaneous Writings* of Mrs. Eddy's human character, her tastes and affections, remembered anecdotes, set pieces on "Voices of Spring" and "Sunrise at Pleasant View," stylistic foibles, echoes from writers she had loved in the past,[39] poems of her own ranging from her greatly loved hymn "Feed My Sheep"[40] to little verses on the Isle of Wight and the "wooings" of "gentle June." One saw her as the students in the Massachusetts Metaphysical College had seen her: a powerful teacher opening up to them a new view of reality, but also a woman with an idiom and idiosyncrasies of her own, costumed and coiffured in the fashion of her day, relaxing into personal reminiscence, sentiment, fancy—and sometimes into unexpected intimacy.

Her style, at its best and at its worst, was *sui generis*. Her articles like her letters usually gave the impression of being written at lightning speed, and she expected Hanna to punctuate and smooth out the grammatical construction before publishing them.[41] He himself took a great deal of delight in her style, writing her typically:

> *There is one thing about your articles that amazes me,—the suddenness with which you stop. But why not, when you have said it all? Wondrous faculty! . . . [I] wish I had it, and more of our contributors.*[42]

This direct, even stripped quality came into evidence when she was most metaphysical—and also when she was most practical. The ornamental "literary" passages belonged much more to her own time and background, and in successive revisions the would-be litterateur often gave way at last to the religious thinker and leader. There is a significance in her instructions to a later editor of the *Journal:*

> *Our periodicals stand for a system to be established and a Science to be demonstrated. They are not to amuse or to entertain so much as to instruct the public. They should contain only what tends to this result. The dabblers in literature are not the ones to fill this demand. We need cultured writers to make the abstract interesting; and sound subjects to make our readers satisfied. . . . Wit and wise repartee are sometimes auxiliaries to this end; and sarcasm blent with love may gain a strong point in human thought. Unlettered novices in C. S. are not the writers that we need.*[43]

What troubled Mrs. Eddy most in the writings of her students was their constant unconscious plagiarism from her works. For years she had insisted that they must quote her less prolifically, must stop writing passages or whole articles that were nothing but paraphrases of her own writings, must develop their own ideas in language not borrowed slavishly from hers.[44] Early in Hanna's editorship she had written him in regard to an article of his which she felt to be correct but unwise:

> *Wait for growth. The Textbooks contain it all—but so arranged as to require growth before it is spoken by those who have not grown to it. The letter killeth; it is the spirit, understanding, behind the words which maketh alive. I doubt not that your article is grand. But it is true that my students are killing to a fearful extent the spirit and effects of my writings by using them so glibly in theirs.*[45]

It is evident from the many references in her letters to this tendency that she saw it not merely as a matter of literary parasitism but as an adulteration of Christian Science. From the evidence of her letters, she seems to have had little complacency as an author but a total faith in the authority of what she was saying, as when she wrote Hanna:

> The effect of my writings is often diluted and sometimes lost by attempting to explain them. It is the seed which once sown springs up, and if seemingly obscure at first, it makes its way in the soil of thought, upward, and though least understood it bears the biggest results of all books.[46]

Except the Bible, she would undoubtedly have added if writing to someone who did not understand her meaning as well as Hanna, for no one believed more fervently than Mrs. Eddy in the first tenet of Christian Science: "As adherents of Truth, we take the inspired Word of the Bible as our sufficient guide to eternal Life."[47] But *Science and Health* as a "key" to the Scriptures belonged in one piece, she believed, and she strongly opposed publishing it in piecemeal selections.[48]

Her strictures on plagiarism therefore regarded it as an abuse of the metaphysical integrity of her work more than of her literary property rights.[49] Hanna brought this out in an editorial comment in the *Journal* on an example which had occurred in an Oregon newspaper:

> The chief objection . . . to these plagiarisms, is that they are unfair attempts to rend into tatters and shreds the garment of Truth, so as to destroy its efficacy by destroying its continuity. Science and Health must be read as a whole, and from every standpoint of its scope and tenor, in order to convey to the reader its full meaning and benefit.[50]

On the other hand, Mrs. Eddy's own writings contained many unidentified quotations and unacknowledged literary borrowings, usually of a trivial sort.[51] When Jessie Gorham asked her about the propriety of identifying a brief quotation from Edward Young,[52] Mrs. Eddy left it to Miss Gorham's judgment as to whether it was necessary, but reminded her that "Chaucer, Homer, Virgil, Shakespeare are quoted with and without quotation marks." The Scriptures, she added, were quoted by Christian writers *ad libitum* without attribution, and this was perhaps wise "since those who read the scriptures recognize it, and those who do not, might accept in that way what they would otherwise reject."[53] She herself constantly wove phrases, terms, images, allusions, and even rhythms from the King James Version into her published and unpublished writings without stopping to label them—so that commentators on her style, less familiar with the Scriptures than she was, have often been comically unaware of her overwhelming literary debt to the English Bible.

When *Christ and Christmas* was published, she had written that it was as "hopelessly original" as *Science and Health,* and the phrase is an apt if wry one. The discovery in recent years, for instance, that Mrs. Eddy had introduced a few phrases and thoughts from Hannah More's eighteenth-century essay on prayer into her own treatment of the subject in *Science and Health* in no way lessened the undeniable originality of that book's chapter on prayer.[54] What did cause a genuine flutter in the dovecotes was the discovery in the 1920's that three out of four paragraphs of a brief message from Mrs. Eddy to the First Members of The Mother Church in 1895 were taken almost verbatim from a sermon by an eighteenth-century divine, Hugh Blair. What was more, the message had been included in *Miscellaneous Writings* when it was published a year and a half later.[55]

There is no evidence to explain this unmistakable borrowing, different in kind from the adaptation and incorporation of stray phrases or figures of speech from other writers. Such minor assimilation is a common enough occurrence among even the best of authors and is often to be accounted for by unconscious mnemonic processes; but no theory of unconscious reproduction is quite sufficient to explain three full paragraphs with only one or two small verbal differences from the original, plus a few changes of punctuation, capitalization, and spelling.[56]

While some of Mrs. Eddy's critics have taken this appropriation as proof that the whole of Christian Science is a vast plagiarism, the passage itself has no trace of specific Christian Science content, except where she changed "The upright man is guided by a fixed principle of mind . . ." to "The upright man is guided by a fixed Principle"—which, in Christian Science terminology, meant guided by God. The passage as a whole is a typical example of high-minded eighteenth-century ethical sentiments, unexceptionable and unexceptional.[57] Ironically enough, the characterization of the "man of integrity" reads in part:

> *He assumes no borrowed appearance. He seeks no mask to cover him, for he acts no studied part; but he is indeed what he appears to be,—full of truth, candor, and humanity. In all his pursuits, he knows no path but the fair, open, and direct one,*

and would much rather fail of success than attain it by reproachable means.[58]

Mrs. Eddy evidently chose this passage for her message to the First Members' meeting in October, 1895, with particular reference to the then burning issue of Foster Eddy, who was still playing a double game with the church.[59] That of itself was perhaps less surprising than her later inclusion of it in *Miscellaneous Writings* without quotation marks or attribution to Blair.

Whatever her reasoning, the passage stands squarely like a block of granite in the way of any future tendency by Christian Scientists to attribute to Mrs. Eddy's published articles the sort of textual or verbal infallibility that biblical literalists and fundamentalists have attributed to the Bible. She could write in *Science and Health* of the infallibility of "divine metaphysics," but her statement of metaphysics left no room for either bibliolatry or mariolatry. Truth was one thing; words, according to her own theory, were at best an approximation.[60]

3

On July 5, 1897, a blazingly hot Monday, all available horse-drawn vehicles in Concord were commandeered to transport more than two thousand[61] Christian Scientists from the city's railroad depot to the lawns and elms of Pleasant View.

The day before had been Communion Sunday at The Mother Church, an occasion marked by the admission of fourteen hundred new members and the normal influx of Christian Scientists from elsewhere who had come to attend the communion service in Boston. Mrs. Eddy's surprise invitation to them to visit her the next day had brought them up to Concord like a host of well-marshaled butterflies, discreetly a-flutter, oscillating between reverence and gaiety.

The event combined the attraction of a religious pilgrimage and a Fourth of July celebration.[62] When Mrs. Eddy came out of the house on the arm of Edward Bates, the crowd greeted her with three rousing cheers. After she had taken her seat on the veranda with a few specially invited guests, the Mayor of Concord, who had been asked to do the honors of the occasion, introduced her to the assemblage and she spoke briefly[63] in a clear voice which carried across the lawn to all but the farthest listeners.

Attired rather magnificently in a dress that had been chosen for her by Augusta Stetson, with one of the fashionable little bonnets for which she had a feminine weakness,[64] Mrs. Eddy wore at her throat the handsome diamond cross familiar from many pictures. Less conspicuous was the small jeweled emblem presented to her when she was made a Daughter of the American Revolution, while—to the surprise of many—"hanging in full view from a gold pin on her gown" was "a pair of eyeglasses."[65] She was, according to the *Boston Herald*, "the picture of health and energy for a lady of her years," and the *Boston Globe* with more particularity reported of her face, "The profile is sharp and keen, and the face in full view is extremely delicate and tender—motherly more nearly expresses it."[66]

Other observers noted the close attention with which Mrs. Eddy listened to the speakers who followed, her face lighting up with pleasure at every touch of wit or eloquence. Particularly effective was the first of the speakers, her forthright cousin General Henry M. Baker, a public figure of some note in New Hampshire—not a Christian Scientist, but a firm admirer of his cousin's good works.[67] Then came Judge Hanna, who, as he listened to Mrs. Eddy's remarks and General Baker's Independence Day zeal, was reminded of one of New Hampshire's heroic women, Mollie Stark, who participated in the Battle of Bennington with her husband General Stark, loading and firing a cannon with patriotic aplomb. Referring to this and by implication applying it to the "motherly" figure on the platform, Hanna quoted from the ballad he had learned in youth:

> The mothers of our forest land,
> Stout-hearted dames were they,
> With nerve to wield the battle-brand,
> And join their border's fray. . . .[68]

Among the other speakers were General Erastus N. Bates, a classical scholar and Civil War hero who, shattered in health by his war service, had been rescued by Christian Science from "what was virtually his grave"[69]; young "Professor" McKenzie, as he was still generally called; the Reverend Dr. George Tomkins, clergyman turned Christian Scientist, who had served as assistant pastor for the famous Charles H. Spurgeon in London's huge Baptist Tabernacle; and the Reverend Irving C. Tomlinson, ex-Universalist minister who, after practicing the social gospel in Boston's slums for some years with growing disillusionment, had found Christian Science, studied with Ira Knapp's wife, Flavia, and joined The Mother Church the day before the Concord gathering.[70]

Minor though they were, these were "names" that seemed to guarantee increasing respectability for Christian Science, and the ladies whose frocks and parasols rivaled the flowers of Pleasant View and the gentlemen who fanned themselves briskly with their panama hats or straw boaters felt properly gratified. Yet, like much else in Mrs. Eddy's life, the scene can be viewed at several different levels.

For one thing, the smiling hostess of Pleasant View wrote the Hannas the following day that previous to July 5 she had been under "such a fire as never before" and consequently at the last moment had prepared a speech to *read*—"a thing I have not done . . . in many years."[71] Probably no one but the members of her household realized at the time how apt was the battle imagery of the verse Hanna had quoted.

Then again, Irving Tomlinson, who wrote that during that day Mrs. Eddy had "radiated light and joy upon all about her,"[72] nearly fifty years later made public a small incident which can stand for a whole class of similar experiences that illustrate a further dimension of her influence.

Seated directly in front of the veranda on which Mrs. Eddy and her guests of honor sat was a Mrs. Jessie Cooper from Kansas City and her two small children. With unabashed curiosity the youngsters gazed up into Mrs. Eddy's face during the speeches, and she, always responsive to children, looked down at them with a smile of warm interest. Mrs. Cooper's emotional account, quoted in part by Tomlinson, describes what happened as she observed this interchange of looks:

> *It was a revelation to me. I saw for the first time the real Mother-Love, and I knew that I did not have it. I had a strange, agonized sense of being absolutely cut off from the children. . . .*
>
> *As I turned . . . and walked toward the line of trees in the front of the yard, there was a bird sitting on the limb of a tree, and I saw the same love, poured out on that bird that I had seen flow from Mrs. Eddy to my children. I looked down at the grass and the flowers and there was the same Love resting on them. . . .*
>
> *I looked at the people milling around on the lawn and I saw it poured out on them. I thought of the various discords in this field, and I saw, for the first time, the absolute unreality of everything but this infinite Love. It was not only everywhere present, like the light, but it was an intelligent presence that spoke to me, and I found myself weeping as I walked back and forth under the trees and saying out loud, "Why did I never know you before? Why have I not known you always?"*[73]

If the description belongs in some ways to that familiar stream of Christian mysticism which extends back through Emerson's *Nature* and Jonathan Edwards's *Personal Narrative* to the visionary lyricism of Vaughan and Traherne, it has the unusual feature of relating equally to the hard Yankee practicality represented by the cure of a boil. For Mrs. Cooper relates that during this experience a large, painful boil on the head of one of the children completely disappeared, leaving the head "as flat as the back of her hand."[74]

This mixture of the visionary and the mundane typifies much that transpired at Pleasant View, where life was lived at a height, depth, diversity, and intensity inconceivable to most of the good Concord folk who saw Mrs. Eddy simply as a distinguished local citizen who was, among other things, a financial asset to the city.

There were some, to be sure, like the caustic Senator William E. Chandler, owner of one of the city's two daily papers, the *Concord Monitor*, who on general principles thought her an unmitigated fraud. On the other hand, the *Monitor's* editor, George H. Moses, despite the respect in which he held Chandler as his political mentor and ideal, developed an affectionate admiration for Mrs. Eddy through his personal and professional dealings with her over the years. In 1929, when he himself had long been a United States Senator, Moses described her to the editor of her own paper, *The Christian Science Monitor*, as "exactly the sort of woman I should have liked my grandmother to have been."[75]

While Mrs. Eddy's secluded life aroused a certain amount of speculative gossip in Concord, the prominent citizens who had direct contact with her in connection with family or public affairs all seem to have admired her personally, whatever they might think of her religious teachings. This was true, for instance, of her lawyer, General Frank S. Streeter, one of the most respected members of the New Hampshire bar; of her cousin Dr. Ezekiel Morrill, a reputable Concord physician whose rugged honesty Mrs. Eddy herself greatly admired; of another cousin and upright New Englander, Fred N. Ladd, treasurer of the Loan and Trust Savings Bank of Concord, who handled many of her financial affairs; and of the Reverend Frank L. Phalen, General Secretary of the New Hampshire Unitarian Association, who came to know her in the latter part of 1897.

Phalen wrote her in November of that year that he was preparing a series of evening lectures, one of which he wished to devote to Christian Science, and that he needed a better understanding of it if he was not to do it an injustice. Mrs. Eddy sent him a friendly reply, commending his disposition to put "the philanthropy and ethics of religion" above "creed and dogma,"[76] and inviting him to come and see her.

The occasional letters that passed between the two after Phalen's subsequent visit illustrate the sort of easygoing relationship which Mrs. Eddy found a pleasant supplement to the more intense responsibilities of her leadership. She could even enjoy Phalen's Unitarian rationalism, his purely humanitarian concern, writing him on one occasion:

> I greatly appreciate the excellence of your Sermon but beg to say, even our Master's agony was not sufficient to cause him to forget his mother in that last supreme moment.
>
> Jesus was not God, Mary was not God. . . . The Infinite alone is God.... To my understanding ... God is quite as much Mother as Father. Your art Mary I prefer to the creedal. Alas! what mistakes creed and dogma, gods and goddesses have entailed. Let the Thinker of to-day do his duty to mankind.[77]

On the rare occasions when Mrs. Eddy entertained friends or visitors who were not Christian Scientists, she never intruded the subject of Christian Science into the conversation,[78] but if they asked her about it she would gladly launch into an exposition. In the same way she found obvious pleasure in responding to Phalen's questions on the level of rational argument, as when she wrote him in February, 1898:

> Christian Science like all Science must be discovered or learned. It is not a native of the senses and cometh not with observation. St. Paul had clear views of this fact. Indeed the testimony of or the evidence before the senses contradict it but not more flatly than they disputed the facts of astronomy and then accepted them through the understanding. . . . It is only more difficult to understand Christian Science than astronomy because the former wars against the whole mortal man and the latter against only a part of him. . . . No man can accept this Science without understanding it in a degree. Mere human ipse dixit is no aid to it and this fact removes it from charlatanism or dogmatism.
>
> Please pardon my prolixity. I never know where to stop on this subject.[79]

Three months later Phalen wrote her that he was glad to see from the current number of The Christian Science Journal "how closely akin our thoughts are upon many points." If he ever succeeded "in the press and stress of other duties" in writing his promised lecture on Christian Science, he was sure she would find it "very sympathetic if not fully confirmatory of your doctrine."[80] Mrs. Eddy, for her part, wrote him with unusual frankness:

> *I am never satisfied with my Christian growth. I can see increase of knowledge yearly, but do not see the spiritual progress that I need more than all else. But the dear God is merciful, and Life is eternal wherein to gain the goal.*[81]

It was a fact that the growing prosperity of Christian Science did not relieve her of the necessity for coping constantly with new complexities. Always it seemed to her that her own progress was not fast enough to keep pace with the need, and that Providence was forcing her through excruciating experience to rise to higher levels of insight and commitment. What she had written several years before to her student Sarah Pine still seemed true: "We are *thrashed* like the corn to make us yield nutriment for ourselves and others." To which she added the unqualified statement: "I have learned through suffering all I have written and taught."[82]

How was she to explain the difference between her students' experience and hers? To Marjorie Colles in England she wrote in 1897:

> *Darling, when will my hour come[?] The students' seem[s] to have come already. They have less and less to combat while I seem to have more and more because of their prosperity. Evil would revenge on me for the prosperity of our Cause. But Love is greater than all.*[83]

To be sure, her students were growing in their appreciation of her mission, she wrote John Linscott, and this "gives the twilight of my years a glow of sunset glory." Now, she commented, the students sat peacefully "in the security of knowing the worst is over with all but me," whereas she had to "work for a larger number if not at the old difficulties."[84]

One of the old difficulties she had finally shed in 1897 was Foster Eddy. When he had removed to Philadelphia at her request to form a new church there, she had continued to give him moral support and he had continued to get into trouble. "You conceal from me all you should tell," she wrote him, "and then when you get into difficulty come to me for help."[85] Finally the Philadelphia church voted to expel him from the Readership and all other offices there, and Mrs. Eddy wrote him that he did not have permission to come to her house "in less than three years from the time you left it last."[86]

In effect, this was a decree of banishment—and of freedom for her from an intolerable burden. For Foster Eddy also it meant freedom of a sort. Idling off to Wisconsin for a lengthy stay with his brother's family, he wrote her several letters (including one from the Yosemite on a sightseeing trip through the West) telling with gusto of his travels and automatically protesting his affection. Mrs. Eddy's view of the letters was summed up in the words she scribbled on the envelope of one of them: "Flattery and pleasure seeking."[87] From that point on, she ceased to regard him as her son.

This development may account for the remarkable burst of energy which followed during the next year and a half. When the house in Concord which she had had remodeled to serve the needs of the local Christian Scientists was completed at the end of 1897, Mrs. Eddy sent a message to be read at the second Sunday service held there:

> *I shall be with you personally very seldom. I have a work to do that, in the words of our Master, "ye know not of." From the interior of Africa to the utmost parts of the earth, the sick and the heavenly homesick or hungry hearts are calling on me for help, and I am helping them. You have less need of me than have they, and you must not expect me further to do your pioneer work in this city.*[88]

Although she preached once at this little hall, on February 27, 1898, and Senator Chandler's *Monitor* reported afterward that "Mrs. Eddy appeared at her best, as sprightly and energetic as a young woman,"[89] her earlier message remained true. The momentum of Christian Science was carrying her far beyond the local and even the national scene.

4

Up to this time, Christian Science had been largely an Anglo-Saxon phenomenon, confined almost entirely to English-speaking followers. Mrs. Eddy's own roots were English and Scots-Irish, and her knowledge of any language other than English was superficial.[90] The King James Version of the Bible was her daily meat and drink. Her admiration for the British throne, and for Queen Victoria in particular, was considerable.

Years before, her cousin Fannie McNeil Potter—niece of Franklin Pierce and his sometime hostess in the White House—had visited the Right Honourable Sir John MacNeill of Edinburgh, described as prominent in British public life and former ambassador to Persia, and had brought back with her a copy of the MacNeill coat of arms. To

Mrs. Eddy she presented an autographed reproduction of the arms with the glad, if incorrect, news that as members of the McNeil family both of them were entitled to use it. As a consequence, it appeared as a crest on Mrs. Eddy's stationery even after Sir John's granddaughter, Mrs. Florence Macalister, in 1904 effectively challenged her right to use it.[91]

In the same way, Mrs. Eddy's statement, "In the line of my Grandmother Baker's family was the late Sir John Macneill . . ." still stands in her autobiographical *Retrospection and Introspection,* published in 1891, a tribute to the romantic veneration for illustrious names she had inherited from her girlhood rather than to any provable connection between the Edinburgh MacNeill and her great-great-grandfather, the John McNeil of Northern Ireland to whom her ancestry is genuinely traceable through her Grandmother Baker.[92]

In *Science and Health* Mrs. Eddy wrote unequivocally: "Jesus acknowledged no ties of the flesh. He said: 'Call no man your father upon the earth: for one is your Father, which is in heaven.' "[93] By contrast she opened *Retrospection and Introspection* with the statement: "My ancestors, according to the flesh, were from both Scotland and England, my great-grandfather, on my father's side, being John McNeil of Edinburgh."[94] The Founder of Christian Science was always strongest when she followed most closely the Founder of Christianity, always weakest when she wrote "according to the flesh." As if in recognition of this fact, she labeled the short chapter in her autobiography dealing with her genealogy "Ancestral Shadows," while in a later chapter entitled "Marriage and Parentage" she suddenly broke off the narrative to say:

> It is well to know, dear reader, that our material, mortal history is but the record of dreams, not of man's real existence, and the dream has no place in the Science of being. It is "as a tale that is told," and "as the shadow when it declineth."

Then, after pointing to the lessons to be learned from doing battle with the false values of this shadow-world, Mrs. Eddy concluded the chapter:

> God is over all. He alone is our origin, aim, and being. The real man is not of the dust, nor is he ever created through the flesh; for his father and mother are the one Spirit, and his brethren are all the children of one parent, the eternal good.[95]

This was the universalism implicit in Christian Science, and it was fully in line with the Christian radicalism of Paul's statement:

"There is neither Jew nor Greek, there is neither bond nor free, there is neither male nor female: for ye are all one in Christ Jesus."[96] But it was one thing to see this in principle; it was another to free oneself entirely from the rooted racist and nationalist assumptions of one's time. Mrs. Eddy was impelled in one direction by the logic of her spiritual convictions but tempted the other way by an age which had exalted racial inheritance as the divinely appointed shaper of history.

The temptress, in this case, was Julia Field-King.

With her somewhat disheveled intellectual liveliness, Mrs. Field-King had become enamored of the Anglo-Israel theory, which held that the Anglo-Saxon "race" was descended from the ten lost tribes of Israel. This fanciful hypothesis suited well the temper of an age in which British imperialism was soon to be joined by American colonial adventurism, and Kipling's touting of the white man's burden made common cause with Admiral Mahan's agitation of the yellow peril.

Mrs. Field-King was particularly taken with a curious work, *Our Race: Its Origin and Its Destiny,* by Lieutenant Charles A. L. Totten, professor of military science and tactics at Yale. This serial exposition of Anglo-Israel theory showed that strange amalgam of religious fervor, symbolism, prophecy, off-beat erudition, florid rhetoric, and intellectual confusion so characteristic of a certain type of military mind engaged in esoteric pursuits unrelated to the disciplines of the drill field and the cavalry charge. Judge Hanna, with his persistent streak of mysticism, had quoted Totten in the *Journal* back in January, 1892.[97] Three years later Mrs. Field-King was carried away by the Yale military man's interpretation of the Apocalyptic "woman clothed with the sun."[98]

More to the point, she was greatly impressed by Totten's genealogical resourcefulness in tracing the British royal line back to David, King of Israel. If Queen Victoria could be proved to be a descendant of the great Hebrew monarch, surely research would disclose a similar lineage for Mary Baker Eddy. As Jesus had been the son of David, so Mrs. Eddy would be shown to be the "Daughter of the King"— and, incidentally, as entitled to the throne of England as "your cousin Victoria."[99]

This extraordinary thesis Mrs. Field-King presented to Mrs. Eddy as an almost proven fact. She had had a researcher in Washington go into the matter thoroughly, and only one final link remained to be established. Mrs. Eddy was swept off her feet by the news. Surely this Davidic descent would convince some otherwise intractable skeptics of the genuineness of her mission. But her common sense reasserted itself to the extent of leading her to urge Mrs. Field-King to be very sure of her facts. As a result, the latter wrote back a week later with a mass of detailed questions about particular ancestors.

Mrs. Eddy at once ordered her to stop the research:

> It is not really in the line of Truth that the thought is forming itself in this investigation but in the line of material origin and this has an end. Now I would turn away from the subject. My reason for asking you to undertake this historical proof was that the people would sooner be convinced perhaps by it of my legitimate mission but I fear it costs you too much to direct your thought so materially and the end will not justify the means.[100]

On the same day, however, Mrs. Field-King wrote her triumphantly, "There is on the way from the Smithsonian Institute and the Great Peabody Library the full proof of your direct descent from David"[101]—and the dramatic possibility persuaded Mrs. Eddy to let the project move forward. Needless to say, the "full proof" proved to be full of holes, and Mrs. Eddy continued to alternate between ardent approval and uneasiness at the evident "materializing" of Mrs. Field-King's thought. Four months later she again told her to do no further research, stop thinking in terms of "matter kinship," and see the descent simply as that of a name:

> No inherent qualities of race exist. Banish the lie from your mind or it will harm you. . . . It is all a "liar from the beginning and Truth abides" not in it."[102]

The subject remained in abeyance until, early in 1896, Mrs. Eddy sent Mrs. Field-King to London to shepherd the English field, a task which she performed with sensational success. Through her teaching and influence, people of social and intellectual prominence turned to Christian Science in increasing numbers, and before long Mrs. Eddy was having letters and visits from Britons with names that recalled the romantic "society" novels of Mrs. Southworth, which she had read so eagerly as a young woman. Among them was the Marchioness of Bath; the Earl and Countess of Dunmore, with their daughters Lady Victoria and Lady Mildred Murray and their son Lord Fincastle; young Lord Abinger, who came to the United States especially to see her before going off to the Boer War; the wife and daughters of Sir James Ramsay, a Scottish historian; the family of the Lord Chancellor of Ireland, and others titled and untitled.[103]

To the danger of making Christian Science the religion of a racial elite was now added the temptation to identify it with a social elite. Mrs. Eddy rightly perceived the indomitable qualities of British character which could bring great strength to the forward thrust of the movement she led. But to equate these qualities with the ethos of a ruling class and a pride of empire destined for progressive obsolescence would be a major strategic error—not to mention a betrayal of the spiritual democracy implicit in her teaching. The erstwhile little farm girl from Bow might look with wide-eyed wonder at the spectacle of "earls, princes and marquises"[104] paying homage to her; the venerable hostess of Pleasant View might greet visiting notables with an accomplished ease which caused them afterward to describe her as a great lady as well as a great leader;[105] but "the discoverer of an eternal truth,"[106] as Mrs. Eddy called herself, needed to look at all such ephemeral circumstances *sub specie æternitatis.*

It was a large order and took time. At first she seriously contemplated the publication of Mrs. Field-King's "genealogy" as a possible support to the movement in England, without any visible recognition of the chauvinism and snobbery it might also encourage among her followers. But even as she tentatively endorsed the project, she warned her persistent student that if the genealogy should be

> *harming or diverting thought from the true issue of this period its publication must stop even as I stopped "Christ and Christmas"*. . . . *It is a great and stupendous point either for or against C. S. and demonstration will prove this.*[107]

Demonstration proved that it would be disastrous. Mrs. Field-King consulted the Lyon King at Arms in Edinburgh and "the best heraldist in the College of Arms" in London, and both agreed that the genealogy was worthless.[108] Having lured Mrs. Eddy into a wild-goose chase for a distinction which, even if it had been genuine, would have been wholly irrelevant to the merits of her position as Discoverer and Founder of Christian Science, the promoter of the scheme now rapidly lost interest in it.

With the formation of First Church of Christ, Scientist, in London in 1897, and with the increasing practical demands of the burgeoning movement in Britain, the Anglo-Israel issue gradually drifted into the background of Mrs. Eddy's thinking. Although she continued to be intrigued by the theory for several years,[109] she kept it resolutely out of her work and her writing on Christian Science. Only in a short poem which makes a plea for Anglo-American moral solidarity does the phrase "Anglo-Israel" occur, but in that context the term seems more metaphorical than historical or ethnic.[110]

Meanwhile, the faint outlines of a wider mission for Christian Science were becoming visible, first in such English-speaking areas as Canada, Australia, New Zealand, South Africa, then in Western Europe, Latin America, the Orient—indeed, wherever a stray individual or family might be studying and practicing Mrs. Eddy's teachings. Demands were beginning to come in for the translation of *Science and Health* into other languages, particularly French and German. In a characteristically sweeping phrase, Mrs. Eddy wrote Carol Norton in 1896 that she was having calls "from all over this planet" asking permission to translate the book, then added, "How deeply I wish that my students would help me."[111]

One or two of the more linguistically knowledgeable students were pressed into service in securing possible translators, examining samples of drafts of short translated portions, and passing judgment on their quality. "I have seen from experience of translations," she wrote Laura Lathrop in New York, "the danger of letting anyone but a thorough student in languages translate this God-given book,"[112] and further experience convinced her that it was equally important that they be thorough students of the "God-given book."

The outcome of several months' work on both French and German versions at that time was not encouraging. While Mrs. Eddy's chief concern was with the metaphysical accuracy of the translated portions, Hanna pointed out to her that there were also legal and copyright problems involved, and added the further comment in regard to a French draft then under consideration: "You are getting so many children on your hands as it is, that I hardly see what you can do with them, and how will it be if an army of French babies is added?"[113]

Shortly after her arrival in England, Julia Field-King had wanted to dash off to Paris in answer to a call for someone to head the work there, but Mrs. Eddy, who knew the difference between the selfless perseverance of a dedicated missionary and the fly-by-night eagerness of a born promoter, held her to the more exacting and legitimate task, while Paris was left to the impartial ministrations of time.

In Germany, however, the work took hold more rapidly, and also more productively. By the end of 1897, Frau Bertha Günther-Peterson of Hannover was listed in the *Journal* as a practitioner, Hans Eckert of Cannstatt was gradually interesting people in the Stuttgart area in Christian Science, and Mrs. Frances Thurber Seal from the United

States had begun her remarkable healing work in Dresden (and, later, Berlin) which would look in time like a chapter from the Acts of the Apostles.[114]

Years before, Mrs. Eddy had told one of her early students, probably the German-born Edward J. Arens, that Germany would be the first European nation to accept Christian Science, and had gone on to say, "Their love of God, their profound religious character, their deep faith, and strong intellectual qualities make them particularly receptive to Christian Science."[115] Ironically enough, Arens himself represented the Germany symbolized by Mesmer rather than by Luther and turned into a bellicose opponent after a short stint as ebullient supporter. The Germany of Evangelical Protestantism did indeed prove receptive to Christian Science—until Hitler (heir of both Mesmer and Bismarck) drove the movement underground. But from the beginning the enormous but ambivalent energies of the national character held out special opportunities and special hazards to the development of Christian Science.

At the very time in 1899 when Mrs. Eddy told Frau Günther-Peterson at Pleasant View, "I look upon the German nation as one of the chief supporters of Christian Science,"[116]—as, indeed, turned out to be the case—the latter's close co-worker, a Fraülein Marie Schön, was nursing within herself a fanatical Germanism that would cause her later to break off and form a nationalist wing of the movement—and eventually try to establish a German origin for Christian Science through an alleged but mysteriously withheld correspondence between two vaguely identified Fichteans.[117]

About this same time, under the continued provocation of police harassment, Mrs. Seal, armed with a letter of introduction from the United States Consul General and accompanied by a Baroness Olga von Beschwitz of Dresden, went to the President of Police in Berlin and challenged him to show anything in German law that would prohibit the practice of Christian Science. The irate gentleman shook in her face a stout volume and gave her the only answer she needed: "This is the criminal code of Germany, and there is not a line in it that prohibits anyone from worshipping God in his own way."[118] From that point on, until the rise of Hitler, the police persecution eased off and Christian Science put down strong roots in Germany, though hard pressed by a privileged state church and a persistent autocratic tradition.

There still remained the problem of language. In 1897, when Mrs. Eddy turned down a French translation of *Science and Health* by one Alice Tournier, she explained to the translator her conviction that the English tongue "will ere long become the universal language,"[119] and the same explanation was given to the prominent Germans[120] who pressed for a German translation. Only toward the end of her life, when she conceived the idea of having the English and foreign-language texts printed on opposite pages, did she authorize a committee to prepare a translation of *Science and Health* into German.[121]

The slow gestation of the project, and of subsequent translations into other European—and eventually Asian—tongues, was an index of Mrs. Eddy's concern for the "purity" of the language in which Christian Science should be presented to the world. "Love," she wrote in *Science and Health,* "is impartial and universal in its adaptation and bestowals,"[122]—but adaptation, as she saw it, did not mean surrender of metaphysical precision in an effort to accommodate Truth to national preferences. Missionary activity must wait upon "scientific" demonstration.

Thus when Julia Field-King, who had been getting into increasing trouble in England,[123] asked to be sent to India, Mrs. Eddy requested her instead to return to her earlier field in St. Louis—where, as it turned out, her old pupils no longer wanted her.[124] All too evidently, Mrs. Field-King's need was to heal her own restless spirit rather than tackle the vast spiritual and temporal woes of the Indian subcontinent. Mrs. Eddy might already be responding in thought to "calls for help" from India, China, and "the interior of Africa," but for a sound development of Christian Science in these far parts of the earth she must first strengthen her base of operations in the United States.

5

By a series of decisive moves Mrs. Eddy made the year 1898 a climactic one for the Church of Christ, Scientist. Seventy-six years old when the year began, she was never more clearly the Founder and Leader.

In January she executed a deed of trust creating a three-member board of trustees to administer the property and run the business of The Christian Science Publishing Society "for the purpose of more effectually promoting and extending the religion of Christian Science."[125] For "special reasons and to prevent unhappy results," she wrote Hanna, "the transaction had to be settled off" in a single night in preparation for a meeting with her lawyer. When she showed him the "woman document" she had prepared, he assured her that there was "nothing incorrect in it," and that was that. "Well," she commented to Hanna afterward, "had I been its author, I scarcely could have believed it. But I was not more the author of that than of S. & H. as I regard it."[126]

Edward Bates, James Neal, and William McKenzie were the three trustees appointed, but once again Bates proved unable to work with others and resigned at the end of July. Characterized by Mrs. Eddy as "the most helpitive student I ever had,"[127] the energetic but sometimes boorish Bates represented business talents which Mrs. Eddy felt could be invaluable if spiritually redeemed. To McKenzie she wrote soon after the appointment:

> *I thank [God] for giving me you and pray that you be kept unspotted from the world; precious James is safe in God even as all are who abide in Him as you two do, and dear Mr. Bates is most useful when in the right line. Help him to keep thus. I never despair of any one till the last hope of their present career is gone and I see that I can do no more for them.*[128]

When Bates a little later asked her whether the time had not arrived to advertise *Science and Health* and the other Christian Science publications in such periodicals as the *Century Magazine,* she answered him, "You may try it and see how it works."[129] But a month later she wrote him again:

> *Now about advertising. Error says go too fast. I have worked thirty years to get an intermediate line of action for that is Christian Science. Now a large expenditure on advertising is useless. The money will be thrown away. The organs that charge such prices go into the hands of people whose hearts are not ready for Christian Science.*
>
> *I never advertised outside of my own volumes and magazine but once and that did no good. I did not advise you to advertise and now you are carrying it to extremes. Hence my advice is to drop advertising altogether except in our own ranks.*[130]

A considerably more effective form of outreach to the general public was the Christian Science Board of Lectureship, which Mrs. Eddy established in January, 1898. Soon public halls were being filled to overflowing with audiences eager or curious to hear the new gospel. At first there were only five lecturers to fill the demands—three ex-ministers, McKenzie, Tomlinson, and Tomkins, plus Edward Kimball and Carol Norton—but before long other able, personable men and women were added to the roster.

It was now that Edward Kimball emerged as an outstandingly successful exponent of Christian Science, impressive not so much through eloquence as through the breadth of his thought and the calm clarity of his presentation. After Kimball had lectured in Kansas City on June 10, Alfred Farlow of that city wrote Mrs. Eddy that the occasion was "a grand success" in every way. The lecture "was logical, clear, and convincing." The entire audience "remained in almost breathless silence until the close of the two-hour talk."[131] And the *Daily Journal* of that city printed the lecture in full—a not unusual procedure in a day when Christian Science was still hot news.

Mrs. Eddy was determined that the lectures, like the publications of the movement, should be presented with dignity and not take on the tone of an evangelistic crusade. To the Linscotts in Washington she had written a little earlier:

> *Christian Science cannot be carried as anti-slavery and temperance are or have attempted to be.* Agitation *injures our Cause. We should always be . . . Christlike. His voice was not heard in the street.*[132]

Her ideal for the lecture work was expressed in an early letter to Tomlinson: "Take the questions uppermost in the public mind and answer them systematically in Science."[133] This was a broader concept of purpose than that held by many Christian Science lecturers in her own day and since, and she welcomed every evidence of their ability to transcend a merely hortatory or proselytizing approach. To Tomlinson she especially commended "Mr. Kimball's method," and of Judge William G. Ewing of Chicago, who was made a lecturer the following year, she wrote that "he does what I require of the Board of Lectureship, *persuades* and convinces by the logic and the tenderness of Christian Science."[134]

As usual, she kept close watch over this new activity, giving practical, detailed criticism where she felt it necessary. On one occasion she wrote Tomlinson, after reading his lecture:

> *In 15 lines "Christian Science" is repeated 4 times and so through the lecture. Pardon me but the lecture is too good and useful to be so dimmed. Eliminate that word sufficiently to give the high toned sentiments a hearing and not stoppage every few lines.*[135]

No advice of hers was to be more systematically disregarded by speakers and writers in her church for the next three quarters of a century. A similar admonition to McKenzie ran equally contrary to the inclination of many of her followers:

> In your lectures when alluding to me please make your allusion short and do not repeat Mrs. Eddy too often. Works, not words, speak most to the point for a pioneer of religion or Science.[136]

This is in line with a notice for the *Journal* which she wrote and then held back from publication at that time:

> Will students be so kind as to use my name less frequently and extravagantly and only when it is unavoidable. Christian Science drops personality whenever it can be merged in generality without dissimulation. The student who has gained the wisdom requisite for his course will see this without being reminded of it.
>
> Many of the panegyrics so wildly and widely pasted on me are too absurd for common sense. Old Time, the centuries' seer, accords due justice even though tardy, and eternity rewards all merit.[137]

It is not altogether surprising that Mrs. Eddy was becoming a figure of legend, even of myth, to some of her followers, who looked with awe on her continuing accomplishments. During 1898 she had taken two more steps which not only gave fresh impetus to the growth of Christian Science but also provided evidence that her own vitality and keenness were undiminished.

One of these steps was the founding of a new periodical, *The Christian Science Weekly,* whose title was soon changed to *Christian Science Sentinel.* The other was the forming of a Board of Education to resume the work of the Massachusetts Metaphysical College and prepare new teachers of Christian Science. The Hannas, already editing the monthly *Journal,* held similar positions on the nascent weekly. The essential members of the Board of Education, after a little preliminary shifting around, were Mrs. Eddy as president, Hanna as vice-president, and Kimball as teacher.

During and after the twelve-month moratorium on teaching which had followed the publication of *Miscellaneous Writings,* Mrs. Eddy had continued to give thought to what was for her a burning question—how to improve the spiritual caliber of Christian Science teachers and teaching. Finally she took an action which turned out to be closely related to her formation of the Board of Education. On

November 15, 1898, she dispatched identical telegrams to seventy individuals—most of them students of hers but some of them especially promising Christian Scientists who had come on the scene more recently. In somewhat mysterious terms they were asked to be present at Christian Science Hall in Concord on the following Sunday afternoon, November 20, to receive "a great blessing," and with two or three exceptions they all made it.

The Hannas and Kimballs were there, and some of her most experienced students, but the really notable feature was the number of younger people, including Neal, McKenzie, Daisette Stocking, Norton, Tomlinson, Knapp's daughter Daphne, and Mrs. Lathrop's son John. As they sat expectantly in Christian Science Hall at four o'clock on Sunday afternoon, Kimball first mounted the platform and read a message from Mrs. Eddy:

> . . . *You were invited hither to receive from me one or more lessons on Christian Science, prior to conferring on any or all of you, who are ready for it, the degree of C.S.D., of the Massachusetts Metaphysical College. This opportunity is designed to impart a fresh impulse to our spiritual attainments. . . . What I have to say may not require more than one lesson, this, however, must depend on results; but the lessons will certainly not exceed three in number.*[138]

Descriptions of what followed abound in Christian Science literature. How Mrs. Eddy appeared with Calvin Frye and stepped up to the platform "with the agility of a child and the grace of a queen," as one exuberant young man put it.[139] How she looked, what she said, what they felt as they listened—all are recorded, sometimes with awe, sometimes with rhapsody, sometimes with quiet exactness.[140] Some of the students' answers to the questions she asked them are also included—for the two-hour session that day and the four-hour session the next were quite as much an examination of those present as instruction of them.[141] Mrs. Eddy was clearly assessing their spirituality as well as preparing them to be better practitioners and teachers.

In this "last class" of hers, the Pentecostal and the matter-of-fact were near neighbors. At one moment she would illustrate a point by a rustic anecdote from her childhood, at another she would insist on a precise metaphysical analysis of a point under discussion, and again she would carry them away on a tide of inspiration as she pointed out, for instance, what it meant to heal through love, to "*be* nothing but love." All accounts agree that her manner was easy, relaxed, "gentle," but she had a "merry twinkle" in her eye when an answer amused her and "tears of joy" on her face when an outpouring of love from her students at the end caused her to say, "Years have rolled off from me while you have been speaking."[142]

This final scene was precipitated by a tribute to Mrs. Eddy which Mrs. Mims of Atlanta[143] tacked on to an interpretation of a scriptural verse which she had just been asked to make. It was a beautiful exegesis, Mrs. Eddy agreed, but it had not been necessary to mention her personally. Mrs. Mims's later report to her own pupils paints the opening of the scene that followed:

> *Then I wish you could have seen that class. One arose with wet eyes and said, "Mother, how could we forget you?" Judge Hanna got up, and it was one of the most heart-rending things I ever heard in my life, as he said:*
>
> *"Mother, let me tell you this. Sometimes all the machinations of evil that are conceivable to the human mind seem to be hurled at us, and sometimes for days the world seems black. Every argument that the ingenuity of evil can suggest whispers, trying to hide your mission, and the light returns only when we see you as you are—the revelator of this Truth."*[144]

Ten years before, Mrs. Eddy had told an audience of four thousand in Chicago:

> *Christian Science is my only ideal; and the individual and his ideal can never be severed. If either is misunderstood or maligned, it eclipses the other with the shadow cast by this error.*[145]

In a very literal way this earlier statement would be proved true a thousand times over in Christian Science history, and Mrs. Eddy now accepted the students' recognition of the inseverability of her message and her mission with gratitude and with tears. But an earlier episode in the same class session indicated her keen awareness of the opposite danger of personal worship.

This incident concerned a virtual newcomer to Christian Science, Judge Joseph R. Clarkson of Omaha, whom Mrs. Eddy had invited to participate in the class because of the exceptional promise of his character and ability. In the course of speaking about the need neither to love nor to hate corporeal personality, she asked him a question, and his reply evidently betrayed to her ear a too personal and adulatory sense of herself. At that point, according to the detailed account of one of those present,

. . . Mrs. Eddy said, in a tone which seemed almost sorrowful, "Judge Clarkson, I trust that no personal sense of me will ever stand between you and Christian Science." Then her voice became illumined, and she went on speaking with deep earnestness, her voice thrilling with love and power. . . . I tried earnestly to follow her words, but became aware that I was not understanding her at all. . . . A feeling of great regret and loss passed over me, and I felt a sense of my own distance from the plane upon which she was speaking. She continued to speak for several minutes, and then paused a few moments and quietly took up her former line of instruction.[146]

Later the writer of these words found that others, too, had failed to understand what Mrs. Eddy said at this point, but they were deeply impressed by her voice and appearance as she spoke—a sort of "transfiguration," as they considered it. And when Judge Clarkson, only two years later, rebelled against her leadership and left the movement, it seemed to them that Mrs. Eddy must have sensed in his attitude on that occasion the personal idolatry that could just as easily turn to personal antipathy—and had been trying to save him from it. But evidently neither he nor they had got the full message.

Interlude: Political

Interlude: Political

At the very time in 1892 when Mrs. Eddy was moving peacefully into Pleasant View, the French anarchist Ravachol was standing trial, in an atmosphere of electric tension, for a series of retributive killings. Before the end of the century, anarchist bombs, knives, and bullets would have claimed, among others, a French President and a Spanish Premier, Empress Elizabeth of Austria and King Umberto of Italy, with the assassination of an American President to open the new century.

When Mrs. Eddy exhorted her followers to "save the victims of the mental assassins,"[1] she was—though referring to a different kind of violence—drawing attention in her own way to the destructive energies seething beneath the complacent surface of the age. "Science only," she wrote in *Science and Health*, "can explain the incredible good and evil elements now coming to the surface."[2] Again this was a metaphysical rather than a sociopolitical judgment, but it challenged the still dominant myth of inevitable linear progress toward universal peace and prosperity.

"This material world is even now becoming the arena for conflicting forces," she warned in a long passage of prophecy. "On one side there will be discord and dismay; on the other side there will be Science and peace."[3] What sort of politics did such a view imply? On one side of *what* would there be Science and peace? Certainly not on one side of the Atlantic, on one side of the class war, on one side of territorial or ethnic or party divisions.

In Mrs. Eddy's metaphysics the basic division lay between two views of reality, each of which must have a practical (though not always recognized) bearing on politics, in the broad Aristotelian sense of the word. One side looked toward material means and methods for ultimate solutions, the other side to pure spirit, to an intelligence above and beyond all human circumstance or instrumentality. To this latter view "Science and peace" were inherent in the divine order of things but, by logical implication, must be demonstrated on the level of interdependent human action as social regeneration. So understood, the metaphysical overview was not a means of escaping politics but of transforming it.

What this meant in practice must be worked out experientially. Mrs. Eddy expected, however, that the leaven of radical spirituality in all areas of human activity would produce a moral fermentation or chemicalization which would make the human situation in many ways worse before it grew better.[4] This was cause for neither pessimism nor optimism, as she wrote in another connection,[5] but it could serve as a call to spiritual arms—and to a better understanding of what was already happening in society.

Through the last decade of the nineteenth century, the cracks in Victorian optimism were beginning to show. The popular faith in automatic material progress and the humanitarian faith in the perfectibility of society could hardly feel entire satisfaction with a ten-year record that included a Russian famine, Italian bread riots, a prolonged American economic depression, the bloody Homestead and Pullman strikes, the march on Washington of Coxey's army of unemployed, the Dreyfus tragedy, the Sino-Japanese war, the Turkish massacre of fifty thousand Armenians, Germany's ominous plans for naval expansion, and that dismal series of *fin de siècle* colonial struggles which held within itself the portent of far worse things to come.

An editorial in the *Christian Science Sentinel* of August 2, 1900, called "The World's Uproar," bore witness to the growing popular unease. Gloomily it took note of the famine in India, then moved on through the current Boer War ("The slaughter of Christian brother by Christian brother thus far in this war, has been awful, and the end is not yet") and the Philippine insurrection in which "our own government is at war with the natives, thus far at a deplorable cost of life," to the "almost continuous series of revolutions" in South America and the atrocity-ridden Boxer uprising in China.

To take note of such events was a small first step toward coming to grips with the metaphysical problem they posed for Christian Scientists.

From its inception in 1898, immediately following the Spanish-American War, the *Sentinel* devoted space to the consideration of public affairs, a function which would later be carried on more professionally by *The Christian Science Monitor*.[6] At the same time, Mrs. Eddy herself was giving thought to public issues which the pressing needs of the movement had earlier crowded into the background of her concern, and with characteristic realism she was learning from events as they occurred. This was particularly evident in regard to the question of war and peace.

She had already in *Science and Health* drawn a relevant distinction between the Jehovah of history and the universal God glimpsed by the Hebrew prophets. "The Jewish tribal Jehovah," she wrote, "was a man-projected God, liable to wrath, repentance, and human changeableness."[7] As she saw it, that terrible though majestic figure still cast its shadow over the God of infinite compassion who had come to light through later revelation:

> *The Jewish conception of God, as Yawah, Jehovah, or only a mighty hero and king, has not quite given place to the true knowledge of God. . . .*
>
> *In that name of Jehovah, the true idea of God seems almost lost. God becomes "a man of war," a tribal god to be worshipped, rather than Love, the divine Principle to be lived and loved.*[8]

To live this principled Love individually, she taught, was to follow in Jesus' footsteps. To live it collectively would require the total effort of the whole Church of Christ. The final goal was clear enough: it was to demonstrate the first Hebrew Commandment— "Thou shalt have no other gods before me"[9]—to the point where all men should come to accept one God, one Mind, as the Principle determining the common good, and she expressed in a single sweeping sentence her vision of what that would mean for the world:

> *One infinite God, good, unifies men and nations; constitutes the brotherhood of man; ends wars; fulfils the Scripture, "Love thy neighbor as thyself;" annihilates pagan and Christian idolatry, —whatever is wrong in social, civil, criminal, political, and religious codes; equalizes the sexes; annuls the curse on man, and leaves nothing that can sin, suffer, be punished or destroyed.*[10]

But in the year of our Lord 1898 the human scene provided much that was self-evidently and even appallingly wrong—much that needed changing, uncovering, punishing, destroying, challenging, rescuing, healing. And no more than any other country was the United States of America prepared to act in these matters on the prescription of Mary Baker Eddy—or, indeed, of Jesus of Nazareth. For that matter, Mrs. Eddy herself was still far from clear as to how to relate her spiritual ideal to the political exigencies of the moment.

On March 20, when the popular clamor for war with Spain was mounting, the *Boston Herald* published a statement by her, "Other Ways Than By War," which contained such unequivocally antiwar statements as, "Killing men is not consonant with the higher law whereby wrong and injustice are righted and exterminated," then concluded somewhat ambiguously, "But if our nation's rights or honor were seized, every citizen would be a soldier and woman would be armed with power girt for the hour."[11]

That Mrs. Eddy did not intend this last sentence to be taken quite so literally as many of her followers subsequently did is suggested by a letter she sent to Mrs. McKinley at the White House ten days later. No greater glory could crown any nation, she wrote the First Lady, than to rebuke but also forgive "so foul a crime" as the blowing up of the American cruiser *Maine* in Havana Harbor. It was her custom, she added, to admonish Christian Scientists in their efforts to defeat repressive laws never to take the sword, metaphorically speaking, but always endeavor to overcome evil with good.[12]

As the war fever mounted, she instructed the Board of Directors on April 14 to pray twice each day that the members of Congress "see the error of making war with Spain and the wisdom of settling this question amicably."[13] To Albert Metcalf, who had written to the President opposing the war, she wrote on the same day:

> *I highly approve of your note to President McKinley. . . . I am astonished at the attitude of Congress! Our Senator Chandler is a bristling man at best and Galliger seems obtuse on this question of war. Our nation never did so blindly before meddle with Spanish America.*[14]

Two days later, however, she sent a further message to the *Boston Herald* which read in part:

> *In order to close the multitudinous questions addressed to me on the subject of the war-cloud and the sober second thought of our chief magistrate, President McKinley, I will say, in my poor opinion it had been better that our friendly nation in the first instance had wiped her hands of Cuba altogether. . . .*
>
> *To coincide with God's government is the proper incentive to the action of all nations. If His purpose for peace is to be subserved by the battle's plan, or the intervention of the United States, whereby Cubans shall learn to make war no more, this means and end will be accomplished.*[15]

Nine days later, on April 25, war was declared. Within a week of that date, Admiral Dewey steamed into Manila Bay and wiped out the Spanish squadron without the loss of a single American life. There was idealism as well as jingoism in the jubilation that followed. Was not this a sign of God's blessing on the country's unselfish purpose to liberate the Cubans? The tribute paid to Dewey's humanity by the defeated commander of the Spanish squadron reinforced earnest hopes that the war might indeed be an expression of American generosity rather than of the naked imperialist ambitions voiced by such men as Beveridge and Lodge.[16]

The flushed atmosphere of that time is reflected in two paragraphs of the annual message which Mrs. Eddy sent to The Mother Church in early June:

> *In your peaceful homes remember our brave soldiers, whether in camp or in battle. Oh, may their love of country, and their faithful service thereof, be unto them life-preservers! May the divine Love succor and protect them, as at Manila, where brave men, led by the dauntless Dewey, and shielded by the power that saved them, sailed victoriously through the jaws of death and blotted out the Spanish squadron.*
>
> *Great occasion have we to rejoice that our nation, which fed her starving foe,—already murdering her peaceful seamen and destroying millions of her money,—will be as formidable in war as she has been compassionate in peace.*[17]

On July 3 the war in Cuba was all but ended by a naval battle off Santiago, and Admiral Sampson's dispatch announced with school-boy panache: "The fleet under my command offers the nation as a Fourth of July present the whole of Cervera's fleet."[18] Not one escaped, he added. Four days afterward the Senate ratified the annexation of Hawaii; by the end of the month Spain asked for an armistice; and five months later the Treaty of Paris transferred sovereignty over the Philippines from Spain to the United States. Americans had joined in the world struggle for power that would come to a head in the smash-up of 1914.

Meanwhile, *The Christian Science Journal* and the new *Sentinel* gave evidence of the learning process that was going on. In a lengthy editorial in the *Journal* of June, 1898, Hanna pointed out that there was no biblical warrant for war if the spiritual meaning of Scripture, as opposed to the literal, was understood. Recalling Moses' song of victory after the drowning of Pharaoh's army, he wrote:

> *These are songs of exultation and victory that would quite adequately express the exuberance of feeling now prevalent in our country over Dewey's great victory at the Philippine Islands. . . . If Deity is to be personalized—as that term is ordinarily under-stood—then we are bound to believe that a personal God person-*

ally gave explicit directions as to the conduct of the ancient battles, and literally acted as commander-in-chief of the armies in much the same sense that President McKinley is now acting as commander-in-chief of our armies.

But the later prophets and, above all, the New Testament had a clear perception of "the non-divinity of war," Hanna continued. Either Jesus meant what he said or he didn't. The only way a genuine Christian could therefore understand the apparent glorification of war in the Old Testament was to see in these accounts a spiritually inspired metaphor of God's destruction of evil beliefs or conditions, not of people. Yet all human action was relative, and some beliefs were better than others—a position summed up by Mrs. Eddy ten years before in her statement: "Wisdom in human action begins with what is nearest right under the circumstances, and thence achieves the absolute."[19] And on that basis Hanna tentatively defended the United States action as perhaps "the most effective means" of righting Cuba's wrongs that could be expected within the "present aggregate understanding" of the United States.[20]

The editorial was an earnest if tortuous effort to think out a problem which comparatively few Christians at that time were willing to tackle. However, with the war drawing to a rapid close and with his weakness for an overliteral interpretation of prophetic Scripture, Hanna backtracked somewhat in the next issue and suggested that there was some ground for believing that "the war is in line with Biblical prophecy." Two months later he had decided that good would unquestionably come from the war, while the fact that it had been ended in the short space of three months "surely is among the evidences of the fulfilling of that prophecy which declares that wars and rumors of wars shall come to an end."[21]

This cheerful assurance did not last long, as it became increasingly evident that the baldest kind of power politics and economic imperialism was involved in the Philippine adventure. Speeches "against imperialism" began to be quoted in the *Christian Science Sentinel.* "Senator Hoar on the Nation's Great Danger" recorded that gentleman's strong opposition to acquiring the Philippines by alleged right of conquest. A lengthy extract from a Carl Schurz speech on "Militarism and Democracy" presented an eloquent argument against America's joining in the old European power game. And in the very week in which the Filipinos under Aguinaldo began their war of independence against the United States, the *Sentinel* ran a column of quotations ironically headed "The Progress of Imperialism":

The Anglo-Saxon advances into the new regions with a Bible in one hand and a shotgun in the other. The inhabitants he cannot convert he gets rid of with the shotgun.—Congressman Sulloway of New Hampshire.

We must hold (permanently) our new possessions under military government.—Captain Mahan.

We have outgrown the Constitution. It is not worth while to discuss it.—General Merritt.

The Constitution must bend . . . —President E. H. Capen of Tufts College.

My plan would be to disarm the natives of the Philippine Islands even if we kill half of them in doing it.—General Shafter.

We will whip them to death.—Senator Carter of Montana.[22]

Mrs. Eddy, during this time, was observing and thinking. In her Communion message to The Mother Church for 1899 she wrote, "I reluctantly foresee great danger threatening our nation,—imperialism, monopoly, and a lax system of religion."[23] However, she was careful at all times not to identify herself with a particular political philosophy[24] or to turn her personal opinions on social and political questions into articles of Christian Science faith. In her messages to The Mother Church as well as in her statements for the secular press, she commented on what she saw as the moral significance of passing events, but she also made it clear that these pronouncements were not to be regarded as papal bulls or official formulations of church policy.

This distinction—which would likewise apply to editorial positions taken by *The Christian Science Monitor* when it came into existence—was evident in the years immediately following the Spanish-American War, when Mrs. Eddy's views on public affairs were evolving as she observed the course of events. In her 1899 message she wrote:

Lean not too much on your Leader. Trust God to direct your steps. Accept my counsel and teachings only as they include the spirit and the letter of the Ten Commandments, the Beatitudes, and the teachings and example of Christ Jesus.[25]

Among similar statements by her in the next few years was one in her message to The Mother Church for 1902 which related her injunction to a brief review of events during the preceding year:

Our nation's forward step was the inauguration of home rule in Cuba,—our military forces withdrawing, and leaving her in the enjoyment of self-government under improved laws....

The world rejoices with our sister nation over the close of the conflict in South Africa; now, British and Boer may prosper in peace, wiser at the close than the beginning of war....

It does not follow that power must mature into oppression.... Competition in commerce, deceit in councils, dishonor in nations, dishonesty in trusts, begin with "Who shall be greatest?" I again repeat, Follow your Leader, only so far as she follows Christ.[26]

Through the remaining years of her life, her concern about war and peace, individual liberty and industrial slavery, continued to grow—as indicated by her marking of the magazines and newspapers she read.[27] But her public mentions of these and other problems were little more than pointers to social ills she felt were in special need of healing, and she left the analysis of them and the political education of her followers to the daily newspaper she was to found in her eighty-eighth year.

For Mrs. Eddy, the healing of the individual was still the basis on which the healing of the nations must rest. "When that [i.e., individual healing] has taken hold of mankind," she had told a socially minded student in 1886, "the other will in time follow as a necessary sequence."[28] She also expected that Christian Scientists in political life or social work would be able to leaven those activities with "the purpose to accomplish the most good for the largest number."[29]

She was cautious, however, about using involvement in public life as a means of furthering Christian Science. When it was mistakenly reported in the press that Sarah Pike Conger, wife of the American Minister to China and an ardent Christian Scientist, had converted the fearsome old Dowager Empress of that country to Christian Science, Mrs. Eddy made public a letter to Mrs. Conger in which she wrote, with a slight overtone of Bret Harte's "The Heathen Chinee" and what might almost have been precognition of the later evolution of Chinese xenophobia under the influence of Marxist materialism and Maoist reeducation:

The report of the success of Christian Science in benighted China, when regarded on one side only, is cheering, but to look at both sides of the great question of introducing Christian Science into a heathen nation gives the subject quite another aspect. I believe that all our great Master's sayings are practical and scientific. If the Dowager Empress could hold her nation, there would be no danger in teaching Christian Science in her country. But a war on religion in China would be more fatal than the Boxers' rebellion. Silent prayer in and for a heathen nation is just what is needed. But to teach and to demonstrate Christian Science before the minds of the people are prepared for it, and when the laws are against it, is fraught with danger.[30]

In reply, Mrs. Conger made it clear that she would have considered it a breach of diplomatic protocol even to mention Christian Science to the ladies of the Imperial Court. Her published letters[31] covering the period of the Boxer uprising, plus her unpublished correspondence with Mrs. Eddy over the years, indicate the way in which events were educating both the Founder and the adherents of Christian Science in world politics.

During the long period when the foreign legation in Peking, with only a handful of armed men to protect them, were under siege by the Boxers and most of the world believed the entire diplomatic corps to have been already massacred,[32] Mrs. Conger was forced pretty drastically to put her faith into practice.[33] But when the siege was finally lifted by an international relief force, her real education began. With the visible evidence of Chinese atrocities everywhere around her, she first wrote her sister:

The awful treachery and base cruelty of the Chinese high officials and the people governed by them are without parallel. Can we ever forgive and forget? The Christ-spirit alone can help us.

After another month her point of view had shifted drastically:

Poor China! Why cannot foreigners let her alone with her own? China has been wronged, and in her desperation she has striven as best she could to stop the inroads, and to blot out those already made. My sympathy is with China. A very unpopular thing to say, but it is an honest conviction, honestly uttered.

After two more months, during which fresh Boxer atrocities had come to light, Mrs. Conger wrote her nephew with a sense of balance rare among Western Christians:

The foreigner has forced himself, his country, his habits, and his productions upon China always against a strong protest. It kept getting worse for China, and she recognized the fact. At length, in one last struggle, she rose in her mistaken might to wipe the foreigner and his influence from her land. Could we, after taking these facts home to ourselves, blame the Chinese for doing what they could to get rid of what they considered *an obnoxious pest that was undermining the long-established customs of their entire country? Their methods, however, are most lamentable.*[34]

All this was a far cry from Concord, New Hampshire, but lines of communication ran between the two. Several years later a well-known reporter of the day, William E. Curtis of the Chicago *Record-Herald,* had an interview with Mrs. Eddy. Since Curtis had been a correspondent in China and knew it well, the conversation turned to the aftermath of the Boxer rebellion. At one point Mrs. Eddy asked for more definite information on a certain question, and then proceeded to take over the topic and discuss it in such unexpected detail "as to quite confound the man."[35]

Michael Meehan, the Concord editor who accompanied Curtis to the interview, wrote later:

> *As we drove from Pleasant View, Mr. Curtis marveled how a woman who so completely excluded the world could possibly know so much about the world's affairs, and particularly how she could have acquired such accurate and comprehensive acquaintance with the history and national habits of the Chinese, a people so little known, and with the court customs and the unpublished intrigues of its rulers. As we parted, he said, "Just one more surprise, one more instance of where we came to preach, and remained to pray."*[36]

In view of the correspondence between Mrs. Eddy and Mrs. Conger, the phenomenon was not quite so mysterious as it seemed to Meehan and Curtis. But it suggests that the subsequent founding of *The Christian Science Monitor* was more deeply rooted in Mrs. Eddy's own consciousness of world happenings than has been generally supposed.

Chapter
V

The Woman and the Serpent

The Woman and the Serpent

The question of Mrs. Eddy's ultimate position within her own movement reached back almost three decades to the rebellion of her early student Richard Kennedy, now a shadowy figure practicing magnetic healing in Boston, forgotten by or unknown to a later generation of Christian Scientists.

But not forgotten by Josephine Curtis Woodbury, an intense, ambitious woman who had first become acquainted with Mrs. Eddy in the late 1870's, later studied with her, became in 1886 a Christian Science teacher, then in 1890 tried to save her own moral reputation by foisting on Mrs. Eddy an outrageous doctrine of "mental conception" to explain the birth of her illegitimate child—after which almost everything Mrs. Woodbury did made a mockery of Christian Science teachings.

From the outset, Mrs. Woodbury seemed to be fascinated by the subject of malicious animal magnetism, and especially by the figure of Richard Kennedy, whom she had never known personally but saw as the epitome of hypnotic power used for malignant purposes.

Her letters to Mrs. Eddy during these years constitute an interesting study in moral ambiguity. Again and again, like Julia Field-King, she abases herself, confesses to unnamed sins, and pours out gratitude for her teacher's "forbearance" and "forgiveness," and for the "severe tenderness" with which Mrs. Eddy has "stripped evil from my eyes."[1] Yet even the most honeyed passages are apt to have a sting in them. "Oh my Mother," she cries in one letter with what seems a touch of murky exhilaration, "I am constantly being blessed by your agony."[2] And it is difficult at times to know whether she is paying a tribute or nursing a resentment, as when she writes:

> *The more I work in public—the more I am convinced that every mesmerist—every hypocrite every sinner every wayward student hates you because they are* afraid of you— *You are the Daniel come to judgment. . . . Sometimes I think it is all they do fear— this exposure by you.*[3]

There was also an obvious desire to wind her way into the intricacies of Mrs. Eddy's mental experience and thus claim a closeness to her which Mrs. Eddy's own letters show was far from being the fact.[4] After encountering some of Kennedy's patients in New Hampshire, in 1888, Mrs. Woodbury wrote her teacher triumphantly, "I saw Richard Kennedy at last!"[5]—by which she apparently meant that she finally understood his mentality by seeing its effects upon his patients. To this she added with some pride, "You know how vivid my experiences have always been—How I stand face to face with those who knew you in the past." And although, as she somewhat dramatically claimed, this mental encounter with Kennedy caused her to drink "the deepest, bitterest cup of poison," her horror was evidently mixed with considerable satisfaction.

A similar ambivalence is detectable in her public utterances of that period, as in the lecture reported in the *Montreal Gazette* of October 8, 1889:

> *The Daniel of this period is the voice of Christian Science, which says to sinners, "Come out from your lazar houses, into the disinfecting sunlight of purity." . . . Did you ever lay open the long grass when you had seen the trail of the serpent? Did you find the serpent there? No, it had gone into still more hidden lairs.*

The sunlight of purity and the lair of the serpent—in these two images Mrs. Woodbury summed up the two attractions which kept her slithering in and out of the long grass for more than a decade. But gradually the fascination of hidden mental power seems to have prevailed over what may have been at one time a genuine if sporadic desire for dedication to an ideal purpose. At any rate, by 1890 the corruption of purpose was fairly complete.

In that year she gave birth to the illegitimate child in question, the fruit of her seduction of one of her male students in Montreal.[6] This awkward development had to be explained away not only to her blindly devoted husband but also to her bewildered students, a number of whom were privy to the fact that the Woodburys had not had sexual relations for the past year or two.[7] Her method of extricating herself from the dilemma showed a moral audacity of a curiously ophidian character.

By claiming an "immaculate conception" for the child, christening him "The Prince of Peace," making him an object of veneration to her students, and then, to crown it all, attributing to Mrs. Eddy an alleged secret doctrine that repetitions of the historic virgin birth were possible to Christian Science women of exceptional purity,[8] Mrs. Woodbury succeeded in doing several things. She quieted and even dazzled further her husband and students, left other Christian Scientists with a feeling of helpless outrage at the mixture of comic opera, blasphemy, and psychopathology into which she had dragged their religion, and suggested to several coming generations of bemused historians that she was really the guileless victim of an idiotic teaching by Mrs. Eddy. The audacity of the claim has blurred the fact that Mrs. Eddy taught the exact opposite of the doctrine attributed to her.[9]

Never in any doubt of the "total depravity"[10] of mortal mind in general or of the dangerous double-mindedness of Mrs. Woodbury in particular, the founder of Christian Science attempted for six more years to wrestle her student back from the abyss. In an emotionally exhausting visit to Pleasant View in 1894, the temporarily or perhaps expediently penitent Mrs. Woodbury confessed that her child, far from being immaculately conceived, had been "incarnated with the devil."[11] A year later she wrote Mrs. Eddy, with the touch of ambiguity that was never absent from her letters:

> Do you know,—way off in that pure realm where you dwell, that the sharpest sting I feel,—is the awful sense of what your disappointment in me is? You say there is a promise of joy ahead if I will trust the dear Mother to guide me, and if I try to do right steadily, but can that Love prevent me from bearing this anguish of regret even to the end? . . . Even now when you know I ought to bear every pang alone without a hint of help from you—and bear it all and without complaint, you come with your soft wing and bear me up lest I fail utterly. You know I could have borne rebuke better than this letting out of your love upon me.[12]

At this time, Mrs. Woodbury was seeking admission to The Mother Church, and although the members were almost solidly against it[13] Mrs. Eddy's feeling that she should be given a chance to rehabilitate herself prevailed, and she was admitted to probationary membership in April, 1895. The reconciliation was short-lived. Stories of malign goings-on continued to reach the Directors' ears, and an unexplained letter from Mrs. Woodbury to Mrs. Eddy on October 2 of that year indicates that the stories were more than idle gossip:

Dear Teacher—
I am ashamed of myself—too ashamed to say anything.
Your student,
J. C. Woodbury[14]

A month later she was dropped from The Mother Church. Although at Mrs. Eddy's request she was reinstated to probationary membership in March, 1896, this time the union lasted for less than two weeks, and on April 4 she was excommunicated from the church forever. Mrs. Eddy explained to Judge Hanna that the *Manual* bylaw providing that a second excommunication of a member should be irrevocable "by no means hinders the salvation of that sinner, for C. S. does not make the church responsible for his salvation as Catholicism does."[15]

It was at this time that one Fred C. Chamberlain brought suit against Mrs. Woodbury for alienating the affections of his wife, who was a pupil of hers. Also, a certain Evelyn I. Rowe applied for a divorce on the ground that her husband gave all his earnings to Mrs. Woodbury for the education and support of the young Prince of Peace. The *Boston Traveller,* in reporting these developments, published interviews with two other indignant gentlemen who asserted that their wives had put pressure on them to buy stock in a highly dubious "air-engine" which Mr. Woodbury was promoting and to make lavish gifts to the immaculately conceived Prince. Mrs. Woodbury thereupon brought suit against the *Traveller* for criminal libel—and lost the case.

Simply glancing back today at her bizarre career, it would be easy enough to write her off as a flighty, confused, possibly unpleasant but slightly comic figure. Nothing could be further from the truth. In her own day Mrs. Woodbury got herself taken very seriously indeed by all who knew her—either as an accomplished, even brilliant woman, grievously misled and wronged, or as a nasty piece of work as strong-minded in her way as the Medeas and Messalinas of antiquity.

A more impressive tribute to her force of mind and will is the somewhat astonishing fact that biographical scholarship for the next three-quarters of a century would almost uniformly transfer the discredit for her sensational involvements to the overburdened shoulders of Mrs. Eddy. Sober doctors of divinity have found it easier to cite her as the authority on what Mrs. Eddy taught about the virgin birth than to examine what Mrs. Eddy actually did teach.[16] In more popular works, Mrs. Eddy's extraordinary patience with her student as revealed in their correspondence has been transformed into a secret envy of the Woodbury flair for the dramatic.[17] Mrs. Woodbury seems almost literally to have hypnotized those who wrote about her.[18]

Evidence accumulated in 1899–1900 in connection with a court case shows dismally the mental slavery in which she held her pupils. They were threatened with sickness, insanity, and death if they broke away from her, for both she and they were firm believers in black magic.[19] Even while on probation in the church, she had warned them ominously against the deceptive blandishments of "the enemy," i.e., the Directors. Even while sending shock waves through The Mother Church by lauding Mrs. Eddy as "the Word made flesh," she was making cynical references in private to "The Mother Mary."[20] As in the case of the soothsaying damsel who cried out after Paul and his companions, "These men are the servants of the most high God,"[21] Mrs. Eddy, like Paul, was "grieved" at what she regarded as the utterance of a blasphemous spirit.

Something of the torment involved in Mrs. Woodbury's state of mind can be glimpsed through the testimony given by Julia Bartlett in regard to a visit the unfortunate woman paid her in 1895.

Though a pillar of New England rectitude, Miss Bartlett combined her transparent honesty with a Christian charity which made even the most errant and rebellious students feel they could confide in her.[22] On this particular morning, Mrs. Woodbury presented herself and explained that she was suffering such agony of remorse that she *must* talk with someone. Miss Bartlett's rather dry, precise account of the visit goes on:

> *She said no one knew the terrible sins she had committed and that it seemed as though she were nothing but evil and that she sometimes said that she believed there was a personal devil and that she was that devil. She also said, at that time, that I had no idea of the number of people she had been the means of putting out of the cause of Christian Science. I said I did know something of what she was doing but she said, "You do not know how many I have caused to leave it." As near as I can remember I asked her if she meant it was through mental influence this was done and she said yes. She then said I did not know what a wicked woman she was and when she realized the enormity of her sins her agony was almost unbearable but fortunately these times did not last long. She repeatedly spoke of Mrs. Eddy's great love and how she had borne with her for so long. As she was going out of the door she said she did not think one would make such a confession, as she had made to me, for the fun of it.*[23]

Depravity is no stranger to traditional Christian theology, but its ambiguities have never been more subtly explored than in the secular literature from Dostoevsky to the present in which moral vision has interpenetrated abnormal psychology.[24] The modern mind has no difficulty in recognizing how deeply the defiant perversity of, for instance, Milton's Satan—"Evil be thou my good"—is rooted in a despairing self-hatred: "Which way I fly is hell; myself am hell."[25] This is the horror that permeates so much of modern literature, the tragic ambivalence summed up in the words of Jesus: "If therefore the light that is in thee be darkness, how great is that darkness."[26] Even the luxury of confession, as Mrs. Woodbury's visit to Julia Bartlett showed, was a recognizable element of the *âme damnée* syndrome.

With the passing of time, the unhappy woman occasionally let her pupils catch a glimpse of a cynical coarseness that nonplussed them, as when she remarked to one of the most adoring of them, Carrie Roach, a maiden lady of irreproachable propriety, "O Carrie, if you'll let a man roll over you once there's *nothing* he won't do for you."[27] On a later visit to her with two equally unworldly fellow pupils Miss Roach was astonished when Mrs. Woodbury "for no apparent reason explained graphically to us what sodomy is and also a crime called buggery, neither of which I had heard of before."[28] It was hard to reconcile these things with a teacher who had preached to them almost hysterically the need for absolute purity.[29]

"How dare you," Mrs. Eddy wrote Mrs. Woodbury shortly before her final excommunication, "how dare you in the sight of God and with your character behind the curtain, and your own students ready to lift it on you, pursue a path perilous?"[30]—a sentence much ridiculed by several biographers in the next century as an example of the "bigoted persecution" of which Mrs. Woodbury complained in a newspaper article she wrote in 1897. Without naming her persecutors, this article went on to say in a tone of meek piety that the writer's only fault had been her willingness to unveil to the world the wicked workings of animal magnetism:

> Not only do serpents poison the crushing heel, but ingratitude stings the beneficent hand; and I have a right to resent the imputation of evil motives to one [i.e., me] whose faults lie in the direction of generosity; but who patiently awaits the verdict of the future, which must sanction her exertions with the signet of Christendom.[31]

So long as she felt there was any chance of recouping her losses in the movement, Mrs. Woodbury abstained from overt attack on Mrs. Eddy.[32] Instead, she praised her in carefully equivocal ways.[33] Her book *War in Heaven* recounted her "sixteen years' experience in Christian Science" in apparently reasonable if thoroughly inaccurate terms. The self-portrait that emerges from the narrative is of a loving disciple humbly devoted to and highly valued by a great religious leader—from whom she has finally been separated by the misrepresentations of less favored disciples jealous of her "intimacy" with the great one. Plausibly presented, the story is belied by the actual correspondence between the two women during those sixteen years.

The deeper struggle beneath the smooth surface of the narrative is suggested by the book's title, taken from Revelation 12:

> *And there was war in heaven: Michael and his angels fought against the dragon; and the dragon fought and his angels. . . . And the great dragon was cast out, that old serpent, called the Devil, and Satan, which deceiveth the whole world.*[34]

Once again, it is not clear who or what Mrs. Woodbury takes the dragon or old serpent to be. But early in her account, after telling of the strange reversals of feeling that followed close upon her first healing, with its "visions of a glorious future" in Christian Science, occurs a passage which may reveal more than the author intended:

> *In my own "chambers of imagery" also there was mental bewilderment. At one moment all seemed surely good; yet the next hour the feeling supervened that wrong was the great ruler, and that mankind might exclaim with Milton's Satan, "Evil, be thou my Good." Over the sky hung a subtle pall. Was there a vision of the two wonders revealed by the angel of the Apocalypse,—the Serpent and the Woman?*[35]

The issue for Mrs. Woodbury was: For which wonder would she finally settle? The issue for Mrs. Eddy was a good deal larger: For which view of life would history finally settle?

2

It was the tree of the *knowledge* of good and evil which lay at the root of the fabled trouble in Eden, Mrs. Eddy pointed out. In her *Unity of Good* she wrote:

> . . . *God forbade man to know evil at the very beginning, when Satan held it up before man as something desirable and a distinct addition to human wisdom, because the knowledge of evil would make man a god,—a representation that God both knew and admitted the dignity of evil.*
>
> *Which is right,—God, who condemned the knowledge of sin and disowned its acquaintance, or the serpent, who pushed that claim with the glittering audacity of diabolical and sinuous logic?*[36]

Mrs. Woodbury's history shows her to have been afflicted by the three classical lusts: the lust for knowledge, the lust for power, and the lust for sensation. It was the first of these that had caused her passionate desire to get into the minds of both Mary Baker Eddy and Richard Kennedy, but inevitably she would have to make a final choice between the two types of mental power they represented to her. When, at the end of 1898, she cast her lot irrevocably on the side of what she herself in earlier years had described as animal magnetism, it was predictable that she would throw her considerable energies into the attempt to discredit and destroy the woman who had written, "Sin is the image of the beast to be effaced by the sweat of agony"[37]—and again:

> *Truth causes sin to betray itself, and sets upon error the mark of the beast. Even the disposition to excuse guilt or to conceal it is punished.*[38]

It was also predictable that Mrs. Woodbury's female animosity would be more deadly than Kennedy's clumsy maneuver in 1878 to pin a "conspiracy to murder" charge on Mrs. Eddy's husband.[39] Early in 1899 newspapers from Bangor, Maine, to Denver, Colorado, began printing derisive little poems, letters, news items, written or inspired by Mrs. Woodbury and aimed at the founder of Christian Science. This first scatter of fire was the prelude to a skillful attempt to build up an image of Mrs. Eddy as herself the embodiment of all that was devious, dishonest, and serpentine. The author of *Science and Health* saw this as an example of the instinct described in a passage in her chapter on the Apocalypse which clearly applies to character assassination as much as to any other form of "killing," and presumptively to Kennedy as well as to Mrs. Woodbury:

> *As of old, evil still charges the spiritual idea with error's own nature and methods. This malicious animal instinct, of which the dragon is the type, incites mortals to kill morally and physically even their fellow-mortals, and worse still, to charge the innocent with the crime.*[40]

The ultimate aim of Mrs. Woodbury's campaign was obviously to destroy any claim of Christian Science to either intellectual respectability or Christian authority. If she could show that Mrs. Eddy's teachings were born in deception, she would be well on the way to dragging them down to the level of her own shenanigans.

Her purpose became clear in an article in the May, 1899, issue of the *Arena*. This socially conscious, mildly radical journal had fallen temporarily out of the hands of its regular editor, Benjamin O. Flower, who enjoyed a quiet distinction as an idealistic crusader, into the clutch of an ardent mind-curer who espoused the cause of "New

Thought, Hypnotism, Occultism, Psychic Research, Will Power," and kindred developments, with a corresponding distaste for Christian Science.

"Eddyism Exposed," the May issue announced, and the exposure took the form of a double-barreled article, "Christian Science and its Prophetess," of which Part I, "The Facts of the Case," was written by Horatio W. Dresser, and Part II, "The Book and the Woman," by Josephine Curtis Woodbury.

Back in 1895, only a few weeks after her admission to probationary membership in The Mother Church, Mrs. Woodbury had sent Mrs. Eddy a copy of a just-published book *The Philosophy of P. P. Quimby* by Annetta G. Dresser. This lady and her then fiancé, Julius A. Dresser, had been patients of the Portland healer Phineas Parkhurst Quimby in 1862 when Mrs. Eddy had gone to him for treatment, and some twenty years later the two Dressers had launched a campaign to establish Quimby as the originator of Christian Science.[41]

In her book, Mrs. Dresser included among the material she quoted from Quimby's manuscripts an 1861 statement which bears interestingly on that contention: "My foundation is animal matter, or life. This, set in action by wisdom, produces thought."[42] While such an assertion was entirely consistent with the evolution of Quimby's thought from his background of mesmeric practice, it was totally inconsistent with Mrs. Eddy's metaphysical premise: "Spirit is God, and man is His image and likeness. Therefore man is not material; he is spiritual."[43]

What the two did have in common was the quality of compassion—what Mrs. Eddy in *Miscellaneous Writings* described as Quimby's "rare humanity and sympathy"[44]—though that humanitarian gentleman could never have written anything remotely like the passage in *Science and Health:*

> *While we adore Jesus, and the heart overflows with gratitude for what he did for mortals,—treading alone his loving pathway up to the throne of glory, in speechless agony exploring the way for us,—yet Jesus spares us not one individual experience, if we follow his commands faithfully; and all have the cup of sorrowful effort to drink in proportion to their demonstration of his love, till all are redeemed through divine Love.*[45]

Now the Dressers' son Horatio, a highly talented young man doing graduate work in philosophy under William James, stepped forward in the *Arena* in partnership with Mrs. Woodbury to champion the claim that Mrs. Eddy had drawn Christian Science from Quimby's psychotherapy rather than from the Bible—a thesis plausible only if one liberally reinterpreted Quimby in the light of Mrs. Eddy's Christian theism and disregarded what might be called the intrinsic or proto-Quimby, as represented by the statement quoted by Mrs. Dresser.[46]

It was the beginning of a thirty-year crusade by Horatio Dresser, but for Josephine Woodbury it was merely a convenient weapon in the private war to which she had now committed herself. The temper of her article is illustrated by the scornful attitude she assumed toward Mrs. Eddy's title of Discoverer and Founder:

> What she has really "discovered" are ways and means of perverting and prostituting the science of healing to her own ecclesiastical aggrandisement, and to the moral and physical depravity of her dupes. As she received this science from Dr. Quimby it meant simply the healing of bodily ills through a lively reliance on the wholeness and order of the Infinite Mind, as clearly perceived and practically demonstrated by a simple and modest love of one's kind. What she has "founded" is a commercial system, monumental in its proportions, but already tottering to its fall.[47]

The summing up of Quimby's theory would have astonished that honest if crude pioneer of mental healing, who started not from the premise of an Infinite Mind but from the clairvoyant and suggestive power of the human mind imbued with the theory or "wisdom" that he finally came to identify with or as God.[48] Similarly, Mrs. Eddy's students read with considerable amazement of the supposed Christian Science doctrine of mental conception through which "maidens have been terrified out of their wits, and stimulated into a frenzy resembling that of deluded French nuns, who believed themselves brought into marital relations with the glorified Jesus."[49]

Within a week or two of the article's publication Mrs. Woodbury's husband died, her willing dupe to the last. Mrs. Woodbury, who underneath her newly displayed rationalism retained a strong faith in black magic and who even claimed credit for a couple of sudden deaths,[50] was said by her intimates to attribute the unexpected event to Mrs. Eddy's malefic powers. On the other hand, her critics had food for thought in the more mundane report that Mr. Woodbury had been embalmed with suspicious haste and without an autopsy, the widow allegedly taking great satisfaction from the continued presence and homage of a handsome, wealthy young man who had recently been living as a member of the Woodbury household.[51]

Mrs. Eddy, however, was less concerned with the questionable details of Mrs. Woodbury's personal life than with what she saw as a problem of far greater proportions. This is summed up in a passage in her chapter on the Apocalypse, which is clearly intended to have a cosmic application extending far beyond any particular illustration of it:

> From Genesis to the Apocalypse, sin, sickness, and death, envy, hatred, and revenge,—all evil,—are typified by a serpent, or animal subtlety. Jesus said, quoting a line from the Psalms, "They hated me without a cause." The serpent is perpetually close upon the heel of harmony. From the beginning to the end, the serpent pursues with hatred the spiritual idea. In Genesis, this allegorical, talking serpent typifies mortal mind, "more subtle than any beast of the field." In the Apocalypse, when nearing its doom, this evil increases and becomes the great red dragon, swollen with sin, inflamed with war against spirituality, and ripe for destruction. It is full of lust and hate, loathing the brightness of divine glory.[52]

The time had come, Mrs. Eddy now felt, when the latest phase of the evil needed denouncing. It was not a matter of counterattacking Mrs. Woodbury, but of exposing the sort of thinking she stood for. Through almost two decades the older woman had struggled to help the younger face and outface her demons, at the same time protecting her from public shame wherever she could. Now when Mrs. Woodbury's determination to destroy what she could not possess had come into the open, her benefactress of past years struck uncompromisingly at the evil that had led to this result.

Three or four weeks after Mr. Woodbury's death, her annual Communion message to her church was read, with its welcome to the many Christian Scientists who as usual had come to Boston for that occasion, its praise of the work of the newly established Board of Lectureship and Board of Education, and its thanks to God "for persecution and for prosecution, if from these ensue a purer Protestantism and monotheism for the latter days of the nineteenth century."[53]

Halfway through the message occurred a passage of mingled prophetic fervor, biblical imagery, and visionary intensity which was, to say the least, startling. Picturing the moral corruption symbolized by the "Babylonish woman" of the Apocalypse, it drew heavily on the language of that book:

> This woman, "drunken with the blood of the saints, and with the blood of the martyrs of Jesus," "drunk with the wine of her fornication," would enter even the church,—the body of Christ, Truth; and retaining the heart of the harlot and the purpose of

the destroying angel, would pour wormwood into the waters—the disturbed human mind—to drown the strong swimmer struggling for the shore,—aiming for Truth,—and if possible, to poison such as drink of the living water. But the recording angel, standing with "right foot upon the sea, and his left foot on the earth," has in his hand a book open (ready to be read), which uncovers and kills this mystery of iniquity and interprets the mystery of godliness,—how the first is finished and the second is no longer a mystery or a miracle, but a marvel, casting out evil and healing the sick. And a voice was heard, saying, "Come out of her, my people" (hearken not to her lies), "that ye receive not of her plagues. For her sins have reached unto heaven, and God hath remembered her iniquities . . . double unto her double according to her works: in the cup which she hath filled fill to her double . . . for she saith in her heart, I . . . am no widow, . . . Therefore shall her plagues come in one day, death, and mourning, and famine; . . . for strong is the Lord God who judgeth her." That which the Revelator saw in spiritual vision will be accomplished. The Babylonish woman is fallen, and who should mourn over the widowhood of lust, of her that "is become the habitation of devils, and the hold of every foul spirit, and a cage of every unclean . . . bird"?[54]

Just what that passage meant was to be the subject of litigation for the next two years. More than that, it would put to the test the durability of Mrs. Eddy's leadership and her credibility as a religious teacher. But for the moment it caused no more than a passing sensation among her followers.

A greater sensation arose from her personal appearance at the annual meeting of The Mother Church, held that year in Tremont Temple where, fourteen years before, she had faced a hostile audience of two thousand. Coming down to Boston by train on the day following Communion Sunday, she spent the night at her old house on Commonwealth Avenue, now the residence of Judge Hanna as First Reader of the church, and while there she had a busy time interviewing directors, trustees, editors, and several others, including Lord and Lady Dunmore and their family. At the annual meeting on Tuesday she sat on the platform, delivered another address which contained no thunderbolts but looked forward to the time when the church militant should rise to the church triumphant, and afterward returned quietly to Concord.

The *Boston Globe* the next day described her appearance on the platform:

> *She looked as she sat there the ideal of the gentle, kindly old lady, who had led an uneventful life and who was enjoying the peace and quiet of a conscience-clear old age. The lines of her face were soft, and there was nothing about her in repose to indicate the force of character and genius which she is credited with possessing.*[55]

The force of her character could, however, be gauged from the violence of Mrs. Woodbury's reaction to the Communion message. First came a story in the *Chicago Inter Ocean,* attributed to an anonymous member of South Side society but ultimately traceable to Mrs. Woodbury in Boston.[56] Chicago Christian Scientists, it stated, were seriously in doubt as to whether Mary Baker Eddy was really alive and on earth. She had appeared in person at none of the recent Boston meetings, according to this report, and the supposed address by her had been delivered by an impersonator.

Quickly an enterprising reporter from the *Boston Journal* presented himself at Pleasant View on the evening of June 20 and asked for an interview. On an impulse Mrs. Eddy granted one, and his story from Concord the next day began with the words: "Am I alive? Why, I haven't felt more sound for forty years." This, he went on, "was the forcible and picturesque response to the question of a *Boston Journal* man as Mrs. Eddy tripped into the parlor of her beautiful home in this city last night at an hour when many younger persons are in bed."[57]

Asked about her daily life, Mrs. Eddy replied in a businesslike way:

> *I rise at six o'clock in the morning . . . and work all day. I retire to my room at nine o'clock but not always to sleep. To-day, I have answered about twenty letters. I take ten minutes for every letter of four pages, read it thoroughly, consider it, and then write or dictate the answers to my private secretary. Of course, there are hundreds of letters that I never answer at all; to-day I have entertained letters from Congo Free State, from several European countries, and answered a letter from the wife of our minister to China. . . . As I toil on I am comforted by the Scripture: "Ye shall run and not weary, walk and not faint."*

Six weeks later Mrs. Woodbury brought suit for libel against Mrs. Eddy and related suits against The Mother Church, the Board of Directors, the Board of Trustees, Hanna as editor, and one or two other assorted officials. All were based on the passage in the Communion message denouncing the Babylonish woman, whom the complainant chose to take as a personal representation of herself rather than as a symbol comparable to the dragon, beast, horsemen, plagues, and other graphic abominations of the Book of Revelation.

Although nominally a libel suit, the action was clearly a propaganda move. In its original form the bill of complaint contained much that was legally immaterial to the libel issue—for instance, the charge that Mrs. Eddy considered herself to be the "woman clothed with the sun" in Revelation 12 and the feminine manifestation of Christ, also that she taught mental conception and attempted mental murder. Even when the complaint was amended and the irrelevancies dropped, it was evident that, despite the multiple suits and defendants, Mrs. Eddy was, as her distinguished Boston attorney Samuel J. Elder put it, "the *only* mark they are aiming at."[58] And Mrs. Eddy not as an individual but as the Discoverer and Founder of Christian Science.

3

Mrs. Woodbury's lawyer, Frederick W. Peabody, was a shrewd, caustic fighter who would devote a good deal of his energy for the next twenty-five years to attempting the total demolition of Christian Science.[59]

Even though the statement of his case, as filed in court, has been described as "more in the nature of an indictment of Christian Science than a statement of Mrs. Woodbury's grounds of complaint,"[60] it probably reflected the division of that lady's own interest between the $150,000 she was seeking in damages and the thorough discrediting of Mrs. Eddy she demonstrably hoped to achieve.

Even after filing the suit, she continued to feed sensational charges to the press, notably in an interview which appeared in the *New York World* on October 15, 1899. Two weeks later Hanna wrote Mrs. Eddy:

> *Woodbury and her attorney are continuing to try their case in the newspapers, and in a conversation with Mr. Elder yesterday, he said that a number of lawyers had spoken to him about the gross impropriety of Peabody's action, and they are contemplating bringing his case before the Bar Association.*
> *Mr. Elder's view is to take no notice of it in the newspapers, but give them rope, and then later on bring the whole proceeding to the attention of the court. W. and her attorney are rapidly uncovering themselves and disgusting more and more decent and thinking people.*[61]

Shortly afterward an action was brought against Mrs. Woodbury for contempt of court, and in a decision rendered on December 28 she was found guilty, fined, and warned that she must not attempt to make use of the newspapers to influence the proceedings in her own libel suit. Thereafter she was more cautious, but a continuous stream of stories favorable to her and unfavorable to Mrs. Eddy continued to appear in the press.

In her Communion message Mrs. Eddy had included a passage that was to mark an important new development in her church:

> *Refrain from public controversy; correct the false with the true—then leave the latter to propagate. . . . I have neither the time nor the inclination to be continually pursuing a lie—the one evil or the evil one. Therefore I ask the help of others in this matter, and I ask that according to the Scriptures my students reprove, rebuke, and exhort. A lie left to itself is not so soon destroyed as it is with the help of truth-telling.*[62]

The help for which she asked had already taken preliminary form in a three-man "Publication Committee" which she charged with the duty of correcting misinformation in the press.[63]

Judge Hanna, who served on the committee for a very short time, produced in 1899 a booklet, *Christian Science History*, which attempted to answer Mrs. Woodbury's Quimby charges. Viewed today, the booklet has a makeshift *ad hoc* quality that is clearly inadequate to the depth and complexity of the subject. Mrs. Eddy was grateful for it but felt that Hanna vastly underrated the seriousness of the Woodbury campaign and of the hitherto latent opposition to Christian Science it was stirring into activity.

For some time Mrs. Eddy had been aware of the effective work her student Alfred Farlow of Kansas City was doing in answering criticisms of Christian Science. He himself had written her in 1893, "God has given me the ability to simplify the Truth to beginners,"[64] and God appeared to have given him also an unusual measure of common sense, balance, and Christian restraint in dealing with popular misconceptions of Christian Science. Mrs. Eddy had commended a lecture of his, printed in the *Journal* of July, 1899, as "clear, simple, sublime, abstract, logical,"[65] and a little later she wrote him that she was readying him for "an important office which needs a true, active, adamant man to fill it."[66]

What she had in mind came to light early in 1900 when she sent a new bylaw to the Directors establishing the Committee on Publication of The Mother Church in essentially its present form and asked them to appoint Farlow to the position. As a one-man committee, he was manager of similar one-man committees in every state of the Union and eventually in all countries where there were Churches of Christ, Scientist.

While often looked upon today as a pioneer venture in public relations, both Mrs. Eddy and Farlow seem to have regarded the Committee on Publication, rather, as a branch of the healing activity of Christian Science. Its purpose was to heal or correct "in a Christian manner"[67] such impositions on public thought as the Woodbury propaganda and thus leave people free to judge Christian Science on its real merits or demerits. Farlow himself never lost sight of that moderate aim, though some of those who worked under him or followed him lapsed into the role of publicist and proselytizer.

Within a year or two, despite his essentially modest character, Farlow would be better known to the general public than almost any other Christian Scientist except Mrs. Eddy herself. But although the necessity for his work grew out of the Woodbury case, he was not personally involved in its legal complexities. And for that he might consider himself fortunate—or so the hard-pressed Hanna might have judged.

For the case came close to being Hanna's Waterloo. At the very beginning he had advised Mrs. Eddy that Peabody planned to commence a suit against her in New Hampshire, where she held property, if he could not find property in her name to attach in Massachusetts. Her personal appearance, Hanna added, could be compelled in New Hampshire as it could not be in Massachusetts, but the whole thing could be forestalled by having counsel appear for her in Massachusetts—"and then whatever is done will be done by us here, and you need not trouble about it."[68]

Mrs. Eddy accepted his recommendation, only to have Peabody go ahead and bring suit in New Hampshire as well as in Massachusetts, thus leaving her saddled with the disadvantages of both situations. After that, Hanna could seem to do nothing right. He published editorials which inadvertently gave aid and comfort to Mrs. Woodbury and an article by a contributor on law and medicine which Mrs. Eddy's attorneys deplored as likely to prejudice the court against her.[69] He sided with the lawyers when her spiritual intuition told her they were wrong, and exalted her in the *Journal* when her common sense told her that this would lead to misunderstanding and censure by the general public.

Poor Hanna, straining to be dutiful, felt under an inexplicable cloud of displeasure. Mrs. Eddy assured him that she did not consider him to be disloyal but rather under the unrecognized influence of m. a. m.[70] It was an unhappy time for them both.

As the legal preliminaries to the trial dragged on through 1900, Mrs. Eddy faced some of her darkest days. Even her lawyers were repelled by the septic stuff that was coming to the surface in their investigation of Mrs. Woodbury's past. In addition, a variety of unsavory dissensions seemed suddenly to be bubbling up in other quarters, so that Mrs. Eddy had to struggle to follow her own advice in *Science and Health* not to be overwhelmed by a sense of the odiousness of sin.[71] As usual, this was reflected in her physical condition, and 1900 saw several entries in Frye's diary that registered the severity of the struggle. Like the one on April 7:

> *Mrs. Eddy had a severe experience all day yesterday being tormented with a sense of evil all day long. . . . An atmosphere of hate & revenge from testimony being taken in Montreal on W suit &c &c. . . . At 3 oclock this morning she called me, and asked me what Love is. I tried to answer her in Science but none of my answers were called correct & she called Laura & she could not do better. She then called Mrs. Leonard & received a better answer & some comfort; she then called Laura again & L. answered her heart yearnings that "Love is selflessness forgetting self & laboring for the good of others &c. this relieved her severe belief of constriction of air passages . . . & she immediately breathed freely.[72]*

Hardest of all to bear was her feeling that even those who wanted most to help her—her legal counsel and her own church officers—were unconsciously influenced by mental suggestion to play into Mrs. Woodbury's hands, with a consequent distrust of what seemed to Mrs. Eddy to be divine directions but looked to them like feminine vagaries. The difficulty this caused on both sides is illustrated by a letter to her from General Streeter, her New Hampshire attorney who had been brought in to handle the suit in that state in coordination with Samuel Elder's preparation of her defense in Massachusetts.[73]

Both Elder and Streeter considered it desirable to file certain interrogatories with the Superior Court which Mrs. Woodbury would be compelled to answer. A letter from Mrs. Eddy instructed Streeter to proceed no further in this direction, since it was clear to her that Mrs. Woodbury was deliberately influencing her counsel through mental suggestion "to show their hand, as she used to call it."[74] Streeter— who, like her other counsel, was not a Christian Scientist—replied:

> *. . . By the last statement, I infer that you think Mrs. W. has "through mental silent suggestion" influenced my mind (as well as that of Mr. Elder) to show our hand,—that is, file the interrogatories,—and when you say "go no further with my consent in that direction," I understand you to instruct me that I am not to see Mr. Elder on your behalf about filing these interrogatories and that the same are not to be filed. Is this what you really mean? If it is, I ought to advise you that you should have counsel whose mental balance cannot be influenced to mismanage your case through the mental silent suggestion of a woman like Madam Woodbury.*
>
> *I, as one of your counsel, am not conscious of being influenced by Mrs. W. to take any action prejudicial to the interests of the case which I, with Mr. Elder, have been employed to defend. I know of but one way to protect your interests and that is to deal with this plaintiff's case in the same way and by the same methods that I would deal with any plaintiff's case in which such a vicious and selfish attack has been made on my client as Mrs. Woodbury has made on you.*[75]

Interestingly enough, later consultation with Elder brought to light further practical considerations which changed the lawyers' views and led them a little sheepishly to agree with Mrs. Eddy's insistence that the interrogatories should not be filed.

A similar turnabout occurred in connection with Streeter's and Elder's views that, because of certain advantages in the New Hampshire libel law, the prosecution should be steered so far as possible from Massachusetts to New Hamphire. Mrs. Eddy again disagreed emphatically. At a conference with them at Pleasant View on January 4, 1901, she held her position in the face of their clear-cut masculine logic but was struck to the quick by the fact that Hanna and Armstrong, who were also present, said not a word in support of her position. The next day she wrote Judge Ewing in Chicago:

> *O that you had been here. I felt so alone. Judge H. Mr. A. and Mr. J. sat with the lawyers in my room [for] hours,—the latter cutting my heart out, the former speechless. I felt as if I were in the presence of headsmen waiting to take me to the scaffold. Why O why are the declining years of a life like mine so haunted hounded soulless unpitied. God only knows!*[76]

Again, however, her views finally won out and appear to have been justified by the events that followed.[77] It was repeated instances of this sort that caused Elder and Streeter, despite the fact that they did not share her religious viewpoint, to develop a frank admiration for her mental ability.

When Elder in later years was asked what he thought of Mrs. Eddy, his invariable answer was to recount an incident which occurred seven years later in connection with another court case. Again a conference was held at Pleasant View, and each of the several lawyers there presented to her the imperative need for taking a certain course of action. Elder's daughter in her biography of her father records what follows:

> *They made no impression. Mrs. Eddy was obdurate. The opposite position was the only one which could be sustained. She spoke quietly and reasonably, but imperiously. Her brilliant black eyes shone with determination. The lawyers were very patient with her. She was an old woman, nearly as old, my father recalled, as his mother. Her person commanded deference, but clearly her legal opinion was valueless. The conference had reached this* impasse *when the hour came for Mrs. Eddy's drive. She dismissed her lawyers, who adjourned to Mr. Streeter's office to continue their discussion.*

In the course of her drive, Mrs. Eddy stopped her carriage outside Streeter's office and sent up for Elder. When he went out to her, she laid her hand on his arm:

> *"Mr. Elder," she said with great impressiveness, looking steadily at him, "you are wrong in this matter which we have been discussing. I wish that you would return to the other gentlemen and ask them to reconsider it. Will you do this?" He assented reluctantly. Then she repeated, "Mr. Elder, you are wrong." Her carriage drove off and Mr. Elder slowly remounted the steps to the office. The situation was awkward, but having given his assent, Mr. Elder could do no less. He returned to the conference, told of Mrs. Eddy's request and insisted that they reconsider their decision, all the time regarding the matter in the same light as did his colleagues. So they went over all their arguments again. The result was that they reversed their decision, followed the lines insisted upon by Mrs. Eddy, and during the trial it became indubitably clear that she had been right.*[78]

Yet neither Elder nor Streeter is likely to have had even a suspicion of what it sometimes cost her to pit her spiritual intuition against their legal expertise.

4

The years of the Woodbury litigation held special difficulties for the officers of the church as well as for Mrs. Eddy.

The suits brought against them caused some worry, even though little action had been taken on them so far and the real target of the attack was obviously Mrs. Eddy herself. Then, too, in the mental stir of the period, her orders often seemed to them arbitrary, inexplicable, querulous, changeable, whereas their response to the situation often seemed to her short-sighted, obtuse, humanly motivated rather than divinely inspired. There were recurrent clashes of male reasoning with feminine intuition.

On December 1, 1900, Judge Clarkson of Omaha had a two-hour interview with her. This comparative neophyte in Christian Science, whom she had invited into her 1898 class,[79] was now serving with considerable éclat on the Christian Science Board of Lectureship. Like many others, he was unable to understand why she was suddenly so down on Judge Hanna, and he reacted to the serious doubts and complaints about her leadership that he had encountered recently in Boston by an equally sudden reversal of his earlier overidealized concept of her.[80]

What Clarkson discussed with Mrs. Eddy on December 1 and again six days later is indicated by a December 7 entry in Frye's diary:

> *Judge Clarkson dined with Mrs. Eddy today & after dinner tried to convince her again that she was mistaken & the cause was going to ruin & the men were essential to take the lead of the cause of C. S. & to assert their rights without her dictation.*[81]

History has already made clear that he failed to persuade her. Instead she shortly afterward wrote an essay, "Man and Woman," the title of which she sent to the copyright office on December 17 but which she then changed her mind about publishing at that time. In its biographical setting, the essay throws light on much that was going on.

It started by pointing out that from the beginning Mrs. Eddy had "uniformly associated man and woman" in her endeavors, though giving "the preponderance to the masculine element in my organizations for carrying out the functions of Christian Science." She cited as example that the Directors and Trustees were all men and there were three men to one woman on the Board of Education, with eleven men and two women on the Board of Lectureship.[82] Nevertheless, Science rested on a God who was both Father and Mother of the universe:

> *The equality of man and woman is established in the premises of this Science. God made them male and female from the beginning, and they were in His image and likeness—not images, but image. In the divine Mind there is no sex, no sexuality, no procreation: the Infinite Mind includes all in Mind.*

The masculine element, she went on, had had precedence in history, but history was temporal, not eternal:

> *The masculine element must not murmur if at some period in human history the verdict should take a turn in behalf of woman, and say,—Her time has come, and the reflection of God's feminine nature is permitted consideration, has come to the front, and will be heard and understood. . . . At such a juncture I would not dislike to be referee;—I would declare that one was not less, nor more, important in God's sight than the other, and that in the divine order they both originated in One and as one, and should continue thus without taint of sexuality.*

The ideal was a perfect balance of masculine and feminine, but as spiritual qualities rather than sexual characteristics:

> *The feminine weakness that talks when it has nothing to say, that gossips, slanders, unwittingly or unconsciously, that envies or scorns where it should only pity, is out of line with being in Science, and in line with the masculine element that robs innocence of purity, and peoples of liberty and life, in the name of the rights of might. These are indeed dark stains on the brighter disk of humanity. . . . But the scene shifts, and behold a woman!— the almond blossom upon her head, busy hands and pen, never leaving the post of duty, but week after week, month after month, and year after year, toiling, watching, praying, and sending forth messages of God's dear love over all the earth.*[83]

With this sudden shift from theory, policy, psychological analysis, to a single vividly felt image, personal yet symbolic, concrete yet archetypal, Mrs. Eddy comes to the heart of the issue which for her lay behind all that was happening at that period. It was the practical matter of spiritual leadership, with its roots in the character of the Godhead itself. The politics of feminism was for her a minor matter compared with the demonstration of principled love for the whole human race.

The issue was little understood, even by many Christian Scientists. In Mrs. Eddy's terminology, the words "woman" and "womanhood" frequently refer not to a particular woman or to women as a sex but to woman as *idea,* or more specifically as that revelatory state of mind in which man is conceived to be the child of God. "No advancing modes of human mind made Jesus," she wrote elsewhere; "rather was it their subjugation, and the pure heart that sees God."[84]

In her hermeneutics, this was the significance of the figurative "woman clothed with the sun" who brought forth a "man child" to rule all nations. On the one hand, she applied this to her own spiritual discovery, which brought forth the Christian Science movement; on the other hand, she saw in it a generic symbol of the way in which revealed truth perceived by the pure in heart must always bring forth a higher expression of humanity.[85] This was the doctrine which she felt Mrs. Woodbury had shamelessly perverted and even reversed in her cooked-up explanation of the all too maculate birth of the little Prince.

There was never any question in Mrs. Eddy's mind that the Christian symbolism of Revelation 12 threw special light on her own experience—the woman travailing in birth "but remembering no more her sorrow for joy that the birth goes on," the dragon standing by to devour her child as soon as it was born, the child caught up to God or "found in its divine Principle,"[86] the dragon's persecution of the woman and her flight into the wilderness. But she also took pains to indicate that it had a larger than personal or denominational meaning for her, a universalism at once Christian and standing above all history:

> *In divine revelation, material and corporeal selfhood disappear, and the spiritual idea is understood.*
> *The woman in the Apocalypse symbolizes generic man, the spiritual idea of God; she illustrates the coincidence of God and man as the divine Principle and divine idea.*[87]

Now, faced by what seemed to her a particularly dragonish effort to pull her down to the level of her detractors, she saw more clearly the danger of personalizing the symbols. This seems to have been at the heart of her temporary but acute dissatisfaction with Hanna. While she had welcomed with gratitude his deep faith in her leadership, along with the mystical biblicism in which he wrapped it, she saw now the peril to herself as well as to him and to the movement in any undue exaltation of her person.[88]

This was pointed up by Mrs. Woodbury's contention that if Christian Scientists considered the woman clothed with the sun to be a person (Mrs. Eddy), then they obviously considered the Babylonish woman to be a person (Mrs. Woodbury), and that was what the libel suit was all about. Mrs. Eddy felt a need for theological no less than legal clarification of the issues.

In regard to the passage that was the basis of the libel suit, she wrote her lawyers:

> *I meant Mrs. Josephine C. Woodbury no more than I meant any other person who is like her. I meant what I think the Revelator means namely that the Babylonish woman is only a symbol of lust, but Mrs. Woodbury has applied this symbol to herself.*[89]

In several unpublished fragments written about this time, Mrs. Eddy also defined more explicitly her concept of the opposing symbol, the woman clothed with the sun:

> *. . . Does not the modern artist, with pencil, brush or chisel, portray a woman crowned with youth, brow sparkling with stars, feet treading upon the dragon, who has subdued the earth—as the woman vividly delineated in the Revelator's vision? Yes, for such was in St. John's concept and such is Jesus' type and such it will be seen after the fulfillment of many days. Today our forms and identifications are but types and shadows of the individual substance and soul of man or woman. I never taught or thought that I was the Woman referred to in the dim distance of St. John's period, nor that the Babylonish woman can be identified or individualized in our time. I have rebuked such a thought and written of this [latter] woman not as an individual but as lust.*[90]

A more elaborate statement is found in an unpublished work of seven short chapters in which she examined various aspects of her career:

> *The Apocalypse like all holy vision, when left to mortals' interpretation or application to identify its meaning, is susceptible of abuse owing to one's ignorance of another's mood and mode of thinking. I am not capable of applying St. John's far-reaching thoughts only as type and shadow. I would as soon undertake to catch a sunbeam in my hand as to run riot on the conclusion he has reached, and do not understand, save as allegory, which symbol or type stands for a quality and not a person. The only safety in translating his vision to the comprehension of mortals must lie in confining his trope and symbol to generalities and not specialities. . . .*
>
> *What St. John saw in prophetic vision and depicted as "a woman clothed with the sun and the moon under her feet" pre-*

figured no speciality or individuality. His vision foretold a type, and this type applied to man as well as to woman. . . . The character or type seen in his vision illustrated purity. The application of this character or type to individuals is left to human conception. "To the pure all things are pure." The purer mind would sooner apprehend and assimilate the qualities typified by the Revelator's figure of "the woman with the moon under her feet, crowned with twelve stars." The impure mind would sooner conceive of and assimilate the opposite type of lust named woman, but no human concept is capable of applying either of the Revelator's types to the present individual. His figures or illustrations of purity and lust are entire, absolute, and who has gained at this age the full conception and the application thereof as depicted in the Apocalypse either of virtue or of vice?[91]

Later she was to authorize Edward Kimball to make a public statement on the subject,[92] for she recognized the need for strong, clear, masculine voices to speak out for her.

Farlow was already doing a notable job. Devoted to Mrs. Eddy heart and soul, he nevertheless had a frank openness in dealing with her that left no room for mystical extravagances. Back in 1893 he had written her about a Sunday School class he had just visited in Kansas City, at a time when such classes were open to pupils of all ages and often included newcomers to Christian Science:

The first question asked was this in substance: "Who is the woman whose price is above rubies." The answer from about a dozen came, "Mrs. Eddy." This seemed to me strong meat for strangers. . . . If students are taught to love Science and Health they are taught to love good, and if they love good they cannot help loving the authoress of this precious book. . . . I have also learned that a constant talking of Mrs. Eddy sometimes becomes obnoxious to the public and only serves to array a. m. against her.[93]

It was this sort of common sense that had caused Mrs. Eddy to choose Farlow for his present position, and a similar respect for Kimball's honesty and ability decided her to bring him to Boston at the beginning of 1901. Several years earlier Edward Bates had written her:

It comes to me that the day is at hand when you will have plenty of good competent business men to carry on your work. . . . When such men as Edward A. Kimball of Chicago and Mr.

Metcalf of Boston are coming into our ranks it will not be long before we shall have plenty of this element.[94]

Bates himself, for all his practical virtues, proved inadequate for the spiritual demands of the two successive positions Mrs. Eddy offered him, and when in 1902 she was to try out another outstanding businessman—Arthur P. De Camp of St. Louis—on the Board of Directors, she found that he, like Bates, was ready to resign after six frustrating months.

Judge Clarkson's belief that the movement would go to wrack and ruin unless the men took over its leadership, retaining Mrs. Eddy only for the authority of her name, receives an ironic comment from an anonymous document, "The Following Scheme of Church Government Is Suggested for Christian Scientists," in the files of The Mother Church. The document may well have been drawn up and submitted by Clarkson himself. After pointing out what the writer considers to be the weaknesses of Mrs. Eddy's organization, it presents its own blueprint, of which the following excerpts are representative:

1. Large cities should represent large districts. . . .

2. The First Church of each district should be built by general subscription from the whole United States in the largest city in the district.

3. These churches would be built when ordered by The Mother Church. . . .

6. The Board of directors of every first church shall be named by the Mother Church. . . .

12. It would be desirable to call in learned and experienced Roman Catholics to advise concerning the details of the scheme as they know more about organization than all the rest of christendom. . . .

14. The Mother Church must own all the First Church edifices and all other societies must be tributary and subordinate to them.

15. This constitutional basis should be adopted during Mrs. Eddy's life time. Her authority is now sufficient to procure its unquestioned adoption. If delayed till after her death no extensive organization will ever be possible and the sect will be split into an hundred heads.[95]

Nothing could make clearer the difference between Mrs. Eddy's concept of the church as a plant to be tended, watered, pruned, protected, cherished, trained upward, and the general approach of the technical expert, the literal-minded, machine-oriented, logic-directed male planner.

But Kimball was a different matter. He shared with Farlow an unshakable conviction of Mrs. Eddy's inspiration, combined with a forthrightness that honored her intelligence by its very matter-of-factness. When the transition from preachers to Readers was made, he wrote her in regard to a rumor that only women would be allowed to read from *Science and Health* at the Sunday services:

> *I think the average state of thought among students is that mortal woman is a higher idea of God than mortal man. This of course is an area of mental malpractice, and so long as it continues will have a repressing influence on the progress of men in scientific endeavor.*
>
> *. . . In my own practice, my great aim is to lead every patient to the understanding of Science and Health, and I have fully as much success with men as with women.*[96]

In 1898 Mrs. Eddy had had all her copyrights transferred to Kimball—an indication of her growing reliance on his integrity—and his subsequent service as a lecturer and as the teacher of the Normal Class under the Board of Education had given evidence of his stature as a Christian Scientist both within and without the movement.

On January 17, 1901, she notified the Directors that she had commissioned him to represent her in all things having to do with the Woodbury case. Two days later Hanna wrote her:

> *I am glad Mr. Kimball is here. We need his fresh, strong thought, and I hope he will remain until it is over. He is not fagged out as are the rest of us. . . . I see also a strong need of greater reliance on the Gospel and less on human law for success in the case.*[97]

It was a generous welcome from a man whose basic desire, like Kimball's, Farlow's, and the Directors', was to help Mrs. Eddy carry forward what they all believed to be the cause of Truth.

5

The Boston atmosphere into which Kimball moved in 1901 was a very disturbed one, as the universal struggled to emerge from the parochial. On January 6, two days after the conference with the lawyers at Pleasant View which had caused Mrs. Eddy such emotional turmoil, William McKenzie had written his fiancée:

*It seems like a state of siege just now, & we scarcely get the
debris from one shellburst [from Concord] cleared up before
there comes another explosion. One thing we shall have to cease
forever, & that is the superstitious worship of a personal leader.
Jesus to John in his Apocalypse said as "the Son of man," "I am
alive forevermore & have the keys of hell & of death." And when
John wished to worship the angel that showed him the doom of
Babylon he was prompt to say "see thou do it not . . . worship
God, for the testimony of Jesus is the Spirit of prophecy." There
has been too much worship of a person, & it is bearing its fruits.
My love is tenderer for the Leader today while I see her in wild
tumult raging with Elizabethan frankness against those who are
serving her with their lives . . . and in general exhibiting the
characteristics of "only a woman"—my love is tenderer, I believe,
than when she was set before me by you as the second Christ—a
greater than Jesus because woman is higher than man.*[98]

This was, to say the least, a healthy revision of attitude, even if
some of the "detonations and Sinaitic flashings" from Pleasant View
of which McKenzie complained in another letter[99] turned out to be
more prophetic than he had thought them to be at the time. An
entry in Frye's diary some months earlier showed that Mrs. Eddy
herself would have approved of the demythologizing process going
on in the minds of those who had shared the assumptions of McKenzie
and his wife-to-be:

*Mrs. Eddy said to me tonight "When I hear people speak of
me or any other mortal as an equal with Jesus it makes me shiver,
for I realize more & more as [I] apprehend his true character &
work his infinite distance above us."*[100]

On the other hand, she felt it essential for her students to understand the nature of her own labors, and she wrote Mrs. Stetson in
February, 1901:

*Mr. [———] has not the knowledge of the past history of
my struggles and . . . the cost of bringing C. S. to this triumphal
hour. My students even know little more of what I have met for
them and still am meeting than the babe in his mothers arm
knows of her travail to bring forth this babe and toil to bring
him up to manhood.*[101]

Kimball, who understood the struggles and made allowance for
the outbursts, quietly pointed out to her the possible choices of action,
confidently accepted her decisions, and efficiently implemented them.

Toward the end of the ordeal, she wrote him, "I have found *you wise, watchful, vigilant*—but none can see what I see[;] hence the wisdom of faith in me."[102] Kimball maintained not only his faith but also his equilibrium.

As the time for the trial neared, the atmosphere heated up. Peabody and Mrs. Woodbury were holding frequent conferences with disaffected students of Mrs. Eddy from the past—Richard Kennedy, Clara Choate, Sarah Crosse, William Nixon. Mrs. Eddy's lawyers were considering whether and how the great mass of damning evidence against Mrs. Woodbury's character which they had accumulated could be introduced into the trial without seeming to support that lady's contention that Mrs. Eddy had meant the Babylonish woman to represent her. Hanna, who had confided to Clarkson earlier his own personal sense of the Revelation symbolism as well as other details that would be damaging in testimony, now learned with dismay that Clarkson, too, was in touch with Peabody; consequently it was decided that it would be wise, as the trial approached, for the Hannas to leave Boston and go off visiting in Pennsylvania.

On April 17 Frye wrote Kimball in regard to Mrs. Eddy, "She is literally living in agony from day to day waiting to have this case called up and disposed of and W. is pouring in her hot shot declaring she cannot live through the ordeal."[103] A month or two earlier, he had written in his diary: "Mrs. Eddy said at supper table today . . . 'If I do not live to see this lawsuit of Ws finished, I can say this[:] Calvin has helped me to live many years.'"[104]

On May 29 Frye noted in his diary, "Libel suit Woodbury vs. Eddy began in Boston Court," and Kimball wrote her the next day:

> *Only one like myself who is on the inside of the whole history can understand how thoroughly Peabody was beaten yesterday on the generalship of the case. All of his hopes and threats to the effect that they would expose Christian Science and reveal its unfavorable workings, were utterly shattered yesterday because the court ruled over and over again that all of those outside matters had no relation to the issue in hand at all. Peabody was in a state of almost constant discomfiture. . . . He has none of the sympathy of the Jury and our lawyers have secured it at once. I do not think the case will last more than ten days.*[105]

Actually it was over in a week. Peabody could find only two witnesses to testify that they had believed Mrs. Eddy's symbolism to refer to Mrs. Woodbury. One of these was Nixon, whose personal hostility to Mrs. Eddy was now as corrosive as Peabody's; he admitted to having had numerous conferences about the case with the latter and to have "accidentally" met and talked with Mrs. Woodbury at three of them. Clara Choate, also called by Peabody, admitted only that she had said at the time of Mrs. Eddy's speech that *if* the passage referred to Mrs. Woodbury she was sorry for her. Hanna, who returned for the last two days of the trial, was asked no questions that he could not answer forthrightly.

The verdict was a clear-cut victory for Mrs. Eddy, even if it left Mrs. Woodbury's transgressions unexposed. The two-year ordeal was over, and after some further delay the cases against the other defendants were dropped without coming to trial. Later, an incident came to light which revealed a curious impression made on the court by Mrs. Woodbury. This occurred during the contempt proceedings at an early stage of the suit.

A young lawyer, Rosemary O. Anderson of Cleveland, Ohio, had come to Boston on legal business and was stopping at the United States Hotel. Judge Braley, who was conducting the contempt hearing, was a fellow guest at the hotel. Falling into conversation with her about the practice of law, he invited her to sit at the same table throughout her stay. During the first conversation he told her that he had "labored a long time with his conscience before deciding to act as judge in the case, as he was intensely prejudiced against Christian Science and thought Christian Scientists were an erratic, unreliable people who were following a delusion," but had since then been impressed with their "honesty of purpose."[106]

Mrs. Anderson herself was able to attend the proceedings on the last day when Peabody received permission for Mrs. Woodbury to speak on her own behalf. As she left the trial table to go forward to the witness stand, Judge Braley, to Mrs. Anderson's astonishment, rose from his seat and moved back a step or two, with a "peculiar expression on his face" and a "penetrating look at her from under his eyebrows"—while "Mrs. Woodbury never removed her eyes from the Judge's face as she step by step advanced toward him."

When Mrs. Anderson remarked on this fact to Braley at dinner that night, he looked surprised and then confided:

> *I am going to tell you something peculiar. I never had such a strange experience in my life before. As that woman started to come forward I felt just as though a snake were coming toward me, but I did not know that I left my seat.*[107]

Others who knew about the case only from what they read in the newspapers tended to see in it nothing but the magnification of a female squabble. As a friendly Concord non-Scientist, Edward A. Jenks, wrote Mrs. Eddy with intended sympathy but obvious amusement, "It strikes me as the most ludicrous bit of malicious litigation of modern times."[108]

What seemed to him comic was for her cosmic. Mrs. Woodbury she saw as both the instrument and the symbol of entrenched materialism's determination to wipe out the possibility of radical spirituality in a demythologized world. It was in that sense a test case.

The issues of spiritual leadership in such a world were suggested in an interview with her in the *New York Herald* of May 1, 1901, several weeks before the judicial decision in the Woodbury case. Joseph Clarke, a well-known *Herald* reporter, had been in Concord for several days unsuccessfully trying to get an appointment with Mrs. Eddy. Antagonized by the refusal of his request, he had written a piece which gathered together all the sensational speculation, rumor, and miscellaneous apocrypha which had been circulating for two years as the result of Mrs. Woodbury's covert campaign. Was the discoverer of Christian Science actually alive? Was she impersonated in her daily carriage drives? Was she mentally and physically enfeebled, palsied, hysterical, drugged? What was the great mystery of Pleasant View?

Through the intervention of Farlow, Clarke was finally granted an interview, and the result was a decided change of attitude. Ironically enough, the speculative and cynical first story appeared four days *after* the responsible second account. Clarke himself was unhappy about the transposition but was willing to leave it for history to sort out.

The account of the actual interview began with his arrival at Pleasant View, and continued:

> *Seated in the large parlor, I became aware of a white-haired lady slowly descending the stairs. She entered with a gracious smile, walking uprightly and with light step, and after a kindly greeting took a seat on a sofa. It was Mrs. Eddy. There was no mistaking that. Older in years, white-haired, and frailer, but Mrs. Eddy herself. The likeness to the portraits of twenty years ago, so often seen in reproductions, was unmistakable. There is no mistaking certain lines that depend upon the osseous structure; there is no mistaking the eyes—those eyes the shade of which is so hard to catch, whether blue-gray or grayish brown, and which*

*are always bright. And when I say frail, let it not be understood
that I mean weak, for weak she was not. . . .*

*"The continuity of The Church of Christ, Scientist," she
said, in her clear voice, "is assured. It is growing wonderfully. . . ."*

*"How will it be governed after all now concerned in its gov-
ernment shall have passed on?"*

*"It will evolve scientifically. Its essence is evangelical. Its
government will develop as it progresses."*

*"Will there be a hierarchy, or will it be directed by a single
earthly ruler?"*

*"In time its present rules of service and present rulership will
advance nearer perfection."*

*It was plain that the answers to questions would be in Mrs.
Eddy's own spirit. She has a rapt way of talking, looking large-
eyed into space, and works around a question in her own way,
reaching an answer often unexpectedly after a prolonged exor-
dium. She explained: "No present change is contemplated in the
rulership. You would ask, perhaps, whether my successor will be a
woman or a man. I can answer that. It will be a man."*

"Can you name the man?"

"I cannot answer that now."

This was a startling announcement that was soon caught up by
other newspapers, even when they ignored the rest of the interview.
But at least one other passage was pivotal to the issue of leadership.
Mrs. Eddy had just remarked that some people had called her a pope
but that her position was more like that of a mother:

*"A position of authority," she went on, "became necessary.
Rules were necessary, and I made a code of by-laws, but each one
was the fruit of experience and the result of prayer. Entrusting
their enforcement to others, I found at one time that they had
five churches under discipline. I intervened. Dissensions are dangerous in an infant church. I wrote to each church in tenderness,
in exhortation, and in rebuke, and so brought all back to union
and love again. If that is to be a pope, then you can judge for
yourself. I have even been spoken of as a Christ, but to my
understanding of Christ that is impossible. If we say that the
sun stands for God, then all his rays collectively stand for Christ,
and each separate ray for men and women. God the Father is
greater than Christ, but Christ is 'one with the Father,' and so*

the mystery is scientifically explained. There can be but one Christ."

Clarke's concluding paragraphs stood in mellow contrast to the sharp skepticism of his pre-interview article:

We talked on many subjects, some only of which are here touched upon, and her views, strictly and always from the standpoint of Christian Science, were continually surprising. She talks as one who has lived with her subject for a lifetime,—an ordinary lifetime; and so far from being puzzled by any question, welcomes it as another opportunity for presenting another view of her religion.

Those who have been anticipating nature and declaring Mrs. Eddy non-existent may learn authoritatively from the Herald *that she is in the flesh and in health. Soon after I reached Concord on my return from Pleasant View, Mrs. Eddy's carriage drove into town and made several turns about the court-house before returning. She was inside, and as she passed me the same expression of looking forward, thinking, thinking, was on her face.*[109]

The statement about a successor, however, brought forth a new crop of speculations. Whom did she have in mind? Since Alfred Farlow had become known to all newspapermen as *the* spokesman for Christian Science—as virtually Mr. Christian Science—his was the name most often mentioned as the man to succeed Mrs. Eddy. The result was a statement which the latter gave to the Associated Press on May 16:

I did say that a man would be my future successor. By this I did not mean Mr. Alfred Farlow nor any other man to-day on earth.

Science and Health makes it plain to all Christian Scientists that the manhood and womanhood of God have already been revealed in a degree through Christ Jesus and Christian Science, His two witnesses. What remains to lead on the centuries and reveal my successor, is man in the full image and likeness of the Father-Mother God, man the generic term for mankind.[110]

In the eyes of its Discoverer and Founder, Christian Science was to bring forth a new *kind* of man.

Chapter
VI

"...remains to be proved..."

Mark Baker of Bow had been a man quarried from the granite of New England Calvinism, not without family affection and kindly concern for the needy, but stern in devotion to the God of Sinai, that Deity so terrible in His wrath, inexorable in His judgment, absolute in His otherness. Mark himself could be unsparing in his denunciation of religious backsliders, obdurate in his Puritan sense of duty.

Something of the adamant in his character he passed along to his youngest daughter, Mary. For all her later motherliness, her sense of logical necessity made her the sort of leader no gentle little old lady could ever have been. She pointedly approved the reason given for the exaltation of Jesus in the Epistle to the Hebrews: "Thou hast loved righteousness, and hated iniquity."[1]

When Henry P. Nunn, a newspaperman from the West Coast, came to Boston to serve on the editorial staff of the *Journal* and *Sentinel,* he learned something of what this meant in his first conference with Mrs. Eddy at which Hanna, Farlow, Tomlinson, and possibly one or two others were also present. His wife has recorded the incident:

> *Mr. Nunn told how, seated by [Mrs. Eddy's] side on the sofa, he was shocked at the rugged, vehement manner in which she talked to the others. (It was only at a later period that he understood she was endeavoring to arouse them from a state of mesmeric apathy in the conduct of certain phases of their work.) Then turning to him with an absolutely changed expression, one of extreme kindness, even tenderness, Mrs. Eddy remarked: "This is strong meat for one so young in the fold as you."*
>
> *Mr. Nunn referred to it as speaking to the older workers "in thundering tones of Sinai," telling them to arouse themselves and break the mesmerism of animal magnetism that was putting them to sleep—that this apathy was exactly what the enemy wanted. At this time Mrs. Eddy remarked: "And you, Judge Hanna, upon whose brow I have placed the laurel—you, too, have given in to*

the enemy," to which he replied: "Well, Mother, I guess you placed the laurel there too soon." At this she seemed to fairly shout at him: "Don't you say that to me." This positive denunciation of the evil, accompanied with great compassion for the individual, relieved them all of the mesmerism that was holding them so that they came away feeling that a master hand had lifted and directed them.[2]

On another occasion when Tomlinson and his sister, Dr. Alfred Baker and his wife, and one or two others had been called by her to Pleasant View, Mrs. Eddy had transacted her business with them, then withdrawn, only to storm back a few minutes later, ordering Calvin Frye and Clara Shannon to confess their "sins" (i.e., shortcomings) to the startled company, then lecturing them all severely on the state of their thinking. Afterward she wrote Tomlinson:

I wish mother could be excused by divine Love from speaking as I did to my fresh happy callers! I thought I was done when I went to my room but the scripture I opened to and the leadings spiritual —sent me back. What I said I no more expected to say than when I wrote S. & H. Afterwards I recalled your kind care of me getting everything ready etc. when I went to Boston and said—O what have I said! I also know that these Sinai detonations make the student grow most rappidly into the holy fitness for every demonstration; or they (under the fire of the enemy) cause him by degrees to dislike mother and keep aloof from her counsel.

The way is strait and narrow. You remember I told you at first of the unseen secret place where few if any enter—holiness. Can I see God and live? Can you?[3]

One had to have moral and spiritual stamina to live in such an atmosphere, even if there were days as relaxed and indeed blithe as Pleasant View itself on a sunny June morning, after a spell of hard weather. At such times it was easy to forget the bitter, bracing winter days and the thundery August squalls rattling across from the Bow Hills, but the spiritual imperatives remained unchanged and life had to be lived at the ready.

Pleasant View had now blossomed into a highly attractive country estate, with its limpid little pond and dappled orchard, its well-groomed lawns and carefully casual flower beds, its utilitarian vegetable gardens, stable, coachhouse, barn, with the rye field and the meadows beyond, which would be a sea of gold by September.

Since 1898 Joseph Mann, one of Mrs. Eddy's personal students, had been in charge of the grounds. Twelve years earlier, at the age of twenty-two and living with his family in the village of Broad Brook, Connecticut, he had been accidentally shot in the breast and the 32-caliber bullet had lodged in the pericardium. Excessive internal bleeding resulted, and four doctors who had been rushed to the scene agreed that nothing could be done to save him.

At that point, as the last doctor pronounced him on the verge of death and telegrams were being prepared to announce his decease to distant friends and relatives, a Christian Scientist turned up on the doorstep, offered to heal him, and in fifteen minutes brought about a complete change in the situation. Three days later, in the words of Mann's affidavit in regard to the episode, he was "up bright and early and about with the family as though the accident had never occurred."[4]

Soon he began healing others, studied with Mrs. Eddy, moved to Boston with his sister Pauline, and became a Christian Science practitioner. Eager to show his gratitude to the discoverer of Christian Science in every way possible, he volunteered to serve as overseer of the Pleasant View estate when he learned that she urgently needed someone for the position. Shortly afterward his sister Pauline was pressed into service as a maid at Pleasant View. Then his brother August and the latter's wife Amanda moved up to the service cottage on the estate and August became Mrs. Eddy's coachman. It was almost a feudal arrangement, with the various family members held to their liege lady by a common bond of loyalty.

Then there was John Salchow, who came to Concord early in 1901 from a farm near Junction City, Kansas, and served for the next ten years as groundsman, handyman, and virtual bodyguard. This simple, powerfully built young man brought up in a family of German immigrants who were both upright and "bitter towards religion,"[5] had learned of Christian Science through Joseph Mann when the latter had come to Junction City to visit his brothers, Christian and Frederick Mann.

Too "proud and shy" to ask about the copy of *Science and Health* he saw in the Mann brothers' house, young Salchow ordered a copy secretly, had an immediate healing from reading it, began its serious study, and left it with design "on the parlor table where everyone could see it." Soon his father was picking it up and reading it when he thought no one was looking, and after three weeks "pulled back his chair at the dinner table one day and announced to the family that he had been a pretty hard old infidel, but he knew this woman had found the truth."

Before long the elder Salchows, John, and a sister had all studied with Joseph Mann, who returned to Junction City briefly to teach a class of neophytes and to organize Christian Science services. Later, when Mrs. Eddy asked Mann to recommend someone who would "stand" if brought to Pleasant View to help with the work, John Salchow leaped to mind as a likely choice. A letter asking him to come arrived at the Salchow farm at ten o'clock in the morning, and by noon of the same day he was on his way to New Hampshire. To Christian Scientists who met him in later years, he was "the man who left his plough in the field and came to serve his Leader."

In Salchow's ingenuous reminiscences, one finds the Pleasant View of planting and mulching, haying and apple picking, drainage problems and carriage repairs, of pigs, cows, and chickens, the farm horses Nelly and Jerry and the carriage horses Prince and Duke, the jokes and gossip of tradesmen and household "help," the daily incidents of a busy little world irradiated by a sense of spiritual purpose.

It is this interpenetration of the inner and outer worlds, of the large and the trivial, that today lends significance to the details of life at Pleasant View. It was Mrs. Eddy's training ground in organizing common life, in relating transcendental authority to empirical need. Every day was an experiment in extending the primacy of Spirit over the heterogeneousness of living. Not surprisingly, the process was often a matter of trial and error.

So long, for instance, as Joseph Mann simply managed the estate, all went reasonably well. But when Mrs. Eddy brought him into the household to serve also as an assistant secretary and metaphysical worker, he found the exacting daily interplay of domestic duties and spiritual challenges more than he could cope with. On several occasions he simply took off for elsewhere, with or without leave. After one of these episodes he wrote Mrs. Eddy that "inability to meet the demand" had driven him to distraction:

> I felt I must hide myself a few days, and so Mrs. Baker found me in [my] brother's quiet home [in Boston]. God bless you and I thank you for sending Mrs. Baker to have me come back. . . . I could at once see how I could be helpful at the cottage at this time, however sad my failures at the house have been, for, though I have kept it from you, dear mother, the cottage and August, in his general management, have needed my constant support.[6]

Mrs. Eddy wrote on the envelope of this letter, "Sad! Sad!" and answered him with a note of her own:

Mother was glad when you returned and would have run out and met you if she were used to running.

Now be happy in the memory of what a good son you have been to mother, think of how many times you have comforted her and how you came to Concord only to help her. After Jesus' temptation in the wilderness angels ministered unto him. Remain near me (if you are willing) and if you are in the Cottage I can call for you in need.[7]

Retiring from Pleasant View in 1904 and leading the life of a busy Christian Science practitioner and teacher in Connecticut for several decades, Mann looked back with both relief and nostalgia to the intensity of his Concord days. It was a familiar feeling to many of those who had served a limited term in Mrs. Eddy's household.

Not so with Salchow, who stayed with her to the end. Behind his service lay a simple, unswerving conviction that if Mrs. Eddy demanded that something be done it *could* be done, no matter how impossible the task might seem by ordinary reckoning.[8] To him at least there was no distinction between the mistress of Pleasant View and the discoverer of Christian Science, and he looked with wonderment on the keenness of her interest in every detail of life there.

"She could see things that no one else did," Salchow wrote in his reminiscences, then gave as an example a time when the house and barn were being painted:

They were working on the barn just as she came out of the house for her drive. As far as I know she did not notice them, and though on her return the painters were still there, she apparently paid no attention to them. I saw her coming up the driveway in the carriage and never once did she seem to glance toward the barn. However, she had no sooner stepped down from the carriage than she turned to August Mann and said, "I wish you would have the painters match the paint a little more closely." I jumped up on the box with August Mann and we drove straight down to the barn, stopping on our way to speak to Mr. Frost, the painter. When August gave Mrs. Eddy's instructions to him he became quite indignant. Frost was a first-rate honest worker and felt pretty badly to have his work criticised. August repeated, "That is what Mrs. Eddy said, and you know what that means." Mr. Frost then got to work and mixed up samples of paint, trying them on a large piece of board which he stood against some shrubs, walking off to get the effect of the color. After studying it a while I heard him exclaim, "By God, it is darker!"[9]

181

Mrs. Eddy, for her part, saw in her "faithful John"[10] an uncomplicated honesty that was as welcome to her as a fresh midsummer shower. From time to time he would be summoned to take care of odd jobs in her apartment, and his own account of those occasions suggests more than it says:

> When I was called to her rooms in this way, I immediately went about the task in hand and never tried to commence a conversation with her. If she chose to talk with me she would do so freely, and she often did, but there were many times when I was in her rooms for hours and never a word was spoken. She frequently told me that I never disturbed her, that when I came in she could feel my presence without knowing that I was near, and that sometimes, when she had been suffering, my thought helped to lift her out of it. I can never begin to tell the joy with which such words filled me. She was always kind and gentle with me.... No mother could have been more kind.[11]

That Mrs. Eddy's concern reached into Salchow's personal life is indicated by her promotion of his marriage.

Obviously in love with a local girl, one Mary McNeil, this rustic Parsifal who had dedicated himself to a life of single-minded service to his Leader resolutely put aside all thought of marriage. Mary—understandably not a Christian Scientist at that time—doubtless thought her own bleak thoughts about the situation, though she protested not very convincingly that the idea of marrying him had not occurred to her despite their protracted and deepening friendship.

Taking on the role of *dea ex machina*, Mrs. Eddy finally had August Mann deliver a letter to Mary's brother, James McNeil, announcing out of the blue that she "approved of the marriage" of his sister and John Salchow. "Naturally we were surprised," Mary wrote demurely in her later reminiscences. "However, John and I obeyed the command."[12] They obeyed it, indeed, only two days after receiving the letter, their alacrity pointing to a fairly delirious coincidence of obedience and desire.

If Mrs. Eddy's concern for the young couple's happiness was as motherly as an old-fashioned farmwife's, her method of showing it had a touch of the stately authority associated with the late Queen Victoria.[13] By the turn of the century she had in fact won an almost regal status in Concord, barring the attitude of such scoffers as ex-Senator Chandler, and she accepted the development with surprising but unsurprised naturalness.

This became evident in her two visits to the Concord State Fair in 1900 and 1901, the first year with Judge and Mrs. Hanna, the second with Judge and Mrs. Ewing.

Her unannounced arrival at the fairgrounds on the afternoon of September 6, 1900, created a sensation. The races on the track were immediately suspended, the band struck up a patriotic air, and "under the escort of mounted police with patrolmen on either side," her victoria "drawn by a pair of handsome bays" passed before the grandstand, which was "filled with five thousand people, and surrounded by three times that number."[14] There was considerable clapping, cheering, baring of heads, waving of handkerchiefs.[15]

She remained there half an hour, watched a race, applauding with the pleasure of a lifelong horse-lover the victory of a particularly handsome trotter, and observed a spectacular eighty-foot dive with the special interest that feats of daring and skill always held for her.[16] As the diver, in devil's costume, plunged through a flaming hoop into the six-foot pool, she was heard to exclaim delightedly to the Hannas, "I beheld Satan as lightning fall from heaven."[17]

The visit a year later was more expected, with a formal speech of welcome to her, more Christian Scientists and more reporters on hand.[18] It was her last appearance at the fair, but each year on a day when children were admitted free to the grounds a rather odd little ceremony took place. Tickets were given out to indigent children which entitled them to a free pair of shoes at W. A. Thompson's store, Mrs. Eddy being both the donor of the shoes and the originator of the idea.

Later, in answer to her own question as to why she liked to "look from her carriage daily on the dear children in Concord," she wrote (in the third person):

> Because she likes to see their feet and hands—the nice fitting of their Thompson boots and the pretty flitting to her of their little hands. The childhood of the one loves the childhood of the other.[19]

It was a toss-up whether Mrs. Eddy's motherliness, masculine strength, or childlikeness would be uppermost on any given occasion.

2

The discoverer of Christian Science held that she could best be understood through her writings. It is at least arguable that the essential Mary Baker Eddy is to be looked for in the book which, in its earliest form, was the fruit of half a lifetime's search for unconditioned being but through the rest of her life was modified, enriched, and clarified by the very developments it called forth. Certainly *Science and Health with Key to the Scriptures* was reshaped by Mrs. Eddy's experience almost as drastically as her experience was reshaped by *Science and Health*.

While the metaphysical substance remained a *given*—"Truth is a revelation"[20]—it was also a fact that spiritual truth must be "reduced" to human comprehension and "adapted" to the needs of the age. If vision must be tested by experience, revision was the imperative of an educational process imposed by the people, books, events, lessons, and practical necessities of her experience as founder. This is illustrated by developments preceding the major revision of *Science and Health* which she undertook in the latter part of 1901.

Sometime not long after the 1899 publication of a little volume entitled *Philosophic Nuggets*, composed of selections from Carlyle, Ruskin, Amiel, and Kingsley, a copy came into Mrs. Eddy's possession and was read by her with unusual interest.

It was her custom to mark the books she read, make marginal notes, or sometimes list page references on the flyleaves, and in this case the notations were abundant. The very first passage from Carlyle that she marked might have served as her own comment on *Philosophic Nuggets* itself: ". . . we admitted that the Book had in a high degree excited us to self-activity, which is the best effect of any book."[21]

Another passage which drew her attention was Carlyle's description of the Koran in his treatment of Mohammed in "The Hero as Prophet":

> *It is the confused ferment of a great rude human soul; rude, untutored, that cannot even read, but fervent, earnest, struggling vehemently to utter itself in words. . . . The panting, breathless haste and vehemence of a man struggling in the thick of battle for life and salvation; this is the mood he is in!* A headlong haste; for very magnitude of meaning, he cannot get himself articulated into words. *The successive utterances of a soul in that mood, colored by the various vicissitudes of three-and-twenty years; now well uttered, now worse; this is the Koran. [Emphasis added]*[22]

Bracketing the penultimate sentence, Mrs. Eddy drew attention to it on the flyleaf by page number and her own added comment: "*S & H. as first written.*"

The "headlong haste" is apparent in almost everything she drafted after her discovery of 1866, but, unlike Mohammed, she revised, rerevised—and took literary advice. Curiously enough, the aid she received on each of the book's major revisions seems to have made it more rather than less her own. It represented her ability to sift, absorb, transform, and distill experience to her own uses—or, as she might have put it, to *demonstrate* the help she needed.

"How seldom will the outward Capability fit the inward," was one of the sentences of Carlyle's that she marked, perhaps ruefully, but her thoughts leaped to meet another passage which found an echo in her next revision of *Science and Health:*

> *The thoughts they had were the parents of the actions they did; their feelings were parents of their thoughts; it was the unseen and spiritual in them that determined the outward and actual. . . .* [23]

There were other echoes from *Philosophic Nuggets* in her writings about this time, but they were inconsequential verbal tags for the most part[24] and were seldom from the passages she marked and commented upon. These markings tell more than the borrowings, for they point to the sentiments that evidently echoed in her heart more than in her ear. None is scored more heavily than Amiel's statement: "And even if I go lonely to the end, I would rather my hope and my dream died with me than that my soul should content itself with any lesser union."[25] This obviously spoke to the very human Mrs. Eddy more than to the Discoverer and Founder of Christian Science. The opposite was true, however, of another sentence by Amiel:

> *To live, so as to keep this consciousness of ours in perpetual relation with the eternal, is to be wise; to live, so as to personify and embody the eternal, is to be religious.*

A sentence in a 1904 speech by Mrs. Eddy picks up this statement, drops Amiel's distinction between the wise and the religious (since Christian Science holds that "No wisdom is wise but His [God's] wisdom" and "God is not separate from the wisdom He bestows"[26]), and adds Mrs. Eddy's distinctive metaphysical "bite":

> *To live so as to keep human consciousness in constant relation with the divine, the spiritual, and the eternal, is to individualize infinite power; and this is Christian Science.*[27]

Back in June, 1898, Mrs. Eddy had struck up a friendship with a minor poet and aesthete of Concord, Edward A. Jenks, and had subsequently consulted him on literary matters and utilized his editorial services on several of her messages to The Mother Church. Not a Christian Scientist, Jenks seems to have been a rather prickly character who, like the earlier Wiggin, combined a general feeling of intellectual superiority with a genuine admiration for his formidable but disarming patroness-client. Early in their acquaintance he wrote her:

> *I somehow received the impression, from my brief conversation with you last week at P. V., that you wanted not merely perfunctory or commonplace criticism, but genuine literary criticism, from some competent person, covering every point,—grammar, rhetoric, literary style and construction, punctuation, etc.,—to the end that from now on Christian Science writings might rank not only as among the ablest, but as among the best religious literature of the world, as they should; and that if you were to have a completely revised and perfected edition of your works prepared, it would be to the same end. Perfect English is perfect English, whether employed in elucidating Christian Science, or in a message of the president to Congress; and it seems to me to be rather more necessary and desirable in the discussions and elucidations of the new cult than in anything else, that "the new tongue" should have no uncertain articulation. I cannot but think that Christian Scientists would as heartily enjoy solid, compact, logical, uninvolved, unobscure, well-rounded English—"perfect English"—as any other people in the world; and Christian Science should be worthy of it.*[28]

As it developed, however, Jenks's help was confined largely to the more ornamental parts of Mrs. Eddy's writing—such rhetorical and descriptive passages as the section on theism and nature worship at the beginning of *Christian Science versus Pantheism,* in which he saved her from confounding *pan* as a Greek prefix with Pan as a mythical deity. His attitude to her warmed with further acquaintance, and she responded with appreciation, if not always with assent, to his somewhat dilettante erudition and genteel taste. But they were too far apart in their basic religious concepts to work together long or deeply.

Early in their association, Jenks had written Mrs. Eddy that he would not dream of "meddling with the more abstruse and scientific portions" of her work.[29] When, following the collapse of the Woodbury suit, she began a revision of *Science and Health* more thorough than any since the fiftieth edition ten years before, she turned for assistance not to Jenks but to two of the ablest writers in her own ranks, Edward Kimball and William McKenzie.

McKenzie and Daisette Stocking had been married at the beginning of August, and the consummation of this long-cherished desire, as well as the successful conclusion of the Woodbury litigation, had restored McKenzie's equanimity as well as his confidence in Mrs. Eddy's leadership.[30] At her request he had been made First Reader of the branch church just formed in Cambridge, across the river from Boston, thus fulfilling the wish that had caused her to send one of her first students there in 1875 in an abortive effort to plant Christian Science in the vicinity of Harvard University.[31]

Kimball, who went over to Cambridge each day to work with McKenzie in his study, described to Mrs. Eddy their *modus operandi* after they received the additions, deletions, changes, and rearrangements that she wished to have made in the text:

> *First I take the copy and study it with a view of detecting any necessary changes. Then Mr. McKenzie takes it and goes over the punctuation and corrects the quotations. After that we go over it together and discuss all changes of every kind and possibly make more and finally each one goes over the complete copy by himself.*[32]

Their suggestions in turn went back to the author, who made the final decisions herself, sometimes after further correspondence with them. In her own way, which was not that of Edward Jenks, Mrs. Eddy was a perfectionist and held each proposed emendation up to microscopic examination. The intensity of her effort for clarified expression over the years had led to her development of a style which, at its best, was characterized by metaphysical pithiness combined with an almost Emersonian shapeliness:

> *The sinner makes his own hell by doing evil, and the saint his own heaven by doing right.*

> *Does divine Love commit a fraud on humanity by making man inclined to sin, and then punishing him for it?*

> *Mortal mind sees what it believes as certainly as it believes what it sees.*

> *We cannot fathom the nature and quality of God's creation by diving into the shallows of mortal belief.*

> *Finite belief limits all things, and would compress Mind, which is infinite, beneath a skull bone.*

> *Allness is the measure of the infinite, and nothing less can express God.*

> *Mortal man has made a covenant with his eyes to belittle Deity with human conceptions.*[33]

Even in her earliest writings on Christian Science and in the impulsive haste of her letters, Mrs. Eddy had shown an aphoristic talent which seems to have been overlooked almost entirely by commentators on her style. These brieflets, to use a word of her own coinage, are scattered through *Science and Health* by the score, and they represent the distillations of someone who—as the *New York Herald* interviewer in 1901 wrote—had lived with her subject for a lifetime:

> *Matter is an error of statement.*
>
> *We tread on forces.*
>
> *The belief of life in matter sins at every step.*
>
> *Discomfort under error is preferable to comfort.*
>
> *To Truth there is no error,—all is Truth.*
>
> *The allness of Deity is His oneness.*
>
> *Asking God to be God is a vain repetition.*
>
> *Sickness is more than fancy; it is solid conviction.*[34]

Through the honing process of criticism and revision, however, Mrs. Eddy had also developed the opposite capacity to present her argument in rounded periods, moving from point to point with apparent ease. While at times she seemed ready to pick up almost any illustration or supplementary argument that lay at hand to support a position already established by logic she worked over certain dialectical passages until they surpassed anything within reach of the literary aides she enlisted to pounce on dangling participles and misplaced subjunctives. For example:

> *When we endow matter with vague spiritual power,—that is, when we do so in our theories, for of course we cannot really endow matter with what it does not and cannot possess,—we disown the Almighty, for such theories lead to one of two things. They either presuppose the self-evolution and self-government of matter, or else they assume that matter is the product of Spirit. To seize the first horn of this dilemma and consider matter as a power in and of itself, is to leave the creator out of His own universe; while to grasp the other horn of the dilemma and regard God as the creator of matter, is not only to make Him responsible for all disasters, physical and moral, but to announce Him as their source, thereby making Him guilty of maintaining perpetual misrule in the form and under the name of natural law.*[35]

A different kind of logic came into play in the final order which the chapters of *Science and Health* took in this edition. There had been a good deal of rearranging of material in the major revisions of earlier years, and for the past decade the book had started off with a chapter, "Science, Theology, Medicine," whose opening words read: "In the year 1866, I discovered the Christ science...."[36]

This was a logical starting point but not a particularly winning one. The author went on in the next sentence to state that God had been "graciously preparing"[37] her for many years to receive this revelation. By now, however, she had come to the conclusion that the reader, too, needed some gracious preparation for such apodictic assertions.

The new arrangement, which remains today, followed a new logic—the logic of her own early development. The first chapter, "Prayer," with its emphasis on "the prayer of fervent desire for growth in grace,"[38] correlates in spirit and intent with her autobiographical statement:

> *From my very childhood I was impelled, by a hunger and thirst after divine things,—a desire for something higher and better than matter, and apart from it,—to seek diligently for the knowledge of God as the one great and ever-present relief from human woe.*[39]

The second chapter, "Atonement and Eucharist," is her answer to the basic theological issue of man's alienation from God which, in its particular Calvinist form, she had challenged as a young girl but which, in its more general "misinterpretation of the Word," she saw as "the underlying cause of the long years of invalidism she endured before Truth dawned upon her understanding."[40]

The third chapter, "Marriage," deals with the related topics of marriage, home, children, divorce, woman's place in society—the problems she herself faced after her first marriage and early widowhood, representative of the disciplines of human living which, she felt, serve "to unite thought more closely to God."[41]

The fourth chapter, "Christian Science versus Spiritualism," explores the crucial distinction between the spiritual values of Christianity and psychic phenomena as represented by the irruption of spiritism in the mid-nineteenth century—when she herself had briefly essayed to "try the spirits whether they are of God"[42]—and by the various occult and paranormal developments with which Christian Science has been confounded ever since.

The fifth chapter, "Animal Magnetism Unmasked," deals with the quintessential difference between reliance on the human mind (suggestion, will power, hypnotism) and on the divine Mind (prayer, spiritual understanding, unselfed love) as the basis of Christian healing—a difference which Mrs. Eddy was forced to sort out after her encounter with Quimbyism in the early 1860's before she could write what now appeared at the beginning of the sixth chapter: "In the year 1866, I discovered. . . ."

One other major innovation marked the revised (226th) edition that came out early in 1902. It was the addition of a final chapter of one hundred pages[43] entitled "Fruitage" and composed entirely of testimony to healings which had resulted from the reading and study of *Science and Health*. At the start of the chapter she put the words of Jesus, "Wherefore by their fruits ye shall know them."[44] The pragmatic test, she implied, was no stranger to Christian kerygma.

3

Since 1899 Edward Kimball as the official teacher[45] of the Christian Science Board of Education had conducted several large Normal and Primary classes in Boston. Through these classes were streaming a host of new names, new faces, new types. It was the first stirring of a new era in Christian Science.

Kimball in his letters to Mrs. Eddy commented with frankness on the students in these classes.

A certain Mlle Demarez of Paris, he wrote, was representative of the French middle class, fairly well educated, honest, self-reliant, brave, although she would not be noticeable if she were not a Christian Scientist. "In the absence of a better leader in Paris she may be relied upon to do fairly well."[46] Mlle Demarez was evidently to be classified as a variant of the many unremarkable students on whom Mrs. Eddy had to rely in earlier days in the United States.

Lord Dunmore, on the other hand, despite a glow of enthusiasm and many admirable traits, lacked "an accurate technical knowledge" of Christian Science and the calmness, deliberation, and maturity of judgment that would "warrant dependence upon him as a leader." Kimball, who was less impressed than Mrs. Eddy by what he called "the effete nobility of Great Britain," nevertheless recognized readily the unusual competence, earnestness, and promise of the two daughters of Lady Ramsay from Edinburgh, who did indeed become outstanding figures in the movement in Scotland.[47]

At the same time, he tended to be a little overgenerous in his estimate of the various ministers and professors in his classes. "Simonsen of Brooklyn," he wrote Mrs. Eddy, "is a grand man, fine looking, benevolent, honest, upright, manly, gentle, humble, teachable." Simonsen in turn wrote in his later book *From the Methodist Pulpit into Christian Science:*

> *I have sat for months in class rooms listening to learned professors and able teachers, but I never supposed it to be possible for any human being to teach and unfold to his students, in the short space of two weeks, all that Mr. Kimball imparted to us. . . . To me he left nothing to be desired. His style was simple, clear, logical, convincing, and illuminating.*[48]

But it was not all mutual admiration. Of Rabbi Max Wertheimer, Kimball wrote Mrs. Eddy that he was insignificant in appearance, sincere, ardent, florid in utterance, dramatic, assertive, alert, well read, industrious—"a poor public speaker but does not know it"—yet promising on the whole. The promise, however, quickly evaporated and Wertheimer sought renown in fields that offered rapid prominence to ambitious converts, though increasing numbers of Jewish disciples were to come into Christian Science during the next decade, some of them doing yeomen service as practitioners, teachers, and lecturers.[49]

Of the several college professors in his classes, Kimball was particularly struck by Hermann S. Hering of Baltimore, who was demonstrating unusual aptitude as well as commitment. "Please keep him in mind," he wrote Mrs. Eddy. "He is splendid—because he has felt the very touch of God and has been born again."[50] In contrast, John B. Willis—described by Kimball as cultured, amiable, well educated, accustomed to good society and good behavior, gentle, kind, unobtrusive, genuine—should not, he thought, be pushed too quickly:

> *At this stage his grasp of C. S. is on the intellectual side although he is naturally spiritually minded.*
>
> *He has not demonstrated much and his chief drawback lies in the fact that he clings much to the idea that the good (?) of mortal mind is very admirable and worthy to coalesce with Science. Mr. Willis will progress rapidly as soon as he learns that what the world calls wisdom is foolishness with God.*
>
> *I like him very much and have great hope concerning him but no student in this class has needed such constant attention on my part or needed as much argument in order to yield & be satisfied.*[51]

Kimball found a good deal of imprecision in the students' understanding of what he called "the technical part" of Christian Science, and his first emphasis in teaching, he wrote Mrs. Eddy, was to present the subject as "exact Science." His second effort was to present "an elaborate uncovering of the claims of error," then to show "the sensible, practicable application" of Christian Science to the destruction of error. Finally, he emphasized the students' need for "the highest conceivable morality, the most tender love, and the activity of mercy, forbearance & forgiveness."[52]

On the one hand, he welcomed the promise of the newer people coming into view, like Bicknell Young of Chicago—"One of the best students of the second generation that I know of"—and George Kinter of Buffalo, of whom he wrote:

> A splendid man . . . a genuine, kind, strong, generous fellow who is too grand in general to be small or mean in particular—sensible, businesslike, effective. Would be a good man for you to have in Boston. So would Mr. Young.[53]

On the other hand, he learned with regret of Mrs. Eddy's decision in June, 1902, to have so tried a veteran as Hanna replaced as editor of the *Journal* and *Sentinel*. "I must have an advocate," she wrote Kimball, "the cause must have an advocate, in those at the head of our publications [who will] not *dodge* when they should fire and not fire when it is unwise."[54] What did Kimball think of his pupil Archibald McLellan, a Chicago attorney and one-man Committee on Publication for Illinois, to serve as editor? Kimball replied: "I grieve much because Judge Hanna has failed to meet your views and the needs, but if there is to be a change, I am indeed inclined to think . . . McLellan would be as good as any."[55]

So Hanna was moved on to the Board of Lectureship and assigned to lecture in the West because, Mrs. Eddy felt, he lacked the "solid learning and culture"[56] required for audiences in the eastern and middle states, while McLellan moved East to take his post and John Willis became assistant editor. At the same time, a new bylaw setting the term of First Reader at three years automatically brought about Hanna's resignation from that office—he had already served seven years—and Professor Hering of Baltimore was appointed by the Board of Directors to take his place.

Another sign of the changing times took place at the church's annual meeting in June, 1902, when ten thousand Christian Scientists voted unanimously to support a motion offered by Kimball and seconded by Judge Ewing:

> Recognizing the necessity for providing an auditorium for The Mother Church that will seat four or five thousand persons, and acting in behalf of ourselves and the Christian Scientists of the

world, we agree to contribute any portion of two million dollars that may be necessary for this purpose.[57]

Four years later the great domed "extension" to The Mother Church would announce to the world the new status of Christian Science, but Mrs. Eddy had no illusions either in 1902 or in 1906 that they had already arrived and could relax the struggle. A few days before the annual meeting at which the vote to build was taken, she had written Kimball:

> *I only wish you could stay with us and be on the Board of Directors but knowing the cost to you I wait on God to see His deliverance. Did you know what I have had to do in every direction, no one ready to help, the Board of Directors asleep, H[anna] ill, nothing ready; and now new officers to train for use, I old, and God my only helper—then the lesson would be learned by you before it is learned.*[58]

As it was, she urged Kimball to remain in Boston and help her train McLellan. "Men generally," she explained, "are more ready to yield to a man than [to] a woman."[59] Kimball, too, was well aware of the rugged discipline required to fit anyone to serve in the front rank of her troops, and this was evident in the caution that tempered his warm approbation of another promising new figure, William D. McCrackan.

McCrackan was a member of the coterie of progressive writers for the *Arena* during its crusading years under Benjamin O. Flower's editorship. Educated at Yale and Heidelberg, brother of the rector of the American Church in Munich, author of a standard history on the rise of the Swiss Republic, friend of Hamlin Garland, Henry George, Lord Bryce, and other politico-literary figures,[60] proponent of various democratic reforms—mild in retrospect but too liberal for the seignorial traditionalism of St. Paul's School at Concord where he taught for a year[61]—McCrackan had become interested in Christian Science at the beginning of 1900, had studied with Mrs. Stetson in April of that year, and was invited by Mrs. Eddy to go through the Normal Class under Kimball two months later.

"I was much pleased with Prof. McCrackan," the latter wrote Mrs. Eddy afterward. "He seems to be gentle, refined, and childlike in his reception of Christian Science . . . and I shall look with affectionate anticipation for a beautiful career." But, he announced firmly, "I do not think that it is best to give Mr. McCrackan a certificate this year."[62] Kimball himself had passed through some years of fiery tempering before he undertook to teach Christian Science to others, and he did not propose to commission a new recruit for a war which was only now beginning to reveal its full dimensions.

4

Back in 1900 when the newly installed Alfred Farlow had been trying to arrange for the appointment of a one-man Committee on Publication in the important state of New York, he had run into a little difficulty with Mrs. Stetson, then dominating the Christian Science scene in Manhattan.

This imposing lady, adept at evangelizing the fashionable and well-to-do, was a positive thinker long before Norman Vincent Peale and saw no reason why Christian Science in New York should expect a bombardment of criticism from the press. Farlow, reporting her views to Mrs. Eddy, commented dryly, "This is well, yet the fact remains that they already have the bombardment on hand, and should be at work to meet it."[63]

Mrs. Eddy entirely agreed, and later she wrote of Farlow to the Directors, "He is doing *well for our* Cause and the Pub. Com. is one of the most important functions in our system of church government."[64] Early in 1901, when he was busy day after day answering adverse Woodbury propaganda in the press, Mrs. Eddy wrote him:

> *When an article on my wrongs appears in our prints it must tell the whole story and have all the muscle and nerve of the Divine Mind ie. all the Truth and Love . . . [that] divine Science and human wisdom can bring to the rescue. I need a strong hand human to lift up mine even as Moses had it. You have done well*[;] *you have learned just the wise ways of meeting the press and would have mastered if m. a. m. had been out of the conflict. You must master that or you can do little for me. I am the target for all the fire.*[65]

As the Woodbury case approached its climax, Mrs. Eddy was even more the target of sensational speculations. "This whirlpool of stuff in the press," she wrote Farlow, "is only to affect the law-suit pending trial. The editors of papers do not know why they are so mesmerized." Then she ended with a slight touch of wonder added to her solicitude: "Be as cool and comfortable as you can[;] you surprise me with your calmness."[66]

The calm would soon be tested. On August 1, 1901, having lost the Woodbury case, Frederick W. Peabody began his official career as chief public castigator of Mrs. Eddy by delivering a vituperative onslaught on her in Tremont Temple. This lecture, published in pamphlet form as *A Complete Exposé of Eddyism or Christian Science and the Plain Truth in Plain Terms Regarding Mary Baker G. Eddy*,[67] set the tone for the criticism of the first decade of the century.

Mrs. Eddy's teaching was described as "unalloyed humbug" delivered by "a rank imposter." *Science and Health* was the product of "an insane mind, a degenerate mind . . . a mind possessed of one overmastering passion to perpetrate a monstrous fraud upon the human race." Was there, Peabody asked with the shocked piety of a nominal believer, "a blasphemy beyond hers? Or a greed beyond hers?"

The documentation adduced to support these pronouncements left something to be desired. An article in *The Christian Science Journal* for April, 1889, was described as an elaborate effort to establish a claim that Mrs. Eddy was the equal of Jesus. In point of fact, the article said the exact opposite.[68] Mrs. Eddy's early manuscript, "The Science of Man," was gratuitously and inaccurately[69] attributed to Quimby, then cited to show parallels with her own—i.e., her other—writings. Her strong statement to a disaffected student: "You would tear my heart out and trample on it," was transposed into a supposed comment by her on the same woman: "I would like to tear her heart out and trample it under my feet."[70] Where there was not even the misshapen shadow of a fact to serve his purpose, Peabody offered speculative answers to nonexistent problems—suggesting, for instance, that if Mrs. Eddy and Calvin Frye were in fact wife and husband, this might be the "most natural explanation" of an "otherwise extraordinary situation."[71]

Archibald McLellan, at that point still Committee on Publication for Illinois, wrote Farlow cautioning circumspection in replying to Peabody, who, he pointed out, was obviously trying to provoke them into actionable language which would permit him to start another libel suit. Mrs. Eddy's lawyers issued a similar warning. Farlow, unsure of Mrs. Eddy's own wishes, wrote Frye on August 7:

> *Following your suggestion I have tried to notice Peabody's stuff as little as possible. . . . There were a number of points in his tirade which I did not take up. After the Boston Journal and Transcript had sent reporters to me I felt it wise that I should go ahead and answer somewhat in the other papers. It was . . . difficult to know what Mother would have us do with it, since in times past she has charged me so particularly to denounce those lies.*[72]

Mrs. Eddy was torn two ways. She wanted to see strong answers, but she did not want to be embroiled in further litigation. Farlow suddenly seemed to her to be fumbling. She was not sure exactly what he should be doing to counter the Peabody attack, but whatever it was, he wasn't doing it.

At that very time, William McCrackan, who was now Committee on Publication for New York, produced two very well-written articles on Christian Science for the dignified *North American Review* in reply to a brace of attacks by J. M. Buckley. This, Mrs. Eddy felt, was the sort of defense she needed, and she wrote McCrackan on October 1:

> *We need you in Mr. Farlow's place. I told him but yesterday the situation had outgrown the incumbent. I like his sturdiness but his education has been not in a literary line which the place demands. . . . Get ready to change your place and come to Boston when the next election to his office is made. Please mention not a word of this and I will make it easy for good Mr. Farlow.*[73]

For a full year she vacillated on this point. At one time she would write McCrackan:

> *I think it is for your interest to remain in the line of your present action ripening as you now are through experience. Is this acceptable to you?*
>
> *Mr. Farlow is regaining his lulled faculties and doing well at present. So I feel not quite justified in removing him while such is the case.*[74]

Two months later the tide would have turned again:

> *Mr. Farlow is a smart business man and a lovely character but he has not the education and literary taste requisite for this responsible office. My* next *choice will be yourself. . . . I want an officer of the Mother Church wise and educated sufficiently to fill his place without my having to look after him in anywise.*[75]

But Farlow's spiritual sturdiness won out over McCrackan's literary grace. When she had first appointed Farlow, Mrs. Eddy had recommended that he find a "literary critic" to help him improve his style; her choice, she added, would have been her old aide Wiggin, except that "they say W[oodbury] has him for her help in writing."[76] Months later Farlow wrote her that he had visited Wiggin some time ago "and while he was kind to me he criticised some of your English called you a very ignorant woman and declared that there was nothing in Christian Science."[77]

This was the kind of blunt honesty Mrs. Eddy would never get from the more polished McCrackan, and in the end she valued it too much to part with it. Also, Farlow had a spiritual grace which showed itself in a feeling for the sensibilities and the limits of comprehension and tolerance of those unfamiliar with Christian Science, while Mrs. Eddy found herself having to write to McCrackan:

> *What you [added] has made your meaning obscure to some readers. None but Scientists can comprehend the fact you stated. . . . Students may speak altogether too metaphysically to others than Christian Scientists. I have often told them of this and shown them the advantage it gives those who sneer at an absolute Science.*[78]

In 1902, just prior to the Peabody attack, an apparent new champion arose in the person of one John Henry Keene, a maverick Baltimore attorney, not a Christian Scientist, who produced a highly polemic manuscript entitled "Christian Science and its Enemies," in which he assailed the clerical critics of the new faith.

Shown some excerpts from the manuscript, Mrs. Eddy wrote the author her enthusiastic thanks and endorsement. But when she read the article in its entirety, she was horrified by its bellicosity, its epithets against traditional theology, its "acrimonious assertions."[79] Could Farlow arrange through Professor Hering to have the objectionable invective removed and the whole piece toned down, so that it could be given wide circulation as a pamphlet? Three days after the Peabody attack she wrote Farlow:

> *I see with the vision of a Seer that this style [Keene's] which I object to is pushed before the public to lessen the shame of Peabody's attack. Now if we go and do likewise it will give our enemies all the advantage over us. . . . His style of attack and pugilism is just the opposite of Christian Science wisdom and will be used as a wedge to split apart the pacification of my Message, and serve as a challenge to further abuse from the press and churches.*[80]

Keene was greatly disappointed, felt the epithets were necessary, and sold twenty thousand copies of the pamphlet on the basis of her earlier endorsement, then yielded to her wishes and withdrew it.[81] With unabated admiration of her and contempt for Farlow, he continued during the rest of Mrs. Eddy's life to offer her unasked and unheeded advice on the right way to deal with published attacks on her.

Particular criticisms should be neither repeated nor refuted, Keene insisted, but dismissed with such lordly assertions as: "An intelligent public will scarcely give even partial credit to such extravagant fables."[82] Sweeping, absolute statements, based on a priori logic, should present her as an inspired metaphysician, rather than as a figure involved in the trials of common humanity. Typical of his objections to Farlow's more commonsense and low-keyed approach is a passage in a letter to her two years later:

> I cannot conceive a more disastrous blow to this budding unfoldment than Farlow's answer to Churchman. I am a patient long suffering reader of twaddle of all kinds daily, but I could not stand this stuff for five minutes. Churchman's letter has a significant tendency towards an atmosphere of rationalistic negation, but Farlow's deals in commonplace, vapid dregs, an unwholesome agglomeration of mere words. Farlow has no one of the gifts of literary expression, no penetrating rationalism, no scholarship, no faculty of philosophic meditation, no large organic or constructive conception of C. S. such as is displayed by many of your lecturers, notably [Bicknell] Young. . . . C. S. is not, as Farlow says, a "competitive" system. It is Christ's.[83]

Mrs. Eddy was unimpressed. To yoke lofty metaphysics with a scornful refusal to answer particular arguments was not the method of Christian Science healing. Farlow remained her man.

At the same time, the "literary" aspect of Christian Science moved into new importance as a world-famous man of letters rode onto the battlefield and, with something between the rebel yell of a Confederate cavalryman and the war whoop of a Comanche brave, ripped into the silver-haired lady of eighty-one whom he would gallantly describe as "that shameless old swindler, Mother Eddy."[84]

Mark Twain—who, like any other woman-worshiping American male of his generation, idolized his invalid wife; who for thirty-two years called his kindly older friend, Mrs. Mary Fairbanks, "Mother" and conferred virtual sainthood on a prettified Joan of Arc before the Holy Office got around to the task officially—found it uproarious that Christian Scientists of that day should bestow the title of Mother on Mrs. Eddy. Also, having married, made, lost, and laboriously recouped a fortune, he found it outrageous that the incessantly busy founder of Christian Science should have earned enough to live during her last years in modest comfort on a pleasant country estate which could not compete in splendor with his own successive mansions in Hartford and Riverdale.

It was as a literary critic of Mrs. Eddy that Mark Twain made some of his most palpable hits, as well as some of his most egregious blunders, but he also usefully tumbled a few attendant shibboleths to the ground. As Mrs. Eddy wrote to several New York newspapers early in 1903, "In his article, of which I have seen only extracts, Mark Twain's wit was not wasted in certain directions."[85] In this matter of the honorific "Mother," for instance. When Mrs. Eddy had complained to Farlow a year earlier of the tendency of the press to refer to her somewhat mockingly as "Mother Eddy," Farlow had replied:

> *The use of the term Mother as applied to you is attributable to Christian Scientists. They use it so much in the Wen. evening meetings, on the street cars and everywhere as to cause this vulgar use of it in the press.*[86]

It took Mark Twain's ridicule, however, to topple the official title which gave occasion for this vulgarization—a title Mrs. Eddy had first resisted, then welcomed.[87] Soon after her letter to the New York papers, she changed the *Manual* bylaw which for several years had insisted that Christian Scientists should reserve the title for her— "except as the term for kinship according to the flesh."[88] In its new form the bylaw read:

> The Title of Mother Changed. *In the year eighteen hundred and ninety-five, loyal Christian Scientists had given to the author of their textbook, the Founder of Christian Science, the individual, endearing term of Mother. At first Mrs. Eddy objected to being called thus, but afterward consented on the ground that this appellative in the Church meant nothing more than a tender term such as sister or brother. In the year nineteen hundred and three and after, owing to the public misunderstanding of this name, it is the duty of Christian Scientists to drop the word* mother *and to substitute Leader, already used in our periodicals.*[89]

Because the mystique died hard, Mrs. Eddy took another step a few years later, when Mark Twain's articles on Christian Science were issued in book form. Included in the book was Peabody's satiric account of his visit with a parcel of awestruck pilgrims to the "Mother's Room" in the Mother Church. This caustic description of it as a "shrine" in which adoring worshipers paid homage to a sanctified leader crystallized Mrs. Eddy's earlier misgivings[90] and she announced in the *Journal* the passing of a new bylaw:

> *The room in The Mother Church formerly known as "Mother's Room" shall hereafter be closed to visitors.*

There is nothing in this room now of any special interest. "Let the dead bury their dead," and the spiritual have all place and power.[91]

The room was thereupon closed to the public in perpetuity, dismantled, and subsequently used for storage and filing purposes. Mark Twain's wit and even Peabody's venom had not been wasted, but neither was the damage yet repaired.

5

If anyone could and should have relished Mrs. Eddy's saltiness, it was Mark Twain, late of Hannibal, Missouri, and nostalgic alter ego of Samuel L. Clemens, Esq., of Riverdale, New York.

Her remark that a refractory student was "so full of animal magnetism that her eyes stick out like a boiled codfish's"[92] displayed the sort of spirited vernacular the creator of Huck Finn would normally have delighted in—if the conventional image of the Victorian lady had not got in the way.

It was the same overidealized image which had weakened his Joan of Arc. The Mark Twain who wrote *Pudd'nhead Wilson* should have had no difficulty in recognizing that Joan's mystical voices and visionary ideals were perfectly compatible with the pungent idiom and peasant realism which befitted a commander of hard-pressed troops. But the same inhibitions that kept him from endowing his ideal Joan with the robust characteristics of a battle-tried campaigner made him complain when Mrs. Eddy said and did things not to be expected of Whistler's mother.

The mistress of Pleasant View made a sizable fortune, for instance, through her writing. It was one thing for a woman to *have* money, like his beloved Livy, but another thing to *make* it, and the inordinately money-conscious Clemens reacted by projecting upon Mrs. Eddy his own passion for wealth, success, display, and applause, then lashing the fantasy figure of his creation.[93] His Mrs. Eddy was, to be sure, a more vivid creation than his idealistic Joan, but no more related to actuality. Clemens was shrewd enough to avoid subjecting himself to any facts that would undermine the mixture of Calamity Jane and Hetty Green which he set up as a counterpoise to his shamefaced attraction toward Christian Science itself. The great humorist (most of his biographers have recognized) was a savagely divided man, as the battles between black rage and high spirits in his last works amply demonstrate.

In a letter to Farlow early in 1903, Mrs. Eddy mentioned that in reading extracts from Mark Twain's recent article she found "an undertone in it which is very complimentary to Christian Science."[94] Peabody, who furnished Clemens with a good deal of ammunition and expected him to be an unqualified ally, had written him shortly before, "I have just read your article in the Dec. North American and, to be perfectly candid, found it somewhat disappointing."[95] Other critics of that day and this have also noted with either disappointment or piqued interest the undercurrent of almost wistful admiration in his treatment of Christian Science and have pointed to such passages of his as the following:

> *The Christian Scientist believes that the Spirit of God (life and love) pervades the universe like an atmosphere; that whoso will study* Science and Health *can get from it the secret of how to inhale that transforming air; that to breathe it is to be made new; that from the new man all sorrow, all care, all miseries of the mind vanish away, for that only peace, contentment and measureless joy can live in that divine fluid; that it purifies the body from disease, which is a vicious creation of the gross human mind, and cannot continue to exist in the presence of the Immortal Mind, the renewing Spirit of God. . . .*
>
> *But there is a mightier benefaction than the healing of the body, and that is the healing of the spirit—which is Christian Science's other claim. So far as I know, so far as I can find out, it makes it good. Personally I have not known a Scientist who did not seem serene, contented, unharassed. I have not found an outsider whose observation of Scientists furnished him a view that differed from my own. . . .*
>
> *For the thing back of it is wholly gracious and beautiful: the power, through loving mercifulness and compassion, to heal fleshly ills and pains and griefs—all—with a word, with a touch of the hand! This power was given by the Saviour to the Disciples, and to* all *the converted. All—every one. It was* exercised *for generations afterwards. Any Christian who was in earnest and not a make-believe, not a policy-Christian, not a Christian for revenue only, had that healing power, and could cure with it* any disease or any hurt or damage possible to human flesh and bone. *These things are true, or they are not. If they were true seventeen and eighteen and nineteen centuries ago it would be difficult to satisfactorily explain why or how or by what argument that power should be non-existent in Christians now.*[96]

Actually Clemens had visited Laura Lathrop in New York sometime in the 1890's and had benefited from the treatments he had from her, afterward recommending Christian Science and/or mind-cure to various friends, and at one point to his daughter Susy.[97]

Then, in the winter of 1898–99 in Europe, emerging from the years of despair which followed his bankruptcy and Susy's death after long medical treatment, he took up his pen and romped briefly into the subject, largely in the spirit of good-natured burlesque.[98] Part of what he wrote at that time appeared in the *Cosmopolitan Magazine* of October, 1899, creating no great stir but adding its ridicule of *Science and Health*[99] to the Woodbury-inspired campaign against Mrs. Eddy then gaining headway in the press.

Three years later he took up the subject again. In December, 1902, he launched the first of four articles on Christian Science in the *North American Review,* with the aim of shaping them into a book to come out in the spring. The first two of them were made up for the most part of the 1899 material which had already appeared in the *Cosmopolitan,* with "corrections" embodied in footnotes which then and since have been largely ignored by his readers.

Mrs. Eddy wrote Farlow after the series had started: "I advise you to take no notice of Mark Twain's effusion of folly and falsehood. Time tells all stories true."[100] However, as Committee on Publication for New York, McCrackan had already got in touch with Clemens, had several long talks with him, and sent him copies of his own two *North American* articles on Christian Science—which, Clemens wrote him, he read "with admiration and with profit."[101] Much of the latter's "violence and anger" had disappeared by the second talk, McCrackan reported,[102] and the two men in fact struck up a pleasant enough friendship, within the limits of their basic disagreement.

At the same time Peabody was working hard to pull Clemens further in the other direction, and although Clemens disliked him as a person, he made liberal and uncritical use of the doctored "facts" furnished him by the tirelessly vindictive lawyer. Nevertheless, he told McCrackan, he had written Peabody "that he did not like his pamphlet, because it showed animus and temper and that the writer should never show temper but should make the reader feel it."[103]

A month later McCrackan, who had been effectively challenging some of the points presented as fact in the *North American* articles, wrote Farlow that Clemens himself was "now showing temper and is attempting to accuse me of actions which I have not committed."[104] Then followed a later report which announced:

I have glad news to tell you. I received a letter from Mark Twain Saturday night, containing a manly statement that he was ashamed of having written me those insulting letters. I at once enclosed them in an envelope and returned them to him so that he can tear them up. I also had a talk with him over the 'phone, and Love has done a great work. I want to thank you for your brotherly help throughout the matter.[105]

The March issue of the *North American Review* carried an article by McCrackan answering some of Mark Twain's criticisms. Earlier there had been an expectation by both men that this would go into the finished book along with the critical articles. Clemens, with typical jocosity, wrote the editor of the *North American,* "I particularly want him in my book, because granting him this courtesy will put me in a position to ask Mrs. Eddy to add my articles to her Science and Health Bible."[106] As McCrackan, however, recognized the intractable ferocity of Twain's personal attack on Mrs. Eddy, he wrote Farlow that he felt it would be a great mistake to keep the projected book afloat by having a serious statement of Christian Science included in it.

Clemens, for his part, refused McCrackan's invitation to go with him to Boston or Concord to talk with some of the men of probity and intelligence who actually knew Mrs. Eddy well—substantial citizens like General Streeter, Samuel Elder, and her cousin General Baker who were not Christian Scientists, as well as believers like Kimball and Hanna who knew her life and thinking from years of intimate association with her. If he went, McCrackan was sure, he would see for himself that these were not men who would be gulled and bamboozled—as Clemens supposed all honest Christian Scientists to be—by a female tyrant cracking her whip from Pleasant View. Nor would they fit into his view of a ruthless "Christian Science Trust" exploiting the credulity of thousands for their own power and profit. He did not propose, however, to inflict the great Mark Twain on Mrs. Eddy.[107]

Clemens had a valid excuse in the illness of his wife, Olivia, for not leaving Riverdale just then. Some of his biographers have speculated that the nervous prostration and heart disease which kept her in isolation during those months, as well as the psychosomatic difficulties of his daughter Clara, may have been in part the origin of his fulminations against Mrs. Eddy.[108] Farlow and McCrackan, on the other hand, saw a woman of a very different sort as playing an unrecognized role in the situation. Not merely was Josephine Woodbury the unseen influence behind much of the bogus information Peabody was feeding Clemens, but she had got into direct contact with the latter, arranged a meeting with him at her New York hotel, and—McCrackan became convinced—was giving him her specific "mental" attention.

In one of their conversations, Clemens told him how time and again he would be roused out of a sound sleep at night by an "impelling force" which would send him downstairs to his library to dash off abusive letters to "the woman in Concord" in a torment of rage. "I generally tear them up, but something forces me to write them," he explained to McCrackan ruefully. "I don't know what it is. It comes to me at night."[109]

Years later McCrackan wrote that it "did not seem possible at the time to explain to him that he was the victim of vulgar hypnotic trickery." Mark Twain's "mental predicament," he added, "was forcibly recalled to my mind by my receiving one of these abusive letters addressed to myself, but evidently intended for the woman in Concord."[110]

This was one of the letters for which Clemens quickly apologized and which McCrackan returned to him without resentment. On another occasion, when McCrackan asked after Mrs. Clemens's health, the despondent husband gave him a gloomy report, then added that he would be only too glad if his friend would give her Christian Science treatment, but "she's such a good Presbyterian she'd rather die than have it."[111]

McCrackan's own attitude to this self-divided man was compounded of liking, dismay, compassion—and incomprehension. In his later recollections of their association, he concluded with a vision of the Mark Twain who might have been if he had been able to free himself from the residual Calvinism (what Bernard De Voto would call the "sophomoric determinism"[112]) of his later philosophy, with its view of "the damned human race,"[113] its anger and outrage and despair:

> *A vision comes to me as I write of a Mark Twain refreshed by the apprehension of the true God, for whom he had always been blindly seeking; a Mark Twain who has found the modus operandi of true justice for others for which he craved. . . . I see him as the Knight clad in spiritual armor fighting against the shams of the world's standards . . . cutting and pounding and hewing, powerful and masterful, dominating with his natural qualities, speaking with authority, flashing his messages, yet doing all this without harming any one, not hurting either the*

oil or the wine, either gladness or inspiration. I see him gentle as a lamb, meek and mighty, simple as a child, grateful, loving and obedient to God, finding his greatest glory in submission to spirit, his best fun in fighting for right. I see him working with instead of working against his best friend, the woman in Concord.[114]

The vision remained strictly a vision. If some of the passages in his writings on Christian Science show Mark Twain momentarily glimpsing with a kind of wonder the possibility of intrinsic good, these glimpses may perhaps be credited to McCrackan's influence. But the cynicism which saw Christian Science healing as merely a variant form of hypnotic suggestion[115] and the Church of Christ, Scientist, as one more proof of a damned human race clamoring to be duped into slavery received attentive nourishment from a Peabody and a Mrs. Woodbury wholly devoid of Mark Twain's own generosity of spirit.

When Harper's decided to postpone indefinitely[116] the publication in book form of his articles, plus supplementary material written in the spring of 1903, the author showed his customary ambivalence. At one moment he was indifferent, at another resentful, and his double-mindedness in regard to Christian Science continued even after the book came out in 1907. In the last year of his life—when, as he wrote with typical extravagance, "I am full of malice, saturated with malignity"[117]—he made two separate statements which sum up his dual attitude.

On the one hand, he remarked to Albert Bigelow Paine, his friend and biographer-to-be, who had just confessed to having been helped by Christian Science treatment:

Of course you have been benefited. Christian Science is humanity's boon. Mother Eddy deserves a place in the Trinity as much as any member of it. She has organized and made available a healing principle that for two thousand years has never been employed, except as the merest kind of guess-work. She is the benefactor of the age.[118]

On the other hand, he wrote to a correspondent in Scotland:

My view of the matter has not changed. To-wit, that Christian Science is valuable; that it has just the same value now that it had when Mrs. Eddy stole it from Quimby; that its healing principle (its most valuable asset) possesses the same force now that it possessed a million years before Quimby was born; that Mrs.

Eddy the fraud, the humbug, organized *that force and is* entitled to high credit for that. *Then with a splendid sagacity she hitched it to the shirt-tail of a religion—the surest of all ways to secure friends for it, and support. In a fine and lofty way—figuratively speaking—it was a tramp stealing a ride on the lightning express. Ah, how did that ignorant village-born peasant woman know the human ass so well? She has no more intellect than a tadpole—until it comes to* business—*then she is a marvel!*[119]

There was something fairly asinine in Mark Twain's own prediction that by 1920 there would be ten million Christian Scientists in the United States, that by 1940 they would be "the governing power in the Republic" and the "Christian Science Trust" would have become "the most insolent and unscrupulous and tyrannical politico-religious master that has dominated a people since the palmy days of the Inquisition"—a master which "after a generation or two" would "probably divide Christendom with the Catholic Church."[120]

Mrs. Eddy's own views were more realistic. The future prosperity of Christian Science, she indicated, was conditional on the demonstration of Christian Science in the lives of Christian Scientists.[121] If Christian Science were not properly taught, lived, and proved, it would disappear from the face of the earth. If she should be deified by her followers, the truth she had expounded would again be lost to the world.[122]

As to her own status, assailed so bombastically by Mark Twain, a single sentence in her published reply to him stated simply: "What I am remains to be proved by the good I do."[123]

Interlude: Semantic

Interlude: Semantic

From the earliest days *Science and Health* has been hailed by its critics as a monument of imprecision. No judgment has been more often quoted than Mark Twain's exuberant dictum that "of all the strange and frantic and incomprehensible and uninterpretable books which the imagination of man has created, surely this one is the prize sample."[1] Less often quoted—in fact, not quoted at all for more than seventy years—is the footnote he added in January, 1903:

> *The first reading of any book whose terminology is new and strange is nearly sure to leave the reader in a bewildered and sarcastic state of mind. But now that, during the past two months, I have, by diligence, gained a fair acquaintanceship with* Science and Health *technicalities, I no longer find the bulk of that work hard to understand.*[2]

More than that, he now found the English "clean, compact, dignified, almost perfect."[3] Nor was this in his opinion merely an indication of improvement in the latest revision. Going back to the third edition of 1883 he found its language "very nearly as straight and clean and competent as is the English of the latest revision"—it "was good at the outset and has remained so."[4] From which he concluded that Mrs. Eddy could not possibly have written *Science and Health*.[5]

While this conclusion was at least as rash and wrong-headed[6] as his first impulsive characterization of the book had been, the change in Mark Twain's estimate pointed toward an experience common to some of Mrs. Eddy's most sedulous students. Convinced at a first reading that *Science and Health* was needlessly obscure, inept, and at times logically contradictory, they found further acquaintance with it revealing virtues—stylistic, semantic, discursive, as well as spiritual—which swept their earlier reservations away and left them confident that they now had a crystalline comprehension of its meaning.[7]

Then, however, would follow a third stage at which they would feel they had barely begun to sound the depths of their "textbook." To the never-ending incredulity of critics entrenched at stage one, these students were apt to speak of Mrs. Eddy as though she were a Kant in petticoats, to be studied with continuous and meticulous attention to the smallest verbal details of her expression.

The publication of an exhaustive concordance to *Science and Health* in 1903 made systematic study of this sort more feasible. Following as it did on the heels of the 1902 revision, this publication marked the beginning of what was to become research in depth into Mrs. Eddy's writings. Enterprising students of Christian Science increasingly found suggestive lines of thought—sometimes astonishing implications—opened up by study of the author's use of key words in varying contexts.

Not only was this true of basic conceptual terms like Truth and Principle,[8] but even of lowly conjunctions and prepositions. The compiler of the concordance, Albert F. Conant, announced in his preface: "This Concordance contains every noun, verb, adjective, and adverb in *Science and Health,* together with certain pronouns, prepositions, and conjunctions, which were deemed of sufficient importance to be introduced."[9] The little word *about* on almost the first page furnishes a piquant illustration.

Christian Scientists then, as now, were apt to speak of "the truth about God" or "the truth about man." But when one consults the concordance for references under *about,* it appears that Mrs. Eddy never used either of these expressions. A little further research discloses the fact that she always referred, instead, to "the truth *of* God" and "the truth *of* man." Noting this, the student could either dismiss the fact as an unimportant oddity of expression or take it as a clue to the meaning of *truth* as she used the word. While the philosophic ramifications of the subject are far too broad for examination here, a few general considerations throw light on both her thinking and her language.

Truth in its primary sense is ontological. A thing is true because it *is.* To affirm the truth of anything, however, is not to establish it as fact. Whatever *is* affirms itself by being what it is, but to be established as fact it must be known for what it is. Truth in this sense is the correspondence of knowing to being. Mrs. Eddy went further and said, it is the identity of knowing with being. In her metaphysical logic, whatever infinite Mind knows derives both its being and its truth from Mind's knowing of it. There is no standard of truth outside of Mind, which itself is the source and determinant of all true being.

"And God said, Let there be light: and there was light. And

God saw [i.e., knew] the light, that it was good."[10]

Here the further identity of truth with good is asserted. If God's being (or, put differently, Mind's knowing) is necessarily good, then all that He brings into existence (or all that Mind knows as idea) must necessarily be good. Being defines good.[11] Truth, as reality-principle, operates in human experience to separate fact from falsehood, substance from shadow, self-existent good from self-assertive evil. "And God divided the light from the darkness. And God called the light Day, and the darkness he called Night."[12] In less metaphorical terms, Mrs. Eddy writes:

> *Truth is immortal; error is mortal. Truth is limitless; error is limited. Truth is intelligent; error is non-intelligent. Moreover, Truth is real, and error is unreal. This last statement contains the point you will most reluctantly admit, although first and last it is the most important to understand.*[13]

From the standpoint of Christian Science, the importance of understanding this final proposition is that it establishes the truth of man as the idea or expression of God, of Truth itself. As understood fact, Mrs. Eddy maintains, this begins at once to bring to light in human experience the "real" man as against the finite, fallible, mortal elements of thought which falsely claim to constitute man. Thus the process is initiated by which the truth *of* God's man and the truth *about* fallacious mortal man are simultaneously and progressively demonstrated.

It is typical of Mrs. Eddy's approach that so small a semantic distinction should involve so consequential an issue. However scandalous her generalizations from the standpoint of the analytical philosophy of a later generation, the interesting fact is that her own ontological-operational analysis of language caused her sometimes to consider a single word closely for several days before choosing it for systematic use in her discursive writing.

Nor did she give any less painstaking attention to critical linguistic details in her analysis of what she called the "false claims" of sin or error. Typical of the hawklike speed with which she swooped down on minute verbal imprecisions which might have large practical consequences is her comment in a letter to Archibald McLellan :

> *In your excellent article* The Question of Omnipotence *you contradict your assertions. Pardon me, but reread it and you will find you wrote that evil is not "something that enjoys,* suffers, *or is real." Then again you speak of evil "as a mirage that misleads the traveler." Who is the traveler that is* misled *and must suffer*

for it? Who but the evil so-called, and does not evil destroy itself through its own lie, namely, a belief in evil, sin, suffering *and death? Yes it does, in belief, and to sever it from this doom would be an evil of itself.*[14]

On one occasion in 1905, Mrs. Eddy called the full Board of Directors and all the editors of the *Journal* and *Sentinel* to Pleasant View to take them to task for a single clause in a *Sentinel* article: " . . . a diseased body is not acceptable to God."[15] According to Christian Science, she pointed out, a healthy *physical* body was no more acceptable to God as the reality of man's being than a sick one, since man was God's spiritual image and likeness.

From that, she apparently went on to discuss the Christ-idea manifest in the life of Jesus as representative of man's nature as the son of God. At one point she referred them to a passage in *Science and Health* which quotes and interprets the verse in Hebrews defining "the Son" as "the brightness of His [God's] glory, and the express [expressed] image of His person [infinite Mind]." The exegesis in *Science and Health* continues:

> *It is noteworthy that the phrase "express image" in the Common Version is, in the Greek Testament, character. Using this word in its higher meaning, we may assume that the author of this remarkable epistle regarded Christ as the Son of God, the royal reflection of the infinite; and the cause given for the exaltation of Jesus, Mary's son, was that he "loved righteousness and hated iniquity."*[16]

Even before pointing out the offending error in the statement from the *Sentinel*, Mrs. Eddy in her interview with the Directors and editors had solemnly charged the former to read the periodicals carefully and help her keep out of them any erroneous or misleading statements that might have escaped the editors' notice. Typically, she related these stern but workaday instructions to the magnitude and urgency of the first chapter of Hebrews. Evidently she felt that the Directors, to the extent that they were to see the brightness of God's glory and be anointed with the oil of gladness above their fellows, must so love righteousness and hate iniquity that they could detect even a small, unconscious error in the statement of Science and understand the disastrous consequences to which it could lead.

In this case, there was a danger that Christian Scientists might come to believe that physical health *of itself* was a sign of grace, i.e., that a well body was more acceptable to God than a sick one. Her statement, "The healthy sinner is the hardened sinner,"[17] was enough to shatter such an assumption. Yet experience had shown her that some naturally robust Christian Scientists were strongly inclined toward a kind of health snobbery, believing themselves spiritually superior to other Christian Scientists (herself, for instance) who might labor at times under severe physical disabilities.[18] Kimball who, despite his extraordinarily active life, experienced occasional periods of acute suffering, wrote with some relief that Mrs. Eddy had told him "we would all be tested and that we might be glad that our temptations came in the way of sickness rather than sin."[19]

Great though the difference is between a pure and an applied science, each requires its own sort of precision. Mrs. Eddy, in her dual role of Discoverer and Founder, rigorously insisted that a similar need for precision was involved in both the study of pure metaphysics and its application to practical experience. While she sometimes used the terms "Divine Science" and "Christian Science" to differentiate between these two aspects of her teaching, she also pointed out that, in the last analysis, the terms were synonymous. "Science," she wrote, "is not susceptible of being held as a mere theory"[20]—and a fragment among her unpublished writings makes the same point with a simple but suggestive metaphor:

> *Five times ten are fifty. This is science. Echo answers: "Five times ten are fifty. This is science." The first statement is true and the latter is untrue. Why? Because one . . . demonstrates Science . . . the other repeats Science. . . .*[21]

Not long before, William James in *The Varieties of Religious Experience* had made a sweeping indictment of theoretical distinctions unrelated to demonstrable effects:

> *If . . . we apply the principle of pragmatism to God's metaphysical attributes, strictly so called, as distinguished from his moral attributes, I think that, even were we forced by a coercive logic to believe them, we still should have to confess them to be destitute of all intelligible significance. Take God's aseity, for example; or his necessariness; his immateriality; his "simplicity" or superiority to the kind of inner variety and succession which we find in finite beings, his indivisibility . . .; his repudiation of inclusion in a genus; his actualized infinity; . . . his self-sufficiency, self-love, and absolute felicity in himself:—candidly speaking, how do such qualities as these make any definite connection with our life? And if they severally call for no distinctive adaptation of our conduct, what vital difference can it possibly make to a man's religion whether they be true or false?*[22]

Metaphysical distinctions did make a difference to Mrs. Eddy. impatient as she might have been with some of those evolved from the subtle disputations of medieval schoolmen. The radical simplicities of a metaphysic resting ultimately on revelation rather than ratiocination were in any case another matter. Here logical confirmation followed on the heels of practical demonstration. As a closed system of ideal propositions, Christian Science might be granted logical coherence, but it was not in fact a closed system. At every point it reached out toward experience. The ideal must be concretized in the actual; revelatory perceptions must prove themselves in new modes of daily living. Only over such empirically unpredictable bridges could reason then move to reconcile fixed absolutes with open-ended, evolving facts.

In her own day, as well as since, Christian Scientists with a speculative turn of mind showed a tendency to elaborate her teachings into an ingenious latter-day scholasticism, increasingly abstract as it soared into the realm of pure but undemonstrated theory.[23] Mrs. Eddy, the evidence shows, was no stranger to those breath-taking upper levels of metaphysical vision in which, as she wrote, "all sense of error forever disappears and thought accepts the divine infinite calculus."[24] But she had small patience with Christian Scientists who were so intoxicated with the vision that they failed to take imperatively needed footsteps toward reifying it in experience. "Your head is way up there in the stars," she admonished one student, "while the enemy is filling your body with bullets."[25]

Like Christianity itself, Christian Science offered a life rather than an argument as its primary answer to what Mrs. Eddy called "the perplexing problem of human existence."[26] But if Christianity was to be scientific, both practical demonstration and reasoned argument were indispensable auxiliaries to the revelation of its basic Principle. In her teaching, accordingly, Mrs. Eddy aimed always to stir thought and stimulate effort, as well as to awaken spirituality.

In an unfinished, undated, and unpublished fragment entitled "Mathematics,"[27] she illustrates this in a curiously untypical way. Its skeletonic structure suggests elements of both an exploratory dialogue with herself and a metaphysical primer for a hypothetical student. While neither purpose is accomplished and Mrs. Eddy understandably abandoned the attempt, the fragment has biographical interest for the light it throws on some of her innermost preoccupations. The abridgment that follows retains the essential elements of the piece, which speaks, however imperfectly, for itself:

Ques. What is the Principle of Metaphysics?
Ans. It is God.

Q. What is the first rule of Metaphysics?
A. Unity.

Q. What is the denomination of Metaphysics?
A. Mind. . . .

Q. With what rule do you begin to learn Metaphysics?
A. The rule of oneness and allness.

Q. What do you mean by this?
A. That there is but one infinite calculus and its infinite manifestation.

Q. Are God and man one?
A. God is one and man is a manifestation of God, therefore . . . they are inseparable as the divine Principle and divine idea. . . .

Q. Is there more than one God?
A. No.

Q. Is there more than one man?
A. No.

Q. Is God infinite?
A. Yes.

Q. Then are you at work in whole numbers or fractions?
A. In one whole number.

Q. Can there be more than one infinity?
A. No.

Q. Is man infinite?
A. Yes.

Q. Is man God?
A. No.

Q. What is man?
A. The reflection of infinity.

Q. Can the reflex idea be unlike its divine Principle?
A. It cannot.

Q. Is the reflection of infinity finity?
A. It is not.

Q. *Then what is the number of God and man?*
A. *One.*

Q. *Is there more than one number in Metaphysics?*
A. *There is not.*

Q. *What is your father and mother, brothers and sisters, husband, wife, and child?*
A. *They that do the will of the Father.*

Q. *What do you mean by this?*
A. *I mean that whatever reflects one Mind is the only reality, the only person, place, or thing which exists.*

Q. *Is God Spirit?*
A. *Yes.*

Q. *What is the reflection of Spirit?*
A. *It must be spirituality.*

Q. *Does matter reflect Spirit . . . in other words, has matter life, substance, or intelligence?*
A. *It has not of its own.*

Q. *Can matter borrow that of God?*
A. *It is generally thought that it can and does. . . .*

Q. *Can we go out of the denomination of Mind to solve the problem of Mind?*
A. *We cannot. . . .*

Q. *How are we to work [out] this problem of being in Metaphysics?*
A. *Just as the Scripture declares, namely, that in "Him (God) we live and move and have our being."*

Q. *What does this mean?*
A. *It means that all our hopes, faith, love, yes, all our tendencies, should be Godward, Spiritward, and away from the human and material to the spiritual and Divine.*

Q. *What do you love? is it a human being?*
A. *Yes it is. . . .*

Q. *Is it Scriptural for you to love aught but God's image and likeness?*
A. *It is not.*

Q. *Then is your human love the love which God demands?*
A. *It is not.*

Q. *Are you a metaphysician?*
A. *I claim to be.*

Q. *Do you abide by the first rule of Being and demonstrate it?*
A. *It seems that I do not.*

Q. *Can you work out the mathematics of metaphysics and not do this?*
A. *I cannot.*

Q. *Do you now see why your demonstration is not perfect?*
A. *I do.*

Q. *Is God Love?*
A. *God is Love.*

Q. *Is God selfish?*
A. *No.*

Q. *Why is He not?*
A. *Because He imparts all that He is by His reflection.*

Q. *Are you as a human being selfish?*
A. *I am.*

Q. *Then do you reflect God?*
A. *I do not.*

Q. *Can you become a metaphysician and be selfish?*
A. *I cannot.*

Q. *Are you working in one whole number or in fractions?*
A. *In fractions.*

Q. *Is this metaphysics?*
A. *It is not.*

Q. *Then will you commence today the demonstration of Divine Metaphysics?*
A. *I will. . . .*

The emphasis here on abstract unity—suggesting in some ways the undifferentiated "block universe" that James attributed to Josiah Royce—is far from typical of Mrs. Eddy, with her rich sense of the variousness and plenitude of life. Taken by itself, it could even lend justification to those Christian Scientists who, from her own day on, have veered off into a kind of generalized ontological euphoria, unrelated to the exigencies of living.

Yet even in this unsuccessful attempt to get down to the bare bones of her systematized vision, it is notable that Mrs. Eddy cannot get away entirely from the humanity, moral energy, and biblical authority which flesh out her absolute metaphysics. As in all her teaching, she starts with God, but she ends with "I will"—and the intervening dialogue makes it clear that the two words imply not an assertion of self but a yielding to God's will. Never, at her most abstract, could the founder of Christian Science forget the imperative, inescapable demand for Christian regeneration.[28]

One final example must stand for a whole class of instances in which she brought home to her students the urgency of this demand.

In the *Sentinel* of October 12, 1899, appeared a question and answer which related to both the theory and the practice of Christian Science. The questioner asked, "If all matter is unreal, why do we deny the existence of disease in the material body and not the body itself?" The editors undoubtedly considered their reply to be in impeccable accord with Mrs. Eddy's "scientific statement of being." Confidently they answered:

"All is Mind and Mind's idea," is the emphatic declaration of Science. Matter, in any form or condition, is but the manifestation of a false mentality called mortal mind. If one admits the reality of matter he must likewise admit the reality of all its conditions. If harmonious matter is real, discordant matter is real also. If health in matter is real, disease in matter is real also. So if one clings to a thought of good in matter he cannot escape the belief of evil in matter, for his sense of discord in matter must of necessity continue to be as real to him as his sense of harmony in matter. It is only as he knows that matter has neither intelligence, substance, nor life, that he is able to heal disease on a scientific basis.

To think of a material body as real while denying the existence of disease in that body, is not scientific practice. A half-way position is neither scientific nor effectual. The great truth that man is spiritual because he is the image and likeness of God, heals sickness and sin. This scientific fact denies the belief of man's materiality, and should be kept before the thought continually, for in the degree that man acknowledges the claims of matter he is in bondage thereto. Mortal man must sacrifice the good that seems to be in matter if he would escape the evil that matter produces, for the one is as real as the other, and no more so.

When she read this, Mrs. Eddy instantly sent a correction to be published in the next issue.

On the face of it, the explanation was unexceptionable as a statement of Christian Science. It was, formally at least, in agreement with the point she herself was later to make with the editors and Directors when she took exception to the assertion that "a diseased body is not acceptable to God." But there was also the point she had made that a statement might be scientific if demonstrated but untrue if merely "repeated." The writer of the editorial seemed to her to be talking away beyond his demonstration. In the language of the analytical philosopher, he was making a pseudo-statement.

The question to which the writer was replying was one which related vitally to the nature of Christian Science treatment. An answer which was no more than an exercise in abstract logic, without power to heal or come to the rescue of the human condition, was of little value in Mrs. Eddy's eyes. It simply lacked the Christianity of which she had written in *Science and Health*: "Science will declare God aright, and Christianity will demonstrate this declaration and its divine Principle, making mankind better physically, morally, and spiritually."[29]

So her own answer to the question propounded the week before took cognizance of the states and stages through which human thought passed as its concept of a material body yielded progressively to a spiritual sense of man's being. To pure Mind matter as a limiting concept could not exist, but to even the most enlightened of mortals the relinquishing of a material sense of things was a process and a discipline, not merely a verbal declaration. If Science must be precise in its statement, it must be equally precise in its application; hence the need for "relative" as well as "absolute" statements in formulating it for the student. When Jesus found his disciples unable to comprehend his statement, "Our friend Lazarus sleepeth; but I go, that I may awake him out of sleep," he said to them plainly, "Lazarus is dead," then *acted* to show what he had meant.[30] With a similar verbal accommodation to the human need, Mrs. Eddy wrote in her correction:

We deny first the existence of disease, because we can meet this negation more readily than we can negative all that the material senses affirm. It is written in "Science and Health with

Key to the Scriptures": "An improved belief is one step out of error, and aids in taking the next step and in understanding the situation in Christian Science" (p. 296).

Thus it is that our great Exemplar, Jesus of Nazareth, first takes up the subject. He does not require the last step to be taken first. He came to the world not to destroy the law of being, but to fulfil it in righteousness. He restored the diseased body to its normal action, functions, and organization, and in explanation of his deeds he said, "Suffer it to be so now: for thus it becometh us to fulfil all righteousness." Job said, "In my flesh shall I see God." Neither the Old nor the New Testament furnishes reasons or examples for the destruction of the human body, but for its restoration to life and health as the scientific proof of "God with us." The power and prerogative of Truth are to destroy all disease and to raise the dead—even the self-same Lazarus. The spiritual body, the incorporeal idea, came with the ascension.

Jesus demonstrated the divine Principle of Christian Science when he presented his material *body absolved from death and the grave. The introduction of pure abstractions into Christian Science, without their correlatives, leaves the divine Principle of Christian Science unexplained, tends to confuse the mind of the reader, and ultimates in what Jesus denounced, namely, straining at gnats and swallowing camels.*[31]

The semantics of Christian Science were, in the last analysis, inseparable from its therapeutics, and those in turn from its hermeneutics. Till the end of mortal history, Mrs. Eddy held, words must be tested by living, as the Word itself had been tested by one historic life.

Chapter
VII

Private Faces, Public Places

The years 1903 to 1906 were years of immense prosperity and growth for Christian Science. Already, in her annual message to the church in 1902, Mrs. Eddy had commented: "With no special effort to achieve this result, our church communicants constantly increase in number, unity, steadfastness."[1] During the next three years membership in The Mother Church increased from twenty-four thousand to thirty-six thousand, while new branch churches were springing into existence every week.

In 1904 Mrs. Eddy wrote the Hannas, "Our cause is *rushing* on, its chariot wheels are heard before the lips can speak its coming."[2] And to Marjorie Colles in London she announced with satisfaction:

> *Our cause grows bigger every moment in the eyes of the people. The churches are turning to consider it more fairly, and the common people hear the glad tidings with joy.*[3]

Yet throughout this period of ebullient progress, she maintained her realism. In an undated memorandum which evidently belongs to 1905, she warned:

> *Although there has been no special organized effort at propagandism in this direction, the growth of the cause of Christian Science seems too rapid to be healthful. As a means for remedying this abnormal condition let there be no proselyting from churches of other denominations for Christian Science teaching. While not prohibiting Christian Science healing to such as are needing and request it, let it not be urged upon them beyond their individual growth in this direction. This accords with the Golden Rule.*[4]

These same years saw an immense amount of church building. The domed extension of The Mother Church, with a touch of both St. Peter's and Santa Sophia about it, was ready for dedication in 1906, when some thirty thousand Christian Scientists flocked to Boston to attend its six consecutive Communion services on June 10. In metropolitan centers in the United States and elsewhere, large, impressive branch churches were being built, many of them in the heavy neoclassical style which was one of the unfortunate legacies of the Chicago Exposition of 1893.[5]

Mrs. Eddy rejoiced in whatever she saw as the spiritual progress of her cause but remained wary of all that would materialize it. A bylaw which prohibited the church's publications from "describing materially Christian Science edifices" concluded with the terse injunction: "Thou shall not make unto thee any graven images."[6] She herself contributed $100,000 toward a handsome Gothic structure for the branch church in her own city of Concord and took considerable interest in its building and furnishing.[7] Yet in her message on the occasion of its dedication on July 17, 1904, she included a quiet reminder:

> At this period, the greatest man or woman on earth stands at the vestibule of Christian Science, struggling to enter into the perfect love of God and man. The infinite will not be buried in the finite. . . . Material theories tend to check spiritual attraction— the tendency towards God, the infinite and eternal—by an opposite attraction towards the temporary and finite. . . . Our proper reason for church edifices is, that in them Christians may worship God,— not that Christians may worship church edifices![8]

In general, it is safe to say that while Christian Science was increasingly becoming associated with an image of middle-class prosperity, Mrs. Eddy herself was far from joining in what William James described as the American worship of the great bitch-goddess Success. In one way or another she made clear her conviction that "success in error is defeat in Truth,"[9] and her own experience had shown her that the perils of prosperity were at least as great as those of adversity. It was in accord with her awareness of the dangers of overreliance on numbers, popularity, the mere trappings of success, that she drew up another *Manual* bylaw prohibiting Christian Scientists from reporting for publication the number of members of The Mother Church and of the branch churches. "According to the Scripture," this bylaw stated with cool indifference to the dawning age of quantification and statistical insatiability, "they shall turn away from personality and numbering the people."[10]

There were times when Mrs. Eddy sounded as though she shared in the American reverence for bigness, but many more when she expressed the basic Christian exaltation of quality above quantity. There was obviously no question in her mind that the real healing inwardness of historical Christianity had suffered grievously from the mass conversions under Constantine. In 1903 she had written of the *Manual* bylaws as necessary "laws of limitation for a Christian Scientist,"[11] and part of their restraint was upon the exuberance that would try to sweep into the church masses of people who were far from ready to accept its disciplines.

To her ever-eager student Captain Linscott in Washington, Mrs. Eddy wrote in 1904 in regard to one of his schemes for promoting Christian Science:

> *Your letter is characteristic, wit and adventure smile together, promise but decoy. Your many students and followers speak well for you. But dear one, if the plan you suggest were wise it would have had its birth in The Mother Church Manual, that is the law of our Gospel—and born of necessity to guide the children of Christian Science.*
>
> *When I started the Mother Church in Boston I said this Church shall be a church without one By-law, each member must be a law to him or herself. But behold the result! Now I say to you and all—abide by the laws of The Mother Church and God will direct your path. Trust in Him and have no other trusts. . . . I can not consent to a single new method outside our Manual.*[12]

Here was the paradox of organization. To prevent its proliferation into meaningless and crippling bureaucracy on the one hand or into frivolous and wasteful experiment on the other, it must be strong enough to safeguard essentials, flexible enough to adapt to circumstances. The test of the *Manual* in the long run would be whether it could prevent the organization from sliding into a self-defeating secularism or freezing into an equally self-defeating ecclesiasticism.

Conservative as the last words of her letter may have sounded to Linscott, for Mrs. Eddy they represented exactly the same radicalism that prescribed purely spiritual means for healing and proscribed the experimental admixture of material means. The purpose of the *Manual,* as she saw it, was not to restrict individual growth but to safeguard it from the top-heavy growth of material organization—the very danger that later characterized the new century—as well as from the religious anarchy that would follow from the breakdown of all established authority.

"I do not believe in much organization in church," she had remarked to Irving Tomlinson in 1902. "The churches are over-organized."[13] The *Manual* was actually designed to keep the organization lean. A cryptic one-sentence message from her in a 1904 issue of the *Christian Science Sentinel* suggests as much, and perhaps a good deal more: "Good deeds overdone numerically, or bad deeds, are remedied by reading the Manual."[14]

Mrs. Eddy saw the Christian churches increasingly dissipating their spiritual energy in worthy endeavors of a basically secular sort—in social clubs, recreational activities, service and charitable functions which in many cases might be equally well or better performed by professional agencies. She had no quarrel with their choice of direction but was deeply concerned that the Church of Christ, Scientist, should preserve its fundamental purpose and identity. Christian Scientists might participate as much as they saw fit in civic, philanthropic, and other such activities, but they should do so as responsible individual citizens rather than as organized groups of Christian Scientists.

When Mrs. Eddy heard of a New York Christian Science Lunch Club composed of businessmen who invited prominent Christian Scientists to address them, she quickly wrote the Lathrops, who had thought the enterprise an admirable one, about the danger of Christian Science organizations separate from the church. "If you go into clubs," she admonished them, "you go out of the church in spirit."[15] Then followed a bylaw on the subject.[16]

The ban seems to have been directed less against the individual Christian Scientist's normal participation in social or professional organizations[17] than against the development of a constellation of self-designated Christian Science activities which would drain the movement's energies away from the sole purpose that would, in her eyes, justify its organization as a church. This purpose, as she reminded the members repeatedly, was Christian healing and regeneration.[18]

An outspoken message which she delivered to her household at this period reveals very clearly what lay at the heart of her concern:

> *The true Science—divine Science—will be lost sight of again unless we arouse ourselves. This demonstrating to make matter build up is not Science. The building up of churches, the writing of articles and the speaking in public is the old way of building up a Cause. The way I brought this Cause into sight was through* healing; *and now these other things would come in and hide it, just as was done in the time of Jesus. Now this Cause must be saved and I pray God to be spared for this work.*[19]

One of the things that differentiated Mrs. Eddy from her followers was her sense of history. The evidence shows that she thought in centuries where most of them thought in years. The gradual paganizing of Christianity in the ancient world was an ever-present reminder to her of the possible secularizing of Christian Science in the future through the attrition of its radical reliance on spiritual as opposed to material means.

While most serious Christian Scientists saw a need to avoid this danger in relation to the practice of Christian Science healing, fewer of them seem to have recognized a similar demand in the way they carried on the organized activities of their church. Again and again Mrs. Eddy issued stern warnings that an adoption of "worldly" ways and means of promoting Christian Science would be fatal to the organization—quite as fatal, she evidently thought, as mixing prayer with drugs would be to successful Christian Science treatment of the sick.

Mrs. Annie M. Knott, who became assistant editor of the *Journal* and *Sentinel*[20] in 1903, recalled in an editorial fifteen years later an occasion when a student in one of Mrs. Eddy's classes had asked to what extent Christian Scientists should attempt to bring the "healing truth" to public attention by printed articles. The editorial described Mrs. Eddy's reply in these words:

> *She began by saying that the silent declarations of truth which heal the sick and transform the sinful may be typified by gold coinage, and the audible declarations of truth by silver coinage. She then explained that published utterances of Christian Science were like paper money which finds its way everywhere and is a wonderful medium of exchange, provided always that it represents the gold.*[21]

The final proviso was all-important and marked the distance in her between the scientist and the rhetorician. In countless ways she emphasized the dictum in *Science and Health*: "The error of the ages is preaching without practice."[22] This was also the burden of some of her most impassioned letters to the Board of Directors, as when she wrote them in 1904:

> *We want the right teaching of C. S. or none at all. I am so disappointed in my students in this respect I have no words to utter myself. . . . It absolutely disgusts me to hear them babble the letter and after that fail in proving what they say! It is high time that they stop talking science or . . . prove their words true.*[23]

In 1903 she had enlarged the Board of Directors to five members, so that Archibald McLellan might serve on it in addition to his editorship of the periodicals. Earlier she had twice asked one or another of the veteran members of the board to resign so that she might put a more experienced businessman in his place, and each time she had found the new man lacking in the spiritual maturity demanded by an office so incommensurable with his accustomed way of operating.

In McLellan a fair degree of worldly experience seemed combined with spiritual modesty, but she now saw the value of retaining all four of the simple but battle-hardened men already serving as directors. Moreover, a five-man board obviously made more sense in terms of avoiding future deadlocks.

A Christmas letter she sent to the Directors in 1903 sums up much that she hoped to see in the conduct of their church responsibilities:

> *May this dear Xmas season be to you a Christ risen, a morn, the break of day. . . . O may your eyes not be holden—but may you discern spiritually what is our Redeemer. I thank you dear ones, for your kind remembrance of me—the most lone and perhaps the most loved and hated of earth! May you watch and pray that you keep the Commandments, and live the Sermon on the Mount this coming year. Watch too that you* keep *the* commandments *that experience has compelled to be written for your guidance and the safety of Christian Science, in our Church Manual.*[24]

The significance of the last sentence is made plain by an earlier letter which she sent to the board that same year. It was to play a crucial role in later events, and with a proper sense of history she asked formally that it be placed on the church records:

> *Never abandon the By-laws nor the denominational government of the Mother Church. If I am not personally with you, the Word of God, and my instructions in the By-laws have led you hitherto and will remain to guide you safely on, and the teachings of St. Paul are as useful to-day as when they were first written.*

> *The present and future prosperity of the cause of Christian Science is largely due to the By-laws and government of "The First Church of Christ, Scientist" in Boston. None but myself can know the importance of the combined sentiment of this Church remaining steadfast in supporting its present By-laws. Each of these many By-laws has met and mastered or forestalled some contingency, some imminent peril, and will continue to do so.*[25]

For the remaining seven years of her life, Mrs. Eddy's greatest effort would be to transfer the government of the church from her personal leadership to the permanent authority of the *Manual.*

2

During these same years, the hostility of the traditional Christian churches to the upstart Church of Christ, Scientist, was mounting visibly in both volume and intensity.

Sermons, pamphlets, and denominational journals presented Christian Science as the work of Satan, a miserable delusion, a dangerous heresy, a damnable fraud.[26] Churches and ministerial associations invited Frederick Peabody to deliver his increasingly vitriolic attacks on the faith and its founder to their congregations and sometimes to huge lecture audiences in municipal auditoriums. To more than a few at that time Mark Twain's prediction that Christian Science would swallow up the Protestant churches seemed to point to a genuine threat.

As Mrs. Eddy had long foreseen, her personal character was the chief issue raised in this polemic storm. In 1904 the intellectually respected Unitarian minister Minot J. Savage hired Peabody to dig into her past and unearth all the discreditable material he could. At the same time Alfred Farlow, and to some extent the ex-Universalist minister Irving Tomlinson, combed her history to find whatever would disprove the Peabody allegations. It was the beginning of two streams of historiography which would produce two entirely disparate Mrs. Eddys—until time, scholarship, and the healing of old acerbities should make possible a more inclusive view.

Farlow and Tomlinson soon found that Mrs. Eddy's own memory of events was a far from infallible guide. She herself had written her student Sarah Bagley as long ago as 1871, ". . . you know my memory *material* is short so it is best for us both to commit things to paper,"[27] and in later years she confessed readily to "misremembering" things on occasion.

In some of Farlow's early letters answering critics, he relied on Mrs. Eddy's recollection of an event but before long realized the value of checking the facts independently to ensure accuracy. In the same way Tomlinson, noting the discrepancy between what the records showed of Mrs. Eddy's New England ancestry and what she had written in *Retrospection and Introspection,* inquired about it and received a letter from Frye:

> Mrs. Eddy says what you said in your lecture . . . is all right
> so far as she knows. She did not correctly state it in Retro. She
> did not mean that her grandfather J. Baker was born in England,
> but that he was of English extraction.[28]

While this cavalier ease in shrugging off factual misstatements
would have shocked those of her followers who held to something like
a doctrine of verbal inerrancy in her writings, to Farlow and Tomlinson it presumably pointed rather to the difference between personal
retrospection and metaphysical introspection.[29] Beside the distortions
of a Peabody, it was only a minor goad to more diligent research.

The whole enterprise had started about the time the Woodbury-
Dresser attack in the *Arena* took place and the Committee on Publication was going into action.

There were preliminary stirrings when it was learned that Henry
M. Goddard, a noted psychologist at Clark University in Worcester,
Massachusetts, was planning to write a "scandalous" book about Mrs.
Eddy. On May 3, 1899, her cousin General Baker had written her
about this, enclosing a copy of a letter which her niece Ellen Philbrook
(daughter of her deceased sister Martha Pilsbury) had sent to Professor Goddard. Although Ellen had turned against Christian Science
and her aunt since the time thirty-two years earlier when the latter had
healed her of what was supposedly a fatal disease,[30] she declined to
have any part in the Goddard effort, as her letter to him suggests:

> *Sir:*
>
> In reply to your letter asking for information in regard to
> Mrs. Eddy I would say I have none to give you along the desired
> lines.
>
> In my childhood I was taught to regard my "Aunt Mary" as
> a suffering saint.
>
> I removed west before Christian Science became the Science
> it is.
>
> In regard to her habits I never knew or heard of tobacco or
> opium; and as to any immoralities I am quite sure there never
> were any.
>
> Yours etc.
> Ellen C. Philbrook[31]

Later Farlow and Hanna had a pleasant visit with Goddard from
which they came away with considerable admiration for his honesty
of intention. He had, they found, simply thought the subject a psychologically interesting one, but when his research failed to support his

initial assumptions he dropped the project, having no desire to shape the facts to suit his thesis.

In December of that same year, Dr. Alvin M. Cushing, the physician who had attended Mrs. Eddy (then Mrs. Patterson) in February, 1866, at the time of her famous "fall in Lynn," gave a newspaper interview in which he denied her account of the accident and the instantaneous healing that followed.[32] The doctor, who vouched for the completeness of his records and the vividness of his recollection, went on to speak of treating Mrs. Patterson again six months after that disputed incident:

> *On Aug. 10, 1866, I was called again to see Mrs. Patterson, this time at the home of a Mrs. Clark in Summer Street, Lynn, and found her suffering from a bad cough. I prescribed for her, and during that month I made her four visits. I fear my treatment at that time was not so satisfactory as it had been on previous occasions, for she left me and was treated by Dr Quimby, who came to see her in either Lynn or Boston.*[33]

This confident circumstantiality in a piqued old gentleman thirty-three years removed from the obscure events in question overlooked one awkward fact. Quimby had died seven months prior to August, 1866, and two weeks before Mrs. Eddy's February accident. As to the alleged detailing of Cushing's own visits in what Peabody would later describe fancifully as the doctor's "record book in which he, at the time, recorded each visit, every symptom and every particular of his treatment,"[34] Farlow, who journeyed to Cushing's home to question him and examine carefully what turned out to be the sketchy jottings in his day book, found this claim to be as mythical as Quimby's post-mortem visit.[35]

Through such experiences, Farlow was learning the value of chasing down each new hare as it bounced out of the bushes. He was particularly assiduous in gathering written accounts and affidavits from former patients of Quimby recounting the actual methods of that pioneer in suggestive therapy.[36]

Even Calvin Frye joined in the search to recover the past, writing to Mrs. Eddy's first student, Hiram Crafts, in 1902:

> *Will you kindly have a typewritten copy made of the manuscript [Mrs. Eddy] gave you [in 1867] when she taught you Christian Science, and certify before a Notary Public to its correctness. Also have the first sheet of your manuscript photographed so as to show Mrs. Eddy's handwriting at that time.*

> *Please have this done soon as possible and send it to Mrs.*
> *Eddy and she will gladly pay for your trouble and expense in*
> *doing this.*[37]

The brief correspondence between Frye and Crafts was concurrent with the somewhat agitated interest at Pleasant View in a copy of Mrs. Eddy's early manuscript "Questions and Answers in Moral Science" which Augusta Stetson had sent Frye for verification. Mrs. Stetson had purchased this relic of the formative stage of Christian Science from one Herbert Dunbar, who in turn had bought it from a lady with the Pickwickian name of Charity Ball, who in 1870 or earlier had received it direct from Mrs. Eddy and now represented it to Dunbar as being in Mrs. Eddy's own handwriting.

Examination soon disproved the latter claim, but this of itself was unimportant, since most of the extant copies of her early manuscripts were in other people's handwriting.[38] More challenging were the traces of Quimbyism in the manuscript, notably its directions for the healer to rub the head of the patient while treating him metaphysically—a practice which Mrs. Eddy decisively banished in 1872.

If, thirty years later, she could have stood off coolly and sorted out the gradual process by which she emerged from Quimby's influence,[39] she might have saved both herself and later historians much trouble. But such retrospective analysis was too much to expect of someone who was throwing her whole energy into the future—into what she saw as her movement's destiny to save Christianity from the otherwise irresistible current of scientific materialism.[40] Confronted now with the evidence of her earlier confusion—as Moses coming down from Mount Sinai with the sixth commandment in the crook of his arm might have been confronted with the caustic reminder that he himself had been an assassin in Egypt—Mrs. Eddy was shaken by this vivid token from the past.

Her first impulse was to repudiate the manuscript entirely. "After seeing it & all night long," Frye wrote in his diary, "she was under great fear & old beliefs asserted themselves."[41] It seems highly probable that she was reminded of the letter she had received two years earlier from Horatio Dresser, by then the recognized champion of Quimby and the emergent New Thought movement:

> *If you come out frankly and acknowledge that the truth in*
> *your "revelation," the method of healing, etc, came from Dr.*
> *Quimby (as your letters show that you know[42]) the world will*
> *respect you and you will go down to history with a reputation. But*

*if it all comes from outsiders, and after your death that which
many are now withholding, it will be a very black record which
will throw you into utter discredit.*

*I know those who have hunted up the whole history, all about
the Lynn boarding house, Mr. Morse and the babe burned in the
store,*[43] *etc, etc. and I know too of those who are preparing the
evidence in regard to your indebtedness to Dr. Quimby, and I
know what will come out, little by little, and that nothing can
stop it. . . .* It is utterly useless to try to head it off. . . .
And so I advise you to make a clean breast of it.[44]

With this letter in mind, along with Peabody's open declaration
of war eighteen months later, it is not too surprising that Mrs. Eddy
should have told Frye, the morning after examining the Charity Ball
manuscript, that the "mental threat" urged upon her by the enemy
was: "You have got to confess that is your Mss & that you got it from
Quimby or you will be damned!"[45]

Inevitably, in a psychologically sophisticated age, this statement
has been read as a classic example of the psychopathology of guilt, and
more particularly as a paranoid projection of the guilt on a fantasied
enemy. But while the theory fits the statement, the facts do not fit the
theory. A more relevant analogy might be the techniques of suggestion
by which eminent prisoners in the Lubyanka Prison have been persuaded to confess to treasonable acts invented by their persuaders.

Mrs. Eddy remained unpersuaded, however, and the facts speak
for themselves today.

First there was the fact that Dresser *had* threatened her with being
damned unless she "acknowledged" that she got Christian Science from
Quimby. There was also the fact that the manuscript was indeed hers.
There was the fact that some of the material in it did represent the
residual influence of Quimby—and that this was the very element she
would eliminate in writing *Science and Health*.[46] Above all, there was
the plain, indubitable, inescapable fact that "Questions and Answers
in Moral Science" was an entirely different manuscript from the
Quimby "Questions and Answers," but that this elementary point was
ignored or obfuscated from the start of the Quimby controversy.[47] In
regard to no other single item in the whole dragged-out dispute has
there been so much ambiguity, misunderstanding, and possibly pre-
varication.[48]

Mrs. Eddy was still far too close to the issues to set the record
straight.[49] It would be as realistic to expect a commanding general in

the midst of a continuing battle to sit down and write a detailed account of the complex events leading up to the outbreak of war as to expect her to have provided painstaking documentation for her generalized statement in *Science and Health* regarding the period between 1866 and 1875: "As former beliefs were gradually expelled from her [the author's] thought, the teaching became clearer, until finally the shadow of old errors was no longer cast upon divine Science."[50]

At times, in relaxed conversation with her household and in fragmentary reminiscences dictated to her secretary, Mrs. Eddy did make reference to the part Quimby had played in her long readying for the discovery of Christian Science.[51] But, like time itself, she was apt to telescope the events of years into something much more fleeting, as when she wrote:

> *I tried him as a healer, and because he seemed to help me for the time, and had a higher ideal than I had heard of up to that time, I praised him to the skies, wrote him letters,—they talk of my letters to Quimby, as if they were something secret, they were not, I was enthusiastic, and couldn't say too much in praise of him; I actually loved him, I mean his high and noble character . . . but when I found that Quimbyism was too short, and would not answer the cry of the human heart for succor, for real aid, I went, being driven there by my extremity, to the Bible, and there I discovered Christian Science; and when I had found it, I deserted Quimby and his scheme of healing just as I had in turn deserted everything else . . . and I have built Christian Science upon the Petra of the Scriptures.*[52]

While serious scholarship would not subject the Dresser-Quimby claim to critical examination for another sixty years,[53] amateur psychobiographers more interested in plausible theories than in plain facts have not hesitated to picture Mrs. Eddy as a woman haunted by suppressed guilt feelings. For that reason the evidence of her unconscious as well as her conscious attitude to Quimby in her later years becomes important to the historian.

During the first decade of the century, Freud's *Interpretation of Dreams* was persuading psychologists of the significance of dreams as an index to the censored secrets of the unconscious. During this time Mrs. Eddy confided to Laura Sargent a dream or "vision" which she had had some time before when struggling to know that "matter was not substance."[54] It takes no dubious Freudian rubric to disclose the psychobiographical—or, better, the metabiographical—significance of a vision so rooted in a unique lifework.[55]

She stood on the bank of a river, across which she saw a city "glittering and grand." From the city came her mother in a small, frail boat:

> When she reached the side where Mrs. Eddy stood, she said, "Get into the boat, Mary"; but Mrs. Eddy said, "Why I should tip it over if I stepped in." Her mother said, "No, you would not. Look there on the sand." Mrs. Eddy said she looked down at the side of where she stood and there lay her own corpse. "Now get into the boat," said her mother, and she stepped in at once and the boat glided across the river. She said she seemed to realize then that the boat was not substance. When they reached the other side her mother took her into one of the buildings. There were different apartments. Her mother had one apartment where little children were and was teaching them; then in another room was her brother Albert and he was teaching adults. His thought seemed to be so occupied he did not seem to see her. In another room she saw Dr. Quimby and he was so glad to see her. In his room she saw Shakespeare and Dr. Quimby said to her, "I can not teach him but you can."[56]

Since girlhood, Shakespeare—"great poet of humanity,"[57] as Mrs. Eddy called him—had represented to her the richness and variety of human life. Quimby, pioneer searcher for a mental science that would banish the simpler human ills, was quite incapable of rising to the height from which he could cope with the full challenge of the human situation. It was Mrs. Eddy's deepest conviction that only a Science built on "the Petra of the Scriptures"—the simple Christianity which had nurtured her childhood—could embrace humanity in the manner she had described in her chapter on the Apocalypse: "John saw the human and divine coincidence, shown in the man Jesus, as divinity embracing humanity in Life and its demonstration,—reducing to human perception and understanding the Life which is God."[58]

But unlike her brother Albert—who represented for her the liberal culture and intellectual eminence she had so greatly admired as a girl—Quimby was "glad" to see in her a higher spirituality than he could approach. He himself had written of woman as possessing a "higher development of God's wisdom" which enabled her to be the spiritual teacher of the race, so that "man stands to woman as a servant to his Lord."[59]

And so it was that in her vision Mrs. Eddy accepted his invitation and "stepped up on the platform and commenced teaching Science."[60]

In a letter to a student some years earlier, Mrs. Eddy had confided the austere disipline which, she felt, her task imposed on her:

I am alone absolutely, *here! No one can know me really, or can see what I have to meet, or meet it for me.*

. . . It is the errors that my students do not see, *neither in themselves nor others, that I am constantly confronting and at war with. If they and the world did see these errors which I see they would take up arms against them, and I could lay down mine.*

But to open the eyes of the blind from paralized optic nerve is nothing, *compared with opening them to see the tendencies of their own human natures even at the* very best.[61]

In the thousands of letters that flowed out from Pleasant View during these years, she dropped hints from time to time of the rigors of her situation, as when she ended a cheerful little thank-you note by sending cordial greetings "from my solitude and workshop," or threw into a business letter a passing reference to her weariness at being "a mere servant and target."[62] And as the movement forged forward confidently in 1903, she wrote another student: "O the amount that I see to be done for all, before Christian Science is established on the Rock 'gainst which the billows beat in vain. . . . My labors are harder now than ever before."[63]

When in that same year the Directors offered to pay her for her long work on a new edition of the *Manual,* she thanked them but explained that she couldn't begin to accept money from the church:

What I do for it no one but myself knows nor could do. . . . This task nothing can compensate but the joy of saving [the members]. *All the money in the world could not prompt me to do it and sometimes I almost think my human life will be the price of my incessant struggle care and perplexity.*[64]

Again in a published message to The Mother Church the next year she expressed the tough-minded, cross-bearing element of her faith, which related it more closely to the granite and gneiss of Puritanism than to the elastic air of Trancendentalism:

Life's ills are its chief recompense; they develop hidden strength. Had I never suffered for The Mother Church, neither she nor I would be practising the virtues that lie concealed in the smooth seasons and calms of human existence.[65]

Perhaps nowhere in her correspondence did Mrs. Eddy more

clearly relate the human cost of her work to what she saw as the infinite promise of her discovery than in a letter to a young man, Calvin C. Hill, who had become a frequent messenger between her, the Directors, and students in the field:

> *"When first I learned my Lord" I was so sure of Truth, my faith so strong in Christian Science as I then discovered it, I had no struggle to meet; but stood on the height of its glory a crowned monarch triumphant over sin and death. But behold me now washing that spiritual understanding with my tears! Learning little by little the* allness *of Omnipotent Mind; and the nothingness of matter, yea the absolute nothingness of* nothing *and the infinite somethingness of* ALL. *O bear with me, loved one, till I accomplish the height, the depth, the Horeb light of divine Life,—divine Love, divine health, holiness and immortality. The way seems not only long but very strait and narrow.*[66]

In the lonely way of spiritual leaders throughout the ages, Mrs. Eddy found that few of her followers recognized the magnitude of the challenge she faced in implementing her own radical defiance of entrenched human positions.[67] Because of her extraordinary resilience and productivity, as well as the equanimity which she customarily showed in public, they took it for granted that she could perform with ease prodigies beyond the utmost reach of their own capacities. To those at Pleasant View she occasionally remarked that someday her followers must know what it had cost her to found Christian Science.

There were nights of mental and sometimes physical agony when Mrs. Eddy struggled to reach a decision or find a solution for a church crisis, or just to find the rest and respite she needed. The metaphysical workers in the household would be called in *seriatim* to pray with and for her.[68] Sometimes a single worker, or "watcher," would be enough to "break the mesmerism." A typical entry in the Frye diary from the days of the Woodbury case records the interplay between Christian confidence and psychosomatic change which seems so bizarre to those for whom all bodily ills demand bodily remedies. On this occasion she had awakened at 3 A.M. in great physical distress:

> *After [our] trying about an hour to help her, she talked with A E B[aker] & then opened S & H [1900 ed.] to p. 208, par 2, 3, 4, which gave her help & courage & she asked Mr. Baker to read it. He called her attention to the last 2 lines on the page & told her of his interest in 2 Thes. last chapter. She read the*

chapter and immediately exclaimed "I have got back my God" &
was comforted & relieved & had a restful sleep from 5:30 to 7.[69]

On May 3, 1903, she had a night of acute suffering which did not
yield to the prayers of the four helpers at Pleasant View or of
Tomlinson, who was summoned from his home in Concord. On
similar occasions in the past she had resolutely withstood Frye's suggestion that she call in her cousin, Dr. Ezekiel Morrill, to have the
difficulty diagnosed medically. This time she consented. Morrill
proved to be out of town and his father, Alpheus, also a physician,
was ill and could not come, so at two in the morning they sent for a
Dr. Conn who responded and after an hour or two called in a Dr.
Stillings for consultation. Their diagnosis was renal calculi, or kidney
stones. At 5 A.M. Mrs. Eddy slept for an hour, but this was followed
by renewed paroxysms, and later that day Ezekiel Morrill, who had
returned to Concord, was sent for and, as Frye noted in his diary,
"gave her a hypodermic" to quiet the pain.[70]

For some years there had been a passage in *Science and Health*
which read: "If Christian Scientists ever fail to receive aid from other
Scientists,—their brethren upon whom they may call,—God will still
guide them into the right use of temporary and eternal means."[71]

This has never been interpreted officially as sanctioning resort to
drug therapy, since another passage in the same book states categorically: "Only through radical reliance on Truth can scientific
healing power be realized."[72] The "temporary means" referred to have
been taken to include crutches, eyeglasses, hearing aids, nursing care
without medication, the setting of a broken bone by a surgeon, and
other expedients obviously not intended to heal the impairment or
diseased condition but to help a person carry on in some fashion until
a genuine healing could take place.

The resort to an injection of morphine on this occasion was self-
evidently for an analgesic rather than a curative purpose, since
nobody could suppose morphine to be a remedy for renal calculi. Possibly the shock of the action was a spur to the renewed efforts of the
metaphysical workers, for within a week or two—during which there
were no more medical visits or injections—Mrs. Eddy had recovered
sufficiently to have business interviews with several non-Scientists,[73] as
well as with various Christian Scientists who came to see her on
church business.

The two physicians initially called in had been summoned for
the purpose of diagnosis, not treatment. Mrs. Eddy subsequently gave
this fact careful consideration, and a week after the attack she sent

to the Directors a new bylaw to go into the revised *Manual* she was preparing: "If a member of this Church has a patient whom he does not heal, and whose case he cannot fully diagnose, he may consult with an M. D. on the anatomy involved."[74] At the same time she sent a notice to the periodicals that the church would not receive its annual message from her that year.[75] However, in a day or two she was as busy as ever with her correspondence,[76] and when the annual meeting season arrived in June she sent off a letter to the church with a short but characteristic message after all.[77]

Going further than that, she invited the assembled members to come to Pleasant View on June 29, and ten thousand responded to the invitation. On that occasion she stood before them on the balcony outside her study, an erect but motherly figure, and addressed them in a voice which reportedly carried clearly and effortlessly to all but a few of the large crowd.[78] The apparent distance between her public triumphs and private struggles was never greater, yet the two were closely bound together at the deepest level of her experience.

During the next three years there was an occasional recurrence of the May 3 seizure, and on several of those occasions one or another of the Morrills was called in to give a hypodermic injection, although in other instances Mrs. Eddy endured almost mortal agony without making this concession.[79] In neither case did she see the condition as a physical one to be healed by material means, but as literally an "attack" on her by the massed materialism which she was challenging in her work for the world. It was the failure of her helpers to recognize this fully, she was convinced, that caused the failure of their efforts to help her on such occasions.

While some Christian Scientists have refused to believe in the possibility that such a situation could ever have arisen, some of Mrs. Eddy's critics have assumed a frequency in the occurrence of the attacks and an addiction to morphine which are entirely unsupported by the evidence.[80]

The Christian Science leader faced a profound dilemma. To try to explain to her followers what she saw as a temporary expedient in a unique situation could cause them consternation and discouragement—which would not be helpful either to their own spiritual progress or, as she saw it, to her finding freedom from the assaults of "the enemy." For those who had exalted her to a pinnacle of human perfection it would not be easy to understand the literalness of the words she had written years before: "Physical torture affords but a slight illustration of the pangs which come to one upon whom the world of sense falls with its leaden weight in the endeavor to crush out of a career its divine destiny."[81]

In the chapter "Atonement and Eucharist" in *Science and Health,* Mrs. Eddy tried to convey something of what she meant, and into her description of the crucifixion of Jesus she poured all that she had learned from her own bitterest experience:

> *The last supreme moment of mockery, desertion, torture, added to an overwhelming sense of the magnitude of his work, wrung from Jesus' lips the awful cry, "My God, why hast Thou forsaken me?"* ...
>
> *The burden of that hour was terrible beyond human conception. The distrust of mortal minds, disbelieving the purpose of his mission, was a million times sharper than the thorns which pierced his flesh. The real cross, which Jesus bore up the hill of grief, was the world's hatred of Truth and Love. Not the spear nor the material cross wrung from his faithful lips the plaintive cry, "Eloi, Eloi, lama sabachthani?" It was the possible loss of something more important than human life which moved him,— the possible misapprehension of the sublimest influence of his career. This dread added the drop of gall to his cup.*[82]

Yet if his experience was representative, it was also unique. Christians could not in the nature of things suffer the depths of his agony, though each was ordered to take up the cross as necessary and follow him at whatever cost. Most of them (perhaps to their loss) were not called upon to suffer the abounding persecutions and infirmities which were the mark of Paul's apostleship—the beatings, imprisonments, shipwrecks, in which he "gloried"; the stubborn thorn in the flesh that was given him "lest I should be exalted above measure."[83]

Nor, Mrs. Eddy might have added, would Christian Scientists be called upon to face all that she had to as the pioneer and leader of this new challenge to a world sunk in materialism. As she put it in *Retrospection and Introspection,* "No one else can drain the cup which I have drunk to the dregs as the Discoverer and teacher of Christian Science; neither can its inspiration be gained without tasting this cup."[84] To which might be added her statement to the church's board of lectureship: "Millions may know that I am the Founder of Christian Science. I alone know what that means."[85]

Yet, if Mrs. Eddy's necessity was not that of her followers, she still faced the categorical imperative that demanded a rule of conduct broad enough to include all instances. So it was that early in May,

1905, she sent to the Directors a paragraph regarding hypodermic injections to be inserted in the next edition of *Science and Health*—a paragraph which was (to the perceptive) both an explanation and a carefully delimited sanction.

One might have expected this to go into the chapter "Christian Science Practice," instead of which she asked to have it on the last page of the chapter "Teaching Christian Science," immediately preceding the crucial "Recapitulation" which is the basis of all Christian Science class instruction. Throughout the chapter on teaching there is an emphasis on the ethics of Christian Science and particularly on the ethical requirements of the Christian Science teacher. As the fountainhead of all such teaching, Mrs. Eddy's own ethical integrity was obviously a matter of the greatest moment to her followers, and only in the context of the preceding and succeeding paragraphs does the statement regarding injections take on its full significance:

> It has been said to the author, "The world is benefited by you, but it feels your influence without seeing you. Why do you not make yourself more widely known?" Could her friends know how little time the author has had, in which to make herself outwardly known except through her laborious publications,—and how much time and toil are still required to establish the stately operations of Christian Science,— they would understand why she is so secluded. Others could not take her place, even if willing so to do. She therefore remains unseen at her post, seeking no self-aggrandizement but praying, watching, and working for the redemption of mankind.
>
> If from an injury or from any cause, a Christian Scientist were seized with pain so violent that he could not treat himself mentally,—and the Scientists had failed to relieve him,—the sufferer could call a surgeon, who would give him a hypodermic injection, then, when the belief of pain was lulled, he could handle his own case mentally. Thus it is that we "prove all things; [and] hold fast that which is good."
>
> In founding a pathological system of Christianity, the author has labored to expound divine Principle, and not to exalt personality. The weapons of bigotry, ignorance, envy, fall before an honest heart. Adulterating Christian Science, makes it void. Falsity has no foundation. "The hireling fleeth, because he is an hireling, and careth not for the sheep." Neither dishonesty nor ignorance ever founded, nor can they overthrow a scientific system of ethics.[86]

At about the same time that Mrs. Eddy wrote the middle paragraph above, she remarked to her young friend Calvin Hill, as he recorded in a diary note:

> The first thing I do in the morning when I awake is to declare I shall have no other mind before divine Mind and become fully conscious of this and then adhere to it throughout the entire day. Then the evil cannot touch me.
>
> I have done it, but am a poor specimen of preservation. But the greatest miracle of the age is that I am alive.[87]

For some years the newspapers had periodically questioned whether she *was* alive, but on that point the members of her household and the officers of her church had no doubt.

4

When Mrs. Eddy was eighty years old and, according to Peabody, in a state of total decrepitude, Joseph Armstrong wrote her:

> I have never known any one who could turn out work and accomplish what you do. It is marvelous even to me who have known you to do many wonderful things. If you had a student who could accomplish half what you do my hope for the establishment of scientific Christianity in the near future would rise proportionately.[88]

Mrs. Eddy's reply was light in tone but serious in its praise of his own diligence:

> I had my laugh over your letter. You are right on my despatch of business and of work. But you should have said as Patt said, "I think a little credit is due to me ownself." You I have found prompt to help.[89]

The Christian Scientists who were called to serve at Pleasant View were apt to be taken aback at first by the merciless quantity of work Mrs. Eddy expected both of herself and of them. Writing in the *Sentinel* in 1903 of his six years of "post-graduate instruction" in her household, Joseph Mann asked with a touch of remorse as well as of tribute, "Who that has spent one hour in the home of Mrs. Eddy has not had his own slothfulness rebuked by her indefatigable labors to bless others?"[90]

Shortly before her crisis of May 3, 1903, Mrs. Eddy sent to the Board of Directors a new bylaw requiring Christian Scientists who should be selected for the purpose to come to Pleasant View to serve for a one-year period. In explanation, she wrote the Directors:

> *When a nation defends itself against wrong it is sometimes driven to accomplish this . . . through its army.*
>
> *Our cause needs defence and its principal* fort *needs fortification. I now call soldiers to supply this need, defend this fort, and the officer working within it for her Church, the field, and the world.*
>
> *When a nation needs more soldiers it necessarily drafts them. I have come to this necessary call for Christian Scientists to hold our fort in God's service. I gladly pay them for their service and give mine; my only sigh is that these soldiers of the cross have not been* volunteers.[91]

A few days after the May 3 attack, she wrote the board in regard to a still further change in the bylaw:

> *. . . some of the students went away from me in my sorest hour of need, and I regret to say it, apparently* heartless *in regard to my dire necessity. This has at times grieved me almost to death. . . . Also before I changed the By-law I deeply pondered the example of our great Wayshower when calling his students and compelling them to leave all for him, and his call was without conditions, imperative. . . . This By-law may be the hobby of my foes and be criticised by my friends, but such has been the case with all of my movements in the first stages of the history of Christian Science. . . . I am watching and praying that I do just His bidding and "hurt not the oil and the wine."*[92]

During this same period Mrs. Eddy sent letters to a number of her older students, probing their competence and readiness to serve in her household. Some came to Concord for interviews and were found insufficiently free from personal ties, personal sense, or physical "claims"[93] to remain; some served for a time but, lacking the long-range vision of their Leader's purpose that would have kept them growing in grace through the rugged as well as the tranquil periods, were later dismissed; others served their full terms or even longer and emerged from the experience with a greatly strengthened and enlarged sense of the cosmic task to which they were committed as Christian Scientists.

Not that normal human needs were overlooked. Kimball's pupil, George Kinter, who became a secretary and metaphysical worker at Pleasant View in 1903 on the basis of the new bylaw, later wrote of Mrs. Eddy's practical concern for the happiness of his wife and small niece (who lived with them as a daughter) during the time that he would be away from them.[94] Peremptory as the bylaw might sound, the evidence shows that she administered it with a good deal of consideration for the families and personal situations it touched.

Kinter, like others in the household, also bore witness to the uncomplaining labors of the man who by August, 1903, had served Mrs. Eddy for twenty-one years with hardly so much as a day off. "I don't know how he does as much as he does," Mrs. Eddy herself remarked of Calvin Frye to young Calvin Hill.[95] She could, to be sure, say to him in exasperation, "Calvin, you are the prince of blunderers"[96]—and even her praise was apt to show a touch of impatience, as in her statement to the household: "When Mr. Frye is himself, he can accomplish the work of fifty men in mental practice, but he is liable the very next day to be off again."[97] Nevertheless, the gifts she gave him on the anniversaries of his first coming to her aid, and her expressions of affectionate gratitude at these and other times, were both generous and obviously genuine.

To the Board of Directors she wrote in August, 1903, suggesting that they remember Frye's faithful service and reward it with a present that would show their conscious appreciation of it. He "has stood by my side to help *our Cause 21 years*," she reminded them. "He has done more practical work in my behalf . . . than any other Student."[98] And to Frye she remarked on another occasion that he had done more for Christian Science than any other person on earth except herself.[99]

A thumbnail sketch of him by a reporter from the *New York Herald* in 1905 serves as a useful corrective to the often reported description of him as a taciturn, pompous little man. He was, according to the *Herald* account,

> . . . a very pleasant-faced man, with hair slightly tinged with gray and with a short gray moustache. Delightful of manners, easy, and graceful, Mr. Frye has a bright smiling eye. He greeted me cheerfully and said that he had read my letter to Mrs. Eddy and that she would see me in her library for a few minutes.[100]

In a letter written after Frye's death, Joseph Mann gave an insider's view of him which is equally far from the widely accepted legend:

> Mr. Frye was a man big enough to do his own thinking, that is, he did not reach conclusions by comparing notes with others, nor even by consulting with himself; for he had within himself a very appreciable element of that good old-fashioned Christian spirit which consulted God. . . . He was no soft-gloved theorist,

but a horny-handed metaphysician; an obedient servant of God, upon whom Mrs. Eddy could call, in her need, for a helpful hand.[101]

Frye had his off moments, sometimes trivial—as when he wrote with good-natured ruefulness in his diary, "Got locked out of front vestibule twice today, then made a dive over balustrade!"[102]—sometimes serious, as in a poker-faced 1905 entry in his diary regarding a "mental collapse" he had one night at nine o'clock:

When Mrs. E. asked me to talk with her when she had just retired I believed I could not & left her without a comforting word, which nearly [killed?] her, but I gave the alarm & called others to her rescue. They watched with her the rest of the night & I was allowed to go to my room and . . . sleep for the rest of the night.[103]

The next day he was partly recovered and after a second night's good sleep he was able to write in his diary, "Mrs. Eddy [and] I both gained our normal condition again."

Another more dramatic instance, which has entered into the folklore of Christian Science, occurred in 1905 and is recorded by George Kinter in his reminiscences.

One winter night the three rings which were Frye's special summons to Mrs. Eddy's room sounded through the house unheeded. Then Kinter's five-ring signal rang out sharply and he flew to answer it. Taking a shortcut through Frye's room, he was surprised to see Calvin in a chair but apparently in a coma. Mrs. Eddy, apprised of this, sent him back to rouse Frye, but Kinter now discovered that the motionless figure was stone cold and rigid, with no perceptible pulse, breath, or other sign of life.

By this time Mrs. Eddy had rung for Laura Sargent, who arrived to find her already out of bed and advancing in her nightdress toward Calvin's room, regardless of the icy cold of the house. Paying no slightest attention to Kinter's and Mrs. Sargent's protests, Mrs. Eddy bent over the sitting figure and began at once to make "bold audible declarations" of truth.

For more than an hour she continued to call upon Frye in one way or another to "wake up and be the man God made!" Mrs. Sargent meanwhile had rung for the maid, who brought a double blanket in which they wrapped Mrs. Eddy, while Kinter with an aching back supported her in the half-stooping position in which she bent over Frye's inert form, completely oblivious of what they were doing for her or of anything except the need to rouse him. At last he moved slightly and began to murmur. They could pick out broken phrases: "Don't call me back. . . . Let me go. . . . I am so tired." To which Mrs. Eddy replied that she would indeed continue to call him back from the dream-state in which he had been—that he loved life and its activities too well to fall asleep, that he was freed from the thralldom of hypnotism and alive to God, his Saviour from sin and death.[104]

In another half hour Calvin had recovered and everybody went to bed. The next morning no mention was made of the night's events. Frye was in his usual place, and life proceeded normally. Several years later an almost identical experience occurred, with the apparently lifeless Frye carried this time into Mrs. Eddy's bedroom.[105]

Shortly after the 1905 episode Gilbert C. Carpenter of Providence, Rhode Island, came to Pleasant View for a year's metaphysical and secretarial service. Greatly given to analysis, he was later to anatomize elaborately every detail of Mrs. Eddy's life (real or apocryphal) that he could pick up, giving it a highly subjective metaphysical interpretation which approaches sheer fantasy at times.[106]

He did, however, glimpse what Mrs. Eddy saw as the essential relation between her rebukes and her healing, as evidenced even in the combination of sharpness and love with which she had addressed the inert Frye. To assume that a cutting rebuke was merely the result of overwrought nerves was therefore to lose its instructional and therapeutic value.[107]

This was certainly the view held by Mrs. Eddy herself, and also by Frye. A typical entry in the latter's diary reads:

> *Mother said this morning that the dangerous error to students is in not seeing error, insensibility to the presence of error. We must see it detect it but see it as unreal and with a true consciousness of the reality of Being destroy [it] but this result will not be gained by stupidity.*[108]

A 1905 entry in the diary gives a mild but characteristic example of instructional reproof:

> *Mrs. Eddy called Mrs. J. D. Prescott, Mrs. M. V. Blain Mrs. L. E. Sargent Mrs. Grace Greene, G C Carpenter & myself into her room this morning & said the moral atmosphere of this house (P. V.) is just perfect there is not a Judas thot in it, but there is yet a lack & I should not be a faithful teacher if I did not tell you this. She waited to see if we would ask her what the need was, but as no one did ask, she reminded us of this lack of inquiry, and said it is a lack of spirituality.*

She then opened the Bible and John 4:10 was the verse she first saw.[109]

To be a member of the Pleasant View household was, according to those who came and went, something between an unremitting discipline and a perpetual revelation.

5

The early, insouciant W. H. Auden has observed that

> Private faces in public places
> are wiser and nicer
> than public faces in private places.[110]

Increasingly there are no private places left in the lives of public figures. Psychologically, electronically, journalistically, bureaucratically, the probing goes on in almost literal fulfilment of the New Testament prophecy: "That which ye have spoken in the ear in closets shall be proclaimed upon the housetops."[111]

If in the middle of an unspecified night of 1906 Mrs. Eddy's personal maid, Caroline Foss, summoned by bell, hurried to the bedside of her mistress only to be told by that eighty-five-year-old lady in a state of sleepy sweetness that she just wanted to kiss her, one can be sure that incident will find its way eventually into the public record along with matters of greater moment.[112] Rather more legitimately, a little-known figure, Anna Machacek, belongs in the record as representative of the various unsung women who gave Mrs. Eddy good service and commonsense devotion.

Anna had fled from her Bohemian homeland, where her father was a prosperous farmer, to escape an arranged but unwelcome marriage. Settling in a large Czech colony in Cedar Rapids, Iowa, the lonely shy girl had been befriended by a Christian Science practitioner and learned with her help to read and speak English by studying the Bohemian Bible in conjunction with the English Scriptures and *Science and Health*.

Recommended to serve as laundress at Pleasant View, she had arrived, blossomed, won everyone's heart with her cheerful readiness to serve and eagerness to learn, been promoted to the role of housekeeper, and finally left to become a Christian Science practitioner in Chicago. A woman who had known her when she was a young immigrant in long, full-skirted calico dress, with a babushka tied over her fair hair, hardly recognized her a few years later on a Chicago street, "trim in her tailored blue suit—smart hat, white blouse and gloves" and "now . . . a busy practitioner."[113]

Pleasant View had been for Anna not the house of mystery portrayed in the yellow press, nor the holy of holies imagined by some Christian Scientists, but a home, a workshop, a group of friends, a place where fruitful convictions grew and an ordinary American success story was transformed into a spiritual adventure. Quite as much as John Salchow, she relates Pleasant View to the common soil of daily life and represents the sort of unselfed help that Mrs. Eddy both needed and appreciated.[114]

Of the other women who served there at various times in a domestic or metaphysical capacity, most were practitioners, some teachers, and many of them called away from demanding work in their local Christian Science fields. They were the background for Mrs. Eddy's accomplishments, ministering to her needs in the traditional role of Martha, but they also drew forth from her in Mary-fashion a constant outflow of ideas, confidences, biblical exegeses and metaphysical instructions, which they then or later recorded in diaries, letters, and written reminiscences.[115]

This large body of evidence amply supports the statement of the otherwise critical British historian, H. A. L. Fisher, that the "great ideas of God, of immortality, of the soul, of a life penetrated by Christianity, were never far from her mind."[116] They also reveal the constant interplay between her writings and her daily life. Hardly for an instant did she cease to be a teacher, but she also learned from observing closely the responses of those around her. Years before, she had written Hanna that it seemed to be her "life-long task to *experiment.*"[117] This was evident in minor household matters fully as much as in major decisions affecting the whole movement.

Nevertheless, it was the larger scene that demanded her greatest care, and a change made by her in 1904 was a further instance of her increasing attention to the long-range interests of her movement. It was also an indication that in organizational matters men still played the dominant role, but always under her final authority.

By 1904 Edward Kimball had been teaching the Normal classes of the Board of Education for several years and had turned out some hundred-and-fifty new teachers. On May 15, 1903, Mrs. Eddy had written him:

> *I write these lines simply to thank you deeply for your dear letter that is a balm for wounds that you never inflicted—and in evidence of my unfaltering faith in you.*

Whatever else befalls I shall never look for your downfall in Christian Science nor a lack of heartfelt fidelity to your Teacher and its Founder.

God bless you and make your exit from sense to Soul, from earth to Heaven here, *gentle.*[118]

Rumors had been stirring as to the nature of Kimball's teaching, together with suggestions that he considered it to be metaphysically in advance of Mrs. Eddy's own—a suggestion which he repudiated with the full force of a notably straightforward character. Two months later he wrote Mrs. Eddy of the opposition of some of the older teachers to the new ones who had come out from his classes. The fact was, he reminded her, that the only two of the "old teachers" who knew at first hand what he taught were Judge Hanna and Mrs. Lathrop, both of whom spoke highly of his teaching.

A month later, an article by him—"The Integrity of Christian Science Literature"—was published in the *Sentinel*[119] condemning the circulation of unauthorized notes, letters, and other writings which purported to present but actually misrepresented what had been taught in authorized (and restricted) Christian Science classes. It was a dilemma with which Mrs. Eddy could sympathize, for she herself had been a victim of the same practice not only in relation to her class teaching but also in regard to her private conversations. As she had written Kimball several years earlier, she sometimes dreaded to have her students visit her, "lest when they leave they report me as saying what they brought out by remarks of their own."[120]

Reports that Kimball's pupils considered themselves superior to hers continued to come from some of her old students, but she seems not to have taken them very seriously. However, the situation did point to the danger of having different interpretations of Christian Science develop and of allowing arguments over the letter of Science to impair the demonstration of its spirit.

Years before, the Reverend William I. Gill had written her in regard to the almost inevitable springing up of factions and sects among the followers of great religious teachers, "I wonder whether you cannot say something clear and strong and striking which shall unfang this serpent."[121] What she had said, in effect, was that *Science and Health* must be the standard for the letter of Christian Science and Christian demonstration the test of its spirit.

On November 26, 1903, she wrote Kimball:

My honored and beloved *Student:*
Do not think that I doubt your loyalty and strict *fidelity. O*

no far from it! . . . But . . . I think, owing to the one you name in this last letter, that it is best for you not to locate at present in Boston, and for the sake of Truth to teach in the Board but two classes annually. This is better than more would be at present. Our cause demands better healers; *and if less teaching classes is enjoined more practitioners will be fitted by the book to heal. I see the need of a healer to be as excluded from other work in Christian Science as for the M. D. . . . I am sorely disappointed in the demonstration of C. S. and it must improve or our cause will float into theory and we will not "show our faith by our works." A chatterer of C. S. is never a healer.*[122]

In a visit with Kimball the following January she expressed continued confidence in him but told him that she intended to limit the term of teacher for the Board of Education to three years. Before she actually did so, he wrote her a letter of resignation in which deep hurt was combined with unwavering loyalty. As usual, too, he was utterly frank:

Three years ago, you told me that you were very desirous of getting Judge Hanna out of office and out of Boston. . . . I resolved that if I ever got the slightest hint of the kind concerning myself I would make short work of it by speedily getting out of the way.

The problem which you had with Judge Hanna was solved by a by-law which terminated his official tenure and precluded by means of the 3 year rule the possibility of his continuance.

Last Saturday, you told me you were going to put into effect the same rule concerning the teacher of the Board of Education and I construe this as a possible hint to me. . . . Considering our educational system which is in great need of uniformity and stability, I hardly think you would provide for frequent changes in the teaching, except because of unusual stress.

The annals of the race make no mention of anyone whose tasks were so severe, so continuous and complex as yours are. . . . I greatly long for your peace, for the more tranquil flow of your life, & I want you to know, my dear dear friend, that there is not an atom of disposition on my part to stand in the way.

You do not need to take any unusual or radical step on my account, dear Mother. I know what it means to ascend the cross and have the nails driven into me. The one who craves position, power or emolument in the Cause of Christian Science is mad. There is nothing that I want except a chance to pray and re-

*pent. . . . Your ways are higher than mine and I do not clearly
see the way. . . .*[123]

But while Kimball continued to feel the termination of his
position with the Board of Education and his return to full-time
lecturing as in some measure a rejection by her—and to suffer from
it accordingly[124]—Mrs. Eddy saw it as a larger necessity for the future
of the movement. "You should see the wisdom of rotation in Teaching
as well as reading in Church," she wrote him.[125]

A statement by her soon followed in the *Sentinel* explaining the
change in just such terms:

> *The Magna Charta of Christian Science means much,* multum
> in parvo,—all-in-one and one-in-all. *It stands for the inalienable,
> universal rights of men. Essentially democratic, its government is
> administered by the common consent of the governed, wherein
> and whereby man governed by his creator is self-governed. The
> Church is the mouthpiece of Christian Science,—its law and gospel
> are according to Christ Jesus; its rules are health, holiness, and
> immortality,—equal rights and privileges, equality of the sexes,
> rotation in office.*
>
> *The long term of the incumbent teacher in the Board of
> Education, Mr. Edward A. Kimball, C.S.D., expires in June next,
> when he retires crowned with honors—his Teacher and Leader
> loving him, his students praising him, and the race benefited by
> his labors. May his successor "go and do likewise."*[126]

The successor was Eugene H. Greene of Providence, Rhode
Island, who had studied with Mrs. Eddy twenty years earlier. A man
who seems to have had considerable grace of spirit[127] though less
teaching ability than Kimball, Greene served acceptably for three
years. Meanwhile Mrs. Eddy took the further drastic step of reducing
Normal instruction to a single term held once every three years, with a
different teacher each time and a class restricted to thirty pupils.

Interestingly enough, her choice for teacher in 1907 was Hanna
and for the next class Kimball. By these two choices she showed her
continued and impartial support of each of the two men and struck
a blow at the tendency in some quarters to speak of two variant
"schools" of Christian Science teaching (sometimes known as the
Boston school and the Chicago school) of which Hanna and Kimball
were presumed to be the chief representatives.[128]

Deeply concerned though Mrs. Eddy was with the proper teaching
of Christian Science, her work as founder necessarily embraced considerations of far greater complexity than the classroom presentation

of its metaphysics. In this respect it resembled Paul's work as a founder of the Christian Church, which had involved much more than the apostolic task of preaching the gospel. "For while one saith, I am of Paul; and another, I am of Apollos; are ye not carnal?" he had asked, then went on to point out to the divided Corinthians that he had planted, Apollos watered, but God gave the increase—indeed, that Paul, Apollos, Cephas, and all things present and to come "are yours; and ye are Christ's; and Christ is God's."[129] At which point of spiritual democracy, doctrine and polity merged.

So far as Mrs. Eddy was concerned, the ultimate teacher of Christian Science was *Science and Health*. The educational system of her church was bigger than any one teacher appointed to conduct a Normal class for the Board of Education. She herself would not always be present personally to make even-handed choice of competent Christian Scientists for that office and to keep any particular emphasis or interpretation of Christian Science from entrenching itself in the church's teaching system. What had seemed to Kimball for a time to be a waning of her full confidence in him was, on these terms, a dawning recognition of the overriding value of rotation in office.

It was one more lesson she had learned from coming to grips with a concrete situation which threatened to divide the field.

Chapter VIII

The World at the Front Door

The World at the Front Door

By June, 1906, Mary Baker Eddy had become a familiar figure in the national press. Her views on war, divorce, politics, heaven, the decline of religion, the death of Pope Leo XIII, and other assorted topics were sought and published by leading newspapers.[1] Her philanthropic contributions to a variety of causes, from the new Dartmouth College library to the victims of the Galveston flood and the San Francisco earthquake, were also a contribution to the developing picture of her as a distinguished, public-spirited elder citizen.[2]

When the International League of Press Clubs brought out a mammoth volume entitled *Bohemia*—hopefully described at the time as one of the supreme triumphs of the printer's and bookmaker's art[3]— Mrs. Eddy was represented in it both as an invited contributor and as the subject of a biographical sketch by Judge Ewing. She was likewise one of the selected few to whom an even more monumental volume, *The Book of the Presidents,* was presented in a specially bound copy which included her picture and biography along with those of the twenty-five variegated gentlemen who had served as Chief Executive of the United States.[4]

The place accorded to Mrs. Eddy in this latter book, the *Boston Herald* noted with an unwonted degree of reverence, was "another of the many evidences of the widening sphere of her spiritual ministry, and emphasizes the patent fact of her growing influence among the intelligent and cultured classes of this and foreign lands."[5]

In 1907, after an exhibit of the Christian Science Publishing Society had won a *Grand Prix* at an international book exposition in Paris, the French government—through Aristide Briand, then Minister of Public Instruction and Fine Arts—was to make Mrs. Eddy an *Officier d'Académie,* and the decoration would be presented to her at Pleasant View by the Commissioner General of the American section of the exposition. That was the year, too, in which she would accept an appointment as *Fondateur* of a new peace society, the Association for International Conciliation, through its American Secretary, Hayne Davis.[6]

For some time Mrs. Eddy's antiwar sentiments had been growing. At the start of the Russo-Japanese War late in 1904, she had issued a statement to the *Boston Globe,* which contained such statements as:

> *Nothing is gained by fighting, but much is lost. . . . War is in itself an evil, barbarous, devilish. Victory in error is defeat in Truth. . . . Whatever brings into human thought or action an element opposed to Love, is never requisite, never a necessity, and is not sanctioned by the law of God, the law of Love.*[7]

The following June she sent a message to the members of her church assembled at the annual meeting in Boston:

> *I request that every member of The Mother Church of Christ, Scientist, in Boston, pray each day for the amicable settlement of the war between Russia and Japan; and pray that God bless that great nation and those islands of the sea with peace and prosperity.*[8]

After two weeks she requested that they stop "special prayer" for peace, explaining in a follow-up statement that this did not mean they should discontinue their general prayer for the peace of nations, which at all times should be part of their daily effort to help establish the kingdom of God on earth. But "a spiritual foresight of the nations' drama" had led her to see that the present need was for "faith in God's disposal of events."[9]

Within three weeks of the publication of this explanation, Russian and Japanese representatives, as a result of the mediatorial efforts of Theodore Roosevelt, had come together for a peace conference in Portsmouth, New Hampshire. God's disposal of events had led not only to the successful intervention of the President of the United States—an accomplishment which won him the Nobel Peace Prize—but also to the selection, out of all the possible sites in the world, of a spot only forty miles from Pleasant View for the peace conference. To many Christian Scientists the geographical propinquity seemed to symbolize the closeness of their leader to the heart of "the nations' drama."[10]

Yet, as Mrs. Eddy drew closer to public events, she withdrew proportionately from public view. During the Russo-Japanese War she gave a brief interview to a *New York Herald* reporter, who described her "motherly expression" and noted that "her face lighted sweetly" as she talked, while "the brightness of the large, full eyes bespoke the owner's mental activity." Her "tall figure," he added in the courtly and somewhat awed tone which marked his whole report, "was exquisitely gowned in black silk of becoming and modish cut." Her welcome was cordial, but he couldn't help feeling that "the exigencies of my quest for facts had not been without their exactions in thus compelling Mrs. Eddy to stand before me to prove that she still lived." Her "grace and charm," however, "softened the difficulty and hardship of that visit." His final conclusion was: "Mrs. Eddy still lives and apparently is enjoying the normal health of one of her years."[11]

Two months later, in May of 1905, Mrs. Sibyl Wilbur O'Brien of the *Boston Herald* was granted an interview which she herself terminated in only a few minutes from a feeling of sheer inability to impose any longer on this woman whom she afterward described as erect, flowerlike, gentle, lovable, but "with a force and decision in every word so gently uttered."[12] The force, she added, was like a command from a mind accustomed to be obeyed. "All that I ask of the world is time," Mrs. Eddy told her, "time to assimilate myself to God." And rather than press her questions on a person "so detached, so luminous," Mrs. O'Brien decided forthwith to leave them in written form with Mrs. Eddy's secretaries so that she might dictate her answers to them at her leisure.[13]

The next day Farlow wrote Gilbert Carpenter:

> *Mrs. O'Brien was just in. I think she is the happiest woman on the earth. She was altogether overcome by her interview with Mrs. Eddy and thinks she is the most wonderful woman she ever saw.*[14]

Several days later, after receiving a letter from Mrs. Eddy with her written answers to Mrs. O'Brien's questions, Farlow wrote back to Pleasant View that he had not let Mrs. Eddy know a hundredth part of the pressure he was under to arrange interviews with her but had already concluded that she must not be disturbed any more with matters of that kind. "You have earned the right to retire," he assured her, "and Mrs. O'Brien's story duly acknowledges this and makes it easier for us to stop this interview business."[15]

The problem, however, was not only reporters but also Christian Scientists. Some of them spoke rapturously of inspiration and healing they had received from catching a glimpse of her as she passed them on her daily carriage drive, and this encouraged others to come to Concord with the hope of receiving similar benefits. Mrs. Eddy recognized this as an unhealthy tendency and felt it as a mental drain on herself.

Accordingly in 1904 she had caused a new *Manual* bylaw to be passed, which read in its final form: "A member of The Mother Church shall not haunt Mrs. Eddy's drive when she goes out, continually stroll by her house, or make a summer resort near her for such a purpose."[16]

In the spring of 1906, as the time for the dedication of the extension of The Mother Church was approaching and preparations were being made in Boston to receive tens of thousands of Christian Scientists from around the world, Mrs. Eddy wrote the Directors, "Now is the time to *throttle the lie* that students worship me or that I claim their homage." The occasion called for "some special reform," and she hoped the Directors would see the need for the notice she enclosed:

> *Divine Love bids me say: Assemble not at the residence of your Pastor Emeritus at or about the time of our annual meeting and communion service, for the divine and not the human should engage our attention at this sacred season of prayer and praise.*[17]

The year before, Hermann Hering's three-year term as First Reader of The Mother Church had come to a close and he had been replaced by William McCrackan, whereupon Mrs. Eddy brought Hering up to Concord to replace Irving Tomlinson as First Reader of the Concord church. Now a special assignment was explained to him in a note from Lewis C. Strang, formerly a Boston drama critic but serving at present as an assistant secretary at Pleasant View. Disregarding Mrs. Eddy's repeatedly expressed wishes, Christian Scientists in droves were haunting her carriage route and peering hopefully across her flower-beds, and Strang wrote:

> *If possible, she would like to have you seek out these thoughtless visitors and bid them spend the time that they are wasting in the worship of personality in careful study of the Church Manual, especially the By-Law, which positively forbids precisely the thing that they are doing.*
>
> *Mrs. Eddy desires that you say to them that Pleasant View is neither a watering-place where they may spend their summer nor a hospital where they can steal their healing.*[18]

Shortly afterward, Mrs. Eddy reinforced this with a *Sentinel* article, "Personal Contagion," which she described to Archibald McLellan as "one of the most important things of thought I ever expressed."[19] Its implications went far beyond the immediate nuisance of ardent gawkers to what she felt had been the undoing of all the world's greatest religions:

> In time of religious or scientific prosperity, certain individuals are inclined to cling to the personality of its leader. This state of mind is sickly; it is a contagion—a mental malady, which must be met and overcome. Why? Because it would dethrone the First Commandment, Thou shalt have one God. . . .
>
> "What went ye out for to see?" A person, or a Principle? Whichever it be, determines the right or the wrong of this following. A personal motive gratified by sense will leave one "a reed shaken with the wind," whereas helping a leader in God's direction, and giving this leader time and retirement to pursue the infinite ascent,—the comprehending of the divine order and consciousness in Science,—will break one's own dream of personal sense, heal disease, and make one a Christian Scientist. . . .
>
> There was never a religion or philosophy lost to the centuries except by sinking its divine Principle in personality. May all Christian Scientists ponder this fact, and give their talents and loving hearts free scope only in the right direction!
>
> I left Boston in the height of prosperity to retreat from the world, and to seek the one divine Person, whereby and wherein to show others the footsteps from sense to Soul. To give me this opportunity is all that I ask of mankind.[20]

Mankind, however, was not inclined to comply with the request. There was still a constant need for Mrs. Eddy to see visitors on church business, to attend to a daily tidal wave of mail, to answer the pleas of those who felt they must see her. To an importunate clergyman who besieged her with letters raising questions he hoped to discuss with her in person, she replied in September, 1906, with a patient negative which carried forward the theme of "Personal Contagion":

> Should I give myself the pleasant pastime of seeing your personal self, or give you the opportunity of seeing mine, you would not see me thus, for I am not there. I have risen to look and wait and watch and pray for the spirit of Truth that leadeth away from person—from body to Soul, even to the true image and likeness of God. St. John found Christ, Truth, in the Word which is God. We look for the sainted Revelator in his writings, and there we find him. Those who look for me in person, or

elsewhere than in my writings, lose me instead of find me. I hope and trust that you and I may meet in truth and know each other there, and know as we are known of God.[21]

Among the skeptical there was speculation that this was a seclusion enforced by ill health, perhaps even by a fatal disease. In the early part of 1906 there had indeed been a return attack of the affliction which had struck her in 1903, but this had been followed by a renewed surge of good health. When Dr. and Mrs. Ezekiel Morrill in the fall arrived back in Concord from a lengthy European trip, Mrs. Eddy wrote them:

October 6, 1906

My dear friends:

I was glad to hear of your return and prosperity. Also have the pleasure of telling you I am well again. Every one of the old symptoms are gone *buried and plucked up by the roots.*

Affectionately yours,
Mary Baker Eddy[22]

The periods of struggle were for her periods of spiritual growth, and to this degree she welcomed them. But most of all she welcomed every evidence that her followers and particularly her helpers were willing to struggle into a greater measure of spiritual dedication and therefore usefulness to the cause. As she wrote to John Lathrop that summer:

Press on, you are in the line of light. Rise to realize the glory of strife; seeking is not sufficient whereby to enter the Kingdom of Harmony. I mourn over the ease of Christian Scientists,—they are not at ease in the pains of sense but are at ease in its pleasures! Which drives out quickest the tenant you wish to get out of your house, the pleasant hours he enjoys in it or its unpleasantness?[23]

There were many pleasant hours at Pleasant View, but before 1906 was over a peculiarly nasty—and therefore, by Mrs. Eddy's reckoning, an especially beneficial—unpleasantness was to knock at its unpretentious front door.

2

As early as November, 1904, a rumor reached Alfred Farlow that *McClure's* magazine, then glorying in what Theodore Roosevelt was pleased to call its "muckraking" reputation, was planning to add Mrs. Eddy and Christian Science to its list of sensational but documented exposés.

At the same time Farlow learned that Mrs. Georgine Milmine Welles, an upstate New York journalist—"with whom," he wrote to Kinter, "we had some dealings a while ago, and all of which was of the most kindly nature"[24]—had been turned against Mrs. Eddy by Frederick Peabody and had changed her mind about the favorable article she had planned to write on the subject for *McClure's*.

During the next eighteen months there were added indications that the magazine was mounting a major offensive. In May, 1906, shortly after the famous palace revolution which caused Ida Tarbell, Lincoln Steffens, and Ray Stannard Baker to leave the editorial staff, Farlow and Cornell Wilson (who had succeeded McCrackan as Committee on Publication for New York) paid a visit to the editorial offices to talk the matter over with S. S. McClure but were fobbed off on Witter Bynner, McClure's new managing editor.

Bynner, whom Farlow described to Mrs. Eddy as "a bright young fellow, with a good face," appeared to be "gratified" with their attitude and "expressed his dissatisfaction with the matter prepared by Miss Milmine"[25]—as Mrs. Welles preferred to be known professionally. They learned that the series she had prepared was now being checked by young Mark Sullivan,[26] and Bynner promised them they would have a chance to see the manuscript before it was published. Two months later they received similar assurances from the still newer managing editor, Will Irwin, who added that the magazine "had no intention of publishing an 'exposé' or an attack."[27]

Meanwhile, however, a Christian Scientist in Chicago had sent them a copy of a letter she had received from her daughter, Martha S. Bensley, a freelance journalist in New York:

> By the way, I have something of interest to say to you, which I think you will probably not be very pleased to hear. Mr. Mc-Clure, who is the owner and editor of McClure's Magazine and of McClure Syndicate . . . has been here a good deal lately; and among other things he has told me that McClure's Magazine is going to start a crusade against Christian Science. They have been at this for some two or three years and have collected as he put it "a whole trunkful of documents," including . . . many letters, some of them originals of Mrs. Eddy's and some of them certified copies, and they have watched the whole course of things for some time with great care. They had people at the convention in Boston a few weeks ago, one of whom I know quite well. As far as I can find out, the first of these articles is to be published in January and they are going on through a large part of the year. They are going

to take up every phase and development of Christian Science and do what they can to ridicule and destroy it. This information is authentic. I heard it from Mr. McClure's own lips. . . . I do not know that there is anything that can be done by any of your people to stop it or interfere with his plans, but sometimes it is worth while knowing these things beforehand.[28]

At the same time another outstanding figure in American journalism was hastening to be in at the kill. With rumors afloat that Mrs. Eddy was either dying or dead and that *McClure's* was digging up sensational facts in her past history, Joseph Pulitzer—now blind and (like Mrs. Eddy) directing his empire from seclusion—convinced himself that it was his public duty to be first to get the story out. During the summer of 1906 his reporters were digging away as determinedly as the *McClure's* staff, which had just been augmented by the still little-known Willa Cather, who was put to work rechecking evidence and doing a certain amount of rewriting of the Milmine text.[29]

Since Mrs. Eddy's public appearances were now confined to her daily carriage drives, any attempt to prove that she was dead or moribund would necessarily have to prove that the slim, upright, smartly dressed figure who smiled and bowed to friends from her carriage—but who was apt to use a small ornamental parasol as a shield from the curious stares of strangers—was an impersonator. And it was just this that Pulitzer's *New York World* was now determined to prove.[30]

On October 14, two *World* reporters named Slaght and Lithchild called at Pleasant View and demanded an interview with Frye. At this interview they informed him that the *World* had received "many letters"[31] declaring that Mrs. Eddy was dead and that Frye was not only the real head of the Christian Science movement but also in de facto possession of her fortune. Slaght explained smoothly that these letters had interested Pulitzer to the point where he had sent the two reporters to establish definitely whether Mrs. Eddy was alive. They were not after a story, he added, as *McClure's* was, and even though they had gathered damaging affidavits from many of Mrs. Eddy's early dissident students, it was not Pulitzer's purpose to use this material if the reporters could satisfy themselves that Mrs. Eddy was still alive.

With this not very subtle mixture of threat and promise, plus the announcement that they had been "informed" that the person in her carriage each day was not Mrs. Eddy, Slaght announced that they would be satisfied if Mrs. Eddy's neighbor, "Professor" John F. Kent,[32] could see the mistress of Pleasant View in their company and identify her as the actual Mrs. Eddy. Frye told them he would let them know her decision by noon the next day, but held back from telling her of the situation until she had returned from her drive about two o'clock on the 15th.

Lewis Strang later sent Cornell Wilson in New York an account of what followed:

> *She immediately sent John Salchow . . . to see Prof. Kent and arranged with him to identify her. [August Mann, the coachman] was sent down to the Eagle Hotel after Messrs. Slaght and Lithchild. They reached Pleasant View about three o'clock. . . .*
>
> *As soon as Prof. Kent arrived, the three men and myself went at once upstairs to Mrs. Eddy's office. She arose and stepped to the middle of the floor to meet them. She spoke to Prof. Kent, saying that she was sorry that he had lost the Principalship of the Concord High School and that she hoped that he would be reappointed. I introduced Mr. Slaght first. She shook hands with him and he said that he was very glad to see her. I then introduced Mr. Lithchild. Mr. Lithchild's name escaped me for the moment, and he was obliged to prompt me. Mrs. Eddy shook hands with him. She explained in a few words that her duties made it impossible for her to receive visitors and that this accounted for her seclusion. She signified that this ended the visit, though I believe that she shook hands again with Prof. Kent before he left the room. I know that Messrs. Slaght and Lithchild preceded me out of the room and down the stairs. Mrs. Eddy remained standing during the entire visit, and as the men left, turned and walked back to her desk in the bay window.*
>
> *When we were going down the stairs, Mr. Lithchild said to me with apparent conviction, "She is certainly a well-preserved woman for her years." Mr. Slaght also gave me to understand that he was thoroughly satisfied as to the soundness of Mrs. Eddy's physical and mental condition. They furthermore led Mr. Mann, who drove them back to the hotel, to understand that they proposed leaving town that afternoon.*[33]

Instead, they stayed for two more weeks, and the story which finally burst into headlines in the *New York World* on Sunday, October 28, 1906, showed what they had been up to. The headlines set the tone for the pages of print that followed:

MRS. MARY BAKER G. EDDY DYING:
FOOTMAN AND "DUMMY" CONTROL HER

Founder of X Science Suffering from Cancer and Nearing Her End, Is Immured at Pleasant View. While Another Woman Impersonates Her in the Streets of Concord.

Mrs. Leonard, Brooklyn Healer, in False Role.

Drives Out Daily in Closed Carriage with Calvin A. Frye, Secretary-Footman, Who is the Supreme Power at the Eddy Home— Founder Estimated to Have Accumulated a Fortune of $15,000,-000, and to Have an Income of $1,000,000 a Year, but Members of Her Coterie Say She Has Spent It All in Charity, Though No Records of Large Gifts Can Be Found.

The story itself, divided into "chapters," showed long preparation and a skill more novelistic than journalistic. Where fact was wanting, fabrication amply supplied the want—as in the creation of an unnamed "cancer specialist" who was described as coming from Boston to Concord "never less frequently than once a week" and being driven "by a roundabout route" to Pleasant View in order to treat Mrs. Eddy for the terminal cancer with which the paper summarily endowed her.[34]

Insufficiently sensational facts could be remedied by simple speculation—as in the newspaper's multiplication of Mrs. Eddy's fortune to fifteen times its actual size—and annoying facts could be reversed by bold theories. To every question about Mrs. Eddy asked of Concord people, the *World* reported, the inevitable answer was: "She is alive and hearty. You can see her every day in her carriage." All the populace joined in the chorus, the paper complained—"citizens of every religious and political creed, city officials, hotel proprietors, tradesmen, professional men, everybody."[35] But the astute *World* reporters offered a spicy explanation: the dying Mrs. Eddy and her sinister "footman"[36] held Concord in the grip of a reign of terror; to criticize her would be to lose one's job, whether one was a high official or a humble cabman.

Again, it was the clever Messrs. Slaght and Lithchild who, a week after their brief but necessary interview with Mrs. Eddy, peeked boldly in the windows of her passing carriage from both sides at once—so that the occupant could not possibly hide behind her parasol from *both* peekers—and decided that the lady was not Mrs. Eddy but a younger member of her household, Mrs. Pamelia Leonard of Brooklyn. To be sure, neither reporter had ever seen Mrs. Leonard, but they had— either through a mysterious feat of precognition or a carefully predetermined plan—brought up to Concord a Brooklyn janitor, John J.

Hennessy, who knew her well by sight and joined in the peeking act, after which he obligingly made the desired identification.

While Hennessy had the pleasure of seeing his name and affidavit prominently displayed in the *World,* the paper did not feel it necessary to print an affidavit made by Mrs. Leonard the day after the story broke:

> *The statement that I have impersonated Mrs. Eddy and ridden in her carriage in her place is entirely false, for I have never stepped inside of her carriage and have never even looked inside of it. . . . At the time Mr. Hennessy claimed to identify me as being down town, I was at home at Pleasant View. Had he taken the pains to come out here to Pleasant View, I would have gladly seen him.*[37]

Lewis Strang also came out with a statement which he amplified and put into affidavit form the next day:

> *One of my duties is to hand Mrs. Eddy into her carriage and tuck her carriage robe about her. I have been doing this since the middle of March, 1906. I therefore speak from positive knowledge when I say that in that time Mrs. Eddy has driven in her carriage daily, with the exception of one day in the early spring, when the roads were so bad that she did not go out.*[38]

The Mrs. Eddy pictured by the *World* would clearly have been incapable of riding out from Pleasant View or even of getting downstairs to her own front door. The paper's description of her—given a fresh lease on life by the Dakin biography twenty-three years later—was done with all the subtlety of a Gothic shocker:

> *Mrs. Eddy looked more dead than alive. She was a skeleton, her hollow cheeks thick with red paint, and the fleshless, hairless bones above the sunken eyes penciled a jet black. The features were thick with powder. Above them was a big white wig. . . .*
>
> *Her weakness was pathetic. She reeled as she stood clinging to the table. Her sunken, faded eyes gazed helplessly, almost pleadingly, at her visitors. The air of the room reeked with the odors of powerful stimulants. In a corner, as though hastily pushed aside, stood a galvanic battery with its surgical basin full of water and a sponge wet from use.*
>
> *To every eye it was clear that the unfortunate old woman had been doped and galvanized for the ordeal of identification. But it*

was equally clear that the utmost stimulation could not keep the tortured woman upon her feet much longer.

Strang glided to her side and held an outstretched arm behind her in readiness for the threatened collapse. But old Mrs. Eddy was nerved to supreme effort.

Her listless eyes were fastened upon Prof. Kent as he stepped toward her. As he bowed formally she released her hold upon the table, swayed toward him, clutched him with her shrivelled fingers, and held on with desperate strength. Had Prof. Kent withdrawn his support she would have fallen.

"My—dear—dear pro-professor!" she cried in the high crackling voice of extreme age. "H-h-how glad I am to see you. Let me co-congratulate you on getting back—your position. I-I am so glad that you are at the head of our sc-school again." . . .

As the visitors were hurried from the room, Mrs. Eddy, surrounded by attendants, was sinking helpless into a pillowed chair.[39]

When the story came out in the Sunday *World*, Concord swung into action. Mrs. Eddy's counsel, General Streeter, collected the mayor of the city, Charles R. Corning, who was also probate judge for Merrimack County, and drove immediately to Pleasant View. Later that day both men gave interviews to the Associated Press. Streeter, who might be considered a prejudiced witness but who also had his professional reputation as a leader of the New Hampshire bar to consider, described the visit:

Mayor Charles R. Corning drove out with me to Pleasant View about four o-clock this afternoon. I sent a note to Mrs. Eddy that we be permitted to call upon her, and the request was almost immediately granted. She arose and most cordially greeted the mayor and myself, exhibiting no appearance of weariness but a physical activity not ordinarily to be found in persons many years younger. The conversation covered a variety of subjects. She spoke briefly, without bitterness, of the false statement being circulated with reference to her health and even death, and said that she was in the hands of an infinite God in whom she had perfect trust, and that He would care for her.

Reference was made to a business transaction of some time ago, about which her memory was exact and accurate. She referred to many details of her daily work and her correspondence and study. She also inquired for a personal friend to whom she had recently sent a valuable present, and expressed her warm affection. . . .

*I can emphatically say that Mrs. Eddy, in spite of her ad-
vanced years, is a remarkably well preserved woman. Her health
and appearance are substantially the same as when I last talked
with her, something over a year ago. Her mind is not only un-
impaired, but she exhibits the same clearness, alertness, strength,
and vigor which have so long distinguished her.*[40]

Corning, both in his Associated Press statement and in a more
extended interview with the *Boston Herald* the next day, spoke
frankly. He had seen Mrs. Eddy in her carriage scores of times but
had never before talked with her in her home:

*I had gone expecting to find a tottering old woman, perhaps
incoherent, almost senile. Instead, when she rose to greet me, her
carriage was almost erect, her walk that of a woman of forty. I
have seen many old ladies, but never one with the vigorous personality of Mrs. Mary Baker G. Eddy. . . .*

*She remembered local incidents and happenings of recent
date, talked family matters with General Streeter, and to try her
mind he asked her concerning the date of her donation of one
thousand dollars annually to the State fair. She remembered within
a few days when the agreement was drawn up two years ago. To
say that she is mentally vigorous is inside the mark. She is wonderful for an octogenarian. Her face is not full, her figure is slight,
but she looks commanding, her eyes are bright, her handclasp is
firm. We talked with her for half an hour, and at the end of that
time, when she rose to bid us good-by, Mrs. Eddy showed no sign
of fatigue.*[41]

Other prominent citizens who had had personal dealings with
Mrs. Eddy for many years, and who received a bow, a smile, and sometimes a few words from her as she passed them on her daily drive came
forward with similar public statements.[42] The issue was clear. Either
the whole of Concord was engaged in a massive cover-up, as the *World*
itself maintained, or else Pulitzer's men had fallen into the trap common to crusading journalists and doctrinaire reformers of making the
evidence fit the hypothesized crime.

From the perspective of today and with the evidence of Mrs. Eddy's
remaining years,[43] it is apparent that the *World* was fantastically off
course. Only a few days before its attack was launched, the Roman
Catholic editor of the *Concord Patriot* had written a personal letter to
Joseph Pulitzer warning that he was being badly misled by the reports
of his determined representatives in Concord—a letter which, as Bates

and Dittemore remark, would have saved that aging gentleman much "fruitless trouble" if he had heeded it.[44] But neither Pulitzer nor the general public knew at that time what the realities of life for the secluded household at Pleasant View might be.

There was plenty of testimony from those who knew Mrs. Eddy, but, naturally enough, nothing would satisfy the reporters flocking into town but an interview with the eighty-five-year-old leader herself. With the help of Alfred Farlow and Cornell Wilson, who had come to Concord, a brief interview was arranged for Tuesday, October 30, at ten to one, just before Mrs. Eddy left for her drive. It was to be confined to the representatives of fourteen leading newspapers and press associations, and it was agreed that she should answer four crucial questions which would be put to her by Sibyl Wilbur O'Brien of the Boston *Herald*.

The publication of the *World* attack two days before had rallied Mrs. Eddy's energies, rather than depressing her. Frye wrote in his diary on Monday, "This morning Mrs. Eddy was in unusually happy spirits when she talked with [the household],"[45] and Strang wrote Hering that she was "in splendid shape," adding that he had "rarely seen her more active and alert since I have been here."[46]

Yet the Tuesday interview was an ordeal. The *World* was not to be represented this time, but "the world"—with all its skepticism, curiosity, incomprehension, hostility—waited for her in the ground-floor drawing room of Pleasant View as she made her way slowly down the stairs, dressed for her drive. She paused for a moment at the drawn portieres—knowing as she later told Laura Sargent, that the Christ went in before her—but when she parted the curtains and stood there for a minute, clinging to them, she visibly shrank from the impact of the scene, and her hands unmistakably shook.

Her replies to the questions put to her by Mrs. O'Brien (or Miss Wilbur, as she was increasingly to be known professionally) were brief. To the first—"Are you in perfect bodily health?"—she answered, "Indeed I am." To the second—"Have you any other physician than God?"—she replied, stepping forward and opening her arms in a sweeping gesture: "No physician but God. His everlasting arms are around me, and that is enough." To the third question—"Do you take a daily drive?"—she gave a simple yes, then turned away to *take* her daily drive. As a result, the fourth question—"Does anyone besides yourself administer your property or attend to your business affairs?" —never got asked.

It has been popular to quote a passage by Fleta Campbell Springer from an otherwise unremarkable biography of Mrs. Eddy to show the diverse reaction of the reporters present at Pleasant View that day. There might have been as many Mrs. Eddys as there were reporters, wrote Mrs. Springer, and then she proceeded to make a loaded but illuminating selection of excerpts from the reports of the interview:

[Mrs. Eddy] "bowed low and with ceremonial precision, reminding one of the entrance of a great diva before an audience made up of fashion and wealth"; "shaking and trembling, she tottered forward, clutching the curtains with palsied hands and paused swaying in the door"; "her eyes, large, dark and lustrous, sought out Mrs. O'Brien, whom she greeted with a smile"; "her faded, lusterless eyes roamed vacantly in space above the heads of the crowd"; "her feebleness seemed only consistent with her great age"; "she stood before them shaking with palsy, a physical wreck, tottering, pallid like a vision from beyond the grave"; "she stood before them erect and upright, nerved for the ordeal"; she wore a black cloak; she wore a cape of white ermine...."[47]

And so on. Mrs. Eddy's own summing up may best be represented by a comment she made in a letter to Annie Knott a week or two later: "Evil is venting itself, and when found out will have done with itself what needs to be done." To which she added the prescription which seemed to her the ethical, metaphysical, and Christian remedy for all the sad phantasmagoria of human life: "Returning good for evil makes good real and evil unreal."[48]

3

The hunt was on. Although the press of the country tended editorially to regard the two interviews as a rather shameful invasion of an aged woman's privacy,[49] the diversity of the reports left enough of a question in public thought to encourage further exploitation of the subject.

On November 4 and 5 the *World* published a caustic two-part article, "How Rev. Wiggin Rewrote Mrs. Eddy's Book," which its author, Livingston Wright, had written from his alleged recollection of Wiggin's confidences before that gentleman's demise six years earlier.[50] Subsequently a measured refutation by Farlow appeared in the *New York American,* whereupon Mrs. Eddy wrote a correction of the refutation which showed that she had lost none of her mental vigor. The opening combined tartness with precision:

Mr. Alfred Farlow's flimsy article in the New York American needs correction. It was a great mistake to say that I employed the Rev. James Henry Wiggin to correct my diction. It was for no such purpose. I engaged Mr. Wiggin so as to avail myself of his criticisms of my statement of Christian Science, which criticisms would enable me to explain more clearly the points that might seem ambiguous to the reader. . . .[51]

Farlow, taken somewhat aback, wrote her gallantly:

The affair may reflect on my reputation for being able to state facts about our beloved Leader, but that is more than compensated by the fact that this letter emphatically shows who is conducting the Christian Science church.[52]

The months that followed were filled with a profusion of polemic articles, pamphlets, books, directed against Christian Science and Mrs. Eddy; and with this gleeful eruption of ill will Harper and Brothers, who for several years had refused to publish Mark Twain's *North American* articles in book form, decided that the atmosphere was now propitious for his bristling extravaganza to appear under their respected auspices.[53]

But first came the *McClure's* series, which commenced with an article in the December, 1906, issue of that crusading journal—an article illustrated by a full-page picture of Mrs. Eddy which turned out to be, in actuality, a photograph of a Mrs. Sarah C. Chevaillier, mother of an 1885 student of Mrs. Eddy's. Farlow, after seeing the picture in *McClure's* advance publicity, wrote them they were making a mistake, but his warning was disregarded and the picture ran with the introduction to the series, while a genuine autograph of Mrs. Eddy under the photograph gave the impression that she had signed it. Later the magazine received letters from a number of people who had known Mrs. Chevaillier[54] expressing astonishment at the mistake, which was a little too symbolic for editorial comfort in a journal that claimed to provide scrupulous documentation for its biographical bombshells.

Various readers who were not Christian Scientists found other flaws in the series' pretensions to unimpeachable accuracy. One man writing in about a sentence in the very first paragraph of the history which read, "Her ancestors, for more than two hundred years, had lived on the New Hampshire hills," noted dryly that since Mrs. Eddy's birth date was 1821 her ancestors "must have been Indians."[55] Another reader commenting on the same installment wrote the editors:

I am not a Christian Scientist, and I cannot say with them "there is no error"; for surely there is one error in the Baker story, and a strong enough one to make me discredit almost any of the balance; and this is the story of Mark Baker mistaking Sunday. . . . Had Mark Baker been living by himself, the mistake might have occurred; but no pious New England housewife and her six children were so devoid of memories as not to have remembered that Saturday's baking day was followed by Sunday.[56]

There were other considerations, however, of more importance than such small slips and implausibilities. The leading German church historian of the early twentieth century, Karl Holl, defined one of these when he described the Milmine biography as "a collection of accusations," and added, "Despite the verifications adduced, most of the statements are readily recognizable as gossip or slander."[57] Miss Milmine herself confessed to some misgivings on this score when she wrote a fellow critic of Mrs. Eddy that the witnesses she and her colleagues quoted were not in every instance "the kind of sources we would have chosen."[58]

A case in point was the lurid story sworn to by Horace Wentworth of Stoughton, Massachusetts, and presented as sober history by the *McClure's* writers and numerous subsequent critics. According to Wentworth, when Mrs. Eddy left the home of his parents in 1870, she departed without notice while they were away from the house, after maliciously slashing the matting and featherbed in her room to pieces and placing live coals on a pile of newspapers in her closet with intent to burn down the house.[59]

The story was later branded false and preposterous by Horace's brother Charles, who had been living as a seventeen-year-old boy with his parents (as Horace was not) when the alleged episode was supposed to have taken place, and their younger sister Lucy described the affectionate parting she had with Mrs. Eddy on the day in question.[60] Although Horace was known as an opinionated and cynical scoffer in his native town, while Charles and Lucy were popularly regarded as honest, good-natured citizens with no ax to grind, *McClure's* collected only such allegations as would support its case.[61] A letter from Horace to S. S. McClure on December 19, 1906, further suggests that his memory may have been helped along a little by both financial and ideological considerations:

Yours of the 17th received. Thank you very much for the check. It came in the right time. I have had bad luck, and it seems like a Christmas present. Shall be glad to assist you what I can, in this work of exposing Eddyism.[62]

After seeing the first article dealing with her family background and early life, Mrs. Eddy wrote Farlow, "What you send me from McClure's Magazine is too much of lies to have given a thought to."[63] Two days later, more deeply disturbed, she wrote him: "Do not reply to this last brutal abuse till the abusers bring out their next threatened article. Then answer both in one article from the Committee."[64] In another three days she had changed her mind again and determined to write a reply of her own for Farlow to circulate.[65]

It was the first and last answer she would give to McClure's. But before she had done with the matter, one final brief flare of hurt and indignation had led her to an impulsive step. When her favorite magazine, the *Literary Digest*, favorably publicized the *McClure's* series, she wrote the Directors that they should insert a request in the church's periodicals that every Christian Scientist who had subscribed to either the *Literary Digest* or *McClure's* discontinue his subscription.

A few days later the Directors answered her letter. They had conferred with Farlow, they wrote, concerning her request and he had stated "that in his opinion it would not be the best thing to do as it might appear to the public to be a boycott of these magazines, and also many others which have advertised McClure's article, and in that way might secure public sympathy for McClure's."[66] The Directors added that they tended to agree with him, and Mrs. Eddy returned their letter with a handwritten note on it:

Beloved Board
I agree with Mr. Farlow and with you that some other means would be better.
Lovingly
Mary B. G. Eddy[67]

During this time, however, her chief energies were given to her Christian Science work. Within two hours of the formidable group interview at Pleasant View, she had a conference with Archibald McLellan on church business,[68] and a steady stream of articles and notices from her continued to appear in the church periodicals. For some time she had been privately gathering and sifting material having to do with the building and dedication of the extension of The Mother Church, together with her articles, addresses, letters, and messages since the compilation of *Miscellaneous Writings* ten years before—all of which was to form the nucleus of her posthumous publication, *The First Church of Christ, Scientist, and Miscellany.*[69]

Through the fall of 1906 and early part of 1907, she gave much time to her last major revision of *Science and Health,* a revision which resulted in innumerable refinements though few large changes. In the preface she revealed that until June, 1907, she had never read through the book consecutively in order to "elucidate her idealism,"[70] though in point of fact she studied it piecemeal almost daily. "To-day," she also wrote of herself in the preface, "though rejoicing in some progress, she still finds herself a willing disciple at the heavenly gate, waiting for the Mind of Christ."[71] And she concluded an article for *The Independent* in November, 1906, with the characteristic comment:

> When I wrote "Science and Health with Key to the Scriptures," I little understood all that I indited; but when I practised its precepts, healing the sick and reforming the sinner, then I learned the truth of what I had written. It is of comparatively little importance what a man thinks or believes he knows; the good that a man does is the one thing needful and sole proof of rightness.[72]

During this period she also had the comfort of receiving many statements of faith and support from both old and new friends who were not Christian Scientists.[73] Among them was her Unitarian friend and ex-critic, Reverend F. L. Phalen, who declared in a sermon toward the end of 1906:

> The assailants of Christian Science reveal their own ignorance, their own wicked hearts, their absolute denial of Jesus Christ. I know Mrs. Eddy, and I do not know one single fact against . . . her purity, honesty, and spirituality. . . . Now let me conclude by saying that when we all become as devoted, as gentle, as earnest, as successful, in our different churches as our Christian Science friends are in their churches, it will then be time to say their religion is a dream.[74]

This contrasted strikingly with the words of an earnest Episcopal rector, Lyman P. Powell, who wrote in a privately printed pamphlet entitled *The Anarchy of Christian Science:*

> Truth can care for itself. . . . But there are in every church good people . . . who have had little or no training in philosophy or science, though sometimes widely read in current literature . . . and the only way to have a care of them is for every minister to make a serious study of Christian Science and thus armed fight it to the death, by public and by private word.[75]

Living up to his own recommendation, Powell published in 1907 a scorching book, *Christian Science: The Faith and its Founder,*[76] which reported that his own extensive researches corroborated the Milmine findings at every point, whereas he found no satisfaction in the parallel but contrasting series of biographical articles by Sibyl Wilbur which were now appearing in an obscure magazine called *Human Life*. On the other hand he stated honestly that he stood ready to revise his book if new evidence should come to light at any time to make revision necessary in the interest of truth.

By one of the many ironies attending Mrs. Eddy's history, Powell was finally to emerge as one of her outstanding champions. Pursuing his own investigation through another two decades, and following leads not provided by the Peabody-Milmine-*World* axis, he came gradually to a reversal of his earlier attitude to Christian Science and its founder,[77] and his 1930 book, *Mary Baker Eddy, a Life Size Portrait,* would for many years be found in Christian Science Reading Rooms next to the Wilbur *Life of Mary Baker Eddy.*[78]

There were anomalies, also, in Miss Wilbur's launching of her *Human Life* series, the half-processed material of her later biography. At the time of her marriage into the Irish O'Briens, she had become a convert—though a lukewarm one—to Roman Catholicism.[79] The overwhelming impression made on her by Mrs. Eddy at their first interview seems to have been a far more vivid religious experience than any she had undergone previously—though more than a whiff of incense remains detectable in her continuing inclination toward hagiography. With all the ardor of a Georgine Milmine but with a very different objective, she now threw herself into the task of gathering fresh evidence. In a letter to Mrs. Eddy on May 22, 1907, she wrote:

> It is a remarkable experience which I am passing through, following in your footsteps, observing the impressions which your acts made upon others and their acts upon your life. . . . I don't know how it is done. I don't know what force or power accomplishes it, but every one of your so-called enemies receives me, answers my questions, and in some way confuses himself in his own falsehoods, or, with amazing frankness, tells the truth. Of these witnesses there are those who have sworn to other statements, and when I have addressed them on certain matters they have allowed the truth to escape, as it were, inadvertently. . . .
> "Atonement and Eucharist" and "Footsteps of Truth" and "Pond and Purpose" were not written by the woman painted in dyes of deception with a brain teeming with worldly design. It is my

intent and desire to make the whole world outside your church realize this.[80]

If Mrs. Eddy's history was strewn with charges, countercharges, voltes-faces, ambivalences, paradoxes, and contradictory evidences, there was something to be said for looking to her writings for the clue to the conundrum.

4

On January 1, 1907, one Ernest Gosselin signed an affidavit which was *not* published in either the *World* or *McClure's*:

> *I, Ernest Gosselin of Amesbury, Mass., a Licensed Chauffeur of Massachusetts, do hereby certify that on Nov. 2 and 3, 1906, three men came to me, whom I afterwards learned to be detectives for the New York World, and tried to have me say that I had taken Dr. Herman Cooper, of this Town, to some place for the purpose of performing an operation on Mrs. Mary Baker G. Eddy. Failing in their purpose on both these occasions, they came again on Nov. 4, 1906 and said if I would take them to the same place that I had taken Dr. Cooper, in an automobile at midnight, to perform said operation on Mrs. Eddy, that money would be no object to them, that they would pay me any amount I would name for my time and labor. And I hereby certify that, as I did not take Dr. Cooper on any such errand, said proposition was refused.*[81]

This abortive attempt to procure false evidence took place only a few days after the inconclusive group interview at Pleasant View, and a short time later James Slaght of the *World* was dispatched to Lead, South Dakota, to enlist the help of Mrs. Eddy's son, George Glover. Obviously a new campaign was already under way, and the potential value of an "estranged" son was not to be overlooked.

When Glover had brought his youngest son, four-year-old Georgie, to visit Mrs. Eddy in 1893, the visit had been all sunshine and flowers. Six years later, in the midst of the Woodbury trial, Mrs. Eddy had presented the Glovers with a handsome mansion in Lead, and had arranged for three of the children to go to St. Joseph, Missouri, to be educated under the care of one of her students, Charles M. Howe.[82] The educational experiment had turned out as unsuccessfully as George's perpetual mining ventures, and the Glovers rattled around in their oversized house with sometimes insufficient funds to keep it properly lighted and heated.

Constant appeals to Mrs. Eddy for money met with something

less than the unlimited indulgence of a doting mother. And when George and his twenty-five-year-old daughter Mary made an unannounced visit to Pleasant View in March, 1903, they were welcomed affectionately but Mrs. Eddy made it clear that she must ration carefully the time she gave them.

Always in the background, it seemed to Glover, was Calvin Frye, whom he suspected—probably with some justification[83]—of keeping from her some of his letters. Here lay the seed of his readiness to be convinced later that Frye was a villain manipulating Mrs. Eddy's person and property to his own advantage, and already in 1903 this incipient suspicion elicited from Mrs. Eddy a letter telling him that Frye was a *real* Christian Scientist:

> [*He*] *does not own a cent of my property, real estate or personal. . . . I have given you a far better house than I occupy myself. I have given you money when you asked for it—thousands of dollars. What have you ever done for your mother? And now you have disgraced yourself by what you said so falsely of her home, your* mother's *home! where you should naturally be with her in her declining years. I have always tried to make my people respect you, and is this your return for it?*[84]

Despite their differences of outlook Glover remained intensely loyal to Mrs. Eddy, as Slaght soon discovered.[85] It was clear that if the simple-hearted and in some ways simple-minded miner was to play the part designed for him by the *World*, he must be thoroughly convinced of Mrs. Eddy's senile helplessness in the clutch of a power-hungry group of men from whom she needed to be rescued by legal action.

The *World* itself later put the matter nicely. Shortly after the paper's initial charge that Mrs. Eddy was "dying" had, to its annoyance, been "clouded in doubt" by "men of solid reputation and prominence" who were somehow "induced" to make public statements in defense of the Christian Science leader and her associates, a group of "public-spirited citizens" had decided that "legal proceedings of the most dignified character were vitally necessary to establish the truth."[86]

These same anonymous public-spirited citizens (easily identifiable today as the publisher and editors of the *World*) then selected and hired ex-Senator William E. Chandler, New Hampshire's most highly placed critic of Mrs. Eddy,[87] to direct the proposed legal proceedings. The plan was to "rescue" her from her church officers and close associates by proving the *World's* contention that she was totally incompetent to manage her own affairs. Now, all that remained to be done was to find a nominal plaintiff. Hence Slaght's visit to Lead, described by the *World* as a "mission of placing before Glover his legal opportunity."[88]

"The prospect of engaging Glover's assistance was not encouraging," the *World* complained, but the bewildered Dakotan was soon persuaded that his mother's welfare and his own financial gain would coincide in the course of action proposed by these flatteringly important and solicitous new friends from the East. The plan was set forth in a letter from Chandler which Slaght brought with him to show Glover:

> *Washington, D.C.*
> *Nov. 22, 1906*
>
> My Dear Mr. Slaght:
>
> *I consent to act as counsel concerning certain questions which arise in connection with Mrs. Mary Baker G. Eddy. It seems clear that there is serious doubt about several points.*
>
> *1. Mrs. Eddy may be detained in the custody of strangers against her will.*
>
> *2. She may be so nearly worn out in body and mind, as a confirmed invalid, that she is incapable of deciding any question whatever according to any will or pleasure of her own, and necessarily, therefore, incapable of managing her business and property affairs.*
>
> *3. Being thus restrained or incapable, and without relatives near her, she may be surrounded by designing men, who either have already sought or may hereafter seek to wrongfully possess themselves of her large property, or induce her to make a disposition of it contrary to what would be her sane and deliberate intentions if she were in perfect possession of her liberty and mental faculties.*
>
> *These doubts have arisen in connection with investigations recently made. Beyond all question, steps should be taken to solve the doubts; to correct wrong, if it exists, and to establish the right in every respect.*
>
> *This new work should be done, if possible in co-operation with Mrs. Eddy's son, or any other relative who may be impressed by his duties in this regard; and if the relatives do not move, it should be done by such right-minded citizens as are in sympathy with the commendable movement.*
>
> *Yours truly,*
> *William E. Chandler*[89]

Before long, Glover was in Chandler's pocket. He and his daughter Mary were brought to Washington, where Chandler practiced law intermittently, and were provided with ample money for a lengthy stay. The lawyer quickly drafted a letter for Glover to send to Mrs. Eddy announcing his desire to visit her with young Mary, and the two of them were carefully briefed on the total debility they might expect to find in the old lady.

Not surprisingly, when the visit was arranged for January 2, 1907, and the two Glovers talked with her for an hour, they saw and found exactly what they expected, even to a buzzing which they attributed to the mythical galvanic battery for which Slaght had prepared them.[90] By the time that same imaginative gentleman had written up the visit for both Glovers to sign, it had much of the Gothic horror of his original interview in the *World,* but it was withheld from publication until the psychological moment should arrive two months later.

Mrs. Eddy may well have shown some agitation in her talk with her son and granddaughter. The second *McClure's* article had just appeared, the household was perturbed by the continuing press attacks, and the induced suspicion and intrigue that had brought her two visitors there could hardly have failed to make itself felt. If so, corroboration arrived five days later in the shape of a letter from one James P. Wilson of Denver, Colorado, a man barely known to Mrs. Eddy and not a Christian Scientist:

> *After reading the McClure article and your reply I take the liberty of addressing this letter to you. I think I see breakers ahead.*
>
> *You perhaps remember me as the atty [attorney] for your son George. I came here three years ago and since then have not been your son's adviser, and we closed our business relations, but we are still very friendly and I think much of him as he has many attributes that command respect. He does not know I'm writing this and has made no request of me to write you, but I write you believing I am doing the proper thing.*
>
> *Your son, Mr. Glover, has many letters from you in his possession—he has kept a copy of all letters written you and has all your replies.*
>
> *You should have all those or many of those letters returned— I need not tell you why but there is a reason why. You are making history—you need some of those letters.*
>
> *Your son is in want, his family is in want, unless you have*

done something for him lately. You built him a fine home—but he had no money to maintain it. You have done much for him but we can't count the cost in dealing with our children. I need not tell you George has made mistakes—my boys make mistakes, but I do want you to meet George and adjust all differences and you to get back many of your letters.

Your son usually followed my advise—when he did he made no mistakes. He sometimes did not take my advise and made some costly mistakes, but I think he will listen to me.

Your work should not be interfered with and no misunderstanding SHOULD ARISE IN THE FUTURE over matters which you can adjust now.

If this is worthy of attention I am pleased to be of some service to you, if not, you can consign this to the waste basket.[91]

Mrs. Eddy knew that in some of her letters to George she had written with a frankness about her own affairs and his which would not be understood if the letters were made public. Now she made immediate efforts through Tomlinson and Farlow to retrieve them from Glover, who first promised to return them but, upon advice of counsel, placed them instead in Chandler's keeping. Even the trust fund for $125,000 which she drew up for Glover and his family, to become operative as soon as the letters were returned, failed to change the purpose of his new advisors, who were aiming at another target altogether.

As it became evident that a greater attack than ever before was building up, Mrs. Eddy wrote Kimball, "To be honest and wise is the acme of Christian Scientists' attainment at this period; I pray importunately for wisdom."[92] That she maintained a measure of equanimity through a period of considerable stress is indicated by the correspondence and reminiscences of that period. Three years earlier young Calvin Hill, after one of his frequent visits to Pleasant View, had written her that the "calm assurance that *God, good* is the *only power,* which I have always seen in you from my first visit, has given me renewed strength and confidence that honesty, fidelity and truth lived, must, will ultimately triumph."[93] Now, on February 21, he wrote her that her last talk with him a few days before had brought him an instantaneous healing of an unnamed difficulty.[94] The woman who could bring this sort of assurance to her helpers was evidently not the terror-stricken Mrs. Eddy which the *World* was again to hold out to the public nine days later.

Through much of February the real Mrs. Eddy had been giving

thought to the creation of a trust to which she could transfer her property, thus divesting herself of the burden of managing her large estate. She considered at least one other plan[95] before settling on the appointment of three trustees—her lawyer cousin General Baker, her banker friend Josiah Fernald, and her leading church officer Archibald McLellan—to whom on March 6 she deeded all her property for their management and disposition subject to the terms of the trust deed.[96]

This decisive action was speeded up, however, by the events which had taken place five days before.

On March 1, Mrs. Eddy had summoned General Baker to Pleasant View, showed him a letter she had just received from George Glover in Washington virtually accusing her of not being competent to conduct her own affairs, and asked him what he thought of it. "George could not write that letter," she stated emphatically, adding that it was "written by an educated man who was skilled in the use of language."[97] Baker replied that it clearly portended some legal action and she would have to await the event.

She did not have to wait long. On the same day a bill in equity was filed in the Superior Court for the county of Merrimack (N. H.) in the name of Mary Baker Glover Eddy by her "next friends," George W. Glover, his daughter Mary Baker Glover, and his cousin George W. Baker[98] against Calvin A. Frye, Alfred Farlow, Irving C. Tomlinson, Ira O. Knapp, William B. Johnson, Stephen A. Chase, Joseph Armstrong, Edward A. Kimball, Hermann S. Hering, and Lewis C. Strang. It was the beginning of what was to prove one of the most bizarre cases in American legal history—and in the history of religious intolerance in the New World.

The *World* once again blazed out with sensational headlines the next day, plus pages of background story which—read with a sufficiently perceptive eye—could have given away the crucial role played by the paper itself in initiating and financing the suit:

RELATIVES SUE TO WREST MOTHER EDDY'S FORTUNE FROM CONTROL OF CLIQUE

Bill in Equity Filed at Concord by Only Son of the Founder of Christian Science, His Daughter and a Nephew—It Alleges That the Enormous Income of Mary Baker Eddy is Wrongfully Withheld from Proper Management—Plaintiffs Declare Her Helpless in the Hands of Calvin Frye, Alfred Farlow and Other Leaders.

*Mrs. Eddy Herself Appears
As Petitioner; Through Others*

Ask for Receiver for Entire Property and for Restitution in Case Funds Have Been Illegally Disposed of—Earnings of More Than a Million from the Boston College and of Vast Sums from Periodicals of the Cult Are Involved—Ex-Senator William E. Chandler Senior Counsel for Petitioners.

Ten days later Ebenezer Foster Eddy and a second obscure Baker cousin[99] joined in the suit with the other "next friends." And once again the *World* acted as procurer.

During the Woodbury trial six years before, Foster Eddy had written Mrs. Eddy with protestations of his "persistent, unswerving loyalty" to her, adding the gratuitous advice: "Be careful, dear One! you are surrounded by vipers! shake them off and put your whole trust in God!"[100] After reading the *World's* opening salvo in the sensational new suit, he quickly wrote Mrs. Sargent that he was wholly out of sympathy with this "diabolical" action against Mrs. Eddy. "I believe her perfect demonstration will be of more value to the world," he added piously, "than all the money in it."[101]

Two or three days later the indefatigable James Slaght arrived at Foster Eddy's Vermont home and in the twinkling of an eye metamorphosed the latter's attitude into a zeal which promised more to both his pocketbook and his wounded pride. Less than a week after writing Mrs. Sargent, the volatile ex-son had been enrolled by Slaght and Chandler in their crusade to save Mrs. Eddy from harm by proving her to be a mental incompetent.

It is clear now, and should have been clear then to any levelheaded observer, that in some degree the *World*, Chandler, and the so-called next friends were all victims of the myth which the newspaper itself had created four months earlier. As Fred N. Ladd, Mrs. Eddy's banker, pointed out, not one of the ten defendants except Frye had anything to do with the management or disposition of any of Mrs. Eddy's property.[102] When the highly reputable accounting firm of Harvey Chase and Company of Boston made a special audit of her books for the fourteen-year period preceding March 6, 1907, they found that Frye had made "all kinds and classes of clerical errors," but the net amount of these errors amounted to $677.41 *against himself,* from which they concluded that he was "an honest agent for Mrs. Eddy although mathematically a poor accountant."[103] Furthermore, it was found that Mrs. Eddy's cash funds and securities amounted to slightly less than a million dollars instead of the fabulous wealth attributed to her by the *World.*[104]

On the face of it, the case was so weak as to be frivolous. There was not a shred of evidence to show that Mrs. Eddy was incompetent to manage her own financial affairs or to choose three responsible trustees to manage them for her. The "next friends" nominally acting on her behalf were, from the start, being financed and stage-managed by a group of men committed to the view that she was a fanatic, a fraud, and a fool. If there was indeed a conspiracy to rob her of her freedom, then the prosecutors needed scrutinizing quite as carefully as the defendants.

5

Frederick Peabody, by now a long-established and increasingly rancorous baiter of Mrs. Eddy, had joined Chandler as junior counsel for the plaintiffs and was drawing to their aid some of the disaffected students who had helped him in the Woodbury case.

Prominent among these was William G. Nixon, Mrs. Eddy's publisher of fifteen years previous, who had now left his wife for a certain Laura May Fullmer of Philadelphia and was desperate for money. Peabody, he wrote Mrs. Fullmer on March 9, had offered him a chance "to make some money with the people he is working for and with in the anti-Eddy litigation"[105]—an interesting characterization of the suit, which showed who was the real target. Soon his letters were peppered with references to "the Senator" and such elegant sentiments as: "I must make some dollars and the place where it seems most easy and likely is my meat." When Chandler was to meet Mrs. Fullmer herself, Nixon wrote her that he trusted the Senator would listen to her "with some measure of the interest and snap he is manifesting in the present case which has developed [into] a real picnic for him and will bring him some additional prestige if he wins."[106]

It was no picnic for Mrs. Eddy, who saw in it a climactic attempt to discredit her whole lifework. The case had once more brought together a battery of eminent lawyers for the defense, among them General Streeter, Allen Hollis, and Edwin Eastman (Attorney General for New Hampshire) as her personal counsel, Samuel Elder as senior counsel for the Massachusetts defendants, and other experienced attorneys like General Baker and Archibald McLellan who were indirectly involved in the proceedings. Again, as in the Woodbury suit, Mrs. Eddy withstood them all on the strategy to be followed—and again her judgment was proved right by later events.[107] What was really under fire, she saw, was not merely her liberty of action but the existence of her church.

At a May 23 hearing on a preliminary motion of Mrs. Eddy's trustees to intervene and be substituted for the alleged "next friends," Chandler based his opposition to the motion on "the incompetency of this aged, palsied woman" to appoint trustees or do anything else of her own free will. "The poor woman is crazy," he announced categorically, adding that the defendants (Frye et al.) were "prepared to inflict any torture on Mrs. Eddy to make her do what they want." As to the trustees, he submitted with sardonic magnanimity that they were "the three most capable trustees to take care of a lunatic that ever were."[108] The motion was denied.

To counteract this sort of burlesque, Mrs. Eddy granted three interviews during the month of June to three outstanding newspapermen.

Arthur Brisbane, then editor of the *New York Evening Journal*, spent an afternoon with her and summed up his detailed account of her appearance and conversation in a single sentence: "It is quite certain that nobody could see this beautiful and venerable woman and ever again speak of her except in terms of affectionate reverence and sympathy."[109]

Edwin J. Park of the *Boston Globe* hopped from subject to subject in his discussion with her, in an effort to test her mental agility, and wrote in his lengthy account:

> *It is true that Mrs. Eddy is not robust physically, and that her hearing is not acute, but her brain is keen and active, and there never is a moment of hesitation in replying to a question nor delay in framing the phraseology in which she answers. The trend of her thoughts remains unbroken, and her alert mind turns instantly from one line of suggested thought to another one put forward to take its place.*[110]

William E. Curtis of the *Chicago Record-Herald* wrote, "I have never seen a woman eighty-six years of age with greater physical or mental vigor," then added:

> *Every one who has come to Concord impressed with the belief that there was some reason or justification for the lawsuit instituted by the so-called "next friends," and who has had opportunities to talk with this remarkable woman, has gone away with the well-defined conviction that among sane people Mrs. Eddy is one of the most sane, that among responsible people she is one of the most responsible, and that among competent and successful business men and women she is one of the most competent and most successful.*[111]

On June 27, one day before Curtis had his interview, Judge Robert N. Chamberlin of the Superior Court appointed Judge Edgar Aldrich as Master of the court to determine Mrs. Eddy's competence "to intelligently manage, control, and conduct her financial affairs and property rights" as of March 1, 1907. Shortly afterward, two co-Masters were appointed to serve with Aldrich: Dr. George F. Jelly, a Boston alienist, and Hosea W. Parker, a New Hampshire attorney.[112]

After more delays, the first hearing before the Masters was held on August 13, and Chandler in his opening speech at last made clear the purpose that lay behind the suit. He was in effect asking the court to find that Christian Science itself was evidence of insane delusion:

> *Mrs. Eddy's book alone is proof that she is suffering from the following systematized delusions and dementia:*
>
> *The first one is the delusion . . . of the non-existence and non-reality of the physical universe, organic and inorganic. All her delusions are built upon this fundamental delusion. . . .*
>
> *The second delusion is that of the supernatural character of the Science she calls her own. . . . She believes as an insane delusion that she was miraculously and supernaturally selected by Almighty God to receive divine revelations. . . .*
>
> *Third, she has been possessed all these years of a delusion as to the cause of all the diseases of mankind; . . . as to the cure of disease; . . . as to the prevention of disease. . . .*
>
> *Fourth—the delusion of the relation of the Science she calls her own to philosophy and Christianity. . . .*
>
> *Fifth—the delusion as to the existence of animal magnetism or malicious animal magnetism. This insane systematized delusion . . . involves the idea of persecution and diabolism. . . .*
>
> *Sixth—the delusion as to the operation of alleged malicious animal magnetism in . . . producing all manner of evil; of poisoning mankind; of producing death itself. . . .*
>
> *These delusions of hers include two well-known systematized delusions—the delusion of grandeur and the delusion of persecution.*

The irony of including these last two evidences of paranoia escaped Chandler.

The "delusion" of grandeur had been charged against every troublesome challenger of religious orthodoxy from the Hebrew prophets and Jesus to Roger Williams and Anne Hutchinson. But it might be considered a more indubitable evidence of such delusion for a

lawyer-politician—the conventional product of a particular culture—
to suppose himself competent to settle in a New Hampshire courtroom
the great metaphysical questions of the ages: the ultimate nature of
reality; the origin of life; the problem of evil; the relation of reason
to revelation, of the empirical to the transcendent, of matter to spirit,
of body to mind; the limits of knowledge; the validity of prayer; the
ambiguity of language; the subjectivity of belief.[113]

Arthur Brisbane, who was no more of a "thinker" than Chandler,
nevertheless showed a more rough-and-ready common sense in his
article in the August *Cosmopolitan*:

> *The Turkish minister of Washington, if any court asked
> him, would say he firmly believes that Mohammed rode up to
> see God on a galloway named Al Borak, that the intelligent Al
> Borak bucked and pranced until Mohammed promised him a
> seat in paradise, that Mohammed studied an interesting angel
> with seventy thousand heads, "in each head seventy thousand
> tongues, and each tongue uttered seventy thousand distinct voices
> at once."* . . .
>
> *The Turkish minister might testify to these things without
> being adjudged insane. He has a right to believe in his religion.
> The ordinary American, not a Christian Scientist, believes that
> God has so arranged matters that great numbers of His children
> will be burned for ever and ever in hell fire. Mrs. Eddy believes
> God has so arranged matters that humanity can cure itself of
> imagined evils, and escape from all suffering, pain, and "error"
> through Christian Science teachings.*
>
> *If the law would refuse to take away the liberty or the prop-
> erty of Christian old ladies because they believe that millions of
> human beings have been damned from all eternity, it is hard to
> understand why that law should take away the liberty or the
> money of Mrs. Eddy because she chooses to believe that eventually
> nobody will be damned at all.*[114]

As to the delusion of persecution from which Mrs. Eddy was said
to suffer, a good many sympathizers at the time asked how it was
possible that a man of Chandler's intelligence could labor under the
fixed delusion that she was *not* being persecuted. And did not this
naked attempt through the courts to have Christian Science labeled
an insane delusion show a purpose, they asked, that reached beyond
Mrs. Eddy's discomfiture to the destruction of her church? Was this
kind of camouflaged attack, perhaps, an example of what she meant

by malicious animal magnetism?[115] Some of those who had been influenced by the earlier *World* attacks were beginning to wonder. Confirmation followed from Dr. Allan McLane Hamilton, a leading alienist of the day,[116] who in 1901 had testified against Christian Science in a New York court case.[117] In spite of this, his professional distinction and reputation for outspoken honesty were such that Streeter recommended that he be employed to make a thorough examination of Mrs. Eddy's mental condition and the facts in the case in order that the counsel for the defense should have the benefit of his expert opinion.[118]

Hamilton's reports both public and private, after a month's investigation in Concord, tell a story which is summed up most simply in an interview he gave *The New York Times* at the conclusion of the case:

> *There really is no mystery about Mrs. Mary Baker G. Eddy. Her case is a perfectly simple one, and the sensational stories which have been disseminated about her have no foundation in fact—although they can be very easily traced to a spirit of religious persecution that at last quite overreached itself. . . .*
>
> *I must confess that I approached this conference with Mrs. Eddy in a decidedly prejudiced state of mind. I had read the current abuse of her that one finds in the magazines and newspapers, and from this reading had become imbued with a distinctly adverse feeling toward Christian Science and its chief exponent. But when I saw and talked with the latter, and read and analyzed her correspondence, I experienced a complete revulsion of feeling, and this to such an extent that I have now become candidly of the opinion that Mrs. Eddy is not only sincere in all she says and does, but I believe, also, that she unselfishly spends her money for the perpetuation of a church which, in her estimation, is destined to play an important part in the betterment of humanity—nor have I found that she is guilty of any extravagant indulgences such as one might look for were her motives less pure. . . .*
>
> *For a woman of her age I do not hesitate to say that she is physically and mentally phenomenal. In the matter of her longevity, some Christian Scientists have gone so far as to assert that she will never die. She herself, however, does not hold to any such ridiculous belief, but refers frequently to the life after death as a state of existence to which she is liable. I fancy that the belief among some of her followers involving the indefinite continuance*

*of her earthly life arises purely from the visible evidence of Mrs.
Eddy's great vitality and absence of any of the usual tokens of
mental breakdown natural to one of her great age.*

*There is certainly no sign yet of the coming of this break-
down. Nor can Mrs. Eddy's religious teachings, strange and unreasonable though they may be, be advanced as a pathological
evidence of mental debility. After all, her teachings are merely a
culmination, a crystallization, of similar systems that have been
cropping up during the last half century under the leadership of
such enthusiasts as Noyes, Cullis, Simpson, Boardman, and a score
of others who, influenced by certain phases of idealistic philosophy, have denied the reality of matter and disease. In this
country everyone is entitled to hold whatever religious belief he
or she may choose; and this being so, there seems to be a manifest
injustice in taxing so excellent and capable a woman as Mrs.
Eddy with any form of insanity.[119]*

The manifest injustice of the charge was shown up by Mrs. Eddy
herself on the second day of the Masters' hearing. At two o'clock in
the afternoon—in deference to her age and frailty but in the face of
bitter protest from Chandler—the Masters, accompanied only by Streeter, Chandler, and a court stenographer, moved from the courtroom
to Pleasant View to interrogate the Christian Science leader in her
library. As they listened to the bright, chatty, entirely lucid answers
and explanations of the erect little figure seated calmly before them,[120]
they could easily have wondered whether the dementia was not actually to be looked for in those who had instigated the suit.

The stenographic report of the hour-long interview speaks for
itself. After the Masters had greeted her and she had welcomed them,
Judge Aldrich began formally:

Q. What was your native town?
*A. Bow, in New Hampshire. My father's farm lies on the banks
of the Merrimack. He did much of his haying in Concord, but
it was in Bow the house was.*

Q. How long have you lived in Concord?
*A. About twenty years; between eighteen and twenty this time—
at this time, do you mean?—since I came here, after my marriage
and residence in Boston.*

Q. Well, the gentlemen present want to ask you some questions—
A. And I beg pardon, my only difficulty is a slight deafness. I can

> see to read common pica but I can't hear distinctly without
> some difficulty. . . .
>
> Q. If you feel fatigued, we want to have you speak of it and let us
> know.
> A. Thank you. I can work hours at my work, day and night, with-
> out fatigue when it is in this line of thought, but when I go to
> worldliness I am sometimes fatigued by it, and yet, these things
> are indispensable and I regard them as sacred.
>
> Q. Did you acquire all this property here at the outset, or did
> you acquire it gradually?
> A. I purchased it at the outset and suggested every construction
> and arrangement of my grounds throughout, and I still attend
> to it. . . . Every one of these trees around here [indicating]
> was planted by myself—that is, not by myself, but by my
> direction.[121]

Later they got to her investments, and she explained why she preferred municipal bonds chosen on the basis of population growth to the speculative uncertainties of the stock market, and why she had finally picked three honest men and true to relieve her of the whole "worldly" responsibility. This led in turn to a question from Dr. Jelly, the alienist, in regard to her religious views, and Mrs. Eddy happily embarked on the subject closest to her heart, including a brief reference to the difference between Christian Science and animal magnetism or mesmerism. She learned early, she told them,

> . . . that God did the healing, and I could no more heal a
> person by mortal mind or will-power, than by cutting off his head.
> I know not how to use will-power to hurt the sick.
> When they began to talk mesmerism first, I began to doubt it;
> and I said to a facetious student, "Hanover Smith, you go into the
> other room and see if I can sit down and tell lies enough to make
> you suffer." He went into the other room, and I commenced
> [arguing] what they said to make folks sick, and I did my best
> talking it and when he came in and I said, "Hanover, do you feel
> ill?" he said, "I never felt better in my life than I do now, I feel
> better than when I went in. I feel rested."
> A Christian Scientist can no more make a person sick than
> they can be a sinner and be a Christian Scientist . . . they have not
> the power to do it. All the power they have comes from on High.
> We have no other power and no faith in any other power.[122]

To all intents and purposes, the next friends suit collapsed with this interview. Chandler was heard to remark to his junior counsel when he returned to the courtroom, "She's smarter than a steel trap."[123] He plowed ahead for three more days in an effort to scrape some small propaganda advantage from an obviously lost cause, but on August 21 moved for dismissal of the suit without asking from the Masters any finding on the question before them.

Streeter immediately rose to his feet and moved that the Masters proceed with the hearing and determine the question of Mrs. Eddy's competency. In a speech both temperate and unsparing, he put the issue on record for history:

> If we are allowed to proceed we should show you that on February 12 Mrs. Eddy began to arrange for the entire management of her property during her life, and to make liberal provision for her kindred during that time. I will not go into the details of these matters excepting to say to you that if your Honors are not already satisfied we should be able to satisfy you beyond question, not only of Mrs. Eddy's absolute competency to deal with her affairs, but that during the last two weeks of February, the last two weeks before this suit was brought, she was dealing with those questions with sagacity so far as her business matters were concerned, and as a noble Christian woman so far as her next of kin were concerned.
>
> Now, your Honors, neither Mrs. Eddy nor her counsel have the power to prevent her so-called "next friends" from trying to persuade Judge Chamberlin to let them dismiss the bill and get out of court. Neither have we the power to prevent their unconditional surrender in the middle of this hearing before the Masters.
>
> They volunteered to begin this wretched assault upon the person, property, and religious faith of an aged citizen of New Hampshire, and now, six months later, when their charges have utterly collapsed, they run to cover. This is their legal right, but I speak of the legal rights of Mrs. Eddy.
>
> Let me temperately review the situation. She is an honored citizen of this state, entitled to the protection of its courts. She is the founder and head of a great religious organization, with many hundred thousand devoted followers. On March 1 last, she was living peacefully in her own home, surrounded by faithful friends of her own choice. She was possessed of a large property, acquired almost solely from the sale of her religious writings. It

will sometime appear that, after providing liberally for her own kin, she has devoted much of her estate to the promotion of the religious views taught by her. She was a good citizen. She was, and is, entitled to the protection of the law.

On that day, March 1 last, this suit was instituted by a great newspaper which had hired and paid eminent counsel to bring it. It was primarily an attack upon the religious teachings of a great religious leader. A son and an adopted son inconsiderately loaned the use of their names as "next friends," and the agent of this newspaper who visited the son at Lead City, Dakota, November 29, and the adopted son at Waterbury, Vermont, March 6, and persuaded them to co-operate, is now writing in the presence of your Honors at the reporters' table.

This suit was brought in her name against ten honest men, alleging, first, that she was incompetent to protect her property, and, second, that these ten defendants have wrongfully misappropriated her funds. Not one of these defendants had ever taken a dollar of her money. They have answered under oath. The truth of their answers is admitted. The suit was based on false pretences. The situation was unique in legal history. Mrs. Eddy, in the eye of the law, was not a defendant, although the proceedings were, in fact, directed solely against her. She was not a plaintiff; the suit was brought against her will. Her trustees, who held and were managing her entire estate under a valid deed, prayed for leave to intervene. Their petition was denied. . . .

You were appointed Masters to pass on the questions submitted in your commission.

Knowing that upon the evidence there could be but one outcome of this hearing, she did not hesitate to submit to your decision. She has co-operated with you to obtain a full investigation. She has assented to every suggestion made by the Masters to enable them to arrive at a just decision. She has submitted herself to your personal examination in the presence of counsel for the alleged "next friends," and the stenographic report thereof, inaccurate in many respects, has been given to the world. She has been asked to submit herself to the examination of hostile alienists, and, for the purpose of enabling you to reach a just conclusion in your own way, she has assented to that. Nothing that your Honors thought would aid in the ascertainment of the truth has been objected to by her or her counsel.

This trial has been proceeding five days, and with the exception of her own examination before you, the only evidence sub-

*mitted is a few letters selected out of thousands written by her,
and a few fragments of her other writings. Upon the charge that
her money has been misappropriated, that her property was not
safeguarded, not one word of testimony has been introduced. The
charge that she is incompetent has utterly collapsed, and now
these altruists who pretended and represented to the court that
they brought this suit as her friends, for her protection and in
her interests, have made their public confession to the world.*

*Under these circumstances, we submit that Mrs. Eddy has a
legal right to a finding of her competency.*[124]

Judge Aldrich replied that "when the party who asserts a lack
of mental capacity withdraws there is really no controversy left; Mrs.
Eddy stands with nothing to answer, as we view it." Though not quite
the explicit legal finding Mrs. Eddy could have wished for, the granting
of Streeter's motion requesting that Mrs. Eddy's trustees be substituted for her in the event that any costs be charged against the defense
was in fact a recognition by the court that she was of full mental
competence when she appointed the trustees on March 6, 1907.

Yet, grieved as she was over the part played by the two Glovers
and Foster Eddy in the long, painful proceedings, almost every visitor
to Pleasant View during those months commented on the lack of
resentment or reproach in her attitude. On the day Calvin Hill hurried from the courtroom to tell her that the battle was over and she
had won, she simply raised her hands from the arm of her chair and
dropped them again, then lifted her head in a movement familiar to
all her household when she prayed or was deeply moved. Almost at
once she turned to her desk and wrote what Hill described as "a letter
of overflowing forgiveness to one of those in whose name the suit had
been brought."[125]

Later she settled $245,000 on Glover and $45,000 on Foster Eddy
in return for their agreement not to contest her will—which, apart
from a few minor bequests, left her entire estate to the church she
had founded.[126] Yet dollars and cents were perhaps the least part of
the whole next friends struggle. The real stake—at least as Mrs. Eddy
saw it—was the survival of Christian Science.

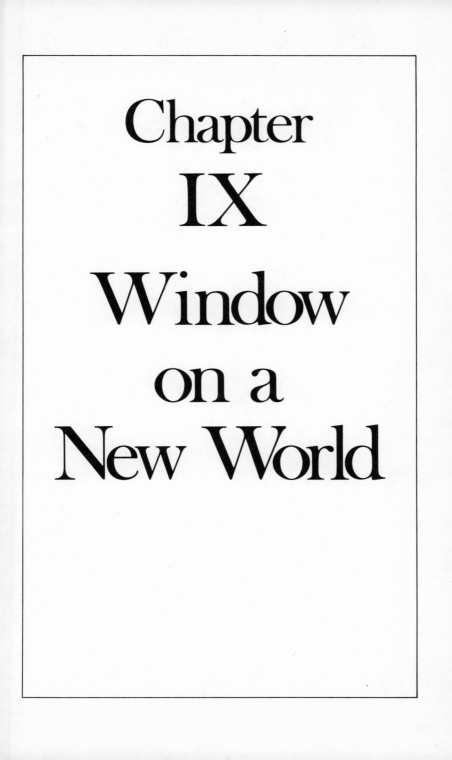

Chapter IX

Window on a New World

While the next friends were assessed the court costs of their abandoned suit, the cost to Mrs. Eddy was of a different kind.

Back on Thanksgiving Day, 1906, she had called the metaphysical workers in her household together and in the course of her talk with them, asked each one what he had to be thankful for. Strang had answered, "for the sense of suffering," and, as Frye recalled her response in his diary that night, "she told him his answer was the nearest right of any we gave, for mortal sense in all its phases is a lie & the sense of suffering is the nearest out of mortal sense."[1]

About that same time she had sent the Directors a new bylaw requiring any Christian Scientist who might be called to serve at Pleasant View to stay there three years at her request. Two months later she wrote them:

> Every statement in "Science and Health" I have gained through suffering. Every step of advancement at my home [—] of my own and . . . of the students [—] is reached in the same "strait and narrow" way.[2]

Through the troubled events of 1907, there had been an unusual stir among the workers at Pleasant View. Joseph Mann, who had come back to help her for several months, was called away by urgent needs at home, and similar domestic appeals took several other valued workers away when they were most needed by Mrs. Eddy. Then Pamelia Leonard, following the unwanted and undeserved notoriety she received from the *World* attack, became severely ill and returned to Brooklyn, where she died on January 7, 1908—just a month after the death of Joseph Armstrong who had been specially singled out for aspersion by Chandler because his illness had kept him from giving testimony as Mrs. Eddy's publisher.[3]

There was also the sad case of Mary Tomlinson, sister of Irving and described by all who knew her as a gentle and lovable young woman. Though the brother and sister lived together in their own house in Concord, they were frequent visitors at Pleasant View and constituted a "Committee on Business"—actually a metaphysical committee to support Mrs. Eddy through the trials of that period. Shortly after the suit was filed, Mary wrote Mrs. Eddy:

> *The first paragraph of your "Miscellaneous Writings" has been very precious to me. To-day it comes to me as applying to you. In the present "storm and tempest" of error you are "safely sheltered in the strong tower of hope, faith, and Love." You are God's nestling, and "He will hide you in His feathers till the storm has passed."*[4]

Only two or three days later the young woman had a complete mental breakdown, wandered off to Boston by herself, and there committed suicide by throwing herself out of a window in the Parker House—from a room directly beneath one in which (the Boston papers reported) Chandler, Peabody, and their associates were at the time in conference, planning their strategy for the next friends suit.

Mrs. Eddy was made of hardier stuff. In the very midst of the legal preparations and maneuvers, she had been busy writing Count Helmuth von Moltke that to have *Science and Health* translated into German would afford her "the keenest satisfaction and joy" (her correspondence with Countess von Moltke had led to the latter's conclusion that a German version was impractical, but Mrs. Eddy would like to have the Count finish his translation of the chapter "Recapitulation" and mail it to McLellan)[5] and telling Augusta Stetson to send no more Christian Science publications to the White House until the new President was elected, and *not then* ("Avoid being identified pro or con in politics. If you do otherwise it will hinder our cause. . . . God alone is capable of government; you are not, I am not . . .")[6] and notifying the Trustees of the Christian Science Publishing Society that she had no recollection of giving permission to the Thinkright Bureau to publish quotations from her copyrighted books ("I have always thought that detached sentences can be made injurious to the real meaning of my writings—I think so now")[7] and snatching a few moments' relaxation with George Kinter, who was doing another short stint of service at Pleasant View and wrote in his diary on May 5, 1907:

> *This is a bright sunny Sunday afternoon. Prompted to call upon our Leader in her study, where I knew she would be at this hour and probably disengaged, I went and just found her finishing some writing: putting up her pen, she greeted me cordially. I offered her some pansies which I had picked . . . and as I laid them down she began talking: soon our conversation turned to the subject of the memory, whereupon she related to me this*

interesting incident [about the farm boy Lyman Durgin whom she had taught to read and memorize Bible verses when she was a girl in Tilton, New Hampshire].[8]

Yet as early as the middle of July Mrs. Eddy felt that the time had come for her to leave New Hampshire, whose courts had failed to protect her from—as it seemed to her—the savage assault of the next friends suit. Secretly during the three months that followed she had McLellan and Farlow look for a suitable property for her in Brookline or Newton, adjacent to Boston. Events were pushing her closer to the point (both geographical and metaphoric) where her church confronted the changing world.

"I want a window in my room like the one here," she wrote Farlow in September, a window from which she could see the street and the carriages passing by. "It relieves my *lonely hours,"*[9] she explained, with a tacit acknowledgment of her isolation from the casual comings and goings of ordinary, heterogeneous human life. Yet the wrench of leaving the familiar and once more launching into the unknown was sharp.

Mrs. Eddy loved Pleasant View dearly, its simplicity and quietude, the elms she had planted years ago, the orchard and flowerbeds she had planned when the place was only a "cow pasture,"[10] the tranquil vistas which she had pointed out with such delight to half a generation of visitors—from lanky James Gilman with his sketchpad to the distinguished jurists and alienists who came to determine her sanity—and the comfortable, familiar rooms through which she made periodic tours of inspection to see that the last plush hassock and beaded lampshade was in order.

There was need for more space as well as new help, for the household had continued to grow despite repeated depletion and the difficulty of finding qualified reinforcements.[11] So the orders were for a larger house than Pleasant View, but nothing pretentious. At one point Mrs. Eddy wrote Farlow:

> *I give up the thought of the estate in —— [sic] for several reasons, one of which is I dislike* arrogant *wealth, a great show of it, and especially for one who* works *as well as preaches for and of the nothingness of matter.*[12]

Early in October McLellan purchased for her a twenty-five-room, gray stone mansion in twelve acres of well-wooded ground in Chestnut Hill, Massachusetts, only a short distance from the Brookline reservoir whose parklike surroundings would provide a pleasant route for her daily drive. Extensive renovations and changes were to be carried out during the next three months, but the name of the new owner would be kept a close secret; nobody should know it until she actually arrived. Even the Pleasant View household was kept ignorant of her intention as long as possible.[13]

It was a demanding period for Mrs. Eddy, and for all of them, as she girded herself for the coming change. John Lathrop, who was in the household for a few months of emergency service, wrote her at one point a letter of gratitude for "the severe, stern, searching, patient, unselfish—the divinely *loving* lessons"[14] which she had been teaching him during that time. Irving Tomlinson, who had moved into Pleasant View as an assistant secretary when Cornell Wilson took off just after the next friends suit, found life there very much harder to take at close quarters than when he had viewed it from his house in Concord.[15]

The lessons Mrs. Eddy herself had learned from the suit had left her scarcely able to bear the lavish tributes that some of her students mistook for the kind of understanding she really needed. To one of them, Annie Dodge, she wrote in November:

> *Your letter . . . was* astounding. *You, that once was calm and wise in your labors for Christian Science, writing like a maniac, more than a Scientist! You an idolater making a god of me! In my article, Personal Contagion, I denounced deeply just what you said in your letter of me[:] beware . . . in turning to a person instead of divine Principle to help in time of need. O that you are blind to this sin seems to me incredible!*[16]

After giving Miss Dodge three days to gather her wits, Mrs. Eddy wrote her again:

> *Has my startling last letter shocked you out of a mesmeric influence that is fatal to all who do not know what causes it? If such is the result I am paid for the great cross I took up when writing thus to you. You do know I love you deeply and so I try to help you in an hour of great need.*[17]

It was a period of many comings and goings in the household, both before and after the move to Chestnut Hill, which took place on January 26, 1908. Tomlinson had been dismissed on January 1 and was replaced by the Reverend Arthur R. Vosburgh, who lasted for only five weeks but who wrote Mrs. Eddy at the end of his stay in the same vein as John Lathrop:

> *I am grateful for the infinite patience, and for the divine impatience with which you deal with your workers' short-comings, and long-goings,—with which you have dealt with mine; and I am*

going, with renewed consecration and resolution, to work for the ideal that is given in Christ Jesus.[18]

When the time came to leave Concord, Lathrop in his diary described the Sunday on which they left as a "beautiful, calm day; sunshiny; snow prophesied; newspapers and world in ignorance [of the move]." Mrs. Eddy, he added, "opened that morning to I Cor. 9:10-14 inclusive and gave us a grand talk."[19] In the afternoon a small cavalcade of carriages took them to the railroad station, where a special train awaited them and Mrs. Eddy appeared suitably spry as she walked across the platform and entered the parlor car provided for her.[20]

No precaution was spared to ensure her safety and comfort. An extra engine preceded them to make sure the tracks were clear. Her cousin, Dr. Alpheus Morrill, accompanied the party—as "the nearest kin at hand," it was later claimed—but stayed with the household members in a separate coach and returned the next day without seeing Mrs. Eddy. The train itself, by a special arrangement worked out with the railroad officials, was deflected outside Boston to the small Chestnut Hill station on another line, so that Mrs. Eddy might avoid the publicity that would inevitably attend her arriving at the terminal in the city.

At Chestnut Hill the party transferred once more to a fleet of carriages, but as the first of these drew up at the entrance to the new home at 400 Beacon Street in the early winter darkness, they were startled to see a large group of reporters and cameramen waiting for them. Word of her move had sped by wire from Concord and the press had quickly discovered her destination. Mrs. Eddy at the end of her trip was obviously no match for the hungry pack about to descend on her, and John Salchow, jumping out of one of the hacks behind her, ran forward, opened her carriage door, swept her up in his arms, and carried her into the house and up the stairs, to set her down laughing in a chair in her own suite.[21]

The change was not all a laughing matter, however. The new house was much larger than Mrs. Eddy expected—a big barn of a place, in her own disconsolate words.[22] On the evening of their arrival, it seemed slightly overwhelming, ablaze as it was with lights and far too warmly heated for even a January night. When she seated herself at her familiar desk the next morning and took stock of her new study, she found it also too spacious by far, with a dark, rich wallpaper instead of the light-colored one she had had at Pleasant View, windows placed wrongly for her to see out to the distant Blue Hills from her chair, and a huge carpet with a rose pattern which caused her to complain that she couldn't wait for her secretary to come to her "across all those roses."[23]

Surveying the scene in which most of her life for the next three years would be lived, she exclaimed with the wry vigor of the Elizabethan she sometimes was: "O splendid misery!"[24]

With equal vigor, however, she proceeded during the next month or two to have the situation rectified. While she moved temporarily into the third-floor room of the resident seamstress, Miss Eveleth, part of her study was walled off and turned into a handily adjacent sitting room for Calvin Frye. A second elevator was installed close to her suite, though the architect who had made changes in the house preparatory to her arrival protested there was no possibility of having it where she wanted it. Mrs. Eddy insisted that it would be possible and not surprisingly it was.

Yet the adjustment from life at Pleasant View was difficult, for her and for the household. It was not just a matter of adapting to new surroundings. Both she and her church faced a change and a challenge that was different from any they had yet encountered.

2

The world in 1908 was only six years from the opening chapter of Armageddon. There was a sunset glow about the period of the first Roosevelt and the seventh Edward that could have been mistaken for an overripe dawn.

In the rosy upper air, great ideals moved majestically as zeppelins. An aged Tolstoy hailed a rising Gandhi. Men like Nicolas Berdyaev and Romain Rolland and Albert Schweitzer saw the spirit of man embracing God, music, revolution, nature, scholarship, so that even cataclysm wore a benevolent face. Thinkers like James and Bergson held out an open-ended universe of inexhaustible vitality, plurality, possibility, while the chilly logic of a Veblen was swept carelessly aside.

It was, in retrospect, an age of somewhat sleazy innocence, soon to be picked to pieces by the semantic demolition squads, the tunnelers in the unconscious, the drilled platoons of scientism, the dialectical plotters, the surrealist planners, the engineers of apocalypse. What rough beast, Yeats would ask after the first crash had come, was slouching toward Bethlehem to be born?

Yet back in the Edwardian years Henry Adams had already predicted a far greater collapse of civilization to follow soon. And earlier even than Adams, Mrs. Eddy had written with more than ecological foresight:

Before error is wholly destroyed, there will be interruptions of the general material routine. Earth will become dreary and desolate, but summer and winter, seedtime and harvest (though in changed forms), will continue unto the end,—until the final spiritualization of all things. . . . The breaking up of material beliefs may seem to be famine and pestilence, want and woe, sin, sickness, and death, which assume new phases until their nothingness appears. . . . This mental fermentation has begun, and will continue until all errors of belief yield to understanding.[25]

The point was that she saw the smash-up of materialism—of materiality itself—within the framework of ultimate spiritual victory, of what she would describe in metaphysical terms as "the translation of man and the universe back into Spirit."[26] This put her in opposition to both the optimists of her own day and the pessimists of ours. Her spiritual affirmations were far from meaningless to a decade that contained such names as Einstein, Rilke, Unamuno, Whitehead, Royce, Jung, Tagore, Keyserling, Jaurès, Smuts, some of whom even had delicate filaments connecting them with Christian Science.[27] But in a curious way she saw more clearly than any of them the black logic of the naturalism summed up in a famous passage by the statesman-philosopher Arthur Balfour:

Man, so far as natural science by itself is able to teach, is no longer the final cause of the universe, the Heaven-descended heir of all the ages. His very existence is an accident, his story a brief and transitory episode in the life of one of the meanest of the planets. . . . We sound the future, and learn that after a period, long compared with the individual life but short indeed compared with the divisions of time open to our investigation, the energies of our system will decay, the glory of the sun will be dimmed, and the earth, tideless and inert, will no longer tolerate the race which for a moment disturbed its solitude.[28]

If matter was in fact the final determinant, then man and the universe deserved the even more poignant elegy of Bertrand Russell:

That man is the product of causes which had no prevision of the ends they were achieving; that his origin, his growth, his hopes and fear, his loves and his beliefs are but the outcome of accidental collocations of atoms; . . . that all the labours of the ages, all the devotion, all the inspiration, all the noonday brightness of human genius, are destined to extinction in the vast death of the solar system, and that the whole of man's achievement

must inevitably be buried beneath the debris of a universe in ruins
—all these things, if not quite beyond dispute, are . . . nearly cer-
tain. . . . Brief and powerless is man's life; on him and all his race
the slow, sure doom falls pitiless and dark. Blind to good and
evil, reckless of destruction, omnipotent matter rolls on its re-
lentless way.[29]

The nucleus of the argument lay in the phrase "omnipotent matter." Ten years before, in 1898, Mrs. Eddy had named as one of the twenty-six topics to be studied by Christian Scientists twice a year in their weekly "lesson-sermons," the question: "Is the Universe, Including Man, Evolved by Atomic Force?" That was the period when every year brought forth dazzling new discoveries and developments in physical science, among them X rays, wireless telegraphy, radioactivity, the electron, radium, quantum theory, the special theory of relativity, along with ultimately related developments in mathematical logic, aeronautics, mutation theory, psychopathology. The whole classical concept of matter, of atomic action, of space and time, of causation itself, seemed to be rushing toward a state of total Heraclitean flux—or perhaps toward the day described in the Second Epistle of Peter "wherein the heavens being on fire shall be dissolved, and the elements shall melt with fervent heat."[30]

There is a curious coincidence to be noted between this period of development in physics and an apparent effort by Mrs. Eddy to make more intelligible what she meant by the "nothingness" of matter. Back in 1904 Alfred Farlow had pointed out in an article in the *Boston Times* the widespread misunderstanding of that particular aspect of her teaching:

> *Recently I have been much impressed with the peculiar man-*
> *ner in which critics undertake to state this Science, by emphasizing*
> *its conclusions, not even mentioning its Principle. . . . For example,*
> *one lately said, "The basic teaching of Christian Science is that*
> *there is no matter," when in fact this abstract statement is a*
> *rather remote conclusion which is neither understood nor accept-*
> *able to the individual unless he first has some knowledge of the*
> *premise upon which it is based. . . . Even a Christian Scientist*
> *would stumble over this . . . if he were not previously prepared*
> *for it.*
>
> *The statement, "there is no matter," standing alone and in-*
> *dependent of any qualification, seems to mean that everything*
> *that we see,—the entire creation,—is non-existent, while in truth*
> *Christian Science teaches that all things, from the least to the*

greatest, are real, though not what they seem to the peculiar sense of those who have not yet learned to perceive them as God made them and as they really are.

The premise of Christian Science is stated in the answer to the first question . . . in . . . "Recapitulation" . . . namely, "What is God?" . . . When we are correctly informed as to what God's creation is we can understand what it is not.[31]

It was in the next year, 1905, that Einstein wrote his first paper on relativity. At the end of the year, in a second paper, he concluded that all energy of whatever sort has mass. It took him until 1907 to "come to the stupendous realization that the reverse must also hold: that all mass, of whatever sort, must have energy"[32]—and twenty-five more years to verify quantitatively the famous 1907 equation $E=mc^2$ in which he expressed this equivalence of mass and energy.

At the end of 1905 and early part of 1906 Mrs. Eddy had been working on her last major revision of *Science and Health*. One small change she made during that time was to add two words to a sentence which in its final form refers to the "warfare between the idea of divine power, which Jesus presented, and mythological material intelligence called *energy* and opposed to Spirit."[33] The two words added in 1905–6 were "called *energy*" (her own italics) and they point to her evident conviction that to identify matter and its claim to intelligence as energy was a useful step toward the further recognition that "Physical force and mortal mind are one"[34]—a false mode of consciousness or misapprehension of being, to be reduced in the last analysis to an impossible limit on Spirit's infinitude.

The Christian Science periodicals for some years had been reporting the scientific developments that were revolutionizing physical concepts of matter. As early as 1896 the *Journal* reprinted, among other scientific items, a newspaper article on "Professor Röntgen's New Force" and the abstract of an address "Defeat of Scientific Materialism" given by a German physicist at a Lübeck convention. From 1900 to 1910 such reports were augmented by original articles contributed by a new breed of Christian Scientist—writers like Judge L. H. Jones of Kentucky, well grounded in philosophy, attentive to the new physics, broad in cultural outlook.

Mrs. Eddy in 1904 had expressed a desire for more contributions of this sort. "Such articles," she wrote William P. McKenzie, "tend to attract the higher class of thinkers and to dignify our cause." As it was, she added, "only Christian Scientists can find food for head and heart in our papers."[35] In comparison with both earlier and later years, however, the *Journal* of the first decade of the century was exceptionally literate in relating Christian Science to current scientific and philosophic thought.

Mrs. Eddy, on the other hand, had no illusion, as some of the *Journal* writers obviously had, that the intellectual sophisticate could be argued into Christian Science. Its inner logic did not lie that close to the surface. To an oversanguine student, she wrote:

> *It is true that generally the scholar is not ready for Christian Science[;] he must slowly study the whole mass just as it is put together in order to advance toward the subject and begin to understand the Science. His thought must become spiritualized before he can comprehend its most simple meaning.*[36]

A good deal of the discussion in the *Journal* articles of that period hinged on the right of Christian Science to be considered scientific. The Reverend James J. Rome, for instance, noting in a 1902 article that scientific development had necessitated an advance beyond the purely empirical or Baconian theory of induction, had quoted from Mill's *System of Logic*:

> *The truths known by intuition are the original premises from which all others are inferred. . . . These general truths will doubtless make their first appearance in the character of hypotheses; not proved, or even admitting of proof, in the first instance, but assumed as premises for the purpose of deducing from them the laws of concrete phenomena.*[37]

Mrs. Eddy, Rome observed airily, has simply "turned to revelation for the hypothesis." But subsequent *Journal* writers were somewhat more enlightening on the relation of scientific discovery to the kind of "revelation" that can be illustrated by Poincaré's realization in a flash that Fuchsian functions were identical with those of non-Euclidean geometry[38] as well as by Mrs. Eddy's sudden realization that the infinitude of Spirit logically ruled out the substantiality of matter.

In his famous essay "Physics and Reality" Einstein was to write:

> *Physics constitutes a logical system of thought which is in a state of evolution, and whose basis cannot be obtained through distillation by any inductive method from the experiences lived through, but which can only be attained by free invention. The justification (truth content) of the system rests in the proof of usefulness of the resulting theorems on the basis of sense experiences, where the relations of the latter to the former can only be comprehended intuitively.*[39]

Here, in terms somewhat scandalous to the experimental researcher and statistical analyst, is a scientific methodology which demands a creative leap akin to the imaginative insight of art and in some degree approaching the revelatory experience of the great religious thinkers. Yet it also demands the kind of empirical verification or justification which separates even theoretical physics from pure mathematics—and which, in a very different context, separates even the metaphysics of Christian Science from a system of abstract idealistic propositions.

While the most effective "proof" of Christian Science lay in its practical utility, its method remained purely deductive, and some of the *Journal* writers were anxious to show the priority as well as the relevance of its metaphysical reasoning to its pragmatic results. Hence the elementary distinctions explored in such articles as Clarence A. Buskirk's "Methods of Reasoning as Used in Christian Science":

> *An experiment is a process for discovering something; a demonstration is a process for accomplishing and thereby proving something. . . . Jesus did not indulge in any such experiments. On the contrary, Jesus applied deductively his understanding of God and of man's relations to God . . . and his "works" proved, or demonstrated, that he was proceeding rightly. . . . Like pure mathematics, Christian Science is a system of deductive reasoning, and when it solves a single problem correctly, such solution, like the solution of a mathematical problem, is a demonstration and not a mere experiment.*[40]

Here the analogy with mathematics is suggestive but oversimplified, since it fails to make a distinction between logical demonstration and empirical confirmation. A later article by Henry R. Corbett entitled "The Genius of Discovery" approached its subject a little more subtly:

> *. . . Coming nearer to our own time, we note the startling discovery of the properties of radium. . . . The discovery which explained and named radium, not only cleared up the exceptional facts, but made waste paper of the libraries previously written on the constitution of matter. To quote again the memorable phrase of Balfour: "It not only explained matter, but explained it away." It seems clear, then, that a discovery may be expected to grow out of the anomalies or problems in its field of thought; to declare a basic law which relates them intelligibly to other knowledge; and furthermore, to show a wider application of the newly discovered*

law, which, while it first disturbs, operates later to illuminate the entire subject. . . .

It may be doubted whether any part of Mrs. Eddy's discovery is more unwelcome to old habits of thought than this classifying of ordinary sense life along with dreams and mesmeric states. A friend of the writer once said almost impatiently: "If you can see no difference between dreams and normal consciousness, we have little common ground for argument." In reply it was suggested that if a botanist should inform us that the moss and the oak belong to the same vegetable kingdom, we might impatiently exclaim that if he saw no difference between the oak and the moss, we lacked a common ground for further discussion. The botanist would probably explain that the two forms were, of course, not identical nor of equal importance; but that in scientific classification they must be placed together in the same field of nature. So Christian Scientists understand, not that the dream and waking state are identical or of equal present importance, but that both belong to the realm of phenomena, the kingdom of appearance.[41]

Although *Journal* articles of this sort tended to quote an impressive array of modern thinkers more or less appositely,[42] the central reference point was nineteen centuries earlier. "Jesus of Nazareth was the most scientific man that ever trod the globe," Mrs. Eddy had written in *Science and Health*. "He plunged beneath the material surface of things, and found the spiritual cause."[43] It might be useful to quote from the *Hibbert Journal* or the transactions of distinguished professional societies,[44] but such material, however apt and agreeable, lacked entirely the vital healing power of the Christian records.

It was the demonstrable contemporaneity rather than the debatable historicity of the New Testament that engaged Mrs. Eddy's followers. What was crucial in scientific Christian discipleship was the evidence of healing in its broadest sense—confirmation by experience, whether the experience was that of first-century apostles or twentieth-century Christian Science Sunday School pupils.

This was where the inductive process came in. "It is true," one of the *Journal* writers commented, "that after [eternal] verities have been arrived at by the deductive process, or after 'works' have been done according to deductive reasoning from them, the inductive process may be employed to persuade mankind of the truth."[45] It was because the physical changes involved in the more startling cases of Christian Science healing stood unexplained and anomalous to the new physics as well as the old physiology that serious consideration must be given to any hypothesis, however radical, which offered these healings as confirmatory data.

"Christian Science must be accepted at this period by induction," Mrs. Eddy herself had written. "We admit the whole, because a part is proved and that part illustrates and proves the entire Principle."[46] Bodily derangement was only a small part of the total "error" to be lifted from human consciousness, but its healing offered essential evidence of the supremacy of spiritual power over material appearance. Such bodily healing, Mrs. Eddy wrote, was "only the bugle-call to thought and action, in the higher range of infinite goodness,"[47] but the need on the highest peaks no less than on the lowest foothills was for a practical, healing dedication to truth, not for an exhilarating exercise of dialectical expertise.

3

If a new world was being born in the arts[48] and sciences, the world of affairs—as usual—lagged behind. Political and economic imperialism, powered by self-confident nationalist and capitalist ambitions, pounded blindly along the collision course set for it by the nineteenth century, like a proud *Titanic* making straight for its clumsy assignation with fate. If this ship should founder, however, it would go down not to the strains of "Nearer My God to Thee" but of "Alexander's Ragtime Band."

The popular press was far less concerned with the hazards of world politics than with the rewards to be gained by dishing out to the public a highly seasoned diet of scandals, scurrilities, crimes, and disasters.[49] As one who had recently seen her lifework endangered by this taste for the sensational, Mrs. Eddy gave renewed thought to the possibilities of a responsible journalism that would aim at clarifying basic issues rather than exploiting ephemeral excitements.

As long ago as 1878, when the infant Christian Science movement was achieving an undesired newspaper notoriety, she had written in *Science and Health*:

> *We have not a newspaper at our command through which to right the wrongs and answer the untruths, we have not a pulpit from which to explain how Christianity heals the sick, but if we had either of these, the slanderer and the physician would have less to do, and we should have more.*[50]

Five years later, when she started *The Christian Science Journal*, she wrote in the first issue:

An organ from the Christian Scientists has become a necessity. After looking over the newspapers of the day, very naturally comes the reflection that it is dangerous to live, so loaded seems the very air with disease. These descriptions carry fears to many minds, to be depicted in some future time upon the body. This error we shall be able in a great measure to counteract, for at the price we issue our paper we shall be able to reach many homes. A great work has already been done, and a great work yet remains to be done.[51]

In 1896 when she revised this passage for inclusion in *Miscellaneous Writings*, Mrs. Eddy changed the word "organ" in the first sentence to "newspaper"—a word clearly inapplicable to the monthly, denominational *Journal*. Two years later, when she started the weekly *Christian Science Sentinel*, several columns of news were regularly included, as well as occasional articles and editorials on public affairs.[52] That she considered this hit-or-miss coverage inadequate is suggested by her somewhat enigmatic statement in a letter of 1902 in regard to Archibald McLellan's becoming editor of the *Journal* and *Sentinel*: "Until I start a widespread press we should have in Boston a born editor."[53]

During these years, she had subscribed to a number of newspapers and magazines, annotating them in her usual fashion and marking items she particularly wished the members of her household to read.[54] The interrelation of these private annotations and her published pronouncements is suggestive at times, as when she wrote in the April 11, 1908, issue of the *Sentinel* a strong antiwar statement which ended with the caveat: "It is unquestionable, however, that at this hour the armament of navies is necessary, for the purpose of preventing war and preserving peace among nations."[55] Twenty-eight months earlier she had underlined a passage in Theodore Roosevelt's State of the Union Message to Congress which observed that "there is more need to get rid of the causes of war than the implements of war" —a sentiment which accorded with her own conviction that it is causes rather than symptoms that need healing. Yet her 1908 *Sentinel* statement differed considerably in tone and emphasis from the suspect pragmatism of Roosevelt's appeal to Congress three days later for increased armaments: "If we desire to secure peace, one of the most powerful instruments of our rising prosperity, it must be known that we are at all times ready for war."[56] Peace to Mrs. Eddy was a moral imperative rather than merely an economic asset or a political convenience.

At this very time she was giving thought to the founding of a newspaper that would present the news in just such a context of moral concern, combining as best it could objective realism with Christian idealism. Her determination had been crystallized by a letter written to her on March 12, 1908, by a local newspaperman and Christian Scientist, John L. Wright, setting forth the desirability of having a Boston daily newspaper run by Christian Scientists. "I am not thinking of a daily official Christian Science paper," he explained, "or one containing in its title the words Christian Science, but of a general newspaper owned by Christian Scientists." The purpose would be to produce a paper that would present the news constructively rather than sensationally and would put "principle before dividends."[57]

On this letter Mrs. Eddy drafted a reply:

> *Beloved Student*
>
> *I have had this newspaper scheme in my thought for quite a while and herein send my name for our daily newspaper*
>
> ### *The Christian Science Monitor*
>
> *This title only classifies the paper and it should have departments for what else is requisite.*[58]

In a number of ways the paper which she had in mind differed from that proposed by Wright, and her decisive announcement of the name she intended to give it emphasized that fact. But she was not yet ready to act. Her note to Wright was probably never sent, nor was another which she drafted on May 3 to McLellan and her publisher, Allison V. Stewart:

> *The time has come when we must have a daily paper entitled Christian Science Monitor. Allow no hesitation or delay on this movement. I will loan you all the money I can raise to help do it. When I proposed having the weekly Sentinel students held back at first; they may hold back this time but I in the name of God direct you to do this. Answer me immediately.*[59]

Urgent as the need now seemed to her, another necessity intervened to cause further delay. The movement's new publishing house was nearing completion, and her Yankee prudence told her it would be unwise to incur additional expense before the building was finished and paid for. By July 28, however, the end was in sight and she wrote the Directors:

Notice. *So soon as the Pub. House debt is paid I request the C. S. Board [of] Directors to start a daily newspaper called* Christian Science Monitor. *This must be* done *without fail.*[60]

The Directors were taken aback. The task seemed immense, and in order to gain time for further consideration of its implications they suggested that the Trustees of the Publishing Society might properly be given the task of getting the paper started. Accordingly on August 8 she sent the latter an unqualified command:

> *It is my request that you start a daily newspaper at once, and call it the Christian Science Monitor. Let there be no delay. The Cause demands that it be issued now.*
>
> *You may consult with the Board of Directors, I have notified them of my intention.*[61]

Even before announcing the project to her church officers, Mrs. Eddy had sensed the opposition it would encounter from both worldliness without and unworldliness within the church. As so often before, the sense of impending stir as she contemplated a major step forward brought on her a bout of ill health, which in turn led to a spate of newspaper rumors that she was dying. On May 15 she had issued a public statement:

> *Permit me to say, the report that I am sick (and I trust the desire thereof) is dead, and should be buried. Whereas the fact that I am well and keenly alive to the truth of being—the Love that is Life—is sure and steadfast. I go out in my carriage daily, and have omitted my drive but twice since I came to Massachusetts. Either my work, the demands upon my time at home, or the weather, is all that prevents my daily drive.*[62]

The next day, the *Christian Science Sentinel* carried a similar signed statement by her for the benefit of Christian Scientists:

> *Since Mrs. Eddy is watched, as one watches a criminal or a sick person, she begs to say, in her own behalf, that she is neither; therefore to be criticized or judged by either a daily drive or a dignified stay at home, is superfluous. When accumulating work requires it, or because of a preference to remain within doors she omits her drive, do not strain at gnats or swallow camels over it, but try to be composed and resigned to the shocking fact that she is minding her own business, and recommends this surprising privilege to all her dear friends and enemies.*[63]

Despite these brave statements, the summer of 1908 was not an easy one for her. On July 14 Frye noted in his diary that she was confined to her bed that day with a sudden attack of intense pain but would not consent to "send for an M. D." to give her an injection when the metaphysical workers failed to relieve her. Two weeks later on July 28 he wrote:

> At about 12 o'clock last night an editor of Boston Herald called . . . and asked at what hour Mrs. Eddy died! He said the rumor on the street is that she is dead. She had been having a series of attacks for over a week which kept her in bed and on the lounge almost the entire time and last night she despaired of living until morning: but when this telephone was rec'd it revealed cause of attack & [she] gained much relief.[64]

It is interesting to note that this climactic episode occurred the night before Mrs. Eddy wrote the Directors asking them to start the *Monitor*. The price of bold leadership, at least in the moral realm, has usually been subjective struggle for the leader at points of crucial decision, and Mrs. Eddy was no exception to this necessity. A week later another attack occurred—this time relieved in forty-five minutes —and it suggests that only through a painful struggle with herself could she bring herself to the assertion of leadership found in a letter which she had her secretary write McLellan the next day:

> Our Leader wishes you would have some thoroughly responsible outside person, write an article to the Sentinel setting forth Mrs. Eddy's unexampled leadership in the interests of Christian Science. . . . Let the article be strong, and carry with it complete conviction as to her ability to lead under divine guidance. . . . You will understand that this article is preparatory to making public her intention of starting a daily newspaper.[65]

While she canceled the request shortly afterward, the appeal may have had its effect on the church officers, for they responded with alacrity and energy to her note three days later asking that there be "no delay" in starting the *Monitor* and that it be "issued now." If her own struggles were, as she saw it, part of the necessary mental preparation for the undertaking, they also emphasized for her the significance of the new step. To certain members of her household she is reported to have said later, "When I established *The Christian Science Monitor*, I took the greatest step forward since I gave *Science and Health* to the world."[66]

Once the enterprise was begun, it moved as though jet-propelled. The just completed Publishing House needed at once to be expanded, new funds to be raised, experienced journalists who were Christian Scientists to be recruited, editorial policies and business procedures to be established. McLellan, chairman of the Board of Directors as well as editor of the existing periodicals, took on the additional editorship as well. The Trustees of the Publishing Society wrote Mrs. Eddy on August 13 outlining the practical steps they would have to take and the magnitude of the task to be accomplished. Yet in just over one hundred days the first issue of the paper appeared—fully professional, distinguished in appearance, already showing evidence of the international daily newspaper it would soon become.[67]

The morning of November 25, the day on which the first *Monitor* was published, was dark and foggy, but Mrs. Eddy announced to the assembled members of her household: "This, in truth, is the lightest of all days. This is the day when our daily paper goes forth to lighten mankind."[68] The claim was a large one, hardly to be justified by the addition of one more newspaper to the world's press. To Mrs. Eddy, however, the paper was a good deal more than this. It was the final link between her church and the whole, great, various, unredeemed world, with its splendor, its wretchedness, its ideal potential. The church was designed to be built on "the understanding and demonstration of divine Truth, Life, and Love," which would heal and save "the world"—not merely the individual—from sin and death.[69] The mission of the church, like that of Jesus, was both individual and collective.[70] Ideally no aspect of the human scene was beyond its healing scope.

Seen in this light, the *Monitor* was the culmination, at least symbolically, of Mrs. Eddy's lifework, and she appropriately though cryptically suggested as much in the scriptural text she selected as a motto for the editorial page: "First the blade, then the ear, then the full grain in the ear."[71] While the early publicity for the paper stressed its "wholesomeness," its freedom from sensationalism, its contructive emphasis—as well as the fact that it was a "real" newspaper covering the whole world, not a merely denominational or local publication—Mrs. Eddy's view of it extended immeasurably further.

In the brief editorial which she wrote for the first issue she announced that the paper's object was "to injure no man, but to bless all mankind"[72]—an admirable if unsurprising aim for a responsible journal. But she also spoke of its purpose "to spread undivided the Science that operates unspent"[73]—a deeper assertion of the place it held in her vision of "Science" as something extending beyond all sectarian, national, and cultural boundaries.

This concept was also reflected in her adamant insistence that the words "Christian Science" be included in the paper's title—a position strongly opposed at first by some of her advisors and church officers, who thought it would be a severe handicap to the paper's winning a nondenominational or secular audience. To Mrs. Eddy, on the other hand, the designated title represented exactly the opposite; it was an identification of the paper with the premise that no human situation was beyond healing or rectification if approached with sufficient understanding of man's God-given potentialities. Nor did the "good news" of Christianity involve the prettification of bad news, but rather, its confident confrontation.

That, at least, was the ideal possibility Mrs. Eddy saw for her newspaper.

Four weeks after its first appearance, an article in the *Sentinel* showed that at least one Christian Scientist had caught a glimpse of what she had in mind. The writer was the wife of her early and now implacably hostile publisher, William G. Nixon. The first effect of the *Monitor*'s publication, Mrs. Nixon wrote, speaking for and to Christian Scientists themselves, had been "to lift one's eyes to an horizon far beyond one's own doorstep." Immersed in their individual healing work, they could no longer pass by the world's collective needs on the other side. "Things we did not like to look at nor think of, problems we did not feel able to cope with, must now be faced manfully, and correct thinking concerning the world's doings cultivated and maintained."[74]

It was not Mrs. Eddy's intention to sacrifice journalistic excellence to the middle-class limitations or prejudices of the paper's Christian Science readership. Two days after the first *Monitor* appeared she asked to have Frederick Dixon, a brilliant London journalist and ardent Christian Scientist, brought to Boston and put in charge of the editorial page.[75] The act symbolized her determination that the paper should have intellectual distinction and not mere popular appeal—a view not always shared by those responsible for its finances.

As Committee on Publication for London and doyen of all Committees on Publication in England, Dixon had been remarkably skillful in answering criticisms of Christian Science in the British press, and Mrs. Eddy had repeatedly praised the effectiveness of his published letters and articles, which were attracting favorable attention to Christian Science in the face of establishment opposition.[76] He had been, she wrote after his arrival, "our star in England" and should be promoted to higher office in America. "He would make a splendid Editor," she wrote the nonplussed McLellan with calculated ambiguity, "but we do not want to change our present chief Editor."[77]

The move to Boston was premature, as it turned out, for the *Monitor* staff was not yet up to working easily with so bright a "star" from across the sea. At the end of April, 1909, Mrs. Eddy returned Dixon to England, explaining that his present opportunities for doing good were greater there than in Boston. Once back, he became District Manager of the Committees on Publication for Great Britain and Ireland, as well as European representative of the *Monitor,* building up a large professional staff for the London office of the paper before returning to Boston in 1914 to serve at last as its editor.[78]

But what Mrs. Eddy valued in Dixon was more than his professionalism; it was his bringing to bear upon current intellectual and cultural trends some of the direct insights of Christian Science. One of the tasks she specifically assigned him when he was first in Boston was the reviewing of books that would allow him to exercise his spiritual talents in this direction. There is no evidence that she expected him to make explicit mention of Christian Science or to use its special language in discussing the ideas of other authors, but she did expect that a knowledgeable Christian Scientist would have something significant, even unique, to contribute to the evaluation of influential ideas and issues—indeed, to the general culture of the day.

Her ideal for the *Monitor* was clearly beyond the scope of most of her followers' comprehension. Some who subscribed for the paper out of loyalty and were proud of the worldwide recognition it soon won, found it rather hard going so far as their own limited interests and tastes were concerned. Others welcomed it as a reassuring bridge between their church and the world of affairs and enjoyed its professionalism, while failing to recognize the larger potential it had for its founder as an instrument of healing in a grievously sundered world.

Nevertheless, the *Monitor* served from the outset as a powerful educational force among Christian Scientists. It was also a visible sign to the world that their church's concern embraced the collective as well as the individual ills of bemused humanity.[79]

4

To John Salchow Mrs. Eddy once remarked of her last residence: "This is not my home. Pleasant View will always be my home."[80] Nevertheless, she gradually felt more settled in it, in accordance with the desire she expressed in a letter to Mrs. Mary Beecher Longyear, whose own Chestnut Hill estate was not far from hers:

> *I came here for quiet, and not to build up a cause. I only*

*desire now to be friendly with all denominations religious . . .
and to drop quietly out of the arena of strife. I was sorry to
disappoint the good people in Concord [by moving]. But I hope
now only to have my giving and good will expressed in a home
life and to give up a public life as fast as possible.*[81]

At first, homesick as she still was for Concord,[82] nothing her
household workers did seemed right to her. On one occasion not long
after the move, Archibald McLellan stood side by side with the young
Englishwoman, Adelaide Still, who had been serving as her personal
maid for the past six months, as they both watched Mrs. Eddy get
into her carriage for her daily drive. McLellan, who knew little of
the workings of the household, asked Miss Still what she did while
Mrs. Eddy was away on her drive.

She had dinner, the young woman replied.

And how long was the drive?

Not more than half an hour these days.

That meant a pretty hurried meal for her, McLellan observed
sympathetically.

"Oh, I wouldn't mind if I never had any dinner," Adelaide burst
out, "if only I could do things right, if only I could please her!"

McLellan shot a keen glance at her, then said quietly: "You can,
Ada. *You can.*"

When Mrs. Eddy returned from her drive that day, her attitude
had completely changed. She was loving, warm, appreciative. Adelaide
salted away the incident,[83] to remind herself from time to time of
what it really meant to *support* Mrs. Eddy. The latter soon afterward
arranged that the young woman should always be present when the
metaphysical workers came to her study for their daily instruction,
and later she gave orders that she should receive the same pay as
these experienced practitioners and teachers, who served in the household as Mrs. Eddy's spiritual aides-de-camp. The maidservant would
outlast them all, and more than half a century later would give a
clear-eyed evaluation of what it was like to spend almost every waking
hour of her life for three and a half years in the presence of the
Discoverer and Founder of Christian Science.[84]

Only two days after the household moved to Chestnut Hill, it
was joined by a new arrival who would make a significant contribution
to both the history and the historiography of Christian Science. Built
like a blacksmith or a prizefighter, endowed with no conspicuous
graces of mind or manner, Adam H. Dickey had the supreme graces
that Mrs. Eddy needed: an unshakable faith in God, an unquestioning

trust in her leadership, and an unswerving determination to serve the cause she led.[85] Of such, in the annals of religious enterprise, are strong lieutenants made. Very soon after he had been installed as her secretary and a member of what he himself described as her metaphysical bodyguard, Dickey became in Mrs. Eddy's eyes a tower of strength for her latter days and an indispensable executor of her purposes.

What this newcomer had to learn, like all the others who came to work for her, was what might be called the Calvinistic realism of Mrs. Eddy's Christian Science. Good was all, evil a lie, she taught—but this was true for the individual *only to the extent that he understood and demonstrated it in his daily life.*[86] Human life as the carnal or mortal mind presented it was riddled with corruption. No Calvinist was more adept than Mrs. Eddy in spotting the tricks and turns of that mind which Paul described as enmity against God and which was to be found doing its hidden dirty work in the lives of saints as well as sinners.

"When I scold," Mrs. Eddy told her metaphysical workers one day, "I cannot see any good in mortal mind, none whatever." Then she added with characteristic realism, "All my students who have left me did so because of my scolding."[87] Again, when she asked them one day, "Is there a real Christian Scientist?" and Dickey replied, "None but you," she quickly told them:

> *Do not except me. When I have demonstrated over old age and the other things that are trying to assail me, then I'm a Christian Scientist; until then I'm only trying to be.*[88]

All evil, she taught, was to be overcome on the basis that it had no legitimacy, no support in the structure of being, no ultimate reality, but its specious claims in their manifold forms first had to be recognized in order to be repudiated. This was where her students seemed to her to be most deficient. The very dissensions that arose in her own household were, she held, an evidence of their failure to identify and handle properly the malicious promptings of "the enemy" —the thinking centered on a fictitious mortal selfhood apart from God. The enemy was, in fact, mortality itself—the "existential anxiety" of a later age, from which sprang the legion of tensions, frustrations, fears, rivalries, and assorted irrationalities that presented themselves disguised as the normal outcome of objective situations.

Take the latest rift in the Chestnut Hill household.

It was a bitter pill for Calvin Frye to find himself superseded in many respects by Dickey. While Mrs. Eddy's affection for Frye grew with the years, he saw the new secretary becoming more and more her confidant. The adaptation to Chestnut Hill was as hard for him as for Mrs. Eddy, and he found it difficult to accept the greater resilience, even ebullience, of some of the newer members of the household. A few weeks after Dickey's arrival, Mrs. Eddy gave the secretary a short note which showed her own recognition of Calvin's need:

> *Mr. Frye needs* encouragement—*despondency is his belief and the dear man has shared my deprivations many years hoping they would cease and so give him release as well as myself. Encourage him to find all happiness in divine* Love *life spiritual here and now.*
>
> *You are able to depict this, for you seem to realize it.*[89]

Another person who saw Frye's need was Alfred Farlow, who joined the Chestnut Hill household for two days at the beginning of June, 1908, but found it impossible to combine his exacting Committee on Publication duties with the arduous responsibility of working metaphysically for Mrs. Eddy during the "night watches." A little later he sent Frye a gift of several smart neckties which his sister had brought with her from Paris. The unworldly Yankee felt he could not accept so dashing a gift, and with typical kindliness Farlow wrote back as to a refractory child:

> *It was unfortunate that I mentioned . . . that the ties came from Paris. . . .* Please *accept them as . . . just a little token of our appreciation of your good faithful work. Now be good and please* us. That *would be* un-*selfish. See?*[90]

Frye yielded, and Farlow then wrote him a letter of thanks for "accepting the little gift which has now become a matter of history." Ironic as the small pleasantry was intended to be, trivialities may indeed have a place in history when they throw inferential light on cloudy matters of greater moment, as do Farlow's further words to Frye in the same letter:

> *Knowing as much as I do about what you have to contend with constantly I am in a position to appreciate your excellent service. For that reason I would be glad to take off my shoes and give them to you any time and walk home bare foot, so please get rid of your exceeding modesty on this subject.*[91]

Most Christian Scientists imagined life at Chestnut Hill to be a sort of heaven on earth. Those intimately acquainted with it knew it to be a life of unending sacrifice.[92] What nerved their efforts and raised their sights was the realization of Mrs. Eddy's own willingness to pay the price that would, as she saw it, enable Christian Science to do the work in history which she envisioned for it. As Adam Dickey put it in his memoirs:

> Many times, while our Leader was working on the problems connected with the government of her church, the physical effects of the discord she wished to overcome seemed to manifest themselves in her body and often she was prostrated with suffering, apparently caused by the chemicalization of the conditions of thought she was endeavoring to meet, and which seemed to culminate in her own thought.
>
> Some of the most important By-laws of The Mother Church formulated themselves in the thought of our Leader while she was under a claim of suffering, which continued until the By-law was ready to be passed upon by the Directors. Then the suffering disappeared and everything went on harmoniously without a single trace of what our Leader had passed through. . . .
>
> Calvin Frye told me that these experiences always came to Mrs. Eddy in this way and that whenever any great revelation came to her, concerning that which seemed necessary for the welfare of our Cause, these struggles appeared in her body.[93]

One of these occasions occurred in June, 1908, when thousands of Christian Scientists poured into Boston for the Communion season and annual meeting of the church. Enthusiasm ran high, as usual. The thoughts of many turned toward Chestnut Hill in a personalized devotion far removed from the spiritual communion with God which the service was designed to further. It was one more example of the tendency of the human mind, given half a chance, to materialize spiritual motives, as it had done so often in Christian history.

Mrs. Eddy had been in pain for several days. Now, struggling with what Dickey would later describe as an "attack of unusual severity,"[94] she suddenly called for him and dictated a bylaw abolishing the Communion season in The Mother Church.[95] By the time he had transcribed it, she had risen from her couch and had begun to work at her desk, as vigorous and cheerful as ever. When she told Frye of the move, however, he took a gloomy view of this abolition of so impressive and massive an annual pilgrimage to The Mother Church and muttered to Adelaide Still as he left the room, "She'll ruin her church!"[96] Possibly as a result of this sort of reaction, Mrs. Eddy explained a little dryly in a public statement a few days later,

"Dropping the communion of The Mother Church does not prevent its distant members from occasionally attending this church."[97]

Through the early months of service, Dickey was learning fast, but not quite fast enough. Gentle as a woman in his dealings with Mrs. Eddy, he sometimes seemed to her to show the male obtuseness that was one of evil's guises. Later in the summer of 1908 when Mrs. Eddy encountered new physical stresses as she pushed forward the *Monitor* project, she sent a note to Frye as to an old and trusted friend:

> *Beloved*
>
> *If you knew with what I am beset continually arguments of dementia incompetence old age etc. it would explain why I am so changed.*
>
> *Mr. Dickey yields to m. a. m. to such an extent he affords me very little help in anything. I have to correct him continually.*[98]

Few if any of her students escaped this sort of censure entirely. Sometimes it seems to have been a momentary relief from exasperation or overburdened nerves. More often it was used with deliberate remedial intent, and she expected them to understand that its purpose was not to fasten a fault on them but to expose it as something foreign to their real nature. The procedure was in accordance with her own dictum: "Speak the truth to every form of error."[99]

For some of them the lesson was a long and hard one. John Salchow later recalled an occasion at Pleasant View when he heard Mrs. Eddy reprimand Laura Sargent "very severely." When next called to the study, Mrs. Sargent was in tears. "Why, Laura," Mrs. Eddy exclaimed in gentle surprise, "I was not speaking to you; I was speaking to the error. You should not take it to yourself."[100]

Now, at Chestnut Hill, Mrs. Sargent showed that at last she had got the message. When the metaphysical workers came to Mrs. Eddy's study one morning for their daily instruction, the oversensitive Laura was in an obvious state of nervous exhaustion—white, shaking, and hardly able to stand. Mrs. Eddy asked her to step forward from the others and immediately addressed her in tones of ringing authority— and severity. This time it was evident that Mrs. Sargent accepted the reproof as meant for the "error" and not for herself, for as she listened she gradually straightened up, her trembling stopped, the color came back to her cheeks, and at the end she stepped back to the others free and normal.[101]

Life at Chestnut Hill might be strenuous; it was never dull. "We live," Mrs. Eddy had written, "in an age of Love's divine adventure to be All-in-all."[102] Some of those adventures might be, in their way, as drastic as the shipwrecks, floggings, and imprisonments, the infirmities, reproaches, and persecutions, in which the Apostle Paul "took pleasure."[103] And to some, at least, of the members of Mrs. Eddy's household even the grimmest of their trials seem to have had the feel of blessedness.

5

The atmosphere of the church in Boston had changed greatly since Mrs. Eddy had left that city twenty years earlier. With denominational success, it was becoming less yeasty, more self-satisfied. There was at least one moment when Mrs. Eddy felt a passing impulse to stir up her church officers to bolder public claims and evangelistic effort, but she quickly reverted to her fundamental conviction that only a deeper spirituality demonstrated through more consistent healing could forward the cause of truth. This was the radical position. Salvation by proclamation was a specious hope.

At times, it seemed to her that the church was full of strangers. To be sure, three of her oldest students were still on the Board of Directors, but William B. Johnson would resign in 1909, to be succeeded by a man she did not even know, and in 1910 Ira Knapp would die in office, leaving only Stephen Chase of the original Directors to serve a year or two longer.

The other two members of the board in 1908, Archibald McLellan and Allison Stewart, represented a different breed entirely from these plain, hardy Yankees. Pupils of Kimball rather than students whom she herself had taught and nurtured through a quarter of a century, the two successful Chicagoans brought to their office broader professional and executive experience but a less tough-fibered spiritual radicalism.

Judge Clifford P. Smith of Iowa, a man in his late thirties and also a pupil of Kimball, was now First Reader of The Mother Church, a Trustee of the Publishing Society, and a rising power in the movement.[104] Even Dickey and William R. Rathvon, a Coloradoan of German extraction who entered the household as an additional secretary and metaphysical worker late in 1908, were Kimball pupils who found it almost impossible to imagine the pioneer days of Christian Science which had produced and molded, for instance, a Calvin Frye.[105]

Mrs. Eddy remained oriented toward the future, even if in the twilight hours when she sat with Frye or Dickey looking out at the passing cars and carriages she reminisced nostalgically about "the golden days"[106] of childhood—which had not seemed nearly so golden in the 1820's and '30's. She knew that change was the essence of human life, and all her deepest thought was given now to how the movement could be fitted to confront the immense changes of the future when she was no longer there to guide it.

Increasingly she refused to make important decisions when the Directors turned to her for advice. They had the *Manual* and her other writings; let them turn to that source for the rules and to the divine Mind for guidance, as they would have to do in the decades and centuries to come if Christian Science was to fulfill the destiny she saw for it. Increasingly, also, she left the answering of letters to her secretaries,[107] while she reserved her strength for the more crucial demands of her remaining years.

There was perhaps symbolic significance in the fact that she never entered the great extension of The Mother Church, whose dome she could sometimes glimpse across the Back Bay Fens on her longer drives. Only once did she ask to be driven to where she could see the church at close quarters, and on that occasion a sudden attack of illness rendered her almost unconscious by the time the carriage drew near the church.[108]

She never repeated the request. The building was to remain for her what she had described it as being in her dedication address in 1906: " . . . a mental monument, a superstructure high above the work of men's hands, even the outcome of their hearts . . . the one edifice on earth which most prefigures self-abnegation, hope, faith; love catching a glimpse of glory."[109]

Meanwhile, however, the building of the *Church Manual* went on.[110] In 1908 Mrs. Eddy abolished the category of First Members (renamed Executive Members several years earlier), which had represented for a time the residual element of congregational democracy in The Mother Church. The following year, on the other hand, she strengthened the democratic self-government of the branch churches by providing in another bylaw that each of them in its internal affairs should be free from interference by any other church—including, by logical necessity, The Mother Church. Through this sort of two-edged clarification, she was articulating for the future the basic federal structure of the organization, with its delicate balance between authority and democracy.

In some respects she was like a military commander strengthening the base of operations for a prolonged campaign which would last far beyond his tenure of personal command. The phenomenal success of Christian Science[111] never for a moment blinded her to the growing intensity of opposition centered on her person but clearly aimed at the force she had set in motion—a force which seemed to many good people at that time to threaten the order of rational science as well as of established religion.

Reports came into Chestnut Hill of both Protestant and Catholic assemblies praying ardently for Mrs. Eddy's death, on the assumption that Christian Science would wither away once its leader was removed. Books, pamphlets, lectures, sermons continued to castigate its theology, its healing work, its literature, its influence on popular thought, even as its Committees on Publication won strenuous legal and legislative battles for the right of Christian Scientists to practice what they preached. Some adherents, lulled by the multiplication of their own numbers, anticipated a rapid conversion of the world, but Mrs. Eddy foresaw increased resistance to the challenge she had flung at organized mortality.[112]

A single example will illustrate the fear as well as the virulence inspired by the spectacular advance of Christian Science at that time. Dr. Stephen Paget, a distinguished British surgeon who had written a critical book entitled *The Faith and Works of Christian Science*,[113] told a Church of England diocesan conference in 1909 that what was needed was a "furious, hating attack" on Christian Science. As reported in the *Church Times*, he had gone on to specify the mode of attack:

> *The doctor and the clergyman must co-operate against Christian Science, not when people were ill, but when they were well. Take a village where the Lady Bountiful was a Christian Scientist. The two men must co-operate to make her faith and works a positive burden to her (laughter and applause). They must ridicule her up and down the place; they must laugh her pretensions to scorn. . . . They must hammer the enemy wherever they could get him—in the pulpit, the press, across the dinner-table, in the market place, all the way round, everywhere.*[114]

While active medical and theological opposition was predictable, the same species of outrage colored the more offhand pronouncements of men of letters and affairs who found the frail octogenarian at Chestnut Hill an intolerable affront to their sense of the fitness of things. Charles Eliot Norton, for instance, could announce with chill Harvardian distaste, "Mother Eddy is the most striking and ugliest figure in New England today," and even so genial a personage as William Dean Howells could write Mark Twain, "Read your Mrs.

Eddy massacre just before I left home and gloated on every drop of her blood."[115]

The lady in question was well aware of the extent of such charitable sentiments, not to mention the invocation of the more livid curses of Deuteronomy 28 by the pious nuns at a St. Joseph, Missouri, convent[116] and the cultivated ill will directed at her from a daunting variety of other sources. Her endeavor was to make all such execrations a means of grace. On one occasion, at a time of stress, she recalled the metaphysical workers to her study to tell them that she had just heard as if a voice had spoken it the biblical verse: "My grace is sufficient for thee." Then, after recalling them once again, she added:

> *I wanted you to know how beautifully that verse concludes: For my strength is made perfect in weakness. When I exhibit material strength then am I weak (will-power, temper, etc.) . . . My enemies . . . have nothing to rejoice over in this present condition.*[117]

Convinced that a proper estimate of her lifework was essential to a proper understanding of her message, Mrs. Eddy from time to time had given thought to the matter of future biographies. In 1903 she had written William D. McCrackan impulsively, "If my history is to be written I hope you will write it,"[118] only to look in another direction two months later when she wrote John B. Willis in regard to an article by him:

> *I* thank you. *My history dolorosa you have depicted, it brought my tears, it will bring others! . . . I am in love with your pathetic style and deep, clear, logical portraiture of cause and effect forming ones life work.*[119]

More seriously she considered both Tomlinson and Farlow as biographers, and the two men spent considerable time in gathering evidence, checking testimony, and chasing down elusive facts.

Farlow actually prepared two books composed largely of documentary evidence, one on the Quimby question and one on Mrs. Eddy's life in general, but in each case she finally decided against their publication[120] as she did also with the documented history of the next friends suit by Michael Meehan.[121] Impressive as much of the evidence in these compilations was, her decision appears to have been a wise one in the long run, since it would have been a tactical mistake to present such important but incomplete primary evidence within so defensive a framework.

As to Tomlinson, she decided in August, 1908, "that he was not broad enough to write her history, but that she would sometime get the right one to write it for her."[122] Only a few days previously, she had exacted from Dickey a solemn promise that after her decease he would make a record of his experiences with her, but in that case she seems not to have had a full-scale biography in mind.[123] At some point she even felt that it might be a hundred years before an adequate biography of her could appear.[124] Once again her sense of history came into play. "Time tells all stories true,"[125] she liked to say, and the developing future would be quite as important as the recorded past in putting her life authentically into perspective.

This whole matter was brought to the fore by the publication of Sibyl Wilbur's *Life of Mary Baker Eddy* in August, 1908. Financed by an Indiana businessman, John V. Dittemore, who had since become Committee on Publication for New York, Miss Wilbur had rewritten and expanded her *Human Life* series into an even more laudatory biography about which Mrs. Eddy had grave reservations even before she read a word of it. In the midst of a physical crisis on August 29 she called in Farlow and directed him to stop the circulation of the book, whereupon she immediately recovered from her prostration.[126] The next day she wrote Miss Wilbur a letter of thanks for acceding to her request to have the book withdrawn from circulation:

> *Please to accept my thanks for your goodness and wisdom in acting so promptly and cheerfully relative to publishing my personal history. I remember your heroism shown in Concord New Hampshire and that same honesty and Divine purpose are governing your life.*[127]

The letter was premature, for on September 10 Dittemore wrote his business partner, William R. Brown:

> *Miss Wilbur has consulted Mr. Elder [Samuel Elder, the Boston attorney] & he is going to undertake to find out for her whether the suppression of the book can be withdrawn. . . . Miss W. seems pretty much worked up & has numerous theories as to "why" things are as they are.*[128]

Faced with the possibility that the disappointed author might take legal action, Dickey asked Mrs. Eddy in a note two weeks later, "As a choice of two evils, do you not think it would be better to waive objection to the circulation of the book, and let them go ahead without your endorsement?"[129] Mrs. Eddy agreed and the sale of the book went forward.

A year later, the Milmine *Life of Mary Baker Eddy*—rewritten, expanded, and even more caustic than the original *McClure's* series—appeared in book form.[130] This seems to have persuaded Mrs. Eddy at last to give the rather cool endorsement of the Wilbur biography which thereafter appeared in that book, preceding the frontispiece and title page.[131] The need for a friendly biography had overridden her misgivings about the shortcomings of the book, misgivings which had been confirmed in the spring of 1909 when Tomlinson read portions of the Wilbur *Life* to her and took note of her objections.[132]

Yet the evidence points to a good deal more than an old lady's touchy concern for her personal reputation. Long before fashionable psychobiography had begun its reinterpretation of life histories in terms of current psychoanalytic theory, she had written in her own auto-biography, "The human history needs to be revised, and the material record expunged."[133] Rather than asking for a sweetening or censoring of established facts, she seems to have been demanding the kind of radical insight into a life that would bring its inner structure to light, as opposed to a mere prowling through the dead lumber of external events. Since the central fact of her own life was Christian Science, some genuine insight into the operation and dynamic of the latter would be a prerequisite to understanding the meaning of her life—and the reverse would also be true.[134]

Thus, despite her desire to see the Peabody–Milmine sort of attack refuted, her common sense kept her aware that a good deal more time would need to elapse before the full facts of her life could be confronted with any depth of realism, and that this would depend on how the structure she had given to the Christian Science movement would have stood the test of the coming years. The best she could hope for in her own lifetime was to prepare her followers by such explanations as her 1907 statement:

> *At this period my demonstration of Christian Science cannot be fully understood, theoretically; therefore it is best explained by its fruits, and by the life of our Lord as depicted in the chapter Atonement and Eucharist, in "Science and Health with Key to the Scriptures."*[135]

The chapter in question dealt with what might be called the Christian depth-dimension of her teachings, and in some ways it was harder for her followers to assimilate than her "absolute" metaphysics. At the heart of Christianity lay the historic sacrifice and triumph of Jesus Christ. In the unique yet archetypal life of the Messiah who was "despised and rejected of men," who was "wounded for our trans-gressions" and "bruised for our iniquities,"[136] was to be found the key to the resistance encountered in some degree by every true spiritual reformer.

At the same time, Mrs. Eddy drew a clear distinction between the lifework of the Founder of Christianity and her own role in discovering and founding Christian Science. He alone from birth to ascension was the immaculate Exemplar for the human race. His life would stand for all time as the ideal but essential exemplification of the Christ in human experience. The same *Manual* bylaw which pointed to him as the perfect model for all Christian Scientists expressly forbade "careless comparison" of him with any other.[137]

In contrast with his, her work had been to discover and teach the structure of law implicit in his demonstration of man's true being. For this age, she held, truth was to take form as a universal science rather than as a personal saviour.[138] The Christ historically demonstrated by one man was to be recognized as the Christ potentially demonstrable by all men. Predictably this revelation would stir up the same sort of opposition as the earlier demonstration of it had[139]— but this time from scientific as well as religious orthodoxies. In both the life of Christ Jesus and the teachings of Christian Science there was, Mrs. Eddy held, a common element intolerable to "mortal mind." As a student in one of her last classes recalled her words:

> She said if Jesus had not declared his divine origin he would not have been crucified. If she had not declared that Science is revealed Truth, mortal mind would be proud of it.[140]

Mrs. Eddy regarded herself as necessarily a student of the science she had discovered[141] and as learning step by step—through trial and error as well as through inspiration—how to apply it to the superhuman task she had been given to do. Her life, as she saw it, was a constant sacrifice to her mission. It was therefore not her life she held out to the world, but her books, her teachings, the church she had founded to lift the world further toward God.

Those of her followers who pictured her as a semidivine creature serenely removed from all ills missed the true magnitude of her achievement. Her strength, as she told her household in 1908, was perfected in weakness, and twenty years before that she had expressed to one of her students what she saw as the meaning and the paradox of her life: "As Mary Baker Eddy, I am the weakest of mortals, but as the Discoverer and Founder of Christian Science, I am the bone and sinew of the world."[142]

Chapter X

Quod Erat Demonstrandum

Quod Erat Demonstrandum

"We err in thinking the object of vital Christianity is only the bequeathing of itself to the coming centuries,"[1] Mrs. Eddy had written in 1901. Nor would the mere temporal and pragmatic success of Christian Science be enough, in its founder's eyes, to justify its self-perpetuation; nothing but progressive demonstration of its profoundly Christian purpose would do that.[2]

In popular thought Christian Science had taken on much of the coloration of the buoyant, optimistic America in which it had surfaced. It was widely regarded as a variant, if not the prototype, of the current success philosophies—and psychologies—that appealed so powerfully to American businessmen. But to Mrs. Eddy, with her roots deep in New Testament Christianity as well as New England Puritanism, success was not to be confounded with salvation. Prosperity might come as the result of demonstrating the love of God for His entire creation, but worldly success on a materialistic basis was far from being a sign of spiritual grace.

In that respect, Mrs. Eddy's teachings differed radically from the popular New Thought pronouncements of Orison Swett Marden, whose magazine *Success* did manage to get quoted in the *Sentinel* occasionally but which properly belonged to a very different tradition. Despite an increasing number of articles on "demonstrating supply" in the Christian Science periodicals in the first decade of the century, Mrs. Eddy was extremely chary of having people turn to Christian Science for the loaves and fishes, and she especially commended an article by Farlow in *The American Business Man*, which said among other things:

> Sometimes individual prosperity is not rightly grounded, and like a house with inadequate foundation, it must therefore be taken down and rebuilded. . . . That which is not rightly done is a misdoing, not a real accomplishment, and, painful as the ordeal may seem to the one concerned, the sooner there is an undoing and a redoing, the better. What appears to be loss under such

*circumstances is not loss but gain. If our riches are not fittingly
acquired they are not really ours, and the sooner we lose them
and learn our actual situation, the better.*[3]

Mrs. Eddy had written that "success in error is defeat in Truth,"[4]
and this would necessarily be as true of the Christian Science movement if it should allow itself to fall into the ways of the world as it
would be of the individual Christian Scientist. The question of
success was therefore related intimately to the question of succession—
of the direction the movement would receive and take when Mrs.
Eddy was no longer on hand to guide it personally.

Both these questions came to a climax in her last three years in
connection with her brilliant, volatile student Augusta Stetson.

Mrs. Stetson had made a raging success of her fashionable aposto-
late in New York City. The wealthy and socially prominent flocked
to her services at First Church of Christ, Scientist, in that city and
sought help from the twenty-five practitioners with offices in the
superbly appointed church building—practitioners to whom Mrs. Stetson gave daily instruction in matters practical and esoteric. Her
philosophy is well expressed in a talk to her pupils in 1902:

> *We need health and strength and peace, and for these we
> look to God. But let us not forget that we also need things, things
> which are but the type and shadow of the real objects of God's
> creating, but which we can use and enjoy until we wake to see
> the real. We surely need clothes. Then why not manifest a
> beautiful concept? Clothes should, indeed, be as nearly perfect
> as possible, in texture, line and color. . . . It is certain, too, that
> we need homes. Then why not have beautiful homes? Our homes
> should express the highest sense of harmony and happiness. . . . We
> have a right to everything that is convenient, most comfortable,
> most harmonious. God made all things, though we only see their
> shadows, and all things are for His children. Everything is ours. It
> does not belong to mortal mind.*[5]

This is the sort of covert materialism of which critics accused Mrs.
Eddy but which is actually a far cry from her teaching. The symbol
she had chosen for Christian Science was a cross encircled by a crown,
but the cross was notably absent from Mrs. Stetson's scale of values.
Through twenty-five years of watching her talented student's development as a Christian Scientist, Mrs. Eddy had alternated between appreciation of her success in building up Christian Science in New
York and a deep concern over her methods, aims, and the quality of
her thinking.

In 1892, on the eve of forming The Mother Church, she had written her "darling Augusta":

> *My heart goes out to you with a prayer—Father keep her, Oh!*
> *keep her in "the paths of thy testimony." If I write but seldom I*
> *never lack this earnest yearning for your growth and welfare. Oh*
> *forget not the shoals on this unexplored coast! and hold . . . your*
> *gaze steadfastly on God and know that if you trust alone in Good*
> *. . . you cannot make shipwreck.*[6]

Although she felt very close to Mrs. Stetson at times and poured out affection and gratitude in her letters, the possibility of shipwreck was always in the background. "You must make strong efforts to save poor Stetson," she wrote Hanna in the mid 1890's, "or m. a. m. will put out her light."[7] The trouble was not merely the worldliness of the self-designated "leader" of Christian Science in New York, her flair for and faith in publicity, her determination to build a church that would surpass in size and splendor all other Christian Science churches, her personal domination of her pupils. What was even more disturbing was her claim to be the only true teacher of Christian Science in New York and closer to Mrs. Eddy spiritually than any other Christian Scientist anywhere.

This inevitably brought her into sharp conflict with many of Mrs. Eddy's students and particularly with the other teachers in New York. In a confidential letter to these teachers in 1899, Mrs. Eddy pointed out the harm that would come from an open split and urged:

> *Keep in fellowship with Stetson and her church. . . . I have*
> *borne much more than you ever can bear from her. She is now*
> *improving under the rod. She is a worker capable of doing great*
> *good and that is why I have held on to her because I loved that*
> *in her and still love it.*[8]

Mrs. Stetson, in return, unquestionably loved Mrs. Eddy after her fashion, which was a highly personalized and even idolatrous one. While Mrs. Eddy found that she could sometimes win Augusta's assent to an unwelcome position by virtue of this emotionalized loyalty, she also saw its danger and warned her repeatedly against the deification of personality. Not only was idolatry abhorrent in itself, but it could also, she recognized, be used as a conscious instrument of self-glorification and personal power by a high priestess serving the deity of her own creating.

On a number of occasions she warned Mrs. Stetson against thinking or speaking of her as a Christ, and in a 1903 letter she pointed out an extension of the same delusion in Mrs. Stetson's basic metaphysics:

> *In your letter to me you spoke of your "divine self." Where do you find such a selfhood outside of God? Nowhere; it is an unscientific statement. You can say your spiritual or God-like self, but divine self includes God, and man is not God—he is His divine reflection, but not a divine selfhood. This expression is one of* Waldo Emerson's *notions, and you beware of m. a. m. filling your thoughts with such* anti-Christian *Science!* . . . *Your material Church is another danger in your path it occupies too much of your attention it savors of the goddess of the Ephesians, the great Diana. O turn ye to one God. I had hoped the interval from Readership would give you a great growth in healing and this is needed more than all else on earth.*[9]

The mention of readership refers to Mrs. Eddy's request in 1902 that branch churches adopt or adapt for their own situations the new bylaw restricting the terms of the Readers of The Mother Church to three years.[10] This had been a great blow to Mrs. Stetson, who had been First Reader in First Church, New York, for many years and intended to continue in that position indefinitely. At first she consulted an attorney (one of her own pupils) as to whether her church could secede from The Mother Church,[11] but as a result of his legal advice and (presumably) her personal loyalty to Mrs. Eddy, she gave up the idea of secession and stepped down from the readership without further ado.

From that time on, however, rumors began to circulate and stories to appear in the press that Mrs. Stetson was expected to succeed Mrs. Eddy as Leader of the Christian Science movement. Though quickly denied by the former, later evidence was to reveal that she was evolving and finally teaching to her inner coterie of pupils a mystical doctrine of spiritual succession, according to which she had been "divinely" appointed by Mrs. Eddy to bring salvation to the world as the sole teacher of Christian Science and to head the movement after Mrs. Eddy had been "translated" into pure spirit.[12]

As long ago as 1895, the founder of Christian Science had complained of "the madness of [Mrs. Stetson's] ambition,"[13] and in its later stages it reached a point of almost literal madness. In her daily meetings with the twenty-five practitioners of her church, she began to hint at a new trinity: Mrs. Eddy as God, Mrs. Stetson as Christ, and First Church, New York, as the Holy Ghost. In 1906, while this insane fantasy was only embryonic and was carefully concealed by her from Mrs. Eddy and from all other Christian Scientists except her own trusted intimates, she wrote a letter which set alarm bells ringing for Mrs. Eddy. Its drift is summed up in a short passage:

> If I thought you could not demonstrate life eternal I would have no courage to go on. If I thought you would ever cease to lead me, I would be utterly hopeless. If I thought there would come an hour when I could not hear you, mentally, or see you through the veil of flesh, as spiritual substance, idea, I could not press forward. . . .[14]

The letter went on with more of the same and Mrs. Eddy dictated an immediate reply:

> I read in your mind an illusion to which you must be awakened, namely, that those, who have departed from a sense of life here, control those who have not departed but are with us in the flesh.
>
> The evil influence that is working against you, to which you alluded in your letter, is instilling this thought in your mind. This illusion is a belief of spiritualism disguised. . . .
>
> Drop forever from your thought the spiritualistic illusion that I am your guiding spirit here or hereafter, for I am not; and you will sink the Principle of Christian Science in personality and ruin your scientific progress, if you continue to believe this lie.
>
> The evil one and the one evil is continually at work on you endeavoring to fasten this hallucination upon your thought; and whatever of good or of evil, which you do under the influence of this belief, is simply self-mesmerism, engendered by hypnotism and its effects upon you.
>
> Now, Augusta, awake from this lie! I am not personally influencing your life one particle. It is only my written word and verbal communications to you, which benefit you or can benefit you, for it is Truth and not personality that guides you aright. . . .
>
> You are never safely guided by personality, your own or anyone else's. I am not your guardian spirit here, and I shall not be hereafter. You have one God, one Spirit, and that God is your Guide, and that Guide is not a person but a Principle. Remember this, and never write to me again nor think again in any other direction, if you would save yourself from the fatal effects of hypnotism.
>
> I am trying to get away from personality, and you are trying

to fasten yourself to personality. Opposites cannot affiliate. You are taking yourself away from my teaching by this course, and I implore you to abandon the views, which you express in your letter to me, and be a Christian Scientist, for you never can be one on the basis that you predicate in your letter. Write to me immediately, and let our love for one another continue steadfast, established on Christian Science, on Principle and not on a person.[15]

After the move to Chestnut Hill, Mrs. Eddy several times wrote Augusta urging her to keep her own and her pupils' thought away from her.[16] Behind the scenes, however, Mrs. Stetson continued on her disaster course, impressing on her dazzled pupils that she was the chosen vessel and mouthpiece of Mrs. Eddy's highest teachings. This was the pattern for later aspirants who would try to capture the church for themselves, as contrasted with defectors like Josephine Woodbury who simply turned against the church and its founder.

Meanwhile, First Church, New York, was flourishing like a forest of green bay trees. On November 30, 1908, the *New York American* announced that in order to take care of its immense overflow congregations, First Church was planning to build a "branch" church on Riverside Drive. This branch of a branch would surpass in size, splendor, and costliness not only First Church, which would finance, plan, and essentially direct it, but also the great Mother Church extension in Boston. It would stand as a monument to Mrs. Stetson's predilection for material magnificence as the supposed symbol of spiritual power. It would also effectively make of its "parent"—First Church, New York—a rival mother church and open the way for it, under Mrs. Stetson's guidance, to develop a whole system of branch organizations.

Mrs. Eddy immediately took action. The *Christian Science Sentinel* for December 5 carried a lead editorial, "Consistency," written mostly by her but (at her request) signed by McLellan. It expressed her often reiterated preference for modesty in church buildings and asked the question: "Are you striving, in Christian Science, to be the best Christian on earth, or are you striving to have the most costly edifice on the earth?"[17]

A second editorial, also signed by McLellan at her request but actually written by Tomlinson under her direction, was entitled "One Mother Church in Christian Science." Its argument can be illustrated by a typical passage:

*The Christian Science movement is in accord with Jesus'
words: "The branch cannot bear fruit of itself, except it abide in
the vine." Were one branch church to depend upon a neighboring
branch for training and support, this action would tend to sever
its connections with The Mother Church. The essential condition
for fruit-bearing is undivided attachment to the parent Vine. On
the other hand, no branch church, however large, is privileged to
oversee or supervise another branch. Such action would violate a
fundamental rule in Christian Science. The Church Manual declares: "The branch churches shall be individual" (Article XXIII,
Sect. 6).[18]*

The *Sentinel* having spoken out officially, Mrs. Eddy now invited
Mrs. Stetson to come to Boston and "take a drive with me around the
Chestnut Hill Reservoir."[19] The two women had not met for more
than two years, and their brief reunion on December 9 was filled with
emotion for both of them. In the course of their drive, Mrs. Eddy
probed Augusta's attitude and found her full of apparent docility,
ready to abandon the plan for the new church if her Leader thought
it unwise—and hastening to assure her that she had never really intended that it be a *branch* of First Church.[20]

When they returned from the cold winter drive, Mrs. Eddy invited her guest to come up to her study for a few moments, then sent
for her again as she was leaving. It was to be the last time they would
meet face to face. As Augusta knelt on the floor at her feet, Mrs. Eddy
took the younger woman's face in her hands, gazed into her eyes long
and searchingly, then said with deep solemnity: "God bless you forever and forever and forever."[21] As events were to show, it was a fare-
well to twenty-five years of patient effort, struggle, hope, and disappointment.

For the moment, however, the crisis was laid. First Church, at
Mrs. Stetson's request, returned to the donors the money already con-
tributed for the proposed Riverside Drive edifice. The *New York
World*, which on December 14 had run sensational headlines—*Mrs.
Eddy Defied in Mrs. Stetson's New Church Plan. Christian Scientists
See in Riverside Drive Project a Scheme to Seize Control of the Cult.
Mother's Frail Condition Denotes a Crisis Is Near*—announced the next
day: "The projected building of a new Christian Science Church in
Riverside Drive . . . has been abandoned temporarily," and quoted Mrs.
Stetson's announcement that "Mrs. Eddy can never have any personal
successor. Her teachings will be her only successor."[22]

After the immediate matter had quieted down, Mrs. Eddy made her first public statement on the subject in an article called "The Way of Wisdom." The most pointed paragraph read:

> *I have crowned The Mother Church building with the spiritual modesty of Christian Science, which is its jewel. When my dear brethren in New York desire to build higher,—to enlarge their phylacteries and demonstrate Christian Science to a higher extent, —they must begin on a wholly spiritual foundation, than which there is no other, and proportionably estimate their success and glory of achievement only as they build upon the rock of Christ, the spiritual foundation. This will open the way, widely and impartially, to their never-ending success,—to salvation and eternal Christian Science.*[23]

This was a concept of success far removed from Mrs. Stetson's. At the end of her *Retrospection and Introspection*, Mrs. Eddy had written, "I am persuaded that only by the modesty and distinguishing affection illustrated in Jesus' career, can Christian Scientists aid the establishment of Christ's kingdom on the earth."[24] But in that same period in the early 1890's, the rebellious William Nixon had warned, "When the founder of Christian Science is taken away, its Christianity will disappear with her."[25]

2

Virgil O. Strickler, First Reader of First Church, New York, was not a pupil of Mrs. Stetson, but by virtue of his office he was invited by her to attend the daily meetings she conducted for the twenty-five practitioners in the church who were her pupils. As he listened to her private instructions to them, his admiration for her was gradually shot through with alarm and he felt it morally imperative to keep a close record of the daily proceedings in his diary. On February 23, 1909, he wrote:

> *Here is her position as she has outlined it today:*
>
> *1. She is working for the destruction of the 2nd, 3rd, 4th, 5th, & 6th churches [in New York City] as well as of the people who compose them.*
>
> *2. No recognition of those churches as being churches will ever take place except over her prostrate form.*

3. Even though Laura Lathrop, John Lathrop and the rest of her enemies in these churches should confess their faults and ask to be forgiven she would not forgive them, but would insist that it would be necessary for them to die and to suffer thru ages before they could be forgiven.

4. In short the issue is that either Mrs. Stetson must be destroyed or else these five churches must be destroyed. Which will it be![26]

During the next six months the moral deterioration continued at a formidable rate. On July 4 Strickler recorded Mrs. Stetson's macabre boast, "I strike to kill!" and then continued:

My reason and my conscience tell me that she understands the letter of Christian Science almost perfectly; that in all matters in which her enemies do not figure she is normal and does much good; but as to all matters relating to her enemies that she is insane. . . . I do not know by what name alienists designate the form of insanity which causes a person to desire to kill everyone against whom they have a grievance. I think it is paranoia. . . . *She works for hours every day to destroy by the use of mental weapons the persons against whom she has real or fancied grievances. . . . She declares that Mrs. Eddy is God and that she is Christ, the "First Born." She asserts that all of her enemies as well as all other people must come to her for spiritual light and that if anyone refuses to recognize her as the First Born they shall die and go out with suffering untold and die on the next plane of consciousness and the next and so on forever until they recognize her as Mrs. Eddy's* first born *and until they atone for the sin of having doubted or opposed her. . . . [July 7] To me these things are nothing more nor less than the vagaries of a disordered mind, but to most of the practitioners they have solemn import. Richard Verrall is the greatest surprise. He seems too intelligent to actually believe the things Mrs. S. stands for, but . . . is leaving no stone unturned in his efforts to make her think that she is Christ.*[27]

Six days later the bedazzlement of the practitioners was made evident in a gift of gold pieces which they gave their teacher together with a composite letter which reached the heights of mystical adoration. "May a purified life," wrote one of them, "attest the endless gratitude I feel for the manifestation of the Christ you have given us, while, with Mary of old I cry, Rabboni—Teacher." Even the sober Richard Verrall could slip into his tribute a phrase that might have come from St. John of the Cross: "In grateful acknowledgment of your example and thinking, we, *as members of your body,* desire to offer this evidence of our intelligent loyalty."[28]

Mrs. Stetson promptly sent the gold and the letter to Mrs. Eddy with a fulsome explanation that "I feel they belong to you, dearest, and are your fruit."[29] Mrs. Eddy in turn forwarded the composite letter to the Board of Directors with a terse command: "Act, and act quickly. Handle the letters according to *Science and Health* and the Mother Church *Manual.*"[30] To Mrs. Stetson she replied:

> *I have just finished reading your interesting letter. I thank you for acknowledging me as your Leader, and I know that every true follower of Christian Science abides by the definite rules which demonstrate the true following of their Leader; therefore, if you are sincere in your protestations and are doing as you say you are, you will be blessed in your obedience.*
>
> *The Scriptures say, "Watch and pray, that ye enter not into temptation." You are aware that animal magnetism is the opposite of divine Science, and that this opponent is the means whereby the conflict against Truth is engendered and developed. Beloved! you need to watch and pray that the enemy of good cannot separate you from your Leader and best earthly friend.*
>
> *You have been duly informed by me that, however much I desire to read all that you send to me, I have not the time to do so. . . . Mr. Adam Dickey is my secretary, through whom all my business is transacted.*[31]

This letter was published in the next issue of the *Sentinel,* a copy of which was handed to Mrs. Stetson while she was conducting the daily practitioners' meeting. Strickler recorded in his diary that one glance at it "was sufficient to transfix her with horror" and, he continued, she became almost hysterical:

> *Her first words were "Oh my God!" Then she held the paper out to me and said in a tone of anguish, "Take it! I can't read it! I can't . . . I don't know what she may have said. She has probably said awful things to me. Students, be prepared for anything. I do not know how she may have rebuked me."*

Strickler looked at the printed letter and told Mrs. Stetson that it was evidently the same one she had received from Mrs. Eddy a few days before:

> *She visibly shuddered at this. When she became somewhat calm I read the letter aloud. . . . In spite of all this . . . she actually*

attempted to make us believe the letter contained evidence of her high standing with Mrs. Eddy and I think about nine tenths of the practitioners are so mesmerized that they believe it.[32]

It was, as Strickler wrote in his diary, the beginning of the end. A week later, when Mrs. Eddy received further reports of Mrs. Stetson's reputed teachings, she drafted or dictated several stiff letters to that lady but sent only the mildest of them, which read:

My dear Student:

Awake and arise from this temptation produced by animal magnetism upon yourself, allowing your students to deify you and me. Treat yourself for it and get your students to help you rise out of it. It will be your destruction if you do not do this. Answer this letter immediately.

As ever, lovingly your teacher,
Mary Baker Eddy[33]

Mrs. Stetson's reply showed that she had learned nothing over the years from Mrs. Eddy's repeated warnings against personal worship. Meanwhile, Mrs. Eddy authorized the Directors to call Stetson to Boston for questioning, take the matter into their own hands, settle it according to the *Manual*, "and leave me out of the question."[34]

At the same time Strickler felt at last compelled to get in touch with a member of the Board of Directors and give him a hint of what was going on in the practitioners' meetings at First Church. At a second meeting with two of them, he tried out on them one of Mrs. Stetson's milder, comparatively "loving" treatments directed by name against the Lathrops, and both Directors were profoundly shocked by it. In his diary afterward Strickler commented: "If these two directors of the Mother Church think that is mal-practice, in God's name what would they think if they only knew some of the bloodcurdling murderous things she has uttered in the practitioners meetings."[35]

By now Mrs. Stetson was hurling her maledictions at all who opposed her, including and particularly the Directors, who, she convinced herself, were persecuting her in direct disobedience to Mrs. Eddy's wishes. Her powerfully uttered commands to them to go "six feet underground"[36] were, she explained to her chosen group, wholly defensive, although Mrs. Eddy herself had explicitly spiked that argument in a 1905 letter to her:

The Golden Rule must guide all your acts. Thirty years ago and over, I taught the Old Testament rules or law of defense. But now I no longer teach the law, but the Gospel in this line, even the rule of our blessed Lord viz. Love your enemies; and return good for evil. And, thank God, I practice these rules daily and hourly, leaving the punishment for mental malpractice alone in His hands who cannot fail in justice or mercy or wisdom.[37]

Mrs. Stetson's own methods were mental malpractice by any reckoning. Some of the earnest practitioners in her group felt deeply uneasy over what was happening but were either too fearful of her vengeance to speak up or allowed themselves to be lulled back to sleep by her strong-willed persuasions; others were so far under her spell that anything she did was ipso facto the work of God. Even Strickler found it painfully difficult to hold out against her play for sympathy when she returned at the end of July, like a wounded martyr, from her first interrogation in Boston.

At the practitioners' meeting later that morning, she began in a confused and halting way, working around little by little to what she wanted the practitioners to say if they should be called to The Mother Church for questioning. Strickler reminded her of some of the things she had often said in these meetings and pointed out that she would be expelled instantly from the church if questions should be asked about these things and they should answer truthfully. His diary entry continues:

> She said "I know it, what shall we do?" She then became almost hysterical and talked rapidly and without much coherence. After a while she said, "we must deny that I ever said any of these things, I deny that I ever said them."[38]

That is exactly what some of the students did when they were examined later in Boston, telling themselves that they were justified in answering "in the absolute"—i.e., denying that something had been said or done, on the ground that error of any kind was only an illusion.[39] This peculiarly dangerous and repellent kind of doublethink was denounced by McLellan in a *Sentinel* editorial a few weeks later,[40] and no issue in the whole Stetson case showed more clearly the moral idiocy, to use Mrs. Eddy's own expression, to which a perversion of Christian Science metaphysics could lead. Twenty years earlier she had written Mrs. Stetson:

> My students are doing more for, and against, C. S. than any others can do. They are the greatest sinners on earth when they

injure it; and are doing more good than all others when they do the best they know how.[41]

Under the circumstances, it is not altogether surprising that on August 2, while the situation was at fever heat, Mrs. Eddy had a return of the old 1903 difficulty and Frye wrote in his diary the next day: "Intense pain last night she requested an M. D. to administer an hyperdermic: called W. H. B." To which he added without comment: "Mother heard an audible voice from God saying 'Leave alone successor contention before it is meddled with.' "[42]

The next day Mrs. Eddy wrote the Directors and asked them to dismiss the charges against Stetson, pointing out that the *Manual* provided for each branch church to discipline its own members.

Mrs. Stetson of course took this as complete vindication, but her jubilee was short-lived. The "mesmerism" was beginning to break for some of the members of her own branch church, including a few of the practitioners in her inner ring of initiates. Troubled complaints, private confessions, and volunteered information in affidavit form were disclosing the situation to the Boston authorities in bits and pieces.[43] Finally Strickler, accompanied by the Second Reader of First Church, read to the Directors portions of his diary which filled in the picture in all its gruesome detail.[44]

With this revelation, the problem could no longer be treated as a matter for branch church discipline. The point at issue was the conduct of a teacher and practitioner authorized by The Mother Church and subject to specific *Manual* bylaws against mental malpractice. Mrs. Eddy was informed, and on September 9 she instructed the Directors to act as befitted The Mother Church when called upon to deal with such "impious conduct."[45] Her name was to be kept out of the proceedings; church discipline was a matter of bylaws, not of persons.

Mrs. Stetson was again called to Boston and examined, and this was followed on September 25 by notification that her right to teach Christian Science had been revoked and her name had been removed from the *Journal* as a practitioner. A committee of inquiry at First Church, composed of her most ardent supporters, reported at a riotous six-hour business meeting on November 4 that they had found her innocent on every point on which the Christian Science Board of Directors had found her guilty, but some of the practitioners who had been trying unsuccessfully to free themselves from her mental hold—including Richard Verrall[46]—found the courage at last to break away.

On November 15 the climax came. On that day the final trial of Mrs. Stetson before the Directors in Boston started. On that same evening a tense meeting at First Church, New York, convened, the lines drawn up for battle. After the opening exercises, the chairman announced that he had a message from Mrs. Eddy and then proceeded to read it:

> *My beloved brethren in First Church of Christ, Scientist, New York City, I advise you with all my soul to support the Directors of The Mother Church, and unite with those in your church who are supporting The Mother Church Directors. Abide [in Truth,] in fellowship with and obedience to The Mother Church, and in this way God will bless and prosper you. This I know, for He has proved it to me for forty years in succession.*[47]

Strickler, who had been heavily under attack from the pro-Stetson faction, wrote in his diary a day or two later:

> *The effect was magical. Bitterness disappeared from the faces of the people and one could feel the relaxation. I stated that I would entertain a motion to adjourn which was voted unanimously and after singing . . . "Shepherd, show me how to go," the meeting was over. . . . As one newspaper reporter put it, "Mrs. Eddy's words were so potent that a meeting which was expected to split the church lasted only 14 minutes and ended in a song."*[48]

When Mrs. Stetson read the letter which had wrought this result, she issued a statement to the press which for the first and only time admitted publicly that she might have been wrong:

> *For 25 years I have gladly obeyed [Mrs. Eddy's] leading in every question. I have always found that by doing this I drew nearer to God. My students know that I have taught them to do likewise, without questioning her wisdom. . . . They will know that it is right for them to unite with those who supported The Mother Church Directors in the judgment rendered against me. I myself have been obeying that judgment, and I shall continue to do so. I shall furthermore obey my Leader by uniting with those who felt it was right to condemn me in their testimony. My leader's letter induces me to believe that I may have been wrong where I felt that I was absolutely right.*[49]

After her three-day trial, Mrs. Stetson was dropped from membership in The Mother Church, and later the same action was taken in regard to those practitioners who continued to defend her position and follow her teachings and guidance. Her moment of meek submission was as ephemeral as, apparently, it was tactical. Quickly she convinced herself that Mrs. Eddy fully supported all that she had done and was only trying to free her from the bonds of organization so that she might build the mystical Church Triumphant on a purely spiritual basis.

From that point on, however, her practical impact on the Church of Christ, Scientist, was effectively ended. In another stormy meeting on January 18, 1910, the members of First Church, New York, elected a new board of trustees free of Stetson influence. The following month the trustees and Readers of the eleven Christian Science churches and societies of Greater New York—"for the first time gathered in one place with one accord"—sent Mrs. Eddy an appreciative but eminently nonmystical letter announcing their intention "to take such action as will unite the churches and societies in this field in the bonds of Christian love and fellowship, thus demonstrating practical Christianity."[50]

3

The Stetson bid for succession had failed, but to Mrs. Eddy as a woman the whole matter was a tragedy rather than a triumph. Her love and hope for her talented, wayward student had been genuine. There was no personal satisfaction to her in discovering how far the worst in Mrs. Stetson had triumphed over the best.

Even after the latter's expulsion from the church and her quick rebound to a position of complete self-justification, Mrs. Eddy hung on for a little to the irrational hope that the chastised student might even now be saved and reinstated. An entry in Rathvon's diary for December 15, 1909, tells the story.

Adam Dickey, Rathvon noted, had not lasted much after nine o'clock on the "watch" that night, but before he was replaced by another member of the household he had done some good work in showing Mrs. Eddy what would happen if Stetson were reinstated. "You would have no church," he had told her flatly. It looked to Rathvon as though the Stetson influence on her were

> making a frantic effort to hang on when its grip is being shaken loose every day. Tonight's experience should give it the last shake and thus free our Leader from its fangs and give her the peace and freedom she deserves if anyone in this wide world does.[51]

That this hope was on the way to realization seems indicated by an entry in his diary ten days later, December 25:

> Mrs. Eddy was in her study earlier than usual and a few minutes afterwards called us to her side. . . . Never did she appear

*more vigorous physically and mentally, nor was her manner ever
more gracious and loving. . . . She also said, impressively, "By
another Christmas there will be great changes. See that you make
them for the better."*[52]

Her work was clearly drawing to a close. However much she may
have grieved personally over the Stetson case, it had brought great
clarification to the succession issue. The future of the church—and
thereby of Christian Science itself—hinged on assuring government by
impersonal law rather than by charismatic leadership. The problem of
authority was to be solved by the spiritual authority of *Science and
Health* in conjunction with the temporal authority of the *Church
Manual*.

At the height of the Stetson controversy, Mrs. Eddy sent a conclusive statement for publication in the *Journal*:

> *I approve the By-laws of The Mother Church, and require
> the Christian Science Board of Directors to maintain them and
> sustain them. These Directors do not act contrary to the rules of
> the Church Manual, neither do they trouble me with their diffi-
> culties with individuals in their own church or with the members
> of branch churches.*
>
> *My province as a Leader—as the Discoverer and Founder of
> Christian Science—is not to interfere in cases of discipline, and I
> hereby publicly declare that I am not personally involved in the
> affairs of the church in any other way than through my written
> and published rules, all of which can be read by the individual
> who desires to inform himself of the facts.*[53]

In the same issue of the *Journal*, one new bylaw and amendments
to three existing bylaws were printed. Taken together they show
clearly the direction Mrs. Eddy's thought was taking. Although obviously occasioned by the Stetson situation, they were powerful moves
toward safeguarding the structure of her church against future
struggles for personal control, as well as toward protecting her teachings from dismemberment by personal interpretation:

> *In order to be eligible to a card in* The Christian Science
> Journal, *churches and societies are required to acknowledge as
> such all other Christian Science churches and societies advertised
> in said* Journal, *and to maintain toward them an attitude of
> Christian fellowship.*

. . . A teacher shall not assume personal control of, or attempt to dominate his pupils, but he shall hold himself morally obligated to promote their progress in the understanding of divine Principle, not only during the class term but after it, and to watch well that they prove sound in sentiment and practical in Christian Science. He shall persistently and patiently counsel his pupils in conformity with the unerring laws of God, and shall enjoin them habitually to study the Scriptures, and "Science and Health with Key to the Scriptures" as a help thereto.

The associations of the pupils of loyal teachers shall convene annually. The pupils shall be guided by the Bible, and Science and Health, not by their teachers' personal views. Teachers shall not call their pupils together, or assemble a selected number of them, for more frequent meetings.

A loyal teacher of Christian Science shall not teach another loyal teacher's pupils, except it be in the Board of Education. Outside of this board each student occupies only his own field of labor. . . .[54]

These same tendencies were reinforced by a letter from Dickey to McLellan in the *Sentinel* of January 15, 1910, setting forth Mrs. Eddy's desire that all branch churches "shall follow the growing tendency to adopt a truly democratic form of church government," and pointing up her meaning with the statement: "She believes that all branch churches that have been controlled by any one teacher, or the students of any one teacher, will find it greatly to their advantage to change to a broader and more liberal form of government."[55]

Mrs. Eddy's own relations with the officers of her church were in a transitional state. While she took an active part in deciding the question of dropping William B. Johnson as Clerk and as member of the Board of Directors in May, 1909,[56] she left it to the Directors to choose his successor, telling them only that she wished them to elect "a scholarly, educated man and a thorough Christian Scientist" to replace him.[57]

When they came up with the name of John V. Dittemore, whom she had met once for a minute or two but could not remember, she told the Directors they would have to appoint him on their own responsibility. Reminded that the *Manual* required her approval of the appointment, she reluctantly gave the needed signature but again emphasized that they must take responsibility for their choice.[58]

Ironically, Dittemore—who played a prominent role in the exposure and trial of Mrs. Stetson—would more than a decade later turn against the church and Mrs. Eddy's leadership and himself be expelled.[59]

On September 22, 1909, Judge Smith—who was acting as special counsel to the Directors in the Stetson affair and would play a somewhat similar role in the later Dittemore case—paid his one and only visit to Mrs. Eddy in company with McLellan. After they had concluded the legal business which had brought them, Mrs. Eddy asked the others present to leave the room and then spoke to Smith for fifteen minutes on the subject of organization.

It was almost, he wrote later, as though she were giving a public address, and she seemed to be a different person as she spoke with authority and precision on the absolute need for organization as a protection to the cause of Christian Science:

> She continued by saying that the organization should fit the occasion; that is, the Christian Science movement needed an organization corresponding to its character and purpose. She spoke of the Christian Scientists who go about saying we need no organization as "not knowing what they are talking about." She also said, in substance, "Organization is a simple matter, for all of its importance. It is simply a matter of doing things by working together."[60]

To some of those around her it seemed that working together under the *Manual* would be anything but simple when Mrs. Eddy was no longer available to supply the authorization or signature required for the functioning of certain existing and essential bylaws. Would not the whole *Manual*, in fact, become inoperable if and when the Board of Directors could no longer obtain her written assent to actions made necessary by these very bylaws?

William Rathvon, as a household member who saw her withdraw further each day mentally from the direction of church affairs, was particularly concerned by this contingency. After consulting with Hanna and Smith—both of them lawyers and both sharing his concern—he came up with a plan for the formation of an advisory council to act in Mrs. Eddy's place if she were unable to give the necessary signature to actions proposed under the bylaws in question.

Dickey, however, refused to present the plan to Mrs. Eddy. There is no evidence that even he recognized at the time how radically such a change in structure would have affected the delicate balance of authority she had provided for the future. But he felt strongly that it would be a mistake to present the plan to her, and finally Rathvon found the reassurance he needed in a conversation with her lawyer cousin, General Baker. "You need not be at all uneasy," Baker emphatically told him when he raised the point about the bylaws which required her signature:

> It is a matter of common law in a case of this kind, where it is physically impossible to carry out specified conditions by the one named, that the next in authority assume that jurisdiction. And in this case the next in authority is the Board of Directors of The Mother Church. Any competent court in the land will uphold the Manual just as Mrs. Eddy intends it to function whether her signature is forthcoming or not.[61]

It is a matter of interest that both Dickey and Rathvon were members of the Board of Directors in 1921 when the Supreme Judicial Court of Massachusetts upheld this position just as Baker had predicted.[62] By that time they were fully agreed that there never had been any need to urge upon Mrs. Eddy so complicating and potentially disruptive a mechanism as an advisory council with veto power over crucial appointments, decisions, and actions of the board entrusted with administering the Manual.

At the same time, the bylaws requiring that certain steps be taken only with her written consent would continue to have additional moral force, as she undoubtedly intended. They would make morally incumbent upon the Directors a careful consideration of the spirit and letter of her instructions before taking a step under any one of these bylaws. Only if it was found that the contemplated action was in full accord with her stated intentions would it have behind it the authority of the Discoverer and Founder of Christian Science and thus fall within the terms of their trusteeship.

To have Christian Scientists look to "the books" instead of to her person was increasingly Mrs. Eddy's aim. In line with this, she asked that the portrait of her which had appeared in some editions of *Science and Health* and *Miscellaneous Writings* be removed and no picture of her appear in any future editions. To her household she remarked:

> In so far as one personalizes thought he limits his spiritual growth. We grow in understanding and if I have ever permitted any personality I have outgrown it.[63]

This remark was made in connection with the marble statue of a "woman in prayer" which had been prepared to go on a pedestal above the organ pipes of The Mother Church extension. Although it bore no resemblance to Mrs. Eddy and was not intended to represent her, the danger that it would be so regarded was obvious. At the very time she was struggling to rise above the turmoil of the Stetson affair, Rathvon wrote in his diary:

> *A Minnesota woman has been at work on this and now notifies the Directors that it is ready for placing. This brought out a strong countermand from our Leader and was the subject of several talks this* PM *on the necessity of impersonalization of thought. Among other things she said, "You will bear testimony that I have of late repudiated the elevating of graven images of personality."*[64]

The Stetson trauma had brought its own blessing to the founder of Christian Science in a deepened sense of what she had written years before in connection with *Christ and Christmas*: "Idolatry is an easily-besetting sin of all peoples."[65]

4

Life was not all bylaws for Mrs. Eddy. Nor all metaphysics. It was small pleasures as well as large demands, interludes of rest as well as intervals of storm, quietude as well as preparation.

There were times when she would call members of the household in to sing the songs she always delighted to hear, when there would be reading aloud or discussion of recent happenings—like Peary's reaching the North Pole or the aviation meet at Squantum which several of the workers had attended.[66] There were pleasant little incidents like that recorded by the indefatigable Rathvon in 1909:

> *The article in the Monitor of yesterday on Luther Burbank and his work was read to our Leader, who enjoyed it greatly and exclaimed, "How I would like to teach that man Science!" AHD[ickey] told her that somewhere Burbank says, "Plants are as responsive to thought as children." "That is Christian Science," said our Leader.*[67]

The next day, by an interesting coincidence, a letter from Luther Burbank ordering two copies of *Science and Health* was received by the book's publisher. Mrs. Eddy was "much pleased," Rathvon noted.

By this time she was definitely at home in Chestnut Hill. "If you cannot make a home here," she told her workers, "you cannot anywhere." But her fuller explanation and later comments were instructive:

Home is not a place, it is a power. Going home is doing
right. . . . I am glad all of you . . . are going with me homeward,
and we will all meet there. . . .

The strongest tie I've ever had, apart from love of God, has
been my love of home. . . .

We can love one another more because we love home most.
. . . I've had to learn. If blessings wouldn't do it, kicking would.
I've had both. . . .

I do not want any of you to leave me. When I get attached
to a person, I stick like a nit.[68]

If she could laugh at herself a little, she could also be coolly
objective. "There is a great gulf between old age and middle age,—a
second childhood," she told them on one occasion. "When a member
of my family is absent now I watch and am anxious for his return
the same as I did when I was a child."[69] It was this strong feeling for
her household "family" that had induced her to allow them to go
on calling her "Mother" after Christian Scientists as a whole had
been forbidden to apply the term to her, but on her eighty-ninth
birthday she called the household together and asked them to discontinue its use. It would be "better and more scientific" not to do so,
she told them.[70]

If there were times when they were discouraged by her physical
and mental condition,[71] they never ceased to be amazed at the way
in which she could rally from indisposition and enter with renewed
vigor into the business of the moment. There were periods of prolonged tranquillity, and such diary entries as Rathvon's for April
9, 1910, were not unusual:

As all hands . . . were assembling in the Pink Room,
AMcL[ellan] arrived and joined us. Then for forty minutes our
Leader held forth in most remarkable fashion at her very best.
She took high ground and held it; she thrust and parried and
had everybody on the run, yet it was all straight Science.[72]

Two weeks later, looking back on her leadership through the
years before he had known her, Rathvon wrote:

I can well understand how she could sway those whose service
or support she needed, for a more lovable person could not be
found in the pages of history or in the hearts of men. If God had
embodied in this remarkable personality all the grace and right-
eousness that He has given to man through it, we would all be
worshippers of the creature instead of the Creator. "But we have

this treasure in earthen vessels, that the excellency of the power may be of God, and not of us."[73]

This biblical application was something that many of her followers would have found hard to understand or even believe. At times the members of her own household found it difficult to reconcile the vision of reality which they had caught from her with the struggles that wracked her, the weakness that beset her, the occasional violent storms that exploded when she was under special stress. But they at least had been taught that their task as healers was not to reconcile such opposites but to destroy the offending errors. On one occasion at the beginning of 1910 she told them:

> *In the New Year see me not sprawled out on the brink but see me about the house as I used to be. See me as God sees me. See only as my spiritual nature devises, directs and demonstrates. And see your wife, your children and all as God sees them, free, upright, perfect.*[74]

This metaphysical demand played havoc with conventional judgments. One trying day when Mrs. Sargent had said or done something which greatly annoyed Mrs. Eddy, the latter burst out afterward to Adelaide Still, "That woman hasn't a scrap of gratitude for all that I've done for her." The shocked Adelaide protested, "You know that isn't so, Mrs. Eddy; it's just animal magnetism that makes you say things like that." Mrs. Eddy pointed sternly to a chair opposite her and said, "Sit down, Adelaide!" Then a brief dialogue followed.

"Did you discover Christian Science or did I?"

"You did, Mrs. Eddy."

"Did you find out about animal magnetism or did I?"

"You did, Mrs. Eddy."

"And do you know more about handling animal magnetism or do I?"

"You do, Mrs. Eddy."

"Well," the discoverer of Christian Science concluded mildly, "never forget it."[75]

With this basic point established, all was well again. A few minutes later, she called Mrs. Sargent back for some small service and addressed her affectionately, with not a trace of the former annoyance. Adelaide quietly absorbed the lesson: one impulsive reaction was not to be cured by another impulsive reaction; she was there to help Mrs. Eddy at moments of stress, not to lecture her; she could do this more effectively by seeing Mrs. Eddy, Mrs. Sargent and, for that matter, herself "as God [saw] them, free, upright, perfect."[76]

She could, in fact, practice the Christian Science she had been taught.

Mrs. Eddy at all times kept before herself the hugeness of the task still to be done. Too much human tranquillity was not good, in her eyes. She deliberately stirred up her household at times, as she often had stirred up the movement. Truth demanded proof at every point of experience, she emphasized; mortal mind—"a murderer from the beginning"[77]—had no intention of letting Christian Science peacefully coexist with its own presuppositions. One or the other, she was convinced, must triumph in the end.

Back in 1908 when a new coachman at Chestnut Hill had been found dead in his bed one morning, she had inserted at the end of the chapter in *Science and Health* called "Christian Science Practice" a clipped command: "Christian Scientists, be a law to yourselves that mental malpractice cannot harm you either when asleep or when awake."[78]

Later in that same year, when she herself was going through an acutely difficult time, she said with impressive gravity to Adam Dickey, "If I should ever leave here, will you promise me that you will write a history of what has transpired in your experiences with me, and say that I was mentally murdered?"[79] Although the request with its defeatist implications was never repeated after her recovery from that particular crisis, she continued to explain the periodic struggles she experienced as resulting from the opposition of entrenched materiality to its destroyer.

On occasion the whole household could be thrown into upheaval by a small misunderstanding. Such episodes, however, were apt to have a dimension that lifted them above the plane of trivial domestic discord or momentary hysteria. This was particularly marked in the case of an emotional cloudburst, with attendant thunder and lightning, caused by the misreporting of a temporary indisposition that kept Mrs. Sargent in bed one morning.

As Mrs. Eddy, following the sudden outburst, sat in her armchair, a little dazed by the small tempest she herself had set in motion, she suddenly roused herself, called Adelaide Still to her side, and dictated to her a brief statement. A few days later she polished the statement further and sent it to the *Sentinel* for publication under the title "A Pæan of Praise." In its final form it read:

> "Behind a frowning providence
> He hides a shining face."

The Christian Scientists at Mrs. Eddy's home are the happiest group on earth. Their faces shine with the reflection of light and love; their footsteps are not weary; their thoughts are upward; their way is onward, and their light shines. The world is better for this happy group of Christian Scientists; Mrs. Eddy is happier because of them; God is glorified in His reflection of peace, love, joy.

When will mankind awake to know their present ownership of all good, and praise and love the spot where God dwells most conspicuously in His reflection of love and leadership? When will the world waken to the privilege of knowing God, the liberty and glory of His presence,—where

> *"He plants His footsteps in the sea*
> *And rides upon the storm."*[80]

It was her Christian Science treatment for the situation that had arisen. In a larger sense, it was her undiminished challenge to what she had elsewhere called "the ghastly farce of material existence."[81]

5

The last year of Mrs. Eddy's life arrived with a light footfall. On January 1, 1910, she called her entire household in and talked to them happily about the fourteenth chapter of John to which she had just opened.[82] After they left, she picked up her pen and quickly composed a little New Year's greeting which she then called them back to hear:

I
O blessings infinite!
O glad New Year!
Sweet sign and substance
Of God's presence here.

II
Give us not only angels' songs,
But Science vast, to which belongs
The tongue of angels
And the song of songs.[83]

Early in February Rathvon noted in his diary: "Those who have been here longest say that not for years has there been such a long period of tranquility as of late."[84] There were days or weeks of severe challenge later, especially in May and September,[85] but the greatest challenge was Mrs. Eddy's growing detachment. William P. McKenzie's account of his visit with her in April, after his not having seen her for several years, tells the story:

*She appeared as one who had been through conflict, showing
evidence thereof, yet remaining victor. Her first question was,
"Did you know me?" My whole heart went out to her in gratitude
as I replied, and once more I saw the light from her eyes which
made her face shine. . . .*

*[Later] I began to tell her of the welfare of the Publishing
Society. I spoke of the many puzzling problems which had come up
in our work so greatly enlarged in scope with the issuing of a daily
newspaper and how much we had wished her both to advise us
and to direct us—how we had asked her for this help a good many
times, but she had not elected to give it and so to the best of
our ability we had to seek earnestly for the guidance of Mind.
Once again I saw her rare smile as with deep earnestness she said
to me, "That is just what I wanted you to do."*

*There must have been a silence for a time. I seemed in that
quiet to newly discern her purpose that all of us in the movement
should be actually manifesting an obedience to God similar to
her own. . . . I know that as I sat quietly in Mrs. Eddy's presence
for the last time, I gained a new sense of the word patience. . . .*[86]

As the weeks went on, she became frailer and more ethereal in
appearance, not taking enough nourishment "to support a kitten,"
as Rathvon noted in his diary.[87] A few days later he added, "It is
hard to say whether our duty lies in urging that more be taken, or
whether it is not best to let the demonstration be made without any
attempt at directing its course."[88] And on July 6 he wrote:

*The most marked change of any since my coming here has
been taking place in the past three months. It portends a meta-
morphosis of some extraordinary nature and which I must believe
is for the good. There is a general softening and broadening. The
nights are quieter than for years and years, I am told, and the
days are full of rest and quiet. I would like to see more vigor
mentally and physically, and more interest in things that were
once the center of thought, but these may be incidental in the
working out of the problem that I feel is under way. There is
little or no physical ailment, the many things that we have had
daily to struggle with having all disappeared into their native
nothingness.*[89]

There was a general sense in the household that Mrs. Eddy was
making toward an unknown destination, a new order of experience,
and she herself clearly had some sort of crucial change in mind. On
August 20 Frye noted in his diary, with his usual lack of comment:

After a peaceful night Mrs. Eddy began singing as soon as she woke this morning at about 7 o clock an old hymn:

"Journeying on journeying on
Bound for the land where our loved ones are gone
See in the distance the bright glowing morn
Journeying on journeying on.[90]

Taken at face value, this could suggest her acceptance of the traditional Christian concept of a heaven to be reached beyond the grave—as, for that matter, might the final stanza of her own "Mother's Evening Prayer," which they had all sung together on New Year's Day:

No snare, no fowler, pestilence or pain;
No night drops down upon the troubled breast,
When heaven's aftersmile earth's tear-drops gain,
And mother finds her home and heavenly rest.[91]

If the metaphor was traditional, the metaphysic that underlay it was not. Mrs. Eddy was by no means retreating into orthodoxy, into the soothing expectation of a compensatory heaven to be gained by dying. Death was the "last enemy that shall be destroyed," as Paul had written,[92] but it was definitely an enemy, a concomitant of the mortal dream to be overcome, not an element of the divine order to be welcomed. Heaven, on the contrary, was a present reality—to be perceived, attained, and demonstrated by living, not dying; it was the state of mind that understood God to be the only life, without beginning and without end.

Almost a quarter of a century earlier, she had written in *Unity of Good* of the "time and immense spiritual growth" required for "complete triumph over death." Then she had gone on to say, in words which reached far beyond denominational and doctrinal considerations to the crucial question of the individual's relation to the truth he lives by:

> *I have by no means spoken of myself, I* cannot *speak of myself as "sufficient for these things." I insist only upon the fact, as it exists in divine Science, that man dies not, and on the words of the Master in support of this verity,—words which can never "pass away till all be fulfilled."*
>
> *Because of these profound reasons I urge Christians to have more faith in living than in dying. I exhort them to accept Christ's promise, and unite the influence of their own thoughts with the power of his teachings, in the Science of being.*[93]

In the intervening years she had many times reiterated this distinction between the fullness of divine Science, as presented in her writings, and the degree to which she might be able to demonstrate it personally in her remaining years on earth. In an undated note in her own handwriting she stated flatly, "Mrs. Eddy has often been asked if she believed she should ever die and always said, There is in reality no death but I have never supposed that I should not pass the transition from this state of existence to another one."[94] Another undated fragment expands on this:

> . . . I have not yet reached the ultimate practical proof of absolute Christian Science, the "full corn in the ear," and may never reach it while remaining visible to the personal senses. But I have written it and my works teach it. God has enabled me—unworthy as I am of such divine Love—to discover and to make known on earth the Divine Science of the divine Principle that heals the sick and saves the sinner through Christ, Truth, Life and Love.[95]

If she could bring her church to the point at which she might safely leave it to advance without her personal presence, she might write Q. E. D. to her forty-five-year mission. But that would not end the need for her own further growth in demonstrating in her personal experience the truths she had taught in her books.[96]

On the other hand, there was no compromise of her metaphysical position in this twilight period of her life. Never, in fact, was she more decisive in regard to the "scientific" statement of truth as a prerequisite to its demonstration. When a Christian Scientist wrote to Chestnut Hill asking whether he was right in referring to himself as an immortal idea of divine Mind (a statement which had been challenged by a fellow Scientist on the ground that he was still living in his flesh) Mrs. Eddy answered in the October Journal:

> You are scientifically correct in your statement about yourself. You can never demonstrate spirituality until you declare yourself to be immortal and understand that you are so. Christian Science is absolute; it is neither behind the point of perfection nor advancing towards it; it is at this point and must be practised therefrom. Unless you fully perceive that you are the child of God, hence perfect, you have no Principle to demonstrate and no rule for its demonstration. By this I do not mean that mortals are the children of God,—far from it. In practising Christian Science you must state its Principle correctly, or you forfeit your ability to demonstrate it.[97]

While the penultimate sentence, with its implicit demand for Christian regeneration, acted as ballast to the statement as a whole, Mrs. Eddy obviously had no intention of modifying the challenge of her radical metaphysics.

At the same time, she continued to be concerned about Christian Scientists who babbled the letter of Christian Science without understanding it as a practical discipline. In a short article entitled "Principle and Practice,"[98] which she dictated to Dickey in September, 1910, she castigated the tendency to accept Christian Science as a mere matter of faith. Healing on such a basis, like any other faith cure, might flourish at first but would inevitably and rightly wither away in time. Science demanded intelligent comprehension, consistent practice. The sharp realism of her warning and the concentrated purpose of the article suggest anything but the pitiful senility attributed by some biographers to the founder of Christian Science in her last months.[99]

Her inner life was, however, increasingly hidden from her associates. There were now days on end when she did not call the household workers together. Sometimes she was alone all day, attended only by Adelaide Still, except for the period of her afternoon drive. This latter ritual, which at one time had been more of a burden than a recreation to her,[100] seems once again to have become a pleasure and now tended to last almost an hour. Yet even that was a working time, and she told Rathvon only two weeks before her passing, "I have uttered some of my best prayers in a carriage."[101]

What was actually going on in her thinking during the days when she remained in solitude is revealed by some of the fragments she dictated to Miss Still in those hours. Among them is one dated simply October, 1910, which tells more than all the diary entries of her male secretaries:

> The deepest hallowed intoned thought is the leader of our lives, and when it is found out people know us in reality and not until then. The surface of the sweetest nut is often a burr, and the thought that guides our life and expresses our being is unseen, except in the outward expressions and actions thereof. Hence the folly of declaring obstinately who is who and what is what, unless we have tested and proven the who and what. The wisdom of the wise is not as much expressed by their lips as by their lives.
>
> I sit quietly alone in my room conversing with the world, and the people thereof answer me intelligibly, the good in man comforts me, affords me pleasure and gives me no displeasure, and

our communings are sincere and sacred. All this has its fulfillment, without a sign dishonest, insincere, ungrateful, unjust. But the opposite of this experience claims as much feasibility and reality as the experience itself. Here learn a lesson of the parable [of] the sower, both sprang up and bore fruit, the good fruit was productive and the evil fruit produced nothing, for good is real and evil is unreal.

The wisdom of this hour and the proper labor of this hour is to know of a certainty the quality of the seed which takes root in our thought . . . in short, the moral life's history is, Be good, do good, speak good, and God, infinite good, cares for all that is and seems to be. . . . Who believes what I have written? He who has the most experience of Good. Who disbelieves it? He who has the most fear of evil. What is the remedy for this belief? It is experience, for every moment, hour and day of mortal existence brings each one of us nearer the understanding of the nothingness of evil in proportion to our understanding of the allness of good.[102]

She was coming back to the heart of the "discovery" she had made in 1866. It was what her students, her church, her movement must demonstrate as she had shown them how to do in her writings. She had provided the framework, the rules, the practical means to carry the work forward; it was up to them to do the rest.

This letting-go brought a strange relaxation to the household—and one that was partly delusory, for within a few weeks they and all Christian Scientists would have to gird themselves for a more lasting challenge than any they had faced in Mrs. Eddy's lifetime. They would have to learn how to carry on the work she had started without her being present any longer to take the main shock of the world's antagonism.

When the good-natured George Kinter came to Chestnut Hill in October to substitute for a few weeks for Dickey, who was called to Kansas City on personal business, he felt and partly misinterpreted the difference in atmosphere between this interlude and his earlier stays with Mrs. Eddy and summed it up in a letter to his friend John Lathrop:

> *. . . Now as to matters here, in which I am sure you are always mightily interested. Things have changed perceptibly and perhaps as much as in any other particular our dear friend's own manner of spending the days. But little reading and scarce any writing,*[103] *a quieter and more peaceful day by all odds than*

ever before, with far greater serenity, and contented reliance upon others to do, at least, as well as may be. All but one may and usually do retire in the evening and are seldom ever called during the night now. [Mrs. Eddy] does not breakfast nearly so early as of yore, and the drive comes at one or as soon thereafter as convenient, generally before half past, but sometimes lasts a full hour, oftener about three quarters. Musicals comprise a frequent means of divertisement and entertainment, sometimes we are all asked to join, but oftenest it is a solo or more by one of the ladies who sings and plays well; the victrola is now in the pink parlor and is frequently brought into requisition. . . .

Perhaps as great as the sort of thing I have related is the increasing release of pressure upon those in attendance; Calvin is quite another person, having, as you doubtless know, much less to do, he is very much more affable, and tractable, more communicative, and far less querulous. Then the folks disport themselves in manners and fashions unknown in days of yore. For example right after breakfast we usually go into the library and look over the daily Boston papers until about 8 o'clock, then each goes his own way, or sometimes two or more go together, one day recently several of us found ourselves in the woods opposite on a chestnut hunt, again Irving took me out to a golf club some miles away with the Ford Runabout, and we spent an hour very agreeably on the links, returning to the house about half past nine.

The Rathvons take the Ford one noon hour and Irving the next; they all go to the neighborhood libraries, and I am now appropriating the new horse Nellie for a drive either morning between half past seven and 9.30 or at noon. . . . [Mrs. Eddy] has gotten over her aversion to having people look into her carriage and rather seems to enjoy it, although I would not advise its being announced [at the] Wednesday night [meeting].[104]

Beneath and beyond these household trivia, other events moved forward. In November Ira Knapp, patriarchal as ever, died in office. For some days Mrs. Eddy took no action on a replacement for him on the Board of Directors. Among the new businessmen and lawyers who were filling church offices efficiently but tending sometimes to think more in terms of executive skill than of spiritual inspiration, she needed someone who had learned from experience with her the nature of the challenge to which they must all rise soon. First she offered the post to Calvin Frye, who wisely refused it, then to Adam Dickey, who on November 21 became a Director.

As she now faced the last enemy, the Church of Christ, Scientist, faced what the sociologist would term the final step from charismatic to bureaucratic leadership. The two challenges, as Mrs. Eddy saw it, were related more than circumstantially.

On November 27 she dictated and signed a single sentence: "It took a combination of sinners that was fast to harm me."[105] Heretofore she had been the focus of the attack on Christian Science. How could she make those who would carry on her work understand the depth of the opposition they would encounter and the height of spiritual demonstration they would have to rise to unless the whole enterprise was to go down in ruins? Some time before, in an effort to shock the members of her household to such an awareness, she had told them that she was living on a plane of thought that would mean instantaneous death to any one of them.[106] Could the officers of her church understand what that meant?

Toward the end of November she caught a severe cold but went out for her drive every day just the same. On Thursday, December 1, as she rode silently beside Mrs. Sargent, her thought seemed far away yet strangely intent. At one point she spoke aloud, as though to herself: "Oh, if the students had only done what I told them, I should have lived and carried the cause."[107]

Upon her return, she had to be carried into the house, and as she lay on her couch it seemed to those around her that she was going. But once again she rallied, called for her writing tablet, and on it set down her last written message: "God is my life."[108] This affirmation spanned forty-five years to the episode of healing in February, 1866, which she had later summed up in a sentence: "That short experience included a glimpse of the great fact that I have since tried to make plain to others, namely, Life in and of Spirit; this Life being the sole reality of existence."[109]

The next day she did not dress but insisted on getting up and going in to her study, where she lay on the couch all day. On the following morning—Saturday, December 3—she stayed in bed but was alert and sent messages to the "watchers." In the afternoon she sat up and for several hours prayed silently for herself; at the end, Adelaide Still noted, she was very much better and sent a message: "Drop the argument; just leave me with divine Love; that is all I need."[110]

After eating her small supper, Mrs. Eddy settled down quietly and that evening at 10.45 passed away without a sound as Dickey and Mrs. Sargent sat beside her.[111] When Miss Still came as usual at seven o'clock the next morning, Frye was sitting outside Mrs. Eddy's bedroom door and said to her simply, "Mother has gone, Adelaide."[112] The medical examiner for the district, Dr. George L. West, who was called in early that morning to issue a death certificate, had his own comment to make to the reporters who questioned him afterward:

> *What struck me most as I looked into the dead face was its extraordinary beauty. . . . The entire countenance bore a placid, serene expression, which could not have been sweeter had the woman fallen away in sleep in the midst of pleasant thoughts. I do not recall ever seeing in death before a face which bore such a beautifully tranquil expression.*[113]

West recorded the death as due to natural causes, "probably pneumonia," and Alfred Farlow, upon further questioning by the press, added that Mrs. Eddy had been indisposed for nine days but critically ill for only two. Later the undertaker who arrived at 8.15 on the Sunday morning gave the church a voluntary statement that throws its own light on Mrs. Eddy's last years:

> *The tissues were remarkably normal; the skin was well preserved, soft, pliable, smooth and healthy. I do not remember having found the body of a person of such advanced age in so good a physical condition. The walls of the arteries were unusually firm and in as healthy a state as might be expected in the body of a young person. The usual accompaniments of age were lacking, and no outward appearance of any disease, no lesion or other conditions common to one having died at such an advanced age were noticeable.*[114]

Later that morning at The Mother Church the Sunday service was carried on as usual, with none of the congregation aware of what had happened the night before, until at the end the First Reader, Judge Smith, made a special announcement. He first of all read them part of a letter Mrs. Eddy had written to the Christian Scientists' Association of the Massachusetts Metaphysical College in 1891:

> My Beloved Students:—*You may be looking to see me in my accustomed place with you, but this you must no longer expect. When I retired from the field of labor, it was a departure, socially, publicly, and finally, from the routine of such material modes as society and our societies demand. Rumors are rumors,—nothing*

*more. I am still with you on the field of battle, taking forward
marches, broader and higher views, and with the hope that you
will follow. . . . All our thoughts should be given to the absolute
demonstration of Christian Science. You can well afford to give
me up, since you have in my last revised edition of Science and
Health your teacher and guide.*[115]

At that point Smith paused for a moment, as the hushed audience
waited, wondering a little; then he continued:

*Although these lines were written years ago, they are true
to-day, and will continue to be true. But it has now become my
duty to announce that Mrs. Eddy passed from our sight last night
at 10.45 o'clock, at her home in Chestnut Hill.*[116]

There were sad faces but few words as the awed congregation
dispersed to the triumphal strains of a Bach toccata from the church
organ. Speculatively they streamed out to a world whose easy assumptions would soon enough be shaken by the first installment of
Armageddon.

Epilogue

Epilogue

In the late twentieth century, questions that were once considered to be metaphysical luxuries have become sharply relevant to the survival of the human race. The ultimate nature of space, matter, life, consciousness, man, language, reality, myth, are seen to have more than a theoretical bearing on the practical decisions of today and tomorrow.

It is not just that we have all become amateur cosmologists and therefore incipient metaphysicians. The very urgencies of global politics, environmental crisis, and technological momentum make impossible an indefinite continuance of the piecemeal empiricism that has brought us so far toward chaos.

In that respect, at least, the brutalitarian planners of enforced utopias are right. Society must seek rescue either by building on an increasingly uncompromising materialism or by discovering radically new possibilities of restructuring experience in the ancient faith that "there is a spirit in man."[1] The choice is stark, the issue crucial. Either the self-destroying energies of matter or the still untried potentialities of spirit will determine humanity's future.

By this time it should be possible to look back across the intervening decades of war, holocaust, revolution, depletion, pollution, across the constantly accelerating cultural change and moral ferment of society, to see Mary Baker Eddy in something other than the terms of either the yellow journalism or the denominational hagiography of her day.

Early in her career as Discoverer and Founder of Christian Science she wrote, "The time for thinkers has come."[2] And again, "As the crude footprints of the past disappear from the dissolving paths of the present, we shall better understand the Science which governs these changes, and shall plant our feet on firmer ground."[3] It is as a thinker that Mrs. Eddy will finally be judged, and as such she may well be accounted the metaphysician who pursued spiritual idealism to its furthest extreme and found it, to her own satisfaction, to be solid realism—found the life of the spirit (in her terminology, the Life that *is* Spirit) to be more concrete, fundamental, demonstrable, determinative, than all the fluctuating phenomena displayed to the physical senses and their instrumental extensions.

Either spiritual values are the mere transient bloom on a passing phase of evolutionary development which itself is an inconsiderable disturbance in the vast, blind realm of spacetime, or they are indications of a different order of being, as it breaks in upon material appearances. Mrs. Eddy, convinced that a Science of Being was even more possible than a science of appearances, nevertheless saw that in human experience all science must be tested *by* experience as well as by reason. This would be true even if its basic data were obtained through the experience of "revelation"—a mode of apprehending reality to be judged not only by its inner consistency but also by its outer results. And it is here that Mrs. Eddy as thinker is inseparable from Mrs. Eddy as doer.

It has been suggested that her unique contribution to world thought was a metaphysic that *healed*.[4] In the same way it might be said that her unique contribution to Christianity was her concept of the lifework of Jesus Christ as an illustration of demonstrable Science rather than a miraculous or magical interruption of the natural (i.e., *true*) order of things. Only demonstrated facts, she insisted, could give authority to words that proclaimed the kingdom of God, the primacy (indeed the allness) of Spirit.[5]

So it is that the Discoverer of Christian Science invited the judgment of history on the Founder of the Church of Christ, Scientist. To rescue the world from its tragic somnambulism, its passage from daydream to nightmare, there must be community, organization, united effort—in short, a church—but the measure of the church's success would not be its size or prestige but the quality of the Christianity demonstrated by its members. From past history the unmatched example of Jesus provided the standard for all time. Future history would have to disclose how far this new spiritual enterprise, presented as science, was bearing witness to the possibility of scientific Christian discipleship in a world devoured by multiplying doubts.

In a very real sense, Mrs. Eddy entrusted the justification of her lifework to her followers. How seriously she would be taken as a thinker in years to come would depend largely on their lives, their demonstrated lovingkindness, their practical intelligence, their radical healing works, their unreserved commitment to the authority of Spirit in the affairs of men. She herself wrote, "What I am remains to be proved by the good I do."[6] The good she did remains to be proved by the church she founded.

If there was any shadow over her last days, it was the recognition that Christian Scientists might have to learn for themselves some of the hard lessons she had hoped to save them from by her teachings and rules—and this need could delay their fuller demonstration of truth to the world, itself in desperate need of spiritual certainty. It could even, she told them, mean the temporary loss of Christian Science to the world.

Yet, as usual, the recognition of human recalcitrance drove her to higher ground. Truth was responsible for its own manifestation. Truth itself was the final authority. Nineteen centuries ago Truth had been lived in its perfection. Now it stood revealed in its Science. Let Truth finish its work: she had done her part. She could say at the end as she had said at a time of crisis more than twenty years earlier: "I rejoice with those who rejoice, and am too apt to weep with those who weep, but over and above it all are eternal sunshine and joy unspeakable."[7]

Appendices
Notes
Index

1892	June 20	Mrs. Eddy moves to Pleasant View.
	September 1	Gives land for church to Christian Science Board of Directors by deed of trust.
	September 23	The Mother Church formally organized.
	September	Hanna made editor of *Journal.*
1893	January	Foster Eddy made publisher of *Science and Health,* Armstrong publisher of *Journal.*
	March	Illustrations of *Christ and Christmas* begun. Armstrong replaces Eastaman as Director.
	April 27	George Glover and son visit Pleasant View.
	September 20	Christian Science Congress at World Parliament of Religions.
	October	Building of The Mother Church begun.
	December 2	*Christ and Christmas* published. Withdrawn January, 1894. Reissued December, 1897.
1894	May 21	Cornerstone of church laid.
	December 19	Ordains Bible and *Science and Health* as pastor.
	December 30	First service in The Mother Church.
1895	January 6	Church building dedicated.
	April 1	Visits church building for first time.
	April 20	Mrs. Woodbury admitted to church on probation; dismissed November 6.
	April	*Pulpit and Press* published. Accepts title of Pastor Emeritus.

	May 26	Delivers first address in The Mother Church.
	Fall	*Manual of The Mother Church* published.
1896	January 5	Delivers second address in The Mother Church.
	February	First permanent public Christian Science services in London begun.
	March 24	Mrs. Woodbury reinstated as probationary member; excommunicated forever April 4.
	August	Sends Foster Eddy away to Philadelphia.
1897	February	*Miscellaneous Writings* published.
	March	All Christian Science teaching suspended for one year.
	July 5	2,500 church members visit Pleasant View.
	July 21	Permanent break with Foster Eddy.
1898	January	Board of Lectureship founded.
	January 25	Deed of trust establishing Christian Science Publishing Society in present form.
	March	First Christian Science church in Germany organized at Hannover.
	September 1	First issue of *The Christian Science Weekly*; renamed *Sentinel* in January, 1899.
	September 29	Board of Education formally announced.
	November 20–21	Teaches last class at Concord.
1899	January 11	Three-man Publication Committee authorized.
	May	Woodbury–Dresser attack in *Arena*.
	June 4	Communion message to The Mother Church.
	June 6	Addresses three thousand in Annual Meeting in Tremont Temple.
	July 31	Woodbury libel suit filed.
	October	First Mark Twain attack in *Cosmopolitan*.

	December 24	Gives new house to Glovers as Christmas gift.
	December 28	Mrs. Woodbury fined for contempt of court.
1900	January 11	Farlow appointed Manager of Committee on Publication under new bylaw.
	September 6	First visit to Concord State Fair.
	December	Clarkson efforts to change leadership.
1901	January 4	Crucial legal conference at Pleasant View.
	January	Puts Kimball in charge of Woodbury case.
	May 1	*New York Herald* interview.
	June 5	Woodbury suit lost by plaintiff.
	August 1	Peabody lecture, "A Complete Exposure of Eddyism," in Tremont Temple.
	August 28	Second visit to Concord State Fair.
	November–December	Work on major revision of *Science and Health*.
1902	January	Revised (226th) edition of *Science and Health* published.
	June	McLellan replaces Hanna as editor of Christian Science periodicals.
	June 18	$2,000,000 pledged by Christian Scientists to build extension of The Mother Church.
	December	First of four Mark Twain articles on Christian Science in *North American Review*.
1903	February	McLellan added to Board of Directors as fifth member.
	March	George Glover and daughter visit Mrs. Eddy.
	April	First foreign-language periodical, *Der Herold der Christian Science,* founded.
	June 29	Addresses ten thousand Christian Scientists from balcony of Pleasant View.
1904	Spring	Kimball resigns from Board of Education.
	July 17	First Church, Concord, dedicated.

1905	May 21	Sibyl Wilbur interview.
	June 17– July 1	Special prayer for end of Russo–Japanese War.
1906	June 10	Dedication of extension of The Mother Church.
	October 15	*New York World* interview with Mrs. Eddy.
	October 28	Sensational *World* attack published.
	October 30	Interview by twelve reporters.
	November	Glover's aid sought by *World* for legal action.
	December	Introductory article of hostile *McClure's* series on Mrs. Eddy.
1907	January 2	Glover and daughter visit Mrs. Eddy.
	February	Considers trusteeship for property. Mark Twain's *Christian Science* published.
	March 1	Next friends suit begun by Chandler.
	March 6	Appoints trustees to care for her property.
	Summer	Interviews by Brisbane, Park, Curtis.
	August 14	Masters' interview at Pleasant View.
	August 21	Next friends suit collapses.
	August 25	*New York Times* interview with Hamilton.
1908	January 6	Stewart succeeds Armstrong as Director.
	January 26	Moves from Pleasant View to Chestnut Hill.
	June	Communion service in The Mother Church abolished as annual gathering.
	August 8	Requests Trustees of Publishing Society to start daily paper.
	August– September	Wilbur *Life of Mary Baker Eddy* published, followed by Milmine *Life of Mary Baker G. Eddy* in 1909.
	November 25	First issue of *The Christian Science Monitor*.
	December 9	Augusta Stetson's last visit with Mrs. Eddy.

1909	May 31	Dittemore replaces Johnson as Director and Clerk.
	September 25	Mrs. Stetson stripped of authority as Christian Science teacher and practitioner.
	November 15	Final Stetson interrogation begins, leading to her excommunication from The Mother Church on November 18.
1910	November	*Poems* published.
	November 21	Dickey succeeds Knapp as Director.
	December 1	Last written words: "God is my life."
	December 3	Passes on in fifth month of ninetieth year.

In September, 1910, less than three months before the end of her life, Mrs. Eddy (then in her ninetieth year) wrote the following article. It was not published until seven years later, in the September 1, 1917, issue of the Christian Science Sentinel *(copyright by the Christian Science Publishing Society). The article, with its sudden, surprising thrust after the conventional opening paragraph, serves as a useful indication of Mrs. Eddy's thinking about the Christian Science movement in her last months.*

The nature and position of mortal mind are the opposite of immortal Mind. The so-called mortal mind is belief and not understanding. Christian Science requires understanding instead of belief; it is based on a fixed eternal and divine Principle, wholly apart from mortal conjecture; and it must be understood, otherwise it cannot be correctly accepted and demonstrated.

The inclination of mortal mind is to receive Christian Science through a belief instead of the understanding, and this inclination prevails like an epidemic on the body; it inflames mortal mind and weakens the intellect, but this so-called mortal mind is wholly ignorant of this fact, and so cherishes its mere faith in Christian Science.

The sick, like drowning men, catch at whatever drifts toward them. The sick are told by a faith-Scientist, "I can heal you, for God is all, and you are well, since God creates neither sin, sickness, nor death." Such statements result in the sick either being healed by their faith in what you tell them—which heals only as a drug would heal, through belief—or in no effect whatever. If the faith healer succeeds in *securing* (kindling) the belief of the patient in his own recovery, the practitioner will have performed a faith-cure which he mistakenly pronounces Christian Science.

In this very manner some students of Christian Science have accepted, through faith, a divine Principle, God, as their savior, but they have not understood this Principle sufficiently well to fulfill the

Scriptural commands, "Go ye into all the world, and preach the gospel." "Heal the sick." It is the healer's understanding of the operation of the divine Principle, and his application thereof, which heals the sick, just as it is one's understanding of the principle of mathematics which enables him to demonstrate its rules.

Christian Science is not a faith-cure, and unless human faith be distinguished from scientific healing, Christian Science will again be lost from the practice of religion as it was soon after the period of our great Master's scientific teaching and practice. Preaching without practice of the divine Principle of man's being has not, in nineteen hundred years, resulted in demonstrating this Principle. Preaching without the truthful and consistent practice of your statements will destroy the success of Christian Science.

Abbreviations Used in Notes

A.	Archives of The Mother Church.
CSJ.	*The Christian Science Journal.*
CSM.	*The Christian Science Monitor.*
CSS.	*Christian Science Sentinel.*

Unpublished writings of Mary Baker Eddy.

A&M.	Articles and Manuscripts.	35 vols.
L&M.	Letters and Miscellany.	94 vols.
LO&VO.	Later acquisitions, unmounted.	

Published works of Mary Baker Eddy:

S&H.	*Science and Health with Key to the Scriptures*
Man.	*Manual of The Mother Church*
Mis.	*Miscellaneous Writings*
My.	*The First Church of Christ, Scientist, and Miscellany*
No.	*No and Yes*
Pan.	*Christian Science versus Pantheism*
Pul.	*Pulpit and Press*
Ret.	*Retrospection and Introspection*
Rud.	*Rudimental Divine Science*
Un.	*Unity of Good*

Unless otherwise indicated, the references to Mrs. Eddy's published writings are always to the latest editions.

Notes: *Prologue*

1. Mark Twain, *Christian Science* (New York: Harper & Brothers, 1907) , p. 102 f.

2. Matthew 7:29.

3. *S&H*, p. 141.

Notes: *Chapter I   Pleasant View, Varying Views*

1. A. Much of the Frye diaries is composed of such unilluminating but useful factual details.

2. A. *L&M* 62–8835. In this letter to Albert Metcalf, Mrs. Eddy indicated that her estate still needed a good deal of development: "When my shrubs and vines, shade trees and flowers are grown you must come again."

3. *My.*, p. 170.

4. *Mis.*, pp. 203 ff.

5. See Jonathan Edwards, *Images or Shadows of Divine Things*, ed. Perry Miller (New Haven: Yale University Press, 1948) . Miller writes (p. 19) of this Berkeleyan-type idealism:

> Once he had grasped that all we know or can know is the idea garnered from the objects of experience . . . Edwards was dedicated to the proposition that the relation of mind to object, of truth to embodiment, is intricate, vital, indissoluble. The tangible world, being experienced as ideal, was intelligible only as idea. The facts of experience became for Edwards . . . the "shadows," and very "images" of divinity. The act of cognition joined together man and nature, whom scholastic psychology had sundered.

Two illustrations of the way in which Edwards blended the optimism of the Enlightenment with the typology of the older past are found on p. 102:

> The late invention of telescopes, whereby heavenly objects are brought so much nearer and made so much plainer to sight and such wonderful discoveries have been made in the heavens, is a type and forerunner of the great increase in the knowledge of heavenly things that shall be in the approaching glorious times of the Christian church.

The changing of the course of trade and the supplying of the world with its treasures from America is a type and forerunner of what is approaching in spiritual things, when the world shall be supplied with spiritual treasures from America.

6. *S&H,* p. 468.

7. A. Frye diaries, August and September, 1892.

8. A. *L&M* 45–5980.

9. A. *L&M* 31–3963. Her reference to the Garden of Eden did not mean that she took the biblical account literally. Her writings consistently refer to the Eden story as an allegory.

10. *Mis.,* p. 158.

11. *Ret.,* p. 23.

12. A. Helen Andrews Nixon reminiscences.

13. Isaiah 52:7; Luke 2:49.

14. By 1906, some thirty years after its first publication, 418,000 copies of the book had been sold—an impressive but not phenomenal number. Neither the facts nor the figures support the assertion sometimes made that Mrs. Eddy required her students to buy a copy of each new revision of *Science and Health.* Since most of the 418 editions (i.e., printings) of the book contained at least a few revisions, such a requirement, if true, would have resulted in the sale of incredible millions of copies by 1906. Since that year, printings have not been numbered.

15. See Robert Peel, *Mary Baker Eddy: The Years of Discovery* (New York: Holt, Rinehart and Winston, 1966, and Boston: Christian Science Publishing Society, 1973) , p. 284; Thomas L. Leishman, *Why I Am a Christian Scientist* (New York: Thomas Nelson & Sons, 1958) , p. 205; and *A Century of Christian Science Healing* (Boston: Christian Science Publishing Society, 1966) , pp. 238 f. and 243 f.

16. A. *L&M* 18–2279.

17. A. *A&M* 13–10386.

18. Matthew Arnold, *Culture and Anarchy* (London: Smith, Elder & Co., 1869) .

19. John Emerich Edward Dahlberg-Acton to Mandell Creighton in 1887. Quoted in *The New York Times,* March 13, 1974.

20. Trust deed of December 17, 1889. Quoted in William Lyman Johnson, *The History of the Christian Science Movement* (Brookline: Zion Research Foundation, 1926) , II, p. 54. It is significant that Mrs. Eddy never surrendered the state charter under which the Church of Christ, Scientist, had been organized in 1879, nor was another charter needed legally at the time of the church's reorganization in 1892. Despite the period of formal disbandment, therefore, the Church of Christ, Scientist, had in some sense had a continuous existence since 1879.

21. While the conflict sometimes seemed to be between the directors and the trustees, the former actually represented Mrs. Eddy's views. As Alfred Lang, one of the trustees, wrote her in March, "It occurs to me that by force of circumstances, not from

choice, touching this question, you are still the power on the throne, not behind it."
(A.) The complexity of the issue is illustrated by the fact that between 1890 and
the spring of 1892 Nixon had served on the board of directors as well as in his other
capacities. Nor were the 1892 directors at first averse to including a publishing house
along with the church building to be erected on the Boston property, as Nixon
desired (see p. 17). Only when Mrs. Eddy put her foot down firmly on this project
and pointed out that it violated the deed which gave the trustees title to the land
did a decisive split occur between the two boards. Dr. Lee Johnson, present Archivist
of The Mother Church, is of the opinion that this was the central issue in the whole
dispute and that Nixon's basic difference with Mrs. Eddy was not over the form of
organization the church should have but over Nixon's "secularist" approach, which
would have subordinated her purpose for the church to his businessman's concern
for the success of his publishing activities. If this is so, as may be the case, it
nevertheless points to his inevitable preference for a form of reorganization that
would vest authority in the membership rather than in a board of directors responsive to Mrs. Eddy's guidance. At that time the ideological issue was by no means
clear to any of the participants except Mrs. Eddy herself, and Nixon's stand was
based on legal and business arguments rather than on the abstract question of
authority.

22. Quoted in Johnson, *History,* II, p. 16.

23. *Mis.,* p. 152 f.

24. *Christian Science Journal,* IX, March, 1892, p. 487. The curious use of the word
"ceremonial" in this passage is explained by the preceding paragraph:

> Our great Master administered to his disciples the Passover, or Last Supper,
> without the prerogative of a visible organization and ordained priesthood. His
> spiritually prepared Breakfast, after his resurrection, and after his disciples had
> left their nets to follow him, was the spiritual Communion which Christian
> Scientists celebrate in commemoration of the Christ. This ordinance is significant
> as a type of the true worship, and it should be observed at present in our
> Churches.

25. One difficulty was that the deed did not have in it the words, "to their heirs,"
which gave the trustees only a life estate in the land on which the church was to be
built. Their proposed remedy for the whole situation was to have the church
brought back to a state of organization so that a deed of the entire property could
be made to it.

26. A. *L&M* 27–3418.

27. A. *L&M* 27–3420.

28. A. *L&M* 26–3287. Cf. her letter a few months later to William B. Johnson, clerk
of the church, member of the board of directors, and along with Knapp one of the
students in whom she put particular trust:

> You are placed by me in a very conspicuous responsible attitude on this
> field of Christian Science. God grant that in one instance of my students, and in
> many a one, the pinnacle does not cause them to cast themselves down!
> You, so far, have been modest and meek, prayerful and watchful, and when

you have blundered by means of [animal magnetism?] have generally heard from me as the mountain pioneer to call you back to the path.

29. *Mis.*, p. 139 f. See Peel, *Mary Baker Eddy: The Years of Trial* (New York: Holt, Rinehart and Winston, 1971), pp. 256 ff. and p. 372, notes 32 and 35.

30. *CSJ*, X, July, 1892, reprinted in *Mis.*, pp. 139 ff.

31. A. F00077.

32. *Mis.*, p. 141.

33. *S&H*, p. 583.

34. See, e.g., *S&H*, pp. 171 and 502. Also *S&H* (first ed.), p. 229, and Peel, *Discovery*, p. 336.

35. See Peel, *Trial*, pp. 186 ff. and 280 ff.

36. William Dana Orcutt, *In Quest of the Perfect Book* (Boston: Little, Brown & Co., 1926), p. 53.

37. This and all following quotations up to the one noted as 38 are from Orcutt, *Mary Baker Eddy and Her Books* (Boston: Christian Science Publishing Society, 1950). That same book contains (pp. 68 ff.) a surprising account of Mrs. Eddy's discussion with Orcutt of William Morris and the *Kelmscott Chaucer*.

38. *S&H*, p. 25. Quoted in Publisher's Note in Orcutt, *Mary Baker Eddy*.

39. Orcutt, *In Quest of the Perfect Book*, p. 53 f.

40. A. James F. Gilman diary.

41. Louise Andrews Kent and Elizabeth Kent Gay, "James F. Gilman," *Vermont Life*, XI, Winter, 1956–57.

42. *Ibid.* Also Catalogue of Gilman Exhibition, Robert Hull Fleming Museum, The University of Vermont, Burlington, 1970.

43. Some of these sketches appeared in the volume, *Pleasant View, Twenty Plates of the Home Surroundings of Rev. Mary Baker Eddy* (Concord: J. F. Gilman and H. E. Carlton, 1894), a book which includes some rather appalling Victorian interiors as well as pleasant surrounding views.

44. A. This and all quotations to the end of this section are from Gilman's diary. The diary is made up in part of letters to a friend, Miss Carrie Huse, which may never actually have been sent to her but which Gilman may have used as a psychological device to spur him into recording his experiences with Mrs. Eddy while they were still vivid in his mind. Printed copies of the diary, which have had a certain underground circulation over the years, capitalize the pronoun "she" whenever it refers to Mrs. Eddy, but the Gilman originals show no such bizarre usage.

45. Actually Mrs. Eddy was seventy-one at that time and of slightly more than medium height. Gilman's lankiness may account for his initial impression that she was "small." Several of her students report in their reminiscences (see Peel, *Trial*, p. 222) that she seemed considerably taller when teaching them than when relaxed in conversation. At moments of special spiritual impressiveness she seemed to some

of them positively to tower above them. At the time she healed Laura Lathrop of an acute heart attack (*Ibid.*, p. 249) she seemed to Mrs. Lathrop to be about seven feet tall as she stood beside her and commanded her to rise from the floor on which she had just collapsed.

46. Mrs. Eddy frequently made such disavowals of personal authorship in her conversation. See also *My.*, p. 115.

47. A different view of the evening is found in a letter Mrs. Eddy wrote to Foster Eddy the next day (A. *L&M* 15–1805) : "Last eve. I worked, and the dear Father's presence was with me and my two guests are sealed for the heaven of Soul, and one is snatched from the jaws of the Lion."

48. This half-formulated plan to hold another Normal class was deferred until 1898. See pp. 124 ff.

49. Psalms 37:5.

50. This has been denied frequently, but a close consideration of all the evidence makes the conclusion inevitable. Even when there were serious misunderstandings between the two as in the next friends suit (see chapter VIII), each placed the blame on third persons who had come between them, and refrained from personal reproaches.

51. A fifth child, George Washington Glover III, was born soon after their return to Lead. In April, 1893, Glover brought little George to visit his grandmother at Pleasant View, and eighty years afterward George III could still recall with pleasure certain vivid details of this visit. Glover also brought his daughter Mary to visit Mrs. Eddy on several subsequent occasions.

52. A. *L&M* 17–2100.

53. A. *L&M* 17–2099.

54. A. Letter of August 1, 1892.

55. A. *L&M* 18–2230.

56. Orcutt, *Mary Baker Eddy*, p. 47.

57. A. *L&M* 15–1801.

58. A. Letter of December 11, 1892.

59. A. Letter of December 13, 1892.

60. Cf. Frye diary for March 18, 1893: "Went to town this morning without first receiving Mrs. Eddy's permission and thereby offended her. Solemnly promised Mrs. Eddy today that I would not leave her and go to town again . . . without first letting her know that I was going." On the other hand, a different side of the picture is suggested by Mrs. Eddy's remark in a letter to Ellen Cross (*L&M* 59–8423) , "It was indeed a test of good nature for you to bear what you did, as you did, from Mr. Frye's peculiarities that I have to meet daily."

61. Mrs. Eddy herself was firmly convinced of this. After receiving a letter from Foster Eddy, dated February 21, 1893, with a bitter complaint relating to something

that had happened on the 18th, she wrote on the back of the letter, "My bad night last Sat. (18th) and Tuesday night (21st) ."

62. A. Gilman diary.

63. A. *L&M* 57–8050.

64. *Mis.* p. 152.

65. See *S&H* 507:3–10.

66. A. *L&M* 20–2573.

67. See *Mis.* 144:32–7.

68. Quoted in *Man.,* p. 130.

69. A. *L&M* 56–7833. The Commissioner of Corporations had ruled that since the 1879 charter had been issued to the Church of Christ (Scientist) and was still in effect, a new charter could not be issued to the church under the name of The First Church of Christ, Scientist.

70. A. *L&M* 1–21.

71. See Peel, *Trial,* p. 257 f.

72. The trust deed of September 1, 1892 (see *Man.,* pp. 128 ff.) established the Christian Science Board of Directors as a corporation or body corporate for the limited purpose set forth in the deed, under the authority of Chapter 39 of the Massachusetts Public Statutes. When the church itself was reorganized on Sept. 23, 1892 (see p. 72 of this book) it was as an unincorporated religious society.

73. Quoted in *Man.,* p. 130.

74. A. *L&M* 32–4152. On September 19 Mrs. Nixon replied:

> There have been so many strange things done which look to me unchristian and unnecessary that I am perplexed.
> But this I can do and am doing. I can wait until Truth shows me where I stand. I feel sure of the Truth of Christian Science and that I am gaining the right understanding of Science and Health.
> May God speedily clear away the many mists from before our eyes!

On October 1 Mrs. Eddy replied (32-4153):

> Oh! do not doubt my confidence in you as Christian. Few of my students have ever impressed me with the faith I have in your hourly Christian life. This is all I need assure you. I have to probe many hearts, to heal them; but love, love only, drives me to do this. I have to talk and write what God bids me, often when I feel myself praying that this cup might pass from me, yet I yield lovingly, or try to, to the Divine will—and do and write and talk as I understand God would have me. This dear one, is my mission, even if it is a cross under which one may faint as did our blessed Master, yet say—"not my will but thine be done" Oh! do not take hearsay whereby to interpret my words or my motives. . . . Kiss the sweet "wee one" for me. Give my love to your husband and dear Paul. . . .

Following this, Mrs. Nixon had what she described in her reminiscences as a "remarkable experience" at a church service:

> During the silent prayer the true understanding of what seemed to be going on in the ranks was unfolded to me. It was as though the leaves of a book were turned over before my vision and I read and understood the workings of error and saw the right course to be pursued. It was perfectly clear that it would have been safe to build with the first title. . . . On October 5, 1892, when we had a church meeting and the first opportunity was given for all to sign for membership, I told what I had been shown and many claimed that their vision was cleared through my help. Mr. Nixon sat beside me and when I finished talking and sat down I looked at him and was amazed at his white face and expression . . . and on the way home he declared that he should never attend another meeting. I did not do this deliberately. Some one told Mrs. Eddy of my action, and she said that if I had asked her advice as to the wisdom of speaking thus publicly she would probably have advised against, but she added, "I am glad you did not ask me."

On November 1 Nixon sent in his resignation as publisher, to take effect on the first of the next year, on which date Foster Eddy succeeded him as publisher of Mrs. Eddy's works, while Joseph Armstrong, a Kansas banker who had studied with Mrs. Eddy in 1887, succeeded him as publisher of *The Christian Science Journal*.

On March 4, 1893, Mrs. Eddy wrote Mrs. Nixon that she would no longer be able to talk with her on private matters, since the two Nixons now disagreed with each other on Christian Science. It was not her policy, she explained, to say anything to a husband or wife that would promote disunity and Mrs. Nixon's place was with her husband: "So I leave you to this straight and narrow way trusting that you both will go to God and Him only for help and find all your questions answered in his love." Let Nixon read this letter, she added, but then drop the thought of consulting her further.

Mrs. Eddy, however, did write her two months later after hearing from Mrs. Nixon's father, Methodist Bishop Andrews of New York, of growing inharmony in the Nixon home. Her letter stressed the moral necessity of fulfilling a wife's full nuptial obligations, and warned Mrs. Nixon, "Never notice the sentiments of those hot-headed students of Christian Science who talk foolishly on the subject of marriage." Despite Mrs. Nixon's immediate compliance with this advice, as well as her devotion to her husband to the end of his days, the situation grew more difficult as Nixon's bitterness toward Mrs. Eddy grew into a kind of rage, while his wife's love for Christian Science and its founder grew steadily stronger. At one point he left her for several years, to return finally a semi-invalid, at which time he resumed his attendance at The Mother Church and turned to Christian Science for help in his last illness.

75. Johnson, *History*, II, p. 38.

76. See Clifford P. Smith, *Historical Sketches from the Life of Mary Baker Eddy and the History of Christian Science* (Boston: Christian Science Publishing Society, 1941), pp. 184 ff., for an account of their functions, the transfer of these functions to the Board of Directors in 1901, and the eventual abolition of their position in 1908.

77. A. *L&M* 77–11043.

1. F00077.

2. For a useful discussion of this subject see the section "Revelation as Discovery" in Stephen Gottschalk, *The Emergence of Christian Science in American Religious Life* (Berkeley: University of California Press, 1973), pp. 27 ff.

3. The only place in her books in which she is referred to as revelator is in the foreword in her posthumously published book *The First Church of Christ, Scientist, and Miscellany.* This foreword, ironically enough, was written in 1906 by Lewis C. Strang, who later left the church and became bitterly hostile to her. The only other use of the word in her writings is in *Mis.*, p. 308:

> Whosoever looks to me personally for his health or holiness, mistakes. He that by reason of human love or hatred or any other cause clings to my material personality, greatly errs, stops his own progress, and loses the path to health, happiness, and heaven. The Scriptures and Christian Science reveal "the way," and personal revelators will take their proper place in history, but will not be deified.

In a number of other places she referred to the writer of the biblical "Revelation of St. John the Divine" as the Revelator, but this was clearly an identification of his authorship, and she was careful to maintain—as he himself did—the distinction between being the recipient and the source of revelation. She always wrote of truth as being revealed *to* her, or alternatively, discovered *by* her.

4. Cf. *S&H*, p. 455: "God selects for the highest service one who has grown into such a fitness for it as renders any abuse of the mission an impossibility."

5. Cf. *S&H*, p. 332: "He was appointed to speak God's word and to appear to mortals in such a form of humanity as they could understand as well as perceive. Mary's conception of him was spiritual, for only purity could reflect Truth and Love, which were plainly incarnate in the good and pure Christ Jesus."

6. Mrs. Eddy consistently identified the Comforter or Holy Spirit with "Divine Science." While making clear that the terms Divine (or divine) Science and Christian Science are synonymous, she added, "It may be said, however, that the term Christian Science relates especially to Science as applied to humanity" (*S&H* p. 127). At times she spoke of her task of reducing divine or Christian Science to human apprehension (*ibid.* 471:23–31; *Mis.* 260:2–5; *Ret.* 26:17–30), but it is clear that both those terms in their absolute sense referred to the eternal laws of God, prior to and independent of any human knowledge or application of them. The term divine Science is usually restricted to this metaphysical sense, whereas Christian Science is commonly used also to designate the institutionalized movement that is its outcome.

7. Mysticism in its primary sense of direct communion with the ultimate ground of being has become so overlaid with suggestions of the mysterious, the occult, the psychologically unhealthy, that it has become virtually unusable in general discourse. It is in the popular sense of the word, which ranges all the way from the overcharged visions of underfed saints to the necromancies of hole-in-the-corner

séances, that Mrs. Eddy utterly repudiated it. In her chapter "Christian Science versus Spiritualism" she wrote, "Science dispels mystery and explains extraordinary phenomena; but Science never removes phenomena from the domain of reason into the realm of mysticism" (S&H, p. 80). Her three criteria for judging truth were revelation, reason, and demonstration, and each must be consonant with the other two. Nor could revelation be wholly a private matter; it must be conjunct with biblical revelation. Repeatedly when she wrote "God has just told me . . ." there is evidence that the conviction had come to her through something read in the Bible. Of her initial "search" of the Scriptures for an understanding of her 1866 healing she wrote:

> I knew the Principle of all harmonious Mind-action to be God, and that cures were produced in primitive Christian healing by holy, uplifting faith; but I must know the Science of this healing, and I won my way to absolute con- clusions through divine revelation, reason, and demonstration. The revelation of Truth in the understanding came to me gradually and apparently through divine power. (Ibid., p. 109.)

Her phrase "in the understanding" is one her Calvinist antecedents could have understood, with their passionate concern for logic and their horror of antinomian subjectivity. It was a natural step from their position to the conviction that revela- tion must be not merely received through faith but understood as science.

8. A. F00077.

9. A. Letter dated April 4, 1894. Cf. Mrs. Eddy's statement in a letter to Foster Eddy (L&M 15–1897): "You and I are not better than Christ Jesus[;] would that we were able to unloose his sandals."

10. A. L&M 18–2278.

11. Davenport (Iowa) Times, April 18, 1903.

12. A. Letter of March 21, 1892.

13. A. L&M 38–4927.

14. A. Letter of July 31, 1891.

15. Ellen Brown Linscott was, like her husband, a student of Mrs. Eddy's and a teacher of Christian Science—a prominent but controversial figure in the Chicago wing of the movement. Later they both moved to Washington, D.C.

16. A. L&M 38–4941.

17. A. L&M 38–4945.

18. A. Letter of February 25, 1893.

19. The Christian Science Journal from January to May, 1892, ran a series of auto- biographical articles by Eastaman entitled "The Travail of my Soul." These ac- counts of adventure on the high seas, of hurricanes, shipwrecks, mutinies, cannibals, and assorted hairbreadth escapes represent Eastaman's own "gracious preparation" for Christian Science. Excerpts from the series are to be found in A Century of Christian Science Healing, pp. 18 ff. and Peel, Trial, p. 286 f. An article in the

July, 1892, *Journal* ("Early Lessons in Demonstration") gives examples of his healing work. See *Century*, p. 21 f.

20. The reference is to an incident during the occupation of Japan in 1946 when MacArthur sent a communication to the Emperor that was described to the press as a request having the force of an order.

21. A. *L&M* 27–3485.

22. A. *L&M* 27–3483. Toward the end of 1893 Mrs. Eddy wrote Eastaman (*L&M* 27–3484) in answer to a letter of his:

> Oh how it carried me back nine years this very month since you entered my class in the College. . . . What varied experiences we all have had since then! It would seem to me that I have lived 20 years instead of nine! The long rushing troubled billows that have flowed over my frail bark have many times threatened to strand it upon another shore. But God was at the helm steering me safely, if roughly, over the dark waters. My dear student, how I have rejoiced that the same Captain of our salvation has brought you with me in the Life boat of Christian Science. And how I do rejoice in the strength of faith and understanding, to know that this dear God will lead us both safely in the port of heaven.

23. A. *L&M* 26–3294.

24. A. *L&M* 56–7876.

25. *CSJ*, X, (March, 1893), pp. 531 ff., reprinted in *Mis.*, pp. 116 ff. Actually this message, entitled "Obedience," had been read before the Christian Scientist Association of the Massachusetts Metaphysical College on February 1, 1893. Frye noted in his diary that it had been sent to the Association to be read just before Mrs. Eddy learned of Foster Eddy's disobedience in conducting his unauthorized and unsuccessful class in Boston.

26. John 5:19, 30.

27. The illustration accompanying this stanza represents a haloed Jesus, in a sitting position, holding the hand of a youthful feminine figure representing Christian Science—also haloed, but standing. The latter figure has sometimes been taken by critics of Christian Science (and by some Christian Scientists) to represent Mrs. Eddy, and was evidently so taken by Julia Field-King when she wrote in September, 1893, "I see that a greater than Jesus is here" (see note 9, p. 389). Mrs. Eddy, while holding that Truth understood as demonstrable Science was greater in scope than Truth perceived solely as a personal Saviour (John 14:12), explicitly denied that the woman in the picture represented a person. She also emphasized her own discipleship in relation to the historical figure whom she repeatedly called "the Saviour" and placed at the center of Christian Science. Cf. *S&H*, p. 31: "Obeying his precious precepts,—following his demonstration so far as we apprehend it,—we drink of his cup, partake of his bread, are baptized with his purity; and at last we shall rest, sit down with him, in a full understanding of the divine Principle which triumphs over death." This passage (as well as *Mis.* 124:32) suggests the possible significance of the fact that the woman in the picture is standing, while Jesus is sitting.

28. Gilman was still in Concord, looking for such art commissions as he could pick up. One day as he was returning, discouraged, from an unsuccessful search for work at St. Paul's School (the Episcopalian boys' academy up the road from Pleasant View) Mrs. Eddy encountered him on her daily drive, stopped the carriage, called him over to her, and told him she would like to talk with him the following evening about some possible work. In his diary that night he wrote that he would never forget "the beautiful picture impressed upon my mind . . . the pure light figure of Mrs. Eddy sitting in her carriage . . . extending her hand to me in her gentle way," with the "smiling face" of an angel "who had intervened just at the right moment."

29. Mrs. Eddy gave a copy of this to Gilman to study, in order that he might realize the quality of the work she wanted done.

30. All quotations in this section, except for those otherwise noted, are from this diary.

31. *Mis.*, p. 107.

32. The search for hidden meanings found its reductio ad absurdum in a huge volume of 980 pages by one Alice L. Orgain entitled *Angelic Overtures of Christ and Christmas* (New York: H. Wolff Co., 1941). This esoteric mishmash rivals in tireless ingenuity some of the more recondite studies of *Ulysses* and *Finnegans Wake*. Mrs. Orgain, a former member of The Mother Church, had taken off on her own some ten years earlier.

33. A year or so later Mrs. Eddy once more essayed to use such symbolism in the stained-glass windows of the original edifice of The Mother Church, but thereafter she promoted no further official experiments in that direction. Music (i.e., hymns, a single solo, organ prelude, offertory, and postlude) and art (in the form of church architecture, usually characterized by simplicity rather than ornateness) played an essential but delimited part in Christian Science worship. Mrs. Eddy specified that the music should be "of a recognized standard of musical excellence" (*Man.*, p. 61) and her letters show an analogous concern for architectural excellence, but she did not want either form of expression to be so striking as to draw attention to itself rather than to the spiritual purpose it was meant to serve. She obviously did not want to see an official symbolism develop (an exception being the simple cross-and-crown emblem stamped on her published works), nor is there evidence that she expected to see a distinctive Christian Science "style" emerge in any of the various forms of art expression. Having made her own experiment she was glad to leave further development of the possibilities to the private initiative, inspiration, skill, style, vision, and demonstration of the individual Christian Science artist. See Robert Peel, *Christian Science: Its Encounter with American Culture* (New York: Holt, 1958), p. 188 f.

34. An example of this occurred when Gilman showed her his sketch of Truth, a white-robed female figure, knocking at the door of a mansion, unheeded by the revelers within. The figure bore in her hand a book intended to represent *Science and Health,* but when Mrs. Eddy pointed out with amusement that this suggested a book agent making a call, they both enjoyed the joke—then decided that a symbolic scroll would be more fitting than a bound volume.

35. Wordsworth's "Ode to Duty." The traditional concept of duty, like the Puritan conscience of New England, was allied to but different from Mrs. Eddy's concept of obedience to Principle as a *scientific* requirement.

36. One of these requirements was money for Gilman's meager expenses. During the period he was working on *Christ and Christmas* Mrs. Eddy paid him only a very small recompense for his work. Whether this was a result of the Yankee parsimony in her background or another form of discipline imposed on him in an effort to force him to rely more radically on divine guidance is not clear. Later on, when he was working on a portrait of her, she told Gilman that she wanted him to get something substantial out of it financially, and added that he didn't look out for his interests enough in this way. It made her sad, she said, to think of him "lonely and destitute," but she nevertheless seems to have withheld from him the charity that she sometimes bestowed on persons considerably less deserving.

37. On this occasion as on one or two others Mrs. Eddy herself struck the position that she felt was appropriate and acted more or less as a model for Gilman, so that he could get the detail right. The most unusual of these instances was when she removed a shoe and stocking from one foot in order that he might draw from it the bared foot of the figure of Truth.

38. *Mis.*, p. 316.

39. Louis Fischer, *The Life of Mahatma Gandhi* (New York: Harper & Brothers, 1950).

40. Louis H. Sullivan, *The Autobiography of an Idea* (New York: Peter Smith, 1949), p. 197.

41. *Mis.*, p. 321 f.

42. See my report on this latter conference in *CSM*, December 1, 1970:

> . . . It is perceptible that when a Muslim speaker quotes extensively from the Koran, when a Roman Catholic speaker lauds Pope John's "Pacem in Terris" or a Jain speaker invokes the Kalpa-Sutra, the assembly as a whole loses interest. . . . There is a general agreement among the delegates that religion today is doomed if it thinks only in terms of self-propagation. . . . The inescapable demand of today, [Archbishop Helder Camara of Brazil] declares with gentle insistence, is for continued and undaunted dialogue—a supreme effort to understand each other's viewpoints. The imposition of one's own convictions on one's fellow beings—what is this but violence? Do not, he sometimes tells his "young Marxist friends," repeat the "terrible mistakes" of church history.

Moving and even saintlike as such an appeal may be, the long history of church conferences (and more recently of interfaith or ecumenical conferences) does not hold out much more hope for unity by dialogue than for unity by violence. Leaving aside the sort of ecumenism that is mere syncretism, the ecumenical ideal of lasting mutual understanding seems to have had a way of escaping the machinery of large-scale conferences. Neither the sharp confrontation of a Nicaea nor the amiable confabulation of an Uppsala or a Nairobi gives evidence of successfully appropriating on a mass scale the prophecy of Christianity's Founder: "Where two or three are gathered together in my name, there am I in the midst of them." In the case of a Chicago parliament of religions or a Kyoto conference on religion and peace, the problem is compounded by the invoked presence of an entire pantheon.

43. A. *L&M* 38–4963.

44. A. *L&M* 53–7416. For background of her comment on the "scholarly thinkers" see her comment to Ellen Linscott in Peel, *Trial*, p. 263.

45. A. Letter of July 31, 1893.

46. A. H00022.

47. *CSJ*, XI, 8 (November, 1893) , pp. 388 ff.

48. See Peel, *Trial*, pp. 155 ff. and Gottschalk, *Emergence*, pp. xv ff.

49. A. Letter of September 22, 1893.

50. A. Letter of September 24, 1893. The expression M. A. M.—or m. a. m., as Mrs. Eddy usually wrote it in later years—was shorthand for "malicious animal magnetism," her name for the conscious enmity, as contrasted with the unconscious resistance, of materialism to spirituality.

51. See p. 41.

52. A. *L&M* 20–2580. Emphasis added.

53. A. *L&M* 38–5027.

54. A. *L&M* 41–5453.

55. A. *L&M* 53–7421.

56. A. *L&M* 53–7429.

57. A. *L&M* 20–2579.

58. A. *L&M* 53–7433.

59. A. Letter of September 30, 1893.

60. A. *L&M* 20–2581.

61. A. Letter of October 5, 1893.

62. A. Letter of October 7, 1893.

63. A. *L&M* 53–7430.

64. A. Letter of October 5, 1893.

65. A. *L&M* 53–7431. There were several efforts by students of Mrs. Eddy to persuade her to publish selected passages or extensive quotations from her works, arranged to illustrate a particular topic or topics, but in each case she refused.

66. A. Cf. Kimball's letter of October 31, 1893, to her:

> I am condemned by you, hated by the pioneers who say that the work and glory of the thing should have been theirs, whereas the only outcome to me at every step has been misery. I have been pushed upon a pedestal, and have fallen, and broken, and am weary and scared and would like to retire to obscurity.

67. A. *L&M* 41–5456.

68. A. *L&M* 38–4990.

69. A. *L&M* 53–7447.

70. Oriental thought had had a considerable influence on the earlier Transcendental movement (see Arthur Christy, *The Orient in American Transcendentalism* [New York: Columbia University Press, 1932]), but the Parliament of Religions at Chicago marked the introduction of Eastern religions to the general American public. Theosophy, already known to Americans, gained added prestige and support from the new Orientalism.

71. Such teachings, Mrs. Eddy had written in *No*, p. 14, were "no more allied to Christian Science than the odor of the upas-tree is to the sweet breath of springtide, or the brilliant coruscations of the northern sky are to solar heat and light."

72. Letter of September 29, 1893.

73. Letter of October 28, 1893. Also, on October 12 and 19, Kimball wrote her in regard to the selections he was making from the addresses at the Christian Science Congress:

It seems to me that when our subject matter is all made up, it ought to show forth the distinctive features of our faith and our works, namely, that Christianity is the religion of Salvation.

That true Christianity is manifested in the imitation of Christ, in healing the sick and casting out evils; that this disappearance of evil is in consequence of the action of the "Mind that was in Christ Jesus" and in perfect accord with natural law, etc. . . .

I aimed to have them all present a gentle and alluring phase of pure Christianity and seem to have caught your own thought somewhat, that we are first to educate the heart.

74. A. *L&M* 77–11031.

75. A. *L&M* 22–2694.

76. A. *L&M* 22–2705.

77. A. *L&M* 39–5159.

78. Reprinted with slight changes in *Mis.*, p. 156. A further notice in the same issue set forth her prescription for the antagonisms which she felt had been needlessly aroused:

I hereby enjoin upon all Christian Scientists that hereafter they refrain from speaking or writing condemnatory of any Christian denomination, and only promulgate Christian Science through correct statement of the science of Christianity, and by its good works.

This alone is consistent with our attitude and the brotherly place accorded us in the Congress and Parliament of Religions in A.D. 1893.

79. *S&H*, p. 141. The full passage reads:

Few understand or adhere to Jesus' divine precepts for living and healing. Why? Because his precepts require the disciple to cut off the right hand and pluck out the right eye,—that is, to set aside even the most cherished beliefs and practices, to leave all for Christ.

80. A. *L&M* 53–7433.

81. It is interesting that even social scientists committed to hard facts have not been immune to the apparent compulsion to explain the institutional phenomena of Christian Science largely through dubious psychobiographical assumptions about its founder drawn from secondary or tertiary sources rather than through the empirical data amply available to them. Christian Scientists have replied that this seems an oddly unscientific procedure. In a letter published in the *Journal for the Scientific Study of Religion*, VI, 2 (Spring, 1966), David E. Sleeper, then Manager, Christian Science Committees on Publication, commented on the edifice of academic theory regarding Christian Science which has been erected on an almost total absence of firsthand acquaintance with it:

> What these gentlemen and others seem to be doing is playing the game of a new sort of medieval scholasticism in which elaborate theories are developed in loving detail with a minimal attention to fact.
>
> There's food for thought in the fact that the "ritualistically repeated denial of objective reality" which Professor Wardwell attributes to Christian Scientists seems to [the latter] to characterize the refusal of these academic critics to subject their stereotypes of Christian Science belief and behavior to comparison with the actual facts.

82. A. Letter of November 23, 1893.

83. A. Letter of December 6, 1893.

84. To one new correspondent from the Middle West who had clearly taken the last step from adulation to apotheosis, Mrs. Eddy replied, addressing her as "My Darling child" (*L&M* 44–5812) : "Your letter startles me! Do not write or say that again. There is but *one* God. If only I reflect this supreme Good it is enough, but I am a poor transparency even."

The same correspondent, nothing daunted, asked in reply, "Was not God hidden from me until you lifted the veil so that I could see Him?" Then adapting for her own purpose the statement from *Science and Health* (p. 6) that "God is not separate from the wisdom He bestows," she instructed Mrs. Eddy: "God is not separate from the wisdom He bestows through you." Amused in spite of herself, the object of this sophistical devotion wrote back, "Your apology is ingenious" (44–5813), but made clear that it definitely was an apology.

85. The best of Mrs. Stetson comes out in her explanation: "I am taking up my cross in daring to write this, and only because I fear you may be made to appear at disadvantage, and because I love you." It took her only two weeks, however, to decide that her move was tactically wrong. On December 21, 1893, she wrote Mrs. Eddy: "That work was an inspiration to me the moment I looked upon its illustrations, and I read volumes and my joy was ecstasy and gratitude beyond words. Then to think I should doubt that whoever did the mechanical work, was not under spiritual guidance."

86. *CSJ*, XI, 10 (January, 1894), p. 430. Reprinted with changes in *Mis.*, pp. 371 ff.

87. A. *L&M* 38–4995. In the January *Journal* Hanna had written of *Christ and Christmas* as "the 'Kohinoor' of all the brilliant cluster [of Mrs. Eddy's works], saving only 'Science and Health with Key to the Scriptures.' It is the Mosaic

Decalogue, the Sermon on the Mount, and 'Science and Health' retouched, reilluminated, reëmphasized." Mrs. Eddy, on the other hand, wrote Julia Bartlett on Jan. 28 (L&M 55–7730) in regard to this sort of laudation of the poem: "It is giving . . . too much credit to a thing of that sort."

88. A. L&M 38–4996.

89. A. L&M 15–1883.

90. CSJ, XI (February, 1894), pp. 471 ff. Reprinted with slight changes in Mis., p. 308.

91. A. L&M 88–13019. To the young woman's teacher, Mrs. Hannah Larminie, she wrote (L&M 35–4524): "Beware of the visionary fabulous idealism that the enemy is sowing in the thoughts of some of my students. Confine yourself to what is written of the Word and neither add nor diminish."

92. This picture, the last in the book, substituted for the ascending Jesus and attendant cherubs the more impersonal symbolism of the cross and crown.

Notes: *Chapter III ". . . designed to be built . . ."*

1. Romans 8:7. See Peel, Trial, p. 114 f.

2. A Church of Christ, Scientist, had been built in Oconto, Wisconsin, in 1886, but it served a purely local need.

3. One problem was the driving of wooden piles below the foundation grade to solid ground. In order to protect them from deterioration, they had to be driven far enough to remain permanently under water and to stay free from atmospheric influence.

4. A. L&M 1–52.

5. A. L&M 1–53.

6. A. L&M 22–2693.

7. Cf. her description of it as "our prayer in stone" (Mis., pp. 141, 320).

8. A. L&M 90–13411.

9. A. Camilla Hanna reminiscences.

10. Mis., p. 144 f.

11. Joseph Armstrong, The Mother Church (Boston: Christian Science Publishing Society, 1897, 1937), p. 29.

12. A. L&M 61–8708.

13. A. L&M 58–8276. Later she agreed to let her students have what they wanted if it would not delay the consummation of the work in 1894.

14. A. Bates reminiscences.

15. A. Letter of October 6, 1895, to Mrs. Eddy.

16. See *My.* 61:21, which relates to a similar situation during the building of the extension of The Mother Church in 1906.

17. A. A year later Mrs. Eddy wrote Knapp in another connection (*L&M* 27–3448): "You will always think you are fully *aroused* to the present need when the glamor is deepest. You are always most safe when you realize you are in need of more conscious truth relative to the lie, and *its action,* and feel sure it is nothing and His strength abounding in you, and see the path of the serpent and handle the error without fear."

18. A. *L&M* 53–7451.

19. A. *L&M* 22–2748.

20. A. Letter of March 15, 1894.

21. *Message for 1901,* p. 11. When the Directors in March, 1895, asked Mrs. Eddy to become permanent pastor of the church, she declined, but added: "If it will comfort you in the least, make me your *Pastor Emeritus,* nominally. Through my book, your textbook, I already speak to you each Sunday" (*Pul.,* p. 87).

22. At the end of his readership, a new bylaw provided that the term of office for each succeeding incumbent should be three years.

23. In a letter to the Directors about this (*L&M* 22–2702), Mrs. Eddy wrote, "I am *sensibly* aware of the wire pulling by the croaking mental messages pouring in on me."

24. *Pul.,* p. 1 f.

25. Henry Rushton Fairclough, *Warming Both Hands* (Stanford: Stanford University Press, 1940), p. 44.

26. A. Letter of August 19, 1932.

27. A. McKenzie reminiscences.

28. Cf. Mrs. Eddy's letter to her student, Mrs. Frame, a fortnight later (*L&M* 87–12837): "While the students were rejoicing in the *Temple* of our God, I was struggling *at home.*"

29. A. Letter of January 25, 1895.

30. A. *L&M* 58–8242.

31. A. *L&M* 27–3488.

32. A letter from Frye to the Bateses in September (A. *L&M* 64–9159) reported her objection to further evidence of an undue Christian Science presence in the neighborhood: "Mother says the influence to induce Scientists to locate near the church in Boston is being carried into extremes and must stop or it will appear similar to a Mormon settlement."

33. A. *L&M* 37–4851.

34. There are widely variant accounts of this episode. That in Hugh Studdert Kennedy, *Mrs. Eddy* (San Francisco: Farallon, 1947), pp. 153 ff., strikes a plausible balance. See brief mention in Peel, *Discovery,* p. 221 f.

35. The wording of the hymn has been slightly changed in the present *Christian Science Hymnal,* but Mrs. Eddy used the older words familiar to her. See Lyman P. Powell, *Mary Baker Eddy: A Life Size Portrait* (Boston: Christian Science Publishing Society, 1950), p. 174.

36. Quoted in *CSJ*, XIII (July, 1895), p. 140.

37. See *Mis.*, pp. 106 ff.

38. A. Johnson (though actually born in England) was by rearing and temperament as Yankee a character as Frye, and more sprightly. Even while he was off the Board of Directors she could address him as "My good boy, Clerk, Student."

39. *Mis.*, p. 107. Cf. *S&H*, 339:11.

40. On January 21, 1896, William P. McKenzie wrote Mrs. Eddy in regard to the "awakening" she had brought to him:

> I used to be very indignant when accused of being a theosophist for I was not even letterly acquainted with the doctrines of theosophy; but I have learned how my whole human mentality with its poetic idealism, aesthetic love, hero worship, pride of seeing hidden things, glory in mental power, had been a subtle spiritualizing of matter—a putting of divine wisdom into human mind. The uncovering was terrible & for a time I seemed to lose my consciousness of Good. Then the intricacies of personality have been revealed as never before & after a long agony I seem to find myself alone with God. I never had any idea before what was unconsciously in mind.

41. Knapp, like the Old Testament prophets, was given to visions which came to him clothed in the imagery of angelology and apocalypse. See Peel, *Trial,* pp. 174 ff., 257 f.

42. On February 10, Mrs. Eddy wrote to the Bateses (A. *L&M* 58–8237): "If you Mr. Bates will take the cup and drink all of it, then I will put you on the Board of C. S. Directors and Mr. Knapp can remain on also. God will one day open his eyes to see the wisdom of my advice, for he is a good man in his way—but has not grown to see what I see." At an earlier period of stress she had written Knapp: "Your face, when I saw you, showed as mine does a weariness or care—that I want you to rise above. . . . Your forgetfulness is not strange with so much as you have to attend to. God loves you for your fidelity to Him and so do I."

43. A. *L&M* 39–5109. Bates had written her earlier, "I do not think that I am of advantage to you, the Church, or myself in my present relation."

44. A. *L&M* 37–4894.

45. A. *L&M* 15–1831. In another letter (16–1962) in which she took him to task, she wrote: "It is love, deep sincere and bleeding that controls my motive in what I have written in this letter, not love for your character and life as known to me in some ways but motherly love that yearns for your true prosperity, happiness, and salvation." And again (16–1975): "At our last interview as you knelt beside me

and prayed for strength I did hope that my faith could mount upward and that I should yet see the travail of my motherhood, joy instead of sorrow, and its pangs cease forever."

46. A. *L&M* 14465.

47. A. *L&M* 18–2285.

48. A. *L&M* 22–2695. To the Directors on one occasion (22–2751) she described him as "so treacherous so sly and untruthful," and added: "I do *fear* him. I see the harm he is doing and he revenges on me if I try to prevent it."

49. A. *L&M* 15–1926.

50. A. *L&M* 21–2664.

51. While the evidence available today leaves some details of the situation obscure, there is no doubt that for whatever reason he may have had Foster Eddy tried hard to keep Mrs. Eddy from knowing that Mrs. Courtney was ensconced in the Publisher's Office.

52. Cf. the fabricated account by Edwin F. Dakin in his *Mrs. Eddy* (New York: Charles Scribner's Sons, 1929), p. 300:

> Next came the story that Bennie was carrying on with a woman in his own office ... the widow [sic] of an old friend. ... Bennie got on a train for Concord within an hour after he himself had heard the story in Boston [actually several days afterward, on April 30, 1895]. He rushed out to Pleasant View, climbed the stairs to Mrs. Eddy's room, found her seated at her desk.
>
> At sight of him, she sprang to her feet, shrieked aloud, and rushed out into the hall. He followed, thinking that she had merely been seized by one of her attacks. Then she screamed "Murder!" Stumbling, falling, dragging herself through the house in terror, she kept up the cries of "Murder!" until she had thrown herself, sobbing, at Frye.
>
> Bennie turned away, left the house, and Mrs. Eddy soon [i.e., one year later, in the summer of 1896] notified him that he was removed from her publishing business. ...

What actually happened when Bennie erupted into Pleasant View on April 30, 1895, is indicated by the letter he wrote her the next day. Addressed to "My Dearest Blessed Mother," it first protested his innocence of any sexual impropriety with Mrs. Courtney, then went on:

> I am sorry now that I disturbed in any manner yesterday you or any of the household. I would not do it now. I beg your pardon—though words seem cold and lifeless. I see that it was error. ... I see the error of having Mrs. C. in our office, but I also declare that I was never in any manner intimate with her. ... I write this with nothing but lots of love for Mama, *am glad you did not see me yesterday.* ... [Emphasis added.]

The Dakin account, which has remained unquestioned by two generations of later writers on Mrs. Eddy, continues:

> Foster Eddy's mind worked slowly. After mulling over the situation three weeks [in May, 1895] he decided that someone must have told Mrs. Eddy that

he wished to kill her. So he went back to the house and besought an interview. [Actually by that time he had already had two visits with her on May 8 and 15, the latter with Knapp, Bates, Armstrong, Hanna, and their wives also present.] Mrs. Eddy was in another mood, a soft, tearful, saddened mood rich with sentiment and loneliness.

She put her trembling, palsied hand into his and begged him never again to leave her. "You know how things are here," she moaned. "I want you to promise me that when you receive an order from me to go away, to do something in another city, do not obey it. Remember, my boy, I shall have been forced to make the order.... Promise me, my son...."

Foster Eddy promised. He left the house wondering. Not long afterward [i.e., fifteen months later, after numerous visits with her and dozens of letters in her own handwriting, evidencing her mental vigor and complete command of the situation] he received an order from Mrs. Eddy to go to Philadelphia and build up a new Church there.

The second visit described by Dakin represents, like the first one, his own elaboration of a sensational report in the *New York World* of March 12, 1907, of an interview with Foster Eddy at a time when the *World* was seeking by all means fair and foul to prove that Mrs. Eddy was a helpless, senile old woman under the total control of Calvin Frye and a designing clique of hard-nosed businessmen running the Christian Science movement. The sober facts are that Foster Eddy knew from his repeated visits with and letters from Mrs. Eddy in 1895–96 exactly what she thought about his going away from Boston. When he pleaded with her to let him stay there, she acceded to his wishes for over a year and even tried him out in several other important offices in the church. At no time did she accept the generally held view that he was having or had had an actual affair with Mrs. Courtney. She did, however, believe that he had been devious and underhanded in this and other episodes and that he was guilty of "mental malpractice" in trying to influence her and others to do what he wanted.

In April, 1896, she wrote John Linscott (*L&M* 77–11047) :

I long to be able to say my warfare is accomplished. For seven almost eight long years [since adopting Bennie] I have had the indescribable, "sharper than vinegar to the teeth," and still have it notwithstanding all that I have done for him, all my prayers and "Mother's evening Hymn" . . . and patience. God help us both to endure to the end.

When she was finally able in August, 1896, to persuade Foster Eddy to go away from Boston, she wrote Hanna: "Today God gave me the *victory*, and Bennie is *saved*."

53. A. *L&M* 2–103.

54. *S&H*, p. 583.

55. A. Letter of May 10, 1895.

56. A. Letter of May 12, 1895.

57. A. Letter of May 10, 1895.

58. A. *L&M* 15–1897.

59. A. Martha Bogue reminiscences. While Mrs. Bogue appears to have been a careful reporter, the word-for-word accuracy of such a passage cannot be guaranteed. The final sentence of the passage is obviously an adaption of Jeremiah 9:1: "Oh that my head were waters, and mine eyes a fountain of tears, that I might weep day and night for the slain of the daughter of my people!"

60. A. Frye diary. This occurs at the end of an entry for May 15, 1895, which describes the scene in which Mrs. Eddy spoke with Foster Eddy, Knapp, Bates, Armstrong, Hanna, and their wives: "She severely rebuked them for lack of love[;] got Dr. to promise he'd leave B[oston] when she said so, & got him to start anew, to do right." This compares interestingly with the latter part of the Dakin passage quoted in note 52, p. 399 f. On October 26, 1895, Frye wrote in his diary, "Speaking about her trials and sufferings over Dr. Foster Eddy, Mrs. Eddy said 'Whatever comes I shall do only what will be for the best interest of that man.' "

61. Some months before her visit, Mrs. Eddy had written her that it was self-mesmerism to "listen for my voice" as she did: "It turns your thought away from the Divine Principle . . . and props your faith in person rather than Principle and the *understanding* of Christian Science. You will hinder your advancement in this way and must abandon it at once" (A. *L&M* 88–18019).

62. A. Daisette McKenzie reminiscences.

63. *Ibid.*

64. A. Letters of October 21, 1893, and various later dates.

65. A. Letter of June 6, 1899. See notes 123 and 124, p. 416.

66. A. F00092.

67. A. F00102.

68. A. *L&M* 38–4930.

69. A. Letter of April 4, 1895.

70. A. *L&M* 58–8213.

71. A. *L&M* 55–7738.

72. A. Frye diary.

73. *Ibid.*, March 31, 1893.

74. *Ibid.*, March 25, 1895.

75. A. *L&M* 17–2127.

76. A. *L&M* 16–1966.

77. A. *L&M* 16–1933.

78. A. Sargent diary.

79. A. Frye diary.

80. *My.*, p. 120.

81. Another book, *The Mother Church* by Joseph Armstrong, appeared in 1897 with a slightly ambivalent endorsement by Mrs. Eddy: "It is prosaic in description, but to builders may prove interesting. Your detailed account is wonderful because of many things, your moral well drawn" (p. xi).

82. *Pul.*, p. vii.

83. See *Pul.*, p. 22:

> If the lives of Christian Scientists attest their fidelity to Truth, I predict that in the twentieth century every Christian church in our land, and a few in far-off lands, will approximate the understanding of Christian Science sufficiently to heal the sick in his name.

84. A. *L&M* 2–153.

85. A. *L&M* 60–8542. Kimball had previously written McKenzie on October 12, 1897, "Our church edifice grows rapidly—but I shall be very glad when the exultant excitement over a beautiful building gives place to the Church of Christ that is within." After the excitement had died down, Mrs. Eddy wrote another student (*L&M* 21–2595): "I hope the church shows are now over.... I recommend to all churches to give no special publicity and particularly no public pictures of their churches. It is too commercial, too cheap looking, too little like things that come in course and to stay; and too like a surprise that one can have a church edifice! These have always been my views on this subject. I felt so even in regard to the Mother Church—although that is an exception to all others."

86. *No*, p. 22.

87. See pamphlet, *The Church Manual—A Source of Strength* (Boston: Christian Science Publishing Society, 1972).

88. *Mis.*, p. 148.

89. *Man.*, p. 74.

90. *My.*, pp. 247, 254.

91. *Peo.*, p. 10.

92. *Pul.*, p. 4.

93. Ecclesiastes 9:15.

94. See Benjamin Sturgis Pray, "The Democracy of Prayer," *CSJ.*, LXIX (July, 1951), p. 351 f. Cf. James 5:15–16, which also links healing of the body ("The prayer of faith shall save the sick") with the healing of the Church: "Confess your faults one to another, and pray one for another, that ye may be healed. The effectual fervent prayer of a righteous man availeth much."

95. *My.*, p. 229 f.

96. *S&H*, p. 40.

97. A. *L&M* 39–5086.

98. *Man.*, p. 19. The quotation continues: "even the understanding and demonstration of divine Truth, Life, and Love, healing and saving the world from sin and death; thus to reflect in some degree the Church Universal and Triumphant."

99. Hebrews 8:5, as quoted by Mrs. Eddy. While Hebrews refers to the Mosaic law, Mrs. Eddy by implication extended the words to both the Sermon on the Mount and the "Science" of Christianity.

Notes: *Chapter IV   Movement with Momentum*

1. A. *L&M* 39–5130.

2. A. *L&M* 22–2776. Cf. her statement in another letter (41–5459) a fortnight later: "Spirituality is so much needed in our ranks that sometimes it is disheartening to go among the oldest students and see its lack."

3. In all her writings she uses the word "enthusiasm" only once. In her definition of "zeal" in *S&H*, p. 599, she first gives (according to her usual custom) its true "spiritual" meaning ("The reflected animation of Life, Truth, and Love") and then its perverted "mortal" meaning ("Blind enthusiasm; mortal will") .

4. See Peel, *Discovery*, pp. 7 ff. and 54 ff.

5. *Mis.*, p. 250.

6. She uses this phrase some dozen times in her published writings, and always in a positive sense. See, e.g., *S&H*, p. 261 f.: "Good demands of man every hour, in which to work out the problem of being."

7. See Laura Lathrop's account of one of these a year afterward in *CSJ*, XIV (February, 1897) , p. 550.

8. *Man.* p. 47.

9. A. *L&M* 39–5218.

10. A. *L&M* 25–3097. When a later editor went to the other extreme, however, Mrs. Eddy wrote him (24–3057) : "I started this great work and *woke the people* by demonstration, not words but works. Our periodicals must have more testimonials in them. . . . Three pages of testimonials are the least to have in the Sentinel." The reference is to the *Christian Science Sentinel*, the weekly magazine she had started in the meantime.

11. James 2:18.

12. A. *L&M* 24–3057.

13. *Ibid.* The intended reference was obviously to "*Hamlet* without the prince."

14. Quoted in Peel, *Encounter*, p. 65. Italics added.

15. See Herbert Spencer's comparison in his *Social Statics* between the "would-be medical hierarchy" and the established church, quoted in Peel, *Encounter*, p. 141.

On the other hand, one must recognize the honest concern of dedicated medical men and women to protect the public from fly-by-night frauds.

16. *Boston Transcript*, March, 1894. Using the field of neurology as an example of the medical advances made in the previous twenty years, James went on to point out the gap that remained between theory and practice:

> But the gain in science has been almost exclusively in the way of anatomy, symptoms, classifications and diagnosis; and the hypnotics, anæsthetics, sedatives and stimulants of various sorts discovered, though brilliantly effective over momentary states, bear little relation to the patient's permanent cure. There is no more epigrammatic instance of that combined greatness and littleness of man's mind, by which Pascal was so much struck, than this particular juxtaposition of wisdom and impotence, than this capacity to give interminable clinical lectures over patients to whom we are radically unable to afford real help. Power and learning do not necessarily go together in this field. The great Charcôt is accused, and probably correctly, of actually manufacturing new types of invalidism by his scientific performances at the Salpêtrière while some common doctor will rescue case after case by using methods which are not medical, but pedagogical and moral, by having a sense for concrete human nature which lets him get at the patient's character.

A more popular estimate of the state of medicine in the 1890's is quoted by Hanna in *CSJ*, XV (April, 1897) , p. 60, from *U. S. Health Reports*. While it has a horse-and-buggy sound to a more sophisticated age, its skepticism may actually be more scientific than the educated credulity of a later public, reliant to a notorious degree on the inconstant permutations of chemotherapy:

> It cannot be denied that there exists a widespread dissatisfaction with what is called regular medical practice, if, indeed, a series of vague and uncertain incongruities deserve to be called by that name. Multitudes of people express an utter want of confidence in physicians and their physic. How rarely do their nauseous medicines do good. How often do they make their patients really worse. How many would have lived had they never touched bolus, granule, tincture, or powder. How many publicly declare that Dr. So-and-so killed their relative or child. Even the regular allopathic and homoepathic practitioners express an utter want of confidence in their remedies. Dr. A. H. Stephenson says: "The older physicians grow, the more skeptical they become in the virtue of their own medicines." And Dr. Bostwick, author of "The History of Medicine," adds: "Every dose of medicine is a blind experiment." We might fill a volume with a list of physicians who condemn the medical science as not only not beneficial, but absolutely injurious and killing in its effects. Is it any wonder, then, that the public demands a system of cure without these murderous drugs, when the physicians themselves condemn them as hurtful?

17. A. *L&M* 67–9586.

18. See *A Century of Christian Science Healing*, pp. 37 ff.

19. A. Neal papers. His correspondence after he moved to Boston shows evidence of continued healings of this sort.

20. A. Historical File and Neal reminiscences.

21. A. *L&M* 28–3524. Quoted also in Lyman P. Powell, *Mary Baker Eddy, A Life Size Portrait* (Boston: Christian Science Publishing Society, 1950), p. 316 f.

22. *Mis.*, p. xii .See Peel, *Trial*, p. 229 f. Cf. her statement to two Canadian students a year earlier (*L&M* 14324) : "At last through Love and infinite wisdom patience and incessant labor I have . . . a little quiet for myself that *needs* it. But the roar of artillery and sound of battle though more distant is not wholly done."

23. Miss Gorham had become known to her through the work she had done as assistant editor of *CSJ* for some time before the Hannas took over that publication.

24. A. *L&M* 18–2240.

25. A. Letter of March 6, 1895.

26. A. *L&M* 56–7974 and 56–7989.

27. A. *L&M* 56–7980.

28. For many years guesswork has incorrectly attached the "copyrighted" title *Repaid Pages* to a manuscript in which Mrs. Eddy described her early footsteps in Christian Science—for no good reason except that the manuscript is untitled.

29. A. *L&M* 22–2807 and 22–2808.

30. A. *L&M* 56–8000. The finale in this case was not reached with the publication of *Mis.*, for she found it full of mistakes. Three months after its appearance she wrote a student (19–2385) : "I have made over 100 corrections . . . since the book came out. This forthcoming edition is the only one I can present willingly to my friends."

31. A. *L&M* 56–8001.

32. A. *L&M* 33–4230. Her friendly encouragement of the Directors gives evidence of what she wrote Armstrong at another time (22–2789) : "Oh, how dear to me the Directors are. We have weathered together hard gales."

33. A. *L&M* 19–2382. *S&H*, p. 568.

34. Mrs. Eddy's usual way of referring to herself in *S&H* is as "the author," and she also uses the simple descriptive term "discoverer of Christian Science" four times, with a lower-case *d*. But when the phrase Discoverer of Christian Science (or Discoverer and Founder) occurs in her other books, the *D* is capitalized to indicate that the term is one of the official titles used for her within her own church. This difference points up her concept of *S&H* as being a book for the world and very much more than a denominational textbook—though it is also that. *S&H* actually preceded the church; her other works were in good part written to forward the mission of the church. In the *Church Manual* she usually refers to herself as Pastor Emeritus.

35. See, e.g., her advice to the church in Lawrence, Massachusetts, found in *Mis.*, p. 155: "Forget self in laboring for mankind; then will you woo the weary wanderer to your door, win the pilgrim and stranger to your church, and find access to the heart of humanity."

36. A. Letter of February 11, 1897.

37. In a letter to Captain Eastaman (A. *L&M* 27–3492) in which she urged him to stick to his healing and not aspire to be a teacher, she wrote:

> As your teacher let me tell you that no one can do as well for the sick who takes classes and teaches this way. The healer is a teacher of his patients but the teacher of classes must take another line of thought in order to teach students. And this makes him lose the line of seeing the sick thought, as he needs to, in order to minister to his patients need. . . . As St. Paul writes each one is for his calling, and I know that your mission is to heal and not take students. We need healers much more than teachers, and have too many teachers already and not enough healers of the sick.

38. A. *L&M* 19–2382.

39. See Peel, *Discovery*, pp. 28, 47, 126.

40. This hymn, better known by its first line ("Shepherd, show me how to go . . ."), is the only poem by Mrs. Eddy to be praised by even her severest critics for its Christian simplicity and sincerity. It is probably also the only one of her hymns to have been sung in a variety of Protestant, Catholic, and interfaith services.

41. A typical letter in 1896 (A. *L&M* 39–5154) appealed to him: "I long to see you punctuate my matter just as you do your own; that is the modern way but I know no rules for it, and leave this to you."

42. A. Letter of January 30, 1894.

43. A. *L&M* 24–3064. In her letters Mrs. Eddy sometimes essayed to play the literary critic, with unfortunate results, as when she compared the language of a certain book to "that of Irving's Pickwick Papers." Only when she criticized *Journal* contributions from a metaphysical or utilitarian standpoint did she speak with authority.

44. See Peel, *Trial*, p. 201.

45. A. *L&M* 38–4995.

46. A. *L&M* 38–4927.

47. *S&H*, p. 497.

48. See pp. 53 and 296.

49. See Peel, *Trial*, note 54, p. 359.

50. *CSJ*, XIII (June, 1895), p. 129.

51. See Peel, *Trial*, p. 185.

52. For Young's influence on her, see Peel, *Discovery*, p. 46 f. and *Trial*, pp. 185 and 355.

53. A. *L&M* 74–10548. This was a dangerous argument which could easily boomerang and be used as one excuse for appropriating her language and ideas without acknowledgment. Her more usual attitude is expressed in *Ret.*, p. 76: "The Bible is not stolen, though it is cited, and quoted deferentially."

54. See chapter on prayer in Hannah More's *Practical Piety,* printed in differing versions in the 1830 and 1838 editions of *The Works of Hannah More* (Philadelphia: J. J. Woodard and New York: Harper & Bros.) and in a still different version as the preface of her *Book of Private Devotion* (New York: Clark & Austin, 1848) :

Practical Piety	*Science and Health*
Prayer is desire. It is not a conception of the mind nor a mere effort of the intellect, nor an act of the memory; but an elevation of the soul toward its maker. . . .	Desire is prayer; and no loss can occur from trusting God with our desires, that they may be moulded and exalted before they take form in words and in deeds.
We do not pray to inform God of our wants, but to express our sense of the wants which he already knows.	God is intelligence. Can we inform the infinite Mind of anything He does not already comprehend?
We murmur that we have not the things we ask amiss, not knowing that they are withheld by the same mercy by which the things that are good for us are granted.	That which we desire and for which we ask, it is not always best for us to receive. . . . Do you ask wisdom to be merciful and not to punish sin? Then "ye ask amiss."

Mrs. Eddy through her early life was a great admirer of Hannah More; but despite these three parallel passages, there is a vast gulf between their respective treatments of prayer. Hannah More's so-called "practical" piety is an earnest but conventional devotion, imbued with the rational moralism of her day. Mrs. Eddy's metaphysical logic gives her far less hortatory chapter a theological "bite" and a character at once luminous and kinetic which may account for the large body of testimony (during the past hundred years) to healings which have taken place from reading it.

55. *Mis.,* 147:14–3. The Blair sermon was known to Mrs. Eddy through an excerpt in *The English Reader* of Lindley Murray, first published in 1798. She had pored over this standard textbook as a schoolgirl and continued to turn to it at intervals throughout her life. It was from the Murray *Reader* that she drew the three paragraphs in question (printed by him as a single paragraph and labeled "The Man of Integrity") . Since the discovery that these paragraphs were not in fact written by Mrs. Eddy, writers for the Christian Science periodicals have not been permitted to quote from them, cite them, or attribute them to her in their articles. This same rule has been applied for a number of years in regard to the article "Taking Offense" in *Mis.,* p. 223 f. Although the curiously ambiguous history of this latter piece (see Peel, *Trial,* p. 185 and note 5) makes a little more understandable how it might have been included mistakenly among Mrs. Eddy's own articles in *Mis.,* it clearly is not hers.

56. In this respect, the "man of integrity" passage and "Taking Offense" differ from the odds and ends of phrases which Mrs. Eddy picked up from various sources, including her early scrapbook (see Peel, *Discovery,* p. 126) and the later anthology *Philosophic Nuggets* (see pp. 184 ff. of the present book) . These shorter borrowings represent the fairly normal and probably unconscious process of assimilation and adaptation to be traced in many reputable writers. If it were not for the two short

articles in *Mis.* taken *in toto* from other sources, there would be no problem in connection with Mrs. Eddy's borrowings. This is a distinction understood better by creative writers than by run-of-the-mill pedants, as the following examples show.

Edgar Allan Poe—always fascinated by the question of plagiarism and undoubtedly guilty of it himself (see Charles D. Stewart, "A Pilfering by Poe," *The Atlantic Monthly,* December, 1958) —wrote in *Godey's Lady's Book* in September, 1845, after giving numerous examples of striking verbal identities among famous poets:

> Of one hundred plagiarisms of this character, seventy-five would be, not accidental, but unintentional. The poetic sentiment implies an abnormally keen appreciation of poetic excellence, with an unconscious assimilation of it into the poetic entity, so that an admired passage, being forgotten and afterwards reviving through an exceedingly shadowy train of association, is supposed by the plagiarizing poet to be really the coinage of his own brain.

Examples of unconscious borrowing are abundant. When William Dean Howells as editor of *The Atlantic Monthly* pointed out to James Russell Lowell that a poem submitted by the latter startlingly resembled one by a Mrs. Akin published in the magazine two years before, Lowell wrote him *(New Letters of James Russell Lowell,* ed. M. A. De Wolfe Howe [New York: Harper & Brothers, 1932]) :

> Last night I found the Atlantic for May, '66, and was astonished at your mildness. You should have cried "Stop thief!" at the top of your lungs. . . . Why Mrs. A. could have brought suit before any court in Christendom. I was taken red-handed and with the goods under my arm. I had utterly forgotten the confounded woman's verses—not that I should have hesitated to bag her idea, *more majorum,* if I had been starving. But I wasn't.

In an 1896 biography of A. J. Gordon, the distinguished Boston preacher who had joined with Joseph Cook in castigating Mrs. Eddy in 1885, his son relates an incident which points to the fact that the homiletic no less than the poetic temperament is subject to such mnemonic tricks:

> On another Sunday [in London] Gordon had the interesting and novel experience of listening to his own words with the slight incidental modifications suitable to differing congregations. . . . For on going to a leading Presbyterian church he was surprised, when the text headings were given out, to note how closely they followed a sermon scheme which he himself had used some months before in Boston. As the sermon progressed from stage to stage, his own illustrations, his own metaphors, his very quotations appeared as on an unfolding panorama. The London minister had, Dr. Gordon afterward conjectured, read the sermon in a somewhat obscure American paper devoted to those prophetic exegeses with which he was closely in touch, and had reproduced it presumably by a process of unconscious cerebration. For when Gordon shook hands with him, introducing himself at the meeting's end, he was invited without the least apparent constraint or embarrassment, which the common ownership of such a secret would naturally involve, to the minister's home, and spent the day with him in pleasant intercourse.

Because of Mark Twain's later strictures on Mrs. Eddy's style and literary ethics, it is especially interesting to see his treatment of a case of unconscious reproduction by Helen Keller at age fourteen, as recorded by Van Wyck Brooks in *Helen Keller: Sketch for a Portrait* (New York: E. P. Dutton & Co., 1958) :

When Mark Twain was carried out of himself by some deep indignation, he would suddenly rise and stand like an eagle on a crag, his plumage all ruffled by the storm of his feeling. So Helen wrote years later, and she might have been recalling his anger over the incident of *The Frost King*. This was a story that Helen had written as a birthday present for Michael Anagnos [Director of Perkins Institute], and it was discovered that somebody else had written it first and Helen had repeated it almost word for word. How had this happened? No one knew until the old story came to light in a house where Helen had heard the story read, after which it had buried itself in her subconscious mind. Her phenomenal power of concentration accounted for it all; but Michael Anagnos, up in arms over what he considered this plagiarism, set up a tribunal to study and report on the question. There were eight judges, four of them blind, in this court of investigation, "solemn donkeys," one and all, Mark Twain said, adding that he "couldn't sleep for blaspheming about it." Connecting Helen with Joan of Arc, about whom he was planning to write a book, he was incensed over this treatment of her. The gallantry of the little girl recalled to him that other child "alone and friendless in her chains, confronting her judges," and he denounced this "plagiarism farce," so "owlishly idiotic and grotesque." He called the court "a collection of decayed human turnips . . . a gang of dull and hoary pirates piously setting themselves the task of disciplining and purifying a kitten that they think they've caught filching a chop." Were they not all plagiarists themselves? Were not most ideas second-hand, consciously or unconsciously drawn from a million outside sources? Had he not himself unconsciously stolen from Oliver Wendell Holmes the dedication for *The Innocents Abroad*, and had not Dr. Holmes told him that he, in turn, had in all probability stolen it from someone else?

This whole subject is potholed with ambiguities and half-truths. Too often simplistic condemnations are met by suspect defenses. It is seldom possible to determine just how conscious or unconscious a particular borrowing is. Plagiarism may be none the less reprehensible for being unconscious, and originality none the less admirable for occasionally borrowing judiciously to serve its purpose. Cf. Rabindranath Tagore, as quoted by Herbert Read in *The Times* (London) , January 10, 1963: "The sign of greatness in great geniuses is their enormous capacity to borrow, very often without ever knowing it; they have an unlimited credit in the world market of culture." Also the thesis of Richard Ellmann (in his *Eminent Domain* [Oxford University Press, 1967]) in regard to the mutual borrowings among Yeats, Wilde, Joyce, Pound, Eliot, and Auden, that "the best writers expropriate best, they disdain petty debt in favor of grand, authoritative larceny." Heine is quoted as saying that the poet "may even appropriate entire columns with their carved capitals, if the temple he thus supports be a beautiful one. Goethe understood this very well, and so did Shakespeare before him." However, such half-ironic literary justifications need the added dimension of Charles Kingsley's commonsense observation: "No earnest thinker is a plagiarist pure and simple. He will never borrow from others that which he has not already, more or less, thought for himself." With Kingsley, a true nineteenth-century moralist, one draws closer to Mrs. Eddy's objection to the plagiarism of her statement of Christian Science by writers who very definitely had not thought out for themselves what she was saying. Basically her objection was metaphysical rather than literary. Cf. *Ret.*, p. 75 f.: "If a student at Harvard College has studied a textbook written by his teacher, is he entitled, when he leaves the University, to write out as his own the substance of this textbook? . . . A student can write voluminous works on Science without trespassing, if he writes honestly, and he cannot dishonestly compose *Christian Science*." Also *ibid.*, p. 30: "The rare bequests of Christian Science are costly, and they have won fields of battle from which the dainty borrower would have fled."

57. The article "Taking Offense" likewise expresses a homiletic ethical humanism which is devoid of Christian Science content but which evidently appealed to Mrs. Eddy as an evocation of the human scene to which the metaphysical insights of Christian Science needed to be applied. See especially the passage:

We should remember that the world is wide; that there are a thousand million different human wills, opinions, ambitions, tastes, and loves; that each person has a different history, constitution, culture, character, from all the rest; that human life is the work, the play, the ceaseless action and reaction upon each other of these different atoms. Then, we should go forth into life with the smallest expectations, but with the largest patience. . . .

There is irony in the fact that whatever immortality this short homily and the "man of integrity" passage may enjoy they will probably owe to Mrs. Eddy's use of them.

58. *Mis.*, p. 147. The less appropriate word "reproachful" in the original has been changed to the more exact "reproachable" in Mrs. Eddy's version.

59. It was not a message to the annual meeting of The Mother Church, as Dakin claims, but to the First Members' meeting, which followed it two weeks later. Dakin's whole picture of a pain-racked, lonely, enfeebled Mrs. Eddy desperately searching for something to say to the church is belied by the fact that she wrote letters to the First Members stressing the special importance of this meeting and telling them that she wished all of them (with the exception of Foster Eddy) to come to Concord to confer with her after hearing the message.

60. See *S&H* 349:13–30.

61. Actually, fifteen hundred arrived from Boston on two special trains, but approximately a thousand others came from various parts of New Hampshire and elsewhere by special conveyances.

62. Since July 4 fell on a Sunday, the fifth was legally observed as Independence Day in 1897.

63. See *Mis.*, pp. 251. ff.

64. Mrs. Stetson, who herself was something of a fashion plate, chose many gowns and bonnets for Mrs. Eddy and sent them to her. Although grateful for this service, Mrs. Eddy sometimes returned them as being too rich or elaborate for her taste. The *Boston Globe* reported that on this occasion, however, she wore "a royal purple silk dress covered with black lace." Dr. and Mrs. Alfred Baker, ex-Quakers from Philadelphia who were seeing her for the first time, were shocked that she was not more simply dressed. When Mrs. Baker confided her distress to her Christian Science teacher, Flavia Knapp, Mrs. Knapp explained that Mrs. Eddy did not have time to shop and had probably had to rely on what Mrs. Stetson sent her for the occasion. Evidently the complaint somehow reached Pleasant View, for after the

Bakers had moved to Concord Mrs. Eddy on her daily carriage drive stopped outside their house one day, sent for Mrs. Baker and—as the latter eyed with approval the simple gray dress and bonnet she was wearing—asked with a twinkle, "How do you like my Quaker costume?" (A. Anna White Baker reminiscences.) If clothes were her one extravagance, the number and variety of her bonnets may have been compensation for the days when, almost penniless but with considerable millinery skill, she could transform an inexpensive straw hat into a very smart little concoction with a few oddments of ribbon or other material. See Peel, *Discovery*, p. 214.

65. A. Irving Tomlinson diary and reminiscences. Tomlinson was told at the time that Mrs. Eddy for some years had used glasses only for very fine print. Later she dispensed with them almost entirely.

66. Quoted in *CSJ*, XV (August, 1897) , p. 263.

67. The August *CSJ* spoke of the "clear, calm and easy conversational tones" in which he spoke. "He dwelt briefly," it reported, "upon the significance of the great Independence Day, in its national and international aspects, emphasized the importance of good citizenship as a necessary condition of good government, and impressed upon his hearers their duty, as apostles of a larger liberty, in the careful and faithful exercise of the elective franchise. He quoted the words of John Robinson, the noted Pilgrim preacher, prophesying that the Lord had more of Light and Truth to impart to His people, and expressed it as his opinion that Christian Science was fulfilling these larger prophecies."

68. A. Hanna papers.

69. From report of General Bates's talk in *CSJ*. He was not related to Edward Bates. See Peel, *Trial*, p. 252.

70. Among the other specially invited guests were a Mrs. Isham of New York who was a granddaughter of Abraham Lincoln, and a couple of additional generals from Concord, where generals seem to have flourished as hardily as colonels in the antebellum South.

71. A. *L&M* 39–5190.

72. A. Tomlinson diary and reminiscences.

73. A. Jessie Cooper reminiscences. Quoted in Irving Tomlinson, *Twelve Years with Mary Baker Eddy* (Boston: Christian Science Publishing Society, 1950) , p. 61 f. Also Will Cooper reminiscences. There are some discrepancies between the accounts of the occasion given by Mrs. Cooper and by her son, Will, who was nine years old at the time and did not write his own reminiscences until 1963, but none of these are irreconcilable and I have drawn on both.

74. A. Jessie Cooper reminiscences. Mrs. Cooper states that for several days it had been impossible for her to comb the little girl's hair, or for the child to bear the weight of her light, daisy-trimmed hat. That morning the situation had been at its worst and the child had wept loudly as her mother tried to make her presentable for Pleasant View. These trifling details may deserve mention, since no statement by Mrs. Eddy has been more often quoted by her critics with derision than one from *S&H*, p. 153: "You say a boil is painful; but that is impossible, for matter without mind is not painful. The boil simply manifests, through inflammation and swelling,

a belief in pain, and this belief is called a boil." Cf. *ibid.*, p. 365: "If the Scientist reaches his patient through divine Love, the healing work will be accomplished at one visit, and the disease will vanish into its native nothingness like dew before the morning sunshine."

75. Willis J. Abbott interview with Moses in *CSM*, June 19, 1929. In May, 1896, Moses wrote Carol Norton (A.) whom he had known from boyhood, regarding the prejudice which had kept the editor of a special "woman's edition" of the *Concord Monitor* from accepting a contribution from Mrs. Eddy: "So far as I am concerned as a journalist I am indignant that the negotiations with Mrs. Eddy should have closed as they did. Had I been the editor of the 'Woman's Edition' I would have seen the kickers go hang before I would have surrendered the control of my pages to their dictation. . . . Mrs. Eddy is easily the foremost woman in New Hampshire, to narrow her to the most contracted sphere which will come into this disputation, and it is folly to bar her from an enterprise of this kind. . . . Mrs. Eddy is too free from guile, and too gentle, to be compelled to undergo such an experience."

76. A. *L&M* 90–13282. In a letter to him the following year (90–13288) she wrote: "You of course have read James Freeman Clark's sermons. His views of matter are as transcendental as mine and his character is a memory of Christlikeness. Theodore Parker, Dr. Peabody, Dr. Bartol, William R. Alger, etc. were my model men."

77. A. *L&M* 90–13283.

78. A. Several members of her household have recorded the impression this made on them, and non-Scientist visitors were frequently charmed by her ability to enter into their interests. Cf. letter from Alfred E. Baker to Mrs. Eddy on Christmas Day, 1900. Baker as usual used the Quaker "thee" in addressing her. "The Salvation Army man was delighted by his visit to thee, and esteemed it as a privilege—he said thee was the most lovely & beautiful woman he had ever seen."

79. A. *L&M* 90–13285.

80. A. Letter of May 9, 1898.

81. A. *L&M* 21–2597.

82. A. *L&M* 44–5874. Cf. her statement in a letter to Nemi Robertson (44–5924) : "Thirty years I have been in the firey furnace and the dross has dropped away from the gold through agony."

83. A. *L&M* 57–8031. Cf. her statement in a letter to the Bateses (58–8254) : "I am in excellent health and spirits this bright morning. . . . God is showing me much and just the opposite of what my students see or understand."

84. A. *L&M* 88–12999.

85. A. *L&M* 16–2004.

86. A. *L&M* 16–2006.

87. A. Letter of June 29, 1897.

88. *My.*, p. 147.

89. William P. McKenzie wrote to Daisette Stocking the next day (A.) : "Her figure has become fuller and expresses more strength. When she spoke her face flushed with the hue of health like that of a child." Tomlinson wrote in his reminiscences: "She spoke for three quarters of an hour, without manuscript or notes, and appeared as free as though preaching to her were an everyday occurrence. . . . She was so natural, so artless in her delivery, that the thought of her auditors was centered wholly on the message and not at all upon the messenger who gave it. . . . The listener felt that the preacher had a burning message to deliver and that her only desire was that this truth, which was so real and precious to her, should become the possession of every hearer."

90. See Peel, *Discovery*, p. 27. She herself wrote of having "forgotten" most of the French she ever knew, while the "smattering" (her own word) of the ancient tongues she had acquired as a girl had long since "vanished like a dream" (*Ret.*, p. 10) .

91. For Mrs. Potter's interest in heraldry and genealogy see Peel, *Trial*, p. 337, note 57. Since she had met Sir John MacNeill, she obviously knew that he was not her "ancestor," but she seems to have been responsible for confusing the Edinburgh family with the McNeils of County Antrim, Ireland, from whom she and Mrs. Eddy were both descended. (A.) The name was spelled differently by various family members and branches of the clan: MacNeill, Macneill, McNeill, McNeil, even McNiel. The *Washington Post* reporter who described Mrs. Potter as a descendant of Sir John McNeil of Edinburgh may have started the whole confusion. After an article in the *Ladies' Home Journal* in November, 1903, had definitely described the MacNeill who had been ambassador to Persia as Mrs. Eddy's great-grandfather, Mrs. Macalister wrote in the London *Truth*: "I am the only married grandchild of the late Right Honourable Sir John MacNeill, G.C.B., of Edinburgh . . . and Mrs. Eddy is certainly not my daughter."

92. This McNeil emigrated to America in 1718. Contrary to Mrs. Eddy's highly impressionistic account of her ancestry in *Ret.*, exhaustive research has established beyond all question (A.) that there had been six generations of Bakers and four generations of McNeils in America before her birth.

93. *S&H*, p. 31.

94. Her great-grandfather on her father's side was actually Lieutenant William Moore of New Hampshire, who married Mary McNeil, daughter of the McNeil who emigrated from County Antrim. It was their daughter, Mary Ann or Maryann Moore, who married Joseph Baker and thus became the paternal grandmother of Mary Baker Eddy. The total confusion of these relationships in the *Ret.* account illustrates the very fallibility Mrs. Eddy so often warned about. In her article entitled "Fallibility of Human Concepts" in *Mis.*, pp. 351 ff., she writes, in the accents of a religious leader rather than a genealogical smatterer: "If one asks me, Is my concept of you right? I reply, The human concept is always imperfect; relinquish your human concept of me, or of any one, and find the divine, and you have gained the right one—and never until then."

95. *Ret.*, p. 21 f. The following brief section entitled "Emergence Into Light" marks the turning point her own life reached in 1866 with the discovery of Christian Science, and the remainder of the little book is written with the sort of authority not to be looked for in the early reminiscences.

96. Galatians 3:28.

97. *CSJ,* IX, S. J. Hanna, "Religious Eras": Lieut. Totten . . . holds that the prophetic Scriptures indicate that the Christian dispensation will end before the close of the present century. He thinks we are near an era of 'infernalness,' such as the world never saw. The *Hartford Courant,* commenting on Mr. Totten's views, says: 'The belief that the present epoch or dispensation is swiftly drawing to a close—that we are even now on the threshold of some strange and momentous crisis in human affairs—is by no means confined to the followers of Edward Irving and Wm. Miller. It is widely diffused among students of the Hebrew and Christian prophetic books in both hemispheres.' "

98. Totten, *Our Race,* Series I, No. 4. A number of Anglo-Israel proponents stressed the prophetic role of woman, possibly because of the liberal use they had to make of the female line of descent in order to make their genealogies come out right. A typical quotation is the following one from an 1893 sermon by the Reverend Joseph Wild, D.D., author of *The Ten Lost Tribes:* "I believe there will come a female who will rule and lead, and her son will be the chief ruler and leader among the nations of the earth, and he will be accepted by God, and he will be accepted by the nations, and she will be accepted as his adviser and director, and they will be of the family of David for a special mission unto the world."

99. A. Letter of April 13, 1895.

100. A. *L&M* 21–2592.

101. A. Letter of March 15, 1895.

102. A. F00022.

103. While this aristocratic bias has persisted to some extent through much of the present century, the base has broadened out greatly to include what sociologist Bryan Wilson calls "a good proportion of office workers, teachers, owners of small business, and the general run of semi-detached dwellers."

104. A. *L&M* 17–2127. The phrase occurs in a letter from Mrs. Eddy to her son, George Glover, telling of her loneliness in the midst of much outward success. The "princes" are a typical epistolary exaggeration. To George Moses she wrote in 1897: "It would seem as if Christian Science were engirdling the earth. London lords and ladies throng to learn its teachings, it is in the White House of our national capital, in Windsor Castle, England, and the leading minds in almost every Christian land are adopting its essential theological points."

105. A. Reminiscences of Lilias and Mary Ramsay, Lady Victoria Murray, Lady Mildred Fitzgerald, etc.

106. *My.,* p. 143.

107. A. F136.

108. A. Field-King letters of February 11 and June 28, 1898, also letter of W. A. Lindsay, College of Arms, to Mrs. Field-King, July 26, 1898. The volatile Julia complained to Mrs. Eddy, "The work in the College of Arms is cold, hard, exact and they hate to deal with probabilities or reckon them at all."

109. As late as 1902 she wrote to the Reverend W. M. H. Milner, Anglican vicar, Fellow of the Royal Geographical Society, and an ardent Anglo-Israelite, who had sent her an inscribed copy of a brochure he had written: "Your work 'The Royal House of Britain an Enduring Dynasty' is indeed masterful: one of the most remarkable Biblical researches in that direction ever accomplished. Its data and the logic of events sustain its authenticity, and its grandeur sparkles in the words 'King Jesus.' "

110. "The United States to Great Britain" (*Poems*, p. 10), written during the Spanish-American War, was first published in the *Boston Herald* on May 15, 1898. It also contains an ambiguous reference to "Judah's sceptered race," which has been duly noted by Anglo-Israel enthusiasts. However, in her January, 1901, poem entitled "The New Century" (*Poems*, p. 22), Mrs. Eddy writes unambiguously and in logical consonance with the universalism of Christian Science:

'Tis writ on earth, on leaf and flower:
Love hath one race, one realm, one power.

111. A. *L&M* 19–2377.

112. A. *L&M* 34–4371.

113. A. Letter of July 20, 1897.

114. See Frances Thurber Seal, *Christian Science in Germany* (Philadelphia: John C. Winston Co., 1931). This vivid account ignores the parallel work of Frau Günther-Peterson, but in other respects is a valuable supplement to the chapter on Germany in Smith's *Historical Sketches*.

115. Quoted in *CSS*, II (January 4, 1900), p. 283, from *Concord Monitor*.

116. A. Günther-Peterson reminiscences.

117. Marie Schön, *Das Unbedingte* (Berlin: Deutscher Verlag der Christlichen Wissenschaft M. Schön G.m.b.H., 1934).

118. Seal, *Christian Science in Germany*, p. 66. The very lively interest in Christian Science in the Imperial Court at this time also played an important part, pro and con, in the situation. *Ibid.*, pp. 59 ff.

119. A. *L&M* 42–5582. In her copy of a book entitled *Anglo-Israel, the Jewish Problem, and Supplement* by the Reverend Thomas Rosling Howlett (Philadelphia, 1896, 5th ed.), one of a very few markings made by Mrs. Eddy was in reference to a passage dealing with the coming universality of English.

120. The most outstanding of these was Count Helmuth von Moltke, nephew of the great Field Marshal and father of the high-minded von Moltke who would later play a leading role in the abortive army plot against Hitler in 1944. Though the German nobility was represented in the early ranks of Christian Science, the movement in Germany—much more than in England—from the beginning rested heavily on the solid burghers who still constitute the bulk of its adherents.

121. The authorization was given on March 31, 1910; the book itself was published two and a half years later. In 1903 Mrs. Eddy had founded *Der Herold der Christian Science*, the first foreign-language edition of a periodical now known as *The Herald*

of Christian Science and published in various languages. As early as September 28, 1900, she had written a letter to William McKenzie as a trustee of the Christian Science Publishing Society, suggesting the system of facing pages of English and German which was ultimately adopted. This read in part:

> I have travailed in Soul for the dear students in Germany and have built up a theory for their relief that I want made practical by our Publishing Society in Boston. It is this: To have the Sentinel and C.S. Journal issued from our House in Boston printed in both the English and German tongue and sent to Germany. That grand nation should certainly have the means for obtaining a knowledge of Christian Science. And this way of providing it will save breaking international law on copyright and dearer far to my heart it will help Frau Gunther-Peterson and Fraulein Schoen to accomplish a great work which they have nobly and patiently inaugurated for the good of their people and the spread of Christian Science.

122. *S&H*, p. 13.

123. The strange duality in Mrs. Field-King's nature, of which she so often spoke in her letters to Mrs. Eddy, was becoming increasingly plainer to the Christian Scientists in London. She herself blamed the recurrent deceitfulness to which she admitted on the "false thinking" she had received from dissident students of Christian Science before studying with Mrs. Eddy, and on the "poison" of suspicion they had instilled in her thought in regard to the founder of Christian Science. Referring to "the horrid things that were started in my very strongest mortal being" by this early teaching, she wrote Mrs. Eddy in February, 1899:

> I have downed them thousands of times and have often thought them destroyed, only to find them staring me in the face and robbing me of my peace. I mean the lying and questions that were back of Mrs. Hopkins' and Mrs. Plunkett's teaching. How long, oh Lord, how long before my release shall come.

124. Mrs. Mary Kimball Morgan of St. Louis, later a Christian Science teacher herself, was a devoted pupil of Mrs. Field-King until (as she told the author c. 1938) she became increasingly aware of what she described as a subtle corruption of thought in her teacher, broke off all connection with her (to the immediate benefit of the mental health of her family), and studied again under Edward Kimball. Mrs. Field-King, faced with the unwillingness of the St. Louis students to accept her mental domination, returned to England, settled down in the countryside, continued to teach *sub rosa*—protesting her loyalty to Mrs. Eddy but introducing doctrines at sharp variance with Mrs. Eddy's teachings—and was dropped from The Mother Church in 1902. In 1917 John V. Dittemore, who was later to become co-author of the Bates–Dittemore *Mary Baker Eddy*, fell heavily under Mrs. Field-King's influence and did his best to have her reinstated in The Mother Church. He was unsuccessful in his effort, a fact which combined with other differences of opinion to take him out of The Mother Church a few years later and into opposition to its founder. The Bates–Dittemore book, written at that time, presents Mrs. Field-King determinedly as "the most tender and loving of all [Mrs. Eddy's] disciples."

125. A. Deed of Trust, Jan. 25, 1898. Quoted in Norman Beasley, *The Continuing Spirit* (New York: Duell, Sloan and Pearce, 1956), pp. 348 ff.

126. A. *L&M* 39–5206, 39–5207. These comments refer, however, to the first draft she drew up early in January. The finished deed, signed on January 25, was considerably more detailed and probably represented further input by her lawyers. Mrs. Eddy later told Neal and Hanna that she had not wanted to set up a separate trust to conduct the church's publishing activities but had been forced to take this step by the then-existing statutory limitations on the earnings of a church.

127. A. *L&M* 58–8199. Bates was replaced by Neal's friend, Thomas W. Hatten, and shortly afterward Mrs. Eddy released Neal from his position, much to his delight, in order that he might devote his whole attention to the healing work.

128. A. *L&M* 37–4870.

129. A. Scribbled on the bottom of his letter to her.

130. A. *L&M* 58–8203.

131. A. Letter of June 30, 1898.

132. A. *L&M* 39–5221. Mrs. Eddy was not alone in thinking this. A year later (April 10, 1899) McKenzie wrote her: "Today the voices of Scientists are being heard through the press, but not always wisely. Papers offer space on condition of so many subscriptions and as in preaching the ill-adapted were most willing to do it, so in contributions to the press, the excited, extreme, or at least untranquilized thought dashes forth unwisely."

133. A. *L&M* 29–3643.

134. A. *L&M* 74–10627.

135. A. *L&M* 29–3727.

136. A. *L&M* 88–13066.

137. A. A7–10271.

138. *CSJ*, XVI, December, 1898, p. 588.

139. A. Edward Everett Norwood reminiscences.

140. See, esp., *We Knew Mary Baker Eddy,* First and Second Series (Boston: Christian Science Publishing Society, 1943 and 1950). Further accounts are scattered through other biographies and unpublished reminiscences.

141. In a special invitation to George Moses to attend the sessions, Mrs. Eddy wrote him (A. *L&M* 89–13163): "It is to be the examination by me of about 50 [actually 67] Christian Scientists preparatory to receiving the degrees of the Mass. Metaphysical College."

142. A. W. P. McKenzie letter to Mrs. Eddy of November 24, 1898. Reminiscences of Emma Shipman, Sue Harper Mims, and others.

143. Mrs. Mims, a woman of considerable charm, character, and ability, was wife of Major Livingston Mims, soon to become a mayor of Atlanta. The daughter of a well-known Mississippi attorney who liked to say of her, "Sue is a better lawyer than I am," she early wrote in the diary which she kept from 1876 to 1887 (portions of which were posthumously published in the *Atlanta Constitution* and the *Atlanta*

Historical Bulletin): "Portia was really the new woman of her time. Why is it so difficult for the world to understand that women can be wise and strong and still gentle?" She herself was one of the best-known hostesses in a South that wanted its women to be charming above all else, but she was also a civic leader and incipient rebel who could confide to her diary: "I much prefer a dinner party when we have the variety of men's views, added to our feminine subleties, to those stupid ladies' luncheons, where . . . trivialities weary the body and soul." After studying with Julia Bartlett, she threw herself wholeheartedly into the work of Christian Science, becoming a practitioner, teacher, and finally lecturer. In this last capacity, she lectured across the country for fifteen years before audiences ranging up to five thousand. A Birmingham newspaper, quoted in the *Atlanta Constitution,* commented after one of these occasions: "Mrs. Mims is one of the brightest minds of the entire South without regard to sex, and Christian Science won its most formidable exponent in this section when she became an advocate of its doctrines."

144. *We Knew Mary Baker Eddy,* II, p. 53 f.

145. *Mis.,* p. 105.

146. A. Daisette S. McKenzie reminiscences. Clarkson wrote Mrs. Eddy a week later assuring her that "no worship of personality entered into my thoughts of you," but going on to explain his view of her in words that still came perilously close to deification.

Notes: *Interlude: Political*

1. *S&H,* p. 447.

2. *Ibid.,* p. 83.

3. *Ibid.,* p. 96.

4. See, e.g., *S&H* 223:25–32 and 96 f.

5. *Mis.* 119:11–21. This is the one time in her writings that Mrs. Eddy used the word "optimism." See also Peel, *Encounter,* p. 127.

6. Hanna, when sending Mrs. Eddy in August, 1898, a dummy of the projected *Christian Science Messenger* (actually issued the following month as the *Christian Science Weekly,* and soon retitled the *Christian Science Sentinel*) had explained to her why he felt it should carry a certain amount of news: "You will observe that we have given some space to current events. It occurred to me that perhaps it would be well to have a newspaper containing items of general interest, sufficient possibly to keep the workers somewhat informed thereof. I thought, too, that our publication might be more apt to reach the outside world if it met it somewhat on its own plane, instead of confining itself exclusively to Christian Science matter." Mrs. Eddy, who before her absorption in the early needs of the Christian Science movement had always had a lively interest in public affairs, found Hanna's suggestion in full accord with her own renewed attention to the larger needs of the world around her.

7. *S&H*, p. 140.

8. *S&H*, pp. 133, 524. On p. 566 she quotes with approval the words put by Scott in the mouth of Rebecca the Jewess:

> When Israel, of the Lord beloved,
>> Out of the land of bondage came,
> Her fathers' God before her moved,
>> An awful guide, in smoke and flame. . . .

> And oh, when stoops on Judah's path
>> In shade and storm the frequent night,
> Be Thou, longsuffering, slow to wrath,
>> A burning and a shining light!

9. Mrs. Eddy described this in *S&H*, p. 340, as her "favorite text" and added that "it signifies that man shall have no other spirit or mind but God, eternal good, and that all men shall have one Mind."

10. *Ibid.*

11. *My.*, p. 277.

12. A. *L&M* 94–14046.

13. A. *L&M* 23–2853.

14. A. *L&M* 62–8840.

15. Quoted in *CSJ*, XVI (May, 1898), p. 77. Reprinted in part in *My.*, p. 278, but combined there with the *Boston Herald* statement of March 20. Mrs. Eddy's various comments on the situation during this period show her developing thought as she sorted out the basic issues involved.

16. After the disappearance of the last frontier of the continental United States, Captain (later Admiral) A. T. Mahan, president of the Naval War College, had written, "Americans must now begin to look outward." Like Mahan, Senators Beveridge and Lodge found their fears and their appetites whetted by what they saw.

17. *Pan.*, p. 14 f.

18. Allan Keller, *The Spanish-American War: A Compact History* (New York: Hawthorn Books, 1969), p. 197.

19. *Mis.*, p. 288.

20. *CSJ*, XVI (June, 1898), pp. 220 ff. Hanna added, however, that if the United States government had been "sufficiently endowed with the Christ-spirit" the war might have been avoided, with "Cuba's sufferings" and "Spain's inhumanities" rectified in some other way.

21. *CSJ*, XVI (September, 1898), p. 450. Cf. *CSS*, II (September 21, 1899), p. 46, in which a question—" . . . is it to be inferred that the *Sentinel* favors the war, or endorses the policy of the administration?"—is answered: "The *Sentinel* is in some sense a newspaper, and because it publishes items of news relating to current events —including some events of the war—it should not be assumed that we favor the

war or endorse war measures. . . . Nevertheless Christian Scientists are a patriotic people and will uphold just government so far as they can."

22. *CSS,* I, February 9, 1899, p. 2.

23. *My.,* p. 129. In a statement published in the *New York World* in 1900 *(My.,* p. 266) she included "industrial slavery" and "insufficient freedom of honest competition" among the dangers she saw confronting the new century.

24. See her statement in the *Boston Post* in 1908 *(My.,* p. 276) : "I am asked, 'What are your politics?' I have none, in reality, other than to help support a righteous government; to love God supremely, and my neighbor as myself." Mrs. Eddy was brought up a Jacksonian Democrat, switched her sympathies to the new Republican Party at the time of the Civil War, managed to sound remarkably like William Jennings Bryan in some of her public pronouncements at the turn of the century, but in general stayed clear of partisan judgments and commitments in her later years.

25. *My.,* p. 129.

26. *Message to The Mother Church, 1902,* p. 3 f. In the books Mrs. Eddy read during this period, her marking of comments on peace and war is of special interest. A passage by Ruskin in *Philosophic Nuggets* (see pp. 184 ff. of this book) which she marked and labeled "Woman & war" condemned women for being too thoughtless to take pains for any creature out of their own immediate circles and addressed them directly:

> You fancy that you are sorry for the pain of others. Now I just tell you this, that if the usual course of war, instead of unroofing peasants' houses and ravaging peasants' fields merely broke the china upon your own drawing-room tables, no war in civilized countries would last a week. I tell you more, that at whatever moment you choose to put a period to war, you could do it with less trouble than you take any day to go out to dinner.

In a book entitled *The Kingship of Self-Control* (New York: Fleming H. Revell Co., 1899) , presented to her by the author, William George Jordan, she marked as "foolish" the following passage: "The greatest triumph of the nineteenth century is . . . the sweet atmosphere of Peace that is covering the nations, it is the growing closer and closer of the peoples of the earth. Peace is but the breath, the perfume, the life of love." Her own anticipations for the coming period of history were considerably less utopian.

27. See Erwin D. Canham, *Commitment to Freedom: The Story of The Christian Science Monitor* (Boston: Houghton Mifflin Co., 1958) , pp. 11 ff.

28. Peel, *Trial,* p. 183.

29. A. *L&M* 38–4922. This passage stands as a wry comment on the involvement of several prominent British Christian Scientists with the ill-conceived appeasement policy of the 1930's and of several American Christian Scientists with the Watergate scandal of the 1970's. At the same time, press efforts to explain these individuals' views and actions as the results of their being Christian Scientists failed to take account of an obvious fact. On the issues involved in both these cases *The Christian Science Monitor* was strongly critical of the position taken by the individuals in

question and was supported in this by the majority of Christian Scientists. Cf. *A Century of Christian Science Healing* [1966], p. 250 f.:

> Like members of other groups, Christian Scientists come from widely diverse backgrounds. All sorts of social and political views are to be found among them. The individual who turns to Christian Science for healing possesses inevitably a whole set of likes, antipathies, convictions, and temperamental characteristics. . . .
>
> Sooner or later it [the study of Christian Science] must result in shaking up those entrenched personal predilections which breed intolerance and are so often mistaken for eternal truths. When Spirit is accepted as the only absolute, the relativity of all human positions becomes gradually evident.
>
> This no more inhibits a Christian Scientist from being an ardent fighter for a particular social cause than it does any other Christian, but it should and can allow him to fight with charity rather than bigotry, with a desire to heal his opponents rather than to crush them. . . .
>
> Whether a Christian Scientist participates in the social battles of our day as a liberal or a conservative, a fighter or a reconciler, a partisan or an independent, a private or a general, his ultimate purpose is to *heal*. Yet most Christian Scientists would probably agree that up to now only a small fraction of the healing dynamic of their religion has been utilized in relation to the urgent collective problems facing the world.

30. *My.*, p. 234.

31. Sarah Pike Conger, *Letters from China* (Chicago: A. C. McClurg & Co., 1910).

32. An interesting footnote to this situation is to be found in Hon. Frances G. Porter reminiscences (A.). Mrs. Porter's father, Lord Ashbourne, formerly Lord Chancellor of Ireland and at that time a member of the British Cabinet, came home to his family one night in 1900 with the somber news that the embassy staffs and families in Peking had all been murdered. Lady Ashbourne, a niece of Mrs. Eddy's student Marjorie Colles and a recent convert to Christian Science, had steadily insisted to her husband that this would never happen, since Mrs. Conger was there and would certainly "make her demonstration." When Lord Ashbourne announced to her that it nevertheless had happened, she replied calmly, "They are not murdered; you will find they are perfectly safe." To which the good gentlemen replied with the slight exasperation of a longsuffering husband and the overconfidence of a minor Tory minister: "Don't be silly, my dear. The information came to the Cabinet, so there can be no mistake." Although a memorial service was held in London for the supposed victims, later events proved Lady Ashbourne—in this case—to be right.

33. For two months of daily terror, Mrs. Conger took a leading role in caring for the wounded, comforting the fearful, organizing life behind the barricades, shepherding the refugees from decimated missions. On July 7 she wrote in her diary: "This morning I made my rounds, then went off in a little nook by myself to read. I opened my Bible to see what lesson was there for me, and turned to Second Corinthians, first chapter. These words . . . were my message: 'For we would not, brethren, have you ignorant of our trouble which came to us in Asia, that we were pressed out of measure, above strength, insomuch that we despaired even of life: But we had the sentence of death in ourselves, that we should not trust in

ourselves, but in God which raiseth the dead: Who delivered us from so great a death, and doth deliver: in whom we trust that he will yet deliver us.' "

34. Conger, *Letters from China*, pp. 168, 176, 188.

35. Powell, *Mary Baker Eddy* (1950 ed.) , p. 200.

36. Quoted in Powell, p. 201.

Notes: *Chapter V   The Woman and the Serpent*

1. A. Woodbury letters of 1880's.

2. A. Letter of September 8, 1889.

3. A. Undated letter, probably circa 1884–85.

4. Twentieth-century writers have repeatedly described her as one of those who was closest to Mrs. Eddy, a myth which is really a tribute to Mrs. Woodbury's later propagandistic efforts to build up exactly that impression. (For the actual situation see Peel, *Trial*, p. 175 f.) In 1887 twenty of Mrs. Woodbury's pupils wrote in a letter to Mrs. Eddy (A.) : "She has often spoken of her faults and failures, the trouble she has given you in consequence, and your persistent forbearance. Repeatedly has she told us of occasions when she has been in error. And how you have reached out your hand drawing her back to Truth and pointing out the way."

5. A. Letter of July 31, 1888.

6. A. Woodbury trial material. The man in question had been happily married for some years, and at the time Mrs. Woodbury exerted her fascination on him his wife was both pregnant and ill. Following this affair, which seems to have come to a climax during a visit to Niagara Falls, Mrs. Woodbury turned on him with remarkable vindictiveness and denounced him to her pupils (without explanation) as the one "through whom she entered hell" and "learned the fullness of Satan's claims." (Statement dictated by her to several pupils on Easter Sunday, 1893.) See also Peel, *Trial*, pp. 268 ff.

7. A. Woodbury trial material. Peel, *Trial*, pp. 262, 270.

8. Much of the discussion at the time made the popular mistake of confounding the "immaculate conception" of Mary with the "virgin birth" of Jesus, but this verbal boner was irrelevant to the point at issue. Mrs. Eddy had made it clear as far back as 1885 that she did not accept the possibility of a present-day recurrence of the event, however it might be labeled. It is a little difficult to understand the often-made claim that Mrs. Woodbury had been "misled" by the doctrine she attributed to Mrs. Eddy. After all, she produced a child. She and her husband had not had sexual relations for more than a year. Was the child, then, fathered by the theory, or was the theory generated by the child?

9. See evidence in Peel, *Trial*, p. 375, notes 83 and 84, including Mrs. Eddy's explicit denial of the possibility in Mrs. Woodbury's presence in 1885. Bates–Dittemore base their claim to the contrary on Mrs. Field-King, who wrote Mrs. Eddy on

April 12, 1896, that after turning to Christian Science she had supposed "in a vague way" that "sufficient spiritual understanding would make such a thing [virgin birth] possible today," and that one of Mrs. Eddy's students, Mrs. Hannah Larminie, had actually taught this to her pupils; but, Mrs. Field-King added, the explicit denial of its possibility in *Ret.*, had disabused her of the assumption. There was plenty in Mrs. Eddy's writings to disabuse her of the assumption, including the flat statement in the chapter entitled "Marriage" in *S&H*: "Marriage is the legal and moral provision for generation among human kind" (p. 56). Mrs. Eddy's consistent teaching that man's true selfhood was spiritual, not material, led always to the necessity in human experience for Christian regeneration, the "new birth" posited by Scripture. Nowhere in her writings was there the slightest ground or justification for a doctrine of physical generation through mental conception or, as Mrs. Woodbury put it in the *Arena*, May, 1899, that "women may become mothers by a supreme effort of their own minds." Bates–Dittemore astonishingly seek to support Mrs. Woodbury's claim by quoting the statement from *S&H* (p. 64) that "the time cometh of which Jesus spake, when he declared that in the resurrection there should be no more marrying nor giving in marriage, but man would be as the angels." Naturally, they add, many of Mrs. Eddy's students felt that they were ready to "enter the angelic state at once." But angels do not give birth to physical children, virginally or otherwise, and if the angelic state ruled out sexuality it equally ruled out procreation. Although the historic virgin birth played a key role in Mrs. Eddy's theology, she saw it as a unique event related to the uniqueness of Jesus' mission. As such, she implied, it played as crucial a part in his demonstration of perfect manhood as did his overcoming of death through the resurrection, but Science enabled one to emulate his example through regeneration and growth in spiritual understanding, not through reproducing the special conditions of his human experience.

10. *Mis.*, p. 2.

11. A. *L&M* 21–2652. See also Peel, *Trial*, p. 271.

12. A. Letter of March 11, 1895.

13. A. Mrs. Eddy's correspondence with the Directors. Only by using her full authority was she able to persuade the First Members to take Mrs. Woodbury into the church even on probation.

14. A. Letter of October 2, 1895.

15. A. *L&M* 14475.

16. Cf. *Notable American Women* (Cambridge: Belknap Press of Harvard University Press, 1971), p. 558: "Mrs. Woodbury was nevertheless admitted to membership in the Mother Church because of her fervent loyalty and because there were some grounds in Christian Science for belief in parthenogenesis." Quite apart from the fact that Christian Science offered no valid grounds for belief in parthenogenesis (see note 9, above), what Mrs. Eddy thought of her student's protestations of "fervent loyalty" is clear from her letters of April 8 and 17, 1895, to Mrs. Woodbury, quoted in part (with slight but unimportant inaccuracies) in Milmine, *Life*, p. 434:

> Now, dear student try one year not to tell a single falsehood, or to practise one cheat, or to break the decalogue, and if you do this to the best

of your ability at the end of that year God will give you a place in our church as sure as you are fit for it. . . .

Now mark what I say. This is your last chance, and you will succeed in getting back, and should. But this I warn you, to stop falsifying, and living impurely in thought, in vile schemes, in fraudulent money-getting, etc. I speak plainly even as the need is.

I am not ignorant of your sins, and I am trying to have you in the church for protection from these temptations, and to effect your full reformation. Remember, the m. a. m., which you say in your letter causes you to sin, is not idle, and will cause you to repeat them, and so turn you again from the church, unless you pray God to keep you from falling into the foul snare.

As usual, Milmine quotes these passages to discredit Mrs. Eddy rather than Mrs. Woodbury, but they make peculiarly gormless the statement that the latter's "fervent loyalty" to the highly moral teachings of Christian Science was a factor in her probationary admission to the church. Such rickety pronouncements are all too typical of the disposition of biographical scholarship since 1900 to accept Mrs. Woodbury's statements at face value. Where guilt and innocence are predetermined by the accepted myths of an age—as, for instance, in the verdicts by learned divines of the sixteenth century against men and women of probity accused of witchcraft— fact is confidently (and often predictably) confounded with fantasy by the supposed guardians of rational inquiry.

17. See, e.g., Dakin, *Mrs. Eddy*, p. 309:

Mrs. Eddy was furious.

Obviously, if anybody was going to achieve a virginal conception in this modern day and age, such a distinction should not come to a mere follower instead of the founder of the system by which such miraculous results could be achieved. And Mrs. Eddy was not at the moment in a mood to believe in miracles concerning any one but herself.

18. This process started early. As editor of *CSJ* during the late 1880's, J. Henry Wiggin was assisted by Mrs. Woodbury, who had a higher degree of literary skill and sophistication than was common at that time among Mrs. Eddy's students. As a man of the world, he was greatly appealed to by what he later described as Mrs. Woodbury's "brain power," witty sarcasm, frankness in discussing "mundane" (i.e., racy?) facts, and capacity for leadership. It seems likely that they found pleasure in a mutual sense of intellectual superiority and that the erosion of his earlier admiration for the author of *S&H* was helped along by his assistant. On the evidence of a panegyrical introduction which he wrote for a volume of Mrs. Woodbury's poems (*Echoes* [Boston: Samuel Usher, 1898]) , it seems clear that she was able to persuade him that the more flamboyant aspects of her life were simply a matter of jealous misrepresentation of her by Mrs. Eddy. Praising Mrs. Woodbury's personality and accomplishments, Wiggin wrote in his introduction of "the opposition encountered by this lady" as deriving from the fact that "nothing so disturbs people as ridicule, especially when merited; intellectual superiority is a sure rouser of jealousy; and dictators seldom enjoy being themselves directed."

19. A. Testimony of James and Mary Landy, Walter and Mary Roach, Elizabeth S. Bangs, and various others. Her most intimate friend, Mrs. Martha E. Burns, who

finally broke loose from her control, testified before the First Members on April 4, 1896: "Mrs. Woodbury often told me that terrible calamities would come to me if I persisted in holding that state of thought to her. . . . She said that my family would be ruined financially and death would come to them. No one who has not been under the influence of such a subtle mind knows anything of how it holds one." Mrs. Landy on the same occasion testified that Mrs. Woodbury "continued up to the time of my last connection with her to hold that the child was of immaculate conception, and that unless I saw this I should not be able to keep well but should get sick and die."

Unsubtle and even ridiculous as such threats sound today, they worked literally like a charm—and Mrs. Woodbury ruled by charm as well as by fear—on the susceptible minds of her pupils. Some of them, though loyal members of The Mother Church, held back from giving evidence for years under what they felt was the alternating attraction and compulsion of her mental sway.

One Charles E. Nash, a solid citizen of Augusta, Maine, and not a Christian Scientist, gave a harrowing, circumstantial account in 1897 of the way Mrs. Woodbury took possession of his young daughter's mind and purse, reduced her at last to an almost mindless state, kept her virtually imprisoned in Boston during her final illness, and allowed the distraught family to take her home only a few days before she died. Two Maine physicians who attended the young woman for the short period before her death furnished written opinions that they believed her to be the victim of protracted, systematic hypnosis. It was a graphic illustration of Mrs. Eddy's statement in *Mis.* (p. 365) that Christian Science was hurt more than all else "by the impostors that come in its name." See *S&H*, p. 235: "Better suffer a doctor infected with smallpox to attend you than to be treated mentally by one who does not obey the requirements of divine Science." Also *ibid.*, p. 459: "Committing the bare process of mental healing to frail mortals, untaught and unrestrained by Christian Science, is like putting a sharp knife into the hands of a blind man or a raging maniac, and turning him loose in the crowded streets of a city."

20. Her sporadic public references to Mrs. Eddy in terms of apotheosis seem to have fooled no one except her own students. The latter term she used with obviously ironic intent as an appended salutation in a note to Mrs. Eddy from Edinburgh in 1896:

> A Miss McNeil who was one of Queen Victoria's favorite ladies in court recently married the Duke of Argyle.
> To The Mother Mary   From J. C. Woodbury

21. Acts 16:16–18.

22. Julia Field-King turned to her similarly when she was in deep and hot waters, and wrote Mrs. Eddy of the comfort and guidance she was getting from Miss Bartlett. See also Peel, *Trial*, p. 179 f.

23. A. Julia Bartlett testimony.

24. Obvious examples are Mann, Gide, Hesse, Camus—writers who are not to be confused with the legion of mere exploiters of the perverse.

25. *Paradise Lost*, Books II and IV. Theology had already advanced closer to psychology since Christopher Marlowe had put into Mephistopheles's mouth the famous rejoinder to Faust:

> Why, this is hell, nor am I out of it:
> Think'st thou that I, who saw the face of God,
> And tasted the eternal joys of heaven,
> Am not tormented with ten thousand hells
> In being deprived of everlasting bliss?

In the age of Eliot's *The Cocktail Party* ("Hell is oneself") and Sartre's *No Exit* ("Hell is other people"), theology and metaphysics (theistic or atheistic) were virtually unthinkable apart from psychology. In such an atmosphere, Mrs. Eddy's definition of hell as " . . . error; lust; remorse; hatred; revenge; . . . self-imposed agony" (*S&H*, p. 588) could be seen as both retrospective and prophetic.

26. Matthew 6:23.

27. A. Carrie Roach testimony.

28. *Ibid.*

29. See Peel, *Trial*, p. 375, note 79.

30. A. *L&M* 21–2652.

31. *Boston Herald, Globe,* and *Post,* March 26, 1897.

32. On a trip to Europe in the summer of 1896 she even sent Mrs. Eddy a cable from London: "Gratitude loyal love Woodbury." A month or two later, the morning after Mrs. Eddy had experienced a night of the sort of physical agony she always attributed to a particularly vicious mental attack on her, another cable arrived, this time from Chamonix, with a one-word message of bland inscrutability: "Greetings Woodbury."

33. See, e.g., her article "Who is to be Mrs. Eddy's Successor?" in her *Christian Science Voices* (Boston: Samuel Usher, 1897):

> Perplexing query, yet not necessarily disloyal.
> Her Gracious Majesty Victoria is still the great Queen-Mother . . . ; nevertheless thought is irresistibly astir over the possible changes in the British Empire. . . .
> Were she to take the most wise step, as is rumored, of voluntarily relinquishing her throne to her successor, by so doing she would but add one more laurel leaf to her already beauteous wreath.
> And what of the Discoverer of Christian Science and her dominion? . . .
> As a discoverer she will be eternally her own successor. . . .
> There need be no re-discovery of the life-giving Tree, when one Mary Eddy has led the way to its umbrageous salvation, where the foliage is falling for the healing of the nations . . . [but] each of these flying leaves may bear a seed, in time to fructify the soil anew, through souls illumined by her revelation.

34. Revelation 12:7, 9. Cf. *S&H* 564:24.

35. Mrs. Woodbury's fascination with the apocalyptic imagery of the serpent and the woman had been evident for years. In 1894 she had brought out an illustrated poem undoubtedly inspired—or provoked—by Mrs. Eddy's *Christ and Christmas,* illustrated in quasi-Beardsley style by her pupil Eric Pape and entitled *The Wonder in Heaven.* The reference was to the "woman" of St. John's vision in Revelation 12:

What woman's form—
O'er Luna queen, star-crowned, sun-clad—
Appeared to him,
Making his heart with rapture glad?
The dragon wroth
With poisoned fang intent to smite
The woman fair,
And all her progeny to blight—

Was Satan named,—
In serpent form, with subtle skill,
His aim unchanged,—
The power of good for aye to kill.
Could John have seen
That Science, when beheld aright,
Is Nature's queen,
Whose royal robes are fringed with light? . . .

36. *Un.*, p. 54.

37. *S&H*, p. 327.

38. *Ibid.*, p. 542.

39. See Peel, *Trial*, pp. 47–58 and 65 f.

40. *S&H*, p. 564. That Mrs. Woodbury had nurtured an unhealthy tendency since her first approach to Christian Science is suggested by her early remark to her brother, General Wendell P. Battles: "I will have Mrs. Eddy's place or pull the whole thing down upon their heads" (see Peel, *Trial*, p. 354, note 68). In the light of this ambition, her final attitude falls into the archetypal pattern of the fallen angel ("Better to reign in hell than serve in heaven") who engineers revenge against the power he has failed to usurp.

41. See Peel, *Discovery* and *Trial*, for a full account of the background and history of the Quimby controversy up to 1891, the year of Julius Dresser's death.

42. Annetta G. Dresser, *The Philosophy of P. P. Quimby* (Boston: George H. Ellis, 1895), p. 87.

43. *S&H*, p. 468.

44. *Mis.*, p. 379.

45. *S&H*, p. 26.

46. See Peel, *Discovery*, pp. 151 ff. and *Trial*, pp. 208 ff.

47. *Arena*, XXI, May, 1899.

48. See Peel, *Discovery*, p. 163 f.

49. *Arena*, May, 1899.

50. A. Woodbury trial material.

51. The young man in question was a brother of the Mrs. Chamberlain whose husband had sued Mrs. Woodbury for the alienation of his wife's affections. Mrs.

Chamberlain, as well as her brother, was for some time a resident of the Woodbury household on Newbury Street, which looked directly across a vacant lot to Mrs. Eddy's Commonwealth Avenue house, then occupied by the Hannas and a center of much official church activity. It was, from Mrs. Woodbury's point of view, a convenient observation post.

52. *S&H*, p. 564 f.

53. *My.*, p. 127.

54. *My.*, p. 125 f.

55. *Boston Globe*, June 7, 1899.

56. Mrs. Eddy had students in Chicago and elsewhere trace, as far as they were able, the origin of various derogatory news items in 1899 and found that the trail repeatedly led back to Mrs. Woodbury. George Moses, editor of the *Concord Monitor*, wrote her early that year that Mrs. Woodbury had showered him for several years with contributions, none of which he had ever published, then added, "I have also had several anonymous letters which I attributed to her, mainly on the ground that the internal evidence pointed to her authorship."

57. *Boston Journal*, June 21, 1899.

58. A. Reported by John Lathrop in undated (1899) letter to Calvin Frye. For Elder's repute, see foreword by William Howard Taft to Margaret M. Elder, *The Life of Samuel J. Elder* (New Haven: Yale University Press, 1925), the presentation speech with which Yale conferred on him the degree of LL.D. as not merely a leader of the Massachusetts bar but "a jurist who influences and guides the development of law" (*Ibid.*, p. 258), and the tributes of fellow lawyers and jurists at the memorial exercises for him in a special session of the Supreme Judicial Court of Massachusetts (*Ibid.*, pp. 332 ff.).

59. Peabody lived on Beacon Street on sacrosanct Beacon Hill, but in no other way could he be considered a "proper Bostonian." His life was lived on the edge of the improper, not to say the spicy. Indicted for libel in 1895 and militantly courting libel charges for the rest of his life, barely escaping censure by the Massachusetts Bar Association on at least one occasion, denied custody of his children by the divorce court, reported in the press to have skipped from his new home after remarriage (leaving behind him unpaid bills and a complaining landlord), defendant in court as often as he was counsel, deserting the bar to launch increasingly sensational lecture and pamphlet campaigns against Mrs. Eddy and Christian Science, Peabody stands out in retrospect as something less than a disinterested champion of human rights and dignity.

60. Edmund A. Whitman contribution to Elder, *The Life of Samuel J. Elder*, p. 192.

61. A. Letter of October 31, 1899.

62. *My.*, p. 129 f.

63. For earlier activity of a similar sort, see Peel, *Trial*, p. 231 f. and 369, note 79.

64. A. Letter of June 11, 1893.

65. A. *L&M* 13–1599.

66. A. *L&M* 13–1600.

67. *Man.*, p. 97. Another *Manual* provision which had a bearing on this situation was Article VIII, Section 3 ("Christ Jesus the Ensample") , one part of which reads: "When it is necessary to show the great gulf between Christian Science and theosophy, hypnotism, or spiritualism, do it, but without hard words. . . . However despitefully used and misrepresented by the churches or the press, in return employ no violent invective, and do good unto your enemies when the opportunity occurs." Additional instructions of the same sort are found in Sections 25 and 26 of Article VIII.

68. A. Letter of August 7, 1899.

69. See Hanna's editorial "Responsibility of All" in *CSS*, II, September 21, 1899, and "A Correction" in issue of September 28. The article in question in *CSJ*, XVII (December, 1899) , pp. 619 ff. began, with unintended but unfortunate relevance, "The way in which agitation in legal circles, intended to secure decisions against Christian Scientists, is resulting in decisions in their favor, suggests an interesting retrospect." At the same time this appeared, young John Lathrop took it upon himself, without consulting Mrs. Eddy, to write to the judge who was conducting the Woodbury contempt case and urge a speedy decision, a step which greatly embarrassed and disturbed Mrs. Eddy's counsel.

70. Shortly before, she had written a new by-law, "Alertness to Duty" (Article VIII, Section 6, of the *Manual*) , which made it a duty for church members to defend themselves daily against aggressive mental suggestion.

71. *S&H*, p. 366. These were the days when Julia Field-King was moving rapidly toward her final separation from the church and causing new trouble in England. In Washington, D.C., a motley crew of dubious gentlemen who might have been boon companions of Mark Twain's Colonel Sellars and were indeed both colonels and lawyers (notably Oliver C. Sabin, editor of the *Washington News-Letter,* and one Nat Ward Fitzgerald of whom Captain Linscott wrote to Armstrong, "He can talk like an angel but he is a *wolf")* had latched on to Christian Science for their own ends and, when Mrs. Eddy discovered their assorted rascalities, had turned wolfishly against her and each other. A brilliant young German-Jewish rabbi, Max Wertheimer, who had gone through the Normal class with Kimball and was complaining because he had not soared at once to the top levels of the movement was on his whirligig way to becoming a fundamentalist preacher and anti-Christian Science pamphleteer. The Reverend George Tomkins remained faithful but vastly embarrassing as the ousted First Reader of the Camden, New Jersey, church, with what the newspapers headlined as "Fist Fight in Church" between the pro- and anti-Tomkins factions. Other less picturesque eruptions, of which Mrs. Eddy had been kept ignorant, caused her to write both to the offenders and to the Board of Directors who had them under discipline by vote of the First Members. To John P. Filbert, for instance, she wrote (A. *L&M* 70–9987) :

> Only yesterday I heard for the first time that you are being reprimanded by my church! My astonishment was indescribable. . . . If you have erred be like all true followers ready to confess you have. It is not necessary that you

repeat an error but only signify your regret and if you are not in the fault say so and all is canceled by my Church and God will do justly in his rewards and punishments.

To the Directors she wrote on the same day (3–242) : "Please pass the enclosed By law and also repeal the votes taken on discipline of J. P. Filbert S. J. Sawyer and Mrs. Graybill of Atchison, Kansas, and all other cases not done under my knowledge." In return William B. Johnson wrote her on May 4: "The Directors are glad to get the word to dismiss *all complaints*. . . . We believe this will do much good, and we shall not have these skeletons haunting us. The slate will be wiped clean and may we hope that it will be kept so."

72. A. Frye diaries. The Mrs. [Pamelia] Leonard mentioned was a student of Mrs. Eddy's who had arrived the day before to serve in the household.

73. Two other lawyers who handled other aspects of the case were William A. Morse and Charles W. Bartlett. Morse, who was able but alcoholic, turned up at Pleasant View one evening decidedly under the influence and was shooed away from the door by a horrified member of the household. Mrs. Eddy happened to look out the window, saw his weaving retreat, and immediately sent after him, had him brought back, cared for lovingly, put to bed, and sent off the next morning clear-headed and with a devotion to her that persisted through the years.

74. A. Quoted by Streeter in his November 1 reply.

75. A. Letter of November 1, 1900.

76. A. *L&M* 90–8531. Some time earlier Judge Ewing had written his wife from Concord that he had just had an unexpected visit from Mrs. Eddy when she came in from her drive. She "embraced and kissed me most affectionately and said 'O! my dear student, I cannot speak my gratitude; others have done valiantly; but you have spoken with more wisdom, judgment and law than all the others. . . .' And as usual I said nothing except a blubber or two." The Mr. J. mentioned in Mrs. Eddy's letter was William B. Johnson, who appears to have supported her position, though feebly. At her request, Johnson brought the situation before the attention of the First Members on January 9. To Armstrong on a similar occasion Mrs. Eddy wrote a fierce rebuke but added: "I thank God for Joseph Armstrong— ie, for giving him to our cause. . . . Mother loves you too much to spare you when you need to be aroused to a sense of need all around you. *Thanks* for your wisdom in not speaking [to Hanna] of what I wrote[;] he is not so well affected by the thunder of Love."

77. Through the indefatigable efforts of William Morse, a new libel law was passed in Massachusetts in the spring of 1901 which gave a defendant the same advantages as the New Hampshire law.

78. Elder, *Life of Samuel J. Elder,* p. 201 f.

79. See p. 126 f. and note 146, p. 418.

80. Clarkson also seems to have stirred up further doubts there. William P. McKenzie, a Trustee of the Christian Science Publishing Society and therefore a defendant in one of the Woodbury suits, wrote his fiancée, Daisette Stocking, on January 9, 1901, in a highly disturbed state of mind. If the suit were lost, he felt,

Mrs. Eddy might well turn the blame on the Directors, Trustees, et al. and make them pay the damages. "I am not forecasting probable loss," he wrote, "but I see some things going on which would disturb one as sincere & honest as Judge Clarkson." In another letter ten days later, he was even more disturbed:

> If anyone induced the lawsuit, she did, & we who published the message did so under her authority. Yet she wished to separate the other suits from hers & make Judge Hanna, Wm Reeder, myself & others meet our suits personally. One of her drastic bylaws is to make the Church not responsible for "private debts"— & from the way these other suits have been spoken of by her, there seems to be no doubt of the intention to sacrifice the faithful workers here if need be.

Since McKenzie went on to quote Clarkson immediately after this, it seems likely that he was responding to the latter's report of the probabilities. In any event, the situation never arose and the fears proved groundless, for when the suit against Mrs. Eddy collapsed in June of that year, it was evident that the other suits would be dropped—as they were, after a little further legal maneuvering.

81. A. Frye diaries. Four days later Clarkson gave a very successful lecture in Concord, but by the end of the month he had resigned from the Board of Lectureship and before long from The Mother Church.

82. Tomlinson in *Twelve Years,* p. 133, quotes from a letter Mrs. Eddy wrote him (between Clarkson's two visits) with reference to a new lecture of his which she had just read: "Dear one, cultivate this tender emotion, have a cell less in the brain and a fibre more in the heart in yourself and it will do much for your lectures and in healing the sick. . . . When lecturing, or addressing the church . . . let this tenderness *appear* and like the dew, it will refresh the parched ear and lonely heart." Her letters show that she expected men and women lecturers alike to demonstrate a blend of those qualities of mind and heart which are often classified respectively as masculine and feminine.

83. A. *A&M* 4–10142B.

84. *Mis.,* p. 360 f.

85. For a sociopolitical application of this doctrine, see p. 63 of *S&H,* especially lines 23–27.

86. The quotations are from pp. 562 and 565 of Mrs. Eddy's chapter, "The Apocalypse," in *S&H.*

87. *Ibid.,* p. 561.

88. Her letters and quotations of this period emphasize that Hanna must agree to write in moderate terms of her, avoid any seeming deification of her, and edit *CSJ* so that "God and not man, Truth and not error" should make clear her significance to the age. A few years earlier she had dictated to Foster Eddy a statement "To All Whom It May Concern" (A. *A&M* 7–10281):

> I am weary of waiting on the involuntary or voluntary motions of the infantile mind in Christian Science to become absolutely right on a single point relating to me. To help settle this problem I will once for all silence

my sensitiveness and give the definition of my present *genus homo,* so far as I understand it. . . .

1st In belief, I am a human being and should be treated as such, and spoken of as such, until I find my place outside this state of being.

2nd So far as I know myself, and history, I am the discoverer and founder of Christian Science. If my claim is unwarranted, show this fact by precedent or proof. Produce a single work before mine which contained *my statement* of Christian Science as in Science and Health, or show this statement incorrect demonstrably, and I will then say that my claim is invalid.

3rd I believe in the Scriptural narrative and the evidence it affords that Jesus of Nazareth demonstrated and taught the divine Principle of Christian Science. But I have no written or verbal evidence that he taught the letter of this Science. . . .

In the flesh I am not what I desire to be; I am not what imagination would make me. I am not a heathen concept or idol. I am not a personality to which others look and are saved, and the world's present ignorance of the place I occupy should suspend its judgment. I am not the Door through which to enter, nor the Rock whereon to build, but what God has spoken to this age through me is the *way* and *sure foundation,* and no man entereth by any other way into Christian Science.

See also her 1906 statement in *My.,* 117:22–27.

89. A. *L&M* 41–5362. In her instructions to the committee whom she appointed to pray daily about the Woodbury suit, she repeatedly emphasized that they *must* keep their work impersonal. They must not hold Mrs. Woodbury in thought in any way as they prayed for a just and principled resolution of the case.

90. A. *A&M* 25–10926.

91. A. *A&M* 16–10408. The unpublished work from which this is taken has been erroneously identified by several writers as "Repaid Pages." See note 28, p. 405. In line with the passage quoted, Mrs. Eddy elsewhere expressed her emphatic desire that, except for her chapter on the Apocalypse in *S&H*, there should be no further interpretation of the Apocalypse by Christian Scientists.

92. In an interview in the *Boston Journal,* June 8, 1901, reprinted in *CSS,* III, June 13, 1901, Kimball answered the question whether Mrs. Eddy considered herself to be the woman clothed with the sun: "She does not. She does not teach or want anyone to teach that. On the contrary, we do not believe that the word 'woman' means any particular woman, but rather refers to conditions of thought, or the revelations of truth." Even Ira Knapp, who is generally associated with Hanna in holding the conviction that Mrs. Eddy was literally the woman in Revelation, was forced to admit under oath during the Woodbury trial that this was not a part of Mrs. Eddy's teaching. The court record speaks for itself:

Peabody: Mr. Knapp, did you know that it was a part of the belief of the people to whom that message was being read, that the author of the message was, herself, a person referred to in the Book of Revelation?

Knapp: I did not.

Peabody: Didn't you then know it to be a part of Mrs. Eddy's teaching, and the belief of the people assembled in the church of that day, that she is what the Book of Revelation calls the "woman clothed with the sun . . ."?

Knapp: I do not know.

Peabody: Did you then know that that was the belief of the other Christian Scientists present?

Knapp: No sir; I did not.

On the other hand, that Mrs. Eddy considered the symbol especially applicable to her own experience is beyond doubt. For instance, the dragon's pursuit of the woman into the wilderness and his sending forth a flood to drown her seemed to her a perfect illustration of her experience, and she drew frequently on its imagery, as when she wrote Mrs. Field-King in 1892 (A. F91) : "Oh how little anyone knows me! The woman in the wilderness, truly! And sometimes I feel that students who put forth such public claims of regard for me burden me more than all the others."

93. A. Letter of May 28, 1893.

94. A. Letter of February 2, 1895.

95. A. Stephen A. Chase file.

96. A. Letter of January 20, 1895.

97. A. Letter of January 19, 1901.

98. A. Letter to Daisette Stocking, January 16, 1901. In a letter to Miss Stocking ten days later, McKenzie's struggle was even more apparent. What was involved was not merely the question of Mrs. Eddy's personal leadership but the whole problem of church organization. "The question of leaving the movement quietly," he wrote his fiancée, "has been much canvassed. Several of us have talked this over, but the decision is to stay." Very early in her experience Mrs. Eddy had found that it was much easier for Christian Scientists to do good healing work on an individual basis than it was for them to demonstrate Christian Science by working together in harmony to heal the larger ills of the human condition. In practice, this meant that it was easier for them to accept her as an inspired revelator and teacher than as the leader of an organized church body made up of disparate individuals with various kinds and degrees of human imperfection. So long as she could be viewed as almost a goddess, it was possible to accept her church and her leadership as a matter of blind faith, but when it was evident that she herself had her share of human weaknesses to surmount in exercising the functions of church leadership, it was tempting to question both the value and the durability of the whole enterprise.

This was the context in which McKenzie—still struggling against the temperamental oversensitiveness of which Mrs. Eddy had warned him—was thrown into anguish by what he could then see only as temperamental instabilities in her character. On the other hand, the outbursts in some of her own letters of the period show that she felt pressed beyond bearing at times by what seemed to her the failure of her followers to understand the stakes and respond to the needs of the hour. (See, e.g., her letter to Judge Ewing quoted on p. 160.) This failure of responsibility, as she saw it, extended to personal and household details. When she most needed to be free to give her full attention to the movement's needs, the cook burned or undercooked her meals, the clothes she ordered did not fit her, the "transformations" that her student Mrs. Frame procured for her in New York did not match her own hair or slipped sideways on her head when she was on her carriage drive. In one moment of exasperation, she even announced in the Christian Science periodicals her need for three bed jackets of certain materials and colors— an apparent irrationality which has caused amazed comment ever since and which brought an embarrassing avalanche of bed jackets to Pleasant View at the time. From her point of view, however, it may have served to remind some of her followers, who expected her to ride with triumphant ease into battles from which they would have fled in terror, that she was not Joan of Arc in shining armor but a veteran eighty-year-old leader who needed all the spiritual and temporal support they could give her.

What few of them seem to have realized was that great leadership requires of the leader a willingness to do battle, at whatever cost to himself, with his own personal limitations as well as with the limitations of objective circumstance. The cost of leading is often the cost of learning, and, as Mrs. Eddy saw it, she learned from struggling with her own as well as others' shortcomings. Mistakes were fatal only when one failed to utilize their lessons. It may have been a glimpse of this fact that carried McKenzie through his brief rebellion to become one of her most unfaltering champions and eventually a member of the Christian Science Board of Directors. Toward the end of his January 16 letter to Miss Stocking he wrote with some astuteness: "How often Mother told us that only by *impersonalization* can the Cause be saved. If she is swept into the extreme of unreasoning personal queenship, maybe it is the very error she foresaw & is now encountering & will conquer." Certainly the crucial lesson of the Woodbury years for her seems to have been the necessity for greater impersonalization of the movement's leadership.

99. A. Letter to Daisette Stocking, July 21, 1901.

100. A. Frye diaries, March 5, 1900.

101. Facsimile letter in Augusta Stetson, *Sermons and Other Writings* (New York: G. P. Putnam's Sons, 1924) , p. 124 f.

102. A. *L&M* 54–7568.

103. A. *L&M* 65–9319.

104. A. Grye diaries, February 27, 1901.

105. A. Letter of May 30, 1901. Kimball's dating of it as May 20 is an obvious typographical error.

106. A. Anderson letter of January 19, 1907.

107. *Ibid.* A few years after the suit ended, Mrs. Woodbury moved to England. In February and March, 1909, Algernon Hervey Bathurst of London wrote Archibald McLellan in Boston several letters in which he told of Mrs. Woodbury's "delivering addresses to people in private houses in and near London," while she herself was staying at Carter's Hotel, Albemarle Street. "She is to be here for some time, and appears to have plenty of money, and is said to be 'very charming.' Her abuse of the Leader, and those at headquarters is so violent . . . that even certain theosophists with whom she is in touch, are beginning to fight shy of her. She is here

ostensibly to start her son in business. . . . One accusation [she makes] against those at headquarters is that they use black magic. . . . Archdeacon Wilberforce was asked to meet her by a Mrs. Albert Lunn. The impression . . . is that she is trying to get in touch with the Church of England." On July 7, 1910, McLellan wrote Frye that he had heard from Frederick Dixon in London that Mrs. Woodbury "has gone under, to use the expression of her friend. Exactly how serious the collapse is I have not been able to discover." Little is known of the rest of her life except that she spent it in Europe and died there in 1930.

108. A. Letter of June 4, 1901.

109. *New York Herald,* May 1, 1901. Reprinted in *CSJ,* XIX, June, 1901. Also in *My.,* pp. 341 ff. It is a curious comment on the ethics of the press that four days after printing these final paragraphs the *Herald* should have run as fact Clarke's earlier collection of Woodbury-inspired rumors, including the allegation that Mrs. Eddy was too feeble to go out in her carriage and was impersonated by a double. Less conspicuously it also ran a second, modified account of his interview, still favorable but with a few touches of the old cynical tone reintroduced. This is illustrated in the final paragraphs:

Among all who have followed her banner no one has shaken her supremacy. She is the absolute mistress, and her manner explains much of it. It is force under gentleness: alertness that seeks not to seem alert; acuteness that is veiled by mysticism; confidence born of success. Perhaps what appealed to me most was her womanliness, whether it was her gentle efforts to please; her little, conscious graces; her pathetic little vanities even. . . . She has the gentle touch and the firm hold. Some one following her with a stronger clutch and a bolder way may smash to flinders the whole fabric she has reared.

In his 1925 autobiography, *My Life and Memories* (New York: Dodd, Mead & Co.) , Clarke combines the two accounts of the interview in his chapter on Mrs. Eddy.

110. This is the version given to the press and reprinted in the June *CSJ.* The version in *My.,* p. 346 f. omits the reference to Farlow.

Notes: *Chapter VI*   " . . . *remains to be proved* . . ."

1. *S&H,* p. 313. Cf. *ibid.,* p. 6: "It is believed by many that a certain magistrate, who lived in the time of Jesus, left this record: 'His rebuke is fearful.' The strong language of our Master confirms this description."

2. A. Nunn reminiscences.

3. A. *L&M* 29–3684. Cf. Frye diary of July 6, 1899, in re Mrs. Eddy's ordering Clara and him "to go to the Library & confess our sins" to the callers: "But instead of doing so I said 'I do not know what to say! the harder I try the more fault is found with me!' Mrs. Eddy rebuked us all sharply, reading to us Matt. 15:8, 9." The next day he wrote the Tomlinsons, Bakers, and one Lemuel Pope:

I feel that it is my duty to write to you about my sin of yesterday morning when I justified myself and alluded to Mrs. Eddy as mistaking. She has so much cause to find fault that it seems to me when I am dark as if she found fault with everything but when it becomes lifted I realize that it is the only successful way she has when malicious mind is darkening me of awaking me and breaking the spell of error. I also know it was for this same reason that she spoke so sharply to us all yesterday morning.

4. This affidavit is quoted in full in *A Century of Christian Science Healing*, pp. 25 ff. See also *We Knew Mary Baker Eddy*, III, pp. 29 ff.

5. This and the quotations in the next two paragraphs are from Salchow's extensive, detailed reminiscences in A.

6. A. Letter of May 1, 1901. As a result of Joseph's initial healing, three brothers and two sisters had become Christian Scientists.

7. A. *L&M* 14618.

8. In his reminiscences, Salchow gives a matter-of-fact example. When a new carriage was delivered in 1904, the iron steps were discovered to be cut in an openwork pattern instead of having a solid surface. Mrs. Eddy, catching her heel in the openwork as she stepped down after her daily drive, promptly directed August Mann to have the situation corrected. New steps were ordered immediately; at the same time the offending steps were hustled to a firm of expert carriage builders for a temporary remedy. After two hours' work the experts had "accomplished nothing, except to spoil the steps." To everyone's relief, the new steps arrived by express before the next day's drive, only to turn out to be duplicates of the openwork ones. At this point Salchow swung into action:

> As a boy my brother and I had rigged up a forge on the farm in Kansas and had gotten so that we could handle iron pretty well. My interest in this work had continued and I had put up a small forge at Pleasant View and collected quite a lot of iron. I told August to start a fire in the forge and I would see if I could work out something. Just then a singular thing happened. It will be remembered that the driveway made a circle to the end of the barn. There was a little piece of lawn there that was mowed regularly each week with the rest of the lawn. Right there I saw a piece of iron about one eighth of an inch thick and long and wide enough to provide just the right surface for a step. Where it had come from I do not know, for I had never seen such a piece of iron around the place before. But there it was, just as if it had been deliberately placed there for me. I had chisels and tools of my own and was able to cut the iron to just the size to fit inside the rim of the step. Upstairs in the barn I found a piece of corrugated rubber which I placed over the iron, riveting it all together with four rivets, so that when completed it made a perfect step.

> Such instances as this had early shown me that error was always trying to tell those who worked for Mrs. Eddy that they could not carry out her instructions. She herself talked with me and taught me how to resist these arguments and to meet the belief of reversal. . . . It was not that what I accomplished was in any way remarkable in itself, because other people could have done as much; it was simply that I had learned to be awake to the error and to protect

myself against it. After her few talks with me, I saw that if I did not meet the arguments that I could not do what was expected of me I would fail Mrs. Eddy and be of no use to her; so I never questioned her instructions but did my best to carry them out.

9. This anecdote, for space reasons, must do duty for a whole category of recorded stories, some of them well attested and some undoubtedly legendary, of similar instances of Mrs. Eddy's extraordinarily acute observation of small physical details around her. Christian Scientists usually explain this faculty in terms of the qualities of thought she detected as contributing to the particular detail of appearance or circumstance.

10. Mrs. Eddy used this term in her inscription in a gift copy of *S&H* to Salchow. There was a touch of mysticism in this practical young man, and one of the "visionary" experiences he recorded was a dream which he had just before receiving his unexpected invitation to come to Pleasant View. It had to do with a boat of his at Clark's Creek in Kansas which, he was told in his dream, he must clean out because Mrs. Eddy wanted to go out in it. He found the boat (greatly enlarged) filled with some fifty people, all quarreling for a place to see her. Willing to forgo that privilege in order to serve her, Salchow went to the stern cabin and took the rudder, but was rewarded by having the door swing open a few inches so that he was able, after all, to see Mrs. Eddy coming toward the boat with a parcel in her hand:

It seemed as if the burden of the whole universe was on her shoulders and as if she would be crushed before she took another step, but still she came on, her eyes looking upward and beyond the world. It was the most sad and heartrending sight I had ever seen. When she reached the spot where the man had spoken to me she caught sight of me through the opening in the door. It seemed then as if the whole scene changed, her burdens fell away and she came tripping directly to the door of the cabin. Without noticing anyone else, she handed her parcel to me (it was a copy of Science and Health) with the words, "To our faithful boy," and then turned and walked away.

Salchow adds that he never told Mrs. Eddy about this dream but found it realized in the inscribed *S&H* she gave him during his early service at Pleasant View.

11. A. In his reminiscences Salchow conveys a sense of normal, quotidian reality which belies or at least supplements the accounts of both rhapsodists and denigrators. Even his clichés help to adjust the balance on a Calvin Frye who "was full of fun and usually entered into almost any kind of a good joke," and who joined Salchow in pulling the leg of a "very serious" Mrs. Sargent as she listened to them with eyes as "round as saucers."

12. A. Mrs. Salchow adds that her brother James "valued his letter for so many had said Mrs. Eddy and Christian Scientists did not approve of marriage. Mrs. Eddy was very happy when she knew we were married . . . and she showed her love to us in many ways." Her reminiscences also include domestic details such as an account of her Roman Catholic friend Theresa who married a French Canadian, then came to work as laundress at Pleasant View and quietly adored the great lady whom she served.

13. Cf. Margaret Elder's comment on her father's attitude to Mrs. Eddy in *The Life of Samuel J. Elder*, p. 202:

> He thought her an unusual and brilliant woman. And, with his courtesy and his gentleness toward all women, and a certain love of hierarchy which was in him, her regal ways called forth a spontaneous chivalry which he gave delightedly, with half-earnest, half-humorous consideration. "Mrs. Eddy was much as usual," he wrote to Mrs. Elder from New Hampshire. "There was no real need of her sending for me so peremptorily. Everything is being done that can be done in her case. But Streeter went off to Europe without seeing her and she commanded my presence much as a queen might have done. Don't laugh. I made a blunder and started off without her blessing. She sent it to me on the staircase."

14. *Boston Globe*, quoted in *CSS*, III, September 13, 1900, p. 24 f.

15. George Moses of the *Concord Monitor* wrote her two days later, "The main thing about your visit is the genuine spontaneity of your reception . . . indicating the real feeling of the people." (A.)

16. Cf. *S&H*, p. 199: "Had Blondin believed it impossible to walk the rope over Niagara's abyss of waters, he could never have done it." This suggests why she arranged to talk with the high diver when she returned to the fair the next year; it was, in a sense, a matter of professional interest.

17. Luke 10:18. No estimate of the influences on Mrs. Eddy's thinking is complete which does not take into account the obvious spontaneity of her constant allusions (direct and indirect) to the Bible—both in her private letters and in daily conversation.

18. *New York Sun* of August 29, 1901, reported:

> The closest scrutiny was possible. Mrs. Eddy looked to be in perfect health for one who bears the weight of four score years. She was dressed in pale lavender with hat of white illusion, and carried a white silk sunshade. Her movements were suggestive of vivacity. She sat upright, held the sunshade firmly in her right hand, and conversed frequently with the two favored guests seated within her carriage.

19. A. *L&M* 20–10554. Salchow mentions that Joseph Mann made up little bags of candies and nuts for her to give to the Concord children with whom she sometimes stopped and chatted during her daily drives. The evidential value of such otherwise trivial details is clear in the light of constant reports that she was incapacitated, moribund, or dead. On June 8, 1900, Henry Robinson, postmaster and former mayor of Concord, wrote to a Mrs. J. J. Post of Seattle, "O, No! The postmaster of this city never said, even in the sheerest jest, that Mrs. Mary Baker Eddy . . . does not exist." After detailing his personal interviews and dealings with her, and his recognition of her on her carriage drives, he added, "She frequently stops near the front of my own home to smile and speak to my little children playing there."

20. *S&H*, p. 117.

21. *Philosophic Nuggets*, ed. Jeanne G. Pennington (New York: Fords, Howard & Hulbert, 1899), p. 3 f. The reference is to the supposed Teufelsdröckh manuscript of *Sartor Resartus*.

22. *Ibid.*, p. 45. An adaptation of Carlyle's statement that Mohammed "was alone with his own soul and the reality of things" is to be found in Mrs. Eddy's *Message for 1901*, 20:8–9. See note 56, pp. 407 ff.

23. Cf. *S&H*, 254:19–23.

24. For the question whether these were conscious or unconscious borrowings, see note 56, pp. 407 ff.

25. For Mrs. Eddy's possible earlier acquaintance with Amiel's *Journal*, see Peel, *Trial*, note 89, p. 381. Other examples of marked passages which evidently had a special personal appeal for her are Carlyle's comment on Dante: "Thought, true labor of any kind, highest virtue of itself, is it not the daughter of pain?" and on Shakespeare: "And now . . . observe his mirthfulness, his genuine overflowing love of laughter. . . . Even at stupidity and pretensions this Shakespeare does not laugh otherwise than genially. . . . Such laughter, like sunshine on the deep sea, is very beautiful to me."

26. *S&H*, pp. 275–76.

27. *My.*, p. 160.

28. A. Letter of June 20, 1898.

29. *Ibid.* He did, however, write an article for the *Arena* of February, 1901, which he described to her as a discussion of certain theological ideas from the standpoint of a Congregationalist, with incidental references to Christian Science. These references, he wrote her, were designed to do Christian Science good as "the testimony of one entirely outside the fold," but were partly critical and "you must prepare yourself for a goodly amount of saintly indignation" (A. Letters of January 17 and February 7, 1901) .

30. See note 80, p. 430, and note 98, p. 433. Mrs. Eddy's encouragement of John Salchow's marriage, and other similar instances, show that she was not "against marriage," as often charged. Her comments on the subject are apt to have two levels of application. To the question: "Is marriage nearer right than celibacy?" she gave the radical answer: "Human knowledge inculcates that it is, while Science indicates that it *is not.*" But she quickly followed this up with the warning that "to force the consciousness of scientific being before it is understood is impossible, and believing otherwise would prevent scientific demonstration" (*Mis.*, p. 288) . With especially promising students, she sometimes expressed a fervent hope that they had reached the point of "scientific being" where they could find fulfillment by giving themselves wholeheartedly and singlemindedly to Christian Science. McKenzie and Miss Stocking had interpreted this expression of hope as an absolute interdict on their marriage, and when they finally decided to go ahead nevertheless, they expected the thunderbolt of her wrath to fall on them. But Mrs. Eddy quickly showed that she took seriously her own statement that to force the issue "would prevent scientific demonstration," and also indicated that she felt it was a matter of weighing the hazards in both directions. To Mrs. McKenzie she wrote (A. *L&M* 88–13025) : "I am glad that you are married to him you love. It was the right time to do so. When first it was contemplated it was not. While I know that marriage rightly understood and thus maintained is a mutual help I sometimes question the ability at present to thus demonstrate it." After the arrival of a son to the

couple, Mrs. Eddy was apt to end even her business letters to McKenzie with such messages as, "Give my love to Mrs. McKenzie and kiss the dear little mortal who comes and goes with a cry" (*L&M* 50–6984). Carol Norton, also unsure of Mrs. Eddy's response to his marriage at about the same time as the McKenzies' (in 1901), did not tell her until after the wedding. Although a bit put out by his secrecy, Mrs. Eddy wrote both him and his bride, Elizabeth, with affectionate support.

31. See Peel, *Discovery*, p. 284 f. In 1904 a new bylaw in the *Manual* permitted members of the academic community who were also members of The Mother Church to form Christian Science organizations at their universities or colleges. Such a bylaw had actually been suggested to Mrs. Eddy by a Harvard student, Wilfred P. Cole, and the Christian Science Organization at Harvard was the first one to be formed, with some five hundred others coming into existence around the world within the next seventy years.

32. A. 32. A. Letter of November 22, 1901.

33. *S&H*, pp. 266, 356, 86, 262, 280, 336, 255.

34. *Ibid.*, pp. 277, 124, 542, 101, 475, 267, 2, 460.

35. *Ibid.*, p. 119.

36. In the last edition (p. 107) this sentence reads: "In the year 1866, I discovered the Christ Science or divine laws of Life, Truth, and Love, and named my discovery Christian Science."

37. See p. 25 of this book.

38. *S&H*, p. 4. The full sentence reads: "What we most need is the prayer of fervent desire for growth in grace, expressed in patience, meekness, love, and good deeds."

39. *Ret.*, p. 31.

40. *Mis.*, p. 169. From a report of a sermon delivered by Mrs. Eddy in the 1880's.

41. *S&H*, p. 57. Cf. p. 486: "Earth's preparatory school must be improved to the utmost."

42. I John 4:1.

43. The first fourteen chapters of *S&H* fill exactly five hundred pages. The eight which follow the six already described are: Physiology; Footsteps of Truth; Creation; Science of Being; Some Objections Answered; Christian Science Practice; Teaching Christian Science; Recapitulation—the last-named being the basis for all Christian Science class instruction. The next section of one hundred pages, subtitled *Key to the Scriptures*, is composed of three chapters: Genesis, The Apocalypse, Glossary [of biblical terms]. The testimonials on pages 600–700 were selected by Kimball and McKenzie from a large number sent to them by Mrs. Eddy, but a few additions and deletions were made in later editions in accord with her wishes.

44. Matthew 7:20.

45. In 1899–1901, Dr. Alfred Baker—ex-physician and ex-Quaker—also taught several obstetric courses under the Board of Education and in close collaboration with Kimball. During that period the Bakers lived in Concord and were in close contact

with Mrs. Eddy, but early in 1902 she dismissed them and they gradually drew away from the organization. Baker had crossed the line between reverence for Mrs. Eddy's leadership and a virtual deification of her as revelator, and like others who did this—including, at one time or another in their teaching or experience, Foster Eddy, Josephine Woodbury, and Augusta Stetson—he ended up in disgrace.

46. All Kimball's comments about students quoted in this section are taken from his letters of June 30, 1900, and July 1, 1901, to Mrs. Eddy. (A.)

47. Both C. Lilias Ramsay and E. Mary Ramsay became Christian Science teachers. The latter, as Committee on Publication for the East of Scotland, was author of the book *Christian Science and Its Discoverer* (Cambridge: Heffer & Sons, 1923; later published by the Christian Science Publishing Society).

48. Severin E. Simonsen, *From the Methodist Pulpit Into Christian Science*, privately printed, 1928, p. 150.

49. See Peel, *Trial*, p. 370, note 3. Wertheimer became a fundamentalist of the variety which anticipates the return of Jesus in physical form on the Mount of Olives to an Israel fully converted to Christianity. As a preacher and pamphleteer, he made occasional reference to his brief flirtation with Christian Science, and in 1916 wrote a much-reprinted pamphlet, "Why I Left Christian Science," which curiously attributed to *Science and Health* several passages that have never appeared in any edition of that book and are completely foreign to Mrs. Eddy's teaching.

50. Hering was professor of electrical engineering in the physics department of Johns Hopkins University.

51. Willis was a Unitarian with theological training who had taught at mission schools in South America, traveled widely in Europe and the Orient, and had then acquired editorial as well as professorial experience in the United States.

52. A. Letter of June 30, 1900. What Kimball called the "technical part" of Christian Science, Mrs. Eddy usually referred to as the "letter." While she repeatedly emphasized the primacy of the spirit over the letter, she was in general accord with Kimball's conviction that Christian Scientists as a whole needed a good deal more exactness in their metaphysical understanding.

53. Young became a prominent practitioner, teacher, and lecturer and Kinter served in Mrs. Eddy's household for several periods, but neither of them moved into careers in the Boston organization. Nor did Kimball for long.

54. A. *L&M* 54–7590.

55. A. Letter of June 3, 1902.

56. A. *L&M* 53–7388.

57. *My.*, p. 7 f.

58. A. *L&M* 54–7591. A month earlier she had asked Kimball to "be prepared to take the position of Editor of the Journal," but had later dropped that idea.

59. A. *L&M* 54–7593. Despite finding the Boston experience a strain on his health and despite his longing to get back to Chicago where he had four hundred applicants for class instruction, Kimball wrote Mrs. Eddy in July, "I am not wise enough to

see my own way & shall do what you tell me is wise for me to do." On further thought, it was clear to her that his primary talents lay elsewhere than in church administration and she released him from a further Boston commitment. But her need at that time is suggested by a letter to the Board of Directors (*L&M* 3–305) :

> With lone and dreary foresight of my tasks I look on this hour unless you help me more in helping new officers know what is best to do and how to do it. But you must help in this or you must give up your office on our Board for I cannot and I shall not do it alone.

Just before writing this letter, Mrs. Eddy had asked Stephen Chase to resign his position on the board in order that Arthur De Camp might serve in his place, and a few months later De Camp would resign and Chase return to the board. Mrs. Eddy's "dreary foresight" seems to have proved true: the new officer found that far from gracing the position automatically with the abilities he brought to it from the past, he was now facing dimensions of experience that called for the development of spiritual talents beyond his present reach. McLellan, on the other hand, seems to have learned his lessons quickly enough to do a satisfactory job.

60. Hamlin Garland's retrospective sketch of him printed in a posthumous edition of McCrackan's *An American Abroad and at Home* suggests the qualities which limited his usefulness as a Christian Scientist as well as a reformer:

> My acquaintance with Will McCrackan began in the early days of the *Arena Magazine,* to which we were fellow contributors. We met on the basis of a mutual interest in Henry George's Single Tax, and in the work and character of William Dean Howells.
>
> Young McCrackan appealed to me at once, both by the charm of his personality and the extent and quality of his knowledge of the Old World. As a reformer, he stood out in notable contrast to the throngs of us who knew only our own country, and not very much of that. He seemed the genial aristocrat, amusing himself with questions of economics, but as I came to know the sincerity of his convictions and his grasp on fundamentals my estimate changed.
>
> His wide studies of Swiss history, folklore and government deepened my liking to admiration. His speech so fine and clear (American in the best sense) arose, I perceived, from contact with highly cultivated men and women at home and abroad, in fact he was all that I was not, and for that reason I particularly valued his companionship. . . .
>
> Of his services to the church of his choice I am not qualified to speak, but of his essential dignity and charm as a Reader I have heard much praise.

During these years Christian Science was touching through here and there to more robust regions of the left. In February, 1902, Mrs. Ewing of Chicago wrote McKenzie that at a recent meeting they had had "most interesting testimonies from Eugene Debs and an associate healed through reading Science & Health" (McKenzie to Mrs. Eddy on March 1, 1902). The interest that Christian Science held for Theodore Dreiser—also a friend of the Socialist leader, Debs—is well known and crops out in *The Genius, A Hoosier Holiday* ("Christian Science . . . somehow hung over this whole tour") and other books, as well as his letters. In a chapter called "The Bowery Mission" in *The Color of a Great City* (New York: Boni & Liveright, 1923) a passing mention reveals the ambivalence of a man attracted to

Christian Science as a philosophy but unfortified by its practice. The mission preacher has just called on one Tommy Wilson in the gallery to sing a hymn, "My Lord and I," and Dreiser comments:

As he sang I could not help thinking of this imaginatively personified Lord of the Universe in all His power and wisdom taking note of this singing shabby ant—of the faith it required to believe that He would. Then I thought of the vast chemistry of things dark, ruthless, brutal—and then of love and mercy and tenderness that is somehow present along with cruelty and savagery. And then I thought of this little shabby reclaimed water rat, this scraping of the mud crawled to the bank who yet could stand there in his shabby coat . . . and sing! What if, after all as the Christian Scientists believe the Lord was not distant from things but here, now, everywhere, divine goodness speaking in and through matter and man. What if evil and weakness and failure were dreams only, evil dreams from which we wake to something different and better—to Omnipotence, to essential unity with life and love? . . . But outside in the cold hard street with its trucks and cars I knew the informing spirit is not quite like that, neither so kind nor helpful, at least not to all.

61. On June 11, 1900, McCrackan wrote Mrs. Eddy: "As a boy I often passed along the road from Concord to St. Paul's School, where I was from 1878 to 1881 and again in 1886–1887 as a teacher. Every part of the road is familiar to me, and the spot where your own 'Pleasant View' is situated comes before my mind as I write." For an amusing anecdote which shows the cloud of misapprehension that veiled Pleasant View from the eyes of the St. Paul's boys, see Cornelius Vanderbilt, Jr., *Man of the World, My Life on Five Continents* (New York: Crown Publishers, 1959) , p. 9.

62. A few months later, however, after McCrackan had begun to prove himself a reasonably doughty warrior, he did receive a certificate.

63. A. Letter to Frye, February 7, 1900.

64. A. *L&M* 3–258.

65. A. *L&M* 13–1617.

66. A. *L&M* 13–1626. About the same time Mrs. Eddy wrote Kimball that the prayers of Christian Scientists in connection with the Woodbury case were evidently too personal and were stirring up too much mentally. If this work was "not carried out *lovingly* and *rightly* so as to avoid the clash of mesmerism," then Kimball should tell them to stop and "leave it to the wise gentle administration of Mr. Farlow and help him in some way. . . . *You* and Farlow work rightly" (54–7559).

67. Privately printed by Peabody a few months later. The quotations in the next two paragraphs are from this edition. A new and enlarged edition was published in 1904 with the word *Exposé* in the title changed to *Exposure* and the epithets stepped up.

68. See Peel, *Trial*, p. 226. See also such statements in the article itself as "Jesus is thus our great High Priest, and he remains that with none to share the office with him, or dispute it through all the ages of eternity." "Christian Science proves that equality with Jesus is the spiritual estate that he showed us the way to enter into. The function of Jesus, his place in human consciousness, is his by acquisition

and consummation; that of the author of Science and Health, and every mortal who follows him, both in the spirit and letter of divine Science, is in the course of accomplishment."

69. See Peel, *Discovery*, pp. 231 ff. and notes 119 and 120, p. 352. Even Bates–Dittemore (*op. cit.*, p. 145), though largely ignoring the implications of their admission, have the grace to acknowledge that the two manuscripts were entirely different and "there was no question of direct plagiarism." See note 47, p. 458 f.

70. A. *L&M* 57–8124.

71. Picking up Peabody's suggestion as fact, several fundamentalist critics have—for the glory of God—launched their attacks against "Mary Morse Baker Glover Patterson Eddy Frye." Peabody included many fundamentalist and evangelical as well as liberal Christian churches on his lecture tours, and more sober critics, too, have accepted without question or examination supposed facts cited by Peabody to support his increasingly reckless charges. By the time the 1904 edition of his pamphlet came out, Mrs. Eddy had become "the most audacious and most successful adventuress, the most mercenary and calculating charlatan, the most vindictive, relentless and cruel woman the enlightened centuries have produced." By 1910 he had progressed to describing her in his book *The Religio-Medical Masquerade* as "mercenary, insincere, shameless, and bold to a degree surpassing that of all other persons who have duped mankind." The line from Woodbury to Peabody to Milmine to Dakin to Bates–Dittemore shows an increase in sophistication but a durable esprit de corps.

72. A. Letter to Frye, August 13, 1901. On the same day Mrs. Eddy had Joseph Mann write Farlow that the blunders he had made in his answer came from the fact that he was blinded "by the incessant malicious argument directly sent to you, as to *all* students, that 'you hate Mrs. Eddy; she has never done you any good; you are not so well off as you were before you accepted Christian Science, etc.' Now take yourself up for this, several times a day, and note the result."

73. A. *L&M* 77–11070. An example of McCrackan's corrective letters is one he wrote to Adolph S. Ochs, publisher of *The New York Times*, on October 5, 1901, which read in part:

> The New York Times has now, for more than a year, been making a practice of misrepresenting Christian Science, and of refusing to print corrections of false statements of fact concerning Christian Science which have appeared in its columns. In this regard The New York Times stands alone among the metropolitan and State papers. Not only have mistakes in matters of fact been made in telegraphic reports, for which there is often some excuse, but after the attention of the editor has been called to these mistakes, they have been repeated, and editorials have been built upon them.
>
> Such terms as "knaves," "reckless and greedy quacks," "humbug healers," "wretched sorcerers," "vampires," "harpies," "cappers," etc., have been freely used; while Christian Science itself has been variously termed a "squalid cult," "Voodooism," "A foul and dismal morass," "A pestilent aggregation of ignorant fanaticism and unscrupulous fraud," etc.
>
> Mrs. Eddy, the Discoverer and Founder of Christian Science, has invariably been referred to in discourteous and false terms. . . .

I have no hesitation therefore in calling your attention, as the responsible publisher of The New York Times, to this attitude on the part of the paper. I have had several conversations with the editor, and he has not seen his way towards making any change in his personal attitude. My appeal, therefore, and that of the vast body of Christian Scientists throughout the State of New York, is directed to you.

At the same time I wish to assure you that I do not question the entire sincerity of the editor. Personally, I have the highest regard for him, and I feel certain that in this I am expressing the sentiment of the great body of Christian Scientists. In spite of his bitter invective, he would find Christian Scientists loyal and true friends if he were to associate with them. The greatest praise is due to The New York Times itself, in every other regard, especially for its admirable tone and its correct news. Christian Scientists would like to be able to read the Times without a constant mental reservation.

There is no evidence that McCrackan received a reply, and if there was any improvement in the paper's attitude during those years, it was minimal.

74. A. *L&M* 77–11080.

75. A. *L&M* 77–11082.

76. A. *L&M* 13–1602.

77. A. Letter of December 1, 1900.

78. A. *L&M* 77–11083.

79. A. *L&M* 76–10809. To Keene she wrote (17–2150): "Recognizing your talent, scholarship, ethics, and marked correctness in logic I admire it. . . . But the scripture 'Love thy enemies' keeps me from eruptions that sometimes bury the good intent and the evil in one grave. Please accept my deep thanks for your *keen* sense of right and wrong."

80. A. *L&M* 13–1639.

81. Stories in the *Baltimore News* and *St. Louis Globe-Democrat* in August, 1902, stated that Keene had turned down an offer from a purchaser who wanted to buy the copyright, publish 100,000 copies of the pamphlet, and distribute it on two continents. Mrs. Eddy was quoted as telling a reporter who asked why she withdrew her endorsement of the pamphlet, "I did this solely because the author's vehemence in denouncing the pulpit's furious attacks on me was not consonant with my Christian sentiment." This was a mark of her development from the 1870's and early 1880's when she could be quite as vehement in public denunciations as Keene now was.

82. A. Keene letter to Mrs. Eddy, January 11, 1907.

83. A. Letter of May 17, 1904. An early example of Farlow's simple, commonsense, but not unskillful type of argumentation is his letter to the *Springfield* (Mass.) *Union*, July 19, 1900. Speaking of the tendency of people in general to attribute a Christian Science healing to anything rather than Christian Science, he commented:

It is not strange that people who have strong faith in medicine should believe that the patient under Christian Science treatment is healed "because the medicine which he formerly used is just taking effect." Neither is it strange that people who do not believe in medicine should say, "It is because you quit taking medicine that you are well." Nor is it strange that those who believe in hypnotism should claim that hypnotism has done the work, and the Spiritualist that Spiritualism has healed the patient. It is but natural that people should attribute results to that in which they believe, rather than to something which has not been satisfactorily proven to them. When Herod heard of the works of Jesus it did not occur to him that Jesus was a new personage. He had already been somewhat convinced of the religion of John the Baptist, hence he said, "John is risen from the dead."

84. The phrase occurs in a letter from Samuel L. Clemens (Mark Twain) to Peabody on December 5, 1902, regarding the articles Clemens was currently writing for the *North American Review*: "I am not combating Xn Science—I haven't a thing in the world against it. Making fun of that shameless old swindler, Mother Eddy, is the only thing I take any interest in." Peabody replied that he intended to publish this letter, adding: "Don't forbid it, for I consider the interests of the public too great for much consideration of personal feelings." Incensed, Clemens replied the next day: "Do you mean to tell me that my private letters are not safe in your hands? You want to go pretty carefully now, and not make any mistakes." A deleted portion of this last letter pointed out to Peabody the seriousness of this "mere private confession that you are proposing to steal the letter—which is my property, not yours." As soon as Clemens had died, however, Peabody did publish the letter in *The Religio-Medical Masquerade*.

85. Reprinted in *My.*, p. 302 f.

86. A. Letter of May 31, 1901.

87. See Peel, *Trial*, p. 109 and note 74, p. 338. The inconsistency pointed out by Mark Twain lies in Mrs. Eddy's oversimplified description of the term as arising in 1895. It first began to be used in the late 1880's and Mrs. Eddy at that time asked her students not to use it. The term continued to crop up, and despite the initial misgivings expressed in her letters she finally began to use it herself. By 1895, when the *Manual* and the bylaw first appeared, it had become general among her followers.

88. *Man.* (2d ed.), p. 15. This bylaw was adopted in its earlier form in July, 1895, ten days before another one which today reads: "No person shall be a member of this Church who claims a spiritually adopted child or a spiritually adopted husband or wife. There must be legal adoption and legal marriage, which can be verified according to the laws of our land." Mrs. Stetson was anxious to tie her talented young protégé Carol Norton to her by an "adoption" both legal and spiritual. As the result of Mrs. Eddy's actions and discussions, the latter project was abandoned, and Mrs. Eddy wrote Mrs. Stetson in November, 1895 (*L&M* 19–2367) :

> . . . do you know what has been saved by avoiding the relationship you contemplated? A child is apt to feel there is no one so little to be obeyed feared or reverenced as his mother!! If this error gets . . . possession of him there is nothing on earth for a mother quite as sharp in its anguish, to bear. This you have been spared. You also do not know . . . how much I have done for Carol to counteract your own errors affecting him and strengthen his *honest* heart in

helping you. I name this . . . merely for you to see . . . that you have God and me always helping you and that *Augusta* does less than she fancies.

A few years later Norton broke loose from Mrs. Stetson's domination.

89. *Man.*, p. 64. This change also served to correct the recurrent tendency among some students to deify Mrs. Eddy. She had taught that God was Mother as well as Father, and it followed that as a religious term that word should be applied to God alone. The fact that Jesus' command to "call no man your father upon the earth" had been disregarded for the best part of two millennia in regard to the Holy Father in Rome offered a precedent but no real justification of the term "Mother" for Mrs. Eddy. The word "Leader" also pointed more clearly to her impersonal authority through the *Manual*. A little later she wrote Farlow (*L&M* 13–1662) :

> That article in the Sentinel relative to Leadership, by the editor in chief, was grand but was too personal, and you are perpetuating the same mistake. The students should take the Manual more for their authority and not personalize so much. This would prevent making me the target on all occasions and would establish a dignified defence on the basis of Principle and not personality. Let the Manual be the *authority* for the *conduct* of the *church members.*

90. See note 87, opposite.

91. *My.*, p. 353.

92. A. Milmine collection. Many of Mrs. Eddy's saltiest comments bear witness to her realistic reading of human nature. On hearing of Mrs. Stetson's desire to adopt Carol Norton, for instance, she remarked laconically, "See how Stetson apes me!" But she could laugh at herself, too, as when she wrote Farlow (*L&M* 14–1689) , "I had not received the reassuring letter of yours when I *growled,* and beg your pardon for it." Or, when a member of her household asked her whether she didn't like the photograph of herself then in *Mis.,* she replied with a little grimace, "No. It looks too confoundedly pleasant!" (John Lathrop reminiscences.)

93. Cf. Justin Kaplan, *Mr. Clemens and Mark Twain* (New York: Simon & Schuster, 1966) , p. 250: "This master of quotidian reality, whose life was a sort of love affair with the transient, gaudy satisfactions the Gilded age offered him, was in the grip of the same benign and transcendent force that raised Grant and Joan of Arc from obscurity to greatness, gave a small man unexpected strength, enabled Jack to kill the giant." Evidently it did not raise Mark Twain high enough to recognize the benign and transcendent force that made a New Hampshire farm girl into the founder of a world religion. In his *Christian Science* (New York: Harper & Brothers, 1907, p. 285) a single paragraph hurling raucous epithets at Mrs. Eddy kills no giants but suggests Tom Sawyer out to make havoc with a pea-shooter:

> Grasping, sordid, penurious, famishing for everything she sees—money, power, glory—vain, untruthful, jealous, despotic, arrogant, insolent, pitiless where thinkers and hypnotists are concerned, illiterate, shallow, incapable of reasoning outside of commercial lines, immeasurably selfish. . . .

This outburst reveals obliquely a good deal more about Mark Twain's own love-hate relationship with the Gilded Age and with himself than it tells us about the author of *Science and Health*. Hence his need to deny that Mrs. Eddy *was* the author. Only psychological compulsion could have driven him, in the face of his own literary astuteness, to project a theory so flagrantly disregardful of the known facts and the plain evidence. See pp. 209–220 of this book.

94. A. Quoted in Farlow letter of January 6, 1903, to McCrackan. Many later critics have noted the same undertone.

95. Peabody letter of December 2, 1902, in Mark Twain Collection, University of California, Berkeley. Cf. the comment of *Harper's Weekly* that the article left one wondering "whether Mark approves Christian Science or not," and the judgment of the *Philadelphia Medical Journal*:

> Mr. Clemens himself comes so near being a follower of Mrs. Eddy that he has not critical insight enough left to see that her claim to be able to abolish disease is the gist of the whole humbug. He already says that Christian Science can abolish *four-fifths* of the disease that afflicts mankind! Clearly, Mark Twain is already four-fifths Eddyite, and of all the blatherskite he has ever written his latest is a little the most senile.

These and other quotations from contemporary reviews are taken from the scholarly edition of Mark Twain, *What Is Man? and Other Philosophical Writings*, ed. Paul Baender (Berkeley: University of California Press for The Iowa Center of Textual Studies, 1973).

96. Clemens, *Christian Science*, pp. 266, 268, 284. Such passages, occurring in a sea of ridicule and invective, bewildered many readers when the book was published in 1907. Professor Baender in his introduction to *What Is Man?* gives useful examples, e.g., the *Nation*'s description of the book as a "skimble-skamble" that could not "be regarded as either a serious or a humorous contribution to the discussion." The *Catholic World* saw in Clemens such irreverence toward religion in general "that no person of religious belief could consider him a suitable candidate for the office of pronouncing a verdict on any cult or creed, even though it be one so grotesque and extravagant as Christian Science." Yet Edward Wagenknecht in his *Mark Twain, The Man and his Work* (Norman: University of Oklahoma Press, 1961), after quoting one of Twain's most sympathetic passages on Christian Science, comments: "It is hard to believe that the writer of these lines did not understand Christian Science. It is harder to believe that he did not understand the spirit of true religion." This diversity of reaction is not surprising in view of the fact noted by one of Twain's most sympathetic interpreters, Bernard De Voto, in his excellent introduction to *The Portable Mark Twain* (New York: Viking Press, 1968), p. 15: "He is usually to be found on both sides of any question he argues."

97. *CSS*, X, March 21, 1908, p. 563 f. Mrs. Lathrop's account of her conversations with Mark Twain does not identify him by name. For his recommendation or commendation of Susy's interest in the subject, see his letter quoted in Wagenknecht, *op. cit.*, p. 184 f., esp. his statement: "I have no language to say how glad and grateful I am that you are a convert to that rational and noble philosophy. Stick to it; don't let anybody talk you out of it. Of all earthly fortune it is the

best, and most enriches the possessor." Cf. Hart Crane's advice to his mother long after he had dropped his early interest in Christian Science:

> I'm glad you have taken up C. S. again. You never should have dropped it. But it seems to me you will have to make a real effort this time—with no half-way measures. It isn't anything you can play with. It's either true—or totally false. And for heaven's sake—don't go to it merely as a *cure*. If it isn't a complete philosophy of life for you it isn't anything at all. It is sheer hypocrisy to take it up when you get scared, and then forsake it as soon as you feel angry about something. (*Letters of Hart Crane and His Family*, ed. Thomas S. W. Lewis [New York: Columbia University Press, 1974], p. 519.)

98. The buffoonery of the early sections, like that in *The Innocents Abroad* and *A Tramp Abroad*, is sometimes hilarious, sometimes banal, but the brief published section on *S&H*, as well as some of the portions written in 1899 but not published till 1902, shows the deeper psychological disturbance that the subject was already beginning to cause him.

99. See p. 209 for comment on his later modification of this ridicule.

100. A. *L&M* 13–1648.

101. Clemens letter of December 15, 1902, to McCrackan. Mark Twain Collection, Berkeley.

102. A. McCrackan letter of December 11, 1902, to Farlow.

103. *Ibid.* That Clemens should object to Peabody's *tone* but not question his facts was in character. As an improvisor-artist, he was more interested in effects than in facts, in capturing impressions than in digging into actualities.

104. A. Letter of January 15, 1903. The accusation probably had to do with McCrackan's returning to Clemens a check which the latter had sent him with a peremptory request that he procure for him a copy of *Mis.*, which he clearly then intended to rip to pieces critically as he had already done with *Ret.* McCrackan, who considered himself neither a book agent nor a flunkey, after further thought saw no reason to act in those capacities, and quietly told Clemens the normal way in which he could order a copy of the book. In one of his quick rages, Clemens pretended to see the whole thing as a conspiracy to keep him from procuring the book. He then proceeded to advertise for a copy, complaining that "Mrs. Eddy's publishing agents" had "refused" to sell the book to him. The whole episode was an example of the petulance—not to say dishonesty—of which the great man was capable.

105. A. Letter of February 9, 1903. This is the incident described slightly inaccurately by Albert Bigelow Paine in *Mark Twain, A Biography* (New York: Harper & Brothers, 1902), III, p. 1187 f.

106. Letter of December 6, 1902, to David A. Munro. Mark Twain Collection, Berkeley.

107. While Mrs. Eddy and Mark Twain might conceivably have hit it off rather well if they had met in a normal way, Farlow felt she had enough opposition to meet without being exposed to possible affront or inquisition.

108. See e.g., Hamlin Hill, *Mark Twain, God's Fool* (New York: Harper & Row, 1973), p. 54 f.

His fear of the power was merely the surface expression of Mark Twain's real concern about Christian Science, however; at a level too deep for comedy, he indisputably saw the relationship of Mrs. Eddy's new science of healing to the illnesses of his own family, a topic he could no longer mock. . . . Mrs. Eddy, in spite of her business instincts, her vanity, and her semi-literate prose, had a solution to the "pains" which Olivia and Clara suffered. Unlike a conscience-stricken and guilt-ridden husband and father, she knew how to heal the ills that originated in his family's minds. And Mark Twain's attack on her and his insistence on the publication of the book became the artistic measure of his own frustration and anguish about his wife's health.

Clara Clemens later became a Christian Scientist, writing about it in two of her own books: *My Husband Gabrilowitsch* (New York: Harper & Brothers, 1938) and *Awake to a Perfect Day* (New York: Citadel Press, 1956).

109. A. McCrackan reminiscences. On February 11, 1903, McCrackan wrote Farlow, "I . . . see that you understood the situation from the start, as was also evident to me, that he was acting under pressure of which he was not conscious."

110. A. McCrackan reminiscences.

111. *Ibid.*

112. *The Portable Mark Twain,* p. 15.

113. The phrase, with its overtones of both Calvinism and atheism, pity and misanthropy, is Mark Twain's own. See also Albert Bigelow Paine, *op. cit.*, III, p. 1153: "He once told Howells . . . how Mrs. Clemens found some compensation, when kept to her room by illness, in the reflection that now she would not hear so much about the 'damned human race.'" This may well have been during the period in 1902–3 when he was writing on Christian Science. Peabody's pamphlet, which he read during this time and described as "bitter, unsparing, and fiendishly interesting," would have done nothing to allay his belief that the human race was damned by its stupidity–and, as he told McCrackan, that a God who would create and permit such a mess was worse than Satan. This attitude found expression during the last decade of his life in *The Mysterious Stranger, What Is Man?* and those miscellaneous writings which only in recent years have been published in such collections as *Mark Twain on the Damned Human Race,* ed. Janet Smith (New York: Hill and Wang, 1962).

114. A. McCrackan reminiscences.

115. A passage in *Christian Science* (p. 267), probably written during the time that Mark Twain was in frequent contact with McCrackan, draws a distinction which the author subsequently failed to maintain:

It is apparent, then, that in Christian Science it is not one man's mind acting upon another man's mind that heals; that it is solely the Spirit of God that heals; that the healer's mind performs no office but to convey that force to the patient; that it is merely the wire which carries the electric fluid, so to speak, and delivers the message. Therefore, if these things be true, mental-healing and Science-healing are separate and distinct processes, and no kinship exists between them.

From *Mark Twain–Howells Letters*, ed. Henry Nash Smith and William H. Gibson (Cambridge: The Belknap Press of Harvard University Press, 1962) , II, p. 658 f., it is clear that Mrs. Howells later persuaded Clemens back to his earlier assumption that hypnotism was the basis of both Christian Science and mind-cure.

116. Harper's implied that they were holding up publication of the book because of Christian Science protests against the unfairness of the *North American* articles. But the hurt feelings of a tiny percentage of the populace would hardly have restrained the publishers if the articles had not been greeted with a notable lack of enthusiasm by the larger reading public. When the sensational *New York World* attack on Mrs. Eddy in 1906, followed by an equally sensational muckraking series by *McClure's*, had aroused a large measure of popular interest, Harper's was quick to take advantage of the situation and bring the book out.

117. Quoted in De Voto's introduction to *The Portable Mark Twain*, p. 14.

118. Paine, *op. cit.*, II, p. 1068.

119. Quoted in *The Portable Mark Twain*, p. 786. "Am I sorry I wrote the book?" he added. "Most certainly not." Then, in reply to his correspondent's statement that there were five hundred Christian Scientists in Glasgow: "Fifty years from now, your posterity will not count them by the hundred but by the thousand. I feel absolutely sure of this."

120. Clemens, *Christian Science*, p. 72 f.

121. See *Pul.*, p. 22: "If the lives of Christian Scientists attest their fidelity to Truth, I predict that in the twentieth century every Christian church in our land, and a few in far-off lands, will approximate the understanding of Christian Science sufficiently to heal the sick in his name." In the next sentence, she looked forward to a millennial period at some unspecified date when "Christ will give to Christianity his new name, and Christendom will be classified as Christian Scientists." But this clearly lay beyond the more limited and provisional prophecy of the first sentence, whose language points chiefly to the United States and to the sort of approximation visible today in the Christian healing movement that has burgeoned in the traditional American churches during this century. For a condensed but balanced summary of the likenesses and differences between Christian Science healing and the various forms of Christian healing carried on in recent decades, see *A Century of Christian Science Healing*, pp. 246–49.

122. See, e.g., *Ret.*, 61:30, *Man.* 44:4, *My.* 197:15 and 117:22-27. Her letters and reported conversations contain many such warnings.

123. *My.*, p. 303. In a very different spirit, Mark Twain held her up to the same pragmatic test and came to the conclusion that she was the most imposing figure since Mohammed:

When we do not know a person—and also when we do—we have to judge his size by the size and nature of his achievements, as compared with the achievements of others in his special line of business—there is no other way. Measured by this standard, it is thirteen hundred years since the world has produced any one who could reach up to Mrs. Eddy's waistbelt. (*Christian Science*, p. 102.)

Notes: *Interlude: Semantic*

1. Clemens, *Christian Science*, p. 29.

2. *Ibid.*, p. 32. The footnote refers not merely to the sentence quoted but to the several pages in which Mark Twain guffaws over *Science and Health* as happily as he does over a medical treatise on the *Encephalic Anatomy of the Races*, whose language—"In the hemicerebrum, the postcentral and subcentral are combined to form a continuous fissure"—is no less foreign to his instant comprehension than the pages of *Science and Health*.

3. Clemens, *Christian Science*, p. 114. Cf. *ibid.*, p. 117 f.: "I wish to say that of Mrs. Eddy I am not requiring perfect English, but only good English. No one can write perfect English and keep it up through a stretch of ten chapters. It has never been done. It was approached in the 'well of English undefiled'; it has been approached in Mrs. Eddy's Annex to that book [i.e., *S&H*]; it has been approached in several English grammars; I have even approached it myself; but none of us has made port."

4. *Ibid.*, pp. 114, 117. In this judgment Mark Twain differs from critics who have asserted—usually without giving any evidence that they have made a comparative study of the various revisions—that the writing in editions prior to the 16th (on which she first received Wiggin's assistance) was uniformly poor. Close examination shows that Twain is nearer the truth but more perverse in the use he makes of it.

5. Edward Kimball, in an article in *Cosmopolitan Magazine*, May, 1907, noted ironically that judged by the same criteria Mark Twain could not be the author of both *Christian Science* and *Personal Recollections of Joan of Arc*. More cogently, it could be argued that Twain missed the whole significance of the difference between Mrs. Eddy's style at its best and at its worst when he pointed out but failed to understand the reason for the stylistic difference between the autobiographical first third (or fourth) of *Ret.* and the metaphysical remainder of that little volume. Willfully he posited two separate authors for the two parts, when the real difference plainly lies between Mrs. Eddy writing about her early personal life (with slips of memory as well as of style) and the Discoverer and Founder of Christian Science writing about the subject that was of infinitely greater importance to her and drew forth her greater powers of concentration and performance. (See Peel, *Trial*, note 101, p. 381.)

6. After Mark Twain's 1899 article on Christian Science appeared in *Cosmopolitan Magazine*, he received a commendatory letter from J. Henry Wiggin, then going blind and nearing his death, who announced himself as the "polisher of Mrs. Eddy's Bible." The polishing was no secret to Christian Scientists, he volunteered in a second letter, and some were even pleased when there wasn't "so much Wiggin" in a later edition. But there was no suggestion in his letters that he or anyone other than Mrs. Eddy was the *author* of *Science and Health* (see Peel,

Trial, p. 187), and this was the point on which Mark Twain went hopelessly astray. Twain also failed to take account of Wiggin's caveat: "I ought to add that in her business relations to myself I found Mrs. Eddy very honourable"—an admission for which "the Woodbury people," he announced in his second letter, "are pitching into me" (Mark Twain Collection, Berkeley). For Woodbury's influence on Wiggin, see note 18, p. 424.

7. The author herself recognized that there were difficulties in a purely literary approach. In an 1897 letter (*L&M* 86–12783) to a newcomer to Christian Science who wished to publish a popularized version of *Science and Health,* she wrote, "One might as consistently transpose and versify Euclid in order to elucidate mathematics as to change the compilation or rendering of that work [*Science and Health*] to elucidate the Science of Christianity."

Cf. Cardinal Newman's *Representative Essays on the Theory of Style*:

> What is true of mathematics is true also of every study. So far as it is scientific, it makes use of words as the mere vehicle of things, and is thereby withdrawn from the province of literature. Thus metaphysics, ethics . . . theology, cease to be literature in the same degree as they are capable of severe scientific treatment.

8. Mrs. Eddy was insistent that the word "principle" when used in connection with Christian Science must always be in the singular. God was not *a* principle, one among many, but Principle itself, the source and condition of all being. Christian Scientists then as now sometimes referred to "Christian Science principles," but Mrs. Eddy was outraged at such usage; it showed, she held, that the user had failed to grasp the fundamental fact that God, Mind, Spirit, was the sole Principle of Christian Science. Cf. *S&H,* p. 334: "Spirit being God, there is but one Spirit, for there can be but one infinite and therefore one God. There are neither spirits many nor gods many." She was not averse, however, to the common, lower-case use of the word when referring to principles of philosophy, mathematics, or physical science.

9. *A Complete Concordance to Science and Health with Key to the Scriptures* (Boston: Joseph Armstrong, 1903).

10. Genesis 1:3, 4. Cf. *S&H,* p. 503.

11. Cf. *S&H,* p. 54, in regard to Jesus: "Through the magnitude of his human life, he demonstrated the divine Life. Out of the amplitude of his pure affection, he defined Love."

12. Genesis 1:4, 5. Cf. *S&H,* p. 503 f.

13. *S&H,* p. 466.

14. A. *L&M* 25–3086.

15. *CSS,* September 30, 1905. A full account of this visit by Annie M. Knott, one of the associate editors, is to be found in *We Knew Mary Baker Eddy,* III, pp. 85–89. To Hanna, Mrs. Eddy had written two years earlier (*L&M* 40–5298A):

> There is a tendency to teach that man is physically as well as spiritually God's son. This error loses the logic of Christian Science. The likeness of God, Spirit, is *spiritual* and in no way allied to matter. Please keep the distinction clear else it follows that sin inseparable from the flesh or physical man is a

part of His image or likeness. *One* defect in divine Metaphysics breaks the link in Science[;] hence our statement of this Science must be consistent.

16. *S&H*, p. 313.

17. *Ibid.*, p. 404.

18. Janette Weller in her reminiscences (A.) quotes her as saying, "I am afraid of a Christian Scientist who is never sick, for, if he is doing his work, he will have plenty to meet."

19. A. Quoted by Kimball in a letter of July 1, 1895, to Mrs. Ruth Ewing.

20. *No*, p. 13.

21. A. *A&M* 18–10436. I have added punctuation in the third and fourth sentences to make the meaning clearer.

22. William James, *The Varieties of Religious Experience* (New York: Random House, The Modern Library), p. 435 f.

23. This tendency reached its *reductio ad absurdum* some forty years later in the schematic elaboration of Christian Science by one John W. Doorly and his followers, notably Dr. Max Kappeler of Zurich. Lining up Mrs. Eddy's seven synonyms for God horizontally in an arbitrary, inflexible order and listing vertically her four metaphorical "walls" of the "city foursquare" of St. John's Revelation (i.e., the Word, Christ, Christianity, Science), they produced a rectangular "matrix" of little squares or boxes representing the stages of development by which one rose, theoretically, from Christian Science to Absolute Christian Science to Divine Science to Science pure and abstract. Everything from the seven days of creation and the four Gospels to the chapter arrangement of *Science and Health*—indeed to the whole of human history—was then forced into this matrix, the process becoming in time an esoteric intellectual game or exercise increasingly unrelated to Mrs. Eddy's demand for practical Christian demonstration. Several other deviant groups which have eschewed such numerological gamesmanship have nevertheless shared the Doorly–Kappeler tendency to regard the Christian or religious nature of Christian Science as something to be left behind for a "scientific" or "absolute" approach. They have also been united in their repudiation of the Church founded by Mrs. Eddy "to reinstate primitive Christianity and its lost element of healing" (*Man.*, p. 17). By one route or another most of these departures from Christian Science as Mrs. Eddy presents it have aimed to reach a state of abstraction which, even when described as pure "being," seems in actuality to be a Nirvana-like state of passivity, empty of experiential content or redemptive influence on human life.

24. *S&H*, p. 520.

25. Powell, *Mary Baker Eddy* (1950 ed.), p. 152.

26. *Un.*, p. 9.

27. A. *A&M* 3–10095.

28. In some ways the schematic formality of this fragment represents the opposite of Mrs. Eddy's actual method of teaching. Though she habitually used the question-and-answer method, in practice she adapted it realistically to the varying needs and

views of her students. The available evidence shows that the give-and-take of her classroom method bore little resemblance to the kind of sustained interior dialogue represented here, though it is a literary device which she did use here and there in her writings in much more abbreviated form.

29. *S&H*, p. 466. In an unpublished article (A. *A&M* 20–10557) she wrote: "Christian Science is not Science unless it be Christian to the highest degree, unless it illustrates and demonstrates the Christianity of Christ beyond all religions. In the language of Scripture this Science is 'God manifest in the flesh, justified in the Spirit, seen of angels, preached unto the Gentiles, believed on in the world, received up into glory.' It is Good disciplining and destroying evil, physically, morally, spiritually."

30. John 11:1–44.

31. *My.*, p. 219 f., from *CSS*, II, 7 (October 19, 1899) , p. 104.

Notes: *Chapter VII Private Faces, Public Places*

1. *'02*, p. 1.

2. A. *L&M* 40–5303.

3. A. *L&M* 57–8044.

4. A. Frye collection. In this memorandum she speaks of the membership of The Mother Church as thirty-five thousand, a figure which points to the year 1905.

5. With the population shift to the suburbs, many of these oversized buildings would be white elephants by the 1970's.

6. This was modified later (*Man.*, p. 48) to permit them to quote descriptions from other periodicals "or give incidental narratives," but there is nothing to indicate that Mrs. Eddy ever changed her mind fundamentally on this issue.

7. The enthusiasm and contributions of Christian Scientists elsewhere soon caused a more elaborate building plan to be substituted for the original one, and the cost soared to something in the neighborhood of $250,000. The builder—E. Noyes Whitcomb, a Christian Scientist from Boston who was chosen also to build The Mother Church extension—was so carried away by his enthusiasm for the Concord project that he personally went into debt to cover the expense of several architectural features which seemed to him imperative for the church. When shortly afterward he died suddenly, his family found themselves unable to meet this unforeseen indebtedness and appealed to the church to meet what they regarded as being the church's moral and financial obligation. Various prominent Christian Scientists, informed of the situation, quietly subscribed the money necessary to pay the debt. Although Mrs. Eddy was kept in ignorance of this situation, it may explain the intuitive emphasis of her dedication message.

8. *My.*, pp. 159 ff.

9. *S&H*, p. 239.

10. *Man.*, p. 48. Cf. *My.*, p. 162: "A small group of wise thinkers is better than a wilderness of dullards and stronger than the might of empires." This is adapted from Ruskin's statement that "a little group of wise hearts is better than a wilderness full of fools," and is one of several sentiments taken from *Philosophic Nuggets* in her dedication message to the Concord church.

11. *My.*, p. 229. See also p. 92 of the present book.

12. A. *L&M* 74–10556.

13. A. Tomlinson diary for January 6, 1902.

14. *CSS*, VII (November 12, 1904), p. 168.

15. A. *L&M* 33–4270.

16. Article VIII, Section 15, "Church Organizations Ample."

17. The prohibition in Section 15 extends only to "organizations which impede [members'] progress in Christian Science." Several years later another bylaw (Section 16) was added as a result of Mrs. Eddy's experience with Hayne Davis of the Association for International Conciliation (see p. 255). This second bylaw, prescriptive as well as proscriptive, stressed the need to promote peace and the general welfare of mankind "by demonstrating the rules of divine Love" rather than by joining societies not specified in the *Manual*.

18. *S&H* 583:14–19, and *Man.*, 19:1-6.

19. A. Lida W. Fitzpatrick notes. Cf. Mrs. Eddy's letter to McKenzie two months later (*L&M* 50–6986):

>   I have much to tell. One thing is—unless there is less teaching, less church making, and better *healing*, and more of it—our denomination will sink into the slough of past sects in having a religion of the letter without the spirit— of doctrine without demonstration.

20. Prior to this appointment, Mrs. Knott, a student of Mrs. Eddy's in 1887 and 1888, had served as a Christian Science practitioner, teacher, and lecturer; in 1919 she would become the first woman member of the Board of Directors. John B. Willis was the other assistant editor in 1903.

21. *CSS*, XX (July 13, 1918), p. 911.

22. *S&H*, p. 241.

23. A. *L&M* 4–383.

24. A. *L&M* 4–369.

25. A. *L&M* 3–325. She added that many times a single bylaw had cost her "long nights of prayer and struggle" but had saved "the walls of Zion" from being torn down.

26. Gottschalk's *Emergence of Christian Science* gives useful examples of some of the earlier and more thoughtful of these criticisms, but takes only cursory note of the flood of pious scurrility referred to here.

27. A. *L&M* 31–3921. In 1901 she wrote Kimball and John B. Willis, "I have no time for aught literary and my memory does not serve me as once it did" (*L&M* 91–13554).

28. A. *L&M* 72-10288. On January 24, 1904, Farlow wrote Mrs. Eddy that his investigation showed conclusively that Sir John McNeill was not her ancestor, though probably both of them had a common McNeil progenitor. Earlier Tomlinson wrote Frye that he and Farlow had visited Tilton, New Hampshire, to examine the Congregational Church records and had found that Peabody was right and Mary Baker was indeed seventeen when she joined the church, rather than twelve as she had written in *Ret.* In her reply to *McClure's Magazine* in 1907 (*My.*, p. 311) Mrs. Eddy offered an explanation of the mistake in her recollection of the event. See Peel, *Discovery*, pp. 26, 50, and 313 (note 64).

29. In 1899 Mrs. Eddy wrote her cousin Rufus Baker, who had done an engraving of her birthplace at Bow, "Affection craves legend and relics." Some of her romanticized memories and mementoes of earlier days certainly fall into this classification, but cf. *Ret.*, p. 22, and *My.*, 117:22–27.

30. See Peel, *Discovery*, p. 215.

31. A. Sent to Mrs. Eddy on May 3, 1899, by Henry M. Baker. Goddard—described by Nathan G. Hale, Jr. in *Freud and the Americans* (New York: Oxford University Press, 1971) as "one of the nation's foremost experts on the feeble-minded and on the new Binet intelligence tests"—was a contributor along with Havelock Ellis, Adolf Meyer, and other up-and-coming psychiatrists, to the influential 1913 compendium *The Modern Treatment of Nervous and Mental Diseases.*

32. For a detailed examination of the evidence regarding this incident, see Peel, *Discovery*, pp. 195 ff. and 344 ff.

33. *Boston Herald*, December 24, 1899.

34. Frederick W. Peabody, *The Religio-Medical Masquerade* (New York: Fleming H. Revell Co., 1910), p. 80.

35. See Peel, *Discovery*, notes 11 and 13, p. 345 f.

36. See *ibid.*, pp. 154–58, 164 f., 169 f., 337 (notes 10–12), 339 (note 39), 340 (notes 52 and 56).

37. A. *L&M* 94–13992. See also *Discovery*, p. 212 f. and 349 f. (notes 60-63). Crafts's visit to Pleasant View in December, 1901, was to make an affidavit about the teachings he had received from Mrs. Eddy in 1867, but he did not go to Concord to deliver the copy requested by Frye, in February, 1902, as alleged by Peabody and Milmine. Instead he merely did what Frye requested in his letter—had the copy made and sent it by mail, receiving in return $4.50 as reimbursement for his expenses.

38. Handwritten copies for circulation were made by such early students as Sally Wentworth and George Barry, though some of these show corrections and revisions in Mrs. Eddy's own hand.

39. It has taken almost one hundred years before this could be done with sufficient, detailed objectivity to make sense out of the apparently conflicting evidence. For

most of that period both sides of the controversy have greatly oversimplified the process, and there is still a tendency among partisans on either side to take a simplistic view. Yet the abundance of new evidence which has come to light in recent years—not to mention the virtually unexamined and unanalyzed evidence which has been available for half a century—makes continued oversimplification inexcusable.

40. See Peel, *Trial*, pp. 16 f., 76 f., and 138 ff. While her realism grappled with a highly indeterminate future, however, her romanticism yearned for a highly selective past. In the midst of daily duties, she found islands of delight in the recurrence in her life of admired figures from early years like Dr. Richard S. Rust (see *Discovery*, pp. 81 f., 91 f., 359), now an octogenarian in Cincinnati, who visited her in 1902 to renew old memories. Of her cousin Hildreth Smith (*Ibid.*, p. 63 f.) who, at the end of an illustrious career as an educator in the South, still looked on her as the great love of his life, she now heard from her student Mrs. Mims in Atlanta and learned with joy that he was studying *Science and Health*—an even happier renascence of the past than singing old gospel hymns at the piano with Dr. Rust when he came to Pleasant View.

Christian Science lecturers traveling around the country reported to her from time to time encounters and conversations they had had with people who had known her in her early or middle years, and these provided a useful counterbalance to the envious gossip that Peabody was so determinedly dredging up. Then there were letters out of the past, like the warm exchange with Fred Ellis of Swampscott (*Ibid.*, p. 203 f.) though she grasped more eagerly at every evidence in her correspondence of ongoing healing and spiritual growth in those who must carry the movement forward.

41. A. Frye diary, February 14, 1902.

42. This reference is to her letters of 1862–66 when she was still under Quimby's direct influence.

43. I am unable to identify these references. Probably they were examples of the wild legends which had grown up about Mrs. Eddy's relatively obscure years from 1866 to 1875, some of which were too obviously fantastic for even Peabody to include in his later catalogue of charges. Dresser at the time he wrote this letter was in close association with Mrs. Woodbury and Peabody.

44. A. Letter of February 3, 1900. In a slightly earlier letter to Hanna, Dresser had written, "Books are being prepared which will inform people, and the Quimby Mss. are being held in reserve as the climax." Actually, they were held in reserve for twenty-one further years before being published, heavily edited by Dresser.

45. A. Frye diary, January 14, 1902.

46. See Peel, *Discovery*, pp. 230–36, 265 f., 268–72, 352 (notes 119 and 120).

47. *Ibid.* Bates–Dittemore on p. 145 of their *Mary Baker Eddy* (1932) made a grudging acknowledgment of this point which seems to have been entirely overlooked by later writers on the subject, probably because the two authors drew a red herring across the trail by repeating the familiar charge of ideological indebtedness:

Owing to the fact that Mrs. Glover's "Questions and Answers" bore the same title as the Quimby manuscript of which she possessed a copy, it has been generally supposed that the two were substantially the same work. Had not Bancroft's book been suppressed, this would have been seen to be a mistake. The method of presentation and the fundamental ideas were, it is true, derived from Quimby, but there was no question of direct plagiarism. In the two manuscripts the emphasis was placed quite differently, Quimby stressing the psychological and practical aspects of his teaching, Mrs. Glover devoting her attention to the metaphysical issues involved.

Apart from the fact that the Bancroft book (*Mrs. Eddy As I Knew Her in 1870*) was easily accessible to any scholarly researcher, the authors miss the fact that Mrs. Glover's "fundamental ideas" were to be found in the very "metaphysical issues" in which she differed so radically from Quimby. For a good brief summary of the Quimby–Dresser contention, see Gottschalk, *Emergence of Christian Science,* pp. 129–38.

48. See Peel, *Trial*, pp. 125–36, 208 ff., 342 ff. (notes 16–44), 361 ff. (notes 77–92). In summation, the following facts are suggestive. When Dresser published *The Quimby Manuscripts* in 1921, he wrote on page 6 that "after February, 1862, copies of his [Quimby's] 'Questions and Answers' were kept in circulation among his patients," and on page 165 that "some of the patients made their own copies." Yet the only patient (except Mrs. Eddy) who is known to have had a copy was Mrs. Eddy's friend, Sarah Crosby, who could easily have copied it from Mrs. Eddy's own copy, as did Mrs. Eddy's later student Sally Wentworth. Apart from Mrs. Eddy's own early and limited use of it, the composition seems to have dropped into oblivion. No mention was made of it, no knowledge of it was shown, by Julius, Annetta, or Horatio Dresser, or by George Quimby, in any of their letters, lectures, or published writings before 1899. In the February 1 *Sentinel* of that year, Hanna quoted extracts from Sarah Crosby's copy of it in order to contrast them with Mrs. Eddy's teachings. In his *Arena* article three months later Dresser commented vaguely, "The extracts quoted from Dr. Quimby in the *Sentinel* are from one of his earlier articles, and do not adequately represent him." The Crosby copy is dated 1865; George Quimby wrote Georgine Milmine on March 13, 1906, that he had the original in his possession "with the date '62 or '63 on it"; and Milmine writing in *McClure's* in 1907 gave its date of composition as June, 1862—four months before Mrs. Eddy met Quimby and four months after the article, according to Dresser, went into general circulation.

The first public mention of Quimby's "Questions and Answers" by name (except for Hanna's 1899 *Sentinel* article) was on July 10, 1904, in *The New York Times*, when an article by an unnamed writer, probably either Peabody or Milmine, compared parallel passages from Sally Wentworth's copy and *Science and Health*. The disingenuous feature in this striking performance was that in some and possibly most cases the writer was actually comparing Mrs. Eddy's own earlier words with her later words. For after Quimby's death, she had tinkered for a while with his manuscript, made small changes in it, added and signed a preface with her own new, unmistakable, and radically different ideas in it, ran the two together in a new version (see Peel, *Discovery*, pp. 231 ff.), then finally abandoned the whole thing to start fresh on her own set of questions and answers, which ended up as "The Science of Man." The Wentworth manuscript quoted in the *Times* article was the hybrid version which included much material by Mrs. Eddy herself, but the writer of the article disregarded this fact and treated all the statements in it as Quimby's. This may account for the uncertainty in George Quimby's letter to Minot J. Savage on August 19, 1904, when, referring to the Wentworth manuscript as quoted in the *Times*, he wrote, "While it is undoubtedly a copy of father's MS, I do not *know that it is*, or how it came in the possession of the present holder [Horace Wentworth]." When Dresser finally published *The Quimby Manuscripts* in 1921, the version of "Questions and Answers" in it was found to differ substantially from the Wentworth copy used by the 1904 writer in the *Times*, as well as having an earlier date assigned to it than had heretofore been the case. Dresser himself remarked as editor, on p. 390: "It is noticeable that in 'Questions and Answers' there is no clear idea of human self, and that other points obscure in that manuscript are obscure in 'Christian Science' also. On the whole 'Questions and Answers' is very obscure."

Much of the mystery, and some of the obscurity, disappears if one assumes that "Questions and Answers" was actually written *after* Mrs. Eddy and Quimby had become acquainted and were having long daily conversations together, as the result of which the composition even in its original form may have taken on a spiritual idealism alien to Quimby's general level of thinking. See Peel, *Discovery*, pp. 179 ff. for a discussion of Mrs. Eddy's influence on Quimby. Also *S&H* (6th ed.), p. 4: "The only manuscript that we ever held of his, longer than to correct it, was one of perhaps a dozen pages, most of which we had composed."

49. It is significant, however, that in her later years she saw the Quimby episode as a step in her "gracious preparation" for the discovery of Christian Science, along with her unhappy experience with Patterson and other equally mixed blessings. When she read the proof of Hanna's 1899 *Sentinel* article, she struck out his statement that far from being a help the Quimby experience had been a hindrance in her advance toward Christian Science.

50. *S&H*, p. 460.

51. At times she seems to have thought of him as a John the Baptist in relation to the coming of Christian Science. See Peel, *Discovery*, p. 180 f.

52. A. *A&M* 6–10242. For her use of the word "Petra," see Peel, *Trial*, p. 257 f.

53. This may be because a thoroughgoing examination of the claims called for a combination of textual, psychological, theological, biographical, and literary analysis that until recently the subject has not been deemed worthy of having. Hence the Dresser thesis has tended to reign unquestioned and undisturbed in academic thought.

54. A. Sargent diaries. Undated.

55. The dangers as well as the attractions of psychobiography are never more apparent than in dealing with a theological or metaphysical subject, and the interpretation of dreams is no substitute for the scrupulous examination of all available evidence in the light of all the known facts. For an illuminating critique of the crucial errors of fact invalidating even so brilliant a psychobiography as Erik Erikson's *Young Man Luther*, see Roland H. Bainton, "Psychiatry and History," *Religion in Life*, XIV, 4 (Winter, 1971), pp. 450–78.

56. A. Sargent diaries.

57. *S&H*, p. 66.

58. *Ibid.*, p. 561.

59. *The Quimby Manuscripts*, ed. Horatio W. Dresser (New York: Thomas Y. Crowell Co., 1921), p. 393 f. There is at least a possibility that some of the wording in this article is a gloss by Mrs. Eddy (then Mrs. Patterson) on a basically Quimby text (see Peel, *Discovery*, pp. 179 ff.). The Ur-Quimby comes out in various earthbound phrases, such as his statement that the higher wisdom which woman is capable of receiving "separates her from matter and brings her into that spiritual state *that rises from all animal life*" (emphasis added). Many of these phrases Dresser omitted (without elisions) when he edited the article for *The Quimby Manuscripts*. For instance, Quimby writes in the manuscript version of this article now in the Library of Congress: "Mind is only another state of matter called life; life is only a state of matter that is purifying itself to receive a higher life that will never end." Dresser, always embarrassed by passages which reveal so sharply the impassable gulf between Quimbyism and Christian Science, prints this on p. 394 of *The Quimby Manuscripts* as: "Mind is only another state called life that is purifying itself to receive a higher life that will never end." Dresser, one might say, has tactically dropped matter in order that the passage might receive a higher meaning.

60. Mrs. Sargent continued her account: "Then the vision disappeared. She did not return to the other side of the river, which would seem significant of the fact that she never returned to the old condition of thought in believing that matter was substance, but could realize clearly afterward that Mind is the only substance." Evidently for Mrs. Sargent, and probably for Mrs. Eddy, the biographical implications of the vision were of less interest than the metaphysical framework within which the classroom incidents took place.

61. A. H00018.

62. A. *L&M* 62–8838 and 37–4869.

63. A. *L&M* 34–4393.

64. A. *L&M* 4–349.

65. *My.*, p. 166. Cf. *S&H* 444:2–4.

66. A. *VO*–3191. Quoted also in *We Knew Mary Baker Eddy* (Third Series, 1975 ed.), p. 95. Cf. her 1902 letter to William B. Johnson: "You say 'when shall we learn the way?' I reply, when you have *all faith* in *Truth* and no faith in error. . . . True I am battlestained; but still I live and give orders that are blessed and foil the enemy" (*L&M* 26–3329). In retrospect, the problems which had beset her in the years immediately after 1866 seemed trivial. (See Peel, *Discovery*, pp. 203 ff. and 229 f.)

67. See *S&H* 28:4–8, 24–31, and 345:26–30.

68. See Frye diary entry, quoted on p. 159.

69. A. Frye diary, January 4, 1901. Baker, a resident of Concord but not a member of the household, was sometimes—like Tomlinson—called in as an auxiliary helper.

70. *Ibid.*

71. *S&H*, p. 444.

72. *Ibid.*, p. 167.

73. A. Frye's diary indicates that among them were her lawyer, General Streeter; her banker, Fred Ladd; the editor of the *Concord Patriot*, George Moses; and Streeter's junior partner, Allen Hollis.

74. *Man.*, p. 47. Since a Christian Science practitioner's "diagnosis" is a wholly mental one and is concerned more with the mental, moral, and spiritual state of his patient than with the physical symptoms and type of disease, he is likely to avail himself only rarely of the permission granted by this bylaw, which goes on to say, "And it shall be the privilege of a Christian Scientist to confer with an M.D. on Ontology, or the Science of being." While leaving this broad statement to individual interpretation, Mrs. Eddy may have been recalling the friendly and no doubt instructive conversations about Christian Science and the healing art which she had had from time to time with her physician cousins, Alpheus and Ezekiel Morrill. The bylaw does not encourage *patients* to seek medical diagnosis, since the result may only increase their fear and make the practitioner's work more difficult; it is the practitioner who may in special circumstances seek such information. An exception is made of cases which are suspected of being contagious, since either the patient or the practitioner then calls in a physician or public health officer to determine whether quarantine is necessary. Mrs. Eddy's own case was unique inasmuch as she was both the patient and the teacher who directed the efforts of her helpers.

75. *My.*, 133:9–20.

76. On May 13, e.g., she wrote McKenzie (A. *L&M* 50–6985), returning the galley proofs of the revised *Manual* and ending with a characteristic message: "Give my love to your wife, kiss the baby for me and know I love it—but I pity it for the inheritance it has to overcome"—by which she meant the general mortal inheritance of the human race, as is shown in a similar message (*L&M* 56–7933) a little later to Mr. and Mrs. George Wickersham: "Kiss the little one for me and know that I love you all; but I must pity the offspring of sense." To Kimball she wrote on May 14 (*L&M* 54–7596): "Each day since your letter came I have endeavored to answer it, but unexpected care, or work, or a *belief* has prevented it. . . . I know not what a day may bring forth." But then she added confidently, "I have accomplished a *great* amount for the present and future of our cause since I saw you."

77. *My.*, p. 133 f.

78. *CSS*, V (July 4, 1903), pp. 696 f., 700. *My.*, p. 170 f. Jewel Spangler Smaus, *Mary Baker Eddy: The Golden Days* (Boston: Christian Science Publishing Society, 1966), pp. 13 f., 166 ff.

79. The archival evidence available indicates that resort to an injection for relief was the exception rather than the rule under even the greatest stress. In regard to Mrs. Eddy's general fortitude, the evidence of diaries, letters, and reminiscences of the 1903–10 period is unanimous. For comment on her 1885 statement in *Mis.*, 248:23–27, see Peel, *Trial*, p. 335, note 26.

80. In 1853 for a short period her doctor prescribed morphine to relieve her pain, but she quickly switched to "cold water and homeopathic remedies" (Peel, *Dis-*

covery, p. 111). In 1866 at the time of her accident in Lynn her doctor prescribed one-eighth of a grain of morphine to lessen the pain of moving her to Swampscott, and her reaction to this dose showed her to be entirely unaccustomed to the drug (*Ibid.*, pp. 195 and 345, note 6). An entry in the Frye diaries indicates that the dose given on the few known occasions in 1903–06 and the three known occasions in 1909–10 when she had injections was one-eighth or one-quarter of a grain. A statement by the Christian Science Board of Directors half a century ago in *CSS*, XXXI, 22 (January 26, 1929), p. 430, and *CSJ*, XLVI (March, 1929), p. 669, presented the essential facts of the later situation, while avoiding use of the word morphine. The statement reads in part:

> As we are informed, Mrs. Eddy did not, at any time after 1866, believe in the use of any drug as a curative agent in connection with the practice of Christian Science. Nor did she, at any time after she became a Christian Scientist, either use a drug or allow one to be used for her, except as she employed, in a few instances, an anæsthetic for the purpose of temporary relief from extreme pain. That she acted consistently with her teaching is shown by her statement about dentistry and surgery in the Christian Science Sentinel for December 6, 1900, and in The Christian Science Journal for January, 1901, and the paragraph in our textbook on the use of an anæsthetic (*Science and Health*, p. 464).

For the passage from *S&H* referred to, see p. 241 of this book.

81. *No*, p. 34.

82. *S&H*, p. 50 f.

83. II Corinthians 12:7.

84. *Ret.*, p. 30.

85. *My.*, p. 249.

86. *S&H*, p. 463 f.

87. A. Calvin Hill diary, April 26, 1905.

88. A. Letter of December 3, 1901.

89. A. *L&M* 23–2922.

90. *CSS*, V (August 8, 1903), p. 775, Joseph G. Mann: "Seventeen Years a Witness."

91. A. *L&M* 4–336.

92. A. *L&M* 4–338.

93. Mrs. Eddy considered it important that the Christian Scientists who came to serve her at Pleasant View not only be free from chronic ailments but also should not have a history of serious disease in the past. She felt that if there was any vulnerability in this respect, it offered a way for "mortal mind" to interfere with their support of her work by causing a relapse under the pressure of the special demands they would encounter in her household.

94. Her concern for Kinter himself is illustrated by a note she sent him one day in 1904 when a brief indisposition confined him to his room (A. *L&M* 70–9999):

"God is nearer than ever before to you. Divine Love *holds you up*. You cannot fall. His arms are around you. If you would like to have your dear wife with you just now be sure and send for her."

95. A. Hill reminiscences.

96. *Ibid.* Frye himself told Hill of this remark.

97. A. Frye diary for April 4, 1902.

98. A. *L&M* 4–352. The gift when it came was a roll-top desk and chair, which greatly pleased Frye. Mrs. Eddy herself had given him a check for $1,000, and the following year presented him with one for $5,000.

99. A. Frye diary, March 7, 1902.

100. *New York Herald,* March 5, 1905.

101. A. Mann letter to William Lyman Johnson, January 24, 1919. That the scope of Frye's interests was larger than has generally been supposed is indicated by the books in his personal library. There were books on astronomy, bookkeeping, algebra, chemistry, law, banking, investment, music, mythology, art, public speaking, argumentation, good English, etiquette, photography, poetry, travel, Latin classics, history. There were anthologies, thesauruses, French, Latin and Greek dictionaries, Lecky's *History of European Morals,* Prescott's *Conquest of Peru,* Thoreau's *Week on the Concord and Merrimack Rivers,* Emerson's *Conduct of Life,* Plutarch's *Lives,* the *Works* of Dickens, *Robinson Crusoe, The Imitation of Christ, The Riches of Chaucer, Book of Common Prayer, Napoleon and His Marshals,* and *First Principles of Natural Philosophy.*

102. A. Frye diary, April 6, 1904.

103. *Ibid,* August 25, 1905.

104. A. Kinter reminiscences.

105. See Tomlinson, *Twelve Years,* p. 58 f. for episode at Chestnut Hill on November 9, 1908. There were also one or two earlier instances which have generally been taken as evidence of cataleptic seizures. Frye himself in a letter to the members of the National Christian Scientist Association dated 1888 told of Mrs. Eddy's rousing him from a state of unconsciousness, and John Salchow in his reminiscences tells of a 1903 occasion when he and his sister (who was then working as a maid at Pleasant View) had been the sole witnesses to Mrs. Eddy's bringing Frye back to consciousness (in about five minutes) after the terror-stricken girl had discovered him crumpled over his desk and, as she supposed, dead. On March 11, 1904, Frye wrote to Tomlinson in regard to Mrs. Mary Munroe who had died in Boston a few hours earlier: "Also if the case was under my care I should make careful examination to find out if there is not a faint *trace of life there,* before removing the remains, by the employment of an expert because the case was peculiar. May it not be a comatose state?"

106. When Carpenter's year of service was over on March 16, 1906, and he returned to his family in Providence, Frye recorded in his diary, "Mrs. Eddy said to him [Carpenter] this morning in presence of the other students at Pleasant View 'Gilbert, it is like taking my heart out to let you go. During the year that you

have been here you have not committed a single moral offense.' " After leaving, Carpenter wrote her on March 27:

> How can I ever thank you for the wonderful year just past. It opens up to me daily more and more. . . . The astronomer looking *into* his little room feels fettered, but when he looks *out*, he finds himself moving about in fetterless space, and so I found more freedom at Pleasant View than I ever before dreamed of.

Shortly afterward, however, Mrs. Eddy wrote him that he must turn his thought away from her and even called him back for a short visit one day to emphasize that dwelling in thought on her and her household as he was doing constituted a species of mental malpractice. This was followed by other letters from him, thanking her for "the splendid lesson and awakening" she had given him and protesting that he would rather lose everything he had "than to willingly or innocently commit that great crime of crimes Mental Malpractice against my best friend. . . . I promise you," he added, "not to trespass for a moment on the dwellers at Pleasant View or anyone else." But Mrs. Eddy's perception of his weakness was shrewder than his own self-knowledge, for during the next few decades his chief thought and energies were to be directed toward collecting, recording, dissecting, interpreting, and "metaphysicalizing" every aspect of life at Pleasant View, in direct contravention of Mrs. Eddy's repeated warnings that this sort of obsessive interest would do neither her nor him any good.

It was an effort to manipulate her life by interpretation—a process which was none the healthier for proceeding from an adulation that attempted to turn even her human shortcomings into examples of suprahuman wisdom. And like all such attempts at glorification, it ended by disregarding her most elementary rights and wishes. For in the 1930's and 1940's Carpenter took it upon himself to print and circulate large numbers of her private letters, unpublished manuscripts, and assorted memorabilia, copies of which he had obtained for the most part from a disaffected Christian Scientist who had stolen them from the church archives and to none of which he held publication rights. Thus in an effort to exalt Mrs. Eddy as the supreme exemplar for future ages (apparently as a substitute for Jesus Christ, whom she herself had declared to be the sole Exemplar for Christian Scientists) Carpenter unwittingly but unwaveringly disregarded her copyrights, her literary property rights, the provisions of her *Manual* and her will, the stated ethics of *Science and Health,* and her often expressed personal convictions. While protesting his own deep loyalty to her and to the church she founded, his actions in effect subordinated her writings to his own exegeses of them, and her legal disposition of her property to his self-appointed role as literary executor. It was a paradox that would hardly have surprised the leader who called him back to show him that even affection when unguided by principle could act as "malpractice."

107. Mrs. Eddy seems to have drawn a distinction between her therapeutic "rebukes" and her moments of sheer impatience. Caroline Foss Gyger tells of a night when Frye, noticing Mrs. Eddy's bedroom door ajar as he passed by, closed it with a jolt that woke her suddenly. Mrs. Gyger (then Miss Foss and acting as Mrs. Eddy's personal maid) wrote:

> As I was asleep at this time I did not hear what she said to Mr. Frye; but the next morning when she was seated in her living room ready to begin

the day's work, she rang the bell for all the household to come to her. . . . Then she told us what had happened in the night. She said that her night had been very poor. That the sudden awakening had disturbed her, and that she had been most impatient with Mr. Frye. Then with great gentleness . . . she told us how sorry she felt that she had had a momentary sense of impatience and that it was that mortal thought which had disturbed her night and not the jarring of the bed.

108. A. Frye diary, June 14, 1896. Cf. an unpublished fragment by her (*A&M* 7–10272) dated March 27, 1899:

My favorite philosopher Josh Billings says, "It won't do to have the harmlessness of a dove till you get the wisdom of the serpent." In my experience the innocence that thinketh no evil, not having the wisdom that Solomon demands of the wise man to "foresee the evil and hide himself'" is but the prey & victim of evil. This innocence is self deceived, and despite itself (or innocence) deceiveth others. It is the blind leading the blind which terminates in both landing in the ditch. . . .

After writing this I opened my Bible & looked upon this verse: "And the Lord commended the unjust steward, because he had done wisely; for the children of this world are in their generation wiser than the children of light." Luke 16:8.

109. A. Frye diary, August 9, 1905.

110. W. H. Auden, *The Orators* (London: Faber and Faber, 1934). Quoted from Random House edition of *Poems,* W. H. Auden (New York, 1962).

111. Luke 12:3.

112. A. This Caroline Foss Gyger reminiscence was first told to me—and fancifully "metaphysicalized"—by Gilbert Carpenter, Jr.

113. A. Isabelle J. Fleming reminiscences.

114. When Anna left Pleasant View temporarily during her three-year stay there, Mrs. Pamelia Leonard wrote her how much the entire household missed her, and how Mrs. Leonard in particular missed reading with her in the morning. "I look for your dear face, and listen for your dear voice, but I do not hear nor see it in the visible, but you are with me in Mind and nothing can separate us there." When the young woman later returned at Mrs. Eddy's request, William B. Johnson wrote her: "Our dear Anna: I am glad to know that you are again with our beloved Leader. She loves you and I know you love her and your willingness to leave all to serve her will be rewarded."

115. Among those who were teachers were Mrs. Sargent; Miss Shannon; Mrs. Leonard of Brooklyn, New York; Mrs. Lida Fitzpatrick of Cleveland, Ohio; Mrs. Ella Peck Sweet of Denver, Colorado; and Mrs. Julia Prescott of Reading, Massachusetts. To meet an emergency need, Mary Armstrong, wife of Joseph Armstrong of the Christian Science Board of Directors, served as cook for some months, and the wife of John B. Willis, assistant editor of *CSJ* and *CSS,* served as a metaphysical worker. The reminiscences of these good ladies can, however, be used only with the greatest care by a conscientious biographer. They were not trained reporters. The many discrepancies and contradictions between their accounts, the almost

inevitable slips of memory, and in a few cases the romanticizing tendencies of writers looking back selectively on long-past experiences, urge caution on the present-day chronicler. This is especially so when an account includes anecdotes of her early life which Mrs. Eddy is supposed to have told the student. Cf. her own statement in *Ret.*, p. 22: "Writers less wise than the apostles essayed in the Apocryphal New Testament a legendary and traditional history of the early life of Jesus." The reminiscences contain abundant valuable evidence for the qualified investigator but hold plenty of pitfalls for ardent disciples looking for tidbits of inspiration.

116. H. A. L. Fisher, *Our New Religion* (New York: Jonathan Cape & Harrison Smith, 1930), p. 60. See also p. 41: "Prayer, meditation, eager and puzzled interrogation of the Bible, had claimed from childhood much of her energy, so that those who met her in later times were conscious of a certain quiet exaltation, such as may come to a woman nursing a secret spiritual advantage."

117. A. *L&M* 39–5151.

118. A. *L&M* 54–7597.

119. *CSS*, V (August 15, 1903), p. 791.

120. A. *L&M* 53–7457. This is presumably the reason why the church today is less than enthusiastic about the circulation of reported notes and reminiscences by those who knew or met Mrs. Eddy. Only meticulous cross-checking through the whole body of evidence available can enable the investigator to sift legend from fact in these varying and often contradictory accounts, sometimes written many years after the event and subject to all the vagaries of which Kimball and Mrs. Eddy complain. Such accounts have been used in this biography only when they could be validated by other substantial evidence, including and especially Mrs. Eddy's own correspondence. History has been poorly served by some of her admirers, as well as her detractors, through the biographical or doctrinal deductions they have drawn from such reminiscences.

121. Quoted in Peel, *Trial*, p. 193.

122. A. *L&M* 54–7602.

123. A. Letter of April 13, 1904, repeating in condensed form the long letter of resignation he had sent her "about January 28" and which Frye informed him had never been received.

124. On May 24 Kimball wrote McKenzie: "Your sweet letter falls into my daily life, as the gentle shower falls on the ground which is accustomed to the fierce blast of heat." The heat continued for some time. Five months later he wrote McKenzie that he had been lecturing constantly through the fall and would keep it up for two more months, then pause for the purpose of renewing acquaintance with his wife and daughter. "I was glad to get even a word from you," he replied to McKenzie's invitation to have dinner with him and Mrs. McKenzie when he came to Boston, "and please bear with me when I tell you that part of the gladness was because of the hope and promise of a square meal.... The Lord seems to delay His Coming in my case and I suppose it is thus with many others whose one virtue—the love of the Christian Science Cause—is linked with many faults."

125. A. *L&M* 21–2613.

126. *CSS*, VI (May 14, 1904), p. 584. Reprinted in part in *My.*, p. 246 f.

127. Greene wrote Mrs. Eddy on November 10, 1904, that he still felt unready and unworthy for the Board of Education teaching, and when his first class started he wrote on December 8 that he felt overwhelmed by the need to reflect the true spirit of Christian Science, but "I appreciate far clearer than ever before what it has cost you to bring this spiritual idea to humanity. I am grateful for the help you are imparting to me. I am conscious of such a spiritual lack and need I can only ask constantly for divine strength and guidance." Greene's wife, Grace, a Christian Science practitioner, served as cook at Pleasant View during part of the three-year period in which he served the Board of Education, and Mrs. Eddy's letters of counsel to him reflect what she was evidently learning about his spiritual needs through observing the "chemicalization" in the mind of the high-spirited but somewhat undisciplined Grace Greene.

128. Actually, Kimball died before the next class (December, 1910) was given, but his pupil and friend Bicknell Young of Chicago was chosen to conduct it instead. In this way Mrs. Eddy maintained the same sort of balance represented by her original choice of Hanna and Kimball for the two successive classes.

129. I Corinthians 3:4–6, 21–23.

Notes: *Chapter VIII   The World at the Front Door*

1. Her tribute to Pope Leo was followed by a reprimand to the Directors for not having The Mother Church join in the tolling of church bells throughout the city at the time of that respected Pontiff's funeral. In her message to the church at the dedication of the new extension on June 10, 1906, she included the statement: "A genuine Christian Scientist loves Protestant and Catholic, D.D. and M.D.,—loves all who love God, good; and he loves his enemies" (*My.*, p. 4). For her unpolitical views on politics, see p. 325 and note 24, p. 420.

2. In her preface to *Mis.*, she quoted with approval the words of the Talmudic commentator: "The noblest charity is to prevent a man from accepting charity; and the best alms are to show and to enable a man to dispense with alms." This conviction did not prevent her, however, from making the normal charitable contributions of a woman of her means: to the Massachusetts Society for Prevention of Cruelty to Children; the Milville (New Hampshire) Orphans' Home; Rutherford College, North Carolina, a Methodist institution where hundreds of clergymen received a free education; the Shaker colony at Canterbury, New Hampshire, following a bad fire; various Congregational, Unitarian, and Methodist churches in New Hampshire beset by special needs; Newton Hospital, Brookline, Massachusetts; the New York Museum of Safety and Sanitation, for its development of industrial safety devices; the New Hampton (New Hampshire) Literary and Biblical Institution; the earthquake victims of Messina, Sicily; the Concord Y.M.C.A.; the New Hampshire Exhibit at the St. Louis Exposition; the Masonic Temple, Washington, D.C.; the New Hampshire Historical Society. The examples given are typical, not exhaustive.

Of the others, some were large, some small, some publicized, some identifiable today only by the letters of thanks preserved in Mrs. Eddy's files. During the Pleasant View years, her contributions to New Hampshire institutions and causes greatly outnumbered all others; charity, for her, evidently began at home.

A small but typical example of her attitude was recounted (A.) by a Methodist minister, E. N. Larmour, who in 1903 was a seminary student and acting pastor of the Methodist Episcopal church at Bow, New Hampshire, Mrs. Eddy's birthplace. Sending out an appeal for funds to repair the church, he received a reply from her offering to give $50 toward a bell if the church could raise enough to meet the balance of the bell's cost. Since they had had no intention of adding such a feature, her suggestion at first caused some derision, but soon others pledged the additional $95 necessary to buy a 900-pound bell. Notified of this Mrs. Eddy sent a check for $100. Young Larmour, puzzled, made a special visit to Pleasant View to ask whether she really meant to send twice as much as she had promised, and she explained to him that $50 was for the bell, $50 for the repairs; having stimulated them to effort beyond their original intention, she was now responding to their original request. On the same occasion, noting the heavy glasses without which Larmour "could not see a thing," she asked him why he was wearing them and added ironically, "For style?" When he returned from Pleasant View, he found himself wholly unable to read until he laid his glasses aside—for good, as it turned out. Fifty years later his wife wrote (A.) that his eyesight was perfect for the rest of his life. Mrs. Eddy's "charities" sometimes took a very unexpected form.

3. Arthur Talmage Abernathy, one of the editors of the book, describes in an unpublished manuscript in A. the way in which the book brought him into contact with Mrs. Eddy. On one later occasion when he arrived unexpectedly in Concord and dropped into Pleasant View to ask for a short interview, she sent down to him a card on which she had written: "I am very busy. I would rather give you a thousand dollars than a minute of my time." His account continued:

> Realizing her cordial good humor, I sent back this inscription on her card: "My initials are A. T. A." Just as I was leaving, a messenger . . . handed me Mrs. Eddy's engraved card on which she had written, "With compliments of"—before her name, and attached thereto was her personal check for $1,000.00! I was stunned! Here was a woman of her word, even to "the half of a kingdom." I felt crude, and wondered what to do with the money. I was too surprised to say another word, and I departed, carrying the check with me, pondering what I should do with it. I felt ashamed of my crude joke. Of course I would not use it for myself. I turned it over to my associates for use in The International League of Press Clubs Journalists' Home Fund, to which fund Mrs. Eddy later donated several thousand dollars additional. And this, too, when the press was most bitter and severe in its unkindly attacks upon her and her work.

Ironically enough, *Bohemia* was dedicated to Joseph Pulitzer, who was to launch the most sensational of all newspaper attacks on her. *The Journalist*, reviewing the book on August 6, 1904, noted with a slip in its general male chauvinism that in addition to contributions from outstanding members of the American press it contained "able articles expressly prepared by the President of the United States Theodore Roosevelt, ex-President Grover Cleveland, President Diaz of Mexico, King Leopold of Belgium, Admiral Dewey, Rear-Admiral Schley, Rear-Admiral Sigsbee, General Miles, Chief Justice Fuller, Cardinal Gibbons, Sir Henry Irving, Mrs. Mary

Baker G. Eddy, Rev. Edward Everett Hale, Rabbi Joseph Krauskopf, Col. William Jennings Bryan, George B. Cortelyou, Secretary of State John Hay, and scores of the world's great men, all of whom have cheerfully joined in the great work under the general direction of the International League of Press Clubs."

4. *The Book of the Presidents,* ed. Charles H. Grosvenor (Washington, D.C.: The Continental Press, 1902).

5. Quoted in *CSJ,* XXIII (August, 1905), pp. 325 ff.

6. This was the one case in which her choice was attributable to the presence of a Christian Scientist in a key position. Hayne Davis was a pupil of Mrs. Stetson's. Later, as Mrs. Eddy grew disenchanted with Davis, her approbation of the organization—though not of its ideals—cooled.

7. *My.,* p. 278 f.

8. *Ibid.,* p. 279.

9. *Ibid.,* p. 280 f.

10. Following the conclusion of peace, one Morris Weber, a Russian of Roseburg, Oregon, wrote Mrs. Eddy that he had tried to view the war from a Christian Science standpoint but had suffered over every Russian reverse. However, he added:

> When you asked us to pray for the conclusion of peace, a sense of utter disability to do so seemed to take hold of me; but from experience I had learned to obey you, and I did then. Great peace came to me in that hour, for I could see the brotherhood of God's children, perfect and eternal, and this conviction ruled out all prejudice and let Love reign supreme. "There is neither Jew nor Greek, there is neither bond nor free, there is neither male nor female, for ye are all one in Christ Jesus."

On the other hand, Mrs. Eddy did not consider a doctrinaire pacifist position practicable as a matter of either national or church policy in a world where material force so largely ruled in collective affairs. In 1908, when the country was divided over Roosevelt's push for a big navy, she issued a statement (*My.,* p. 286) that was closer to the ideal of armed force serving a defensive police function under international law than to unilateral disarmament:

> For many years I have prayed daily that there be no more war, no more barbarous slaughtering of our fellow-beings; prayed that all the peoples on earth and the islands of the sea have one God, one Mind; love God supremely, and love their neighbor as themselves.
> National disagreements can be, and should be arbitrated wisely, fairly; and fully settled.
> It is unquestionable, however, that at this hour the armament of navies is necessary, for the purpose of preventing war and preserving peace among nations.

Since she shared the general American faith in the Monroe Doctrine, which unconsciously presupposed the power of the British Navy as a shield against New World colonial adventures by European powers, it might be considered a step in realism to support the growth of American sea power to a point commensurate with the commitments of United States hemispheric policy and with the inevitable time-limits on British naval hegemony.

11. *New York Herald,* March 5, 1905. Mrs. Eddy wrote Farlow (A. *L&M* 14–1678) that the article would be useful in contradicting the recent report "sent through the press viz. that Mrs. Eddy died of pneumonia three or four months ago." Four days later she wrote him (14–1681), "Please say and do no more on this silly subject of my decease."

12. *Boston Herald,* June 11, 1905, and Wilbur, *Life of Mary Baker Eddy,* p. 341.

13. The written answers were remarkable chiefly for their brevity. For instance, to the question: "Is poverty a disease of society or the individual?" Mrs. Eddy replied laconically, "Of both."

14. A. Letter of May 22, 1905.

15. A. Letter of May 27, 1905.

16. *Man.,* p. 48.

17. *My.,* p. 26 f.

18. A. *L&M* 84–12350.

19. A. *L&M* 25–3115.

20. *My.,* pp. 116 ff.

21. *Ibid.,* p. 119 f.

22. A. *L&M* 62–8871.

23. A. *L&M* 33–4290.

24. A. Letter of November 9, 1904.

25. A. Letters of May 15, 1906 (to Mrs. Eddy) and of May 18, 1906 (to the Directors).

26. Sullivan's later account of this in his autobiography, *The Education of an American* (New York: Doubleday, Doran & Co., 1938), shows a serene unconsciousness of any bias in the Milmine manuscript.

27. A. Farlow's letter of July 15 [?], 1906, to the Directors. Cornell Wilson wrote Farlow on July 18: "My impression is that what was said to Mr. McClure during our call the other day had little effect, except to make him cautious and determined to keep within the bounds of such statements as he can verify by living witnesses and documents of record. On the other hand, I believe . . . Mr. Irwin and others would prefer, if they could, to prevent the appearance of such an article [sic] on Christian Science." On November 23 McClure himself wrote John V. Dittemore, a businessman of Indianapolis and New York, that they were not going to publish an "attack" on Mrs. Eddy: "We are giving a clear, documentary history of Christian Science, such a history as no one would possibly object to unless he objects to the simple truth." A clearly apocryphal story attributed to Bynner is found in Peter Lyon, *Success Story: The Life and Times of S. S. McClure* (New York: Charles Scribner's Sons, 1963), p. 300. According to Lyon, three Christian Science spokesmen

appeared in the office during Bynner's brief managing editorship and demanded to see McClure. Admitted to his office, they "stood on chairs and closed the transoms over the two doors to the room. Then they made their demand: the series must not be published." Apart from the inherent implausibility of the transom detail, the story is contradicted in virtually every particular by the correspondence of the period.

28. A. Enclosed in letter of July 10, 1906, from Mrs. Augusta B. Bensley to John B. Willis.

29. Elizabeth Shepley Sergeant in her *Willa Cather: a Memoir* (New York & Philadelphia: Lippincott, 1953) speaks of the finished articles (or book) as a "composite, not Willa Cather's personal work," and adds that it "bears little mark of her own style"—a judgment which contrasts with the eminently nonliterary pronouncement of Peter Lyon (*op. cit.*) that "her hand is evident in every line." Lyman Powell, who was in close contact with both women from 1906 to 1910, stated in a 1932 memorandum to William P. McKenzie (A.) that Willa Cather always minimized her part in the editing of the Milmine biography, and this is borne out by a letter from Miss Cather to Mrs. Genevive Richmond (A.) dated December 8, 1933:

> I had to do with Miss Milmine's "Life of Mrs. Eddy" only in an editorial capacity. That is, I cut out passages that were too rambling, coordinated the material and in some instances rewrote a few paragraphs to make the English more concise and clear. To credit me with the authorship is incorrect. I did exactly the same kind of work on "The Story of Montana," published serially in McClures, just as Miss Milmine's biography of Mrs. Eddy was published serially. I think I never even saw Miss Milmine's biography after it was put into book form. I had no interest in it beyond making it as presentable for the magazine as possible—presentable, I mean, from purely a technical point of view, as a readable narrative. When she published the book, Miss Milmine may have restored the passsages I cut out.

30. On October 4, 1906, Farlow wrote the Directors that recently *McClure's* had sent a man to Concord to find out whether or not Mrs. Eddy was still living and they had learned "that she was really alive!"—to which he added, "I only wish the rest of us were as much alive." This seems to indicate that the *McClure's* representative preceded the *World* reporters in Concord by only a week or two. The *Concord Patriot* lumped them all together when it wrote editorially on December 5:

> The men who came to Concord did not have for their purpose the ascertainment of facts; they did not want the truth as known to Concord people, but ardently desired to have preconceived notions confirmed and slanderous insinuations and statements endorsed.
>
> A citizen of Concord, a trusted and honored official, said to one of McClure's representatives after some questions had been asked and answered, and the bent of the interviewer's mind had been made apparent, "There is little to gain by continuing this conversation; you are not after what I know; you desire that I should approve guesses. It is clear to me that your purpose is to write Mrs. Eddy down regardless of what her neighbors and those who know her best may say."

31. A. Strang memorandum of October 27, 1906.

32. Kent, who had been principal of the Concord High School until his voluntary or involuntary retirement a few years earlier, had been recommended to Slaght and Lithchild as Mrs. Eddy's bitterest enemy in Concord. His rancor stemmed in part from a dispute over the paving of the road that ran before their two houses. By Concordians he was usually given the courtesy title of Professor. For his later reaction to the *World's* attack on Mrs. Eddy, see note 99, on p. 482.

33. A. Strang memorandum of October 27.

34. The *World* quietly dropped this charge when it became clear that there was not a scrap of evidence to support it. Dakin, who twenty-three years later revived, applauded, and even embellished the *World* account as a whole, carefully abstained from repeating this particular blunder. *The New York Times* recalled at the time of the *World* interview that an anonymous novel published by Appleton in February, 1905, entitled *The Mother Light,* had "described a cult so similar to the Christian Scientists, with a high priestess so resembling some of the popular notions of Mrs. Eddy" that it had caused the Committee on Publication to protest to the Appletons, though Christian Science was nowhere mentioned by name. *The Times* went on to say:

> In the fiction story, a beautiful and virtuous young woman in hard luck was taken to the home of the Mother Light, priestess of the cult, when the priestess was dying, made up to resemble the priestess, and trained in the part. It being necessary for the faithful to think that no true believer could die, when the high priestess's death did occur, she was buried in the cellar by the inner circle of three who lived on the profits of the cult. Her substitute took her place, and although at first rebellious, grew to like the power she wielded and made a very acceptable high priestess, indeed. The chief plotter in the novel was the real high priestess's private secretary, whose appearance, except for the addition of a venerable white beard, was not dissimilar from that of the footman-secretary of Mrs. Eddy.

Some of the more lurid features of the *World* story may well have been suggested by this novel, which was later learned to have been written by David Graham Phillips. Curiously enough, Phillips had been on the staff of the *World* from 1893 to 1902 but had fallen out with Pulitzer when he wrote a muckraking novel about a ruthless individual who gained control of a New York newspaper.

35. A typical denial is that of Josiah E. Fernald, president of the National State Capital Bank and respected Baptist layman, to whom Mrs. Eddy once remarked, "Mr. Fernald, you are a better Christian Scientist than many of my students, because you are a better Christian" (A. Hering reminiscences). To Cornell Wilson, Fernald wrote on October 2:

> I was informed there is a report in circulation, coming from persons outside of Concord, that the person whom I meet every few days driving and to whom I am always pleased to bow is not the Reverend Mary Baker Eddy but some other person.
> Now I have known Mrs. Eddy for a number of years and have had business relations with her since she came to Concord and made her home at Pleasant View, which relations extend up to the present time. I have also

visited her in her home so that I can state from personal knowledge that it is Mrs. Eddy, and no other person, whom I see riding in her carriage. I will also state that she stands high in this community. I do not find those who speak evil of her in this her home city, and I believe those who come here with evil reports come with malicious intentions.

I am not a follower of the Christian Science faith but make this statement as a citizen of Concord who wishes to see the things that are true, the things that are honest and the things that are just prevail.

36. Each day when Mrs. Eddy went out on her drive, Frye sat on the box beside the coachman, both of them in livery. This extraordinary custom presented the secretary-majordomo to the public in a menial guise quite as misleading as the supposition that he was the grey or even black eminence of Pleasant View.

37. A. Leonard affidavit, October 29, 1906.

38. Strang statement to press, October 28, quoted in Michael Meehan, *Mrs. Eddy and the Late Suit in Equity* (Concord: privately printed, 1908), p. 19. On the same day, Hermann S. Hering, First Reader of the Concord church, issued a statement (Meehan, *loc. cit.*):

This is to certify that Mrs. Eddy stopped at my residence, 91 North State Street, this city, shortly after one o'clock to-day, and I had several minutes' conversation with her. The carriage door was open and she shook hands with me cordially. I have known Mrs. Eddy for a number of years, and I know that she is the same person with whom I spoke to-day. She was very evidently in excellent health and strength. I have also known Mrs. Pamelia J. Leonard for a number of years, and although I have seen Mrs. Eddy's carriage on State Street almost daily, I have never seen Mrs. Leonard occupy it. The occupant has always been Mrs. Eddy herself.

John Salchow in his reminiscences states that during his ten-year stay with Mrs. Eddy, she did suggest on a few occasions that Mrs. Sargent or one of the other women in the household should take her place when she "did not feel like going out" and thought that one of the "family" would enjoy the "brief period of relaxation," but he adds: "I know that no deliberate attempt was made to deceive the public into believing that Mrs. Eddy was in the carriage on such occasions, for none of these ladies closely resembled Mrs. Eddy"—for one thing, they were a generation younger—"neither did they dress like her, nor attempt to conceal their faces." However, these few instances were evidently enough to start the rumors.

39. *New York World,* October 28, 1906. Bates–Dittemore, who abstain carefully from questioning the paper's motives, nevertheless concede (*op. cit.*, p. 398), "In the light of subsequent events, one may safely say that no more misleading interview was ever published."

40. Meehan, *op. cit.*, p. 17.

41. *Boston Herald,* October 30, 1906, quoted in B. O. Flower, "The Recent Reckless and Irresponsible Attacks on Christian Science and its Founder," *The Arena,* 37 (January, 1907), p. 50.

42. The statement by George Moses, editor of the *Concord Monitor* (Meehan, *op. cit.*, p. 20) is of particular interest because of the close relations between that

senator-to-be and his publisher, ex-Senator Chandler, who was soon to lead the legal attack on Mrs. Eddy's sanity:

> I have had the pleasure of knowing Mrs. Eddy for more than ten years, and I have had frequent occasion to correspond with her and to meet her with reference to matters of public importance in this community. These relations with her still continue, and within a very short time I have received from her long letters written from beginning to end in her own handwriting, which, from long acquaintance, is perfectly familiar to me, and that she is indubitably alive, both physically and mentally, is well attested by these communications.
>
> Moreover, I see Mrs. Eddy driving in her carriage through our streets almost every day, and I have, within a very few days, met her carriage and spoken to her as she drove past. That the occupant of the carriage was Mrs. Eddy *in propria persona* is accurate testimony which I am very glad to give, and had any of the newspaper representatives to whom you allude taken trouble to call upon me during their stay in Concord, I would have freely told them as I now write you.
>
> While it would be futile to assert that Mrs. Eddy is wholly without critics or opponents in Concord, it is entirely within the bounds of accuracy to say that by the vast majority of all our people, and most emphatically by those who by their position in the community are most entitled to represent that intangible spirit which we call public opinion, she is regarded as our foremost citizen. Her numerous good works, her constant and consistent charities here, her keen interest in all that makes for the betterment of the community, and her blameless, laborious, and useful life among us, all contribute to make her beloved and respected by the people of Concord, and we all hope that she may live long in her present full possession of physical, mental, and spiritual power to continue her good work among us.

43. The continued vigor of Mrs. Eddy's letters and articles, her handling of the next friends suit, her carefully considered move to Boston, her founding of *The Christian Science Monitor,* the decisive changes she made in church policies in the last three years of her life—all these show a triumph over her debilities which points to the frivolity of the *World* thesis. That Dakin twenty-three years later should have been able to reanimate the thesis and present the *World* story as incontrovertible fact, and that so widely respected a church historian as Charles S. Braden should have been able after another three decades to describe Dakin's *roman à thèse* as "probably the ... most thoroughly documented biography that has yet appeared" (*Christian Science Today* [Dallas: Southern Methodist University Press, 1958]), is perhaps a mordant comment on the triumph of animus over noesis.

44. Bates–Dittemore, *op. cit.,* p. 396. Meehan's letter to Pulitzer not only referred to his personal talks and encounters with Mrs. Eddy in her home and on her carriage drives but also appealed to Pulitzer's sense of chivalry:

> My dear Mr. Pulitzer,—You are a comparatively old man, and your years, your character, and your accomplishments entitle you to the respect and kindly regard of your fellows. That which is due you, and which you have a right to expect at the hands of men, is due from you and yours to others under like or similar conditions. ...
>
> This letter to you is not occasioned by any special zeal on my part in the cause of Christian Science, nor is it occasioned by any blind adherence to or

worship of persons or advocacies, but solely in a spirit of justice, truth, and square dealing—a becoming regard for brains and respectability as well as reverence for age and motherhood.

45. A. Frye diaries, October 29, 1906.

46. A. Strang letter of same date.

47. Springer, *According to the Flesh* (New York: Coward-McCann, 1930), p. 413 f. Strang wrote Farlow on October 31:

> The interview yesterday afternoon seemed to be fairly treated as far as the Boston papers were concerned with the exception of the Globe. The position was a very difficult one for our Leader, and although I told her to step right into the room and face the newspaper people there squarely, the mental blast seemed to beat her back momentarily when she reached the door, and so the effect was not quite so positive as we could have wished. At the last moment, too, Mrs. Eddy ordered from the top of the stairs that the portiere of the door be drawn while she came down, which from my personal standpoint as a newspaper man seemed to me a mistake. The [*Globe*] statement that I was anywhere near Mrs. Eddy during the interview . . . was false, for I was outside the house with the carriage.

The following day (November 1) Harlan C. Pearson, local representative of the Associated Press, and Michael Meehan were invited out to Pleasant View to watch Mrs. Eddy (though unseen by her) as she came downstairs alone and stepped into her carriage. From their vantage point they heard her remark casually, "It is a little colder than yesterday but still pleasant" (A. Clara McKee reminiscences), and Pearson commented to Meehan that she looked "25 per cent better than she did when all the reporters were out here" (*Boston Post*, November 2). Strang replied that she was no longer under the strain which the interview had put upon her, so the difference was natural.

48. A. *L&M* 36–4757.

49. A typical editorial comment was that of the *Chicago Evening Post* of October 31:

> . . . It remained for one of New York's representatives of degenerate journalism to invade the privacy of Mrs. Eddy's home, in Concord, to print an alleged interview with her and to say certain things about her that another New York newspaper—openly opposed to Mrs. Eddy's teachings— has shown to-day to have been unqualifiedly false. . . .
>
> The New York *Sun* prints the result of their visit to-day. The *Sun* is unfriendly to Mrs. Eddy's teachings, yet what it says to-day bears the impress of truth and fairness. Mrs. Eddy stood during the interview, steadying herself by holding onto a portiere curtain; her voice trembled slightly, but was remarkably level and deep; her face was white, her head and hands trembled, her features were thin and pointed; at the close of the interview she walked to her carriage with "stately, languid grace, hardly suggestive of old age." In a word, the visitors discovered that a woman 85 years of age had the ordinary appearance of being old.

How many persons of 85 could have conducted themselves as Mrs. Eddy did during this trying newspaper inquisition? To attain such an age, to carry it gracefully, to be able to go for a drive daily, to walk with a "stately, languid grace," usually means to have lived a clean and wholesome life.

50. See Peel, *Trial*, p. 378, note 45.

51. *New York American*, November 22, 1906. Reprinted in *CSS*, December 1, 1906, with omission of the word "flimsy," and in *My.*, pp. 317 ff., with omission of any reference to Farlow.

52. A. Farlow letter to Mrs. Eddy, November 22, 1906. On the same date he wrote to Strang:

> You can imagine my surprise and chagrin to find our beloved Leader's letter in the N. Y. American. . . . I have thought all the while that Wiggin actually undertook to help her diction. I believe now that she should see all of Wright's article so she can see just what they are claiming.

53. Mark Twain's brief preface to the book *Christian Science* is dated January, 1907, but seems to have been written in 1903. Like all the rest of the book, it throws total confusion over what parts were written when.

54. This included an affidavit from her son in Texas and another from a Boston shorthand reporter who had boarded with her for many years. One amusing letter came to *McClure's* from E. J. Thompson of Lynn, who had known Mrs. Eddy when they were both officers of a temperance organization in that city. This plain-spoken Yankee who had no truck with Christian Science wrote: "Yours received. You ask me if I would like to know about Mrs. Eddy. Why, Mr. Gauss, I knew her very well when she was Mrs. Patterson, in 1865–1866, years before your magazine was born! If you do not do better with her life than you have with her picture, I fear it will not be a success, for it is certainly not her picture that you have sent me." For his feeling about the *McClure's* series after it appeared, see Peel, *Discovery*, pp. 188 and 343, note 124.

55. A. Milmine collection.

56. *Ibid.* Another letter from a non-Scientist pointed out that in describing the stay of Mary Baker and her first husband, George Glover, in Wilmington, the article had moved that sizable city from North to South Carolina, where there is no Wilmington. No one caught, however, the boner by which Glover was turned into a "bricklayer" by a casual fusion of his roles as building contractor and Mason—i.e., Freemason. Such minor inaccuracies would be hardly worth mentioning if it were not for the extravagant claims made for the accuracy of the *McClure's* opus and the continued censure of every venial slip discovered in Mrs. Eddy's recollections.

57. Karl Holl, "Der Szientismus," *Gesammelte Aufsätze*, III, pp. 450 ff. See Peel, *Discovery* and *Trial*, for examples indexed under Milmine and *McClure's*.

58. Powell, *Mary Baker Eddy*, p. 6.

59. Bates–Dittemore, who accept many of Horace Wentworth's charges, grant (*op. cit.*, p. 126) that his account of this episode in the Milmine *Life* is "so intrinsically improbable as to be very difficult of belief," while they describe the account in the

Wilbur *Life* as "far more credible" though "a little too smooth." They show no knowledge or at least make no mention of the later statements and affidavits by other members of the Wentworth family which completely discredit the account by Horace. Some of this is quoted in Kenneth Hufford, *Mary Baker Eddy and the Stoughton Years* (Brookline: Longyear Foundation, 1963).

60. Hufford, *op. cit.*, pp. 32 ff. Also Wentworth material in A.

61. A granddaughter of Horace Wentworth who, as a girl in her late teens, lived with him and his wife between 1916 and 1921, described him fifty years later (A. Mrs. Grace H. Black statement) as a bitter, foul-mouthed man who was nevertheless generous and goodhearted beneath his truculent manner. More surprisingly, on every Sunday before breakfast he would assemble the family and "read out of Mary Baker Eddy's book." Later in the morning, they were free to go to any church they wanted to, but this was his own mandatory religious service. It was an unlikely development in a man whose earlier interviews and correspondence show him full of rancor toward Mrs. Eddy and Christian Science, but it is one more evidence of the deep impression the founder of Christian Science made on some of those who fought most bitterly to discredit her.

62. A. Milmine collection. There is evidence that financial considerations entered into some of the more scurrilous testimony furnished to Peabody, the *New York World*, and *McClure's*. Six weeks after Wentworth's letter, his former friend and neighbor Mary Crafts (widow of the by then deceased Hiram) wrote Mrs. Eddy (see Peel, *Discovery*, p. 218) that she was being "teased to death" to make a statement about Mrs. Eddy's stay at the Crafts's home, that she would like to have some money from Mrs. Eddy to "keep my mouth closed," but that she would talk to "the one that will pay me the most money." Mrs. Eddy ignored the letter, and Mrs. Crafts—through her brother—furnished *McClure's* with the affidavit they wanted. Another person who saw an opportunity for financial gain in the situation was Mrs. Eddy's former publisher William G. Nixon (see p. 282). See also p. 275 for an abortive attempt to procure perjured evidence from a witness through bribery.

63. A. *L&M* 14–1707.

64. A. *L&M* 14–1708.

65. A. *L&M* 12–1560. The lengthy reply, published in *CSJ*, January, 1907, is to be found in *My.*, pp. 308 ff. and culminates in her more than rhetorical question: "Who or what is the *McClure* 'history,' so called, presenting? Is it myself, the veritable Mrs. Eddy, whom the *New York World* declared dying of cancer, or is it her alleged double or dummy heretofore described?"

66. A. Letter of December 31, 1906.

67. A. *L&M* 5–522.

68. *CSJ*, XXIV, 9 (December, 1906), p. 569 f.

69. This book, with additional material added from the last three years of her life, was published in 1913. The foreword, often supposed to be hers, was written by Lewis Strang, and was first published as a letter by him in *CSS*, VIII, 35 (April 28, 1906), p. 552.

70. *S&H*, p. xii.

71. *Ibid.*, p. ix. Although this statement appeared in the fiftieth edition in 1891, Mrs. Eddy retained it to the end as applicable to her continuing situation.

72. *My.*, p. 271. This article was sent to *The Independent* in Mrs. Eddy's own handwriting, with an accompanying letter, which the magazine reproduced in facsimile as evidence of the comparative vigor of her chirography.

73. For a statement issued at this time by her cousin, Hildreth H. Smith of Atlanta, see Peel, *Discovery*, p. 63 f. Frye also received letters of support from family and old friends. His cousin, Judge N. P. Frye of Lawrence, Mass., not a Christian Scientist, wrote him (A.) on November 15, 1906, in regard to the *New York World* and *Boston Globe* reporters who had pressed him for details that would support their case:

> I told them of your good character, that I had known you ever since we were children and played together in good old Andover, that I had never caught you in a mean act, and that I did not believe you would do a wrong thing in your present position, and I am satisfied I told them correctly. . . . Stand by Mrs. Eddy until the end for she is a worthy woman.

An exchange of letters between Frye and his brother Oscar and the latter's wife Ori at this time showed the family bridging a gap of many years' standing with evident affection and mutual respect.

74. Reprinted in *Concord Monitor,* December 20, 1906, from *Fairhaven* (Massachusetts) *Star.* For Mrs. Eddy's friendship with Phalen, see pp. 111 ff. of this book.

75. *Op. cit.,* from foreword, signed at St. John's Rectory, Northampton, Massachusetts, November 15, 1906.

76. New York: G. P. Putnam's Sons, 1907. Though the book is harsh in its denunciations of both the faith and its founder, Powell already shows something of Mark Twain's ambivalence in a few passages—e.g. (p. 8) :

> Some of the purest souls alive to-day are Christian Scientists. They have done much good. . . . To an age grown weary and impatient of ecclesiasticism and machinery, Christian Scientists have brought something of the warmth and glow, the freshness and the spontaneity, the poise and the sincerity, the gladness and the other worldliness which suffused the Apostolic age and made it all alive with spiritual power.

77. Powell, forty years old in 1906 and described by his own biographer as "a Ritschlian with touches of Schleiermacher," was one of the founders of the Emmanuel Movement, an Episcopalian healing movement which started in Boston in the first decade of the twentieth century as an endeavor to counter Christian Science by combining religion with psychology and medicine. Powell's *The Emmanuel Movement in a New England Town* was published in 1909, the same year as his *Heavenly Heretics* (a study of Jonathan Edwards, John Wesley, William Ellery Channing, Horace Bushnell, and Phillips Brooks) . In 1911 he was chosen to write the "neutral" article to accompany a critical and a favorable article on Christian Science for the great *Schaff-Herzog Encyclopedia of Religious Knowledge* and in 1921 to write an objective analysis of *Science and Health* for the *Cambridge History of American Literature,* to replace a caustic one by Woodbridge Riley. The research

for these two articles, together with Powell's increasing acquaintance with Christian Science and Christian Scientists, led to the gradual but (in the end) total revision of his view of Mrs. Eddy. The final result showed more goodwill than insight.

78. First published by Macmillan, the book was taken over by the Christian Science Publishing Society a few years later and remained on their list until 1974.

79. In a letter of July 18, 1907, to Mrs. Eddy, Miss Wilbur spoke of "your goodness and tenderness to me, a Catholic, touched by this higher thought." (A.) Curiously enough, the editor of *Human Life* was also a Roman Catholic, but his interest in the series seems to have been wholly commercial.

80. A. Wilbur letter of May 22, 1907.

81. A. Gosselin affidavit.

82. Howe was also in charge of the building of the house in Lead for the Glovers. Later the family complained bitterly about his behavior in both these undertakings, but it is not clear from the evidence available today whether it was really he or the willfulness of young Mary Baker Glover that was at the bottom of this ill feeling.

83. On May 20, 1904, when Mrs. Eddy was (in Christian Science jargon) having "a problem to meet," George Kinter wrote Judge Ewing in regard to an article on Christian Science for the *New Standard Encyclopedia* which the latter had just written and sent to her for comment. "We have not taken her anything in the shape of MS for some time, and very little mail of any kind for some days past . . . but this in my judgment is so well calculated to rest her, and please her, that I shall have a certain happiness in doing it"—if, he added, "I can get past Mr. Frye with it." (A.) Mrs. Eddy was greatly pleased with the article, made a few editorial emendations, and wrote Judge Ewing a letter expressing her pleasure and gratitude, but Kinter's half-jocular phrase about Frye does point to that gentleman's sometimes overanxious efforts to spare Mrs. Eddy what he considered unnecessary burdens.

84. A. *L&M* 17–2136.

85. The *Detroit Free Press* of March 7, 1907, quoted Glover as saying: "I most sincerely believe in Christian Science. I believe in it because I know that my life was saved by my mother while I was in the army and she was hundreds of miles from me. . . . The fact that she saved me from death . . . when doctors had given me up, makes her dearer to me than most mothers are to their boys."

86. *New York World,* March 2, 1907.

87. See p. 111.

88. *World,* March 2, 1907.

89. *Ibid.* Slaght's name was omitted when the letter was published in the *World,* since the newspaper took great care to conceal its own role in initiating the suit that followed.

90. Mrs. Eddy had written shrewdly in *S&H* (p. 86) , "Mortal mind sees what it believes as certainly as it believes what it sees"—and this may be as good an

explanation as any of the galvanic battery which the *World* reporters alone of all those who visited or stayed at Pleasant View ever "saw." Even Bates–Dittemore dismiss it as a palpable fiction. What may conceivably have suggested the possibility to Slaght or Lithchild was "that loud buzzing that is apt to be during high winds" (A. *L&M* 51–7103) of which Calvin Frye complained in a letter to McLellan full of household details, explaining that it was caused by the electric cable which ran between the house, the stable, and the cottage. Frye suggested having a cable laid underground in order to eliminate the noise.

91. A. Letter of January 7, 1907. A Mrs. Mabel Goodman of Des Moines, Iowa, wrote Mrs. Eddy on June 18, 1907, that she had met Wilson the preceding fall and he had told her that he had frequently written letters for George Glover to his mother and that a very pleading one when George was hard up had brought a check for $1,000 by return mail, but that although Mrs. Eddy was generous he believed Frye, Howe, and others stood between mother and son.

92. A. *L&M* 54–7609.

93. A. Letter of May 6, 1904.

94. A. Hill added, in comment: "This manner of healing is on a par with the accounts of the way Jesus healed."

95. A. A Frye memorandum of February 14, 1907, to Mrs. Eddy commended her suggestion to transfer her property to a proposed "Christian Science Association of Home and Foreign Missions." He pointed out that she would be able to draw on this for whatever money she might need.

96. For full text of the deed, see Beasley, *The Cross and the Crown*, pp. 618 ff. A detailed account of the March 6 meeting with the lawyers and trustees at which Mrs. Eddy signed the trust deed is to be found in the affidavits of Fred N. Ladd and Josiah Fernald in Meehan, *op. cit.*, pp. 82 and 96 f. Ladd described her reading of the deed to them:

> She then proceeded to read the deed aloud, word for word, from the beginning to the end, and her manner of reading showed that she thoroughly understood all its provisions. During the reading she paused from time to time and made comments on certain of the provisions and expressed her views. I remember that when she had read Article Fourth . . . she stopped and, with emphatic voice and gesture said, "That is just what I want." I remember that once she stopped and said, "You will note that I am reading this without glasses, and I do not have to hold it way off either."

George Kinter, who was also present, tells in a memorandum in A. how she asked at the end, with a good-natured smile, whether they would judge her to be "of sound and disposing mind" and competent to transact business, to which they answered with some amusement and a decided affirmative.

97. Henry M. Baker affidavit quoted in Meehan, *op. cit.*, p. 88.

98. For George Baker's early relations with Mrs. Eddy, see Peel, *Discovery*. He was clearly in the suit now for what he could get out of it and as the result of Slaght's and Chandler's persuasion. Two letters (A.) which Baker wrote his cousin Mary Baker Glover on January 30 and September 29, 1909, indicate the care with which Chandler manipulated his puppets:

I do wish, Mary, that I could have met you, when you have been East. I proposed such a meeting to Mr. Chandler, but, while he heartily "wished it might be" . . . he never arranged to let me know of the visit of your father and yourself in such a way as to allow of a meeting. Sometimes I've wondered why.

———————

I don't *care*, Mary; I have no *claim* on Aunt Mary's *property* at all; but I was a party to that first suit, and it was at first represented to me that I was the *only* one to bring the suit, and upon that basis I "put in" because I believed, *as I do now*, that Frye was the backbone of the lies.

In somewhat mellower retrospection, Baker wrote the same cousin on February 18, 1923:

Of my father's three sisters I had a Boy's love for my aunt Mary that I did not have for either of the others, and for years we corresponded very regularly; while she lived in Lynn . . . I seldom went to Boston without going to Lynn for a visit with her; her success in Christian Science was, at the first at least, a source of gratification to me, and because of that success I was rather proud of my relationship to her. But after she opened her "Metaphysical College" . . . I never saw her; her letters to me entirely ceased, and even by appointment . . . I was not allowed to see her. The sycophant who was for so many years her secretary, footman, general factotum, and, in a way, perhaps ruler, suppressed all my letters . . . and it was he who refused me admission to her twice in Boston. . . . For Aunt Mary personally, I always held a lively affection, and I do not think she felt otherwise for me. . . . But she did tell me at one time [when he wanted to argue with her] that "I would never be good enough for a Christian Scientist!" There was no anger or impatience in her remark, either—it was all in perfect good nature, and we parted as good friends as we ever were. I can see her smile and hear her laugh as she said it, to this day, and in those days I used to think she had the sweetest smile and the most musical laugh of any woman I knew!

99. This was Fred W. Baker of Epsom, New Hampshire. On March 13, 1907, the *Boston Post* ran an interview with Mrs. Joseph P. Emond, sister of Fred and second cousin of Mrs. Eddy. This lady reported that Chandler had spent an entire evening trying to persuade her into the suit. Not only did she refuse, but she also expressed amazement that her brother had accepted the proposition. "I know nothing about Mrs. Eddy's personal affairs, nor her money matters, and care less," she stated. "The very fact that all those . . . in the case are actuated by revenge or mercenary motives" was enough to keep her out. The preceding summer, during a visit to Concord, she had stopped by Pleasant View one morning. "She was busy at the time, but they urged, fairly begged, me to call during the afternoon, when Mrs. Eddy would be at leisure, and told me she would be delighted to see me . . . as she always was to see those of her relatives who really cared for her and not for her money." Two months later when Fred Baker saw how thoroughly he had been misled as to the suit, he withdrew from it.

He was not the only one to suffer disillusion. Mrs. Eddy's hostile neighbor, John F. Kent, was not a party to the suit but had been in touch with Peabody for some time and at first was very much in sympathy with the Chandler–Peabody effort. On March 30, 1907, however, the *Boston Evening Record* carried a story: "Kent

Goes Over to Mrs. Eddy, Says Plaintiff Used Him Falsely." In the story he was quoted as saying: "I could not go as far as the enemies of Mrs. Eddy desired that I should.... What little information I did give was distorted and magnified. It was made to appear that I was an accuser of Mrs. Eddy, while as a matter of fact I had gone no farther than to express distrust of some of the persons who had gained her confidence." Kent's casual reference to "the enemies of Mrs. Eddy" shows his own estimate of her "next friends." The report in the *Boston Record* concludes: "Finding himself placed in what he considered a false position, Mr. Kent has decided to side henceforth with the defendants."

100. A. Letter of February 28, 1901.

101. A. Letter of March 4, 1907.

102. Meehan, *op. cit.*, p. 83 f.

103. A. Affidavit by Harvey S. Chase, May 16, 1907, and report by Harvey Chase & Co. to the trustees of Mrs. Eddy's estate.

104. The headlined "vast sums" she was said to receive from the Christian Science periodicals were wholly mythical, since she did not receive a penny from the periodicals or the Christian Science Publishing Society but only from the sale of her own books. On the other hand, in a memorandum to Mrs. Eddy (A.) on April 1, 1907, Frye pointed out that she herself was partly responsible for the inflated notion of her wealth. While she was a realistic businesswoman, she had a wishful tendency to let statistics balloon in recollection. Reminding her of her impressionistic estimate that she had taught some four thousand students in the Massachusetts Metaphysical College, Frye pointed out that if she had taught even half that number at $300 a head she would have been a vastly wealthier woman than she was. The records show that actually she taught no more than a thousand at the most (many of them at reduced or no fees) and this figure is supported by collateral evidence in her correspondence.

105. A. Fulmer affidavit of August 13, 1908 and Nixon letters. Nixon had dinner with S. S. McClure on Christmas Day, 1906, and later conferences with Miss Milmine and Miss Cather, but he appears to have found this less profitable than the next friends suit. On March 18 he wrote Mrs. Fullmer the first of a number of letters regarding his meetings with Chandler and *World* representatives.

106. A. Letter of April 28, 1907. Cf. Fulmer affidavit: "Nixon stated to me on many occasions that he would receive from the [Eddy] litigation a large sum of money."

107. See p. 161.

108. *Boston Journal,* May 25, 1907.

109. *Cosmopolitan Magazine,* August, 1907. Brisbane describes her as slender, frail, erect, with a firm handshake, a clear skin, "a face made very beautiful by age, deep thought, and many years' exercise of great power." When he picked up a copy of *CSJ* at one point, opened it at random, and asked her to read a passage from it aloud, she did so. In a little book entitled *Mrs. Eddy As I Knew Her* by Hugh A. Studdert-Kennedy (San Francisco, 1931), the author contrasted Brisbane's comment on this performance with Dakin's highly imaginative reconstruction of an interview held a month or two later. Brisbane wrote:

If any Christian Scientists have worried about Mrs. Eddy's health and strength, that reading would have ended the worry, could they have heard it. Among young public speakers there are few with voices stronger, deeper than the voice of Mrs. Eddy at eighty-six years of age. She read the ordinary magazine type without glasses, as readily as any woman of twenty-five could do, and with great power of expression and understanding.

Dakin, necessarily drawing his details out of thin air and undocumented speculation, created the fantasy figure on which later psychological analyses of her have been based:

> She seemed almost to be acting a well-learned part—a voice high-pitched and unmodulated . . . only the nervous flutter of her eyes and fingers occasionally betraying her anxiety. . . . Her eyes lost their focus. She moistened her lips. . . . Mrs. Eddy craned forward slightly, clutching her lace shawl with palsied hands. . . . "Thank you," replied Mrs. Eddy in her singsong soprano—her voice had lost the sonority of its earlier years.

110. *Boston Globe,* June 16, 1907.

111. *Chicago Record-Herald,* July 19, 1907. See p. 140 for further reference to this interview.

112. The original appointment on July 5 was of Jelly and another alienist, Dr. G. Alden Blumer of Providence, Rhode Island. Blumer refused to serve, and Parker was then appointed instead.

113. It is ironic to find Chandler's biographer describing the suit as a "purely legal dispute." See Leon Burr Richardson, *William E. Chandler: Republican* (New York: Dodd, Mead & Co., 1940) , p. 697:

> The most amazing feature of this long contest was the evidence which it afforded of Chandler's skill as a practicing and forensic lawyer. . . . Now, at this advanced age, out of touch, it would seem, with the routine of courts and with the development of the law, he suddenly became chief counsel in a purely legal dispute, bristling with technicalities and with nice distinctions, litigation which was attracting attention throughout the nation, with counsel on the other side composed of the most successful, adroit and highly esteemed members of the bar that the State had to offer, led by his political opponent, General Streeter. It is true that he had most efficient assistants and that he profited by their advice, but at no time was he in any other position than that of command. In these circumstances he was never at loss, he was never in a position in which he was not contending with the learned counsel opposed to him upon terms of entire equality, he showed complete familiarity with all the technicalities of the law; he was ingenious and plausible, and he seems to have made no mistakes. It was a remarkable example of the versatility of the man.

The admiring biographer goes on to say, "Chandler, small-boned, erect, without an ounce of superfluous flesh, was cocky, confident, never at loss for retort, never in doubt of his ability to hold his own no matter who his opponent might be." By 1912, however, his cocky confidence had led his hapless client, George Glover, into enough fruitless litigation to eat up a good deal of the final settlement which Mrs. Eddy made on him.

114. It was predictable that if an attempt were made in the United States to have a particular religious belief branded judicially as ipso facto evidence of insane delusion in the believer, the attempt would be directed against a new, small, relatively powerless yet threateningly successful sect. The very slight disguise assumed by the attackers, when the attempt was finally made, is illustrated in the argument of one of the associate counsel for the next friends, DeWitt C. Howe, on the third day of hearing: "I am not attempting to show that Christian Science, *per se*, is an insane delusion. I am attempting to show that insane delusions strictly, which have now become designated as Christian Science, are nevertheless insane delusions regardless of the name by which they are called." Even militant atheists have not attempted to bring such charges against the deeply held beliefs of powerful, established churches. Twentieth-century scientific humanism, for instance, simply dismisses the doctrine of transubstantiation as a primitive magical belief surviving into the present age through its manipulative value to a long-established church hierarchy. But even in a predominantly Protestant and secular America, the weight of Catholic influence (supplemented by Anglican and Lutheran acceptance of the "real presence" in a variant form) has restrained public attack on this doctrine; no one has been foolish enough to argue in a court of law that belief that a piece of bread could become God was evidence of a mental derangement which disqualified the believer from transacting his normal business affairs.

115. On August 3, 1907, Streeter—who, like Chandler, was a rationalistic Unitarian— wrote Mrs. Eddy from Boston:

As you know, depositions were begun here on Thursday afternoon. Most of the day yesterday was taken up with the cross-examination of Mr. Farlow on the general subject of malicious animal magnetism. I think I ought to say to you that Mr. Farlow's statements on this subject were clear, sane and convincing. Every one present, including Mr. Elder, Mr. Morse, Mr. Eastman and myself, felt that Mr. Farlow had added a splendid contribution to the literature on that subject. . . . Archibald McLellan who has been with us here at the Parker House practically all the time since Thursday afternoon . . . instructs me to express his very confident belief that these depositions which the enemy are taking will be of great value to us.

Actually the suit collapsed before most of the depositions could be introduced, so Farlow's explanation was not entered on the court record. Not that Chandler is likely to have wanted to use it. But in his own "explanation" to the court of what he supposed Mrs. Eddy to mean by malicious animal magnetism—i.e., the crudest kind of black magic—Chandler unwittingly furnished an illustration of what she really did mean by it. "Now this [m. a. m] is a part of Mrs. Eddy's whole life," he announced, "and we have shown you that she believes that it has taken possession or will take possession of her son, George Glover, and *lead him to break her will*." (Italics added.) That, of course, was exactly what Glover was led to attempt after his mother's death—and led, not surprisingly, by Chandler—despite the fact that he had signed an agreement a year or two earlier that he would not contest the will. Mrs. Eddy knew perfectly well that her son bore her no real malice and that he had no inherent desire to thwart her plans for the church she had founded. But she also knew that he was extremely suggestible and could all too easily be persuaded to act as the tool of those who did hope to destroy the church—that, in short, he left himself open to the operation of "malicious animal magnetism."

The reminiscences (A.) of Eva Thompson, a Christian Scientist of Burlington, Iowa, who was a good friend of the Glovers, throw light on George Glover's state of mind under the influence of Slaght and Chandler. On June 16, 1907, while on a visit to the East, Miss Thompson had an interview with Mrs. Eddy, who during the course of their talk wrote a short note for her to take to George:

> I love you, my only child. Why do you allow yourself to be used to bring this great grief and trouble on your own aged mother!
> As ever affectionately,
> Mary B. G. Eddy

When she arrived in Lead, Miss Thompson was greeted by the Glovers with considerably less cordiality than usual:

> I, however, made nothing of it, and delivered to Mr. Glover the letter which his mother had written. He retired with other members of the family to read the message and left me with Mrs. Glover. On his return, Mr. Glover asked me if Mr. Fry hadn't gotten hold of me. I assured him that I hadn't even seen Mr. Fry, but that through Mr. Hering, had obtained an interview with his mother, that all the advances had been made by me, and that unsolicited, I had gone to Concord seeking ways and means of reaching his mother in order to get help for him. But Mr. Glover did not believe a word I said.
>
> After a short conversation, the situation began to ease a little.... After that there seemed to be a kind, receptive thought, and I spent a very pleasant and profitable two weeks.
>
> I would like to mention the physical conditions I found there. Mr. Glover was in a very dazed condition all the time, constantly falling asleep during a conversation, and later going sound asleep during the church services. Mary manifested a very angry eruption on her face. After a few days of reading the Lesson morning and evening and lovingly correcting the suspicions and misconceptions in regard to his mother, these physical errors gradually disappeared....
>
> During all the time I was in the home, every day and part of the evenings, a young man from New York would visit them. He said that he represented a group of wealthy people in New York who wished to help Mr. Glover develop his mine. However, with all this talk, he took no steps toward that end.... He seemed to have convinced Mr. Glover that he was his friend and was there to help him.... I recognized him as being a regular detective and agent of Mrs. Eddy's enemies, and told Mr. Glover so in no uncertain terms. The thought I held to all the time was, "Mental malpractice cannot put man to sleep to his best interests." After that Mr. Glover was wide awake both mentally and physically, and would listen to what I had to say without falling asleep.

At breakfast the last morning, the Glovers read aloud to her the short letter from Mrs. Eddy that she had brought to them two weeks earlier, whereupon she promptly burst into tears until finally "the whole family was in tears." Glover ended by telling her he would do everything possible to end the suit, and a few days later he left for the East with intent to do just that. But the rugged Dakotan was no match for Chandler, and it was Mrs. Eddy's interview with the Masters in August rather than Miss Thompson's contagious tears in July that brought an abrupt end to the suit.

116. Grandson of Alexander Hamilton, member of the American Neurological Association, founder and first president of the Psychiatrical Society, Fellow of the Royal Society at Edinburgh, consulting physician in the Manhattan State Hospital for the Insane, professor of clinical psychiatry at Cornell University, writer on nervous diseases and medical jurisprudence, art collector, theater lover, friend of Max Beerbohm, Stanford White, John Hay and a host of other variegated notables, Hamilton was called in as an expert in most of the prominent cases of his day involving questions of insanity, including the trials of Guiteau and Czolgosz, assassins respectively of Presidents Garfield and McKinley.

117. This was the Brush Will Case, in which certain pupils of Augusta Stetson perjured themselves by answering questions "in the absolute," in accordance with Mrs. Stetson's private instructions—a practice which was one of the contributing causes to her excommunication from the church when the facts eventually came to light. See pp. 340 ff.

118. An alienist, Dr. Edward French, for many years superintendent of the Massachusetts Hospital for the Insane at Medfield, was also asked to make an expert, critical report to Mrs. Eddy's personal counsel. After an examination of her on July 10, during which he asked her to write a letter in his presence and found her replies to his questions "fully sane and above the average in intelligence and directness," he reported that "there was not the least evidence of mental weakness or incompetence." (A.) The letter she wrote for him read in part:

> I rise at about 6 o'clock A.M. eat my breakfast at about 7 A.M. Open my Bible and read whatever I open to with a mental invocation that the divine Lord give me grace, meekness, understanding and wisdom for each hour of this day. . . .
> I daily look into the rooms of my house to see that neatness and order are preserved and afternoons I take my daily drive.

Counsel for the next friends also engaged an expert, Dr. Henry R. Hopkins, who turned out to be an early morning jogger in an age not accustomed to elderly joggers, thereby causing a brief wonderment and scandal in Concord. A headline in the *Patriot* of August 22 tells the story: "Wasn't Crazy. He Was Out for an Early Morning Run. Dr. Henry R. Hopkins. Of Buffalo, N. Y. Who is in Concord at the Expense of Next Friends Mistaken for an Inmate of Hospital for Insane." Upon his return to Buffalo, Dr. Hopkins spoke to a family of his acquaintance with such astonished respect of the deep impression which Mrs. Eddy had made on him that a daughter of the family formed a lifelong devotion to Christian Science, studying its literature though never becoming an avowed Christian Scientist. This stray piece of information came to me through a casual social conversation in the mid-1950's with Mrs. Miles Wambaugh of Hingham, Massachusetts, who turned out to be the daughter concerned.

119. *The New York Times,* August 25, 1907. In his official report (A.) Hamilton wrote also of the "inherent evidences of mental vigor" and "intellectual good order" in the large number of recent and current letters by Mrs. Eddy which he had examined. Her handwriting, he added, was "remarkably firm for a person of her age, and there are no mistakes; neither are there omissions. Her words are well formed, and although there is a slight tremor, not uncommon in old people, and possibly because her mind travels faster than her pen, I do not regard this in any way as pathological." In the same way he found in her conversation "no visible indication of any motor symptoms of insanity or nervous disease." In his autobiography

Recollections of an Alienist (New York: George H. Doran Co., 1916), he adopted a slightly more patronizing personal attitude toward Mrs. Eddy on the score of her intellectual limitations and added Quimby to the list of her ideological predecessors. This sort of faint backtracking was "not uncommon" in those whose firsthand (and in this case professional) impressions of the Christian Science leader were later modified by the prevailing value judgments of their normal intellectual environment.

120. Bates–Dittemore (*op. cit.*, p. 413) write: "She greeted her visitors with the air of a gracious hostess, and, despite their efforts to maintain the frigid decorum of a court-room, she soon carried the interview into the easy atmosphere of an afternoon call." Cf. Dakin's attempt (see note 109, p. 483) to turn her into a quavering senile figure on this occasion. While the two biographies share a common reductionist—not to say lethal—purpose, the difference in tactics is instructive.

121. When Mrs. Eddy was given the opportunity to edit the stenographic record of the full interview before its publication in the Meehan book, one of the few changes she made was to delete the reference to her slight difficulty in hearing. The full transcript of course remained a part of the court record.

122. Bates–Dittemore (p. 416) describe this incident as "highly imaginative," state that she did not meet Hanover Smith until 1882 "eleven years after she had commenced her attacks on mesmerism," and conclude that "her present denial of the power of mesmerism was contradicted by a thousand statements from her pen or tongue and would be contradicted many times again." Their claim is inaccurate on several scores. She taught Hanover Smith in May, 1880, the year she took up special, intensive "research" into the question of mesmerism or mental malpractice (see Peel, *Trial*, pp. 75 ff.) . Nor did she ever vary from the position that the practice of genuine Christian Science was incompatible with the use of hypnotic suggestion to harm another. This was the very thing that Chandler claimed Christian Scientists did attempt to do and was obviously the reason for her telling the story. As to the use of malicious suggestion by those who accepted the power of mind but rejected the disciplines of Christian love and spiritual humility, she was again insistent in maintaining that such malpractice could produce results only to the degree that its mental influence was undetected and unrejected by those against whom it was aimed. Cf. *S&H*, p. 234: "Evil thoughts, lusts, and malicious purposes cannot go forth, like wandering pollen, from one human mind to another, finding unsuspected lodgment, if virtue and truth build a strong defence."

123. A. John M. Tutt and Minnie A. Scott reminiscences. One account attributes the remark to Chandler as he left Pleasant View and the wording differs slightly, but he may well have made the comment to more than one person. I have telescoped the two accounts.

124. The full speech is included in Meehan, *op. cit.*, pp. 217 ff. Five or six weeks later Streeter dropped his opposition to dismissal of the suit, possibly because Mrs. Eddy judged it better to leave well enough alone than to prolong the ordeal.

125. A. Hill reminiscences. Also quoted in *We Knew Mary Baker Eddy*, III, p. 55. What and to whom she wrote at that moment is not known, but on August 30 she wrote Foster Eddy, addressing him as Benny once again and telling him that she now had a little leisure and would "be pleased to see your dear face once more for a chat with you after the old way." Benny never took her up on this, but it is

interesting that she was willing even to invite Chandler to come and talk with her after the suit was over. Streeter, however, dissuaded her from this, writing her on September 30:

> I think I thoroughly know W. E. Chandler. I have carefully observed his attitude of mind with reference to yourself personally and this case. The objection to your plan is that he strongly disbelieves in you and in your system of healing and in your religion. He has convinced himself that the claims of yourself and your followers with reference to healing the sick, are arrant humbuggery. . . .
> The differences between you and Chandler are fundamental. His only purpose in going to your house would be to get some advantage over you. He would not meet you with the same spirit with which you would receive him. I advise you not to invite him. . . .
> Let me add that your policy of dignified silence with reference to these enemies of yourself has commended itself to the strong men who have talked with me and who have not the pleasure of knowing you personally. With warm expressions of approval they have referred to the personal dignity of character which you have shown and the dignified way in which this litigation has been carried on in your behalf.

The *New York American* of August 26 carried an interview with her by W. T. MacIntyre, reprinted in *CSS*, IX, 53 (August 31, 1907), p. 999 f., which reflected something of this widespread feeling:

> No one who has talked with Mrs. Eddy can doubt her deep spiritual nature. No one who has met her can fail to be profoundly impressed by her nobility of character.
> Mrs. Eddy is old, very old in years and wisdom—yet her heart is still young, for she herself so told me. Indeed she imparted that interesting information with so pretty a smile that youth itself seemed to shine forth from the snow-capped face with the clear blue eyes, and while youth and old age blend in a charming way in the Leader of Christian Science, it is also indisputably true that she is entirely mistress of her mentalities and both physically and mentally a phenomenon. With the exception of a slight deafness she is a woman in full possession of her faculties. . . .
> Tears filled her eyes when I told her that there were legions who were not Christian Scientists who rejoiced that the suits against her had collapsed and that her persecution was ended.
> In a voice slightly quivering, but of indescribable softness, Mrs. Eddy leaned forward and said:—
> "Truth and right will always prevail. Persecution cannot last forever. There is always a reaction. But I hold no enmity. Those who have attempted to injure me have gained nothing.
> "But why would they persecute me? All that I ask in the remaining years of my life is peace and quietude. . . .
> "There is a tremendous amount of good in the world, and it will not harbor resentments against those who have inflicted ill upon [one]."

126. George Glover had never taken advantage of the trust fund of $125,000 which Mrs. Eddy had provided for him back in February, subject to his agreement to return her letters. Ten months later, on December 19, 1907, McLellan wrote Mrs. Eddy that her own trustees had agreed upon a settlement of $140,000 with the "nexters" (in-

cluding Foster Eddy) and that he looked for agreement on details that day or the next. At that point Mrs. Eddy balked at what she saw as a kind of blackmail, and it was almost two years before agreement was finally reached. The original trust fund, which Glover had refused under Chandler's suggestion of far greater riches to be won, was upped to $150,000 and thrown in with the sum agreed upon in the abortive settlement of 1907. The result is summed up in the headlines of the *Boston Traveler* of November 10, 1909: "Sons Get $290,000 from Mrs. Eddy. Head of Christian Science Church, in Agreement Announced Today, Pays Geo. W. Glover $245,000 and Ebenezer J. Foster Eddy $45,000 to Release All Their Claims. Final Chapter in 'Next Friends' Suit." The terms of the agreement included the signatories' written agreement never to contest any will Mrs. Eddy might leave, and the *Boston Herald* announced that "Chandler Declares Terms are Entirely Satisfactory to Him"—but only, as later events would show, until Mrs. Eddy's death cleared the way for new litigation.

Notes: *Chapter IX   Window on a New World*

1. A. Frye diary, November 29, 1906.

2. A. *L&M* 5–524.

3. Armstrong lived next door to William D. McCrackan, who as First Reader of The Mother Church at that time occupied Mrs. Eddy's old house at 385 Commonwealth Avenue. During the first half of 1907 McCrackan, who was reading proof for Mrs. Eddy's last major revision of *S&H*, came closely in contact with Armstrong as publisher of *S&H* and later described him (A.) as

> . . . a tall, powerful man with a long beard such as we are accustomed to see in pictures of John Brown. By nature he was rugged, but through Science was as compassionate and gentle as a woman. Many Scientists from all over the field were in the habit of asking his help, and he did not fail them, even while seemingly overpowered by the many duties required of him by Mrs. Eddy.

Two years before, Mrs. Eddy had written Armstrong (*L&M* 24–2995) that the last time she saw him "I read in your mind what startled me!" He must, she wrote, "meet and break the spell of m. a. m. to ruin you, and *you can*." Two days later she assured him (24–3009) that she was "sorry if I gave you a single unnecessary care for yourself. But since the death of Mr. Whitcomb when I see the image of an evil one in the mind of any one it startles me! But this should not alarm you. . . . Because you have met and mastered this before you can again and *always can* for God is all and there is no other mind." The correspondence does not show what the particular difficulty was.

4. A. Letter of April 14, 1907.

5. A. *L&M* 94–14083. See also p. 415, note 120.

6. A. *L&M* 91–13516.

7. A. *L&M* 52–7259.

8. A. Kinter diary. For Durgin story, see Peel, *Discovery*, p. 53 f.

9. A. *L&M* 14–1719.

10. See p. 9.

11. Calvin Hill wrote Mrs. Eddy on August 27, 1907, that he would start the next day to investigate some persons whose names the Business Committee had secured as prospective helpers for Pleasant View. Mrs. Eddy wrote him on the reverse side of his letter: "Darling I thank you. Please wait till I get breath over Mr. Wilson leaving me. I have now to watch and to qualify a new Sec. The persecution of your leader is far from being over."

12. A. *L&M* 14–1721.

13. Tomlinson recorded in his diary (A.) that on September 10, 1907, when Mrs. Eddy called the metaphysical workers into her study, she gave them her morning greeting, then opened the Bible at random in her customary way and read aloud a passage from Romans 15 which included the words: ". . . having no more place in these parts . . . I take my journey into Spain." Tomlinson comments: "She said in substance that she could not tell us the import of the words, that they were in perfect harmony with what she had been dwelling upon the entire morning. I asked what was meant by 'Spain' and she only smiled."

14. A. Letter of December 29, 1907.

15. His correspondence with Mrs. Eddy during the next year, as well as references to him in her letters to McLellan and in Frye's diary, show a series of ups and downs in their relationship. As he experienced the daily discipline of living in the house and not merely being an occasional visitor to it, he "chemicalized" to the point where on several occasions Mrs. Eddy sent him away to cool off. On January 11, ten days after one dismissal, she wrote him (*L&M* 91–13530) :

> Your suggestion to return to me seemed nothing but a lack of faith in what I had before tenderly and honestly as usual *explained* . . . and you agreed with me afterwards and said so. Now the tempter turns you back to your old temptation to doubt either the honesty or the spiritual understanding of [Mrs. Eddy]. . . . If I should have you return to me I should disobey God for I know what He teaches me and you do not know it and even disbelieve me when I tell you.

On the following February 20 she wrote him (30–3876) to return to her for four weeks and added, "Do not fail to come and then if you and God and I think best you can arrange perhaps to remain here." From that point on he remained, with only a few brief periods of exile.

16. A. *L&M* 91–13479.

17. A. *L&M* 74–10530.

18. A. Letter of February 5, 1908.

19. A. Lathrop diary for January 26, 1908.

20. Lyman Powell, *op. cit.*, pp. 211 ff. Also Salchow and other reminiscences in A.

21. *Ibid.* Confirmed to me by M. Adelaide Still, who was present on the occasion and especially noted Mrs. Eddy's amusement.

22. A. Still reminiscences, plus personal account to me.

23. *Ibid.*

24. *Ibid.* Cf. her statement dictated to Adam Dickey (A. A10346) : "The house that I now occupy was purchased for me before I saw it or had any correct idea of its dimensions and expense. When, after leaving Concord and arriving at Chestnut Hill, I looked on the house I now own, I was shocked, and went to my room and wept. Had I seen the house before purchasing it, I should not now be occupying it."

25. *S&H*, p. 96.

26. *Ibid.*, p. 209.

27. Einstein showed a slight but recurrent interest in Christian Science in his later years, having been introduced to *S&H* (apparently for the first time) by the actress Elisabeth Bergner, an old Berlin acquaintance, when they met in Princeton following World War II. Rilke's wife was a Christian Scientist. Whitehead in his Harvard classes sometimes pointed out how his process philosophy "explained" the possibility of Christian Science healing. Jung wrote with a kind of dogmatic ambivalence that in Christian Science "the Christian religion, which represents a high cultural level, is used for magic cures. The poverty of the spiritual content is appalling, but Christian Science is alive; it possesses a thoroughly earth-rooted power and has worked those wonders which we look for in vain in the official churches." (Quoted in Quincy Howe, *A World History of Our Own Times*, Vol. I [New York: Simon & Schuster, 1949].) Keyserling in his *America Set Free* (New York: Harper & Brothers, 1929) strikingly compared Christian Science as the representative of "American spirituality" with the Christian sects stressing self-denial, suffering, and passivity which represent "Russian religiosity," and he set both in equal contrast to the cultural norms of traditional European Christianity. The Keyserling discussion is also quoted at some length in Peel, *Encounter*, pp. 200 ff. An odd cultural potpourri is suggested by a news item in the *New York Herald* of May 23, 1908, to the effect that the works of Emerson, Huxley, Maeterlinck, Felix Adler, and Mary Baker Eddy were to be studied the following year in a course at the Yale Divinity School on "Christianity and Modern Thought" by Professor Ambrose White Vernon, to acquaint students with "modern views of the world which have become influential in the present time."

28. Arthur Balfour, *Foundations of Belief*, quoted in Henry Steele Commager, *The American Mind* (New Haven: Yale University Press, 1950) , p. 104.

29. *Basic Writings of Bertrand Russell (1903–1959)*, ed. Robert E. Egner and Lester E. Denonn (New York: Simon & Schuster, 1961) , pp. 67, 72.

30. II Peter 3:10–12.

31. Quoted in *CSS*, VI (June 11, 1904) , p. 645. In an article, "Do Christian Scientists Ignore the Material Universe?" quoted from the *Greensburg* (Pennsylvania) *Star* in *CSS*, VII (September 17, 1904) , p. 38, Farlow developed the subject further:

> As a matter of fact, a Christian Scientist, having some insight into the spirituality of God's creation, beholds in nature a new beauty and satisfaction.

As one grows spiritually, the things on earth will not disappear, but will become more vivid, even as an object beheld through a veil presents fairer and stronger outlines when the covering is lifted. The perishable, imperfect things which we now view will be discerned in all their spirituality, beauty, and perfection as our erroneous, human concepts disappear. Nature will be seen bearing the imprint of the divine Mind, the Supreme Being. Paul seems to have had this idea when he said, "For if that which was done away was glorious, much more that which remaineth is glorious."

In *CSS*, VIII (February 10, 1906), p. 374, Edward Kimball is quoted from *The Interior* to similar effect: "Mrs. Eddy knows that the statement, 'There is no matter,' is a negation and not a 'first principle.' She does not assert that Christian Science is founded on such a statement or discovery. The only Principle that she acknowledges is God, and the entire structure of Christian Science rests on the allness of God as Spirit, as omniscience, omnipresence, and omnipotence."

32. Banesh Hoffman, *Albert Einstein, Creator and Rebel* (New York: Viking, 1972), p. 81.

33. *S&H*, p. 534.

34. *Ibid.*, p. 484.

35. A. *S&M* 37–4877. To McLellan she wrote in 1904: "... there must be better literature and more interesting in the Sentinel.... The last two issues' articles on the first pages are shockingly wanting in quality."

36. A. *L&M* 86–12783.

37. *CSJ*, XX (July, 1902), p. 200.

38. Other scientists and mathematicians, including Einstein, have recorded a similar revelatory "moment of truth" (of a kind the very opposite of Hemingway's bullfighters') in which a long-sought solution has arrived "of itself," by an unpredictable leap of understanding. It is interesting that Poincaré's often-quoted account is included as a religious experience in Victor Gollancz's remarkable anthology, *From Darkness to Light* (New York: Harper & Brothers, 1956), p. 355. A *New York Sun* story (reprinted from the *London Globe*) is quoted in *CSS*, VIII (April 14, 1906), p. 520, re Poincaré's article "The End of Matter," in which the mathematician argued that there is no true matter, only holes in the ether. The newspaper writer went on to say: "But Professor Poincaré . . . declares in his 'Science and Hypothesis' that 'a day will come when the ether will be rejected as useless.' If, then, the atoms are merely holes in the ether, they too will be abolished." The day would come when Poincaré's friend and fellow mathematician, William Rivier, in a series of little known but provocative books (*Le Problème de la Vie* [Paris, 1937]; *Les Deux Chemins* [Brussels, n.d.]; *Le Pouvoir de l'Esprit* [Neuchâtel, 1957]) would argue learnedly for the unreality of space itself, explicitly linking his views with Mrs. Eddy's.

39. Albert Einstein, *Out of My Later Years* (New York: Philosophical Library, 1950), p. 96.

40. *CSJ*, XXII (October, 1904), p. 404 f. Cf. Einstein's statement in his *Essays in Science* (New York: Philosophical Library, 1934), p. 18:

Experience may suggest the appropriate mathematical concepts, but they most certainly cannot be deduced from it. Experience remains, of course, the sole criterion of the physical utility of a mathematical construction. But the creative principle resides in mathematics. In a certain sense, therefore, I hold it true that pure thought can grasp reality, as the ancients dreamed.

Substitute "metaphysics" for "mathematics" and the statement could stand for the Christian Science position, with its twin emphasis on revelation and demonstration. Cf. also the description of Einstein's position by a philosophic commentator (Albert William Levi, *Philosophy and the Modern World* [Bloomington: Indiana University Press, 1959], p. 160) :

> The position is moderate: science would be empty if the propositions of its conceptual system were not firmly rooted in sensory experiences, but at the same time the conceptual system does not derive from experience and it has its own rules of system, logic, and order. There is a dualism here, which sees mathematics and experience as joint sources of the systematic edifice of science.

In Christian Science, metaphysics (i.e., revelation developed in terms of system, logic, and order) demands validation by experience (i.e., practical demonstration through Christian healing and living). An editorial in *CSJ,* XX (February, 1903), p. 711, quoted from the recently published *Varieties of Religious Experience* James's reference to the noted materialist Sir Henry Maudsley: "Not its origin, but *the way in which it works on the whole* is Dr. Maudsley's final test of a belief. This is our own empirical criterion; and this criterion the stoutest insisters on supernatural origin have also been forced to use in the end."

41. *CSJ,* XXVIII (April, 1910), p. 19 f. An earlier reference to Balfour's bon mot occurs in an editorial by John B. Willis in *CSS,* VII (September 17, 1904), p. 40, re Balfour's address as President of the Association for the Advancement of Science. Willis wrote: "The latest investigations of the Curies, Professor Thomson, and others, which go to prove that 'Matter is but a condition of energy' and wholly phenomenal, are accepted as the basis of his [Balfour's] very pertinent and paradoxical declaration that to-day 'Matter is explained, and is explained away.' " Balfour had gone on to say that the situation suggested a "certain inevitable incoherence in any general scheme of thought which is built out of the material provided by natural science alone" (which sounded like P. W. Bridgman) and that in the course of time such a scheme must be grounded in "an idealistic interpretation of the universe" (which sounded like Arthur Eddington). Later Christian Science writers and speakers sometimes fell into the trap of taking such philosophically idealistic interpretations as Eddington's as literal confirmation of the Christian Science position, not seeing that they were objectionable on the same grounds as Berkeleyan metaphysics: they simply transformed the material universe *with all its built-in imperfections and limitations* into a necessary system of ideas. From the Christian Science point of view in its strictest sense, this concept had no more redemptive power than the old scientific model of the universe as a self-operating machine.

42. This tendency reached a culmination in *CSJ,* XXV (March, 1908), with a substantial article by M. G. Kains, "A Physical Scientist's View of Christian Science," and an even longer (fifteen-page) article by Martha R. White, "The Outer World and the Inner Man," which moved from Bacon's *Instauratio Magna* to Herbert

Spencer's *Principles of Sociology* to Max Müller's *Science of Language* to Kant's *Inaugural Dissertation* to William James's *Psychology* to Huxley, Balfour, Chesterton, Oliver Lodge, and various others.

43. *S&H*, p. 313.

44. Mrs. Eddy herself took a look from time to time at the *Journal of Transactions of the Victoria Institute* (of which she was a life associate member). A passage she marked in an article on Confucianism in Volume 37 is suggestive:

> It may be mentioned that with idle scholars he [Confucius] would have nothing to do. "I do not open the truth," he said, "to anyone who is not eager after knowledge, nor do I help anyone who is not anxious to explain himself. When I have presented one corner of a subject and the listener cannot learn from it the other three, I do not repeat my lesson."

But while Mrs. Eddy found confirmation and/or stimulation in thoughts picked up from many sources, her basic attitude is expressed in a letter to the Reverend Jesse L. Fonda: "The Bible supplies me with learning and research for all time. All other books may come and go but that lives on forever." (A. *L&M* 43–5722.)

45. *CSJ*, XXII (October, 1904), p. 406.

46. *S&H*, p. 461.

47. *Rud.*, p. 2.

48. Even before World War I the new era was beginning with the emergence of such names as Stravinsky, Schönberg, Braque, Kandinsky, Picasso, Gide, Mann, Proust, Pound, and Lawrence. The artist's sensibility was already registering earthquake tremors from the scientific revolution, psychology's plunge into the unconscious, and the drift toward total flux.

49. Of the two outstanding names in popular American journalism, it is paradoxical that the more reputable, Joseph Pulitzer, should have launched the major newspaper attack on Mrs. Eddy (though staff members of *The Christian Science Monitor* would later win Pulitzer prizes for excellence in journalism), while the less reputable, William Randolph Hearst, issued strict orders that there should be no attacks on Christian Science in any Hearst paper. This latter phenomenon arose from the overnight healing of Hearst's baby son by a Christian Science practitioner after the "best doctors in the world" had been unable to keep the infant from wasting away "to an actual skeleton" as the result of its being born with a closed pylorus which prevented it from taking and holding so much as "a teaspoonful of milk or even water." Hearst's later account of the healing (*Los Angeles Examiner*, July 17, 1941) adds: "The child is now a little over six feet tall, and weighs 180 pounds, and runs a newspaper considerably better than his father can."

50. *S&H* (2d ed.), p. 166.

51. *CSJ*, I (April, 1883), p. 3. Reprinted in changed form in *Mis.*, p. 7.

52. See p. 132.

53. A. *L&M* 54–7593.

54. See Erwin D. Canham, *Commitment to Freedom: The Story of The Christian Science Monitor* (Boston: Houghton Mifflin Co., 1958) , pp. 11 ff.

55. Reprinted in *My.*, p. 286. When Hayne Davis sent a copy of this statement to the President, Roosevelt replied, "I wish that all other religious leaders showed as much good sense." (A.)

56. Quoted in Canham, *Commitment to Freedom*, p. 11.

57. A. Quoted at greater length in Canham, p. 18 f.

58. A. *L&M* 50–6998.

59. A. *L&M* 51–7146.

60. A. *L&M* 6–596.

61. A. *L&M* 52–7268.

62. *My.*, p. 275.

63. *Ibid.*, p. 276.

64. A. Frye diary.

65. A. Dickey to McLellan, August 5, 1908.

66. A. Quoted by Dickey at a *Monitor* meeting in Second Church, Boston, in 1924. Charles E. Heitman of the Christian Science Board of Directors told me some ten years later that he had talked with three different members of Mrs. Eddy's household who assured him that she had made similar statements to them. However, because of the hearsay nature of the evidence and perhaps because of excessive use of the statement by the advertising and circulation departments of the *Monitor* in the 1920's, the Directors in 1934 decided that it should not be quoted officially thereafter. Since Dickey himself was only repeating what he had heard secondhand from other household members, the board's caution is understandable. But with this caveat and the recognition that Mrs. Eddy was comparing single steps she had taken (as contrasted with the series of steps which resulted in the formation of the church and the *Manual*) , the statement seems to me both credible and in accord with her view of the *Monitor's* function as the link between her church and the affairs of the world at large. The Archivist dissents from this judgment.

67. A month earlier, on October 17, an editorial in *CSS* had announced the coming publication of "a strictly up-to-date newspaper, in which all the news of the day that should be printed will find a place, and whose service will not be restricted to any one locality or section, but will cover the daily activities of the entire world."

68. Tomlinson, *Twelve Years*, p. 107.

69. *Man.*, p. 19. See also p. 93 and note 98, p. 403, of this book.

70. See *S&H* p. 18.

71. Mark 4:28 (ASV).

72. *My.*, p. 353.

73. *Ibid.* See Peel, *Encounter*, p. 171.

74. *CSS*, XI, 17 (December 26, 1908), p. 324. Also Peel, *Encounter*, p. 172 f. Cf. Farlow in his letter of July 30, 1910 (A.) to Mrs. Eddy: "It is wonderful what the Monitor is doing as a missionary. . . . It is a better missionary than the Christian Scientists because it does not talk too much; it does not commit Christian Science unwisely, and does not disgrace us by unwise answers to insincere questions of critics."

75. Not all members of the staff then or now were Christian Scientists. Mrs. Eddy preferred to have Christian Scientists on the paper whenever possible, but she felt that the first consideration should be that its editors and writers be good news-papermen. Dixon's own comment in the *Outlook* (London) two years later gives a useful picture of her concern with such matters: "Mrs. Eddy herself took the utmost interest in everything, and, from the moment the first number was issued, actively guided the policy and destiny of the paper as it rapidly grew into an organ with a great circulation embracing every country in the world." The first sheet of the editorial page taken off the press each day was sent out to Chestnut Hill imme-diately, with the writers of the editorials indicated on it for her information.

76. An example of his low-keyed polemic—reprinted in *CSS*, X, 31 (April 4, 1908), p. 606 f., from the *Onlooker* of London—gives a useful indication of the qualities in his writing which Mrs. Eddy admired and wished to see utilized in the *Monitor*. Questioning whether "Luke really did travel with Paul as a sort of physician-in-ordinary," as a critic of Christian Science had implied, Dixon wrote in part:

> That Luke was a physician before he became a Christian may perhaps be granted. . . . There are to-day in the Christian Science movement numbers of men who have given up medical practice, but to pretend that, because they are still known as doctors, they are still practising in accordance with their old theories, would be ridiculous. . . .
> The whole weight of inference is on the side of Professor Harnack in writing, "His medical profession seems to have led him to Christianity, for he embraced that religion in the conviction that by its means, and by quite new methods, he would be enabled to heal disease, and drive out evil spirits." To begin with, there are more miracles recorded by Luke than any other New Testament writer. Quite apart from those performed by Jesus, there is the long catalogue recorded in Acts. Yet we are asked to believe that the man who chronicled all these had himself recourse to the pharmacopœia of Pliny. Pliny himself was particularly candid in his criticism both of doctors and their remedies. . . . "It is," he says, "at the expense of our perils that they learn, and they experiment by putting us to death, a physician being the only person that can kill another with sovereign impunity." It may be asked whether the man who recorded the raising of Jairus's daughter, the raising of Dorcas, and the raising of Eutychus, would be likely to have turned back to the methods of such a company as this.
> The simple fact is that the more closely the prescriptions recorded by Pliny are studied, the more impossible it becomes to believe that Luke, the Christian, would have meddled with them. . . . Jesus referred to this when he said that those who believed in him should "take up serpents." Now the remedies for snake-bites were innumerable. You might "hold the animal that had inflicted the injury (if you could catch it) on the end of a stick over the steam of boiling water," you might "burn it and use the ashes as a liniment"; or you

might "boil it in a shallow pan, in water seasoned with dill," and then make tabloids out of it. Harnack has shown with tolerable certainty that the viper which came out of the fire on Melita actually did bite Paul, and that was why the barbarians "looked when he should have swollen or fallen down dead." It was, perhaps, as well for Paul that he understood the power of Truth, and so could "take up serpents," instead of having to wait while Luke went to find a shallow pan and some dill.

77. A. *L&M* 25–3212.

78. He lasted in the position only seven years. During a disruptive but determinative period of litigation between the Trustees of the Publishing Society and the Directors of the church in 1919–21, Dixon supported the Trustees in their challenging of the authority of the *Church Manual.* At the collapse of their suit, he left first the paper, then the church, dying two years later with what most of his friends described as a broken heart. Erwin Canham gives an admirably balanced view of Dixon's accomplishments and failings in *Commitment to Freedom,* pp. 136–51, 162–74. While Mrs. Eddy's plans for Dixon show the sort of excellence she hoped to see on the paper and in the movement, her sending him back to London in 1909 may indicate that she had found him lacking in the spiritual maturity or stamina necessary to cope with the Boston headwinds.

79. For a further discussion of this point, see Peel, *Encounter,* pp. 173 ff., and *A Century of Christian Science Healing,* p. 250 f.

80. A. Salchow reminiscences.

81. A. *L&M* 41–5402.

82. To Gilbert Carpenter in Providence she wrote on March 15, 1908: " . . . I cannot give the time just now to anything new. I am so homesick to get accustomed to my new home hence there is no hurry to have a new carriage" (91–13473). Two months later she could write the worker in charge of her grounds: "I hereby tell you that no garden or flowers shall be cultivated on this place. Make no road for me to see such things on this place; the road to Heaven is not one of flowers, but it is strait and narrow, it is bearing the cross and turning away from things that lure the material senses, denying them, and finding all in Spirit, in God, in good and doing good" (63–8961). The austerity was temporary, however, for later there were flowers.

83. Recounted to me by Miss Still in 1960. M. Adelaide Still (the M. conceals a Minnie) was usually called Ada by other members of the household, but at Chestnut Hill Mrs. Eddy switched to Adelaide.

84. Miss Still committed some of her reminiscences to writing, but during the last years of her life in the late 1950's and early 1960's I spent many hours in conversation with her and profited from her intimate knowledge of the details of Mrs. Eddy's life from 1907 through 1910. Both at Pleasant View and Chestnut Hill, Mrs. Eddy always wished her to be in the same room with her or in the next room with the door open, so that she could call her easily if she wanted anything done. The estimate of Miss Still by her fellow workers at Chestnut Hill is summed up in a diary entry by William R. Rathvon (see p. 320): ". . . her understanding of Christian Science has been clear and from the first she has been an invaluable

member of the household. Being trained as a personal maid before coming to this country, she understands the technical part of her duties thoroughly, and is proving herself true as steel and loyal as the most faithful of the old or new." In the years when I knew her, Miss Still had the uncommon virtues of total honesty as well as scrupulous accuracy in recalling the small details of the past. In every case in which I was able to check these against other existing evidence, I found them to be fully supported by the facts.

85. Canadian by birth, Dickey came to Chestnut Hill from Kansas City, where he and his wife had been Christian Science practitioners. Dickey had given up a promising business career to become a Christian Science practitioner. In a biographical sketch of him (A.) , William D. McCrackan wrote:

> He gave the impression of a plodder, of great determination and devotion to any task to which he set himself, and his personal history shows that he pursued what his sense of duty indicated with unflagging zeal. . . . He had brilliant opportunities to enter business under the most favorable circumstances, but he preferred to follow the star of his choice whithersoever it might lead, and . . . there were times when he and his good wife did not know where their next dollar was coming from. He was tested and tried from every angle as to his absolute trust in God.

86. Cf. her statement to her household as recorded in Rathvon's diary (A.) for January 11, 1909: "I have no use for the smiling kind who say with their lips 'God is all' and sit with folded hands doing nothing in the way of proof. It is a lie to say that which implies proving, if we prove it not."

87. A. Rathvon diary, April 20, 1909. Rathvon also tells of an occasion in one of her early classes in which Mrs. Eddy asked the class whether they knew anyone who fully understood her writings. One man answered that he did know such a one— "Mrs. Eddy herself." To which she replied decisively: "She does not. She understands only what she has demonstrated, and that is no further than the A.B.C."

88. *Ibid.*, October 15, 1909.

89. A. *L&M* 76–10867.

90. A. Letter of July 29, 1908.

91. A. Letter of August 3, 1908.

92. One of the metaphysical workers at Chestnut Hill was Mrs. Ella W. Hoag, a practitioner and teacher who later became an associate editor of the Christian Science periodicals. When a gushing Christian Scientist said to her years afterward, "How *wonderful* it must have been to live in our Leader's home!" Mrs. Hoag replied laconically with a quotation from Mrs. Eddy's *Christian Healing*: "Heaven's favors are formidable."

93. A. Dickey, *Memoirs of Mary Baker Eddy* (Boston: privately printed, 1927) .

94. *Ibid.*

95. Twice yearly, when the weekly Bible lesson is on "Sacrament," Christian Science congregations in all branch churches kneel for a few moments' silent "communion" toward the close of the service, in addition to the regular period of prayer. At The

Mother Church, this "Communion service" in June had become linked with the annual meeting of the church which followed two days later, and the joint attraction had drawn numbers of Christian Scientists to Boston each year. In abolishing the special communion season at The Mother Church, Mrs. Eddy met with some criticism from those who looked forward eagerly to this annual pilgrimage to Boston, and she wrote Judge Smith: "I sought God's guidance in doing it, but the most important events are criticized. The Mother Church communion season was literally a communion of branch church communicants which might in time lose its sacredness and merge into a meeting for greetings" (*My.*, p. 142). However, as a purely religious occasion, the Communion service continued to be observed twice yearly in the branch churches, as Mrs. Eddy intended.

96. Recounted to me by Miss Still in 1961.

97. *My.*, p. 140.

98. A. Frye diary for July 2, 1908.

99. *S&H*, p. 418.

100. A. Salchow reminiscences.

101. A. Tomlinson reminiscences, supplemented by verbal accounts I have heard from both Tomlinson and Adelaide Still.

102. *My.*, p. 158.

103. II Corinthians 12:10. See also *Mis.*, pp. 199 ff.

104. Judge Smith, who in 1914 became the second Manager of Christian Science Committees on Publication, had written a letter back in 1903 in which he analyzed the legal position of Christian Scientists, concluding: "I believe that our fight for the protection of human law must, sooner or later, be fought out in the legislatures. The protection of human law will come to us through 'the quickened sense of the people' (*Science and Health* 343:13)." This view was given further study by a special committee appointed by the Board of Directors, composed of Smith himself, Kimball, and Hanna, and was subsequently adopted as policy for the Committee on Publication. But in equating legislative action with "the quickened sense of the people" there was a very real danger of losing sight of the fact that favorable statutes were only as good and as lasting as the general climate of thought that sustained them. Thus Farlow's percipient emphasis on correcting public misapprehensions of Christian Science was sometimes lost sight of in the exhilaration of legislative victories.

105. Rathvon's diary (A.) is sprinkled with such comments as his entry on October 1, 1909: "Yesterday at breakfast CF wore a large, dark-colored grouch, the outcome of the experiences of the night before which were troublous. As usual the condition to his notion was due to the 'pouring in of error,' 'someone is at work to break her down,' etc." In addition to what seemed to him Frye's undue negativism, he felt that the latter's twenty-six years of service in the household had circumscribed his outlook, as an entry the next day noted:

It came to me that CF is different from the rest of us, among other things, in this. We have two aims in our work here: first, to protect our Leader; and second, to protect the Cause. CF has shown his are: first, to protect our Leader; and second, to protect our Leader. The Cause never appears to enter his considerations and hence he is always ready to sacrifice its interests. He has never done any field work and really does not know to what the movement outside his little spot of action really amounts.

106. A. *L&M* 86–12649.

107. Sometimes she sent or drafted a letter in her own handwriting; sometimes she dictated it and signed the typed copy; sometimes she told a secretary in a general way how she wanted a letter answered, leaving him to write and sign it with an explanation that "Mrs. Eddy has asked me to tell you that . . ."; sometimes, when they did not want to bother her with a flood of letters of no great importance, the secretaries would answer them on their own, explaining that she was too busy to reply and possibly adding a comment of their own on the subject in question.

108. A. Frye diary.

109. *My.*, p. 6.

110. In the summer of 1908 Judge Smith helped Mrs. Eddy rearrange the provisions of the *Manual* in a more orderly sequence. On July 31, the seventy-third edition was adopted and later in the summer was made the authority for all succeeding editions, together with such revisions as Mrs. Eddy might subsequently approve.

111. By the end of her life, the movement was growing at the rate of two new churches a week. Articles by Farlow, Hanna, Tomlinson, Dixon, Kimball, and other prominent Christian Scientists were appearing in both popular magazines and respected journals, among them tributes to Christian Science by a noted English surgeon (Dr. Walter F. W. Wilding), an American surgeon of equal standing (Dr. Edmund F. Burton), a highly successful Broadway playwright (Charles Klein), and a wide assortment of minor notabilities. Christian Science might be controversial; it was certainly news.

112. See, e.g., *S&H* 534:24–26 and 97:21–25.

113. This book was brought out by Macmillan in an English and an American edition in 1909 and attributed to "The Writer of 'Confessio Medici,'" itself published anonymously. Paget freely admitted to authorship of both books, however. The preface of the book announced confidently (on the basis of the Milmine, Powell, and Mark Twain books) "that in America the Church of Christ, Scientist, is passing, or will soon pass, from consolidation to disintegration." But, he added gloomily, it might take twenty-five years for it to be eliminated from England.

114. *Church Times*, May 21, 1909. William James found something comic in the fact that even the disputed new "science" of psychoanalysis found it necessary to denounce Christian Science. When Sigmund Freud in 1909 made his celebrated visit to Clark University at Worcester, not far from Chestnut Hill, James wrote Theodore Flournoy in Geneva: "A newspaper report of the congress said that Freud had condemned the American religious therapy (which has such extensive results) as very 'dangerous' because so 'unscientific.' Bah!" *Letters of William James*, ed. Henry James (Boston: Atlantic Monthly Press, 1920), II, p. 328.

115. *Mark Twain–Howells Letters*, II, p. 847. Mark Twain, who grieved over the martyrdom of the Maid of Orleans but considered it manly sport to roast old ladies,

replied, "If Mrs. Eddy would try martyrdom it would make her cult permanent; & besides, I would be her friend."

116. Two letters (A.) from a Christian Scientist employed as a music teacher in a convent school record the writer's horrified astonishment at overhearing these maledictions uttered in unison by the ordinarily genial sisters at a private service in the chapel and directed by name against Mrs. Eddy. Dickey was sufficiently interested to write her after the first letter and ask for further particulars, which she then sent.

117. A. Tomlinson diary, August 25, 1908.

118. A. L&M 14412.

119. A. L&M 91–13551.

120. The equable Farlow wrote back to Mrs. Eddy (A.) on July 13, 1909, after the second volume, "Historical Facts Concerning Mary Baker Eddy and Christian Science," had been turned down:

> While I earnestly wish that the public knew what my document contains I have no desire to resort to means of placing it before the people that would not be effectual. I have no desire in the matter at all but leave it to your wisdom which I have never found wanting. If you find odd moments enough to run over the manuscript. I should like your judgment as to its correctness.

This manuscript volume is not to be confused with Farlow's pamphlet "Christian Science: Historical Facts," published in 1902.

121. See Powell, *Mary Baker Eddy: A Life Size Portrait* (1950 ed.) , p. 209 f.

122. A. Frye diary.

123. Dickey delayed pulling his scattered notes together until the last year or two of his life. In 1927, following his death, his widow had his sketchy memoir printed and copies sent to all his pupils. At the Board of Directors' request these copies were later recalled, and the copyright of the book was acquired by the Directors. It was their contention that Mrs. Eddy had asked Dickey to "write" a history of his experiences with her but not necessarily to publish it, and that to have deposited a copy of the memoirs in the church archives for the use of future full-scale biographers would have satisfied her request. The nub of the problem was evidently the unreadiness of the Christian Science field at that time to accept a less than idealized picture of Mrs. Eddy's life, plus the fear of what critics of Christian Science would make of Dickey's incomplete sketch. What they would make of it was soon evidenced by Dakin and Bates-Dittemore, and later by other biographers, who inevitably got hold of copies of the book and made the most of it for their own purposes. Half a century later, the general drift and salient details of the Dickey account are common knowledge and can be judged in the perspective of today's fuller comprehension of the subject. Like all other personal memoirs, it contributes to the general picture but needs some correction from the diverse accounts by other participants in Mrs. Eddy's last years.

124. Reported to me by Adelaide Still. In regard to propositions made to write her life while she was still alive, Dickey records in his memoirs: "Her reply to proposals of this kind was, 'The time has not yet come for my history to be written. The person to whom this important work should be intrusted is not here yet and I

will not give my consent to its being done at this time.' This was the nature of the reply she invariably made whenever some of her loving students proposed to her that her life history should be written."

125. See p. 202.

126. A. *L&M* 14–1771, plus Tomlinson diary and letter to McLellan. Mrs. Eddy's early opposition to the book seems to have been based on her conviction that her life demanded more understanding than Miss Wilbur or anyone else at that time could bring to it. (See note 124, opposite.) That the book's prospective publication made her ill doubtless confirmed her conviction.

127. A. *L&M* 63–9007. This letter was later reproduced in facsimile in the Wilbur biography, where it appeared to be an expression of gratitude for the author's writing the book instead of gratitude for her willingness to withdraw it, as the archival material makes plain. When the facts about it came to light, it was withdrawn from the book in 1976.

128. A. Dittemore, Brown, and a third partner financed and published the book, using the name Concord Publishing Company. The printing was done by the University Press, headed by Mrs. Eddy's old friend William Dana Orcutt.

129. A. Note of September 24, 1908.

130. Willa Cather surmised that Miss Milmine restored some of the passages which she (Miss Cather) had cut out of the *McClure's* series. Certainly the book was even more intemperate than the series, as Miss Wilbur's book was more adulatory than her *Human Life* series.

131. Of particular interest in this endorsement is Mrs. Eddy's statement: "I briefly declare that nothing has occurred in my life's experience which, if correctly narrated and understood, could injure me."

132. Some of the points she mentioned to him were picayune, and in some cases she herself evidently "misremembered" the facts, but in general the portions of the book he read to her seem to have struck her as too bland a portrayal of her "life dolorosa."

133. *Ret.,* p. 22.

134. In some ways, Mrs. Eddy remained to the end of her days a Victorian lady with a strong regard for the amenities and proprieties, and at that level she did sometimes show the sort of wishful revisionism that can be read into the quoted statement from her autobiography. But cutting across that was the spiritual radicalism which, in the two paragraphs that follow, repudiated the "legendary and traditional history of the early life of Jesus" for the Jesus of Paul—"Who for the joy that was set before him endured the cross, despising the shame, and is set down at the right hand of the throne of God." To which she added, as the spirited warrior she remained to the end: "It may be that the mortal life-battle still wages, and must continue till its involved errors are vanquished by victory-bringing Science; but this triumph will come!"

135. *My.,* p. 136.

136. Isaiah 53:3–5.

137. *Man.*, 41:3–5.

138. See, e.g., *Mis.*, p. 163 f. and *My.*, 346:29. That Jesus himself expected a further unfolding of truth to the world was (Mrs. Eddy held) evident from such statements of his as, "He that believeth on me, the works that I do shall he do also; and greater works than these shall he do; because I go unto my Father. . . . And I will pray the Father, and he shall give you another Comforter, that he may abide with you for ever, even the Spirit of truth. . . . Howbeit when he, the Spirit of truth, is come, he will guide you into all truth." (John 14:12, 16, 17, and 16:13.)

139. *S&H* 28:22–31, 474:4–15, 534:24–30.

140. A. Martha Bogue reminiscences.

141. Cf. her statement in a letter (A. *L&M* 43–5722) to a Protestant minister: "I long for less to do as a leader and more time to be a student."

142. A. Emma Shipman reminiscences.

Notes: *Chapter X   Quod Erat Demonstrandum*

1. *Message for 1901*, p. 30.

2. See, e.g., *Mis.*, 365:10–12, *No* 12:1–6, *S&H* 449:3–6.

3. *The American Business Man*, II, 5 (May, 1908), pp. 155 ff. Cf. Farlow letter in *Boston Times*, quoted in *CSS*, X, 22 (February 1, 1908), p. 429:

> . . . One of the principal dangers in praying for material things is that of erring in judgment. We are likely to ask for that which we really ought not to have, for that which would in reality be an injury to us. Therefore, we can do no better than to heed Jesus' admonition, "Seek ye first the kingdom of God, and his righteousness; and all these things shall be added unto you."

Also Clarence A. Buskirk, "Poverty and Riches," *CSS*, XII, 31 (April 2, 1910), p. 599:

> It is a serious mistake to suppose that the belief of poverty needs to be overcome, but that the belief of riches does not. Both alike need the ministry of Christian Science. . . . They may differ more or less in aspect, but their primary origin is the same. . . . Not only are the needs of the individual sufferer to be regarded from this view-point, but likewise the needs of society and political government. The social and governmental ills which come from both of these beliefs are widespread throughout the earth. Class hatred, class jealousies, class antagonisms, proceeding from both beliefs, cannot be safely disregarded.

Gottschalk, *Emergence of Christian Science*, pp. 249–59, contains an excellent discussion of this whole subject.

4. *S&H*, p. 239. See also *Message for 1900*, 10:1, and *My.* 278:26.

5. From the records of one of her students. Quoted in Altman K. Swihart, *Since Mrs. Eddy* (New York: Holt, 1931), p. 43 f.

6. A. H00016.

7. A. *L&M* 38–5035.

8. A. *L&M* 19–2446. A little earlier she had written to Tomlinson (29–3644) : "I love poor Stetson and have rebuked her more severely than almost any other student and am still trying to save her." To Stetson herself she wrote in 1904 (H00088) : "Do not doubt my *love* for you, my faith in you, and my faithful rebuke if need be. . . . [I love] you just as tenderly in giving you His rod as His staff. . . ."

9. A. *L&M* 20–2565.

10. See p. 192.

11. A. George DeLana affidavit. DeLana stated that she also consulted him about the possibility of secession when Carol Norton, who had committed the unforgivable sin of breaking with her, was appointed Committee on Publication for New York.

12. In support of this claim, Mrs. Stetson read her students (and later printed in her books) all those letters or parts of letters in which Mrs. Eddy praised her, while carefully omitting the stern warnings, reprimands, and corrections which were the other side of Mrs. Eddy's affection for her.

13. A. *L&M* 60–8510.

14. A. Letter of August 2, 1906.

15. A. *L&M* 20–2568. A year later Mrs. Eddy again found it necessary to write her (20–2569) : "At all times let your trust be *in God not in* ME. Personal contagion comes of thinking of me as a person to bear your sins or be a personal medium of your salvation for *I* am *not*. All that I do for you is by means of my *pen* and *teachings*. I can do *nothing more.*"

16. Typical of these is the note she sent Mrs. Stetson after receiving another of the latter's lavish gifts: "*Do not* send me another thought or thing material. My treasures are spiritual and laid up in Heaven." (A. H00125)

17. The editorial referred to the Chestnut Hill house as being too large and not what Mrs. Eddy wanted, "but it is a plain house, and its furnishings are not extravagant. Mrs. Eddy has continued to declare against the display of material things, and has said that the less we have of them the better. Since God has taught her that matter is unreal and Spirit is the only reality, any other position would be unscientific." This statement is adapted from her own words quoted in note 24, p. 492, plus her further statement: "I have always declared against the display of material things & said the less we have of them the better. Since God taught me that matter is unreal and Spirit is the only reality any other position is unscientific."

18. *CSS*, XI, 14 (December 5, 1908) , p. 270. Eleven years earlier, Mrs. Eddy had written Tomlinson, then a relative newcomer to Christian Science, in regard to Mrs. Stetson, "Beware! never come under *her influence.*"

19. A. *L&M* 91–13518.

20. Mrs. Stetson had nevertheless allowed the *New York American* story to stand without contradiction.

21. Mrs. Stetson's account of this incident, quoted in Swihart, *Since Mrs. Eddy*, pp. 62 ff., adds that Mrs. Eddy followed these words with the statement: "This is the happiest hour of my life—the very happiest hour of my life, *on earth*." For the credibility of Mrs. Stetson's reports of her own and others' words, see note 39, p. 507.

22. On the same day Mrs. Stetson wrote Mrs. Eddy a letter which does not sound as though she had definitely abandoned her hope for a new church building that would be bigger and better than them all:

> . . . we had not even considered what the structure would be; our attention having been directed entirely to securing the lot. Still we knew the edifice would be worthy of our Cause and its Leader. We shall wait on God. . . . Then the children of Israel . . . will go forward to reveal a church edifice which will manifest in phenomenon the unity and love of our people,—a symbol of the "Church Triumphant," in the beauty, outline, form, color, and substance of Divine Mind. . . . The words of the Poet come to mind right here:
>
> > Build thee more stately mansions, O my soul,
> >   As the swift seasons roll.
> > Let each new temple, mightier than the last,
> > Shut thee in heaven with a dome more vast,
> >   Till thou at length art free,
> > Leaving thine outgrown shell by time's unresting sea.

23. *CSS*, XI, 20 (January 16, 1909), p. 390. Later, when Mrs. Stetson was expelled from The Mother Church with Mrs. Eddy's full knowledge and concurrence, the banished disciple went back to this paragraph—and particularly to the words "they must begin on a wholly spiritual foundation"—to develop her theory that Mrs. Eddy was thereby telling her secretly that she, Mrs. Stetson, had risen above the need for a human organization and was to build and lead a purely spiritual church that would supersede The First Church of Christ, Scientist, in Boston.

24. *Ret.*, p. 94.

25. A. Reported by Mrs. Eddy in a letter to Hanna as having been stated by Nixon "under his own signature."

26. A. Strickler diary.

27. *Ibid.*

28. A. Stetson material.

29. A. Letter of July 10, 1909.

30. Bates–Dittemore, *Mary Baker Eddy*, p. 432.

31. *My.*, p. 357 f.

32. A. Strickler diary, July 16, 1909.

33. *My.*, p. 359 f.

34. A. *L&M* 6–614. In another letter to the Directors, Mrs. Eddy made a statement which has significance beyond the Stetson case: "Do not name me as your

authority, but my published works, and say that I abide by them and approve all that is done according to them" (6–618).

35. A. Strickler diary, July 28, 1909.

36. A. Dittemore letter to Dickey, August 12, 1909.

37. A. H00102. A little earlier Mrs. Eddy had written Mrs. Stetson: "You asked what I meant by 'doing nothing in secret that you would not do openly'? This was my meaning. To keep your thoughts right in God's sight. It is one of my greatest struggles to guard the unseen consciousness so that the visible shall always bless myself *and others.*" To another student she wrote (LX–8524): "Never teach a student to try to hurt another in their own self-defense . . . for that is doing evil that good might come. It took me many years to learn never to make a mistake in trying to do right. . . ."

38. A. Strickler diary, July 31, 1909.

39. In the later Boston hearings, it emerged that these same besotted students had used this same criminal casuistry in the Brush Will Case in New York in 1901, perjuring themselves in the witness box by giving testimony "in the absolute." No single piece of evidence was more damning to Mrs. Stetson's moral character and teaching. It is an interesting question why, in the light of these long-known facts, so many critics of Mrs. Eddy have accepted in toto Mrs. Stetson's version of her dispute with the church. A partial exception is Bates—Dittemore, undoubtedly owing to the fact that in this one instance Dittemore was on the inside of the events described and knew what actually went on.

40. *CSS,* XII, 3 (September 18, 1909), p. 50. The editorial abstained from any mention of the Stetson affair for obvious reasons and presented the issue in generalities:

> From time to time Christian Scientists have been charged by critics of this denomination with being double-minded; that is, it is claimed that in their statements concerning themselves and their affairs, they make certain mental reservations in order that these statements shall coincide with an individual concept of what they term "absolute" Christian Science, rather than with the phenomena of sense perception with which they are dealing. . . .
>
> It can be safely said . . . that no true Christian Scientist will knowingly lay himself open to such a charge, for he fully understands that to make the perfection of Christ, of man in the image and likeness of God, a cloak for deception of any kind, whether it be the blackest of sins or the "white lies" of conventionality, is to commit an enormity; it is . . . stealing "the livery of the court of heaven to serve the devil in."

41. A. H00042.

42. A. Frye diary. W.H.B. was Mrs. Eddy's student, W. H. Bertram, who in 1888 had left the Massachusetts Metaphysical College with several other students to study at a medical college in order that they might fit themselves to act as qualified obstetricians as well as Christian Science practitioners in cases of childbirth. Later that year they had turned against Mrs. Eddy and left the Boston church. (See Peel, *Trial,* p. 240 f.) Bertram had gone on to become a homeopathic doctor, but by 1907 had begun to hanker for Christian Science again and had written Mrs. Eddy of his

continuing gratitude to her. Since he lived in Charlestown, just across the Charles River from Boston, it was natural that when a doctor was called to administer a hypodermic on three occasions of acute crisis in Mrs. Eddy's last two years, this friendly homeopathist should have been the one to be asked. On one or two other occasions in that period he was summoned by Frye to stand by overnight in case of need, but was not used. Dickey put his foot down finally after a seizure in the spring of 1910 had caused two injections to be given within a few days—a dangerous dependence, he felt, which had not been evident since the earliest attacks. There should be no more injections, he ruled, and there were not. There were also no further attacks of the old complaint.

43. In conversation with Strickler on August 11, John Dittemore stated that the Directors already had fifteen affidavits but that Mrs. Stetson's hold on her students was so absolute she could undoubtedly by mere fiat produce many more in rebuttal.

44. The two were also accompanied by Margaret Beecher White, a granddaughter of Henry Ward Beecher and a devoted pupil of Mrs. Stetson, who had finally recoiled from the latter's excesses and corroborated the testimony of the two Readers in every particular.

45. A. *L&M* 6–622.

46. On September 20 Verrall had gone to Boston with the full intention of informing the Directors that he had told them various untruths when he was there in July with Mrs. Stetson and wanted now to tell them what really went on in the practitioners' meetings at First Church. But Mrs. Stetson got wind of this purpose, and her mental control of Verrall was sufficient to make him reverse himself when he got there. However, he continued to try to break loose, and the day after the business meeting he wrote Mrs. Eddy that he finally understood what she meant by her warnings against sinking Principle in personality and allowing animal magnetism to deceive one into deifying a particular personality.

47. *My.*, p. 360. When this letter was republished in *CSS*, December 4, 1909, the words "in Truth" were added at Mrs. Eddy's request in order to clarify her meaning to the literal-minded.

48. A. Strickler diary.

49. This qualified penitence was short-lived. Mrs. Stetson soon took the tack not merely that she was right but that Mrs. Eddy was secretly supporting her, all private letters and published statements to the contrary notwithstanding. The letters were dismissed as forgeries, the statements as the work of church officials who mysteriously kept their Leader unaware of what they were publishing over her name in the *Journal* and *Sentinel*. For contrast with Mrs. Stetson's attitude, see Emma C. Shipman, "Requirements in Christian Science Practice," *CSS*, XII, 9 (October 30, 1909) , p. 165:

> ... the requirements for practising this Science are not superficial. They must reach to the depths of one's nature and exact the final destruction of all that is not Christian, not based on divine Principle.
> The first necessity is honesty, absolute integrity of thought.... There are two ways in which one must know himself. He must be able to recognize his faults, weaknesses, and sins. He must also comprehend in some degree the actuality of his true being as the perfect expression of divine Mind, God's own image and

likeness. This knowledge of himself enables one to overcome human weaknesses and manifest in their stead the qualities of God. . . .

The practitioner must prove by his work that Christian Science is not personal magnetism. . . . Worldly success and high-sounding talk do not bear witness to a real Christian Science practitioner, neither do mock humility and puritanical pretense. The witness to true success is healing—disease banished, grief assuaged, discordant homes made happy, and sin overcome. In the serene activities of good and in the eradication of every thought of self-aggrandizement, the Christian Science practitioner gains dominion over human beliefs.

50. *CSS*, XII, 24 (February 12, 1910) , p. 471. Also *My.*, p. 362.

51. Rathvon diary, December 15, 1909.

52. *Ibid.* Rathvon in his reminiscences added the comment: "She was in such a cheerful mood that it is not reasonable to suppose that she had in mind what was to occur before the next year passed."

53. *My.*, p. 358 f.

54. *CSJ*, XXVII (November, 1909) , p. 560 f. Also *Man.*, pp. 74, 83 ff.

55. *CSS*, XII, 20 (January 15, 1910) , p. 390.

56. The other members of the board had for some time been restless over the undue confidence which Johnson put in his son, William Lyman Johnson, who in turn seems to have been somewhat under the spell of Mrs. Stetson; but that the elder Johnson's resignation was not entirely for this reason is suggested by Mrs. Eddy's reply to his letter informing her of the move (A. *L&M* 94–14031) :

I thank you deeply for your dear loving letter. I think it is for your good that you take the step you name. Having no office work to meet in a business way will give you a better chance to attend to yourself, and we all must do this sometime or the weeds will choke the growing grain. . . . You have named to me in confidence certain needs of your own. Now dear one, attend persistently to them and you will conquer and be blessed in all ways.

57. A. *L&M* 26–3232.

58. A. Dickey notes.

59. It is one more irony of Christian Science history that the man who financed the Sibyl Wilbur biography should in time have collaborated with Ernest Sutherland Bates on so unremittingly iconoclastic a book as their *Mary Baker Eddy* (1932) . Writing to Frederick Remington four years later (A. Letter of May 23, 1936) , Dittemore noted in regard to the latter book:

Its sales & royalties have become quite small, for which, in a way, I am really not sorry. I realize that if I had it to do over, I should insist on eliminating, not documented facts, proving the *human* side of Mrs. Eddy's character, which it is folly, I feel, to try to deny or camouflage, but certain unfortunate deductions & implications, which Bates . . . demanded should be included as inescapable.

The next year, on March 23, 1937, after years of bitter attack against The Mother Church, Dittemore wrote the Directors a letter which gives the final turnabout to a career that ended not long afterward:

As the result of experience over a period of years and a great deal of serious study devoted to the science of government, I have come to the humble conclusion that I made a great mistake in allowing personal differences of opinion and the feelings that developed therefrom, to influence me to the extent which they evidently did after Mrs. Eddy passed on.

We were all greatly affected by her demise and held divergent views regarding the policies to be pursued when she was no longer here to direct us. And while I acted upon convictions which I regarded as right at the time, I have since been led to see, and am anxious to go on record as admitting it, that I was wrong in letting personal opinion and matters of policy induce me to depart from Principle.

God's law does not divide and separate men, it unites them, enabling them to work together and perpetuates this unity. Personal differences that appear irreconcilable disappear as we grow in the understanding of His law and the ability to demonstrate it. Man is properly self-governed only as he enthrones this mighty law in his heart and mind. It annihilates everything unlike itself and I find it has destroyed all sense of personal animosity, all desire to justify self, and brought instead the sincere desire to acknowledge my mistake in organizing what was apparently regarded as an opposition movement, opposed to the Cause of Christian Science, to Mrs. Eddy and her teachings.

I recognize and revere her as having restored to humanity primitive Christian healing and acknowledge The First Church of Christ, Scientist, in Boston, Mass., as the first church in history to stand for the spiritual and scientific significance of the life of Christ.

I am happy to forward you this letter to use as you may see fit and to sincerely announce as my fervent desire that the Cause which you represent may continue to grow and prosper under your direction.

60. "An Interview with Mrs. Eddy," *Permanency of The Mother Church and Its Manual* (Boston: Christian Science Publishing Society, 1954), p. 10. Smith's part in the trial was related to his *Manual* function as First Reader of The Mother Church. His visit to Chestnut Hill was in connection with his approving a change in the trustees of her personal estate.

61. Quoted in Rathvon's "Interview with General Henry M. Baker," *Permanency of The Mother Church*, p. 13.

62. *Eustace* vs. *Dickey*, 240 Mass. Rep. 55: *Dittemore* vs. *Dickey*, 249 Mass. Rep. 95.

63. A. Tomlinson diary, December 13, 1909.

64. A. Rathvon diary, December 13, 1909.

65. *Mis.*, p. 307.

66. Mrs. Eddy showed the liveliest interest in this latter event in September, 1910, which involved an exhibition flight by the English aviator Graham White—the first ever held in Boston. She wanted a detailed report from those who went, yet in the end she found the possibilities of "material" flight considerably less engaging than those of spiritual exploration. In a fragment entitled "Soaring," which she dictated to Dickey, the changed mood shows clearly:

To fly materially is animal, to fly spiritually is divine. . . . Flying materially is a sport that may become engrossing. . . . The elevation worth obtaining or

possible to obtain in Science is spiritual ascent, thought soaring above matter. . . .
Oh when will the age plant its discoveries on spiritual cause & effect, on that
which is not only capable of going up but is ascending, physically, mentally and
spiritually. Almost one century of experience has caused me to say, How long, O
Lord, how long!

67. A. Rathvon diary, February 13, 1909.

68. *Ibid.* Entries in February, July, August, and November, 1910.

69. A. Frye diary, October 26, 1909.

70. A. Tomlinson diary, July 16, 1910.

71. The picture of a house filled with constant gloom and struggle is as fallacious
as the picture of a house filled with perpetual sunshine and serenity. There is
limited evidence to support both views; but the first has been built on a comparatively
few (though pungent) entries in the Frye diaries and on the general tone of the
Dickey *Memoirs,* while the rose-colored view has necessitated a disregard of the
clear indications Mrs. Eddy herself has given in such passages as *My.,* 136:3–8, taken
in conjunction with *S&H* 48:10 to 54:28 and 463:32 to 464:20.

72. Rathvon's zest often makes an interesting contrast with Frye's low spirits. But
cf. his entry for April 30, 1910:

> It was a shining sign of the times to see CF after a difficult night and under
> conditions which would ordinarily have made him in the past grouchy and
> sore come down chipper and jovial as the rest of us. It looks to me as though
> he was seeing a great light and is becoming converted to the efficacy of team
> work.

73. A. Rathvon diary, April 22, 1910.

74. A. Tomlinson diary, undated.

75. Told to me by Miss Still on February 6, 1960. She also referred me to Mrs.
Eddy's words in *Mis.,* 121:6–11.

76. Still, February 6, 1960. See *Mis.,* 353:7–10. In my last conversation with Miss Still,
a few days before her death at a very advanced age, she told me of the wonderful
"unfoldments of truth" she was having as she studied and prayed, and that she
kept wishing, "Oh, if I had only understood that fifty years ago!"

77. John 8:44.

78. *S&H,* p. 442, final version.

79. A. Dickey memoirs.

80. *My.,* p. 355 f. Detailed background of the incident from Miss Still. Mrs. Sargent,
who was removed from the house for a week's rest at the Hotel Beaconsfield in
Brookline, returned at the end of that time in good health.

81. *S&H,* p. 272.

82. A. Sargent notes, Rathvon diary, etc.

83. *My.*, p. 354.

84. A. Rathvon diary.

85. See note 42, above, for the situation in May. The condition in September seems to have been one of extreme weakness and weariness rather than pain.

86. Quoted in Smith, *Historical Sketches,* p. 100 f.

87. A. Rathvon diary, June 13, 1910.

88. *Ibid.,* June 18, 1910.

89. *Ibid.,* July 6, 1910. Two days later Rathvon wrote of Mrs. Eddy's calling "all hands" in for an especially long session in which she was "at her best" in "poise, acumen, and graciousness" and "kept us all busy answering questions." The entry concluded: "I never saw a better or more wonderful exhibition of clear skill."

90. A. Frye diary. Mrs. Eddy seems to have recalled literally dozens of hymns from her early years and loved to have them sung for her.

91. *Mis.,* p. 389. This poem had been written in 1893.

92. I Corinthians 15:26. Although Mrs. Eddy had asked McLellan as early as 1908 to reserve a lot in Mount Auburn Cemetery for an unnamed purpose, her repudiation of death as a part of God's plan for man was never more vigorous than during her last three years.

93. *Un.,* p. 43.

94. A. A6–10240.

95. A. A6–10217.

96. Her words in *S&H* 291:5–11 and 292:1–6 obviously apply to herself as well as to all other members of the human race.

97. *My.,* p. 242. Also in *CSS,* V, 13, September 3, 1910.

98. See Appendix B.

99. Bates–Dittemore ask rhetorically of her contemplative hours, "Was this a kind of senile coma, or was she, as the faithful believed, communing with Moses and the prophets?" This choice of communicants is evidently to be attributed to the sardonic imagination of Bates (see note 59, p. 509 f.).

100. Dickey in his *Memoirs* tells of an occasion a year or two earlier when she said to him as she prepared to go out: "Mr. Dickey, I want you to know that it does me good to go on this drive. I do not mean that the physical going for a drive does me good, but the enemy have made a law that it hurts me to go on this drive, and they are trying to enforce it." Evidently the "enemy" failed of its purpose.

101. A. Rathvon diary, November 20, 1910.

102. A. A8–10355.

103. In her last months, nearly all her writing was done by dictation rather than by her own hand.

104. A. Letter of October 13, 1910.

105. A. V03121.

106. A. Dickey memoirs.

107. A. Still reminiscences. Told to Miss Still by Mrs. Sargent. The two women lived together as companions in the Chestnut Hill house for several years after Mrs. Eddy's passing.

108. A. *L&M* 6–637.

109. *Mis.*, p. 24.

110. A. Still reminiscences.

111. The official report and the later reminiscences of Rathvon and Tomlinson speak of the two latter, plus Frye and Mrs. Ella Rathvon, as also having been present at the end. The transition was apparently so gentle that it was difficult to be sure whether her breathing had stopped before or after these others were called in.

112. A. Still reminiscences.

113. A. *New York Herald,* December 5, 1910.

114. A. The rest of this written statement by the undertakers is also of evidential value:

December 6, 1910.

To Whom it may Concern:

We were called to the residence of Mrs. Mary Baker Eddy in Chestnut Hill, Mass., at 8-15 A.M. Sunday December 4, 1910, to care for her body. We found it in an excellent state of preservation when first called, and also fifty eight hours after death. No preserving compounds were used until that time. . . .

In the process of embalming we found the body at sixty hours after death, in as good condition of preservation as we always find at twelve to twenty-four hours after death.

This is our voluntary statement made without solicitation or influence of any kind.

Frank S. Waterman
George A. Pierce
Katharine M. Foote

115. *Mis.*, p. 135 f.

116. The funeral service was not held until the morning of Thursday, December 8, in order to allow time for George Glover and his family to come from South Dakota. The service was a simple one, attended by some fifty people (including a former governor of Massachusetts), and contrary to the usual Christian Science custom the casket was left open so that those present might file by and see for themselves that the figure within it was indubitably that of Mary Baker Eddy. The coffin was then taken to the general receiving vault at Mount Auburn Cemetery in Cambridge, where it was carefully guarded until the completion of a special tomb at the site of the present monument, and for added security a telephone line was extended to the guard until the transfer was made and the tomb sealed. This normal safety precaution was given a lurid significance by Augusta Stetson's announcement to the

press that she fully expected Mrs. Eddy's imminent resurrection from the grave. As a result, Farlow explained in an official statement:

> While Christian Scientists believe the Scriptural teaching that the time will come when there will be no more death, they take the common-sense view that centuries may pass meanwhile before this exalted spiritual estate is reached.
> Christian Scientists believe the Scriptural teaching concerning the resurrection, that it means a putting off of mortality and a putting on of immortality. In other words a gradual spiritual growth wherein the individual makes a transition from a material condition to a spiritual condition.
> They believe that the resurrection begins in this life and continues here or hereafter until perfection is attained. This is the belief that they entertain concerning Mrs. Eddy. They do not look for her return to this world.

Nevertheless, the myth-making tendency remains strong even among those who pride themselves on their hard-headed respect for facts, and the legend still persists that "the Christian Scientists have a telephone in Mrs. Eddy's tomb." Sober historians at Harvard who only need to stroll over to Mount Auburn or pick up their own telephone to find out the real facts, have preferred ever since 1910 to repeat the allegation as a droll dinner-table story of unimpeachable authority. As a result, Farlow's successors have had to deny printed reports of the myth at least a dozen times a year for the past seven decades. This stands as an ironic final comment on the "denial of reality" attributed to Mrs. Eddy by some of these same historians.

Notes: *Epilogue*

1. Job 32:8.

2. *S&H*, p. vii.

3. *Ibid.*, p. 224.

4. This is the conclusion of Henry W. Steiger in his academic study *Christian Science and Philosophy* (New York: Philosophical Library, 1948) .

5. See chapters "The Pragmatic Test" in Peel, *Encounter,* and "Christian Science and the American Pragmatic Orientation" in Gottschalk, *Emergence.*

6. *My.*, p. 303.

7. *Mis.*, p. 279.

Index

Abbey, Edwin, 43
Abernathy, Arthur Talmage, 469n3
Abinger, Lord, 117
Acton, Lord, 16
Adams, Henry, 300
Adoption, 24–26, 79, 446n88
Africa, 114, 121
Aguinaldo, Emilio, 136
Alcott, A. Bronson, 98
Aldrich, Edgar, 284, 287, 291
Alger, William R., 412n76
American Business Man, The, 329
Amiel, Henri, 184, 185, 439n25
Anarchy of Christian Science, The (Powell) , 273
Anderson, Rosemary O., 171
Angelic Overtures of Christ and Christmas (Orgain) , 391n32
Angelico, Fra, 61
Anglo-Israel theory, 116–119, 414n98, 415n10
Animal magnetism, 67, 80, 83, 150, 189–190, 288, 338–339, 350, 367; *see also* Malicious animal magnetism, Mesmerism, and Hypnotism
Arena, 150, 151, 193, 230, 423n9, 459n48
Arens, Edward J., 120
Armstrong, Joseph, 80, 82, 100, 101, 103, 160, 242, 387n74, 400n52, 401n60, 405n32, 430n76, 490n3; named to Board of Directors, 41; construction of Mother Church, 68, 70–71, 402n81; next friends suit, 280; death of, 295
Armstrong, Mary, 100, 466n115
Arnold, Matthew, 16
Ashbourne, Lord, 421n32
Asia, 421n33
Association for International Conciliation, 255
Atlanta, Ga., 417n143, 458n40
Auden, W. H., 247
Augusta, Me., 425n19
Authority, 4–5, 13, 16, 32–34, 42, 68,

90–92, 225, 228–229, 346–347, 447n89, 506n34

Bacon, Francis, 494n42
Bagley, Sarah, 229
Baha'i, 57
Baker, Albert (brother) , 235
Baker, Dr. Alfred, 178, 237, 410n64, 412n78, 461n69; teacher of obstetrics class, 440n45
Baker, Fred W., 482n99
Baker, George W. (nephew) , 280
Baker, Gen. Henry M. (cousin) , 109, 230, 280, 282, 457n31
Baker, Joseph (grandfather) , 230
Baker, Mark (father) , 177, 271
Baker, Mary Ann (Maryann) Moore (grandmother) , 115, 413n94
Baker, Ray Stannard, 261
Baker, Rufus (cousin) , 457n29
Balfour, Arthur, 301, 305, 494n41
Ball, Charity, 232, 233
Baltimore, Md., 191, 197
Baptism, 10–11
Barrows, J. H., 51, 53, 54
Barry, George, 457n38
Bartlett, Charles W., 430n73
Bartlett, Julia, 32, 33, 396n87, 418n143, 425n22; on Mrs. Woodbury, 147
Bartol, Cyrus A., 412n76
Bates, Caroline (Mrs. E. P.) , 71, 85
Bates, Edward P., 71, 72, 75, 82, 93, 102, 103, 104, 108, 166, 167, 397n32, 400n52, 401n60, 412n83; on Board of Directors, 78, 398n42; trustee of Publishing Society, 122, 417n127
Bates, Gen. Erastus N., 109, 411n69
Bates, E. S., 267, 458n47, 474n39, 509n59, 512n99
Bath, Marchioness of, 117
Bathurst, Algernon Hervey, 434n107
Battles, Gen. Wendell P., 427n40
Beardsley, Aubrey, 43, 426n35

Chicago Inter-Ocean, 49, 50, 155
Chicago Record-Herald, 283
China, 121; Christian Science in, 138–139
Choate, Clara, 170, 171
Christ, 5, 15, 20, 60, 93, 138, 173–174, 252, 325–326, 336–337, 394n79, 507-n40; see also Christianity and Jesus
Christian Science: Christianity and,
Christian Science: Christianity and, 325–326, 455n29; disciplines, 30; discovery of, 25, 37, 189, 234, 413n95, 440n36; and disease, 212–213, 218–220, 462n74 (see also Healing); and Divine Science, 38, 104, 213, 355, 388n6; Doorly-Kappeler schematic approach to, 454n23; and Eastern religions, 50–51, 57–58, 394nn70 & 71; in English-speaking countries, 114–119, 414n104; vs. faith healing, 356, 377–378, 501n111; in Germany, 119–121, 415nn114 & 118 & 120–121; hostility to, 57–59, 229–235, 285, 321–323, 395n81; healing as art of, 62 (see also Healing); influence of, 50, 88–89, 255, 402n83; legal position of, 98–99, 500n104; "letter" of, 441n52; Mark Twain on, 3–4, 32, 198–206, 209, 229, 270, 322, 446nn84 & 87, 477n53, 452-n26, 501n115; methodology, 304–307; organization of, 13, 16–18, 33, 346; perpetuation of, 329–336; practitioners, 30, 101, 508n49; promotion of, 14–16, 39, 48, 54, 89, 121, 122, 223–227, 334–336, 455n7; publication activity, 14, 15, 103, 121–122, 124, 132, 227, 307–314, 352–353, 382n21, 418n6; publicity, 59, 75, 89, 98, 158, 172–174, 257–259, 331, 397n32, 402n85; on resurrection, 514n116; sociopolitical implications, 115–116, 118, 131–140, 224–225, 329–330, 420n29, 442n60; teachers and teaching, 30, 104, 124, 190–194, 227, 241, 248–252, 344–345; tests of growth in, 59, 394n73; understanding of, 112, 304; universalism of, 13, 115–116; see also Metaphysics
Christian Science Board of Education, 168, 248, 251, 252; established, 124; term of teacher, 250
Christian Science Board of Lectureship, 122–124, 162, 192; established, 122
Christian Science Committee on Publication, 157–158, 192, 194–198, 230, 261, 313, 314, 317, 324, 500n104; see also Alfred Farlow
Christian Science Congress (Chicago,

1893), 49–52, 57, 224; see also World's Parliament of Religions
Christian Science Journal, The, 14, 17, 18, 37, 38, 39, 41, 42, 48, 55, 56, 59, 61, 62, 69, 72, 84, 91, 97, 99, 102, 104, 105, 112, 116, 119, 124, 157, 158, 177, 192, 195, 199, 212, 227, 303–308, 341, 355, 405n23, 406n43, 416n121, 508n49; "Deification of Personality," 63; Eastaman articles, 389n19; testimonials in, 98–99
Christian Science Messenger, 418n6
Christian Science Monitor, The, 111, 420n29, 495n49; founded, 307–314, 319, 352–353, 496n66, 497nn74 & 76; public issues covered by, 132, 137, 140; staff of, 497n75
Christian Science Publishing Society, The, 255, 483n104; Board of Trustees created, 121–122, 417nn126 & 127
Christian Science Sentinel, 177, 192, 212, 218, 226, 227, 242, 251, 258, 308, 310, 313, 329, 334, 335, 338, 340, 345, 351, 377, 403n10, 416n121, 459n48, 460n49, 493n35, 508n49; founded, 124; public issues covered by, 132–137, 418n6, 419n21; "The World's Uproar" (editorial), 132
Christian Science: The Faith and its Founder (Powell), 274
Christian Science Weekly, The, 124, 418n6; see also Christian Science Sentinel
Christianity, 4, 30, 44, 54, 60, 67, 219, 225, 227, 235, 248, 259, 329, 331, 336, 343, 394n78; and Christian Science, 325–326, 455n29
Church buildings, 75, 89, 224, 334–336, 402n85
Church Manual, see Manual of The Mother Church
Church of Christ, Scientist: Board of Directors, 80, 81, 82, 89, 134, 193, 212, 227, 244, 272, 309–310, 320, 338, 339, 341, 358, 399n48, 405n32, 442n59, 456n20, 496n66, 502n123; Board of Directors and construction of Boston church, 68–71; Board of Directors established, 32, 386n72; Board of Directors enlarged, 228; branch churches, 34, 334–335; Christian Science college orgs, 440n31; Christian Science organizations separate from, 226; federal system of church government for, 32–33; goals and functions, 30; name selected, 32; organization of

517

Eddy, Mary Baker (*cont.*)
from students, and her reaction, 126–127, 418n146; antiwar views, 132–140, 256, 470n10; politics of, 420n24; Josephine Woodbury and *Woodbury vs. Eddy* libel suit, 143–174, 194, 275, 443n66; Dresser-Woodbury campaign to discredit, 151–152; "Babylonish woman," 153–154; at Mother Church annual meeting (1899) , 154–155; Publication Committee formed, 157–158; difference with lawyers, 159–161, 167, 430n76; Clarkson attack on feminine leadership, 162, 430n80; her view of womanhood and biblical prophecy, 162–166, 432n92; dissatisfaction with Hanna, 164, 431n88, 433–n98; Kimball brought in, 166–170; *New York Herald* interview, 172–174; on her successor, 173–174; at Concord State Fair, 182–183; seen through her writings, 183–190; dismisses Hanna, 192; praises Committee on Publication, 194; Peabody attack on, 194–197, 199, 200, 201, 202, 443n67, 444–n71; criticizes but retains Farlow, 196–198; Mark Twain's attacks on, 198–206; Twain's revised view of her style, 209; (*see also* Twain, Mark) ; her linguistic usage, 209–220; attitude to material growth, 223–226; to Christian Science secularism, 226; to worldly means, 227; her sense of history, 227–228; solemn charge to the Board of Directors, 228–229; opposition to, by traditional Christianity, 229–235; Lynn accident (1866) , 231, 464n80; Quimbyism, 231–235; her struggles, 236–242, 461n66; temporary means, 238–242, 462nn74 & 79 & 80; household discipline, 242–244; gratitude to Frye, 244; healing of Frye, 245–246; her women helpers, 247–248; dismisses Kimball, 248–251; named *Fondateur* of Association for International Conciliation, 255; made an Officier d'Académie, 255; prayer for peace, 256, 308, 470n10; newspaper interviews, 256–257; condemns personality cult, 257–260; *McClure's* and *New York World* attacks, 260–275; 471–479nn27–77 passim; *World* "interview," 262–266; group interview, 268–269; *McClure's* biography, 270–272; Powell and Wilbur contributions, 273–275; *World* approach to George

Glover, 275–278; next friends suit, 280–291, 295, 323, 385n50; disposition of estate, 280, 291, 481nn95–96, 489–n126; charitable contributions, 255, 468n2, 468n3; move to Chestnut Hill, Mass., 297–300, 314–315, 498n82; and physical science, 302–307, 492–495–nn27–44 passim; founding of *The Christian Science Monitor*, 307–314; life at Chestnut Hill, 310–311; 314–320; Boston atmosphere, 320–321; new attacks on, 321–323; biographers of, 323–326; Stetson bid to succeed Mrs. Eddy, 330–343; result of Stetson defeat, 343–348; life with household "family," 348–352; final year, 352–360; challenge to the "last enemy," 354–359, 512n92; passing of, 359–361, 513nn111 & 114 & 116; assessment of, 365–367—writings, 18, 61–62, 91, 455–n29, 499n87, 506n34; *Christ and Christmas*, 43–47, 59–64, 107, 348, 390–n27, 391nn28–35, 392nn36–37, 395–nn84–87, 396nn91–92, 426n35; *Christian Healing*, 499n92; *Christian Science versus Pantheism*, 186; "Deification of Personality," 63; "Fallibility of Human Concepts," 413n94; *The First Church of Christ Scientist, and Miscellany*, 272, 388n3; "Man and Woman," 162; "Mathematics," 214; *Miscellaneous Writings*, 101, 102–108, 151, 272, 308; "Mother's Evening Prayer," 354; "The New Century," 415n110; "Obedience," 42, 390n25; "Other Ways Than By War," 133; "A Pæan of Praise," 351; "Personal Contagion," 258–259; "Pond and Purpose," 10, 23, 46; "Principle and Practice," 356, 377–378; *Pulpit and Press*, 88; "Questions and Answers in Moral Science," 232, 233; *Repaid Pages*, 103, 405n28, 432n91; *Retrospection and Introspection*, 115, 229, 240, 336; "The Science of Man," 195; "Shepherd, show me how to go," 406n40; "Soaring," 510n66; "Taking Offense," 407nn55–56; "The United States to Great Britain," 415n110; *Unity of Good*, 149, 354; "The Way of Wisdom," 336; *see also* Church of Christ, Scientist: *Manual of the Mother Church*; Mother Church, The: annual messages to, Communion messages to; *Science and Health with Key to the Scriptures*

Eden allegory, 12, 382n9
Edinburgh, Scotland, 114, 115, 190
Education: through the church, 30, 34, 93; teaching Christian Science, 247–252; variant schools of Christian Science teaching, 251; see also Christian Science Board of Education
Education of an American, The (Sullivan), 471n26
Edwards, Jonathan, 10, 43, 111; idealism of, 381n5
Einstein, Albert, 301, 303, 304, 492n27, 493nn38 & 40
Elder, Samuel J., 156, 159, 160, 161
Eliot, T. S., 426n25
Elisha (prophet), 70
Elizabeth of Austria, 131
Ellis, Fred, 458n40
Ellis, Havelock, 457n31
Ellmann, Richard, 409n56
Emerson, Ralph Waldo, 102, 429n27
England: Christian Science in, 114–119, 414n104
English Reader, The (Murray), 407n55
Erikson, Erik, 460n55
Eveleth, Miss, 300
Ewing, Ruth, 89
Ewing, Judge William G., 123, 160, 182, 192, 255, 430n76

Fairbanks, Mary, 198
Faith and Works of Christian Science, The (Paget), 322
Fall River, Mass., 32
Farlow, Alfred, 123, 166, 168, 172, 174, 177, 199, 257, 268, 269, 279, 297, 317, 329, 360, 504n3, 514n116; Manager of Committees on Publication, 157–158, 194–198, 202, 203, 500n104; answers critics of Mrs. Eddy, 229–231, 302, 323, 445n83, 492n31, 502n20; Mc-Clure's attack, 260, 261, 270, 272, 471-n27; next friends suit, 280, 485n115
Fernald, Josiah, 280, 473n35
Field-King, Julia, 18, 37, 143, 390n27, 422n9, 425n22, 433n92; adulation of Mrs. Eddy, 38, editor of *Christian Science Journal*, 38, 39; Anglo-Israel theory, 116–117; in England, 117–119, 121, 414n108, 416n124; dual nature of, 84–85, 416n123; dropped from Mother Church, 416n124
Filbert, John F., 429n71
Fincastle, Lord, 117
First Church of Christ, Scientist, The, in Boston, Massachusetts: see Church

of Christ, Scientist, and Mother Church, The
Fisher, H. A. L., 248, 467n116
Fitzgerald, Nat Ward, 429n71
Fitzpatrick, Lida, 466n115
Florence, Italy, 20
Flournoy, Theodore, 501n114
Flower, Benjamin O., 150, 193
Fonda, Jesse L., 495n44
Foss, Caroline, see Gyger, Caroline Foss
Fra Angelico, 61
Frame, Mrs. Caroline W., 397n28
French, Dr. Edward, 487n118
Freud, Sigmund, 234, 501n114
From the Methodist Pulpit into Christian Science (Simonsen), 190
Frye, Calvin A., 9, 11, 12, 28, 58, 75, 84, 85, 103, 125, 159, 162, 169, 170, 178, 195, 229, 231–232, 237, 238, 310, 311, 318, 341, 353, 385n60, 397n32, 398n38, 400n52, 428n58, 435nn3 & 107, 479-n73, 500n105, 511n72, 513n111; on Foster Eddy, 81, 83, 86, 401n60; at Pleasant View, 244–246, 464nn98 & 105, 465n107; and *New York World* attack on Mrs. Eddy, 262; next friends suit, 280, 281, 283; at Chestnut Hill, 316–317; personal library, 464n101
Fullmer, Laura May, 282, 483n105

Gandhi, Mahatma, 46
Garland, Hamlin, 193
George, Henry, 193
Germany: Christian Science in, 119–121, 415nn114 & 118 & 120–121
Gill, William I., 249
Gilman, James F., 28, 56, 80, 297; Christian Science and, 21–24; *Christ and Christmas* illustrations, 43–47, 61, 64, 390n27, 391nn28–29 & 34, 392-nn36–37; diary of, 384n44
Glover, Evelyn (granddaughter), 25
Glover, George Washington II (son), 25–26, 79, 275, 414n104, 481n91, 485-n115, 489n126, 513n116; next friends suit, 275–282, 291
Glover, George Washington III (grandson), 275, 385n51
Glover, Mary Baker (granddaughter), 25, 278, 280, 385n51, 480n82, 481n98
Glover, Nellie (Mrs. George), 25
God: as Life, 359; as Love, 133; as Mind, 37, 162, 210–212, 470n10; as Mother and Father, 112, 115, 162, 174, 447n89; as Person, 259; as Principle,

Morris, William, 384n37
Morse, William A., 233, 430nn73 & 77
Moses (Prophet) , 135, 194, 232
Moses, Sen. George H., 111, 412n75, 414n104, 417n141, 428n56, 438n15, 462n73, 474n42
Mother Church, The (The First Church of Christ, Scientist, Boston) , 146, 339, 340, 341, 360, 410n59, 506n23, 510n59; annual messages to, 135, 137–138, 223, 236; beginnings in Boston, 13–18, 29–34, 386nn69 & 72; bell tower chimes, 75; Communion messages to, 137, 153–154, 157; Communion season abolished, 318–319, 499n95; construction of, 67–72, 396nn3 & 7; cornerstone laid, 69; Christian Science neighborhood around, 397n32; date of founding, 33; dedication (1895) , 73–74; early development and organization, 29–34; Easton named pastor, 41–42; Mrs. Eddy's first two visits to, 75–78; her last visit to, 97; enlargement of building, 192–193, 223–224, 258, 272; First Members and their functions, 33–34, 91, 321, 387n76, 410-n59, 423n9, 425n19; form of service for, 72–73; growth and development, 320–326; Hanna as pastor and First Reader, 72–73; membership in, 34; vs. mother figure, 29; Mother's Room, 75, 76, 77, 88, 199–200; prayers for peace, 256; Readers, 332; readership term of office, 397n22; suspending summer services, 89; Woodbury suit against, 155
Mount Auburn Cemetery, Cambridge, Mass., 512n92, 513n116
Müller, Max, 495n42
Munroe, Mary W., 32, 464n105
Murray, Lindley, 407n55
Murray, Lady Mildred, 117
Murray, Lady Victoria, 117
Mysticism, 18, 32, 57, 110–111, 116, 388-n7, 437n10

Nash, Charles E., 425n19
National Christian Scientist Association, 12
Neal, James, 125; healings by, 100–101, 404n19; trustee of Publishing Society, 122, 417n127
New Thought movement, 329
New York American, 269, 334
New York City: First Church of Christ, Scientist, 330, 332, 334, 336, 342, 343;

Lathrops (Second Church) in, 119, 202, 226, 337
New York Evening Journal, 283
New York Herald, 172, 174, 188, 244, 256, 435n109, 492n27
New York Sun, 493n38
New York Times, 286, 444n73, 459n48
New York World, 156, 335, 400n52; "exposé" of Mrs. Eddy, 260–282
Newman, Cardinal, 453n7
Next friends suit, 280–291, 295, 323, 385n50
Nicaea, Council of, 392n42
Nixon, William G., 13–16, 39, 41, 170, 282, 336, 383n21, 483nn105–106; and legal status of Boston church, 29–30; resignation as publisher, 387n21
Nixon, Helen Andrews (Mrs. W. G.) , 14, 33, 386n74; on The Christian Science Monitor, 313
No Exit (Sartre) , 426n25
Norcross, Lanson P., 40
North American Review, 196, 202, 203, 270, 446n84
Norton, Carol, 103, 104, 119, 123, 412-n75, 440n30, 447n92
Norton, Charles Eliot, 19, 322
Norwood, Edward E., 125, 417n139
Noyes, Caroline, 53
Nunn, Henry P., 177

"O little town of Bethlehem" (Brooks) , 43
Obedience, 40–41, 42, 53, 56, 59
O'Brien, Sibyl Wilbur, see Sibyl Wilbur
Ochs, Adolph S., 444n73
Oconto, Wis., 396n2
"Ode to Duty" (Wordsworth) , 391n35
Omaha, Neb., 126, 162
Onlooker (London) , 497n76
Orcutt, William Dana, 19–21, 384n37, 503n128; on Foster Eddy, 27
Orgain, Alice L., 391n32
Our Race (Totten) , 116
Outlook (Boston) , 497n75

Paget, Dr. Stephen, 322, 501n113
Paris, France, 119, 194, 255, 317
Park, Edwin J., 283
Parker, Hosea W., 284
Parker, Theodore, 412n76
Paul, Saint, 112, 115, 147, 240, 252, 320, 406n37, 493n31, 497n76
Peabody, Frederick W., 156, 158, 170, 171, 428n59, 432n92; campaign against Mrs. Eddy, 194–197, 200, 201, 202,

Sawyer, S. J., 430n71
Schön, Marie, 120, 416n121
Schurz, Carl, 136
Schweitzer, Albert, 300
Science and Health with Key to the Scriptures, 14, 18, 20, 24, 44, 50, 55, 64, 71, 76, 88, 93, 100, 103, 104, 108, 115, 131, 133, 150, 151, 153, 159, 168, 174, 195, 202, 212, 219–220, 227, 233, 234, 238, 240, 241, 249, 306, 307, 311, 325, 338, 347, 348, 351, 395n84, 437n10, 448n93, 454n23, 458n40, 459n48, 500-n104, 511n71, 512n96; authority of, 344; advertising of, 122; authorship of, 23, 42, 43, 62, 84, 107, 184–187, 407n54; concordance to, 210; no piecemeal publication of, 57, 106, 393n65; as "pastor" of Mother Church, 72–73, 81; popularized version, 453n7; printings of, 19, 382n14; revisions of, 25, 184, 187, 189–190, 273, 303, 440-n43, 490n3; style of, 187–188, 209; as teacher of Christian Science, 252; translations of, 119–121, 296; Mark Twain on, 209
Scott, Sir Walter, 419n8
Seal, Frances Thurber, 119, 120
Shakespeare, William, 98, 235
Shannon, Clara, 12, 75, 76, 103, 178, 466n115
Sheba, Queen of, 73
Simonsen, Severin E., 190
Sino-Japanese war, 73, 132
Slaght, James, 262, 263, 275, 276, 277, 278, 281
Slavery, industrial, 138
Sleeper, David E., 395n81
Smith, Judge Clifford P., 320, 346, 360–361, 500n104, 501n110
Smith, Hanover, 288, 488n122
Smith, Hildreth (cousin), 458n40, 479-n73
Smuts, Jan, 301
Social Statics (Spencer), 403n15
Solomon, 73
Southworth, Mrs. E. D. E. N., 117
Spanish-American War, 132, 133–135
Spencer, Herbert, 403n15, 494n42
Spinoza, Baruch, 24
Spiritualism, 189
Springer, Fleta Campbell, 268
Spurgeon, Charles H., 109
Stark, Mollie, 109
Steffens, Lincoln, 261
Stetson, Augusta E., 48, 50, 99, 103, 108, 169, 193, 194, 232, 410n64, 447n92; on

Christ and Christmas, 61, 395n85; materialism, 329–330, 335–336; relations with Mrs. Eddy, 331–335, 505–506-nn8–22 passim; deterioration and expulsion, 336–343, 506nn23 & 34, 507-nn37 & 39–40, 508nn43–49 passim, 509n56, 513n116
Stewart, Allison V., 309, 320
Stewart, Charles D., 408n56
Still, M. Adelaide, 315, 318, 350, 351, 356, 359, 360, 492n21, 498nn83–84, 502n124, 511nn75–76
Stillings, Dr., 238
Stocking, Daisette, 74, 125, 186, 413n89, 430n80, 433n98; first meeting with Mrs. Eddy, 83–84
Strang, Lewis C., 258, 268, 388n3; next friends suit, 280
Streeter, Gen. Frank S., 111, 159, 160, 161, 266, 267, 282, 287, 289, 462n73
Strickler, Virgil O., 336, 338–339, 342
Studdert-Kennedy, Hugh, 398n34, 483-n109
Stuttgart, Germany, 119
Sullivan, Mark, 261
Swampscott, Mass., 458n40
Sweet, Ella Peck, 466n115

Taft, William Howard, 428n58
Tagore, Rabindranath, 409n56
Tarbell, Ida, 261
Theosophy, 57, 394n70, 398n40
Thompson, E. J., 477n54
Thompson, Eva, 486n115
Tilton, N.H., 457n28
Tomkins, George, 109, 123, 429n71
Tomlinson, Irving, 109, 110, 123, 125, 177, 178, 226, 229–230, 238, 258, 279, 295, 298, 323, 324, 325, 334, 410n65, 411n73, 464n105, 513n111; next friends suit, 280
Tomlinson, Mary, 295–296
Toronto, University of, 74
Totten, Lt. Charles A. L., 116, 414-nn97–98
Tournier, Alice, 121
Transcendentalism, 236, 394n70
True Awakening (Edwards), 43
Truth (London), 413n91
Twain, Mark, 408n56, 429n71; on Christian Science, 3–4, 32, 201–203, 205–206, 229, 446n84, 448nn95–98, 449-n103, 450nn108 & 115, 451n119; on Mrs. Eddy, 3, 198–206, 209, 446nn84 & 87, 447n93, 449nn104 & 107, 450-n113, 451n123; on *Science and Health*,